Politics and Empire in Victorian Britain

A Reader

Edited by

Antoinette Burton

palgrave

First published 2001 by
PALGRAVE™
175 Fifth Avenue, New York, NY 10010 and
Houndmills, Basingstoke, Hampshire, England RG21 6XS.
Companies and representatives throughout the world.

Palgrave is the new global publishing imprint of St. Martin's Press LLC Scholarly and
Reference Division and Palgrave Publishers Ltd (formerly Macmillan Press Ltd).

ISBN 0–312–22997–6 (cloth)
ISBN 0–312–29335–6 (paper)

Library of Congress Cataloging-in-Publication Data
Politics and empire in Victorian Britain : a reader / [compiled by] Antoinette Burton.
    p.   cm.
  Includes bibliographical references and index.
    ISBN 0–312–22997–6 — ISBN 0–312–29335–6 (pbk.)
    1. Great Britain—Colonies—History—19th century—Sources.   2. Great Britain—
Politics and Government—1837–1901—Sources.   3. Great Britain—Social conditions—
19th century—Sources.   I. Burton, Antoinette M., 1961-

JV1017.P65   2001
909'.0971241081—dc21   2001019448

Design by Letra Libre, Inc.

First Edition: October 2001
10   9   8   7   6   5   4   3   2   1

Printed in the United States of America.

Politics and Empire in Victorian Britain

WITHDRAWN

Contents

Part I
Shaping the Imperial Body Politic, 1829–1857

A. EMANCIPATION, REPRESENTATION, AND EMPIRE

B. CULTURES OF SERVICE, ANTI-SLAVERY, AND REFORM

C. Imperial Britons at Midcentury

Part II
Liberalizing Imperial Democracy: Midcentury and After

A. Imagining an Imperial Polity

B. Women, Politics, and Empire

C. Varieties of National and Imperial Patriotism

Part III
At Home with Imperial Culture: Toward the Twentieth Century

A. Empire's Civilizing Missions

B. Work, Race, and Politics: Centers and Peripheries

C. The Boer War and the New Century

Timetable of Select Events

1829	Catholic Emancipation
1832	First Reform Act
1833	Slavery Abolition Act
	Factory Act
1834	Poor Law Amendment Act
1837	Aborigines Protection Society and New Zealand Association founded
	Queen Victoria ascends the throne
1838	The People's Charter
	Apprenticeship system in the West Indies abolished
1839	The "Opium War"
	London Missionary Society founded
1842	Treaty of Nanking; Hong Kong ceded to Britain
	Mines Act
1843	Daniel O'Connell launches the Repeal Movement
	Maori Wars begin
1845	Onset of the Irish famine
1846	Repeal of the Corn Laws
1848	Chartist demonstration, Kennington Common
1851	The Great Exhibition at the Crystal Palace
	Australian gold rush
1854	The Crimean War
1855	New South Wales, Victoria, and Newfoundland granted responsible government
1856	Oudh annexed
1857	Mutiny in India
1858	Jews admitted to the House of Commons
1859	Charles Darwin, *Origin of Species*
1860	Siege of Peking; treaty of Peking
1864	First Contagious Diseases Act
1865	Uprising in Morant Bay, Jamaica
	John Stuart Mill elected MP
1866	Hyde Park "riots"
1867	Second Reform Act
	British North America Act; creates Dominion of Canada

Declaration of an Irish Republic; failure of Fenian insurrection
Lily Maxwell casts a parliamentary vote at Manchester
1868   William Gladstone elected Prime Minister
1869   National Society for Women's Suffrage founded
Opening of the Suez Canal
1871   Charles Darwin, *Descent of Man*
1872   Secret Ballot Act
Disraeli's Crystal Palace speech
1873   Home Rule League founded, Dublin
1875   Charles Stewart Parnell enters Parliament
1876   Benjamin Disraeli created Earl of Beaconsfield
Royal Titles Act (Queen Victoria, Empress of India)
1877   British annexation of the Transvaal
1879   Michael Davitt founds the Land League
1881   First South African War; British defeat at Majuba Hill
1882   Arabi uprising, British occupation of Egypt
Phoenix Park Murders
1884   Third Reform Act
Siege of Khartoum
Establishment of the Fabian Society
1885   Foundation of the Indian National Congress
Death of General Gordon at Khartoum
Helen Taylor attempts a parliamentary seat for Camberwell
1886   Indian and Colonial Exhibition
Irish Home Rule defeated at Westminster
Repeal of the Contagious Diseases Acts
1887   Queen's Golden Jubilee
"Bloody Sunday," Trafalgar Square
1889   Dock laborers' strike
1890   Cecil Rhodes becomes Prime Minister of Cape Colony
Charles Parnell cited in Kitty O'Shea's divorce case
1892   Dadhabai Naoroji elected to Parliament
1893   Foundation of Independent Labour Party
1897   Queen's Diamond Jubilee
1899   Anglo-Boer War
1900   Siege of Ladysmith
1901   Death of Queen Victoria
Commonwealth of Australia established
1903   Foundation of the Women's Social and Political Union
1904   Royal Commission on Physical Deterioration
Vida Goldstein's senate candidacy
1905   Alien Immigration Act
First convention of Sinn Féin

Preface

‏‏‎ ‎

In 2000 the Runnymede Trust published a 400-page report on "The Future of Multi-Ethnic Britain." Among the authors were Lord Parekh, a Labour peer and political scientist, and Stuart Hall, a critical race theorist and one of the founders of Cultural Studies in Britain. The report called for the establishment of a human rights commission, an end to racially discriminatory search policies on the part of the police, and the abolition of the voucher system for asylum-seekers. The failure of the state-supported educational system to include the story of Britain's imperial dominance in school curricula also came under fire: the authors recommended that the history of the United Kingdom be revised in order to account for the impact of empire, ex-colonial migration and nonwhite communities and constituencies on contemporary British life. In a section on "the future of Britishness," the report questioned the implicit equation of Englishness with whiteness and, in the process, argued that "Britishness" should be dispensed with because it was a "racially coded" identity that was no longer accurate (had it ever been) for describing Britain's multicultural character. A storm of protest followed from Tories and Labour leaders alike, as did calls for "native" Britons to defend their right to the integrity of the designation "British." The Home Secretary, Jack Straw, announced that he was proud to be British. "Unlike the Runnymede Trust," he declared, "I firmly believe there is a future for Britain and a future for Britishness."[1]

Such is the pressure that the legacy of British imperialism continues to exert on the public imagination—and on the very category of "Britishness" itself—in Britain on the threshold of the new millennium. *Politics and Empire in Victorian Britain: A Reader* engages directly with these questions by offering students and teachers of British history alike the opportunity to construct a narrative of the nineteenth century that maps the impact of imperialism in its many guises on society, politics, and culture in the Victorian period. Readers will find that the volume combines a discussion of the social and political developments of the Victorian era with an examination of Britain's role as a global imperial power—both formal and informal—in India, Africa, Ireland, Australia, and East Asia. Its uniqueness lies in its commitment to keeping "high politics" in play while exposing students to the social, economic, and cultural

---

1. Alan Travis, "'British' a Term of Coded Racism, says Report," *Guardian Weekly* October 19–25, 2000, p. 11.

impact of political decisions and debates that animated the years 1829–1905. That this is a period bounded by Catholic Emancipation on one end and the Alien Immigration Act on the other suggests how fruitfully we might reimagine the Victorian era beyond the traditional Whig narrative—as well as how consistently questions of citizenship and political belonging turned on ethnic and religious identities in the shifting contexts of imperial confidence, retrenchment, and reform. Indeed, the reader tracks the ways in which imperial expansion, Irish nationalism, and the rhetoric of the civilizing mission all helped to shape the terms of political debate, as well as to reconfirm the white male character of democracy in Victorian Britain. White women's attempts to participate in political and social reform, to vote and to influence Britain's imperial projects are dealt with throughout, as is the presence of colonial and other "nonwhite" peoples in the metropole where documents are available. Special attention is also paid to the impact of empire on the daily life and cultural attitudes of Britons across the empire in this, Britain's so-called "imperial" century.

The chief purpose of *Politics and Empire in Victorian Britain: A Reader* is to introduce students to the intersections of "home" and "empire" so that the effects of imperialism on Victorian politics and society can be more fully appreciated. Understanding that Britons' encounter with empire at home did not begin with the influx of post-1945 colonial immigrants but has a long history rooted in the nineteenth century (and before) will, hopefully, allow undergraduates to imagine new connections between past and present and to reevaluate Britain's investment in "the Island Story" as well. This is perhaps of special importance for Americans drawn to British history. For despite the influence of multiculturalism in the U.S., many American students still view Britain as a place shorn of racial tension and only dimly recognizable as the home of a lost, once-great empire. Understanding how and why the Victorian period anticipated the debates about multiculturalism that have raged at this century's end will help students of all nationalities and political persuasions to interrogate American exceptionalism: to realize, in other words, that the United States has not been unique in its confrontation with racial questions and the challenges of ethnic pluralism produced in part by colonial encounters from within and without. Recognizing both the reality and the fantasy of that "splendid isolationism" for which Britain has long been famous will result equally, I hope, in a more nuanced and critically engaged appreciation for Britain's imperial past and its postcolonial present as well.

Many people have helped to make this volume a reality, and I am grateful to them all. The scholarship of Peter Fryer, Catherine Hall, Ron Ramdin, and Rozina Visram has been a constant source of inspiration to me as I tried to put together a reader that would address the influence of imperial power and its histories on Britain "proper." Their belief in the possibility of a different history of and for Britain is in large measure what has made this collection imaginable. Heloise Brown, Catherine Candy, Ann Curthoys, Nadja Durbach, Ian Fletcher, Madhavi Kale, Lara Kriegel, Philippa Levine, Laura Mayhall, Douglas Peers, Fiona Paisley, Barbara Ramusack, George Robb, Mrinalini Sinha, Kevin Switaj, Susan Thorne, and Angela Woollacott each helped me to identify sources, track down citations and finalize the biographical and historical details necessary for undertaking the project and seeing it to completion. Not everything they suggested or helped me with made the final cut but I appreciate their time and effort nonetheless. Raka Nandi spent hours in the University of Illinois library digging up materials, always efficiently and cheerfully, for which I thank her. Françoise Labrique was instrumental in the final stages and so thanks are due to her as well. Students in my Victorian Britain course at the University of Illinois offered their opinions on the benefits of some documents over others, and I hope they will recognize their influence in the final selections. Pamela Wilson and her staff at the University of Illinois obtained the necessary permissions, without which the volume would not have been what it is. Liz Gaugler and Charlotte Mayne at Sencor were unfailingly helpful where the complexities of digitilization were concerned. Paul Arroyo's technical interventions remain as astonishing as they are essential, down to the very last—for which I am eternally grateful.

Permissions

Selections from *Mafeking Diary: A Black Man's View of a White Man's War by Sol T. Plaatje* (Ohio University Press, 1990) are reprinted with the permission of Ohio University Press, Athens, Ohio.

Selections from Ian Schapera, ed., *Livingston's Missionary Correspondence 1841–1856* (Berkeley: University of California Press, 1961), are reprinted with permission.

Edinburgh University Press has graciously agreed to allow the reprint of selections from Iain McCalman, ed., *The Horrors of Slavery and Other Writings of Robert Wedderburn* (Edinburgh: Edinburgh University Press, 1991).

Selections from *The History of Mary Prince* (1831), edited with an introduction by Moira Ferguson (Ann Arbor: University of Michigan Press, 1992) have been reprinted with permission.

Part I

Shaping the Imperial Body Politic,
1829–1857

A. Emancipation, Representation, and Empire

~ঞ্চ~

Daniel O'Connell (1775–1847)—known to contemporaries as "The Liberator," "The Coun-sellor," "The Uncrowned King of Ireland," and the "Big Beggarman"—was elected MP for Clare in 1828 but could not take his seat because he was a Catholic. In the speeches below he makes the case for the removal of religious disabilities for both Catholics and Jews.

~ঞ্চ~

Daniel O'Connell, "Speech at the Bar" (1829)

Mr. O'Connell then proceeded to address the House. He said he thought he could not be accused of affectation when he stated that he was very ignorant of the forms of that House, and therefore he required the kind indulgence of the House if he should hap-pen to violate them. He said he was there to claim his right to sit and vote in the House as the representative of the county of Clare, without taking the Oath of Supremacy. He was ready to take the Oath of Allegiance provided by the recent statute, entitled "An Act for the Relief of His Majesty's Roman Catholic Subjects." He was desirous to have that oath administered to him, and of course must be prepared to verify his qualifica-tion in point of property; and whether the House should be of opinion that he ought to be permitted to take the new oath or not, he respectfully required to be allowed to take the qualification oath. If he was allowed to take that oath, be it then at his own hazard to sit and vote in the House. If he were allowed only to take that oath, he was content to run the risk of sitting in the House. His right to sit and vote in that House was in its nature perfectly plain. He had been returned duly elected by the proper of-ficer. It appeared by that return, that he had had a great majority of the legal voters of the county of Clare, who voted for his return; and that return had since been con-firmed by the unanimous decision of a committee of the House. He therefore had as good a right to sit and vote in the House, according to the principles of the constitu-tion, as any of the right . . . hon. gentlemen by whom he was surrounded. The voice of the people had sent him there. He was a representative of the people. The question, as it affected his right to sit and vote in the House, could not, he said, arise at common law, but only on statute law. It was a question of statute law, whether a representative of the people was bound, before he entered on the execution of his duty to his constituents, to take oaths of any description. . . .

He would not detain the House by going minutely through the Act [for the Relief of . . . Catholic(s)]. He would rest his claim upon the tenth clause, which conferred the right of exercising every civil right upon Catholics. If he should be asked, whether the right of sitting and voting in Parliament were a civil right, he would reply, if it might be permitted, by asking another question—namely, "If it be not a civil right, what is it?" He had looked through the law books, and he found that Blackstone divided the entire law into rights and wrongs, and amongst the civil rights he classed the privileges of sitting and voting in Parliament. But he would appeal to the common sense and understanding of men. Was it not a civil right? Must it not be a civil right? In this very statute itself civil and military rights were contradistinguished. Thus there was in the act itself a clue to the meaning of the act. If he went out of the act, and referred to those authorities which decided the meaning of words in the English language, he found that the words "civil rights" included every right of the description for which he was now contending. "Civil," according to Dr. Johnson, was an adjective which meant "relating to the community; political; relating to the city or government." Now, political and civil were just the same thing, only that one was derived from the Latin, and the other from the Greek. What he claimed was a political right. No man could deny that it was a political right to sit and vote in Parliament. One of the examples which Dr. Johnson gave showed that "civil" and "political" bore the same meaning. The example was—"But there is another unity which would be most advantageous to our country, and that is your endeavour after a civil, a political union in the whole nation." This definition proved that the tenth clause necessarily included such a right as that which he claimed. He now came to the definition of the word "right." Dr. Johnson said it was a noun substantive, meaning, first, a "just claim;" next, "that which justly belonged to one;" next, "property, interest;" next, "power, prerogative;" next, "immunity, privilege." In short, there was not one of those significations which was not more comprehensive than he desired it to be. In reference to the signification of "just claim," Dr. Johnson gave this definition: "The Roman citizens were by the sword taught to acknowledge the Pope their Lord, though they knew not by what right." There was a plain definition of the meaning of the language of the tenth clause where it spoke of "civil right." It could not mean "franchise;" for that was already included. It could not mean "property," for that was already included under the twenty-third clause, which provided, "that from and after the passing of this act, no oath or oaths shall be tendered to, or required to be taken by, his Majesty's subjects professing the Roman Catholic religion, for enabling them to hold or enjoy any real or personal property, other than such as may by law be tendered to and required to be taken by his Majesty's other subjects." It was evident, therefore, that the words of the tenth clause did not mean franchise or property, but a just claim to protection, privilege, and immunity of any kind whatever. Thus, then, common sense showed what the law sanctioned, that the phrase "civil rights" must necessarily include the right to speak and vote in that House.

I now turn round and respectfully ask, why I am not to be allowed to exercise my rights? Let it be remembered that my case cannot be drawn into precedent: it can never occur again; and I ask the House, in construing the act, whether it intends to make it an outlawry against a single individual? (Hear, hear.) If the act were meant to meet my case, why was not my case specified in it? It existed when the act was passed; it was upon the records of the house, for a committee had sat while the bill was pending, and had given in its report upon oath. Why, I ask again, was not my case specified? Simply, because it was not intended to be included. Where, then, is the individual who would think it ought to be included? Let me call the attention of the House to the recital of the statute: "Whereas, by various Acts of Parliament certain restraints and disabilities affecting Roman Catholics;" and proceeds—"And whereas it is expedient that such restraints and disabilities shall be henceforth discontinued: and whereas by various acts certain oaths and certain declarations . . . are or may be required to be taken, made, and subscribed by the subjects of his Majesty as qualifications for sitting and voting in Parliament, and for the enjoyment of certain offices, franchises, and civil rights: Be it enacted . . . that such restraints and disabilities shall be from henceforth discontinued." All are to be discontinued. What do I claim? That they shall be discontinued. It is a maxim of law that the recital of a statute shall not control the enactments; but with this qualification, that, although a particular recital cannot control a general enactment, there is no rule of law that a general recital shall not explain a particular enactment. But I have a general recital, and a general enactment, too, in my favour. If to sit and vote be not a civil right, what civil right was intended by the word; for every other is provided for? Why should this be excluded? Look at the recital and look at the intention of the statute, and shall I then be told that a doubt can arise as to the right to sit and vote? If I have not that right, what is to be done? Is the statute of Charles II, enabling the house to exclude me, still in force? What is to become of me? Am I to remain the representative for Clare? Will the House not let me in, and is it not able to turn me out? What, I ask again, is to become of me? I call the attention of the house to that—what is to become of me? (Hear, and a laugh). The statute of Charles II imposed penalties for not taking the oaths and signing the declaration; among others there was a pecuniary penalty, and it continued in force until the Union with Ireland. The first question I would ask the lawyers of the House, then, is this—did the Union Act continue those penalties? I take upon me to say it did not. Then, I ask, can any penalty or punishment be continued on a free-born British subject, when an Act of Parliament, like that of the Union, is silent, and contains no enactment as to penalty? That is a question of constitutional law; and if I were sued tomorrow for the penalty of £500 in a court of justice, I should, of course, instantly demur. If I am right in that position—if the penalty of £500 could not be recovered, shall the greater infliction remain? When courts of justice would refuse to enforce the fine, shall this House take the law into its own hands, and deprive me of what ought to be infinitely more precious—the right to sit and vote as the representative of a divided, a disinterested, and, I had almost said, a martyred people? The Union statue, I apprehend, would alone be sufficient, but I do not stand on that merely. This Relief Bill has abolished the oaths and declaration, and abolished with it the punishment for not taking the one and subscribing the other. If the declaration be abolished, does the pecuniary penalty remain? I answer, no; and if the pecuniary penalty do not remain, does the heavier penalty of exclusion continue? Certainly not; and I respectfully submit to the House that it has not now jurisdiction to prevent the exercise of my civil right of sitting and voting here. . . .

The question is: is it not my right, on this return, to take the seat to which I have been duly elected? Is the question free from doubt? If there be a doubt, I am entitled to the benefit of that doubt. I maintain that I have a constitutional right, founded on the return of the sheriff and the voice of the people; and if there be a doubt on the subject, it should be removed. The statute comes before us to be construed from the first clause. I did—and I am not ashamed to own it—I did defer to the opinion of others, and was averse from calling that construction; and if it had not been for the interests of those who sent me here, my own right should have been buried in oblivion. But now I require the House to consider it. Will you decide that a civil right does not mean a civil right? And if this case of mine be not excepted, will you add it as an additional exception? It might have been said by some of those who supported the bill, that it was intended by that measure to compensate a nation for by-gone wrongs, and to form the foundation stone of a solid and substantial building, to be consecrated to the unity and peace of the empire. But if what is certain may be disturbed; if what words express may be erased; if civil rights may be determined not to be civil rights; if we are to be told that, by some excuse or by some pretext, what is not uncertain may be made so, we shall be put under an impossibility to know what construction we must hereafter place on the statutes. I have endeavoured to treat this House with respect. My title to sit in it is clear and plain; and I contend that the statute is all-comprehensive in its intention, in its recital, and in its enactments. It comprehends every principle and measure of relief, with such exceptions as are thereinafter excepted. But while I show my respect for this House, I stand here on my right, and claim the benefit of it.

The hon. and learned gentleman then bowed to the house and withdrew, amidst loud and general cheering.

Daniel O'Connell,
On a Bill for the Removal of Jewish Disabilities (1830)

Mr. O'Connell said, he was proud of the opportunity of supporting the measure. He supported it both on principle and sympathy. The time had but recently gone by, when the Catholics were assailed by clamours which he would refute that very evening by his conduct. They had been assailed by a cry which might be very satisfactory to some Christians, who thought that no others were right in argument or good sense but themselves. The cry then raised was Protestant—now it was Christian. To persons who now raised that cry against this measure, he would say that they avoided or evaded the true principles of Christianity, which were liberality and charity. On the former occasion, these persons said that the Catholics were the advocates of bigotry. Who were the advocates of bigotry now? Christian charity, with such people, was a good thing to talk of, but when they came to the point they refused to put it in practice. Who were before the House now in the character of claimants for rights? They were not foreigners—they were not Poles—nor Russians—nor Turks—nor Frenchmen. They were men born in England—men entitled to hold property in England—to inherit property from their ancestors in England—in short, they were Englishmen. They were debarred from some of the privileges of Englishmen because they refused to take an oath of a particular kind, and therefore they were shut out of that House. They were excluded, as it was said, because the safety of our institution demanded their exclusion. But the House might be asked whether it would admit the unbeliever? It did admit the Mahometan. The Mahometan might, perhaps, refuse the oath, "on the faith of a Christian." Yes, that was true, the Mahometan might be considered excluded; but would they laugh at him now, when he asked them what sanction had they against the Atheist or the Deist? Against any man who did believe in a God, or professed a particular religion, they had a protection, but they had no check upon the man who had no religious faith. It was said that the Jews had sympathies elsewhere. In the same manner, it had been said, that the Catholics had sympathies elsewhere. He did not mean to disavow that he and they carried spiritual homage to another than the King of England; but his own Sovereign received his undivided political homage. So it was with the Jews; he might still remember the traditionary home of his fathers, but he was obedient to our laws. Let them not, therefore, talk of the name of Christianity, when it was used to do evil instead of good. In such a case he scorned the name; he desired the substance. Christianity was charitable; charity was the precept of Jesus Christ their Saviour himself. He was charitable to all men, even to his murderers; he prayed even for them, saying—"Father, forgive them, they know not what they do." In France they had a Christian Legislature, and the Jews were ranked with the other citizens of the State. Perhaps it might be denied that the French Legislature was Christian; for one mark of a Christian Legislature they had not—they had not a boroughmongering system—they had not one lord with ten retainers, who, after sitting with the Côte Gauche, went over just at the critical moment to the Côte Droite, carrying his ten retainers with him. Certainly that was not the case in France; and yet he imagined, notwithstanding its disadvantage in this respect, it might be said to have a Christian legislature. But both there and in the Netherlands, Jews were appointed judges, magistrates and legislators, and performed their duties in the most efficient and most honorable manner; and at the moment at which he was speaking, one of the secretaries of the Sorbonne was a converted Jew. Conversion was prevented in this country by our own system of laws.

Affect to scorn a man for his opinions, or to deprive him of civil power on their account, and he became wedded to them more firmly than ever. Such had been the case with the Catholics, and such would be the case with the Jews, and with all other people in similar circumstances. They had been told that the same reason did not hold for admitting the Jews as for admitting the Catholics. It was true, for there were more reasons against the admission of the Catholics than against that of the Jews. It was because the Catholics were so numerous that they ought not to have been admitted; for if their belief were dangerous to the State, their numbers only rendered it doubly dangerous. That was not the case with the Jews, whose numbers were insufficient to create the least degree of alarm. Then it was said the Catholics were a proselytising race; that made them more dangerous still, though, perhaps they could gain but few proselytes, for they could offer but few pecuniary advantages; and, as an hon. member had said the other night, if the road to heaven were not paved with gold, nobody would have taken the trouble to discover it. He should support the bill on the universal principle of toleration, if that were not an improper word to be used on such an occasion—perhaps he ought to have said the principle of right. That right was not to be infringed either by an inquisition which inflicted torture, as in Spain, or by laws which, as in England, imposed privation. Man had a right to inflict neither the one nor the other; Christianity had spread itself—not by the force of temporal power, not by the efforts of Christians, nor by the labour of Christian legislatures, but by virtue of its own truth, and its mild and benevolent influence on the human heart. It had expanded itself, not only without the assistance of temporal power, but against the most formidable opposition; and where was the Christian that would tell him that the arm of God was short, and needed the aid of any of His creatures?

—※—

Thomas Babington Macaulay (1800–1859) was a member of Parliament (for Calne in 1830 and Leeds in 1832) and a Whig historian who also served as the Law Member for India in the

1830s (see below). Here he makes the conservative case for political reform, arguing that change is necessary in order to preserve English traditions of government.

Thomas Babington Macaulay, "Parliamentary Reform" (1831)

It is a circumstance, Sir, of happy augury for the motion before the House, that almost all those who have opposed it have declared themselves hostile on principle to Parliamentary Reform. Two Members, I think, have confessed that, though they disapprove of the plan now submitted to us, they are forced to admit the necessity of a change in the Representative system. Yet even those gentlemen have used, as far as I have observed, no arguments which would not apply as strongly to the most moderate change as to that which has been proposed by His Majesty's Government. I say, Sir, that I consider this as a circumstance of happy augury. For what I feared was, not the opposition of those who are averse to all Reform, but the disunion of reformers. I knew that, during three months, every reformer had been employed in conjecturing what the plan of the Government would be. I knew that every reformer had imagined in his own mind a scheme differing doubtless in some points from that which my noble friend, the Paymaster of the Forces, has developed. I felt therefore great apprehension that one person would be dissatisfied with one part of the bill, that another person would be dissatisfied with another part, and that thus our whole strength would be wasted in internal dissensions. That apprehension is now at an end. I have seen with delight the perfect concord which prevails among all who deserve the name of reformers in this House; and I trust that I may consider it as an omen of the concord which will prevail among reformers throughout the country. I will not, Sir, at present express any opinion as to the details of the bill; but, having during the last twenty-four hours given the most diligent consideration to its general principles, I have no hesitation in pronouncing it a wise, noble, and comprehensive measure, skilfully framed for the healing of great distempers, for the securing at once of the public liberties and of the public repose, and for the reconciling and knitting together of all the orders of the State.

I consider this, Sir, as a practical question. I rest my opinion on no general theory of government. I distrust all general theories of government. I will not positively say, that there is any form of polity which may not, in some conceivable circumstances, be the best possible. I believe that there are societies in which every man may safely be admitted to vote. Gentlemen may cheer, but such is my opinion. I say, Sir, that there are countries in which the condition of the labouring classes is such that they may safely be intrusted with the right of electing Members of the Legislature. If the labourers of England were in that state in which I, from my soul, wish to see them, if employment were always plentiful, wages always high, food always cheap, if a large family were considered not as an encumbrance but as a blessing, the principal objections to Universal Suffrage would, I think, be removed. Universal Suffrage exists in the United States without producing any very frightful consequences; and I do not believe, that the people of those States, or of any part of the world, are in any good quality naturally superior to our own countrymen. But, unhappily, the labouring classes in England, and in all old countries, are occasionally in a state of great distress. Some of the causes of this distress are, I fear, beyond the control of the Government. We know what effect distress produces, even on people more intelligent than the great body of the labouring classes can possibly be. We know that it makes even wise men irritable, unreasonable, credulous, eager for immediate relief, heedless of remote consequences. There is no quackery in medicine, religion, or politics, which may not impose even on a powerful mind, when that mind has been disordered by pain or fear. It is therefore no reflection on the poorer class of Englishmen, who are not, and who cannot in the nature of things be, highly educated, to say that distress produces on them its natural effects, those effects which it would produce on the Americans, or on any other people, that it blinds their judgment, that it inflames their passions, that it makes them prone to believe those who flatter them, and to distrust those who would serve them. For the sake, therefore, of the whole society, for the sake of the labouring classes themselves, I hold it to be clearly expedient that, in a country like this, the right of suffrage should depend on a pecuniary qualification.

But, Sir, every argument which would induce me to oppose Universal Suffrage, induces me to support the plan which is now before us. I am opposed to Universal Suffrage, because I think that it would produce a destructive revolution. I support this plan, because I am sure that it is our best security against a revolution. . . .

To say that such a system is ancient is no defence. My honorable friend, the Member for the University of Oxford challenges us to show, that the Constitution was ever better than it is. Sir, we are legislators, not antiquaries. The question for us is, not whether the Constitution was better formerly, but whether we can make it better now.

But these great cities, says my honorable friend, the Member for the University of Oxford, are virtually, though not directly, represented. Are not the wishes of Manchester, he asks, as much consulted as those of any town which sends Members to Parliament? Now, Sir, I do not understand how a power which is salutary when exercised virtually can be noxious when exercised directly. If the wishes of Manchester have as much weight with us as they would have under a system which should give Representatives to Manchester, how can there be any danger in giving Representatives to Manchester? A virtual Representative is, I presume, a man who acts as a direct Representative would act: for surely it would be absurd to say that a man virtually represents the people of Manchester, who is in the habit of saying No, when a man directly representing the people of Manchester would say Aye. The utmost that can be expected from virtual Representation is that it may be as good as direct Representation. If so, why not grant direct Representation to places which, as every body allows, ought, by some process or other, to be represented?

. . . Under such circumstances, a great plan of reconciliation, prepared by the Ministers of the Crown, has been brought before us in a manner which gives additional lustre to a noble name, inseparably associated during two centuries with the dearest liberties of the English people. I will not say, that this plan is in all its details precisely such as I might wish it to be; but it is founded on a great and a sound principle. It takes away a vast power from a few. It distributes that power through the great mass of the middle order. Every man, therefore, who thinks as I think is bound to stand firmly by Ministers who are resolved to stand or fall with this measure. Were I one of them, I would sooner, infinitely sooner, fall with such a measure than stand by any other means that ever supported a Cabinet.

My honorable friend, the Member for the University of Oxford, tells us, that if we pass this law, England will soon be a republic. The reformed House of Commons will, according to him, before it has sat ten years, depose the King, and expel the Lords from their House. Sir, if my honorable friend could prove this, he would have succeeded in bringing an argument for democracy, infinitely stronger than any that is to be found in the works of Paine. My honorable friend's proposition is in fact this; that our monarchical and aristocratical institutions have no hold on the public mind of England; that these institutions are regarded with aversion by a decided majority of the middle class. This, Sir, I say, is plainly deducible from his proposition; for he tells us that the Representatives of the middle class will inevitably abolish royalty and nobility within ten years: and there is surely no reason to think that the Representatives of the middle class will be more inclined to a democratic revolution than their constituents. Now, Sir, if I were convinced that the great body of the middle class in England look with aversion on monarchy and aristocracy, I should be forced, much against my will, to come to this conclusion, that monarchical and aristocratical institutions are unsuited to my country. Monarchy and aristocracy, valuable and useful as I think them, are still valuable and useful as means, and not as ends. The end of government is the happiness of the people: and I do not conceive that, in a country like this, the happiness of the people can be promoted by a form of government in which the middle classes place no confidence, and which exists only because the middle classes have no organ by which to make their sentiments known.

. . . The question of Parliamentary Reform is still behind. But signs, of which it is impossible to misconceive the import, do most clearly indicate that, unless that question also be speedily settled, property, and order, and all the institutions of this great monarchy, will be exposed to fearful peril. Is it possible that gentlemen long versed in high political affairs cannot read these signs? Is it possible that they can really believe that the Representative system of England, such as it now is, will last till the year 1860? If not, for what would they have us wait? Would they have us wait merely that we may show to all the world how little we have profited by our own recent experience? Would they have us wait, that we may once again hit the exact point where we can neither refuse with authority, nor concede with grace? Would they have us wait, that the numbers of the discontented party may become larger, its demands higher, its feelings more acrimonious, its organisation more complete? . . .

Have they forgotten how the spirit of liberty in Ireland, debarred from its natural outlet, found a vent by forbidden passages? Have they forgotten how we were forced to indulge the Catholics in all the licence of rebels, merely because we chose to withhold from them the liberties of subjects? Do they wait for associations more formidable than that of the Corn Exchange, for contributions larger than the Rent, for agitators more violent than those who, three years ago, divided with the King and the Parliament the sovereignty of Ireland? Do they wait for that last and most dreadful paroxysm of popular rage, for that last and most cruel test of military fidelity? . . . Turn where we may, within, around, the voice of great events is proclaiming to us, Reform, that you may preserve. Now, therefore, while every thing at home and abroad forebodes ruin to those who persist in a hopeless struggle against the spirit of the age, now, while the crash of the proudest throne of the continent is still resounding in our ears, now, while the roof of a British palace affords an ignominious shelter to the exiled heir of forty kings, now, while we see on every side ancient institutions subverted, and great societies dissolved, now, while the heart of England is still sound, now, while old feelings and old associations retain a power and a charm which may too soon pass away, now, in this your accepted time, now, in this your day of salvation, take counsel, not of prejudice, not of party spirit, not of the ignominious pride of a fatal consistency, but of history, of reason, of the ages which are past, of the signs of this most portentous time. Pronounce in a manner worthy of the expectation with which this great debate has been anticipated, and of the long remembrance which it will leave behind. Renew the youth of the State. Save property, divided against itself. Save the multitude, endangered by its own ungovernable passions. Save the aristocracy, endangered by its own unpopular power. Save the greatest, and fairest, and most highly civilised community that ever existed, from calamities which may in a few days sweep away all the rich heritage of so many ages of wisdom and glory. The danger is terrible. The time is short. If this bill should be rejected, I pray to God that none of those who concur in rejecting it may ever remember their votes with unavailing remorse, amidst the wreck of laws, the confusion of ranks, the spoliation of property, and the dissolution of social order.

Edward Gibbon Wakefield (1796–1862) helped to found the South Australian Association in 1834 and was the London agent of the New Zealand Land Company from 1839 to 1846. In 1829 he wrote the first of a series of "Letters from Sydney" to the Morning Chronicle, a leading London daily, under the name of Robert Yonger, in which he articulated the views of a fictional colonist. The Australian press responded by insisting that its author had never been to Australia.

Edward Gibbon Wakefield, A Letter from Sydney (1833)

As the Australasian settlements are known indifferently by several names, I must introduce the following account of their condition and prospects, by requesting you to understand that, by Australia, I mean the large island of which one half is called New Holland, and the other New South Wales; and that, by Australasia, I mean Australia and all the smaller islands in its neighbourhood, including Van Diemen's Land.

In the first place, I have to give you, in general terms, my opinion of Eastern Australia, and of the prospects which this penal settlement offers to emigrants of a class above "convicts, labourers, mechanics, and desperate or needy men."

. . . The soil of New South Wales is not particularly fertile. The plains of the Ganges, and of the great rivers of China, the lowlands of the West India islands, the swamps of the Gulf of Mexico, and even the marshes of Essex, produce crops of which the people here have no conception; but then, as we are without great masses of alluvial deposit, so are agues and intermittent fevers absolutely unknown. In point of natural fertility, I am inclined to compare this soil to that of France; and I have no doubt that, if the same quantity of agricultural labour as is employed in France, were here bestowed upon an area equal to the French territory, the quantity of produce would fully equal that of France. But hundreds of years must elapse before land, here, will be cultivated as well as in the most barbarous countries of Europe. Having regard, however, only to the natural powers of the soil, this account will probably satisfy you. Timber, coal, iron, and other useful minerals, abound; the harbours and rivers teem with fish; cattle of all sorts thrive and multiply with astonishing rapidity; every fruit that flourishes in Spain and Italy comes to the highest perfection; and Nature fully performs her part in bestowing upon man the necessaries, comforts, and luxuries of life.

. . . I did not, you know, intend to become a farmer. Having fortune enough for all my wants, I proposed to get a large domain, to build a good house, to keep enough land in my own hands for pleasure-grounds, park, and game preserves; and to let the rest, after erecting farm-houses in the most suitable spots. My mansion, park, preserves, and tenants, were all a mere dream. I have not one of them. When, upon my first arrival, I talked of these things to some sensible men, to whom I was recommended, they laughed in my face. I soon found that a house would, though the stone and timber were to be had for nothing, cost three times as much as in England. This was on account of the very high wages required by mechanics; but this was not all. None of the materials of a house, except stone and timber, are produced in the colony. Every pane of glass, every nail, every grain of paint, and every piece of furniture, from the kitchen copper to the drawing-room curtains, must have come from England. My property is at a distance of nearly seventy miles from the sea, and there is no road, but a track through the forest, for two-thirds of that distance. Everything, even the food of the labourers, must have been transported from afar. Log-houses must have been built for the labourers; and the cheapest way of providing for them would have been by the establishment of a farm, in the first instance, to produce enough for their subsistence. Lastly, though none of these obstacles had existed, the whole colony did not contain as many masons, carpenters, glaziers, painters, black and whitesmiths, and other mechanics, as I should have required. You may believe most statements of fact respecting the colony; but beware how you draw conclusions!

Of course, I soon abandoned all thought of building a mansion. As for a park, my whole property was a park, and a preserve for kangaroos and emus. The grand object was to dispark it as soon as possible. I clung for some time to the hope of having tenants; but you will readily see that what deterred me from building a mansion presented numerous obstacles to the erection of farm-houses. Besides, even though I had forced circumstances, and had, at an enormous cost, placed a dozen good homesteads on my land, where was I to find tenants? There is no such class as a tenantry in this country, where every man, who has capital to cultivate a farm, can obtain one of his own for nothing. I soon found that what little my twenty thousand acres had cost me would be entirely lost, unless I turned farmer myself, and endeavoured, by my own exertions, with the assistance of convict servants, to extract something from the soil. Believe statements of fact—but beware how you draw conclusions!

Settling

I bore my disappointment as well as could be expected; and, to use a colonial phrase, "took boldly to the bush." I dare say you fancy that it was very agreeable, but I assure you that it was not. The novelty of the thing pleased me at first; but I soon tired of the clear Italian sky, the noble forests, and the sublime solitude of the untrodden wilderness. People in a highly civilized country, like England, are not aware of their own wants. The wants exist, but most of them are supplied as soon as they are formed. In England, when you want to eat, you eat, and there is an end of the want; when you are sleepy, you go to bed; when your clothes are wet, you change them; when you are tired of talking, you take a book; and when you are tired of reading, you begin to talk. But, in the desert, almost every want is severely felt before it is supplied. Everything, from the very beginning, has either to be created or brought from a great distance. Try to reckon the number of your physical wants, which are every day supplied without any effort on your part, and you may form some idea of the physical deprivations of a settler. As for mental wants, talking and reading are out of the question, except it be to scold your servants, and to con over a Sydney newspaper, which contains little else but the miserable party politics of this speck upon the globe, reports of crime and punishment, and low-lived slang and flash, such as fill the pot-house Sunday papers of London.

However, the settler's attention is pretty well diverted from his wants, physical and mental, by the necessity of watching over his property. I bought herds and flocks, horses, ploughs, carts, carpenters' tools, and all sorts of implements of husbandry. My only servants were convicts. My own man, who had served me for eight years in England, and had often sworn that he would go the wide world over with me, seeing that I was the best of masters, never reached my new abode. He had saved about £150 in my service; and I had advised him to take the money out of a London Savings' Bank, under an idea that he might obtain ten percent for it at Sydney. He followed my advice. About a month after our arrival I missed him one morning. Before night I received a letter, by which he informed me that he had taken a grant of land near Hunter's River, and that he "hoped we parted friends." He is now one of the most consequential persons in the Colony, has grown enormously fat, feeds upon greasy dainties, drinks oceans of bottled porter and port wine, damns the Governor, and swears by all his gods, Jupiter, Jingo, and Old Harry, that this Colony must soon be independent.

But to return to my convicts. One of them was a London pickpocket, and a more mischievous animal I never had to contend with. The others were country bumpkins, transported for poaching, whom I had obtained with much trouble, supposing that they would serve my turn much better than Londoners; but if they were better able to work than the cockney, they were not a bit more willing. Perhaps he corrupted them; but, be this as it may, they altogether led me the life of a dog. My sheep and cows were continually lost, and it was nobody's fault; my effects were often stolen, though most of them could be of no use to the thieves. I grumbled and threatened; but these men, all round, declared their innocence, and called Heaven to witness that they had not wronged me of a "dump." I stopped some of their extra allowance until the goods should be produced. No more work was done; one was ill—another had hurt his hand—a third "would see me damned first"—and there was I, planted, as the French say, at the distance of twelve miles from any sort of assistance. It seemed necessary, however, to quell this rebellion. I rode, therefore, to the magistrate, got a constable, and sent the whole gang to prison; but the next day I was but too glad to fetch them back; for harvest had just begun, and my maize would have rotted on the ground, had I been long deprived of their labour, such as it was. I might have had them flogged, or, in colonial language, had "their backs scarified," whereby I should have punished them without losing their labour. This is the ordinary, because the most economical, mode of correcting our slaves; but, thanks to Fortune, I was not compelled to adopt it, being rich enough to indulge some foolish sentiments of tenderness and respect for all my fellow-creatures, not to mention tenderness and respect for myself. A necessary consequence, however, of this my abstract humanity and selfish pride, was, that I became the slave of my slaves. Can you imagine a more hateful existence? Meanwhile, I had built a house—so called here, but, properly speaking, a shed. It is well I have abstained from marriage. What should I have done for a delicate woman, bound to me by sacred ties? And if I had had children, and those children had happened to be daughters? Why, I should have done like others, who carry women and children out of civilized society to inhabit the wilderness. I should have made my tender wife a drudge, and my children little savages. Could 20,000 acres of valueless desert have compensated for such misery?

Disgusted with my convict servants, I sent to England for shepherds, ploughmen, carpenters, a blacksmith, a bricklayer, and other useful labourers. The men arrived in high spirits, having been hired from a part of the country where I was well known, and having, most of them, worked for me in England. They knew that they could depend on the high wages that my English agent had promised them; their passage had been paid for by me; and the sailors had told them that in New South Wales they would live like fighting cocks. Being in the desert when I received notice of their arrival, I hastened to Sydney, having first got rid of my convicts, for fear that they should contaminate the new-comers. The latter, who, my Sydney agent informed me, had, when they were put ashore, spoken in raptures of the 'Squire, received me with gloomy looks. They were already contaminated, notwithstanding my precaution. One of them, a harness-maker from Salisbury, acted as spokesman for the party, and told me flatly that they had been imposed on. I stared, and asked in what respect?—"They had not been told," he said, "what high wages a man could get in New South Wales—they were told now they could not live on the wages which had been promised them, and they hoped I should take their case into my consideration." I had not bound them by indentures, for I was weak enough to think that free agents would prove better servants than bondsmen. I desired them to "take into their consideration" the cost of their passage; but in the long discussion that ensued, they carefully avoided that point, and dwelt with dogged pertinacity on the wages which honest men, like them, could obtain at or near Sydney. I was completely in their power. By dint of flattery, appeals to their honour, and promises of comfort, I induced the mere peasants to observe their agreement and follow me to the wilds; but the mechanics were impracticable. They had already engaged with masters at Sydney and Parramatta, at double the high wages that I had promised; and I could make no impression on them. I retired to the woods with my clodhoppers, whom I found very serviceable during a whole year; but at the end of that time they began to grumble and fidget. Other persons had settled in my neighbourhood. Some of these had been convicts, and afterwards emancipated servants. They persuaded my men to become settlers also. In less than two years each of my servants saved wherewith to stock a small farm, and one by one they all left me. At last I was glad to obtain a fresh supply of convicts. Under these circumstances, my estate did not produce largely. My herds and flocks, however, had rapidly multiplied: and in the last year of which I speak, I reaped one hundred and forty acres of corn. This was thought immense doings; but as my free labourers were gone, I had no such prospect for the future; and as for the flocks, their increase in number was not a proportionate increase of property to me. The wool produced something; but the flesh was worth nothing, unless taken to market, and then it would scarcely repay the cost of the journey. Here, there are no drovers or jobbers in cattle to come between the farmer and the butcher. In short, there is little division of labour, and you may roll in plenty, without possessing anything of exchangeable value. You must do almost everything yourself; and flocks in the wilderness are not worth much more than the wilderness itself, of which you may obtain nearly any quantity for all but nothing. Under an idea that cheese would be easily transported, and would fetch a good price in Sydney, I thought at one time of establishing a dairy. But I ought to have known better.

My cows were as wild as hyenas, and almost as wicked. I had no milkmaids, no dairy-women, no churns, no any thing that was wanted for the purpose; and, above all, I wanted industry, skill, economy, and taste, for any such pursuits, or, at least, a drudge of a wife to supply those wants. At length my impatience got the better of a certain stupid vanity that had led me to fancy myself qualified to become a settler. I wrote to my friends at Sydney acknowledging that I was sick of the bush, and that their prophecies of my ill success had been fulfilled to the letter. By their assistance I made over my estate for twenty years, with everything upon it, to a tough Scotch farmer, on condition of receiving one-third of its produce. This third produces me less than 3 per cent interest on what I have expended; but I am, comparatively speaking, a happy man, living upon my English income, in a place where at least books, and men and women, such as they are, are not quite wanting, and where money will supply the more pressing wants of civilized life.

<hr>

Convict Experiences (1837–38)

The passages below are taken from the *Report of Select Committee on Transportation*, 1837–38, and detail conditions on the chain gang, in the penal settlements, and in the experience of transportation in the Antipodes.

<hr>

The Chain Gang

In 1834 the number of convicts in the chain-gangs of New South Wales was about 1,000, and in those of Van Diemen's Land in 1837 about 700; this description of punishment is a very severe one. Sir G. Arthur said, "as severe a one as could be inflicted on man." Sir R. Bourke stated, "that the condition of the convicts in the chain-gangs was one of great privation and unhappiness." They are locked up from sunset to sunrise in the caravans or boxes used for this description of persons, which hold from 20 to 28 men, but in which the whole number can neither stand upright nor sit down at the same time (except with their legs at right angles to their bodies), and which, in some instances, do not allow more than 18 inches in width for each individual to lie upon on the bare boards, they are kept to work under a strict military guard during the day, and liable to suffer flagellation for trifling offences, such as an exhibition of obstinacy, insolence, and the like; being in chains, discipline is more easily preserved amongst them, and escape more easily prevented than among road-parties out of chains. This description of punishment belongs to a barbarous age, and merely tends to increase the desperation of the character of an offender. The nature of the duty imposed upon the military in guarding the chain gangs has the worst effects upon the character and discipline of the soldiers. Colonel Breton, who commanded a regiment in New South Wales, stated to Your Committee, that it produced the greatest demoralization among the troops, and the men became reckless; the demoralization arose, he said, partly from drunkenness, of which there was much amongst the troops in that country; he had no less than 16 soldiers transported to Norfolk Island, all of them from being drunk on sentry; demoralization was likewise produced amongst the troops by their intercourse with the prison population, which could not be prevented, because many of the men found their fathers, brothers, and other relations, amongst the convicts.

Penal Settlements

For crimes of greater magnitude convicts are re-transported. The penal settlements of New South Wales are Norfolk Island and Moreton Bay; at the former, the number of convicts in 1837 were about 1,200; in the same year the number at Moreton Bay did not exceed 300, as the establishment there has been considerably diminished, and only offenders under short sentences were sent there. Moreton Bay is likewise a place of punishment for convict females, who are re-transported for offences committed in the colony. The number of convicts at the penal settlement of Van Diemen's Land, Port Arthur was, in 1835, 1,172. Norfolk Island is a small and most beautiful volcanic island, situated in the midst of the ocean, 1,000 miles from the eastern shores of Australia, and inaccessible, except in one place, to boats. Port Arthur is on a small and sterile peninsula, of about 100,000 acres, connected with Van Diemen's Land by a narrow neck of land, which is guarded, day and night, by soldiers, and by a line of fierce dogs. All communications, except of an official nature, between these places and the settled districts are strictly forbidden; the penal settlements of Norfolk Island and Port Arthur are inhabited solely by the convicts and their keepers. "The work appointed for the convicts," to use the expression of the chief superintendent of convicts in Van Diemen's Land, "is of the most incessant and galling description the settlement can produce; and any disobedience of orders, turbulence or other misconduct is instantaneously punished by the lash."

The condition of the convicts in these settlements has been shown to Your Committee to be one of unmitigated wretchedness. Sir Francis Forbes, chief-justice of Australia, stated, in a letter to Mr. Amos on the subject of transportation, that "The experience furnished by these penal settlements has proved that transportation is capable of being carried to an extent of suffering such as to render death desirable, and to induce many prisoners to seek it under its most appalling aspects." And the same gentleman, in his evidence before Your Committee, said, "that he had known many cases in which it appeared that convicts at Norfolk Island had committed crimes which subjected them to execution, for the mere purpose of being sent up to Sydney; and the cause of their desiring to be so sent was to avoid the state of endurance under which they were placed in Norfolk Island; that he thought, from the expressions they employed, that they contemplated the certainty of execution; that he believed they deliberately preferred death, because there was no chance of escape, and they stated they were weary of life, and would rather go to Sydney and be hanged." Sir Francis Forbes likewise mentioned the case of several men at Norfolk Island cutting the heads of their fellow prisoners with a hoe while at work, with a certainty of being detected, and with a certainty of being executed; and according to him, they acted in this manner apparently without malice, and with very slight excitement, stating they knew they should be hanged, but it was better than being where they were. A similar case was mentioned by the Rev. Henry Stiles, in his Report to Sir Richard Bourke on the state of Norfolk Island. And

Sir George Arthur assured Your Committee that similar cases had recently occurred at Port Arthur. Sir Francis Forbes was then asked, "What good do you think is produced by the infliction of so horrible a punishment in Norfolk Island; and upon whom do you think it produces good?" His answer was, "That he thought that it did not produce any good;" and that, "If it were to be put to himself, he should not hesitate to prefer death, under any form that it could be presented to him, rather than such a state of endurance as that of the convicts at Norfolk Island."

Transportation as Slavery

Transportation, though chiefly dreaded as exile, undoubtedly is much more than exile; it is slavery as well; and the condition of the convict slave is frequently a very miserable one; but that condition is unknown, and cannot be made known; for the physical condition of a convict is generally better than that of an agricultural labourer; the former is in most cases better fed and better clothed than the latter; it is the restraint on freedom of action, the degradation of slavery, and the other moral evils, which chiefly constitute the pains of transportation, and of which no description can convey an adequate idea to that class in whom Transportation ought to inspire terror. . . . A criminal sentenced to transportation may be sent to New South Wales, or to Van Diemen's Land, or to Bermuda, or even to Norfolk Island; in each colony a different fate would await him; his chance of enduring pain would be different. In New South Wales, or even under the severer system of Van Diemen's Land, he might be a domestic servant, well fed, well clothed, and well treated by a kind and indulgent master; he might be fortunate in obtaining a ticket of leave, or a conditional pardon, and finish his career by accumulating considerable wealth. Or he may be the wretched . . . slave of some harsh master, compelled by the lash to work, until driven to desperation, he takes to the bush, and is shot down like a beast of prey; or for some small offence is sent to work in chains, or to a penal settlement, where having suffered till he can endure no longer, he commits murder in order that he may die. Between these extremes of comfort and misery, there are innumerable gradations of good and evil, in which the lot of the convict may be cast. But even if all this were known to the evil-disposed, as well known, as it is to all, who have perused the Evidence taken before Your Committee, the uncertainty of the punishment would destroy its effect, and prevent the suffering, which in many instances is inflicted, from producing apprehension. For it should be carefully borne in mind, that punishment is meant for those persons, who are inclined to evil, and its effects are to be estimated with regard to them alone. Now, the mind of a person disposed to commit a crime is precisely that of a gambler; he dwells with satisfaction on every favourable chance, overlooks every adverse one, and believes that that event will happen, which is most in accordance with his wishes. He hopes, that, if he commit a crime, he will escape detection; that, if detected, he will escape conviction; that, if convicted, he will be pardoned or get off with a few years in the hulks or Penitentiary; that, if transported, he will be sent to New South Wales; that if sent to New South Wales, he will be as well off, as are some of his acquaintances, and make a fortune. It is by diminishing the number of chances in the criminal's favour, not by increasing the amount of contingent evil; in other words, it is far more by the certainty, than by the severity of punishment, that apprehension is produced, and thus Transportation sins against the first and acknowledged principles of penal legislation.

———

Macaulay (see p. 7) was head of the Indian Law Commission from 1835 to 1838. In his now infamous Minute on Education, designed as part of a debate about government responsibility for colonial education, he argued that "we must at present do our best to form . . . a class of persons, Indian in blood and colour, but English in taste, in opinions, in morals, and in intellect."

———

Thomas Babington Macaulay, Minute on Education in India (1835)

As it seems to be the opinion of some of the gentlemen who compose the Committee of Public Instruction, that the course which they have hitherto pursued was strictly prescribed by the British Parliament in 1813, and as, if that opinion be correct, a legislative act will be necessary to warrant a change, I have thought it right to refrain from taking any part in the preparation of the adverse statements which are now before us, and to reserve what I had to say on the subject till it should come before me as a member of the Council of India.

It does not appear to me that the Act of Parliament can, by any art of construction, be made to bear the meaning which has been assigned to it. It contains nothing about the particular languages or sciences which are to be studied. A sum is set apart "for the revival and promotion of literature and the encouragement of the learned natives of India, and for the introduction and promotion of a knowledge of the sciences among the inhabitants of the British territories." It is argued, or rather taken for granted, that by literature, the Parliament can have meant only Arabic and Sanskrit literature, that they never would have given the honorable appellation of 'a learned native' to a native who was familiar with the poetry of Milton, the Metaphysics of Locke, and the Physics of Newton; but that they meant to designate by that name only such persons as might have studied in the sacred books of the Hindoos all the uses of cusa-grass, and all the mysteries of absorption into the Deity. This does not appear to be a very satisfactory interpretation. To take a parallel case; suppose that the Pacha of Egypt, a country once superior in knowledge to the nations of Europe, but now sunk far below them, were to appropriate a sum for the purpose of 'reviving and promoting literature, and encouraging learned natives of Egypt,' would anybody infer that he meant the youth of his pachalic to give years to the study of hieroglyphics, to search into all the doctrines disguised under the fable of Osiris, and to ascertain with all possible accuracy the ritual with which cats and onions were anciently adored? Would he be justly charged with inconsistency, if, instead of employing his young subjects in deciphering obelisks, he were to order them to be instructed in the English and French languages, and in all the sciences to which those languages are the chief keys?

. . . The admirers of the Oriental system of education . . . conceive that the public faith is pledged to the present system, and that to alter the appropriation of any of the funds which have hitherto been spent in encouraging the study of Arabic and Sanskrit, would be down-right spoliation. It is not easy to understand by what process of reasoning they can have arrived at this conclusion. The grants which are made from the public purse for the encouragement of literature differed in no respect from the grants which are made from the same purse for other objects of real or supposed utility. We found a sanatarium on a spot which we suppose to be healthy. Do we thereby pledge ourselves to keep a sanatarium there, if the result should not answer our expectation? We commence the erection of a pier. Is it a violation of the public faith to stop the works, if we afterwards see reason to believe that the building will be useless? The rights of property are undoubtedly sacred. But nothing endangers those rights so much as the practice, now unhappily too common, of attributing them to things to which they do not belong. Those who would impart to abuses the sanctity of property are in truth imparting to the institution of property the unpopularity and the fragility of abuses. If the Government has given to any person a formal assurance; nay, if the Government has excited in any person's mind a reasonable expectation that he shall receive a certain income as a teacher or a learner of Sanskrit or Arabic, I would respect that person's pecuniary interests—I would rather err on the side of liberality to individuals than suffer the public faith to be called in question. But to talk of a Government pledging itself to teach certain languages and certain sciences, though those languages may become useless, though those sciences may be exploded, seems to me quite unmeaning. There is not a single word in any public instructions, from which it can be inferred that the Indian Government ever intended to give any pledge on this subject, or ever considered the destination of these funds as unalterably fixed. But had it been otherwise, I should have denied the competence of our predecessors to bind us by any pledge on such a subject. Suppose that a Government had in the last century enacted in the most solemn manner that all its subjects should, to the end of time, be inoculated for the small-pox: would that Government be bound to persist in the practice after Jenner's discovery? These promises, of which nobody claims the performance, and from which nobody can grant a release; these vested rights, which vest in nobody; this property without proprietors; this robbery, which makes nobody poorer, may be comprehended by persons of higher faculties than mine.—I consider this plea merely as a set form of words, regularly used both in England and in India, in defence of every abuse for which no other plea can be set up.

The fact that the Hindoo law is to be learned chiefly from Sanskrit books, and the Mahomedan law from Arabic books, has been much insisted on, but seems not to bear at all on the question. We are commanded by Parliament to ascertain and digest the laws of India. The assistance of a law Commission has been given to us for that purpose. As soon as the code is promulgated, the Shasters and the Hedaya will be useless to a Moonsiff or Sudder Ameen. I hope and trust that before the boys who are now entering at the Madrassa and the Sanskrit college have completed their studies, this great work will be finished. It would be manifestly absurd to educate the rising generation with a view to a state of things which we mean to alter before they reach manhood.

But there is yet another argument which seems even more untenable. It is said that Sanskrit and Arabic are the languages in which the sacred books of a hundred millions of people are written, and that they are, on that account, entitled to peculiar encouragement. Assuredly it is the duty of the British Government in India to be not only tolerant, but neutral on all religious questions. But to encourage the study of a literature admitted to be of small intrinsic value, only because that literature inculcates the most serious errors on the most important subjects, is a course hardly reconcilable with reason, with morality, or even with that very neutrality which ought, as we all agree, to be sacredly preserved. It is confessed that a language is barren of useful knowledge. We are to teach it because it is fruitful of monstrous superstitions. We are to teach false History, false Astronomy, false Medicine, because we find them in company with a false religion. We abstain, and I trust shall always abstain, from giving any public encouragement to those who are engaged in the work of converting natives to Christianity. And while we act thus, can we reasonably and decently bribe men out of the revenues of the state to waste their youth in learning how they are to purify themselves after touching an ass, or what text of the Vedas they are to repeat to expiate the crime of killing a goat?

It is taken for granted by the advocates of Oriental learning, that no native of this country can possibly attain more than a mere smattering of English. They do not attempt to prove this; but they perpetually insinuate it. They designate the education which their opponents recommend as a mere spelling book education. They assume it as undeniable, that the question is between a profound knowledge of Hindoo and Arabian literature and science on the one side, and a superficial knowledge of the rudiments of English on the other. This is not merely an assumption, but an assumption contrary to all reason and experience. We know that foreigners of all nations do learn our language sufficiently to have access to all the most abstruse knowledge which it contains, sufficiently to relish even the more delicate graces of our most idiomatic writers. There are in this very town natives who are quite competent to discuss political or scientific questions with fluency and precision in the English language. I have heard the very question on which I am now writing discussed by native gentlemen with a liberality and an intelligence which would do credit to any member of the Committee of Public Instruction. Indeed it is unusual to find, even in the literary circles of the continent, any foreigner who can express himself in English with so much facility and correctness as we find in many Hindoos. Nobody, I suppose, will contend that English is so difficult to a Hindoo as Greek to an Englishman. Yet an intelligent English youth, in a much smaller number of years than our unfortunate pupils pass at the Sanskrit college, becomes able to read, to enjoy, and even to imitate, not unhappily, the compositions of the best Greek Authors. Less than half the time which enables an English youth to read Herodotus and Sophocles, ought to enable a Hindoo to read Hume and Milton.

To sum up what I have said, I think it clear that . . . we are not fettered by any pledge expressed or implied; that we are free to employ our funds as we choose; that we ought to employ them in teaching what is best worth knowing; that English is better worth knowing than Sanskrit or Arabic; that the natives are desirous to be taught English, and are not desirous to be taught Sanskrit or Arabic; that neither as the languages of law, nor as the languages of religion, have the Sanskrit and Arabic any peculiar claim to our engagement; that it is possible to make natives of this country thoroughly good English scholars, and that to this end our efforts ought to be directed.

In one point I fully agree with the gentlemen to whose general views I am opposed. I feel with them, that it is impossible for us, with our limited means, to attempt to educate the body of the people. We must at present do our best to form a class who may be interpreters between us and the millions whom we govern; a class of persons, Indian in blood and colour, but English in taste, in opinions, in morals, and in intellect. To that class we may leave it to refine the vernacular dialects of the country, to enrich those dialects with terms of science borrowed from the Western nomenclature, and to render them by degrees fit vehicles for conveying knowledge to the great mass of the population.

Sidney and Beatrice Webb (1859–1947 and 1858–1943, respectively) were early members of the Fabian Society and were committed to collectivist ideals and the gradual evolution of a so-cialist society in Britain. They drafted the Minority Report of the Royal Commission on Poor Laws (on which Beatrice served, 1905–1909). Their account of Poor Law reform is valuable for the contemporary sources it cites around the eighteenth and nineteenth century debates, as well as for their belief that the monies paid out for poor relief were "but a modest premium against a social revolution."

Sidney and Beatrice Webb, from *English Poor Law History*, v. 1 (1929)

To the propertied class in the first quarter of the nineteenth century the foremost scan-dal of the English Poor Law was its steadily rising cost. The annual expenditure by the Local Authorities on the relief of destitution, which had risen from two millions sterling in 1784 to four millions in 1803, gradually mounted in the next ten years to over six and a half millions; and in 1818 it reached, exceptionally, nearly eight millions. To a generation unaccustomed to public expenditure, such a sum seemed stupendous. It worked out at 13s. 3d. a year for every inhabitant—man, woman and child—and nearly equalled the entire peace expenditure of the National Government (apart from the bur-den of debt) in all its civil departments, omitting the army and navy . . . the rates were exacted, not from those who were receiving the rapidly rising rents, royalties and prof-its, but, in accordance with the Elizabethan legislation, from "every occupier of lands, houses, tithes . . . or appropriations of tithes, coalmines and saleable underwoods;" in-cluding, therefore, the farmer with the innkeeper and the village blacksmith or shop-keeper, the rector or vicar in his glebe with the squire in his park, each in proportion to the assessed annual value of his holding. Even more unequal and oppressive was the local incidence of the parochial rates. The fifteen thousand separate parishes and townships, each one having to maintain its own poor, varied in area from a few score acres to thirty or forty square miles; in the number of inhabitants, from a few dozen to tens of thou-sands of households; in financial resources, from a barren common to the densely con-gregated residences, shops, banks, warehouses and wharves of the parishes in the City of London. . . . Hence, whilst the more prosperous manufacturing districts often escaped with a Poor Rate of a few shillings, rates were rising in rural parishes to over twenty shillings, and, in a few instances, to as much as thirty shillings in the pound; thus in-volving not infrequently a payment to the rate-collector that exceeded the total sum levied by the landlord and the tithe-owner themselves.

The Inadequacy of the Relief

To the general body of wage-earners, comprising five-sixths of the whole community, the scandal of the Poor Law seemed to be the insufficiency of the relief afforded to those brought down to destitution. . . . if we [consider] the hosiery workers, the handloom weavers and other operatives in course of supersession by new machinery, or thrown out of employment by the recurring slumps of trade dependent on production for a world market, we see them in a condition of constant indigence, misery and helplessness, all the more striking from its contrast with the affluence characteristic of the growing class of capitalist employers. The "National Dividend" was, indeed, rising by leaps and bounds. In these very decades the number of persons productively employed was steadily increasing; the new machine-industry, especially in textile manufactures and every kind of engineering, was enormously augmenting the output of commodities; the mines of coal, ironstone, copper, lead and tin were annually producing a larger supply of the materials which industry was fashioning for the most varied service; the system of internal transport was reaching, by canals and turnpike roads, an efficiency in speed and regularity never before dreamed of; agricultural improvements were yielding an ever-growing food supply; an extremely profitable exchange of commodities between England and the countries of North and South America, India and the Far East, the Baltic and the Mediterranean was continually enlarging the market of the British manufacturer; whilst the rapidly extending commerce of the whole world was being carried, in the main, by British ships, was being organised principally by the merchants of London and Liverpool, Bristol and Glasgow, and was being financed and insured almost exclusively by British bankers and British underwriters. All this meant, in the first quarter of the nineteenth century, in spite of the losses of the Napoleonic War, an aggregate production of wealth to the nation as a whole which, although comparative statistics are lacking, must have far surpassed, per head of population, anything that the world had ever before witnessed. . . . When we remember that the statisticians estimate the nation's annual income in the third decade of the century at somewhere about three or four hundred millions sterling, and that there were, at the time, no public services other than those of the Poor Law available for the five-sixths of the community who were wage-earners, the payment of seven or eight millions annually—being no more than two per cent of the total—will seem but a modest premium against a social revolution.

. . . The revolutionary changes in Poor Law policy, and in the structure of Local Government, brought about by the Poor Law Amendment Act of 1834, were, however, not the outcome of mere fear, anger and greed on the part of the propertied classes. This deliberately planned and persistently executed social reform was rooted in theories firmly held by a new school of thought then dominant among the ablest and most enlightened members of the ruling class. The leading tenets of this school of thought, so far as they concerned the treatment of the poor, may be easily summarised.

1. That the public relief of destitution out of funds raised by taxation—as distinguished from the alms of the charitable—devitalised the recipients, degraded their character and induced in them general bad behaviour.

2. That the operation of the Malthusian Law of Population, accentuated by the Theory of a Wage Fund, rendered all such relief not only futile in diminishing the miseries of the poor, but actually harmful in the creation of a wider pool of destitution.

3. That it was imperative for the National Government to direct and control the action of the Local Authorities, so as to impose on them a policy calculated to bring about the "greatest good of the greatest number"

. . . It was not until the general demobilisation on the Peace of 1815, and the extensive unemployment involved in the ensuing slump in trade, that we find any considerable expression of opinion in favour of the abolition of all compulsory provision for the poor in order to allow the fullest possible scope for voluntary charity. The chief propagandist in this movement was the Rev. Thomas Chalmers, the famous Scottish Presbyterian minister, who regarded himself as a political economist, and was much honoured by the Court and the aristocracy. From his voluminous writings we quote the following: "Now, it should be recollected, that it has all along been our main object to show, that the poor-laws of England are the result of a very bungling attempt on the part of the Legislature, to do that which would have been better done had Nature been left to her own free processes, and man to the unconstrained influence of such principles as Nature and Christianity have bestowed upon him. We affirm, that the great and urgent law of self-preservation ought not to have been so tampered with; that the instincts of relationship ought not to have been so impeded in their operation; that the sympathies, and the attentions of neighbourhood, ought not to have been so superseded; that the powerful workings of generous and compassionate feeling ought not to have been so damped and discouraged, as they have in fact been by this artificial and uncalled-for process of interference." But Dr. Chalmers did not stand alone. Many of the most experienced of English administrators of the Poor Law were of the same opinion. Thus Thomas Walker, who was a prominent Poor Law reformer, stigmatised pauperism as a disease of society which must be rooted out in order to save the nation from bankruptcy: "Pauperism, in the legal sense of the word, is a state of dependence upon parochial provision. That provision, so far as it is necessary to supply the demand for labour, is a tax upon wages; beyond that amount, it is a tax upon property, and operates as a bounty to improvidence. Where labourers, with an ordinary degree of prudence, cannot maintain themselves and their families without parochial relief, such relief is part of their own wages, kept back to be doled out to them as emergency requires. . . . With respect to that celebrated statute 43rd Elizabeth, the leading one on the subject, it would have been difficult, a priori, to have shown its defects, or even to have withheld that approbation which till latterly has been universally bestowed upon it. But the principle is assuredly erroneous: it is the admission of a Moral Pestilence, to which it is in vain to say—'thus far only shalt thou go'. It never has been—it cannot be—confined to infancy, age, or infirmity; to morbid subjects, or to obscure quarters—it attacks and paralyses the young and the vigorous—it seizes whole families—it becomes hereditary—it pervades the city and the fields—it is found in the most flourishing, as well as in the poorest districts, and, as long as it is permitted to infest the land, it will have its periods of devastating violence" . . .

We pass to the consideration of the second article of faith contributing to the initiation and general acceptance of the Poor Law legislation of 1834: the famous "Principle of Population," from which was deduced the dogma that any relief of destitution, far from diminishing the miseries of the poor, was actually harmful in the creation of a still wider morass of poverty.

We need not inquire too curiously as to the paternity of this principle, seeing that, in so far as the development of the English Poor Law is concerned, the author was without doubt the Rev. T. R. Malthus. As originally stated, this Principle of Population consisted of two premises: (1) "that food is necessary to the existence of man; (2) that the passion between the sexes is necessary and will remain in its present state." "These two laws," he continues, "ever since we have had any knowledge of mankind, appear to have been fixed laws of our nature; and, as we have not hitherto seen any alteration in them, we have no right to conclude that they will ever cease to be what they now are, without an immediate act of power in that Being who first arranged the system of the universe; and for the advantage of His creatures, still exercises according to fixed laws, all

His various operations." But there was a third premiss to the Malthusian theory of population; a premiss derived from a study of the past history of the human race. Whilst there was no practical limit to the multiplication of the human species except the attainable amount of food, there were limits, and limits which would be rapidly reached, to the capacity of the extra men to extract additional food from the earth's surface. Following the topical fashion of political arithmetic, Malthus gave a quantitative expression to this "law"; population increases in a geometrical ratio, whilst subsistence lags behind according to an arithmetical ratio, with the consequence that population presses, and always will press, closely on subsistence. The only checks to this tragic tendency are famine, war and pestilence, or, to state it in a more general way, vice and misery. "The view which he gives of human life," the author writes in the third person in his preface to the first edition, "has a melancholy hue; but he feels conscious that he has drawn these dark tints from a conviction that they are really in the picture, and not from a jaundiced eye or inherent spleen of disposition."

It thus followed logically that any relief of destitution, whether by compulsory or by voluntary charity, in adding to the temporary subsistence of the poor, merely enabled them to multiply their numbers, and therefore failed to diminish their poverty. . . .

This gloomy forecast of the inevitable misery, past, present and future, of the workers of all countries and all races, shocked public opinion by throwing doubts on the beneficence of an all-powerful Creator. Hence, in the second edition of the Essay on the Principle of Population, published in 1803, Malthus introduced a third check on increase, namely, moral restraint; that is, abstinence from propagation unless means of subsistence for the prospective child are clearly available. "One of the principal reasons," we are told by Malthus in subsequent editions, "which have prevented an assent to the doctrine of the constant tendency of population to increase beyond the means of subsistence, is a great unwillingness to believe that the Deity would by the laws of nature bring beings into existence, which by the laws of nature could not be supported in that existence. . . . If it appear that, by a strict obedience to the duties pointed out to us by the light of nature and reason, and confirmed and sanctioned by revelation, these evils may be avoided, the objection will, I trust, be removed, and all apparent imputation on the goodness of the Deity be done away with." This ray of hope does not seem to have altered the effect of the Principle of Population on the controversy about the Poor Law. Thus, in the Letter to Samuel Whitbread, M.P., on his proposed Bill for the Amendment of the Poor Laws, Malthus objects that "The compulsory provision for the poor in this country has, you will allow, produced effects which follow almost necessarily from the principle of population. The mere pecuniary consideration of the rapid increase of the rates of late years, though a point on which much stress has been laid, is not that which I consider as of the greatest importance; but the cause of this rapid increase, the increasing proportion of the dependent poor, appears to me to be a subject as truly alarming, as in some degree to threaten the extinction of all honourable feeling and spirit among the lower ranks of society, and to degrade and depress the condition of a very large and most important part of the community. . . . It is your object, and I trust that of the nation, to diminish the proportion of dependent poverty, and not to increase it; but the specific evil I fear from your Bill, as it stands at present, is an increase of it." And in his speech on the Poor Laws in the House of Commons (February 1807) Samuel Whitbread acknowledges the influence of Malthus in creating a great revolution in public opinion. "Till within a very few years of the period in which I am speaking, the 43rd of Elizabeth was, if I may be allowed the expression, considered as the bible on this subject. Many persons observing the rapid increase of the bur-thens imposed by that statute, have projected plans of reform, and the legislature has adopted many new Acts: but they have all proceeded upon the same principle. No one ever ventured to surmise that the system itself was radically defective and vicious. . . . One philosopher in particular has arisen amongst us, who has gone deeply into the causes of our present situation. I mean Mr. Malthus. His work upon Population has, I believe, been very generally read; and it has completed that change of opinion with re-gard to the poor laws, which had before been in some measure begun. . . . This philosopher has delivered it as his opinion, that the poor laws have not only failed in their object, but that they have been productive of much more wretchedness than would have existed without them: that 'though they may have alleviated a little the in-tensity of individual misfortune, they have spread the evil over a larger surface'. Many persons, agreeing in this position, have wished that the whole system was well ex-punged from our statute book; and perhaps I should not go too far in saying, that such is the prevailing sentiment." "Of all the applications of the doctrine of Malthus," says . . . [one] student of his work, "their application to pauperism was probably, at the time, of the greatest public interest. . . . These three chapters in the later Essay on Pop-ulation have influenced public opinion and legislation about the destitute poor almost as powerfully as the Wealth of Nations has influenced commercial policy. Malthus is the father, not only of the new Poor Law, but of all our latter-day societies for the or-ganisation of charity."

Harriet Martineau (1802–76) was a reformer and public intellectual with a wide variety of in-terests (see also below). Her *Poor Laws and Paupers Illustrated* captures some of the dynamics of the pre-reform Poor Law system (of which she was a supporter) and offers a fictional glimpse into relations between the overseer, the squire, and the petitioner for relief.

Harriet Martineau, from *Poor Laws and Paupers Illustrated* (1833)

Pay Day at Thorpe.

"Bless me, squire! what brings you here, I wonder?" exclaimed farmer Goldby, on squire Manning taking his stand opposite to Donkin, the overseer, who was preparing to pay the paupers, to whom the doors were about to be thrown open. "I thought, squire, that you and I saw enough of these people at home, and that you would leave it to Donkin to deal with them to-day."

"I might as well ask what you come for," observed the squire: "but, of course, you will say it is to see how your money goes. You keep a sharp look out upon Donkin, I know, and make him answer for every sixpence he pays away."

"I wish some other people did so too, and then mine would be an easier office than it is," observed Donkin. "Mr. Goldby and I together are a pretty good match for the paupers; but when you come, squire, or, what is the same thing, when you send Woollerton. . . ."

"Aye, Woollerton! Where's Woollerton? That is one of the things I came to ask," observed the squire. "I want to see him."

"You have only to wait a few minutes, if, as is most likely, he happened to see you turn in here. He will be sure to pay his respects to your worship and the people without."

"Poor Woollerton! It seems mighty hard that he should always be sneered at by you overseers, when he gets ready so much of your work to your hand."

"There is no denying that he does that," replied Donkin, laughing. "He and you cut out plenty of work for the overseer."

"Woollerton is in duty bound to do so, if the squire wishes it," observed Goldby. "Who gave *poor* Woollerton his office, hey, squire?"

"The vestry, of course. The vestry made him their clerk, and appointed him his salary. It does not follow that he is at my beck and call because I thought him a fit person to be vestry-clerk. But what I came for is to speak to you about the widow Brand. She has taken an odd fancy into her head. She wants to give up her pay to-day."

"Well, that is an odd fancy," observed Donkin.

"Do let one speak, Mr. Donkin. She comes to me to ask to be rated, that she may open a beer-shop. I tell her she does not know what she is about in undertaking such a thing; and it is my belief that it will be her destruction. What is she to do, I ask her, with half-a-dozen fellows, when they get merry over their beer? much more when they grow quarrelsome. And then her family— . . ."

"O, leave all that to her," cried Goldby. "It is no concern of ours whether she turns out a tipsy customer herself, or gets a stout neighbour to do it. Let us only slip her and her three children off the rate, and she may settle the rest."

The squire felt it his business, whatever Goldby might think, to prevent a poor widow, if he could, from entering upon a speculation which was likely to ruin her and hers, soul, body, and estate. He had hoped to keep the parish free from the nuisance of a beer-shop; but it was in vain to hope that no one else would set one up, if widow Brand did not, now that the notion was abroad that such a thing must answer. But he must make one more attempt to show the widow that she had best "let well alone," and go on respectably and comfortably, as she had done from her husband's death till now; and he looked to Donkin to bear him out in what he said.

Donkin smiled at the idea of the respectability and prosperity of living in part on parish pay, as the widow and her children had done since poor Brand's death. He agreed, however, that, judging of a beer-shop by what beer-shops were in other places, it was a fearful undertaking for a lone woman, with young people who might be corrupted. He was far from desiring to cast her off the rate as he would cast off a stout labourer, and was willing to give her his best advice. Widow Brand, being in waiting outside, was called in.

She came curtseying, and looking by far too bashful to be fit for her proposed occupation. She hoped the gentlemen would not take it ill that she came to give up her pay.

No fear! farmer Goldby assured her; particularly if she proposed to assist the rate instead of living upon it.

She must endeavour to do so, the widow replied, as it was necessary to her undertaking, though there was one of her children—the one whose hand she held—that was likely to be always a burden, and for whom she should be glad to have an allowance still; but she feared that could not be, if she was rated. . . .

"Yes, sir; [Mr. Blogg] is my landlord. He offered me a choice between the middle house of the row, and this one on the common; and I chose this, (though the rent is higher by thirty shillings,) because it has a large room below, where people may sit and take their beer."

"And have a room to knock one another under the table; hey, dame?" added the squire.

"And because," continued Mrs. Brand, "one gets on better with the neighbours if any thing of the nature of a public-house stands apart, in case of such a thing as a quarrel, or of singing that any one might think too loud."

"So you expect some trouble of that sort," observed Donkin. "Since you do, and yet have made up your mind, there is nothing more to be said. But you have done wisely in not taking one of the cottages in the row—at least, if you have made sure of yours being better built and drained."

. . ."You have taken pay for three children, I think," said the overseer to the widow. "You managed to live upon this and your own allowance, and the little you earned."

"Just managed, sir. With one more child I should have been pretty comfortable."

"The devil you would," cried Goldby. "So you and your neighbours have children to be made comfortable out of our pockets."

The widow hoped no offence, and went on to relate that she must dispose of a part of her family, in order to make room for her customers.

"And to get your young people out of harm's way, I hope," observed the squire. "What do you do with your sister? She is so much younger than you, you must re-member, that you ought not to reckon on her being so steady."

"I had that in my mind early, sir; and Jemima has got a very good service with Mrs. Blogg, who takes in washing, and keeps a person always employed under her. Jemima will be there from early in the morning till late at night, when my house will be cleared; so that the only help I have to ask is for my daughter Ruth. If the parish will find her a place, I shall be very glad to be relieved of her."

Farmer Goldby was sure she must want Ruth at home to help her to draw beer, and keep the scores, and clean the house after the many feet that would be going and com-ing; but the widow declared her little son Peter to be equal to a part of this business, and that she must take the rest upon herself, or hire help, rather than run the risk of unfit-ting Ruth for a respectable service, by making so young a girl wait in a beer-shop. Donkin thought the widow was right, and asked Goldby whether he did not want such a girl as Ruth in his kitchen or dairy, adding, that he believed her to be a well conducted, intelligent girl.

"If you would please to ask the governess, sir," interposed the widow, "she would tell you that Ruth is considered a credit to the school; and I am sure you would look long among the children in the workhouse before you would find one that that would make you so good a servant."

Goldby merely replied that he did not want such a servant at present.

"You remember," added Donkin, "you must take your share of the boys and girls who are to be put out next week. It is ten to one that you get such a lass as Ruth."

"And you certainly mean to take charge of her among those who are seeking service?"

"Certainly," the squire decided. "You cannot do less for Mrs. Brand, in consideration of her taking herself and her family off the rates."

"Well, then, as Ruth must be a parish girl, and as I must take a parish girl, I may as well take her instead of standing the chance of a worse. But it is very hard when I have too many servants already; and so my good woman will tell me when she hears of it. Now, mind ye, Donkin, don't put another upon me for a long time to come; for I take this girl purely to serve the parish."

"And me, I am sure, and I own it with many thanks," said the widow, curtseying and withdrawing on the entrance of other persons who had business with the overseer. . . .

—⟊—

According to one historian, "The great potato famine of 1845–49 opened an abyss that swallowed up many husbands of thousands of impoverished Irish people." T. C. Foster was one of many observers who recorded their accounts of the poverty-stricken landscape, registering both his sympathies for and his prejudices about Ireland and the Irish.

—⟊—

T. C. Foster, "Letters on the Condition of the People of Ireland" (1847)

I date my letter from the centre of the hills in the north of Donegal, where, ten years ago, there was not a road,—where scarcely anything but bogs and heather and rocks were to be seen for miles,—where the people held the land in rundale, and did as they liked,—paid no rent, and lived on potatoes and the produce of illicit distillation. I write from the centre of an estate where the subdivision of farms had gone on to such an extent, that about seven years ago it was sold to its present owner, Lord George Hill, on the advice of the then agent of the late owner, who was my informant as to this fact, because the rents were so small and numerous and difficult to collect that they were not worth the expense and trouble of collecting. Yet I now write from an inn as comfortable as any in England,—comforts the value of which you learn doubly to appreciate from the miseries you endure before you arrive here from Donegal, should you be compelled to stop a night on the road. Luxuriant crops surround the inn; industry and cleanliness begin to mark the people; each man has his own squared farm and a decent cottage, and there are good roads. . . . It will be the chief object of my letter to-day to show what landlords of an opposite kind effect; what men who extract as much rent as they can, and never spend a shilling on their estates,—who make no efforts to improve either their tenants or their land,—accomplish in the misery and barbarity of their countrymen, and in the waste of the capabilities of their country.

Let no political partisan—because I will not hesitate to state the truth—take it into his head that I come here to write a tirade against landlords. I intend to give them every credit for all that they may do for the benefit of their estates and of their tenants, whenever I see such examples. I do not think it is the part of a good citizen, or of an honest man, to shield the misdeeds of those who so use their property that they are a curse to their country, and to whom are to be attributed all the social evils under which Ireland groans.

I intend giving you to-day a sketch of my journey from Donegal to this place,—the accuracy of which may be tested by any one who pleases to take the same course. My motive for taking this route was, because I heard in Donegal, and read in the evidence of the Land Commission, that the total neglect and bad management of large tracts of land between this place and Donegal had led to an extent of subdivision of farms and of misery almost unparalleled.

Now, this is not hearsay or imagination. I walked a couple of miles from Glenties amongst the farmers' cottages, with a guide,—the Vice-President of the Poor Law Union there,—and I will shortly describe to you the condition of the farmers, as I had it from their own lips, and noted it down at the time.

The land is not let by the acre, but by what is termed a "cow's grass"—so many "cows' grass" to a farm. A "cow's grass" is a measure of land; usually it means as much mountain grazing-land as will keep a cow during the summer, and as much arable-land as will keep the cow-house in fodder during the winter. The size of the farms varies from six to twenty acres, and larger, by the measurement of acres. The rent of arable-land is about 30s. an acre. It is sandy soil and bog mixed, on a granite rock foundation. The grazing mountain-land is let at about 2s. 6d. an acre. The farmer pays his rent and rates by disposing of his butter, pigs, eggs, beef, hay, and oats,—and milk, when he can sell it. He usually sells the whole of his produce, except potatoes, and in dear seasons even part of his stock of potatoes, and buys meal on credit, in order to pay his rent. . . . If the tenant lives near a town where he can sell his milk he sells that also, and the common drink to their potatoes then is an infusion of pepper—pepper and water, as being more tasty than water. . . . If a farmer is so well off as to have milk to his potatoes, or to be able to buy a few sprats, he is what they term here "thokey"—that is, in independent circumstances. The farmer who gave me this information pays 16l. rent . . . [and] holds seven cows' grass. . . . The grazing is so poor that last year these seven cows produced only two firkins of butter, which he sold for 6l.; he sold two pigs for 5l., and he could hardly tell how he scraped up the rest of the rent from the sale of his oats and some potatoes. This farmer assured me that for the half of this year, whilst his cows gave no milk, he had to subsist on pepper and water and potatoes. He could not afford to eat butter. "Not a bit of bread have I eaten since I was born," said this man; "we must sell the corn and the butter to give to the landlord. I have the largest farm in the district; some don't pay more than 3l. to 5l. rent, and I am as well off as any in the country." This man gave me his name, but did not wish it to be published, as it might do him an injury with the agent. This man also assured me that many of the tenants have no beds, and lie on a "shakedown" of straw or hay on the ground in their cottages, with but a blanket or a rug to cover five or six of the family. "The people," he said, "do what they can to improve, but the landlord does nothing, and they have not the ability to improve. They are tenants at will; and if they improve their rent is raised accordingly at the next valuation. The only good thing we have is plenty of turf to keep us warm. We never taste meat of any kind, or bacon, unless a pig chances to die of some disorder and we cannot sell it, and we would not taste that if we could sell it." I asked him if he would show me the cottage of any small farmer who lived in the way he had described. He took me immediately to the cottages of John and Charles McCabe, who lived across a field close by. I state this case to you because it is a sample of the subdivision which is permitted to go on. The father rented four cows' grass, for which he paid 5l. 10s. rent. He was so pressed by poverty and distress in 1842 that he sold the tenant-right of half his farm for 15l. to another man, who came in, built a cottage, and occupied it as tenant. His son had married, and having a family growing up, he divided the half of his remaining farm with his son, and father and son are now subsisting with their families on a cow's grass of land each. Into these cottages I entered. They were stone-built, and well roofed—but the mud-floor was uneven, damp, and filthy. In one corner was a place for the pig, with a drain from it through the wall to carry off the liquid manure, like a stable. Two chairs, a bedstead of the rudest description, a cradle, a spinning-wheel, and an iron-pot constituted the whole furniture. An inner room contained another rude bedstead; the mud-floor was quite damp. In this room six children slept on loose hay, with one dirty blanket to cover them. The father, mother, and an infant slept in the first room, also on loose hay, and with but one blanket on the bed. The children were running about as nearly naked as possible, dressed in the cast-off rags of the father and mother; the father could not buy them clothes. They had not been to mass for a twelvemonth for want of decent clothes to go in. Both these men assured me that their whole food was potatoes, and if they had a penny to spare they bought salt or a few sprats, but very seldom these. Instead of buying salt they sometimes bought pepper and mixed it with the water they drank. This they called "kitchin"—it gave a flavour to their food. Both cottages were in the same wretched condition, and the rent of the farm had been twice raised; last time from 48s. to 5l. 10s. If their rent was not punctually paid, their cattle and everything they had was immediately distrained. From these men I went to another small farmer's house. He was mowing. His name is Menus McGinty. He has two cows' grass, for which he pays 3l. 8s. There has been no improvement on his farm for the last twenty years; but his rent was recently raised from 2l. 5s. . . .

I [then visited] a village called Labgarroo, containing twenty-four cottages, and almost the whole of its shockingly destitute and half-naked shoeless population immediately swarmed out and surrounded me, begging me to go into their cottages—such of them, at least, as could speak English—and look at their misery. Some thrust scraps of paper into my hands with petitions written on them, praying for assistance to keep them from starving, for medical assistance, to have their rents reduced, and so on: such an assemblage of wretched beggar-like human beings I never saw. Picture to yourself the beggars who sometimes on Sundays lie about the pavements in the streets of London, dressed up to excite commiseration, and who write with a piece of chalk on the flags "I'm starving," and then lay themselves down beside this scrawl crouched up in a violent shivering fit as the people pass them from church, and you have an exact fac-simile of the kind of looking people around me—the tenants of the Marquis of Conyngham! I asked one man—a cobbler—who spoke English, to show me into one or two of the cottages near. I entered that of Nelly Gallagher; she pays 30s. rent for one cow's grass. She was preparing her dinner of potatoes, and—what, think you?—sea-weed. They gather, I was told by some twenty of them (and I saw them using it), a kind of sea-weed called "dillisk," which they dry, and boil as "kitchin" with their potatoes. It boils down to a kind of gluten with the potatoes, and the salt in it, they say, makes the potatoes more palatable. In winter they gather the common sea-weed,—the sea-rack which grows on the rocks,—and which they call "dhoolaman," in Irish, and cutting off the thin leaves at the extremities of the weed, boil these when they cannot get "dillisk," which is a better kind of sea-weed. They showed me how they used it, and above a dozen of them told me the same story; in fact, every one that I asked about it confirmed it. My guide, the coast-guard man, and a respectable seaman, assured me that the tenants on the mainland in the same manner lived on sea-weed part of the year, and that they used it, as he called it, a "kitchin," to make their potatoes more palatable, and in aid of their potato food. Some of these tenants had quantities of land as small as the fourth part of a cow's grass. Their cottages are stone-built, with mud-floors, no chimneys, rarely any furniture in them, usually hay on the floor for a bed, with a rug or old clothes for bed covering. I walked over the whole island and saw many such, and rarely any in the least degree better. There is a Roman Catholic chapel on the island, and a school is talked of being built, but there is not one at present. Some kelp-burning is going on now, and this has helped the people a good deal. At times I was informed, and I can well believe it from what I saw, that their destitution is horrible. They are, however, but a degree worse than the tenants on the mainland opposite. . . .

In this letter to Lord John Russell, the planter William Archibald implores the Tory statesman to extend his "saving hand to the disheartened and sinking planter" whose economic fortunes were in peril in the wake of emancipation. Archibald's detailed plan for improving the lot of English planters revolves around making sugar both more profitable for plantation owners and more affordable for English consumers.

W. A. Archibald, "The Sugar Question" (1847)

. . . To the Right Honorable, the Lord John Russell.
My Lord,

Upwards of twenty years experience as a planter (my family possessing extensive estates in the Island of Porto Rico) and as a refiner, has put me in possession of several very interesting facts, relative to the Sugar question, (learnt by visiting the most important Sugar countries in existence), which facts I take the liberty of laying before your Lordship, believing that a consideration of them may possibly point out to your Lordship, the practical means of realizing the following paramount objects, viz.:—

1. To save the British planter from the danger of ruin to which he will be exposed, by the admission of foreign Sugars.

2. To prevent three-fourths of the estates, in the West Indies, from being thrown out of cultivation, a circumstance now almost certain to occur.

3. To furnish Great Britain with English Sugar, at a price that will probably quadruple the present consumption.

4. To ensure, perhaps, four times the revenue now received from Sugar.

5. To treble the number of English ships now employed in the West India trade.

6. To secure . . . by the free will of the foreign planter, and through the means of the English free labourers, the emancipation of foreign slaves, and the total extinction of the slave trade.

The facts I allude to, my Lord, are these:—

1. That it is a truth, not to be questioned, that the salvation of the British planter, and the preservation of the English West India Colonies from destruction, now depend entirely on the adoption of some improved method of raising the cane, and of manufacturing Sugar.

2. That two formidable obstacles oppose the efforts of the planter, to accomplish those objects, namely:—first—the absence of labourers,—secondly—the want of the means of procuring the necessary machinery for improving and augmenting his produce.

3. That the expense of fitting an estate, with new machinery, being from £7,000 to £10,000—three-fourths of the planters, not having at their disposal even one half of that sum, will be forced to abandon their estates.

4. That so discouraged and alarmed are the West India merchants, that they will advance no money fitting up new machinery, and even now hesitate at sending out the usual supplies.

5. That there is uncultivated land enough, in the British West Indies, (especially in British Guiana, Trinidad, and Jamaica, with what is under cultivation), to furnish, by applying a new mode of manufacturing Sugar, more of that article, and that too at a very reduced price, than England is likely to consume; and to leave a large surplus to supply the continental markets to the exclusion of slave-made Sugar.

6. That it has been demonstrated and proved, that the cane contains 18 per cent. of Sugar, while, by the system now followed, not more than about 5 to 6 per cent. can be obtained.

7. That by the present mode of manufacturing Sugar, in the English, as well as the foreign colonies, only about one-half of the juice obtained is converted into Sugar, (and a considerable quantity of that, of so inferior a quality that it requires to be refined), and the other half into molasses. . . .

10. That by the adoption of an improved and more rational mode of operating in the West Indies, more particularly in purifying the juice, not only would the above losses be avoided, but nearly the whole of that part of the juice, which is converted into molasses, would be transformed into superior Sugar, thus giving an increase of at least 50 per cent. out of the canes now raised; while the operations would be attended with less expense of labour, fuel, and time, and, viewing the product, with considerably less cost.

. . . 14. That, on this fact becoming generally known, Havannah Sugar will, there can be no doubt, be preferred for general consumption; and above all, for ordinary household purposes, to English brown Sugar, for, not only is it as white as refined Sugar, but it will be found to be considerably more economical than brown Sugar, as 112 lbs. of white Havannah will cost 58s., whereas 160 lbs. of brown Sugar (its equivalent in saccharine matter), will cost (@ 50s. per cwt.) 71s. 6d.

Such are the facts, my Lord, and they prove two things:—first, that the only resource left to the English planter, to obviate total destruction, is to adopt some means that will enable him, at the same time, to improve the quality of his produce, and to convert more of his juice, than he now does, into Sugar. Secondly,—that in doing so, not only will he (by obtaining out of the same quantity of canes that yield 100 lbs. inferior Sugar to the foreigner, 150 or 180 lbs. of superior Sugar), be enabled to compete successfully with slave labour Sugar, but to exclude it entirely from the English and Continental markets, and thereby to force the foreigner to emancipate his slaves.

. . . Now the English planter would, in adapting an improved mode of (above all), purifying his juice, and of making Sugar, obtain out of the same quantity of canes, that yield the above result, at least 150 lbs. of Sugar, and that too would be equal in whiteness, and far superior in purity, to the best white Havannah, so that where the Cuban and Brazilian planters get only 35 lbs. of white, (it is out of their power to procure more by their present system), the English planter would be able to bring into the market, against them, 150 (probably, I repeat, 180 lbs.) of Sugar of an incomparably larger and finer crystal, and of better quality, and that too at less expense.

The Cuban and Brazilian planters take 30 or 40 days to prepare their Sugar, whereas, the English planter could have his ready in less than ten days. It is thus quite obvious, that if the English planter had the means of improving his produce, by a process that would at the same time augment the quantity, he would be able to furnish brown or white Sugar at a considerably less price than the foreigner.

But, besides this my Lord, to the English planter, who has not the means of saving himself from annihilation, by the improvement of his Sugars, another less expensive, more simple, practical and beneficial resource, holds out the hand of salvation, while, it at the same time offers him the certain means of securing himself from competition with slave Sugar.

This consists in his ceasing to make Sugar altogether, in the Colony, and in his shipping the whole of the product of the cane, in a state of concentrated juice, to be converted into Sugar in England. . . .

The advantages to be derived from this mode of shipping colonial produce, would be as follows:—

1. That the planter, who may be unable to establish new machinery for the improvement of his Sugar, would still have it in his power to continue his cultivation with greater advantage.

2. That, with the present apparatus the canes could be ground one day, and the whole of its product shipped the next, instead of, as now, only one half at the end of three and four weeks.

3. That the Ships, instead of being detained, as now, two to four months in the Colonies, at an useless expence, would be enabled to load and quit in a few days.

4. That the produce would arrive some two or three months earlier than usual, which would give an incalculable advantage, to the English, over the foreign planter. . . .

11. That the revenue would unquestionably gain very considerably, inasmuch as a much larger quantity of produce would be subjected to duty.

12. That by shipping his produce, in the state referred to, the English planter would secure to himself, for this article, the chief, if not the entire monopoly of the English, and Continental markets, and, by that means, the exclusive supply of sugar;—for, from certain local, and other difficulties, the Brazilian and Cuban planters would be unable to furnish it, except, to a most limited and insignificant extent, at a much higher price.

13. That with such a system as this, and more labourers to raise the cane, operating with English capital and talent, applied at home, England would become, for Sugar, what she is for cotton goods, the mistress of the world; and thereby, as it would be entirely impossible for other countries to furnish Sugar at the low price that she could do it, render slave labour Sugar unsaleable; and consequently secure the Emancipation of the foreign slaves, and the total extirpation of the Slave trade.

Such, my Lord, are the advantages that this mode of importing colonial produce would yield to the country at large, but they are to be obtained only by the aid and co-operation of her Majesty's Government, to be afforded in the shape of encouragement to the importation of the material alluded to. That encouragement could be given by granting a premium on the article, in a way that would not prejudice the revenue, and by fixing a duty on concentrated cane juice, according to the Sugar and molasses that the planter could obtain from a given quantity, imported always at a certain stipulated density; so that on its arrival, it may not be subjected to difficulty and delay at the Custom House, and to an erroneous and capricious mode of ascertaining the duty which it ought to pay. Without some measure of this kind, my Lord, the article will not be imported; and unless the planter be encouraged to ship his produce in that state, or be furnished the means of improving it in the West Indies, three-fourths of the estates will inevitably be thrown out of cultivation, and the West India trade become annihilated; for it is a delusion to hope, that, should the present merchants cease to furnish means, for continuing the cultivation of the estates, others will be found, under present circumstances, and, above all, seeing the price at which white Cuban and Brazilian Sugar can be furnished, to advance £30,000 to £100,000, to pay off the mortgages, and from £7,000 to £10,000, more to fit up new machinery to improve the Sugars.

By stretching out, while it is yet time, your saving hand to the disheartened and sinking planter, not only would you, my Lord, have secured to England a boon, but your Lordship, after having shattered the manacles of the English slaves, would have acquired the enviable renown of having used him as a lever to raise his brethren from slavery and oppression, and as an instrument to save his former master from ruin, and to secure his future fortune;—How many tongues would, my Lord, sound to heaven a blessing on your Lordship's name?

I have the honour to be, with profound respect,
My Lord,
Your Lordship's obedient, humble servant,
W. A. ARCHIBALD.

Sir Robert Peel (1788–1850) presided over the passage of the repeal of the Corn Laws in 1846 and with it, a split in the Tory party over the question of free trade. Here an anonymous contributor to the *Edinburgh Review* reflects on Peel's last ministry and the centrality of empire to Britain's treasury.

Anonymous, "The Ministry and the New Parliament" (1848)

We have just entered on the first session of a new parliament, and the second session of a new ministry, which had previously not commanded a majority in either house of parliament. Besides, the commencement of a new era in our commercial legislation may be almost dated from the year 1846. Political parties, broken up, thrown into confusion, and almost pulverised by the events of that year, have not hardened again into a new and compact adhesion. The seeds of new combinations and new measures, perhaps even of new opinions, are floating about at random in the political chaos, and await the organising hand of the statesman, who is to separate the discordant elements, and shape them into a new and more regular form. At such a period as this, it may not be devoid of use, if we trace an outline of the principal events of our internal history during the last few years, for the purpose of ascertaining the existing position of parties and opinions, and the political state of the country, and of considering what is the policy which is best suited to our present social condition.

In the debates which preceded . . . [his ministry] Sir Robert Peel . . . and his chief supporters in the House of Commons . . . did little to inflame the anti-free-trade feeling, and they carefully abstained from the use of expressions which committed them to the perpetual maintenance of protective duties on corn. . . . But although he did little to increase the anti-free-trade cry, he did not repudiate it; by his silence at so critical a moment he permitted his followers to believe that he shared their opinions; he maintained the necessity of a protective duty on corn; and by heading the attack upon the government, and subsequently succeeding to the office of prime minister, he certainly took advantage of their strenuous and combined exertions in favour of the principle of protection.

However, soon after his accession to power, Sir R. Peel began to show that he was not prepared to purchase the support of the agricultural interest by any extraordinary concessions to their wishes. The revised corn law which he proposed at the commencement of the session of 1842, mitigated, in some degree, the previous protection, and lost him the adhesion of the Duke of Buckingham, who left the cabinet from dissatisfaction with the new measure. The alterations of the tariff proposed in the same year, and in 1844, (particularly the remission of the duties on foreign cattle and meat), and even the Canada corn law of 1843, were more decided movements in the direction of free trade, and created much alarm and discontent among the agricultural party. . . .

Sir R. Peel's adoption of a more liberal policy than had been anticipated of him, appears to have arisen mainly from his consciousness, when in government, of the necessity of adapting his measures to public opinion, and of not falling short of a standard which had been practically established by his predecessors. Having assumed the leadership of the reformed parliament, and being placed in a position where he could closely watch the course of public events, and the effects of new legislation, he felt the convenience and also discovered the safety and practical good working of a liberal system of administration. Enlightened by experience, he discarded many traditional opinions which he had hitherto retained from habit, and without sufficient examination.

In this state of mind he received, during the autumn of 1845, the first accounts of the failure of the potato crop, which began then to show itself to a considerable extent over the whole United Kingdom, but which was, for obvious reasons, most formidable in Ireland. Influenced by the example of Belgium and other foreign countries which had already opened their ports to foreign grain, he came without delay to the conclusion that the utmost facilities ought to be given for the importation of corn. Accordingly, on the first of November he proposed to the cabinet that 'the duties on the import of foreign grain' should be suspended for a limited period, either by order in council or by legislative enactment; parliament, in either case, 'being summoned without delay.' He considered this proposition as involving the necessity of a reconsideration of the laws imposing restrictions on the import of foreign grain, and thought that 'any new laws to be enacted should contain within themselves the principle of gradual reduction and final repeal.' To this proposition the cabinet did not accede; only three of Sir R. Peel's colleagues supported him in this prompt and decisive though judicious policy. Nothing, therefore, was said or done publicly. Near the end of the month appeared Lord J. Russell's letter to the electors of London, in which he complained of the inaction of the government at so critical a moment, expressed his opinion that the time for a compromise was past, and declared himself in favour of the total though not necessarily immediate abolition of the corn duties. 'The imposition (he said) of any duty at present, without a provision for its extinction within a short period', would but prolong a contest already 'sufficiently fruitful of animosity and discontent'. The struggle 'to make bread scarce and dear, when it is clear that part, at 'least, of the additional price goes to increase rent, is a struggle deeply injurious to an aristocracy which (this quarrel once removed) is strong in property, strong in the construction of our legislature, strong in opinion, strong in ancient associations and the memory of immortal services.'

The cabinet reassembled on the 26th of November, and agreed to the issue of an extraordinary commission for the relief of distress in Ireland. Shortly afterwards Sir R. Peel renewed his proposition to the cabinet, with the exception of the order in council. The events which had occurred since the beginning of the month had modified the views of the former majority, and on this occasion Lord Stanley stood alone in his opposition. Lord Stanley had been willing, from the first meeting of the cabinet, to consent to a temporary suspension of the corn duties, but he refused to consent to their prospective abolition. After taking a short time for consideration, he decided to tender his resignation; and in this step he was supported by one of his colleagues, whom he did not feel at liberty to name, but who subsequently joined Sir R. Peel. Upon this Sir R. Peel's government was broken up, and his resignation was accepted by the Queen on the 6th of December. As Lord Stanley was not prepared to undertake the formation of a government, the Queen, of her own choice, then sent for Lord John Russell. . . .

The practical question at issue between Sir R. Peel and Lord Stanley, when the latter, at the end of November, stood alone in his opposition, and broke up the government, was whether the Corn Laws should be suspended temporarily, upon an understanding that the duties should revive after the suspension; or should be suspended temporarily, with a view to their ultimate though gradual repeal. The question is thus stated by Sir R. Peel, in his speech of May 15th.

'It was quite impossible for me, consistently with my own convictions, after a suspension of import duties, to propose the re-establishment of the existing law with any security for its continuance. Well, then, the question which naturally arose was this— shall we propose some diminished protection to agriculture; or, in the state of public feeling which will exist after the suspension of restriction, shall we propose a permanent and ultimate settlement of the question?'

Afterwards he adds: 'I think you could have continued this law, notwithstanding these increased difficulties, for a short time longer; but I believe that the interval of its maintenance would have been but short, and that there would have been, during the period of its continuance, a desperate conflict between different classes of society; that your arguments in favour of it would have been weak; that you might have had no alternative at an early period, had the cycle of unfavourable harvests returned—and who can give an assurance that they would not?—that you might at an early period have had no alternative but to concede an alteration of this law under circumstances infinitely less favourable than the present to a final settlement of the question. . . . It was the foresight of these consequences—it was the belief that you were about to enter into a bitter and, ultimately, an unsuccessful struggle, that has induced me to think that for the benefit of all classes—for the benefit of the agricultural class itself—it was desirable to come to a permanent and equitable settlement of this question.'

The same line of argument had been pursued by Sir R. Peel in his speech of the 16th February.

'After the suspension of the existing law, and the admission of foreign importation for a period of several months, how do you propose to deal with the existing Corn Laws?

That is the question which a minister was bound to consider who advised the suspension of the Corn Laws. Now, my conviction is so strong, that it would be utterly impossible, after establishing perfect freedom of trade in corn for a period of seven or eight months, to give a guarantee that the existing Corn Law should come into operation at the end of that period, that I could not encourage the delusive hope of such a result. I know it may be said, that after a temporary suspension of the law, the law itself would revive by its own operation—that there would be no necessity for any special enactment to restore its vigour. But I think it is an utter misapprehension of the state of public opinion to suppose it possible, that after this country, for eight months, should have tasted of freedom in the trade of corn, you could revive, either by the tacit operation of the law itself, or by new and special enactment, the existing Corn Law. Surely the fact of suspension would be a condemnation of the law. It would demonstrate that the law, which professed, by the total reduction of duty on corn when it reached a certain price to provide security against scarcity, had failed in one of its essential parts.' . . . As the more unreasoning and selfish portion of the Conservative party—those who really believed that their rents depended on the sliding-scale, and who voted in order to keep up their rents—not only separated themselves from Sir R. Peel, but heaped every species of rancorous vituperation upon his head; it was impossible for a man of honourable feelings to remain minister under such circumstances, even if by some concession he could have purchased their future allegiance. It was, therefore, evident that Sir R. Peel's restored ministry would not long survive the repeal of the Corn Law. . . . The breach between him and the main section of his followers was complete. They would not be led by him; he did not wish to lead them. Neither of the two parties to the quarrel was willing to be reconciled. He could not apologise for a deliberate act; and they were too angry to accept any apology, or even to wish for one.

The result has been the lasting separation of all the leading and more intelligent portion of the Conservative party from the majority. The seceders hold an intermediate station, but visibly inclining towards Liberal opinions. They are unpledged, and free to act according to their individual views on all political questions: but recent events have clearly shown that they have a much stronger affinity with the Liberal than with the Protectionist party. Many occurrences, both during the last session and the late elections, have proved that the repulsion between Protectionists and free trade Conservatives is sufficiently strong to drive the latter towards the opposite scale of the balance.

The members of the Anti-Corn-Law League probably little thought what important political consequences would flow from their victory. They not only contributed greatly to the repeal of the Corn Law, but they have produced a permanent schism in the Conservative party, which has paralysed it for all active purposes.

. . . Whatever may be the evils of an organised system of popular agitation, like that of the Anti-Corn-Law League, such a body is naturally called into existence by the obstinate adherence of politicians to unjust and impolitic laws; and its effects are less detrimental than the abuse which is attacked. The worst consequence of such a body is, that it may create a vested interest in agitation, and prolong the existence of the combination beyond the occasion which gave it birth. Lord Stanley, even so late as the 25th of May, 1846, predicted, in the House of Lords, that this confederacy would not dissolve itself, although the Corn Law was repealed. "When, my lords, (he said) was an 'organised agitation' put down by concessions extorted from its 'opponents?' Depend upon it, that when this body shall have 'once tasted the cup of political power', the draught will be too 'sweet' to induce them to relinquish it. I agree with my noble 'friend' that this is only one of the measures which, one after 'another, will be the object of the Anti-Corn-Law League.'" Notwithstanding this confident prediction, we know that the Anti-corn-law League has been dissolved, both nominally and really, since the settlement of the Corn-Law question; and that the leaders of that powerful body had, like Washington, the virtue, as well as good sense, to abdicate at the moment of their greatest power. In this respect they have exhibited a striking contrast with the Catholic association of Ireland, which, having, under the leadership of Mr. O'Connell, done much to procure the repeal of the Catholic disabilities, did not, when this legitimate object had been attained, surrender its power, but was revived, under the same leader, for the mischievous and impracticable purpose of detaching Ireland from England, and destroying the integrity of the empire.

. . . Our extensive colonial empire, consisting of numerous communities, distant from each other, and dissimilar in laws, manners, climate, population, and language,— is necessarily exposed to many casualties. At present, however, it is in a state of quietude, and requires only the ordinary attention of the mother country. The colonial administration of Lord Grey has given satisfaction, so far as its results have been hitherto developed, and we have seen with much joy his departure from the practice of appointing military officers to conduct the civil government of colonies. India, likewise, after having lately caused so much anxiety, and so many conflicts, is now pacified; and we trust that the able governor-general—not selected on any narrow party ground—who has recently gone out, will be able to cultivate with success those arts of peace, which are so much needed in the vast territories under his control. The cost of the civil government of the dependencies of the English crown is principally defrayed from the local revenues; their chief expense to the mother country consists in their naval and military defence. We perceive that the attention of the government has been directed to the diminution of the latter head of expense, by affording means in some colonies for the organisation of a native armed force. The total expense of our large colonial possessions to the imperial treasury is, however, considerably less than the small and comparatively worthless settlement of Algeria causes to France.

. . . Nothing would more conduce at present to the public welfare than a prevailing disposition to recognise certain maxims of legislation, not derived from a blind and passive tradition, but forged anew, by actual labour, out of recent facts, and adapted to the exigencies of our modern societies. No mistake can be greater than to suppose that an unchanging is necessarily a conservative policy, or that new dangers can be always averted by old securities. A fortification which was impregnable by the spear and the arrow, may be worthless against cannon. While society is changing its aspect around us, the principles by which society is governed must be renovated by assiduous inspection. It is true, that even if such guides to legislation were generally admitted, there would still be much difficulty in applying them in practice; but discussions in parliament would be more likely to lead to a useful result, if there were more agreement about principles. The present is a favourable time for prosecuting such researches. The fanaticism about political forms, and the tendency to expect that good laws will be produced mechanically by a good constitution of the legislature, is greatly diminished. People have begun to see, that though some governments are nearly always bad, none are always good. There is neither a royal nor a democratic road to perpetual good government. This, however, only renders it the more necessary to use all practicable means for insuring a progressive improvement of our laws and institutions, and not to imitate the sluggish folly of the Roman emperor, of whom Tacitus says, that he thought by postponing the remedies, he could drive off the evils themselves.

B. Cultures of Service,
Anti-Slavery, and Reform

Robert Wedderburn (1761–1835) was the son of a slave woman and a Scottish planter who came to Britain at the age of 17. After navigating the poverty and racism of the "immigrant underworld" of London, he became a tailor, a beggar, and a thief as well. His conversion to Methodism aided his transition to radical politics—which he insisted must be linked to abolitionism. In *The Horrors of Slavery* he recalls the very public forum in which he sought to reclaim his family history.

Robert Wedderburn, "The Horrors of Slavery" (1824)

To William Wilberforce, Esq. MP
    Respected Sir,
    An oppressed, insulted, and degraded African—to whom but you can I dedicate the following pages, illustrative of the treatment of my poor countrymen? Your name stands high in the list of the glorious benefactors of the human race; and the slaves of the earth look upon you as a tower of strength in their behalf. When in prison, for conscience-sake, at Dorchester, you visited me, and you gave me—your advice, for which I am still your debtor, and likewise for the two books beautifully bound in calf, from which I have since derived much ghostly consolation. Receive, Sir, my thanks for what you have done; and if, from the following pages, you should be induced to form any motion in parliament, I am ready to prove their contents before the bar of that most Honourable House.

I remain, Sir,
Your most obedient, and
and most devoted servant
Robert Wedderburn.
23, Russell Court,
Drury Lane.

Life of the Rev. Robert Wedderburn.

The events of my life have been few and uninteresting. To my unfortunate origin I must attribute all my miseries and misfortunes. I am now upwards of sixty years of age, and therefore I cannot long expect to be numbered amongst the living. But, before I pass from this vale of tears, I deem it an act of justice to myself, to my children, and to the memory of my mother, to say what I am, and who were the authors of my existence; and to shew the world, that, not to my own misconduct is to be attributed my misfortunes, but to the inhumanity of a MAN, whom I am compelled to call by the name of FATHER. I am the offspring of a slave, it is true; but I am a man of free thought and opinion; and though I was immured for two years in his Majesty's gaol at Dorchester, for daring to express my sentiments as a free man, I am still the same in mind as I was before, and imprisonment has but confirmed me that I was right. They who know me, will confirm this statement.

To begin then with the beginning—I was born in the island of Jamaica, about the year 1762, on the estate of a Lady Douglas, a distant relation of the Duke of Queensbury. My mother was a woman of colour, by name ROSANNA, and at the time of my birth a slave to the above Lady Douglas. My father's name was JAMES WEDDERBURN, Esq. of Inveresk, in Scotland, an extensive proprietor, of sugar estates in Jamaica, which are now in the possession of a younger brother of mine, by name, A. COLVILLE, Esq. of No.35, Leadenhall Street. . . .

My father's name, as I said before, was JAMES WEDDERBURN, of Inveresk, in Scotland, near Musselborough, where, if my information is correct, the Wedderburn family have been seated for a long time. My grandfather was a staunch Jacobite, and exerted himself strenuously in the cause of the Pretender, in the rebellion of the year 1745. For his aiding to restore the exiled family to the throne of England, he was tried, condemned, and executed. He was hung by the neck till he was dead; his head was then cut off, and his body was divided into four quarters. When I first came to England, in the year 1779, I remember seeing the remains of a rebel's skull which had been affixed over Temple Bar; but I never yet could fully ascertain whether it was my dear grandfather's skull, or not. Perhaps my dear brother, A. COLVILLE, can lend me some assistance in this affair. For this act of high treason, our family estates were confiscated to the King, and my dear father found himself destitute in the world, or with no resource but his own industry. He adopted the medical profession; and in Jamaica he was Doctor and Man-Midwife, and turned an honest penny by drugging and physic[k]ing the poor blacks, where those that were cured, he had the credit for, and for those he killed, the fault was laid to their own obstinacy. In the course of time, by dint of *booing* and *booing,* my father was restored to his father's property, and he became the proprietor of one of the most extensive sugar estates in Jamaica. While my dear and honoured father was poor, he was chaste as any Scotchman, whose poverty made him virtuous; but the moment he became rich, he gave loose to his carnal appetites, and indulged himself without moderation, but as parsimonious as ever. My father's mental powers were none of the brightest, which may account for his libidinous excess. It is a common practice, as has been stated by Mr. Wilberforce in parliament, for the planters to have lewd intercourse with their female slaves; and so inhuman are many of these said planters, that many well-authenticated instances are known, of their selling their slaves while pregnant, and making that a pretence to enhance their value. A father selling his offspring is no disgrace there. A planter letting out his prettiest female slaves for purposes of lust, is by no means uncommon. My father ranged through the whole of his household for his own lewd purposes; for they being his personal property, cost nothing extra; and if any one proved with child—why, it was an acquisition which might one day fetch something in the market, like a horse or pig in Smithfield. In short, amongst his own slaves my father was a perfect parish bull; and his pleasure was the greater, because he at the same time increased his profits.

I now come to speak of the infamous manner with which JAMES WEDDERBURN, Esq. of Inveresk, and father to A. COLVILLE, Esq. No.35, Leadenhall Street, entrapped my poor mother in his power. My mother was a lady's maid, and had received an education which perfectly qualified her to conduct a household in the most agreeable manner. She was the property of Lady Douglas, whom I have before mentioned; and, prior to the time she met my father, was chaste and virtuous. After my father had got his estate, he did not renounce the pestle and mortar, but, in the capacity of Doctor, he visited Lady Douglas. He there met my mother for the first time, and was determined to have possession of her. His character was known; and therefore he was obliged to go *covertly* and *falsely* to work. In Jamaica, slaves that are esteemed by their owners have generally the power of refusal, whether they will be sold to a particular planter, or not; and my father was aware, that if *he* offered to purchase her, he would meet with a refusal. But his brutal lust was not to be stopped by trifles; my father's conscience would stretch to any extent; and he was a firm believer in the doctrine of 'grace abounding to the chief of sinners.' For this purpose, he employed a fellow of the name of Cruikshank, a brother doctor and Scotchman, to strike a bargain with Lady Douglas for my mother; and this scoundrel of a Scotchman bought my mother for the use of my father, in the name of another planter, a most respectable and highly esteemed man. I have often heard my mother express her indignation at this base and treacherous conduct of my father—a treachery the more base, as it was so calm and premeditated. Let my brother COLVILLE deny this if he can; let him bring me into court, and I will prove what I here advance. To this present hour, while I think of the treatment of my mother, my blood boils in my veins; and, had I not some connections for which I was bound to live, I should long ago have taken ample revenge of my father. But it is as well as it is; and I will not leave the world without some testimony to the injustice and inhumanity of my father.

From the time my mother became the property of my father, she assumed the direction and management of his house; for which no woman was better qualified. But her station there was very disgusting. My father's house was full of female slaves, all objects of his lusts; amongst whom he strutted like Solomon in his grand seraglio, or like a bantam cock upon his own dunghill. My good father's slaves did increase and multiply, like Jacob's kine; and he cultivated those talents well which God had granted so amply. My poor mother, from being the housekeeper, was the object of their envy, which was increased by her superiority of education over the common herd of female slaves. While in this situation, she bore my father two children, one of whom, my brother James, a mill-wright, I believe, is now living in Jamaica, upon the estate.

. . . After the death of Lady Douglas, who was brought to England to buried, James Charles Sholto Douglas, Esq., my mother's master, promised her her freedom on his return to Jamaica; but his covetous heart would not let him perform his promise. He told my mother to look out for another master to purchase her; and that her price was to be £100. The villain Cruikshank, whom I have mentioned before, offered Douglas £10 more for her; and Douglas was so mean as to require £110 from my mother; otherwise he would have sold her to Cruikshank against her will, for purposes the reader can guess. One Doctor Campbell purchased her; and in consequence of my mother having been a companion of, and borne children to my father, Mrs. Campbell used to upbraid her for not being humble enough to her, who was but a doctor's wife. This ill-treatment had such an effect on my mother, that she resolved to starve herself to death; and, though a cook, abstained from victuals for six days. When her intention was discovered, Doctor Campbell became quite alarmed for his £110, and gave my mother leave to look out for another owner; which she did, and became the property of a Doctor Boswell. The following letter, descriptive of her treatment in this place, appeared in 'BELL'S LIFE IN LONDON,' a Sunday paper, on the 29th February 1824:—

To The Editor of *Bell's Life in London.*
February 20th, 1824

SIR,—Your observations on the Meeting of the Receivers of Stolen Men call for my sincere thanks, I being a descendant of a Slave by a base Slave-Holder, the late JAMES WEDDERBURN, Esq. of Inveresk, who sold my mother when she was with child of me, HER THIRD SON BY HIM!!! She was FORCED to submit to him, being *his Slave,* THOUGH HE KNEW SHE DISLIKED HIM! She knew that he was mean, and, when gratified, would not give her her freedom, which is the custom for those, *as a reward,* who have preserved their persons, with Gentlemen (if I may call a Slave-Dealer a Gentleman). I have seen my poor mother stretched on the ground, tied hands and feet, and FLOGGED in the most indecent manner, though PREGNANT AT THE SAME TIME!!! her *fault* being the not acquainting her mistress that her master had *given her leave to go to see her mother in town!* So great was the anger of this Christian Slave-Dealer, that he went fifteen miles to punish her while on the visit! Her master was then one BOSWELL; his chief companion was CAPTAIN PARR, who *chained a female Slave to a stake, and starved her to death!* Had it not been for a British Officer in the Army, who had her dug up and proved it, this fact would not have been known. *The murderer was sentenced to transport himself for one year.* He came to England, and returned in the time—this was his *punishment.* My uncle and aunt were sent to America, and sold by their father's brother, who said that he sent them to be educated. *He had a little shame,* for the law in Jamaica allowed him to sell them, or even had they been his children—*so much for humanity and Christian goodness.* As for these men, who wished that the King would proclaim that there was no intention of emancipation—Oh, what barbarism!—

Robert Wedderburn.
No.27, Crown Street, Soho

I little expected, when I sent this letter, that my dear brother, A. COLVILLE, Esq. of No.35, Leadenhall Street, would have dared to reply to it. But he did; and what all my letters and applications to him, and my visit to my father, could not accomplish, was done by the above plain letter. The following is the letter of Andrew, as it appeared in the same paper on the 21st of March last, with the Editor's comments:—

BROTHER or NO BROTHER—'THAT IS THE QUESTION?'
. . . To The Editor of *Bell's Life in London*

SIR,—Your Paper of the 29th ult. containing a Letter signed ROBERT WEDDERBURN, was put into my hands only yesterday, otherwise I should have felt it to be my duty to take earlier notice of it.

In answer to this most slanderous publication, I have to state, that the person calling himself Robert Wedderburn is NOT a son of the late Mr. James Wedderburn, of Inveresk, who never had any child by, or any connection of *that kind* with the mother of this man. The pretence of his using the name of Wedderburn at all, arises out of the following circumstances:—The late Mr. James Wedderburn, of Inveresk, had, when he resided in the parish of Westmoreland, in the Island of Jamaica, a negro woman-*slave,* whom he employed as a cook; this woman had so violent a temper that she was continually quarrelling with the other servants, and occasioning a disturbance in the house. He happened to make some observation upon her troublesome temper, when a gentleman in company said, he would be very glad to *purchase* her if she was a good cook. The *sale accordingly took place,* and the woman was removed to the residence of the gentleman, in the parish of Hanover. Several years afterwards, this woman was delivered of a mulatto child, and as *she could not tell who was the father,* her master, in a foolish joke, named the child Wedderburn. About twenty-two or twenty-three years ago, this man applied to me for money upon the *strength of his name,* claiming to be a son of Mr. James Wedderburn, of Inveresk, which occasioned me to write to my father, when he gave me the above explanation respecting this person; adding, that a few years after he had returned to this country, and married, this same person importuned him with the same story that he now tells; and as he persisted in annoying him after the above explanation was given to him, that he found it necessary to have him brought before the Sheriff of the county of Edinburgh. But whether the man was punished, or only discharged upon promising not to repeat the annoyance, *I do not now recollect.*

'Your conduct, Sir, is most unjustifiable in thus lending yourself to be the vehicle of such foul slander upon the character of the respected dead—when the story is so improbable in itself—when upon the slightest enquiry you would have discovered that it referred to a period of between sixty and seventy years ago, and *therefore* is not applicable to any argument upon the present condition of the West India Colonies—and when, upon a little further enquiry, you might easily have obtained the above contradiction and explanation.

'I have only to add, that in the event of your not inserting this letter in your Paper of Sunday next, or of your repeating or insinuating any further slander upon the character of my father, the late Mr. James Wedderburn, of Inveresk, I have instructed my Solicitor to take immediate measures for obtaining legal redress against you.

'I am, Sir, your humble Servant,

A. Coville
35, Leadenhall Street, March 17th, 1824.

To The Editor of *Bell's Life in London*

SIR,—I did not expect, when I communicated my statement, as it appeared in your Paper of the 29th ult. that any person would have had the temerity, not to say audacity, to have contradicted my assertion, and thereby occasion me to PROVE the deep depravity of the man to whom I owe my existence. I deem it now an imperative duty to reply to the infamous letter of A. COLVILLE, alias WEDDERBURN, and to defend the memory of my unfortunate mother, a woman virtuous in principle, but a Slave, and a sacrifice to the unprincipled lust of my father.—Your Correspondent, *my dear and affectionate brother,* will, doubtless, laugh, when he hears of the VIRTUES of SLAVES, *unless such as will enhance their price*—but I shall leave it to your readers to decide on the *laugh* of a Slave-Dealer after the picture of lust and cruelty and avarice, which I mean to lay before them. *My dear brother's statement* is FALSE, when he says that I was not born till several years after my mother was sold by my father:—but let me tell him, that my mother was preg-nant *at* the time of *sale,* and that I was born within four months after it took place. One of the conditions of the sale was, that her offspring, your humble servant, was to be free, from its birth, and I thank my GOD, that through a long life of hardship and adversity, I have ever been free both in mind and body: and have always raised my voice in behalf of my enslaved countrymen! My mother had, previously to my birth, borne two other sons to JAMES WEDDERBURN, Esq. of Inveresk, Slave-Dealer, one of whom, a mill-wright, works now upon the family estate in Jamaica, and has done his whole life-time; and so far was my father from doubting me to be his son, that he recorded my freedom, and that of my brother JAMES, the millwright, himself, in the Government Secretary's Office; where it may be seen to this day. *My dear brother* states that my mother was of a violent temper, which was the reason of my father selling her;—yes, and I glory in her *rebellious* disposition, and which I have inherited from her. My honoured father's house was, in fact, nothing more than a *Seraglio of Black Slaves,* miserable objects of an abandoned lust, guided by avarice; and it was from this den of iniquity that she (my mother) was determined to escape. A Lady DOUGLAS, of the parish of St. Mary, was my mother's pur-chaser, and also stood my godmother. Perhaps, *my dear brother* knows nothing of one ESTHER TROTTER, a free tawny, who bore my father two children, a boy and a girl, and which children my inhuman father *transported to Scotland,* to gratify his malice, because their mother refused to be any longer the object of his lust, and because she claimed sup-port for herself and offspring? Those children *my dear and loving brother* knows under the name of Graham, being brought up in the same house with them at Inveresk. It is true that I did apply to *my dear brother,* A. COLVILLE—as he signs himself, but his real name is WEDDERBURN—for some pecuniary assistance; but it was upon the ground of *right,* according to *Deuteronomy,* xxi.10, 17.

'If a man have two wives, one beloved and another hated, and they have borne him chil-dren, both the beloved and the hated, and if the first-born son be her's that was hated;

'Then it shall be, when he maketh his sons to inherit that which he hath, that he may not make the son of the beloved first-born before the son of the hated, which is, indeed, the first-born;

'But he shall acknowledge the son of the hated for the first-born, by giving him a dou-ble portion of all that he hath, for he is the beginning of his strength, the right of the first-born is his.'

I was at that time, Mr. Editor, in extreme distress; the quartern loaf was then 1s. 10«d., I was out of work, and my wife was lying in, which I think was some excuse for applying to an *affectionate brother,* who refused to relieve me. He says that he knew noth-ing of me before that time; but he will remember seeing me at his father's house five years before—the precise time I forget, but A. COLVILLE will recollect it, when I state, that it was the very day on which one of our *dear* father's cows died in calving, and when a butcher was sent for from Musselburgh, to *kill the dead beast,* and take it to market—a perfect specimen of Scotch economy. It was seven years after my arrival in England that I visited my father, who had the inhumanity to threaten to send me to gaol if I trou-bled him. I never saw my worthy father in Britain but this time, and then he did not abuse my mother, as my dear brother, A. COLVILLE, has done; nor did he deny me to be his son, but called me a *lazy fellow,* and said he would do nothing for me. From his cook I had one draught of small beer, and his footman gave me a cracked sixpence—and these are all the obligations I am under to my *worthy* father and *my dear brother,* A. COLVILLE. It is false where my brother says I was taken before the Sheriff of the County—I applied to the Council of the City of Edinburgh for assistance, and they gave me 16d. and a travelling pass; and for my passage up to London I was indebted to the Captain of a Berwick smack.

In conclusion, Mr. Editor, I have to say, that if *my dear brother* means to *show fight* before the Nobs at Westminster, I shall soon give him an opportunity, as I mean to publish my whole history in a cheap pamphlet, and to give the public a specimen of the inhumanity, cruelty, avarice, and diabolical lust of the West-India Slave-Holders; and in the Courts of Justice I will defend and prove my assertions.

I am, Sir, your obedient Servant,

Robert Wedderburn
23 Russell Court, Drury Lane.

Mary Prince (b. 1788) was born in Bermuda and spent much of her young life in domestic servitude on the islands, eventually securing her freedom in London in 1828. *The History* she wrote of her life may be counted as the first known autobiography by a British ex-slave, as well as a powerful testimony to the abuses of British slavery. In the selections below we have the opportunity to hear her narrative of the journey from the Caribbean to Britain, as well as an account of how her story came before the public eye.

Mary Prince, from *The History of Mary Prince* (1831)

Preface

The idea of writing Mary Prince's history was first suggested by herself. She wished it to be done, she said, that good people in England might hear from a slave what a slave had felt and suffered; and a letter of her late master's, which will be found in the Supplement, induced me to accede to her wish without farther delay. The more immediate object of the publication will afterwards appear.

The narrative was taken down from Mary's own lips by a lady who happened to be at the time residing in my family as a visitor. It was written out fully, with all the narrator's repetitions and prolixities, and afterwards pruned into its present shape; retaining, as far as was practicable, Mary's exact expressions and peculiar phraseology. No fact of importance has been omitted, and not a single circumstance or sentiment has been added. It is essentially her own, without any material alteration farther than was requisite to exclude redundancies and gross grammatical errors, so as to render it clearly intelligible.

After it had been thus written out, I went over the whole, carefully examining her on every fact and circumstance detailed; and in all that relates to her residence in Antigua.

I had the advantage of being assisted in this scrutiny by Mr. Joseph Phillips, who was a resident in that colony during the same period, and had known her there.

The names of all the persons mentioned by the narrator have been printed in full, except those of Capt. I——and his wife, and that of Mr. D——, to whom conduct of peculiar atrocity is ascribed. These three individuals are now gone to answer at a far more awful tribunal than that of public opinion, for the deeds of which their former bond-woman accuses them; and to hold them up more openly to human reprobation could no longer affect themselves, while it might deeply lacerate the feelings of their surviving and perhaps innocent relatives, without any commensurate public advantage.

Without detaining the reader with remarks on other points which will be adverted to more conveniently in the Supplement, I shall here merely notice farther, that the Anti-Slavery Society have no concern whatever with this publication, nor are they in any degree responsible for the statements it contains. I have published the tract, not as their Secretary, but in my private capacity; and any profits that may arise from the sale will be exclusively appropriated to the benefit of Mary Prince herself.

Thomas Pringle
7, Solly Terrace, Claremont Square,
January 25, 1831

. . . I was born at Brackish-Pond, in Bermuda, on a farm belonging to Mr. Charles Myners. My mother was a household slave; and my father, whose name was Prince, was a sawyer belonging to Mr. Trimmingham, a shipbuilder at Crow-Lane. When I was an infant, old Mr. Myners died, and there was a division of the slaves and other property among the family. I was bought along with my mother by old Captain Darrel, and given to his grandchild, little Miss Betsey Williams. Captain Williams, Mr. Darrel's son-in-law, was master of a vessel which traded to several places in America and the West Indies, and he was seldom at home long together.

Mrs. Williams was a kind-hearted good woman, and she treated all her slaves well. She had only one daughter, Miss Betsey, for whom I was purchased, and who was about my own age. I was made quite a pet of by Miss Betsey, and loved her very much. She used to lead me about by the hand, and call me her little nigger. This was the happiest period of my life; for I was too young to understand rightly my condition as a slave, and too thoughtless and full of spirits to look forward to the days of toil and sorrow.

My mother was a household slave in the same family. I was under her own care, and my little brothers and sisters were my play-fellows and companions. My mother had several fine children after she came to Mrs. Williams,—three girls and two boys. The tasks given out to us children were light, and we used to play together with Miss Betsey, with as much freedom almost as if she had been our sister.

My master, however, was a very harsh, selfish man; and we always dreaded his return from sea. His wife was herself much afraid of him; and, during his stay at home, seldom dared to shew her usual kindness to the slaves. He often left her, in the most distressed circumstances, to reside in other female society, at some place in the West Indies of which I have forgot the name. My poor mistress bore his ill-treatment with great patience, and all her slaves loved and pitied her. I was truly attached to her, and, next to my own mother, loved her better than any creature in the world. My obedience to her commands was cheerfully given: it sprung solely from the affection I felt for her, and not from fear of the power which the white people's law had given her over me.

I had scarcely reached my twelfth year when my mistress became too poor to keep so many of us at home; and she hired me out to Mrs. Pruden, a lady who lived about five miles off, in the adjoining parish, in a large house near the sea. I cried bitterly at parting with my dear mistress and Miss Betsey, and when I kissed my mother and brothers and sisters, I thought my young heart would break, it pained me so. But there was no help; I was forced to go. Good Mrs. Williams comforted me by saying that I should still be near the home I was about to quit, and might come over and see her and my kindred whenever I could obtain leave of absence from Mrs. Pruden. A few hours after this I was taken to a strange house, and found myself among strange people. This separation seemed a sore trial to me then; but oh! 'twas light, light to the trials I have since endured!—'twas nothing—nothing to be mentioned with them; but I was a child then, and it was according to my strength.

I knew that Mrs. Williams could no longer maintain me; that she was fain to part with me for my food and clothing; and I tried to submit myself to the change. My new mistress was a passionate woman; but yet she did not treat me very unkindly. I do not remember her striking me but once, and that was for going to see Mrs. Williams when I heard she was sick, and staying longer than she had given me leave to do. All my employment at this time was nursing a sweet baby, little Master Daniel; and I grew so fond of my nursling that it was my greatest delight to walk out with him by the sea-shore, accompanied by his brother and sister, Miss Fanny and Master James.—Dear Miss Fanny! She was a sweet, kind young lady, and so fond of me that she wished me to learn all that she knew herself; and her method of teaching me was as follows:—Directly she had said her lessons to her grandmamma, she used to come running to me, and make me repeat them one by one after her; and in a few months I was able not only to say my letters but to spell many small words. But this happy state was not to last long. Those days were too pleasant to last. My heart always softens when I think of them.

At this time Mrs. Williams died. I was told suddenly of her death, and my grief was so great that, forgetting I had the baby in my arms, I ran away directly to my poor mistress's house; but reached it only in time to see the corpse carried out. Oh, that was a day of sorrow—a heavy day! All the slaves cried. My mother cried and lamented her sore; and I (foolish creature!) vainly entreated them to bring my dear mistress back to life. I knew nothing rightly about death then, and it seemed a hard thing to bear. When I thought about my mistress I felt as if the world was all gone wrong; and for many days and weeks I could think of nothing else. I returned to Mrs. Pruden's; but my sorrow was too great to be comforted, for my own dear mistress was always in my mind. Whether in the house or abroad, my thoughts were always talking to me about her.

I staid at Mrs. Pruden's about three months after this; I was then sent back to Mr. Williams to be sold. Oh, that was a sad sad time! I recollect the day well. Mrs. Pruden came to me and said, 'Mary, you will have to go home directly; your master is going to be married, and he means to sell you and two of your sisters to raise money for the wedding.' Hearing this I burst out a crying,—though I was then far from being sensible of the full weight of my misfortune, or of the misery that waited for me. Besides, I did not like to leave Mrs. Pruden, and the dear baby, who had grown very fond of me. For some time I could scarcely believe that Mrs. Pruden was in earnest, till I received orders for my immediate return.—Dear Miss Fanny! how she cried at parting with me, whilst I kissed and hugged the baby, thinking I should never see him again. I left Mrs. Pruden's, and walked home with a heart full of sorrow. The idea of being sold away from my mother and Miss Betsey was so frightful, that I dared not trust myself to think about it.

We had been bought of Mrs. Myners, as I have mentioned, by Miss Betsey's grandfather, and given to her, so that we were by right *her* property, and I never thought we should be separated or sold away from her.

When I reached the house, I went in directly to Miss Betsey. I found her in great distress; and she cried out as soon as she saw me, 'Oh, Mary! my father is going to sell you all to raise money to marry that wicked woman. You are *my* slaves, and he has no right to sell you; but it is all to please her.' She then told me that my mother was living with her father's sister at a house close by, and I went there to see her. It was a sorrowful meeting; and we lamented with a great and sore crying our unfortunate situation. 'Here comes one of my poor piccaninnies!' she said, the moment I came in, 'one of the poor slave-brood who are to be sold to-morrow.'

Oh dear! I cannot bear to think of that day,—it is too much.—It recalls the great grief that filled my heart, and the woeful thoughts that passed to and fro through my mind, whilst listening to the pitiful words of my poor mother, weeping for the loss of her children. I wish I could find words to tell you all I then felt and suffered. The great God above alone knows the thoughts of the poor slave's heart, and the bitter pains which follow such separations as these. All that we love taken away from us—oh, it is sad, sad! and sore to be borne!—I got no sleep that night for thinking of the morrow; and dear Miss Betsey was scarcely less distressed. She could not bear to part with her old playmates and she cried sore and would not be pacified.

The black morning at length came; it came too soon for my poor mother and us. Whilst she was putting on us the new osnaburgs in which we were to be sold, she said, in a sorrowful voice, (I shall never forget it!) 'See, I am *shrouding* my poor children; what a task for a mother!'—She then called Miss Betsey to take leave of us. 'I am going to carry my little chickens to market,' (these were her very words) 'take your last look of them; may be you will see them no more.' 'Oh, my poor slaves! my own slaves!' said dear Miss Betsey, 'you belong to me; and it grieves my heart to part with you.'—Miss Betsey kissed us all, and, when she left us, my mother called the rest of the slaves to bid us good bye. One of them, a woman named Moll, came with her infant in her arms. 'Ay!' said my mother, seeing her turn away and look at her child with the tears in her eyes, 'your turn will come next.' The slaves could say nothing to comfort us; they could only weep and lament with us. When I left my dear little brothers and the house in which I had been brought up, I thought my heart would burst.

Our mother, weeping as she went, called me away with the children Hannah and Dinah, and we took the road that led to Hamble Town, which we reached about four o'clock in the afternoon. We followed my mother to the market-place, where she placed us in a row against a large house, with our backs to the wall and our arms folded across our breasts. I, as the eldest, stood first, Hannah next to me, then Dinah; and our mother stood beside, crying over us. My heart throbbed with grief and terror so violently, that I pressed my hands quite tightly across my breast, but I could not keep it still, and it continued to leap as though it would burst out of my body. But who cared for that? Did one of the many bystanders, who were looking at us so carelessly, think of the pain that wrung the hearts of the negro woman and her young ones? No, no! They were not all bad, I dare say, but slavery hardens white people's hearts towards the blacks; and many of them were not slow to make their remarks upon us aloud, without regard to our grief—though their light words fell like cayenne on the fresh wounds of our hearts. Oh those white people have small hearts who can only feel for themselves.

At length the vendue master, who was to offer us for sale like sheep or cattle, arrived, and asked my mother which was the eldest. She said nothing, but pointed to me. He took me by the hand, and led me out into the middle of the street, and, turning me slowly round, exposed me to the view of those who attended the vendue. I was soon sur-rounded by strange men, who examined and handled me in the same manner that a butcher would a calf or a lamb he was about to purchase, and who talked about my shape and size in like words—as if I could no more understand their meaning than the dumb beasts. I was then put up for sale. The bidding commenced at a few pounds, and gradually rose to fifty-seven, when I was knocked down to the highest bidder; and the people who stood by said that I had fetched a great sum for so young a slave.

. . . My new master was a Captain I——, who lived at Spanish Point. After parting with my mother and sisters, I followed him to his store, and he gave me into the charge of his son, a lad about my own age, Master Benjy, who took me to my new home. I did not know where I was going, or what my new master would do with me. My heart was quite broken with grief, and my thoughts went back continually to those from whom I had been so suddenly parted. 'Oh, my mother! my mother!' I kept saying to myself, 'Oh, my mammy and my sisters and my brothers, shall I never see you again!'

Oh, the trials! the trials! they make the salt water come into my eyes when I think of the days in which I was afflicted—the times that are gone; when I mourned and grieved with a young heart for those whom I loved.

It was night when I reached my new home. The house was large, and built at the bot-tom of a very high hill; but I could not see much of it that night. I saw too much of it afterwards. The stones and the timber were the best things in it; they were not so hard as the hearts of the owners.

. . . I got a sad fright, that night. I was just going to sleep, when I heard a noise in my mistress's room; and she presently called out to inquire if some work was finished that she had ordered Hetty to do. 'No, Ma'am, not yet,' was Hetty's answer from below. On hearing this, my master started up from his bed, and just as he was, in his shirt, ran down stairs with a long cow-skin in his hand. I heard immediately after, the cracking of the thong, and the house rang to the shrieks of poor Hetty, who kept crying out, 'Oh, Massa! Massa! me dead. Massa! have mercy upon me—don't kill me outright.'—This was a sad beginning for me. I sat up upon my blanket, trembling with terror, like a frightened hound, and thinking that my turn would come next. At length the house be-came still, and I forgot for a little while all my sorrows by falling fast asleep.

The next morning my mistress set about instructing me in my tasks. She taught me to do all sorts of household work; to wash and bake, pick cotton and wool, and wash floors, and cook. And she taught me (how can I ever forget it!) more things than these; she caused me to know the exact difference between the smart of the rope, the cart-whip, and the cow-skin, when applied to my naked body by her own cruel hand. And there was scarcely any punishment more dreadful than the blows I received on my face and head from her hard heavy fist. She was a fearful woman, and a savage mistress to her slaves. . . .

Poor Hetty, my fellow slave, was very kind to me, and I used to call her my Aunt; but she led a most miserable life, and her death was hastened (at least the slaves all believed and said so) by the dreadful chastisement she received from my master during her preg-nancy. It happened as follows. One of the cows had dragged the rope away from the stake to which Hetty had fastened it, and got loose. My master flew into a terrible pas-sion, and ordered the poor creature to be stripped quite naked, notwithstanding her pregnancy, and to be tied up to a tree in the yard. He then flogged her as hard as he could lick, both with the whip and cow-skin, till she was all over streaming with blood. He rested, and then beat her again and again. Her shrieks were terrible. The consequence was that poor Hetty was brought to bed before her time, and was delivered after severe labour of a dead child. She appeared to recover after her confinement, so far that she was repeatedly flogged by both master and mistress afterwards; but her former strength never returned to her. Ere long her body and limbs swelled to a great size; and she lay on a mat in the kitchen, till the water burst out of her body and she died. All the slaves said that death was a good thing for poor Hetty; but I cried very much for her death. The manner of it filled me with horror. I could not bear to think about it; yet it was always present to my mind for many a day.

After Hetty died all her labours fell upon me, in addition to my own. I had now to milk eleven cows every morning before sunrise, sitting among the damp weeds; to take care of the cattle as well as the children; and to do the work of the house. There was no end to my toils—no end to my blows. I lay down at night and rose up in the morning in fear and sorrow; and often wished that like poor Hetty I could escape from this cruel bondage and be at rest in the grave. But the hand of that God whom then I knew not, was stretched over me; and I was mercifully preserved for better things. . . .

For five years after this I remained in his house, and almost daily received the same harsh treatment. At length he put me on board a sloop, and to my great joy sent me away to Turk's Island. I was not permitted to see my mother or father, or poor sisters and brothers, to say good bye, though going away to a strange land, and might never see them again. Oh the Buckra people who keep slaves think that black people are like cattle, without natural affection. But my heart tells me it is far otherwise.

We were nearly four weeks on the voyage, which was unusually long. Sometimes we had a light breeze, sometimes a great calm, and the ship made no way; so that our provisions and water ran very low, and we were put upon short allowance. I should almost have been starved had it not been for the kindness of a black man called Anthony, and his wife, who had brought their own victuals, and shared them with me.

When we went ashore at the Grand Quay, the captain sent me to the house of my new master, Mr. D——, to whom Captain I——had sold me. Grand Quay is a small town upon a sandbank; the houses low and built of wood. Such was my new master's. The first person I saw, on my arrival, was Mr. D—, a stout sulky looking man, who carried me through the hall to show me to his wife and children. Next day I was put up by the vendue master to know how much I was worth, and I was valued at one hundred pounds currency.

My new master was one of the owners or holders of the salt ponds, and he received a certain sum for every slave that worked upon his premises, whether they were young or old. This sum was allowed him out of the profits arising from the salt works. I was immediately sent to work in the salt water with the rest of the slaves. This work was perfectly new to me. I was given a half barrel and a shovel, and had to stand up to my knees in the water, from four o'clock in the morning till nine, when we were given some Indian corn boiled in water, which we were obliged to swallow as fast as we could for fear the rain should come on and melt the salt. We were then called again to our tasks, and worked through the heat of the day; the sun flaming upon our heads like fire, and raising salt blisters in those parts which were not completely covered. Our feet and legs, from standing in the salt water for so many hours, soon became full of dreadful boils, which eat down in some cases to the very bone, afflicting the sufferers with great torment. We came home at twelve; ate our corn soup, called *blawly*, as fast as we could, and went back to our employment till dark at night. We then shovelled up the salt in large heaps, and went down to the sea, where we washed the pickle from our limbs, and cleaned the barrows and shovels from the salt. When we returned to the house, our master gave us each our allowance of raw Indian corn, which we pounded in a mortar and boiled in water for our suppers.

 . . . Oh the horrors of slavery!—How the thought of it pains my heart! But the truth ought to be told of it; and what my eyes have seen I think it is my duty to relate; for few people in England know what slavery is. I have been a slave—I have felt what a slave feels, and I know what a slave knows; and I would have all the good people in England to know it too, that they may break our chains, and set us free. . . .

I think it was about ten years I had worked in the salt ponds at Turk's Island, when my master left off business, and retired to a house he had in Bermuda, leaving his son to succeed him in the island. He took me with him to wait upon his daughters; and I was joyful, for I was sick, sick of Turk's Island, and my heart yearned to see my native place again, my mother, and my kindred.

 . . . After I left Turk's Island, I was told by some negroes that came over from it, that the poor slaves had built up a place with boughs and leaves, where they might meet for prayers, but the white people pulled it down twice, and would not allow them even a shed for prayers. A flood came down soon after and washed away many houses, filled the place with sand, and overflowed the ponds: and I do think that this was for their wickedness; for the Buckra men there were very wicked. I saw and heard much that was very very bad at that place.

I was several years the slave of Mr. D——after I returned to my native place. Here I worked in the grounds. My work was planting and hoeing sweet-potatoes, Indian corn, plantains, bananas, cabbages, pumpkins, onions, &c. I did all the household work, and attended upon a horse and cow besides,—going also upon all errands. I had to curry the horse—to clean and feed him—and sometimes to ride him a little. I had more than enough to do—but still it was not so very bad as Turk's Island.

My old master often got drunk, and then he would get in a fury with his daughter, and beat her till she was not fit to be seen. I remember on one occasion, I had gone to fetch water, and when I was coming up the hill I heard a great screaming; I ran as fast as I could to the house, put down the water, and went into the chamber, where I found my master beating Miss D——dreadfully. I strove with all my strength to get her away from him; for she was all black and blue with bruises. He had beat her with his fist, and almost killed her. The people gave me credit for getting her away. He turned round and began to lick me. Then I said, 'Sir, this is not Turk's Island.' I can't repeat his answer, the words were too wicked—too bad to say. He wanted to treat me the same in Bermuda as he had done in Turk's Island.

He had an ugly fashion of stripping himself quite naked and ordering me then to wash him in a tub of water. This was worse to me than all the licks. Sometimes when he called me to wash him I would not come, my eyes were so full of shame. He would then come to beat me. One time I had plates and knives in my hand, and I dropped both plates and knives, and some of the plates were broken. He struck me so severely for this, that at last I defended myself, for I thought it was high time to do so. I then told him I would not live longer with him, for he was a very indecent man—very spiteful, and too indecent; with no shame for his servants, no shame for his own flesh. So I went away to a neighbouring house and sat down and cried till the next morning, when I went home again, not knowing what else to do.

After that I was hired to work at Cedar Hills, and every Saturday night I paid the money to my master. I had plenty of work to do there—plenty of washing; but yet I made myself pretty comfortable. I earned two dollars and a quarter a week, which is twenty pence a day.

During the time I worked there, I heard that Mr. John Wood was going to Antigua. I felt a great wish to go there, and I went to Mr. D——, and asked him to let me go in Mr. Wood's service. Mr. Wood did not then want to purchase me; it was my own fault that I came under him, I was so anxious to go. It was ordained to be, I suppose; God led me there. The truth is, I did not wish to be any longer the slave of my indecent master.

Mr. Wood took me with him to Antigua, to the town of St. John's, where he lived. This was about fifteen years ago. He did not then know whether I was to be sold; but Mrs. Wood found that I could work, and she wanted to buy me. Her husband then wrote to my master to inquire whether I was to be sold? Mr. D——wrote in reply, 'that I should not be sold to any one that would treat me ill.' It was strange he should say this, when he had treated me so ill himself. So I was purchased by Mr. Wood for 300 dollars (or £100 Bermuda currency.)

. . . While we were at Date Hill Christmas came; and the slave woman who had the care of the place (which then belonged to Mr. Roberts the marshal), asked me to go with her to her husband's house, to a Methodist meeting for prayer, at a plantation called Winthorps. I went; and they were the first prayers I ever understood. One woman prayed; and then they all sung a hymn; then there was another prayer and another hymn; and then they all spoke by turns of their own griefs as sinners. The husband of the woman I went with was a black driver. His name was Henry. He confessed that he had treated the slaves very cruelly; but said that he was compelled to obey the orders of his master. He prayed them all to forgive him, and he prayed that God would forgive him. He said it was a horrid thing for a ranger to have sometimes to beat his own wife or sister; but he must do so if ordered by his master.

. . . The Moravian ladies (Mrs. Richter, Mrs. Olufsen, and Mrs. Sauter) taught me to read in the class; and I got on very fast. In this class there were all sorts of people, old and young, grey headed folks and children; but most of them were free people. After we had done spelling, we tried to read in the Bible. After the reading was over, the missionary gave out a hymn for us to sing. I dearly loved to go to the church, it was so solemn. I never knew rightly that I had much sin till I went there. When I found out that I was a great sinner, I was very sorely grieved, and very much frightened. I used to pray God to pardon my sins for Christ's sake, and forgive me for every thing I had done amiss; and when I went home to my work, I always thought about what I had heard from the missionaries, and wished to be good that I might go to heaven. After a while I was admitted a candidate for the holy Communion.—I had been baptized long before this, in August 1817, by the Rev. Mr. Curtin, of the English Church, after I had been taught to repeat the Creed and the Lord's Prayer. I wished at that time to attend a Sunday School taught by Mr. Curtin, but he would not receive me without a written note from my master, granting his permission. I did not ask my owner's permission, from the belief that it would be refused; so that I got no farther instruction at that time from the English Church.

Some time after I began to attend the Moravian Church, I met with Daniel James, afterwards my dear husband. He was a carpenter and cooper to his trade; an honest, hard-working, decent black man, and a widower. He had purchased his freedom of his mistress, old Mrs. Baker, with money he had earned whilst a slave. When he asked me to marry him, I took time to consider the matter over with myself, and would not say yes till he went to church with me and joined the Moravians. He was very industrious after he bought his freedom; and he had hired a comfortable house, and had convenient things about him. We were joined in marriage, about Christmas 1826, in the Moravian Chapel at Spring Gardens, by the Rev. Mr. Olufsen. We could not be married in the English Church. English marriage is not allowed to slaves; and no free man can marry a slave woman.

When Mr. Wood heard of my marriage, he flew into a great rage, and sent for Daniel, who was helping to build a house for his old mistress. Mr. Wood asked him who gave him a right to marry a slave of his? My husband said, 'Sir, I am a free man, and thought I had a right to choose a wife; but if I had known Molly was not allowed to have a husband, I should not have asked her to marry me.' Mrs. Wood was more vexed about my marriage than her husband. She could not forgive me for getting married, but stirred up Mr. Wood to flog me dreadfully with his horsewhip. I thought it very hard to be whipped at my time of life for getting a husband—I told her so. She said that she would not have nigger men about the yards and premises, or allow a nigger man's clothes to be washed in the same tub where hers were washed. She was fearful, I think, that I should lose her time, in order to wash and do things for my husband: but I had then no time to wash for myself; I was obliged to put out my own clothes, though I was always at the wash-tub. . . .

About this time my master and mistress were going to England to put their son in school, and bring their daughters home; and they took me with them to take care of the child. I was willing to come to England: I thought that by going there I should probably get cured of my rheumatism, and should return with my master and mistress, quite well, to my husband. My husband was willing for me to come away, for he had heard that my master would free me,—and I also hoped this might prove true; but it was all a false report.

The steward of the ship was very kind to me. He and my husband were in the same class in the Moravian Church. I was thankful that he was so friendly, for my mistress was not kind to me on the passage; and she told me, when she was angry, that she did not intend to treat me any better in England than in the West Indies—that I need not expect it. And she was as good as her word.

When we drew near to England, the rheumatism seized all my limbs worse than ever, and my body was dreadfully swelled. When we landed at the Tower, I shewed my flesh to my mistress, but she took no great notice of it. We were obliged to stop at the tavern till my master got a house; and a day or two after, my mistress sent me down into the wash-house to learn to wash in the English way. In the West Indies we wash with cold water—in England with hot. I told my mistress I was afraid that putting my hands first into the hot water and then into the cold, would increase the pain in my limbs. The doctor had told my mistress long before I came from the West Indies, that I was a sickly body and the washing did not agree with me. But Mrs. Wood would not release me from the tub, so I was forced to do as I could. I grew worse, and could not stand to wash. I was then forced to sit down with the tub before me, and often through pain and weakness was reduced to kneel or to sit down on the floor, to finish my task. When I complained to my mistress of this, she only got into a passion as usual, and said washing in hot water could not hurt any one;—that I was lazy and insolent, and wanted to be free of my work; but that she would make me do it. I thought her very hard on me, and my heart rose up within me. However I kept still at that time, and went down again to wash the child's things; but the English washerwomen who were at work there, when they saw that I was so ill, had pity upon me and washed them for me.

After that, when we came up to live in Leigh Street, Mrs. Wood sorted out five bags of clothes which we had used at sea, and also such as had been worn since we came on shore, for me and the cook to wash. Elizabeth the cook told her, that she did not think that I was able to stand to the tub, and that she had better hire a woman. I also said myself, that I had come over to nurse the child, and that I was sorry I had come from Antigua, since mistress would work me so hard, without compassion for my rheumatism. Mr. and Mrs. Wood, when they heard this, rose up in a passion against me. They opened the door and bade me get out. But I was a stranger, and did not know one door in the street from another, and was unwilling to go away. They made a dreadful uproar, and from that day they constantly kept cursing and abusing me. I was obliged to wash, though I was very ill. Mrs. Wood, indeed once hired a washerwoman, but she was not well treated, and would come no more.

. . . About this time, a woman of the name of Hill told me of the Anti-Slavery Society, and went with me to their office, to inquire if they could do any thing to get me my freedom, and send me back to the West Indies. The gentlemen of the Society took me to a lawyer, who examined very strictly into my case; but told me that the laws of England could do nothing to make me free in Antigua. However they did all they could for me: they gave me a little money from time to time to keep me from want; and some of them went to Mr. Wood to try to persuade him to let me return a free woman to my husband; but though they offered him, as I have heard, a large sum for my freedom, he was sulky and obstinate, and would not consent to let me go free.

This was the first winter I spent in England, and I suffered much from the severe cold, and from the rheumatic pains, which still at times torment me. However, Providence was very good to me, and I got many friends—especially some Quaker ladies, who hearing of my case, came and sought me out, and gave me good warm clothing and money. Thus I had great cause to bless God in my affliction.

. . . At last I went into the service of Mr. and Mrs. Pringle, where I have been ever since, and am as comfortable as I can be while separated from my dear husband, and away from my own country and all old friends and connections. My dear mistress teaches me daily to read the word of God, and takes great pains to make me understand it. I enjoy the great privilege of being enabled to attend church three times on the Sunday; and I have met with many kind friends since I have been here, both clergymen and others. The Rev. Mr. Young, who lives in the next house, has shown me much kindness, and taken much pains to instruct me, particularly while my master and mistress were absent in Scotland. Nor must I forget, among my friends, the Rev. Mr. Mortimer, the good clergyman of the parish, under whose ministry I have now sat for upwards of twelve months. I trust in God I have profited by what I have heard from him. He never keeps back the truth, and I think he has been the means of opening my eyes and ears much better to understand the word of God. Mr. Mortimer tells me that he cannot open the eyes of my heart, but that I must pray to God to change my heart, and make me to know the truth, and the truth will make me free.

I still live in the hope that God will find a way to give me my liberty, and give me back to my husband. I endeavour to keep down my fretting, and to leave all to Him, for he knows what is good for me better than I know myself. Yet, I must confess, I find it a hard and heavy task to do so. . . .

—☙—

A cabinetmaker and toolmaker respectively, William Lovett and John Collins addressed their pamphlet "to the working classes of the United Kingdom, and more especially to the advocates of the rights and liberties of the whole people as set forth in the 'People's Charter.'" Committed to securing "to all classes of society their just political power," the authors display their desire to be included in the political nation and their determination that Chartism be seen as the fulfillment of Britain's long-standing traditions of civil and political liberty.

—☙—

William Lovett and John Collins, "Chartism: A New Organization of the People" (1840)

Being desirous of exerting the humble abilities God has given us towards procuring for our brethren equality of political rights, and placing them in such a social condition as shall best develop and preserve all their faculties, physical, moral, and intellectual, we have presumed to put forth the following pages for their consideration, containing our opinions of the best means of accomplishing those important objects. Believing that the proposed act of parliament, entitled "The People's Charter," is calculated to secure to all classes of society their just share of political power, and forming one of the most important steps to all social improvement, we are desirous of seeing the energies of all peacefully concentrated to cause that measure to be enacted as one of the laws of our country. Unhappily, the conflicting opinions entertained by some portion of the working-classes regarding the means of accomplishing that object have hitherto greatly retarded it; but we trust that experience, the great teacher of mankind, has led them to perceive that no other means are likely to be so effective as a peaceful combination of the millions, founding their hopes on the might and influence of intellectual and moral progress. . . . Various propositions have been made at different times for educating the whole people, none of which have been, nor deserve to be, adopted, on account of their exclusive or sectarian character. There is also so much evil to be apprehended from placing the education of our children in the hands of any government, especially of an irresponsible one, that it becomes one of the most important duties of the working and middle classes, to take the subject into their own hands, and to establish a just and liberal system of education, lest the power of educating their own children be taken from them by the arbitrary act of a corrupt and exclusive government. If, therefore, we should succeed in arousing the attention of the millions to the great importance of the subjects treated of in this pamphlet, we think we shall not have suffered twelve months' imprisonment in vain.

. . . According to the "Constitution," the Commons' House belongs to the common people. History informs us, that, at different periods, they have adopted different modes of choosing it, from the Universal Suffrage to that of individual choice; and if they find their present mode an improper one; they have surely a right to change it for a better, without the interference of those who belong to the other parts of the Constitution. If those they once elected as servants have gradually assumed the mastery, and by the power they were first invested with have rendered the People's House a corrupt and subservient instrument for party and faction to plunder and oppress the industrious with impunity, it is indeed time to talk of radical reform, in order that the people's portion of the Constitution may be placed in its original position; fairly to "balance" all the others. But if those sticklers for our Constitution, who are industriously opposing the efforts now making to reform the House of Commons, fail to recognize in their reading of that Constitution the right of Universal Suffrage; it will remain for them to prove its great and superior excellence to the satisfaction of the multitude. And great must be their ingenuity if, in these inquiring times, they can persuade them that universal labour and universal taxation do not fully entitle them to Universal Suffrage.

The supposition that Universal Suffrage would give the working classes a preponderating power in the House of Commons, is not borne out by the experience of other countries. They are far from possessing such a power even in America, where wealth and rank have far less influence than with us, and where the exercise of the suffrage for more than half a century have given them opportunities to get their rights better represented than they are. But wealth with them, as with us, will always maintain an undue influence, till the people are morally and politically instructed; then, indeed, will wealth secure its just and proper influence, and not, as at present, stand in opposition to the claims of industry, intellect, merit, freedom, and happiness. . . .

The assumption that the working classes would elect "violent and designing men" is equally absurd and groundless, as their public conduct on several occasions testifies. For, setting aside, as altogether worthless, the idea our opponents entertain, that all who differ from them in politics are "violent and designing," we maintain that, taking into account the whole of the political or municipal contests of the last seven years, the candidates who have been elected by the multitude by a shew of hands, have been better qualified for their respective offices, both intellectually and morally, than those who were subsequently elected by the privileged class of voters. It would be invidious were we to mention names, and draw parallels in proof of this assertion; but if any man of unbiased mind will contrast the cases that have come within the range of his experience during that period, he will agree with its general correctness. Whether such discrimination in working men betrays the "want of political information," and proves the superior mental qualification of electors, can only be partially proved, and that by examining the meritorious acts of the successful candidates. It would be well, however, if those who taunt the industrious classes with their "political ignorance," had first reviewed their political struggles during the last ten or twelve years. If they had considered their efforts to establish the rights of free discussion, to open mechanics' institutions, establish reading rooms and libraries, form working men's associations, and others of a like character; and, above all, their sufferings and difficulties in establishing a cheap press, by which millions of periodicals are weekly diffusing their enlightening influences throughout the empire; and then, if those scoffers at the ignorance of the millions had considered their present efforts to obtain their political rights, we think they would have reserved their illiberal taunts for others than the working classes.

. . . But, fellow workmen, while we ought to be anxious for the co-operation of good men among all classes, we should mainly rely on our own energies to effect our own freedom. For if we fail in activity, perseverance, and watchful exertions, and supinely trust our liberties to others, our disappointment will remind us of our folly, and new burthens and restrictions place our hopes at a still greater distance. Benevolent and well-intentioned individuals of all classes have warmly espoused our principles, and have zealously laboured to extend them; and thousands, we trust, will yet be found equally ardent and effective. But when we consider the various influences of rank, wealth, and station, which are continually operating to deter all those above our own sphere from becoming the open and daring advocates of our rights; and consider, moreover, the numerous links of relationship, professions, business-connection, interest, and friendship, which bind them to our present system; we should be the more readily convinced of the necessity of self-reliance, and the more firmly resolved by the concentration of every mental and moral energy nature has given us, to build up the sacred temple of our own liberties. The means are within our grasp, if we judiciously apply them, and no power on earth can prevent the consummation of so glorious an achievement. Then shall we the better appreciate what we have intellectually and morally erected; then shall we stand on its threshold erect, and enter its precincts rejoicing—possessing rights and feelings which no earthly power can confer, and inspired with a mental devotedness to use them for our country's welfare. And when we shall be no more, then may our children proudly point to that edifice raised by their hard-working progenitors when they were depressed by poverty, weakened by toil, and cursed by corrupt and plundering oppressors. Let our hopes then be built on our own united exertions, and let those exertions be proportioned to the magnitude of our object, and success will soon yield us a bountiful reward.

. . . The most important questions that, we conceive, have engaged our attention during the last twelve months are these:—How can we best create and extend an enlightened public opinion in favour of the People's Charter, such as shall peaceably cause its enactment; and how shall that opinion be morally and politically trained and concentrated, so as to realize all the social happiness that can be made to result from the powers and energies of representative democracy? While we have no disposition to renew the unwise and unprofitable discussion regarding "moral" and "physical" force; and while we maintain that the people have the same right to employ similar means to regain their liberties, as have been used to enslave them, we are anxious, as we have ever been, to effect our object in peace. And though we incurred no small share of censure from the most ardent of our brethren, for contending for the superiority of our moral energies over our physical abilities, we think the disposition we evinced, and the part we performed, both in and out of the Convention, towards carrying all and every righteous measure into effect likely to promote the passing of the Charter, will sufficiently exonerate us from any charge of cowardice, as well as from any selfish predilection in favour of our own opinions. And, however we may regret, we are not disposed to condemn, the confident reliance many of our brethren placed on their physical resources, nor complain of the strong feelings they manifested against us, and all who differed in opinion from them. We are now satisfied that many of them experience more acute sufferings, and daily witness worse scenes of wretchedness, than sudden death can possibly inflict, or battle-strife disclose to them. For, what worse can those experience on earth who, from earliest morn to latest night, are toiling in misery, yet starving while they toil—who, possessing all the anxieties of fond parents, cannot satisfy their children with bread—who, susceptible of every domestic affection, perceive their hearths desolate, and little ones neglected, while the wives of their bosoms are exhausting every toiling faculty in the field or workshop, to add to the scanty portion which merely serves to protract their lives of care-worn wretchedness? Men thus steeped in misery, and standing on the very verge of existence, cannot philosophise on prudence; they are disposed to risk their lives on any chance which offers the prospect of immediate relief, as the only means of rendering life supportable, or helping them to escape death in its most agonizing forms. When we further reflect on the circumstances which have hitherto influenced the great mass of mankind, we are not surprised at the feeling that prevails in favour of physical force. When we consider their early education—their school-book heroes—their historical records of military and naval renown—their idolized warriors of sea and land—their prayers for conquest, and thanksgivings for victories—and the effect of all these influences to expand their combative faculties, and weaken their moral powers, we need not wonder that men generally place so much reliance on physical force, and undervalue the superior force of their reason and moral energies. Experience, however, will eventually dispel this delusion, and will cause reformers to hold in reserve the exercise of the former, till the latter has been proved to be ineffectual. Nor can we help entertaining the opinion, that recent experience has greatly served to lessen the faith of the most sanguine in their theory of force, and caused them to review proposals they once spurned as visionary and contemptible. While we never doubted the constitutional right of Englishmen to possess "arms," we have doubted the propriety of placing reliance on such means for effecting our freedom; and further reflection has convinced us, that far more effective and certain means are within our reach.

. . . As some persons, however, may imagine that such important results are not within the compass of practicability, while others may suppose that the numerous objects embraced in such a plan are calculated to place our political emancipation at a greater distance, we proceed at once to submit the following "Plan, Rules, and Regulations," for the consideration of our brethren; hoping we shall hereafter be able to demonstrate its practicability, and prove it to be the nearest means towards the accomplishment of our great object—that of securing to all men their equal political and social rights.

The legislative reform of industrial conditions began in 1802 with the Health and Morals of Apprentices Act; subsequent Factory Acts (1819 and 1833) were limited to work in textile mills. The 1842 Mines Act followed upon the Report of the Royal Commissioners on mining conditions. In addition to prohibiting women and girls and boys under the age of 10 from being employed underground, the Act also authorized the appointment of Inspectors.

Children's Employment Commission:
Appendix to the First Report of Commissioners—Mines (1842)
Part II: Reports and Evidence from Sub-Commissioners.

Iron Workers and Collieries in Glamorganshire, Wales
GRAIG COLLIERY, parish of Merthyr, Glamorganshire, Wales—Messrs W and R
Thomas, Occupiers.
Persons employed:—

	MALES	FEMALES
Adults	28	4
Under 18	13	3
Under 13	2	

No. 49. Mr Thomas Howell, Overseer to Graig Colliery:

"The Coal in the Graig is worked for the London market, which we ship from Cardiff. We employ about 50 persons, out of which 10 are under 18 years of age; one third are females. I have been acquainted with this district many years, and have had many colliers under my charge at this and other works. The colliers in this part take both sexes down at very early ages; sometimes to assist in uncutting, trapping, or getting extra drams [carts] of work; the latter are claimed for children, although worked by the parents. Females are employed on the bank at drawing coals. Many come to work from service, as it [is] less restraining, and more money is gained; but it acts much to their injury, as amongst the mining men they acquire the habits of swearing and drinking, and soon lose that character for sobriety by which this part was characterized for centuries. Men who drive the heads in mines are subject to short breath and spit much; this disease reaches them at 40 to 45 years of age. Friendly societies have much increased, and though the men cry out against the bastardy clause, yet they avail them more of the opportunity, and the women are certainly more reckless, especially those who work in mines and iron-works. Accidents are rare in this part; have only had one fatal within two years. Ann Jenkins, a girl of 12 years of age, fell down the pit and died on the spot; the shaft is 60 yards deep; it is supposed she incautiously lay against the dram as it descended. The children are shamefully ignorant in the neighbourhood of Merthyr; the early age proprietors allow them admission entirely places them out of the pale of instruction."

No. 50. Mary Price, 17 years old, unloader:

"Unloads coals from the mouth of the pit, and wheels to the canal. The weight of coal in the drams is 8 cwt; sometimes less. Three drams count the ton; cannot say how many hundred-weight in the ton, or pounds in the hundred-weight. When the coals come up the shaft, I unlock the cage, and wheel the dram to canal-boat, and cast the coals over. The work is very hard, but am used to none other, as I was taken below the ground when seven years old to keep trap-doors. I once fell asleep when minding the trap-doors, and rolled on the tram, and a cart passed over me and broke my leg, which caused me to stay away from work some time yet. I go to a Welsh Sunday-school; am trying to make my letters; cannot read any yet. They have never told me anything of Jesus Christ, nor do I know who he is. I cannot knit; mother has taught me to mend my stockings."

No. 51. Jane Davies, 12 years old, wheels drams:

"Began to wheel drams of coal two years ago. never did any kind of work before, except fetch the water for mother to wash clothes with. Father is a boatman, and earns 18s to 20s a-week. Three children at home younger than self: do not know their ages. Never been to day-school; on Sundays go to Mr. Evan's chapel to learn the letters [knows four letters in the Welsh alphabet]. I hear the preaching sometimes, but do not know what the preacher means. I go because I am told it is good to go, and that it will prevent me from telling lies and swearing. I do not tell lies or swear; indeed I do not know who Jesus Christ is. My father never told me who made me. Mother seldom goes to chapel. I play after work is over, and wash myself always before I go to bed. I earn 14s a month. Sometimes my father slashes [beats] me."

No. 52. Ann Davis,
14 or 15 years old, wheels drams:

"Been unloading coals at Graig Colliery five weeks. Earns 18s a-month. Was at road-cleaning in the Plymouth Mine for near two years. Never was at school. Sometimes goes to chapel where Mr. Jones is preacher; he tells me to be a good girl, and not to swear, as the good go to heaven and the bad to hell. Have heard something about Jesus Christ; can't say who he is; indeed I do not know who God is—no, nothing do I know about him. Never heard what prayer means; have seen people on their knees; thinks they ask to go to a good place; do not know who they ask. Father is a collier; mother a collier's daughter. When I get home they send me to buy things for eating. Sometimes I buy things by the pound; I think there are two halves in the pound; can't say how many ounces or quarters. Sometimes I buy linen and flannel with mother, but I do not know how many feet are in the yard. The pit-shaft is 60 yards deep; so they tell me; can't say how many feet."

53. Charlotte Chiles,
19 years old, lander and weigher of coals:

"I draw, land, and weigh coals: have done so for two years. Was kitchen-maid at Lord Kensington's, near Carmarthen, I prefer this work, as it is not so confining, and I get more money. My wages are 40s a-month; as a servant I only earned 60s or 70s for the year's service. I cannot save money now; but I can get more dress and more liberty. I work 12 hours daily. I was six years at a free school at Pembroke, and was taught to read, write, and cipher [all of which she does well, and is well acquainted with Scripture]. My brothers are ironstone-miners, and work near to me. The work, though very hard, I care nothing for, as I have good health and strength."

No. 54 John Evans David, 42 years old, collier:

"Been upwards of 35 years in mines about this quarter of Wales. Has suffered much from asthma, which he considers has been caused by the air of the mines, and smoke which gathers after blasting. Spits a black fluid; has done so five years; does so if off work a month or more. The fluid thrown up is like black paint; and many miners are affected with the complaint; should think one in ten are touched after they arrive at 40 years. Scarcely ever drinks spirits, nor do the colliers about here do so; the new beer is preferred. Always clothes in flannel close to skin, and takes meat generally for dinner. Works 10 to 12 hours. The gunpowder consumed in blasting in my work costs about 1s to 1s 6d weekly. Have brought my boy to work; he is eight years of age; the Sunday-school teachers are instructing him in his letters."

. . . Dinas Colliery,
parish of Yshadgvogodog, Glamorganshire.
Walter Coffin, Proprietory.
Males Employed:

Adults	301
Under 18	32
Under 13	81

No. 94. Walter Coffin, Esq, proprietor

"The workings here are ventilated in the mode common to the collieries in the north of England. They are entered by shafts. NO loss of life has ever occurred in our mines by the machinery. No ropes are used except in sinking new pits; chains, which are safer, are generally used. The mainways are about five feet high, and the thickness of the seam of coal we are now working is about three feet; about 42 fathoms from the surface of the earth. We have some inflammable gas in our pits, but no accidents have arisen either from fire-damp or choke-dam; one man was killed within the last two years; it was in sinking a new pit; he fell off a stage in the middle to the bottom of the pit."

"We have no females employed in our workings, nor do we use the girdle and chain. . . . The youngest age at which children are employed with us is eight years of age, and their occupation is generally attending the air-doors; they appear healthy, but they certainly should not be employed at an earlier age. . . . There is a school attached to the colliery; a payment of 2d in the pound is stopped at the pay-table for the support of that school, and 1d in the pound is stopped for the medical gentleman who attends the workplace."

No. 103. William Isaac, 11 years old, air-door keeper:

"Has to keep the air-doors in the coal-mine; goes down the shaft at four or five in the morning, and returns at five and six at night; works frequently at night. Been four years below ground; was burned by fire-dam 20 months since, and laid idle 18 months; only returned to pit two months since. The accident took place from a collier incautiously entering an old working with his candle near the roof; several were burned, and the horse which brought up the train of carts was killed. Takes bread and cheese down. Was at day-school before at work in coal-mine; had learned the reading; has forgotten all now, or nearly so [cannot read]; has lately been at Sunday-school; the teachers instruct the children in the Welsh language, and few are beyond the spelling." [Neglected; the whole skin of the face burned, and had a very disagreeable appearance the eyes much inflamed].

No. 104. Llewellyn Powell, 14 years old, collier:

"Assists his father; has done so six years; when idle above is sent to school, to Mr. Jenkins's; can read Welsh, and write a few words; goes to Methodists' chapel on Sundays; never was taught English; father and mother speak only [Welsh]; earns 6s, and sometimes 8s in the week." [Very little scriptural knowledge.]

No. 105. Matthew Lewis, 11 years old, collier:

"Began to work at seven years old; works 12 hours daily, sometimes longer; is wrought near to 30-inch vein. Was burned by fire-damp three years ago, when at the air-door, and laid aside six months; was attended by Mr. Evan Davis; the medical attendant was, he believes, paid by Mr. Caffin. The pain was very great; several others were burned at the same time, one almost to death; feels very sore at times from the new skin being very tender. Spells a little Welsh; does not understand a word of English; no scriptural knowledge."

In this, the official Repeal Year (1843), Daniel O'Connell passionately argues for an end to the Act of Union.

Daniel O'Connell, Speech at Mullinger (1843)

My first object is to get Ireland for the Irish (*loud cheers*) . . .

Nobody can know how to govern us as well as we would know how to do it ourselves—nobody could know how to relieve our wants as well as we would ourselves—nobody could have so deep an interest in our prosperity, or could be so well fitted for remedying our evils, and procuring happiness (loud cheers). That is what I am struggling for (*hear, hear*). What numberless advantages would not the Irish enjoy if they possessed their own country? A domestic parliament would encourage Irish manufactures. The linen trade, and the woollen would be spreading amongst you. An Irish parliament would foster Irish commerce, and protect Irish agriculture. The labourer, the artizan, and the shopkeeper would be all benefited by the repeal of the union; but if I were to describe all the blessings that it would confer I would detain you here crowding on each other's backs until morning before I would be done (*laughter*). In the first place I ask did you ever hear of the tithe rent charge (*groans*). Are you satisfied to be paying parsons who do not pray for you (*no, no*). It is time, therefore, that they should be put an end to (*hear, hear*). The people of England do not pay for the church of the minority. I would thus do you two pieces of service by the repeal of the Union. I would relieve the poor without the imposition of poor rates, and I would prevent you from paying any clergy but your own (*loud cheers*). I should not have used the word prevent, because if any of you wished to pay both you might do it if you pleased (*laughter*). I often asked Protestants how would they like to pay for the support of the Catholic clergy by force, and they always said they would not like it at all; and why should the Catholics like it one bit the better (*hear*)? [He would abolish the grand jury, cess, and the treasury, not poor farmers and tenants who would pay for public words, roads and bridges.] I want that every head of a family, every married man and every householder should have a right to vote for members of parliament. They say that I would have an interest in that, because I would then have more votes; but my answer is, if I would it is because the people know I am acting honestly by them, and everybody else who does the same will be equally supported. The landlords now persecute those who vote differently from their wishes, but I would institute the ballot-box. Every married man should have a vote, and any blackguard who could not get a wife anywhere I would not pity him to be without the vote (*cheers and laughter*). The good landlord would then be sure to be supported by his tenants; but if he were a scoundrel, whether he was a Catholic, a Protestant, or a Presbyterian, he would deserve to be turned out (*hear, hear*). If he was serving notices to quit, or holding up his head in the street, and not looking his tenants in the face and speaking to them, or if he was a man who would not salute their wives and children as he passed them, or if, when he sat upon the bench, he was always fining, fining, fining (*loud laughter*), the tenant would always have the advantage of using the ballot-box against that fellow (*hear, hear, and cheers*). . . . You know that the landlords have duties as well as rights, and I would establish the fixity of tenure (*loud cheers*) to remind them of these duties. I will tell you what my plan is, and you can consider it among yourselves. My plan is that no landlord could recover rent unless he made a lease for twenty-one years to the tenant—no lease or no rent say I (*loud cheers*). Unless he made a lease, he would have no more business looking for his rent than a dog would have barking at the moon (*cheers and laughter*).

They would not leave Dublin till they would agree to an Act of Parliament to establish a domestic legislature, household suffrage, vote by ballot, fixity of tenure, and a law against absentees having estates in the country. Many estates would then be sold, in lots and purchased by those who would become small proprietors; and it was a fact well ascertained that in proportion as the owners in fee were numerous in any country, so in proportion were the people prosperous (*hear, hear*). It was truly said by Mr. Martin, their chairman, that if they had their own parliament, taxation would be diminished to almost nothing. . . .

Harriet Martineau (see above) traveled over the course of her life, to Egypt, Palestine, Ireland, and the United States. Although she was not able to attend the Women's Rights Convention in America in 1851, her letter, below, attests to the transatlantic nature of abolition in the Victorian era.

Harriet Martineau,
Letter to the American Women's Rights Convention (1851)

MY DEAR MADAM: I beg to thank you heartily for your kindness in sending me the Report of the Proceedings of your 'Woman's Rights Convention.' I had gathered what I could from the newspapers concerning it, but I was gratified at being able to read, in a collected form, addresses so full of earnestness and sound truth as I found most of the speeches to be. I hope you are aware of the interest excited in this country by that Convention; the strongest proof of which is the appearance of an article on the subject in *The Westminster Review* (for July,) as thorough-going as any of your own addresses, and from the pen (at least, as it is understood here,) of one of our very first men, Mr. John S. Mill. I am not without hope that this article will materially strengthen your hands, and I am sure it cannot but cheer your hearts.

As for me, my thoughts and best wishes will be with you when you meet in October. I cannot accept your hearty invitation to attend your Convention, as my home duties will not allow of my leaving my own country. But you may be assured of my warm and unrestricted sympathy. Ever since I became capable of thinking for myself, I have clearly seen—and I have said it till my listeners and readers are probably tired of hearing it—that there can be but one true method in the treatment of each human being of either sex, of any color, and under any outward circumstances—to ascertain what are the powers of that being, to cultivate them to the utmost, and *then* to see what action they will find for themselves. This has probably never been done for men, unless in some rare individual cases. It has certainly never been done for women: and, till it is done, all debating about what woman's intellect is—all speculation, or laying down the law, as to what is woman's sphere, is a mere beating of the air. *A priori* conceptions have long been found worthless in physical science, and nothing was really effected till the experimental method was clearly made out and strictly applied in practice, and the same principle holds most certainly through the whole range of Moral Science. Whether we regard the physical fact of what women are able to do, or the moral fact of what woman ought to do, it is equally necessary to abstain from making any decision prior to experiment. We see plainly enough the waste of time and thought among the men who once talked of Nature abhorring a vacuum, or disputed at great length as to whether angels could go from end to end without passing through the middle; and the day will come when it will appear to be no less absurd to have argued, as men and women are arguing now, about what woman ought to do, before it was ascertained what woman can do. Let us once see a hundred women educated up to the highest point that education at present reaches—let them be supplied with such knowledge as their faculties are found to crave, and let them be free to use, apply and increase their knowledge as their faculties shall instigate, and it will presently appear what is the sphere of each of the hundred. One may be discovering comets, like Miss Herschel; one may be laying upon the mathematical structure of the universe, like Mrs. Somerville; another may be analyzing the chemical relations of Nature in the laboratory; another may be penetrating the mysteries of physiology; others may be applying Science in the healing of diseases; others may be investigating the laws of social relations, learning the great natural laws under which society, like every thing else, proceeds; others, again, may be actively carrying out the social arrangements which have been formed under these laws; and others may be chiefly occupied in family business, in the duties of the wife and mother, and the ruler of a household. If, among the hundred women, a great diversity of powers should appear, (which I have no doubt would be the case), there will always be plenty of scope and material for the greatest amount and variety of power that can be brought out. If not—if it should appear that women fall below men in all but the domestic function—then it will be well that the experiment has been tried; and the trial had better go on forever, that woman's sphere may forever determine itself, to the satisfaction of everybody.

It is clear that Education, to be what I demand on behalf of woman, must be intended to issue in active life. A man's medical education would be worth little, if it was not a preparation for practice. The astronomer and the chemist would put little force into their studies, if it was certain that they must leave off in four or five years, and do nothing for the rest of their lives; and no man could possibly feel much interest in political and social morals, if he knew that he must all his life long, pay taxes, but neither speak nor move about public affairs. Women, like men, must be educated with a view to action, or their studies cannot be called Education, and no judgment can be formed of the scope of their faculties. The pursuit must be the life's business, or it will be mere pastime or an irksome task. This was always my point of difference with one who carefully cherished a reverence for woman—the late Dr. Channing. How much we spoke and wrote of the old controversy—INFLUENCE *vs.* OFFICE! He would have had any woman study any thing that her faculties led her to, whether physical science, or law, government and political economy; but he would have had her stop at the study. From the moment she entered the hospital as physician, and not nurse; from the moment she took her place in a court of justice in the jury-box, and not the witness-box; from the moment she brought her mind and her voice into the legislature, instead of discussing the principles of laws at home; from the moment she . . . administered justice, instead of looking upon it from afar, as a thing with which she had no concern—she would, he feared, lose her influence as an observing intelligence, standing by in a state of purity, 'unspotted from the world.' My conviction always was, that an intelligence never carried out into action could not be worth much; and that, if all the action of human life was of a character so tainted as to be unfit for woman, it could be no better for men, and we ought all to sit down together to let barbarism overtake us once more. My own conviction is, that the natural action of the whole human being occasions not only the most strength, but the highest elevation: not only the warmest sympathy, but the deepest purity. The highest and purest beings among women seem now to be those who, far from being idle, find among their restricted opportunities some means of strenuous action; and I cannot doubt that, if an active social career were open to all women, with due means of preparation for it, those who are high and holy now would be high and holy then, and would be joined by an innumerable company of just spirits from among those whose energies are now pining and fretting in enforced idleness or unworthy frivolity, or brought down into pursuits and aims which are any thing but pure and peaceable. In regard to this old controversy—of Influence *vs.* Office—it appears to me that, if Influence is good and Office is bad for human morals and character, Man's present position is one of such hardship as it is almost profane to contemplate; and if, on the contrary, Office is good and a life of Influence is bad, Woman has an instant right to claim that her position be amended. . . .

Isabella Beeton (1836–65) wrote her *Book of Household Management* because she believed that "there is no more fruitful source of family discontent than a house-wife's badly cooked dinners and untidy ways." Her response was to offer the middle-class lady of the house strict instructions on the benefits and possibilities of careful domestic engineering. She died shortly thereafter at the age of 28 from complications following the birth of her fourth child.

Isabella Beeton, from *The Book of Household Management* (1861)

1. As with the Commander of an Army, or the leader of any enterprise, so is it with the mistress of a house. Her spirit will be seen through the whole establishment; and just in proportion as she performs her duties intelligently and thoroughly, so will her domestics follow in her path. Of all those acquirements, which more particularly belong to the feminine character, there are none which take a higher rank, in our estimation, than such as enter into a knowledge of household duties; for on these are perpetually dependent the happiness, comfort, and well-being of a family. . . .

2. Pursuing this Picture, we may add, that to be a good housewife does not necessarily imply an abandonment of proper pleasures or amusing recreation; and we think it the more necessary to express this, as the performance of the duties of a mistress may, to some minds, perhaps seem to be incompatible with the enjoyment of life. Let us, however, now proceed to describe some of those home qualities and virtues which are necessary to the proper management of a Household, and then point out the plan which may be the most profitably pursued for the daily regulation of its affairs. . . .

4. Cleanliness is also indispensable to Health, and must be studied both in regard to the person and the house, and all that it contains. Cold or tepid baths should be employed every morning, unless, on account of illness or other circumstances, they should be deemed objectionable. The bathing of children will be treated of under the head of "Management of Children."

5. Frugality and Economy are Home Virtues, without which no household can prosper. . . . The necessity of practising economy should be evident to every one, whether in the possession of an income no more than sufficient for a family's requirements, or of a large fortune, which puts financial adversity out of the question. We must always remember that it is a great merit in housekeeping to manage a little well. "He is a good waggoner," says Bishop Hall, "that can turn in a little room. To live well in abundance is the praise of the estate, not of the person. I will study more how to give a good account of my little, than how to make it more." In this there is true wisdom, and it may be added, that those who can manage a little well, are most likely to succeed in their management of larger matters. Economy and frugality must never, however, be allowed to degenerate into parsimony and meanness.

10. Good Temper should be cultivated by every mistress, as upon it the welfare of the household may be said to turn; indeed, its influence can hardly be over-estimated, as it has the effect of moulding the characters of those around her, and of acting most beneficially on the happiness of the domestic circle. Every head of a household should strive to be cheerful, and should never fail to show a deep interest in all that appertains to the well-being of those who claim the protection of her roof. . . .

14. Charity and Benevolence are duties which a mistress owes to herself as well as to her fellow-creatures; and there is scarcely any income so small, but something may be spared from it, even if it be but "the widow's mite." It is to be always remembered, however, that it is the spirit of charity which imparts to the gift a value far beyond its actual amount, and is by far its better part.

. . . Visiting the houses of the poor is the only practical way really to understand the actual state of each family; and although there may be difficulties in following out this plan in the metropolis and other large cities, yet in country towns and rural districts these objections do not obtain. Great advantages may result from visits paid to the poor; for there being, unfortunately, much ignorance, generally, amongst them with respect to all household knowledge, there will be opportunities for advising and instructing them, in a pleasant and unobtrusive manner, in cleanliness, industry, cookery, and good management. . . .

17. Engaging Domestics is one of those duties in which the judgment of the mistress must be keenly exercised. There are some respectable registry-offices, where good servants may sometimes be hired; but the plan rather to be recommended is, for the mistress to make inquiry amongst her circle of friends and acquaintances, and her tradespeople. The latter generally know those in their neighbourhood, who are wanting situations, and will communicate with them, when a personal interview with some of

them will enable the mistress to form some idea of the characters of the applicants, and to suit herself accordingly. . . .

18. In obtaining a Servant's Character, it is not well to be guided by a written one from some unknown quarter; but it is better to have an interview, if at all possible, with the former mistress. By this means you will be assisted in your decision of the suitableness of the servant for your place, from the appearance of the lady and the state of her house. Negligence and want of cleanliness in her and her household generally, will naturally lead you to the conclusion, that her servant has suffered from the influence of the bad example.

The proper course to pursue in order to obtain a personal interview with the lady is this:—The servant in search of the situation must be desired to see her former mistress, and ask her to be kind enough to appoint a time, convenient to herself, when you may call on her; this proper observance of courtesy being necessary to prevent any unseasonable intrusion on the part of a stranger. Your first questions should be relative to the honesty and general morality of her former servant; and if no objection is stated in that

Table of the Average Yearly Wages

	When Not Found in Livery	*When Found in Livery*
The house steward	From £40 to £80	—
The valet	From £25 to £50	From £20 to £30
The butler	From £25 to £50	—
The cook	From £20 to £40	—
The gardener	From £20 to £40	—
The footman	From £20 to £40	From £15 to £25
The under butler	From £15 to £30	From £15 to £25
The coachman	—	From £20 to £35
The groom	From £15 to £30	From £12 to £20
The under footman	—	From £12 to £20
The page or footboy	From £8 to £18	From £6 to £14
The stableboy	From £6 to £12	—

	When No Extra Allowance Is Made for Tea, Sugar, and Beer	*When an Extra Allowance Is Made for Tea, Sugar, and Beer*
The housekeeper	From £20 to £15	From £18 to £40
The lady's-maid	From £12 to £25	From £10 to £20
The head nurse	From £15 to £30	From £13 to £26
The cook	From £14 to £30	From £12 to £26
The upper housemaid	From £12 to £20	From £10 to £17
The upper laundry-maid	From £12 to £18	From £10 to £15
The maid-of-all-work	From £9 to £14	From £7 to £11
The under housemaid	From £8 to £12	From £6 to £10
The still-room maid	From £9 to £14	From £8 to £12
The nursemaid	From £8 to £12	From £5 to £10
The under laundry-maid	From £9 to £14	From £8 to £12
The kitchen-maid	From £9 to £14	From £8 to £12
The scullery-maid	From £5 to £9	From £4 to £8

respect, her other qualifications are then to be ascertained. Inquiries should be very minute, so that you may avoid disappointment and trouble, by knowing the weak points of your domestic. . . .

21. The [preceding] Table of the Average Yearly Wages paid to domestics, with the various members of the household placed in the order in which they are usually ranked, will serve as a guide to regulate the expenditure of an establishment:

These quotations of wages are those usually given in or near the metropolis; but, of course, there are many circumstances connected with locality, and also having reference to the long service on the one hand, or the inexperience on the other, of domestics, which may render the wages still higher or lower than those named above. All the domestics mentioned in the above table would enter into the establishment of a wealthy nobleman.

While he echoes some of Beeton's concerns, this observer of Australian society also addresses the problems that "service" posed to household management in a white settler colony—including the relative value of "colonials" versus Irish servants.

Richard Twopenny on Servants in Australia (1883)

. . . Where mistresses are many and servants are few, it goes almost without saying that large establishments are out of the question. Given equal incomes, and the English mistress has twice as many servants as the Australian, and what is more, twice as competent ones. . . . I don't suppose there are a hundred households in all Australia which keep a butler pure and simple, though there must be several thousand with what is generically known as a man-servant, who gets twenty-five shillings a week, all found. A coachman's wages are on the average about the same. The "boy" gets ten shillings. Man-cooks are rare. A decent female cook, who ranks out here as first-class, earns fifteen shillings to a pound a week. For this sum she is supposed to know something about cooking; yet I have known one in receipt of a weekly guinea look with astonishment at a hare which had been sent to her master as a present, and declare that it was "impossible to make soup out of that thing." After a little persuasion she was induced to try to make hare-soup after Mrs. Beeton's recipe, but the result was such as to try the politeness of her master's visitors. This lack of decent cooks is principally due to the lack of establishments large enough to keep kitchen maids. Would-be cooks have no chance of acquiring their art by training from their superiors; they gain their knowledge by experiments on their employers' digestions; never staying long in one place, they learn to make some new dishes in each house they go to, and gradually rise in the wages-scale.

Directly you come to incomes below a thousand a year, the number of servants is often reduced to a maid-of-all-work, more or less competent according to her wages, which run from seven to fifteen shillings a week. At the former price she knows absolutely nothing; at the latter something of everything. She cooks, washes, sweeps, dusts, makes the beds, clears the baths, and answers the door. All is grist that comes to her mill; and if she is Jill-of-all-trades and mistress of none, one must admit that an English-bred servant would not be one quarter so suitable to colonial requirements. Of course she is independent, often even cheeky, but a mistress learns to put up with occasional tantrums, provided the general behaviour and character are good. When we were first out here we used to run a-muck with our servants about once a week; but now we find it better to bear the ills we have than to fly to others which we know not of. Our present Lizzie is impertinent to a degree when reproved; but then she can cook decently, and she is the first decent cook we have had since we have been out here. When you have lived on colonial fare for a few months, a good plain dinner covers a multitude of sins.

Unfortunately, four-fifths of our servants are Irish,—liars and dirty. These Irish are less impertinent than the colonials; but if you do get hold of a well-trained colonial, she is worth her weight in gold on account of her heterogeneity. Your Irish immigrant at eight and ten shillings a week has as often as not never been inside any other household than her native hovel, and stares in astonishment to find that you don't keep a pig on your drawing-room sofa. On entering your house, she gapes in awe of what she considers the grandeur around her, and the whole of her first day's work consists of ejaculating "Lor" and "Goodness!" We once had a hopeful of this kind who, after she had been given full instructions as to how a rice-pudding was to be made, sat down and wept bitterly for half an hour, till—her mistress having told her to "bake"—the happy thought struck her to put a dish full of rice in the oven, *sans* milk, *sans* eggs, *sans* everything. Another Biddy, engaged by a friend of ours, having to make a yeast-cake, put it under her bed-clothes "just to plump it a bit." A third, having been given a bill-of-fare for the day, put soup, meat, and pudding all into one pot, and served them up *au pot-pourri.*

. . . When there are children in a middle-class family, a nurse-girl is generally, but by no means always, kept. Hers is the lowest of all the branches of service, and is only taken by a young girl just going out into the world. Trained nurses, such as are common at home, are in great demand, and are almost unobtainable. They can earn a pound a week easily, and at such wages a man whose income only runs into three figures is forced to put up with a nurse-girl. She undertakes no responsibility, her duties being confined to carrying the baby and screaming at the other children if they attempt to do themselves any bodily harm. If you wish to understand what the average nurse-girl is like, you have but to walk through any of the public gardens; you will see babies without number left in the blazing sun, some hanging half-way out of their perambulators, others sucking large painted "lollies" or green apples. The elder children, if they are unruly, are slapped and sent off to play by themselves, while the nurse-girls hold a confab on a neighbouring bench. Not that these girls are necessarily bad, but they lack the supervision and training of a head-nurse; they have been taught to look upon nursing as derogatory, and never stay long enough as nurses to get any experience in handling children. A few months of this, the lowest stage of servant-galdom, and then they pass into the maid-of-all-work class. Thus it is that many mothers prefer undertaking the duties of nurse themselves, and devote themselves to their children at the expense of their husbands, and certainly of all social relations. . . .

The great redeeming-point about the servant-girl is the power she acquires of getting through a large and multifarious quantity of work. She has frequently to do the whole house-work, cooking, washing, and ironing for a family of six or seven, and unless the mistress and her daughters are particularly helpful, it is out of all reason to expect that any of those things can be well done. Of course there are some good servants, but, unfortunately for their employers, the butchers and bakers generally have a keen eye for such, arguing with great justice that a good servant is likely to make a good wife.

The greater part of the high wages which servants get is spent on dress. If ever they condescend to wear their mistress's left-off clothes, it is only for work in the house; but the trouble they take to copy the exact fashion and cut of their mistress's clothes is very amusing. One girl we had frankly asked my wife to allow her to take a dress she admired to her dressmaker, in order that she might have one made up like it. Whilst girls in the upper and middle classes are very handy with their fingers, and often make up their own hats and dresses, the servant-class despise to do this, and almost invariably employ milliners, who often cheat them dreadfully, knowing that they appreciate a hat or a dress much according to the price they have paid for it, and the amount of show it makes. In hats and bonnets this is specially noticeable; I have often seen our servants with hats or bonnets on, which cannot have cost them less than three or four pounds.

The shortest and upon the whole the best way to get a servant is by going to one of the numerous registry offices. Some of these exist merely to palm off bad servants upon you; but there are always offices of good reputation, which will not recommend a girl they know absolutely nothing about.

The needlewoman is little in vogue here; but as nearly everyone washes at home, washerwomen are plentiful; their wages run from four to five shillings a day, according to their capabilities, food being of course included.

In spite of constant shipments from England, servants are always at a premium, and I need scarcely point out what an excellent opening these colonies afford for women-servants. Unfortunately, but a very small proportion of the daughters of the poorer colonial working-class will go into service. For some inexplicable reason, they turn up their noses at the high wages and comparatively light work offered, and prefer to undertake the veriest drudgery in factories for a miserable pittance. At a recent strike in a large shirt-making factory in Melbourne, it came out that a competent needlewoman could not make more than eighteen shillings a week even by working overtime, and that the general average earnings of a factory girl were only eleven to thirteen shillings a week. But so great is the love of independence in the colonial girl, that she prefers hard work and low wages in order to be able to enjoy freedom of an evening. It is in vain that the press points out that girls whose parents do not keep servants are accustomed to perform the same household duties in their own homes that are required of them in service; that work which is not degrading at home cannot become degrading in service; and that they will be the better wives for the knowledge of household work which they acquire in service. They might as well preach to the winds; and there are more applications for employment in shops and factories than there is work for, whilst mistresses go begging for lady-helps. There is a sad side to this picture as regards the social condition of the colonies, in addition to the inconvenience to people who keep servants. The girls who go into shops and factories, and have their evenings to themselves, necessarily undergo a great deal of temptation, and it is undeniable that they are not at all delivered from evil. The subject is out of keeping with these letters, but unless some means can be found to reconcile colonial girls to service, I fear an evil is growing up in our midst which is likely to be even more baneful in its effects upon the community than the corresponding tendency to "larrikinism" amongst colonial youths.

C. Imperial Britons at Midcentury

Lieutenant John Ouchterlony's book was among the first detailed accounts of the military side of the First Anglo-Chinese War (1839–43), a war prompted in the first instance by the confiscation of all the opium stored by British merchants in Cantonese warehouses but which was in fact the outcome of two decades of attempts by the Chinese emperor to quash the British import trade. Among the postwar settlement provisions was the opening of five long-desired ports to the British and the secession of Hong Kong to the British Crown.

Lieutenant John Ouchterlony, from *The Chinese War* (1844)

... Gloom had now overcast the political horizon in China, and affairs had, in the commencement of 1841, approached that crisis whence no extrication could be hoped, consistent with the dignity and honour of the British nation, save by a display of that power which the ignorant Chinese had so long affected to despise. During the early part of the past year, the position of the British community remained nearly unchanged, very few individuals venturing to trust their persons within the reach of the Imperial commissioner, and the greater number residing on board merchant vessels at the anchorage of Toong-Koo, near the island of Lintin; a few remained, with their families, at Macao; and beyond the anxiety attending the uncertainty of their position among the Portuguese, and that caused by the extensive gathering of troops in the vicinity of the settlement, their residence was not rendered so precarious and unpleasant as it had been found in the latter part of the preceding year. Early in January, appeared an edict of the Emperor, expressing his satisfaction at the stoppage of all British trade; and this gave public confirmation and approval of the extraordinary and almost desperate proceedings of Lin. The tone which he adopted was now undisguisedly hostile, defiance was hurled in his own edicts against the British, and a large bounty was set upon their heads, to excite the populace along the sea-coast to expel and destroy them as noxious reptiles. All thought of compensation for the opium surrendered, and for the serious losses which the merchants had suffered during the tumult at Canton, and their expulsion from the factories, was repudiated, as well as all idea of abandoning their right to seize and execute foreigners, whenever the savage laws of the empire should demand life for life.

However, it would appear that about this time Lin had some misgivings as to the course which it was proposed to pursue, for he ordered the release of Captain Gribble, who had been seized by the crew of a mandarin's boat, while on his passage from Macao to Canton, an outrage which Captain Smith, the senior naval officer on the station, had immediately resented, by moving her Majesty's ships towards the Bogue, and threatening a blockade of the port in the event of the prisoner's detention.

. . . While affairs continued in this critical and unsatisfactory state in China, active measures were preparing in India for the hostile attitude which the unbearable and despotic conduct of the Chinese government had rendered indispensable. Early in the year, orders were received from England by the Governor-General of India, to organize a small but efficient force for service on the coast of China, and to prepare the transports for its conveyance, to start from Calcutta and Madras as soon as the verge of the northerly monsoon should approach. An order in council was also issued, declaring an embargo on all Chinese vessels, and directing reprisals to be made in the seas of China, while at the same time a royal commission was entrusted to Rear-Admiral Elliot, C.B., as chief, and to Captain Elliot, R.N., as second, for the purpose of making a communication to the imperial government regarding the differences and difficulties which had led to the existing unhappy state of public affairs in the southern districts of the empire.

The novel war which was thus in a measure proclaimed was not very popular in England, since there were many who could not divest their minds of the erroneous idea that it was undertaken to enforce upon the Chinese the continuance of a traffic whose tendency upon the morals and welfare of the people was of the most pernicious kind, and that it was a domineering and disgraceful attempt to compel the importation of an article strictly forbidden by their own laws; and further, that the sordid motives which had influenced the British government to appeal to arms in support of the unrighteous cause of the opium dealers, ought to be held in abhorrence as wholly unworthy of that standard which was now about to be unfurled against a race whose sole offence was a desire to maintain their own institutions, and to withdraw from all intercourse with a people who had spared no exertion to overturn and set them at defiance.

. . . Early on the morning of the 10th October, a strong column of infantry and artillery was landed upon a sandy beach far to the right or eastward of the Chinese position, and made a circuit round the base of the hills on which the main body of the enemy were posted, so as to get well in their rear, while their attention was diverted by the attack of another column which was landed near the mouth of the river, and by the fire of the men-of-war and steamers, which were anchored as close in shore as the shoaling of the water would allow, in order to demolish the defences of the citadel, and to throw shells into the batteries and entrenchments on the heights. A small detachment of sappers and miners, under Captain Cotton, of the Madras engineers, having been attached to Sir William Parker's column, the naval portion of the force was assigned the duty of carrying all the enemy's works on the left, or west bank of the river; and accordingly, after a brisk and effective cannonade of the works of the citadel, the boats of the squadron pushed in shore with the small-arms men and marines, who, scaling the rocky heights on which they were situated, entered by a gate already partially ruined by the well-directed fire of the Wellesley, and speedily made themselves masters of the position, from which the Chinese fled as they approached. The scaling-ladders were then planted against the ramparts of the city at a point favourable for escalade, and the naval column was speedily in possession of the place, no resistance being offered by the enemy, whose discomfiture on this side the river was now complete.

In the meanwhile, a dreadful scene of slaughter was enacting on the right bank of the river, where the Chinese troops, retiring before the advance of the centre column, under Sir Hugh Gough, in the hope of retreating across the river by a bridge of boats which had been left uninjured a short distance up the stream, came suddenly upon the head of the left column, which, having overcome all opposition in its course, had completed the circuit of the hills, and was debouching upon the banks of the river, so as effectually to intercept the retreat of the dense mass which was then crowding towards the bridge.

It is not difficult to conceive the scene which ensued. Hemmed in on all sides, and crushed and overwhelmed by the fire of a complete semicircle of musketry, the hapless Chinese rushed by hundreds into the water; and while some attempted to escape the tempest of death which roared around them, by consigning themselves to the stream, and floating out beyond the range of fire, others appeared to drown themselves in despair. Every effort was made by the general and his officers to stop the butchery, but the bugles had to sound the "cease firing" long and often before the fury of our men could be restrained. The 55th regiment and Madras rifles, having observed that a large body of the enemy were escaping from this scene of indiscriminate slaughter along the opposite bank of the river, from the citadel and batteries which the naval brigade had stormed, separated themselves, and pushing across the bridge of boats, severed the retreating column in two; and before the Chinese could be prevailed upon to surrender themselves prisoners, a great number were shot down or driven into the water and drowned.

The loss of the Chinese was immense in killed and wounded; a vast mob of prisoners was captured, besides numerous pieces of cannon, many of which were brass, an immense quantity of camp equipage, ammunition, arms, and stores of all descriptions, and a considerable number of junks and armed boats. The prisoners were all set at liberty on the following day, deprived of course of their arms, and some also of their tails, which, though an accident easily remedied by the humblest of their tonsors (by plaiting a new tail into the root of the old one), was a mark of disgrace that did not fall to the province of the victors to inflict, and was a wanton outrage on the feelings of the Chinese, which could only serve to exasperate them against their invaders. Sir Hugh Gough, when informed by an officer of what was taking place, sanctioned his interference, and ordered that the prisoners should be merely disarmed, and released without degradation of any kind. When, however, this gentleman, who had followed Sir Hugh Gough in a boat, reached the shore, the last man of the Chinese detenus was under the hands of the operator, a tar, who, upon being hailed to cease his proceedings, hastily drew his knife across the victimized tail, exclaiming that it was a pity the fellow should have the laugh against the rest.

. . . As the city had been taken possession of without resistance, every precaution was adopted to prevent plunder, while a rigid search was instituted after public treasure in such buildings as were considered likely to contain the coveted store, that it might be made available as legitimate prize-property. No great amount of bullion was, however, found, but several extensive stores of cash, a small thin copper coin, of which 100 equal a dollar, were discovered inside the city; as, however, there was a doubt about their being the property of the government, some informants alleging that the owners were merchants or bankers of the place, a difficulty arose touching the right of appropriation in the minds of the prize-agents, who had to decide questions of legality in regard to plunder. It was finally settled by taking a portion only, a sort of percentage on the whole, as a tax or insurance, in return for the security in which the remainder was kept under a British guard. A vast quantity of rice and other grain was found in the public granaries, and as this was not required for the use of the force, whose magazines were already well supplied, it was sold to the Chinese, who were allowed to take away as much as one man could carry for the sum of one dollar, a load which was in many instances almost miraculous, and for which the price demanded was not unfrequently paid in coin of a most doubtful character; several hundreds of counterfeit dollars were, in fact, received during the sale of the grain.

Some serviceable little ponies which were found in paddocks and in stables attached to the barracks of the city, were appropriated for the service of the artillery, and before long were rendered most useful as draught-animals, and for the transport of ammunition boxes and other necessary appendages of a field train. Shortly after the occupation of the town, the light-draught steamers were dispatched up the river to examine its course, to inquire into the condition of the province, and to ascertain what indications there might be of the assembling of large bodies of troops in the neighbourhood of the frontier towns. Nothing, however, was discovered which led the reconnoitering party to suppose that the Chinese meditated any aggressive operations against Ningpo; and as the chiefs of the expedition intended no further hostilities along the coast, the troops employed themselves in constructing fire-places in their barracks and in the guard-houses on the ramparts, improving the windows, planking the floors, and adopting all the measures of precaution against winter and foul weather which the experience of the older campaigners suggested.

The extensive buildings comprising the residence and offices of the Taou-tae, in which were included the prisons of Mrs. Noble and her fellow-captives, being situated too near the heart of the city to render them a desirable military post in an unfriendly place, they were abandoned, and some joss-houses and mandarins' residences near the north-west angle of the ramparts, were taken possession of as a cantonment for the whole force. The old quarters were condemned as the fuel store for the winter, (a few old bricks, a little wood, and half-a-dozen old Chinese matchlocks, made up an excellent grate in half-an-hour,) and long before the cold season had passed, its beams, rafters, doors, and windows had been consigned to the fire-places of the barrack-rooms, and nothing but the ruined walls of the capacious building remained. . . .

———

Chinese emigrant labour circulated throughout the British empire because the imperial economy was dependent on all kinds of nonwhite laborers, as this *Times* brief and the observations of Robert Thomson from Australia both illustrate. Whether concerned with statistics or the conditions of immigrant workers, Victorian observers were preoccupied with what they perceived as the cultural and racial characteristics of Chinese and Indian immigrants, and with what those meant for the future of the British Empire.

———

London *Times*, "Chinese Emigration" (1866)

CHINESE EMIGRATION.—During the season 1864–65 the number of emigrants who left China for British Guiana, Trinidad, and Honduras was 2,858, to British Guiana, 1,776, of whom 414 were women; to Trinidad, 612, of whom 187 were women; and to Honduras, 480, of whom 14 were women. To this number are to be added 15 born on the voyage, making a total of 2,873; the number of deaths on the voyage was 115, equal to 4 percent, which, the Emigration Commissioners say, cannot be considered large, considering the length of the voyage (about 102 days), and the impossibility of entirely excluding men whose constitutions have been enfeebled by opium eating. The emigration agent of Trinidad, in speaking of the Chinese as who arrived in that colony in the season of 1861–65, says that, with few exceptions, they have been more subordinate than was expected; that some of the gangs have not only worked well for wages, but have surrounded themselves with gardens, and have acquired pigs and poultry; and that the women are nearly all industrious and quiet. There are, however, exceptions, he adds, to this description, some of the gangs being idle and unmanageable. The Chinese are more difficult to manage than the Indians, and require temper and discretion on the part of the overseers; they have no respect for courts where corporal punishment is not inflicted, and are much given to petty thefts. The Chinese imported into Cuba are said to be more honest and trustworthy, and the immigration agent is of opinion that a severer discipline, including corporal punishment, would have a good effect on their first arrival. Imprisonment with hard labour they regard without apprehension. During the season 1865–66, 1,250 Chinese immigrants were ordered for British Guiana and 750 for Trinidad, in accordance with an arrangement which had been made by British Guiana and Trinidad for placing in a somewhat more permanent footing the immigration from China to those colonies. It was provided that British Guiana and Trinidad should take between them not less than 2,000 emigrants in the year, of whom five-eighths were to be sent to the former colony, and three-eighths to the latter. Two ships are reported as having been despatched from China for Trinidad carrying 613 emigrants, of whom six were women; and three for British Guiana carrying 1,278 emigrants, of whom 36 were women. The Emigration Commissioners have received intelligence of the arrival at their destination of three ships, conveying 1,106 emigrants; the number of deaths on the voyage was 22. . . . In one of the ships for British Guiana, the Pride of the Ganges, a mutiny broke out the day after the vessel sailed, the master and the purser were thrown overboard, and the mutineers compelled the first mate to land the passengers at Hainau. The ship was afterwards taken to Hong Kong by the mate, and sailed again for British Guiana with 305 emigrants, of whom 29 were women.

Robert Thomson on the Chinese in Australia (1888)

The question whether it is an advantage or injury to this country that "the rubbish of the Celestial Empire should continue to be shot on these shores" has already been sufficiently investigated, and more people have agreed, that it is decidedly an injury to it. Yet they who have so agreed, have hitherto argued as if they were mere sojourners in the land, whose sole object in being here was to get a living in a comfortable, moral, and respectable manner. On the other hand there is a minority—chiefly employers of labour—that maintains that though amongst the Chinese who come here certain vices are more prevalent than amongst Europeans, yet they are, as a rule, a peaceable, industrious, and, above all, a "Cheap people," and hence a benefit to the country—to the country, meaning to the employers of labour. This dictum of the minority, from its point of view, is apparently unimpeachable, though it is really not so. However, that is not a point to be discussed at present. The former of these opinions on the Mongolian influx may be aptly described as that of *a citizen of the British Empire;* the latter as that of *a cosmopolite or citizen of the world.* But there is another light in which the subject must be viewed by our people, and that is, from an Australian standpoint.

The Australian cannot look at the question in the same light as a man who is essentially a colonist, that is, one who goes to a new country to improve his condition in life, and cares for that country principally as affording him scope for obtaining an easier and better livelihood than he could expect "at home." But *this* country is the Australian's home. He knows no other. It is not for him a place for making money or for obtaining a living only. It is his native land, where in good or evil report he will live and die; and he owes it no divided allegiance, but that sacred and indissoluble attachment due from every man, savage or civilised, to the land of his birth. It may here be remarked that this attachment is always more perceptible in small or young democratic countries, for every native of the soil in such cases feels himself a more important unit in the sum total of his nation, than any single citizen of a long-established, populous country could consider himself. . . .

It will be evident from the foregoing, that the question whether the Chinese who come here are moral or immoral is a matter of comparative indifference to an Australian. Their crime is that they are a cheap race—cheap to a degree that is destructive to the white race. And, as we proudly hope that Australia shall one day be the seat of a mighty independent nation of the Anglo-Saxon race, to which Britain shall look in the far-off future with eyes full of trustful love and pride, it is our bounden duty as loyal and patriotic natives of the soil, to use every effort in our power to prevent the calamity which would bring about the one result, and so destroy our hopes and prospects of the other. In fact, it would be little short of treason to our land to stand by and see a cancer in her breast, which, though small at present, grows daily stronger in vitality, taking deeper and deeper root, and slowly but surely sending its noxious parasitical fibres hither and thither throughout our land.

. . . So far from thinking a Chinese war would be a calamity to Australia I fervently believe it would be the greatest blessing we could possibly receive. For it would give us an excuse to clear out every yellow alien from our midst; and there would be such an uprising of patriotism in Australia as has seldom been seen in Anglo-Saxon annals; for the Australian is more enthusiastic and excitable than his fathers. At the first threat of approaching danger, the youth, the young men and the old men of the continent would lay down their pens, their tools and their whips, and pick up whatsoever in the shape of a rifle or musket was available to their hands, and there would be a sound of shooting and of drilling and of martial command in every hamlet, township and city of the country. The whole land would ring with the shout of preparation, and in the general outburst of warlike enthusiasm the women even would not be idle. Never a girl would look at her lover did he not bear on his arm or breast the badge of Australian defence, and in every home in Australia fair women with sparkling eyes and warm hearts would be broidering the colours of the local companies or making the wherewithal to comfort those whom they loved but who soon might lay [*sic*] cold or wounded on a patriot's field. Yes, a Chinese threat of invasion would do all that and it would do more—far more: it would immediately federate our states into one nation; it would give us a permanent national government; and, baptised with the certain halo of a glorious victory in a truly righteous and holy cause, the flag of our new-born nation, the blue banner of the Southern Cross, would be an emblem that henceforth to all time would inspire the sons of our country with patriotic pride and a firm resolution to live true to her, and, when necessary, to die for her. No longer would our land hang doubtfully on the fiat of others. She would have arisen from the tutelage and the milk of dependence into the clear light of manhood and independence. No longer would the hated word "Colonial" be cast at our heads: but as citizens of the Sovereign and Independent States of Australia our people and their representatives could rightfully claim a free and equal admittance into the family of nations. . . .

In his moral character John Chinaman is like his den and his yard. He has, saving a species of ant-like industry, but one virtue, and that is the effect of the training of ages. He has a kind of regard for his progenitors. That is the single good point in the Mongol's moral side. As against this, he has no ideas such as prevail among Caucasian races of what is due from man to man. John Chinaman will leave his comrade to die in a ditch, or cast him upon the tender mercies of the whites. He has no wife; but merely a toy or a slave— a thing to gratify his lusts or a creature to be silent and obey. If he has more children than he requires, he either kills them in infancy—a practice which is recognised by his Government—or he sells them into slavery without the slightest compunction. John has no ideas in his language which are analogous to sin or morality in ours. If he sins more than usually, he never regrets the wrong—but merely the bad policy. In short, he has no ideas in common with Europeans on the subject of right and wrong. Everything is simply a question of good and bad taste. In the matter of lying, John is without a rival: but he is never troubled about his lies except when they are discovered, and then he grieves sorely because he overdid the thing. . . . the fact is the "Chinkie" generally knows all the filth that a mind with not a single moral principle in it could possibly imbibe, long before he leaves sight of the teeming dens and hovels of Canton or Hong Kong.

Such is the law-abiding, virtuous race of citizens that takes the fancy of some of our philanthropists and philosophers. I would advise these kind of gentlemen to take the Mongols to their own bosoms first, and to nurse them to be their daughters' husbands, and then, when they have well tested the matter in that-wise, I will certainly say they have some right to recommend John Chinaman to others.

Caroline Chisholm (1808–1877) worked for thirty years to assist single women and families in migrating to and settling in Australia. Her home for female immigrants in Sydney is best known, though she also founded a school for soldiers in Madras—indicating the wide geographical scope of her interests. Here, in her famous letter to Early Grey, she expressed the hope that her firsthand testimony and experience among emigrants would persuade the government that a "mature and immediate deliberation of the Imperial Parliament" on the subject of "a respectable system of female emigration."

Caroline Chisholm,
"Emigration and Transportation Relatively Considered" (1847)

My Lord,

If the subject which I am desirous of advocating be not of sufficient importance to plead my apology for thus addressing you, there is nothing which I could say that would make the act excusable.

At a season of such unparalleled misery and distress—at a time when England groans with the burden of her redundant population—the subject which I have chosen increases in importance and responsibility. The system so long pursued of peopling Australia with prisoners, naturally raised strong prejudices against free emigration, and which nothing but the extraordinary success and prosperity of her people could have removed; but the period has now arrived when a free passage to these Colonies is eagerly sought for by honest men and respectable families. It must be left to common sense to solve the financial question, as to whether it is better to endeavour to support the overburdened labour market of the United Kingdom by the instrumentality of Government works which are not required, and by an augmentation of the poor rates; or whether it would not be more in accordance with the sound spirit of political economy to give a free passage to her Majesty's Colonies, to such eligible families as should voluntarily come forward and solicit this boon.

. . . The demand for labour in New South Wales, Port Phillip, and South Australia, is urgent and increasing. Is it not a lamentable thought, then, my Lord, that deaths should daily result from starvation among British subjects, while in this valuable colony good wheat is rotting on the ground for the want of hands to gather it in;—that tens of thousands of fine sheep, droves after droves, thousands upon thousands of fat cattle are annually slaughtered there and "boiled down," in order to be rendered into tallow for the European market, while the vast refuse is cast into the fields to be devoured by dogs and pigs, and yet no effort is made by England to provide for her struggling people by a humane system of colonization? Let me then, in the name of suffering humanity, entreat of your Lordship to take into mature and immediate consideration, this demand for labour—this fearful waste of human food, and withal the vast capabilities of our Australasian Colonies, (nearly equal in size to all Europe); and let me hope that the result of your Lordship's deliberation, and that of other friends of humanity, will be to give to some of our starving peasantry a passage to a country admirably adapted to the hardworking man. I am aware that one Noble Lord has said, that we have land enough to support our population, and from a national feeling of vanity I wish to believe this true. Waste lands are to be cultivated by the poor! An undertaking which our capitalists do not deem a safe investment, is proposed as a wise measure for a half-famished population! To give a poor man the chance of getting good land, is a proposal that has never been made; surely, it can never be said that one of the strongest impediments in the way of emigration, is the dread that the poor would too soon become rich? . . . The love of possessing land is so strong a feeling in man's bosom, that it requires caution on the part of a Government lest it should be charged with feeding a spirit of thriftless speculation. It appears to me, however, that a very safe principle to go upon, is to meet the demand of the money market. If this were done, the cry of "No funds" would soon cease, for the labour market of New South Wales at this time is positively glutted with the small capitalists; but at the mere mention of a farm, the cry immediately is, "We should have Ireland the Second." Much do I wish to see this groundless dread removed; the absurdity of which, I am certain, your Lordship has too much discernment to participate in. . . .

. . . Transportation, as it is conducted in the present day, cannot be viewed as a punishment; for, to give a man disposed to work (supposing he is a common labourer) a free passage to any of the Australian Colonies, is equal to placing the interest of £1150 at his disposal! A highly respectable gentleman at Port Phillip, and who is an advocate for the renewal of transportation, in speaking of that splendid Colony, calls it "the Rogues' Paradise." Intimately acquainted as I am with the feelings of the emancipists and "ticket-of-leave men," I am compelled, in common justice to a British public, to state, that the general feeling amongst them is one of deep gratitude for having been sent to a Colony wherein they can procure abundance of food and every reasonable comfort. Often, my Lord, have I heard the emancipist, at family prayer, return thanks to Almighty God that his children were not in a country where they might be tempted by hunger to perpetrate crime. Any attempt, therefore, to deter men from the commission of crime by speaking of the horrors of transportation under the present "exile" system, is like frightening little babies to sleep by telling them "the boo-man will take them away." In making this admission in favour of the Colony, supported, as I can corroborate it, with the voluntary statements of the Australians, emigrants, ticket-of-leave men, and emancipists, I make no allusion to those unhappy men who have become victims to an ill-devised system; men whose hearts had been hardened by harshness; whose domestic feelings had been destroyed, until they have sunk into a state more like beasts than human beings. Their deplorable condition has at length been made a subject of humane consideration and enquiry by Her Majesty's Government. In all the systems, and every system which has hitherto been tried, I do not, as far as my observation has gone, see much to approve; on the whole, I am bound to say, that the ease with which men can earn a living honestly, has done more for the reformation of the prisoner than any other observable cause. One of the most demoralizing evils of the old system, has been the separation of the men from all domestic influence—rending for ever asunder the links of nature. The spirit of British justice never contemplated to sever for ever those whom "God had joined together;" nor is it in accordance with the dictates of religion and pure morality, that such a state of things should exist, as to doom men to be for years incarcerated together by hundreds, like a menagerie of wild beasts, or to live a solitary hopeless life in the bush; but so it is, thousands upon thousands are thus victimized, and destined to undergo all the frightful and deteriorating effects of this more than savage life.

. . . No individual, perhaps, has had so many opportunities as I have had of becoming acquainted with the people of New South Wales. Wandering for hundreds of miles in search of suitable homes and eligible employment for the emigrant families and ticket-of-leave men, I had been accustomed at nightfall to find shelter at the nearest hut; as one of the family I have shared in the hospitality of all classes, whether rich or poor; consequently, I have had opportunities of gaining an intimate knowledge of the peculiarities and feelings of the people, and these justify what might otherwise appear uncalled for— my recording here my humble testimony to the sterling worth and exemplary conduct, as a body, of the emancipists of New South Wales. . . . When engaged at one time in providing for some emigrant families in the interior, I was accommodated at a farm-house, where both the heads of the family happened to have been sent out by Her Majesty's Government; neither could read or write. Here I found a man engaged as teacher; certainly not the person you would wish to see trusted with the tuition of a promising young family of boys and girls. Their parents, a few weeks previous to my seeing them, had sent a few bushels of wheat to market, just to find them tea and sugar, until they could go to Sydney to sell their regular crop; they sold to the amount of 35s; sixteen shillings of this sum were expended on books and stationery for their children. The books were handed to me by the mother, who remarked; "they cost a good bit, but we could not do better with our money." One of the books was the life of———; the hero of this tale distinguished himself by his prodigies of adroit exploits in Newgate and its environs,—a wild story of facts and fiction. I remarked that I had been informed it was a dangerous book; that it made what was bad look like good; was particularly enticing to youths of a certain turn of mind. "Now, do you say so? How glad Jack will be you called—what a Providence!" and before I could even be aware of her intention, it was in flames on their hearthstone. It never entered into her mind it could be exchanged, re-sold; that my opinion might be wrong; but, at the mere mention of apprehended danger, the book was destroyed. It was dashed into the fire, as if a venomous reptile had clung to a part of her garments. Is not this, my Lord, a bright example for imitation? . . .

You have heard enough, my Lord, of the horrors that have resulted from the Penal system; a system which has doomed thousands and tens of thousands to the demoralizing state of bachelorism. Calmly consider the evil which has thus been created, and in common justice to the virtuous part of the community there, remedy it, by giving a due encouragement to a respectable system of female emigration. Think you, my Lord, that the most abandoned of the female race are fit companions for the children of such men; a class of men who are, perhaps, more sensitively alive than any other to connecting their families in marriage to doubtful characters. No one more fully appreciates virtue than the reformed. I repeat, what I have frequently stated, that to send abandoned women to our Colonies is an act of cruelty to them. Few, indeed, will be sought for as wives; respectable families will not receive them as servants. If Her Majesty's Government be really desirous of seeing a well-conducted community spring up in these Colonies, the social wants of the people must be considered. If the paternal Government wish to entitle itself to that honoured appellation, it must look to the materials it may send as a nucleus for the formation of a good and a great people. For all the clergy you can despatch, all the schoolmasters you can appoint, all the churches you can build, and all the books you can export, will never do much good, without what a gentleman in that Colony very appropriately called "God's police"—wives and little children—good and virtuous women. Oh! it is frightful to look upon the monster evil which our penal policy has entailed upon that country, and which the Emigration Rules have in some degree cherished. It is full time that a subject of such high national and religious importance should occupy the attention of all well-thinking men, and that the regulations affecting emigrants should not be dictated by those who deem cheap labour as the chief consideration. . . .

The subject, then, of resuming emigration to the Australian Colonies, is one which imperatively demands the mature and immediate deliberation of the Imperial Parliament, or a species of slavery will creep into our British possessions. Gentlemen, and men of large capital, having their all at stake, must and will have labour from some where. The neglect attending the urgent want of the labour market did much in former days to rivet the chains of slavery. Free emigration and slavery cannot for any length of time have being in the same country; the presence of one gradually does away with the other; it is the safe, the cheap, the natural mode pointed out by Providence; and though it may not be considered prudent policy to enrich a rival State, still the sacred cause of humanity pleads strongly in this case. We hear the wailings of our fellow beings, and their aspirations for the full right of man, liberty. Emigration, then, systematically and judiciously pursued, to Canada, will do much for the slaves in the United States; it will loosen the links, by lowering the value, of slave labour; and thereby draw out one of the strongest staples, which now holds fast in accursed thraldom a large portion of the human race.

I have the honor to be,
My Lord,
Your obedient humble Servant,
Caroline Chisholm.

William Rathbone Greg (1809–1881) is probably best known for the provocative query he posed in a 1862 periodical article called "Are Women Redundant?" (though the idea of redundancy as applied to women had been coined by Harriet Martineau several years before). A mill-owner and a commissioner of customs, here he lays out the pros and cons of a different question, addressing everything from the financial costs to the racial composition of Britain's imperial "burden."

William Greg, "Shall We Retain our Colonies?" (1851)

Our colonial empire—independent of the vast possessions of the East India Company; independent, also, of the Hudson's Bay Company's territory, and the uncivilised parts of North America—stretches over an area of nearly four million square miles, and includes a population of more than six million souls; of whom two millions and a half are whites, and one million and a half are of British birth or descent. The distribution of these numbers may be seen more minutely in the following table, where our colonies are classed into groups. The figures for Africa do not include our last acquisitions at the Cape, nor on the Gold Coast. The East Indian colonies mean Mauritius and Ceylon. The population is given for 1846, the last year for which we have any accurate returns. Since then, of course, a very considerable increase has taken place, both by immigration and by natural multiplication.

We have been taught to believe that our colonial empire, 'on which the sun never sets,' is about the most important element in our national greatness, and that these vast dominions in every part of the world add incalculably, though in some mysterious way, to our imperial dignity and strength. And such vague declamation as the following is given us in lieu of argument. The extent and glory of an empire are solid advantages for all its inhabitants, and especially for those who inhabit its centre. Whatever the possession of our colonies may cost us in money, the possession is worth more in money than its money cost, and infinitely more in other respects. For, by overawing foreign nations and impressing mankind with a prestige of our might, it enables us to keep the peace of the world, which we have no interest in disturbing, as it would enable us to disturb the world if we pleased. The advantage is, that the possession of this immense empire by England, causes the mere name of England to be a real and mighty power; the greatest power that now exists in the world. If we give up our colonies England would cease to be a power; and in order to preserve our independence we should have to spend more than we now do in the business of our defence. Mr. Cobden and his party argue on the other hand, and with much force, that this 'prestige of empire' is a hollow show, which other nations as well as ourselves are beginning to see through; that outlying dependencies which require to be garrisoned in time of peace and protected in time of war, draft off from this country the forces which are needed for our defence at home; dissipate our army and navy in forty or fifty isolated and distant quarters; and waste the funds which should be devoted to the protection of the mother country. It is idle, they affirm, to pretend that a system which gives us such a vast additional territory to defend without giving us any additional means of defending it, can be other than a source of dangerous weakness; that if we had no dependencies, we should be impregnable and invulnerable at home; and that half our navy and a fourth of our army would suffice for the protection of our hearths and homes. If, indeed, the colonies paid tribute into our treasury, if they furnished contingents to our military force, and supplied a fixed quota of ships and stores toward the augmentation of our navy—the case might be different. But they do nothing of all this: over-taxed and overburdened England pays for a great part of their civil government, and nearly the whole of their naval and military requirements; the impoverished and struggling peasant of Dorsetshire—the suffering artisan of Lancashire—the wretched needle-women of London—all have to pay their contribution to the defence and the civil rule of the comfortable Australian farmer, the wealthy Canadian settler, and the luxurious Jamaica negro. . . .

Lastly, we govern them ill; and, governing them as we do from a distance, and having such an immense number and variety of them to govern, we cannot govern them otherwise than ill. They are perpetual sources of difficulty and dispute; they are always quarrelling with us, and complaining of us, and not unfrequently breaking out into open rebellion; they yearn for independence, and would gladly purchase immunity from our vexatious interference and ignorant control by encountering all the risks and difficulties to which a severance of the Imperial connexion might expose them. . . . Since, then, the colonies are commercially as free as America or Spain; since they are no longer favoured or enforced customers for our productions; since they would be at least as available to our emigrants if independent as if still subject to our rule; since they refuse to help us by relieving us of our convict population; since they are sources of weakness and not of strength to us in times of peril or of war; since they pay no part of the expenses of the mother country, and only a small portion of their own; since we mismanage their affairs and impede their progress; and since they themselves wish to be set free from a fettering and galling yoke;—what argument, which will bear the test of close investigation, can be adduced to warrant our retaining them in tutelage?

. . . The cost, fairly calculated, to Great Britain of her colonial empire, is . . . something less than two millions yearly. There was a time, unquestionably, when it was far greater. In the old days of protection the arguments of those, who are for abandoning our colonies on the score of their costliness, might have been based upon far stronger and more startling facts. At a time when the protective duties on the produce of our sugar colonies alone were calculated to cost us 5,000,000l. a year, and those on Canadian timber at least 1,000,000l. more, it would have been difficult to maintain that these dependencies did not cost us more than they were worth, and more than we could easily or wisely pay.

In the first place, not a single one of our colonies is inhabited by a homogeneous population. In none, is the British race the sole one; in scarcely any, is it the most numerous. Some of the dependencies have been taken from savage tribes; others have been conquered from other European nations. In Trinidad we have seven distinct races; in the Cape colony at least five; in Canada four; in Mauritius four; in Ceylon at least three; in Australia and New Zealand two. The Australian colonies are the only ones which, from the unimportance of the native savages, we can venture to consider as peopled by a purely British race. In Lower Canada, the French form five-sevenths of the population; and taking the whole of our North American provinces together, more than one-fourth of the inhabitants are of French origin or descent. In the West Indian group the whites are only one in fifteen of the whole; the remainder are, mainly, recently emancipated slaves, still retaining (as the late visitation of cholera brought painfully into view) much of the ignorance of their African origin, and many of the feelings of their servile condition. The population of the Cape, in 1847, is stated at 170,000, of whom 72,000 were whites, and of these 52,000 were Dutch; the rest were Caffres, Hottentots, and Negroes. The population of Mauritius was, in 1845, 180,000, of which number (though we have no certain record later than 1827), probably not more than 10,000 at the outside were whites, the remainder being Coolies and Negroes. In Ceylon the estimate for 1847, gave 1,500,000 as the number of the native or immigrant coloured races, chiefly Cingalese, and 5,572 as the number of the Whites, some of these being Portuguese, and many being Dutch, from whom we took the island. In New Zealand, the natives, a hardy, intelligent, and noble race, amount, it is calculated, to 120,000, and the inhabitants of European descent to not more than 18,000, at the latest dates.

Now, with what show of decency or justice could England abandon to their own guidance and protection countries peopled by such various, heterogeneous, and often hostile races,—even if any considerable number of their inhabitants were unwise enough to wish it? What inevitable injustice such a step must entail upon one or other section of the colonists, what certain peril to the interests of them all, and of humanity at large! Let us follow out this inquiry in the case of two or three of them. We will assume that Canada would go on without any serious disturbances, now that the various populations which inhabit it have been so much more amalgamated than before by being pressed together into one legislature. We will suppose that the Australian colonies would be able to stand on their own feet, and to maintain their own interests, and would manifest that marvellous faculty for self-government and social organisation which has always been the proud distinction of the Anglo-Saxon race. We will concede that the settlers in New Zealand would succeed in civilising the wild tribes around them, and would make them friendly fellow-citizens, and useful subjects and auxiliaries; though we should not be without some apprehension as to the result, since with a warlike, shrewd, and energetic people seven to one is fearful odds. But what would be the result in Jamaica, in Mauritius, at the Cape, and in Ceylon, where the Blacks outnumber the Whites in overwhelming proportion, and where the Whites themselves belong to disunited and hostile nations? In Jamaica, and our other West Indian possessions, one of three results would follow,—either the Whites would remain as now, the dominant class, and would use their legislative power for the promotion of their own interests, and for the compression of the subject race;—would induce large immigration, would prohibit squatting, would compel work; would tax the necessaries of life rather than their own property or their own commerce,—perhaps might even strive to restore a modified slavery: or, the Blacks, easily excited, but not easily restrained when once aroused by their demagogues and missionaries, would seize upon the supreme power, either by sudden insurrection, or by gradual and constitutional, but not open force; and in this event few who know the negroes well, who have watched them during the prevalence of cholera in Jamaica, or who have the example of Haiti before their eyes, will doubt that another Haiti would ere long, though not perhaps at once, be the issue of the experiment: or, lastly, the Whites, fearing the second alternative, and finding themselves too feeble to enforce the first, would throw themselves into the arms of the United Sates, who would, as we are well aware, receive them with a warm welcome and a covetous embrace, and would speedily reconvert 800,000 freemen into slaves. This we think far the most probable alternative of the three. But is there one of the three which any philanthropist, any Briton, any friend to progress and civilisation, could contemplate without grief and dismay? Or is there any fourth issue of the abandonment of these colonies which bears even the shadow of likelihood about it? Whether the Negroes subdued the Whites, and established a black paradise of their own, or the Whites, with the help of the Americans, reduced the Negroes to slavery, the result would be almost equally deplorable. All the hopes which England has nourished of civilising and redeeming the African race must be abandoned, and all the sacrifices she has made so ungrudgingly for this high purpose will have been thrown away. But, apart from this consideration, we have simply no right to abandon the Blacks to the possible oppression of the Whites, nor the Whites to the dubious mercies of the Blacks. We cannot do so without a dereliction of duty, amounting to a crime. Towards both races we have incurred the solemn obligations of protection and control; both have acted or suffered under a tacit covenant, which it would be flagrant dishonesty to violate; towards both we have assumed a position which we may not without dishonour abdicate, on the miserable plea that it would be convenient and economical to do so.

Colonies with mixed and aboriginal populations such as these, then, we simply could not abandon; colonies, with a population exclusively or overpoweringly British, come under a different category. But even with these, we think it is not difficult to see that the interests of civilisation will be far more effectually served by their retention than by their abandonment,—by still maintaining them as integral portions by the British Empire,—than by casting them adrift to run the chances of a hazardous voyage unassisted and alone. They would 'go ahead' far faster, we are told, if independent, than if still subject to the hampering rule of the mother country; and the example of the United States is triumphantly appealed to in confirmation of the assertion. We reply, that we can well believe that they would go ahead far faster if free than if fettered, but not than they will now, when colonial legislatures have been created and endowed with the powers of managing all strictly colonial concerns. There is scarcely an advantage, conferrable by freedom, possessed by the United States since their separation from Britain, that will not now be enjoyed in an equal degree by our North American and our Australian dependencies.

. . . We hope we have succeeded in making it clear that our colonies are far too valuable portions of our empire to be lightly laid down or put away; and that if they should not continue to be so, the fault will lie in some and mismanagement of our own. Many of them, in simple justice to the native population, or to those British subjects who have settled there on the faith of the Imperial connexion, we could not possibly abandon. Others the interests of civilisation and humanity compel us to retain. All of them ought to be, and will be if we govern them aright, sources of strength and pride to us. The very interests of that free and enlightened commercial policy for which we have fought so long and sacrificed so much, forbid us to entertain the thought of severing the time-hallowed connexion between Great Britain and the communities which have gone forth from her bosom. Nor is there any call or motive for such a step: the cost of our colonies, though less by one half than it has been represented, we could easily sustain were it twice as great: the affection of the colonists it is easy to preserve, or to recover where, through misjudgment or misunderstanding, it has been shaken or impaired. By ruling them with forbearance, steadiness, and justice; by leading them forward in the path of freedom with an encouraging but cautious hand; by bestowing on them the fullest powers of self-government wherever the infusion of British blood is large enough to warrant such a course; in a word, by following out the line of policy announced and defended by Lord John Russell in his speech on the introduction of the bill for the government of the Australian colonies in February of last year—we may secure the existence and rivet the co-hesion of a vast dominion blest with the wisest, soberest, most beneficial form of liberty which the world has yet enjoyed, and spreading to distant lands and future ages the highest, most prolific, most expansive development of civilisation which Providence has ever granted to humanity. To abandon these great hopes—to cast our colonial empire to the winds, with the sole aim of saving two millions a year—is a line of policy which, we sincerely think, is worthy only of a narrow and a niggard school; which will be coun-selled only by men who are merchants rather than statesmen, and whose mercantile wis-dom even is confined, short-sighted, and unenlightened; one, which, we feel assured, can never be adopted by England till the national spirit which has made her what she is, shall have begun to wane and fade away.

In this novel written to commemorate—and satirize—the Great Exhibition, the journalist Henry Mayhew (1812–1887) views the opening of the Crystal Palace through the awestruck eyes of two average English visitors. Troubadours, Barnum and Bailey, Eskimos, and Poor Law Commissioners mingle in this kaleidoscopic vision of the opening day of the "GREAT EXHI-BITION OF ALL NATIONS."

Henry Mayhew, *1851: or, The Adventures of Mr. and Mrs. Cursty Sandboys*

THE GREAT EXHIBITION was about to attract the sight-seers of all the world—the sight-seers, who make up nine-tenths of the human family. The African had mounted his ostrich. The Crisp of the Desert had announced an excursion caravan from Zoolu to Fez. The Yakutskian Shillibeer had already started the first reindeer omnibus to Novo-gorod. Penny cargoes were steaming down Old Nile, in Egyptian "Daylights;" and "Moonlights," while floating from the Punjab, and congregating down the Indus, Scindian "Bridesmaids" and "Bachelors" came racing up the Red Sea, with Burmese "Watermen, Nos. 9 and 12," calling at the piers of Muscat and Aden, to pick up pas-sengers for the Isthmus—at two-pence a-head.

The Esquimaux had just purchased his new "registered paletot" of seal-skin from the great "sweater" of the Arctic Regions. The Hottentot Venus had already added to the graceful ebullitions of nature, the charms of a Parisian crinoline. The Yemassee was busy blueing his cheeks with the rouge of the backwoods. The Truefit of New Zealand had dressed the full buzz wig, and cut and curled the horn of the chief of the Papuas. The Botocudo had ordered a new pair of wooden ear-rings. The Mariposan had japanned his teeth with the best Brunswick Black Odonto. The Cingalese was hard at work with a Kalydor of Cocoa-Nut-Oil, polishing himself up like a boot; and the King of Da-homey. . . [with his] gaiters and epaulets, was wending his way towards London to ten-der his congratulations to the Prince Consort.

Nor was the commotion confined alone to the extremes of the world—the metropolis of Great Britain was also in a prodigious excitement. Alexis Soyer was preparing to open a restaurant of all nations, where the universe might dine, from sixpence to a hundred guineas, off cartes ranging from pickled whelks to nightingales' tongues—from the rats á la Tartare of the Chinese, to the "turkey and truffles" of the Parisian gourmand—from the "long sixes, au naturel," of the Russian, to the "stewed Missionary of the Marquesas," or the "cold roast Bishop" of New Zealand. Here, too, was to be a park with Swiss cottages, wherein the sober Turk might quaff his Dublin stout; and Chinese pagodas, from whose golden galleries the poor German student, dreaming of the undiscoverable noumena of Kant, might smoke his penny Pickwick, sip his Arabian chicory, and in a fit of absence, think of his father-land and pocket the sugar.

St. Paul's and Westminster Abbey ("in consequence of the increased demand") were about to double their prices of admission, when M. Jullien, "ever ready to deserve the patronage of a discerning public," made the two great English cathedrals so tempting an offer that they "did not think themselves justified in refusing it." And there, on alternate nights, were shortly to be exhibited, to admiring millions, the crystal curtain, the stained glass windows illuminated with gas, and the statues lighted up with rose-coloured lamps; the "Black Band of his Majesty of Tsjaddi, with a hundred additional bones;" the monster Jew's harp; the Euhurdy-gurdyehon; the Musicians of Tongoose; the Singers of the Maldives; the Glee Minstrels of Paraguay; the Troubadours of far Vancouver; the Snow Ball Family from the Gold Coast; the Canary of the Samoiedes; the Theban Brothers; and, "expressly engaged for the occasion," the celebrated Band of Robbers from the Desert.

Barnum, too, had "thrown up" Jenny Lind, and entered into an agreement with the Poor Law Commissioners to pay the Poor Rates of all England during one year for the sole possession of Somerset House, as a "Grand Hotel for all Nations," under the highly explanatory title of the "Xenodokeion Pancosmopolitanicon;" where each guest was to be provided with a bed, boudoir, and banquet, together with one hour's use per diem of a valet, and a private chaplain (according to the religious opinions of the individual); the privilege of free admission to all the theatres and green-rooms; the right of entrée to the Privy Council and the Palace; a knife and fork, and spittoon at pleasure, at the tables of the nobility; a seat with nightcap and pillow in the House of Commons, and a cigar on the Bench with the Judges; the free use of the columns of "The Times" newspaper, and the right of abusing therein their friends and hosts of the day before; the privilege of paying visits in the Lord Mayor's state-carriage (with the freedom of the City of London), and of using the Goldsmiths' state barge for aquatic excursions; and finally, the full right of presentation at the Drawing-room to her most gracious Majesty, and of investiture with the Order of the Garter at discretion, as well as the prerogative of sitting down, once a week, in rotation, at the dinner-table of His Excellency General Tom-Thumb. These advantages Mr. Barnum, to use his own language, had "determined upon offering to a generous and enlightened American public at one shilling per head per day—numbers alone enabling him to complete his engagements."

While these gigantic preparations for the gratification of foreign visitors were being made, the whole of the British Provinces likewise were preparing extensively to enjoy themselves. Every city was arranging some "monster train" to shoot the whole of its inhabitants, at a halfpenny per ton, into the lodging-houses of London. All the houses of York were on tiptoe, in the hope of shaking hands in Hyde Park with all the houses of Lancaster. Beds, Bucks, Notts, Wilts, Hants, Hunts, and Herts were respectively cramming their carpet bags in anticipation of "a week in London." Not a village, a hamlet, a borough, a township, or a wick, but had each its shilling club, for providing their inhabitants with a three days' journey to London, a mattrass under the dry arches of the Adelphi, and tickets for soup ad libitum. John o'Groats was anxiously looking forward to the time when he was to clutch the Land's End to his bosom—the Isle of Man was panting to take the Isle of Dogs by the hand, and welcome Thanet, Sheppy, and Skye to the gaieties of a London life—the North Foreland was preparing for a friendly stroll up Regent-street with Holy-Head on his arm—and the man at Eddystone Lighthouse could see the distant glimmer of a hope of shortly setting eyes upon the long looked for Buoy at the Nore.

Bradshaw's Railway Guide had swelled into an encyclopædia, and Masters and Bachelors of Arts "who had taken distinguished degrees," were daily advertising, to perfect persons in the understanding of the Time Tables, in six easy lessons for one guinea. Omnibus conductors were undergoing a Polyglott course on the Hamiltonian system, to enable them to abuse all foreigners in their native tongues; the "Atlases" were being made extra strong, so that they might be able to bear the whole world on top of them; and the proprietors of the Camberwell and Camden Town 'Busses were eagerly watching for the time when English, French, Prussians and Belgians should join their Wellingtons and Bluchers on the heights of "Waterloo!"

Such was the state of the world, the continent, the provinces, and the metropolis. Nor was the pulse that beat so throbbingly at Bermondsey, Bow, Bayswater, Brixton, Brompton, Brentford, and Blackheath, without a response on the banks of Crummock Water and the tranquil meadows of Buttermere. The long-looked-for first of May, 1851, had at length arrived, and the morning was ushered in with merry peals from almost every steeple; afar off the drone of the thousand bells sounded like the boom of a huge gong—the signal, as it were, for the swarming of the Great Hive.

For miles round all wore a holiday aspect; the work-people with clean and smiling faces, and decked out in all the bright colours of their Sunday attire, were up and about shortly after daybreak, and, with their bundle of provisions on their arms, were soon seen streaming along the road, like so many living rays, converging towards the Crystal focus of the World.

It was the great Jubilee of art and industry, to which almost every corner of the earth had sent some token of its skill and brotherly feeling, and to which the inhabitants of the most distant climes had come, each to gaze at the science and handicraft of the other. Never was labour—whether mental or manual, whether the craft of the hand or of the brain—so much honoured—the first great recognition, perhaps, of the artistic qualities of the artizan.

With the first gleam of daylight, the boys of London, ever foremost at a sight, had taken up their places in the trees, like their impudent counterparts, the London sparrows, and men and women grouped round the rails, determined at least to have a good place for seeing the opening of the World's Show. Hammers were to be heard on all sides, fastening the timbers of the wooden stages that were being set up by the many who delight in holidays solely as a matter of business. Some were pouring in at the Park-gates, laden with tables and chairs for the sight-seers to stand upon. Others again, came with the omnipresent street provisions—huge trucks filled with bottles of ginger beer—baskets of gingerbread and "fatty cakes"—and tins of brandy-balls and hardbake—while from every quarter there streamed girls and women with round wicker sieves piled up in pyramids with oranges. Then there were the women with the brown-looking trotters, spread on white cloths, and the men with their ham sandwiches, as thin as if made out of whitey-brown paper; while at the gates and all along the roads, stood men with trays of bright silvery looking medals of the Crystal Palace, and filling the air with the cheapness and attractions of their wares. Nor were the beggars absent from the scene, for in every direction along which the great mass of people came pouring, there were the blind and the crippled, reaping their holiday harvest.

As the morning advanced the crowds that came straggling on, grew denser and denser, till at last it was one compact kind of road, paved with heads; and on they went—fathers with their wives and children, skipping jauntily along, and youths with their gaily-dressed sweethearts, in lively-coloured shawls and ribbons—and many—early as it was—munching apples, or cracking nuts as they trudged on their way.

All London, and half the country, and a good part of the world, were wending their way to see the Queen pass in state on her way to open the

GREAT EXHIBITION OF ALL NATIONS,

The Great Exhibition of the Industry of all Countries is the first public national expression ever made in this country, as to the dignity and artistic quality of labour.

Our "working men," until within the last few years, we have been in the habit of looking upon as mere labourers—as muscular machines—creatures with whom the spinning-jenny and the power-loom might be brought into competition, and whom the sense of fatigue, and consequent demand for rest, rendered immeasurably inferior "as producers," to the instruments of brass and iron.

It is only within the last ten years, perhaps, that we have got to acknowledge the artistic and intellectual quality of many forms of manual labour, speaking of certain classes of operatives no longer as handicraftsmen—that is to say, as men who, from long habit, acquired a dexterity of finger which fitted them for the "automatic" performance of certain operations—but styling them artisans, or the artists of our manufactures. It is because we have been so slow to perceive and express this "great fact"—the artistic character of artisanship—that so much intellectual power has been lost to society, and there has been so much more toil and suffering in the world than there has been any necessity for.

Had we, as a really great people, been impressed with the sense of the heavy debt we owed to labour, we should long ago have sought to acknowledge and respect the mental operations connected with many forms of it, and have striven to have ennobled and embellished and enlivened the intellect of those several modes of industry that still remained as purely physical employments among us. Had the men of mind done as much for the men of labour, as these had done for those, we might long ago have learned how to have made toil pleasant rather than irksome, and to have rendered it noble instead of mean.

. . . Had we striven to elevate ploughing into an art, and the ploughman into an artist—teaching him to understand the several subtle laws and forces concerned in the cultivation of every plant—and more especially of those with which he was dealing—had we thus made the turning up of the soil not a brute operation, but an intellectual process, we might have rendered the work a pleasure, and the workman a man of thought, dignity, and refinement.

. . . The Great Exhibition of the 'Works of Industry and Art of all Nations' is, then, the first attempt to dignify and refine toil; and, by collecting the several products of scientific and æsthetic art from every quarter of the globe into one focus, to diffuse a high standard of excellence among our operatives, and thus to raise the artistic qualities of labour, so that men, no longer working with their fingers alone, shall find that which is now mere drudgery converted into a delight, their intellects expanded, their natures softened, and their pursuits ennobled by the process.

Of all the tributes to Florence Nightingale at her death (1910), Harriet Martineau's is among the most unsentimental. Her verdict nicely sums up the qualities that made the Lady with the Lamp a true heroine for many Victorians: "She was no declaimer, but a housewifely woman; she talked little, and did great things."

Harriet Martineau on the death of Florence Nightingale (1910)

. . . Florence Nightingale had perhaps the highest lot ever fulfilled by woman, except women Sovereigns who have not merely reigned but ruled. She had the highest lot that the remedial function admits of. The loftier creative . . . function is so rare, and so few human beings have as yet been adequate to it, that it is no wonder if there is no female exemplification of it in the history of the world. It is no small distinction to our time that it produced a woman who effected two great things: a mighty reform in the care of the sick and an opening for her sex into the region of serious business, in proportion to their ability to maintain a place in it.

. . . We think of her dressing wounds, bringing wine and food, carrying her lamp through miles of sick soldiers in the middle of the night, noting every face and answering the appeal of every eye as she passed. We think of her spending precious hours in selecting books to please the men's individual wish or want, and stocking her coffee-house with luxuries and innocent pleasures to draw the soldiers away from poisonous drinks and mischief. We think now of the poor fellow who said that he looked for her coming in hospital, for he could at least kiss her shadow on his pillow as she passed.

We think to-day of the little Russian prisoner, the poor boy who could not speak or be spoken to till she had taken him in and had him taught and made useful; and how he answered when at length he could understand a question. When asked if he knew where he would go when he was dead, he confidently said: "I shall go to Miss Nightingale."

. . . In early childhood Florence Nightingale heard a good deal of a different class of sufferings from that to which she devoted herself at last. She was the granddaughter of William Smith, the well-known member for Norwich, who for a long course of years sustained the interests of the Dissenters in Parliament, and was a prominent member of the anti-slavery party there. She was not near enough to the daily life of the abolition clique to incur the danger expressed in the maxim that the children of philanthropists are usually heartless; and the spectacle of eminent men taking a world of trouble to get slavery abolished, as they had already put an end to the legal slave trade, may, naturally, have disposed the grandchildren of the abolitionists to consider, at least, the case of any suffering class.

It was William Smith's daughter Frances who married Mr. Nightingale—born Shore, of the Yorkshire family of Shores, and assuming the name of Nightingale, with the estates which made him a wealthy man. The marriage was an early one, and the young people went abroad, to spend two or three years—a proceeding less common then than it is now. Their first child (afterwards Lady Verney) was born at Naples, and was called

Parthenope. The next, and only other, was born on May 15th, 1820, at Florence, and named accordingly.

. . . The sisters grew up unspoiled, and thoroughly exercised in the best parts of middle-class education, while living in an atmosphere of accomplishment, such as belongs to a station and a family connection like theirs. Their grandmother refused a peerage; their father refused a peerage; yet, as we have all seen, Florence had as familiar an acquaintance with the world's daily work as any farmer's or shopkeeper's daughter. She was never quite happy, in fact, till she had escaped from the region of factitious interests and superficial pursuits and devoted herself to stern, practical toil, appropriated to a benevolent end.

. . . The first step which fixed the attention of the world was her undertaking the management of the sanatorium for sick ladies in Harley-street. It is instructive, though humiliating, to recall the hubbub that arose in London society when Florence Nightingale became matron of that institution. It was related at the time by persons who appreciated the act that if she had forged a bill, or eloped, or betted her father's fortune away at Newmarket, she could not have provoked a more virulent hue and cry than she did by settling herself to a useful work in a quiet way, in mature age, and without either seeking or deprecating the world's opinion. Her object was to retrieve the institution, which was in debt and disorder. She stipulated for power, and she achieved the work. She set about it like an accountant; looked into things like a housekeeper; organized the establishment like a born administrator, as she was; nursed the inmates like a Sister of Charity; and cheered the sufferers by the indescribable graces of the thoroughly developed and high-bred woman.

. . . The next call made upon her was the well-known appeal of Mr. Sidney Herbert in that letter which was treacherously stolen and made public by an officious person who subjected the friends to ungenerous criticism, and to imputations of vanity and self-seeking, purely absurd to all who had any knowledge whatever of Florence and her friends. All that matters little now; but it should be simply recorded, because no picture of her career can be complete which omits the oppositions she had to encounter.

From the formalists at home who were shocked at her handling keys and keeping accounts to the jealous and quizzing doctors abroad who would have suppressed her altogether, and the vulgar among the nurses who whispered that she ate the jams and jellies in a corner which were meant for the sick, she had all the hostility to encounter which the great may always expect from those who are too small to apprehend their minds and ways.

She had a strong will and a clear purpose in every act of her life, and she was not troubled with a too acute self-consciousness, nor with any anxiety about the popular judgment on her course. To her it was "a small thing to be judged by man's judgment" while the sick were suffering before her eyes; and nothing but her freedom and egotism could have left her mind clear and open for the study how to extend the benefits of good nursing to the greatest number. So she went on her own way, and the critics and maligners were left far behind, where they never found any considerable number to listen to them.

In October, 1854, Florence Nightingale set out for the seat of war in the East, accompanied by her friends, Mr. and Mrs. Bracebridge, and leading a company of thirty-seven nurses. We all remember how they were received in France, from the landing, when the Boulogne fish women insisted on carrying their luggage, and the innkeeper on feasting them without pay, to the generous farewells at Marseilles. We remember, only too painfully, the difficulties to be got over at Scutari, and the horrors to be witnessed and the delays to be endured. The two pictures—of Scutari hospital before the reforms, and the same place afterwards—were burnt in upon the brain of the passing generation; and Florence Nightingale was throughout the prominent figure.

. . . Before she was believed in on the spot, we see her using her strong will—pointing to a locked door, and ordering, on her own responsibility, that it should be broken open, to get at the bedding within. We see her obtaining a gift of five refused "cases" after a battle—soldiers hopelessly wounded, on whom it would be wrong to spend the surgeon's time—feeding them by spoonfuls all night, so that they were in a condition next day to be operated upon, and were saved. We see her silent under aggressive inquiries into her religious opinions, obedient to medical orders, and constraining others to the same obedience, and gradually obtaining the ascendency she deserved, till not only were the hospitals in a state of unhoped-for order and efficiency, but the medical and military officers were almost as vehement in their admiration of her as her patients.

We see again the rising up of the kitchen, "Miss Nightingale's kitchen," which was to save more lives than any amount of medicine and surgery could do without it; and some of us foresaw at the moment a reform of soldiers' food, and therein of their health and morals, throughout the Empire, and through coming generations, beginning from the saving of life at Scutari—from the punctuality and nourishing and palatable quality of the meals sent out from that kitchen. Success carried all before it; in a short time all good people were helping; and before the close of the war the British soldiery in the East were in a condition of health and vigour excelling that of any class of men at home.

Many of the wisest of men and women have said that talk about the powers and position of women is nearly useless, because all human beings take rank, in the long run, according to their capability. But it is true, and will remain true, that what women are able to do they will do, with or without leave obtained from men. Florence Nightingale encountered opposition—from her own sex as much as the other; and she achieved, as the most natural thing in the world, and without the smallest sacrifice of her womanly quality, what would beforehand have been declared a deed for a future age.

She was no declaimer, but a housewifely woman; she talked little, and did great things. When other women see that there are things for them to do, and train themselves to the work, they will get it done easily enough. There can never be a more unthought-of and marvellous career before any working woman than Florence Nightingale has achieved; and her success has opened a way to all others easier than anyone had prepared for her.

Though dozens of portraits were put forth as hers during the Crimean War which were spurious, or were wholly unlike, her general appearance was well known—the tall, slender figure, the intelligent, agreeable countenance, and the remarkable mixture of reserve and simplicity in her expression and manner, with the occasional sparkle of fun on the one hand and the general gravity, never degenerating into sentimentality, on the other.

She was the most quiet and natural of all ladylike women; presenting no points for special observation, but good sense and cultivation as to mind, and correctness in demeanour and manners. One would fain linger on these particulars; for this is the only way now left to retaining their very traces. She is gone, and we can only dwell on what has been.

———❦———

Mary Seacole (1805–1881) is less well known than her contemporary Florence Nightingale, but her work earned her an elaborate gravestone in a London cemetery in which she is commemorated as a "notable nurse who cared for the sick and wounded in the West Indies, Panama, and on the Battlefields of the Crimea." Here she details her origins, her work in the Crimea, and her experience of battle.

———❦———

Mary Seacole,
from *The Wonderful Adventures of Mrs. Seacole in Many Lands* (1858)

I was born in the town of Kingston, in the island of Jamaica, some time in the present century. As a female, and a widow, I may be well excused giving the precise date of this important event. But I do not mind confessing that the century and myself were both young together and that we have grown side by side into age and consequence. I am a Creole, and have good Scotch blood coursing in my veins. My father was a soldier, of an old Scotch family; and to him I often trace my affection for a camp-life, and my sympathy with what I have heard my friends call 'the pomp, pride, and circumstance of glorious war.' Many people have also traced to my Scotch blood that energy and activity which are not always found in the Creole race, and which have carried me to so many varied scenes: and perhaps they are right. I have often heard the term 'lazy Creole' applied to my country people; but I am sure I do not know what it is to be indolent. All my life long I have followed the impulse which led me to be up and doing; and so far from resting idle anywhere, I have never wanted inclination to rove, nor will powerful enough to find a way to carry out my wishes. That these qualities have led me into many countries, and brought me into some strange and amusing adventures, the reader, if he or she has the patience to get through this book, will see. Some people, indeed, have called me quite a female Ulysses. I believe that they intended it as a compliment; but from my experience of the Greeks, I do not consider it a very flattering one.

It is not my intention to dwell at any length upon the recollections of my childhood. My mother kept a boarding-house in Kingston, and was, like many of the Creole women, an admirable doctress; in high repute with the officers of both services, and their wives, who were from time to time stationed at Kingston. It was very natural that I should inherit her tastes; and so I had from early youth a yearning for medical knowledge and practice which has never deserted me. When I was a very young child I was taken by an old lady, who brought me up in her household among her own grandchildren, and who could scarcely have shown me more kindness had I been one of them; indeed, I was so spoiled by my kind patroness that but for being frequently with my mother, I might very likely have grown up idle and useless. But I saw so much of her, and of her patients, that the ambition to become a doctress early took firm root in my mind; and I was very young when I began to make use of the little knowledge I had acquired from watching my mother, upon a great sufferer—my doll. I have noticed always what actors children are. If you leave one alone in a room, how soon it clears a little stage; and, making an audience out of a few chairs and stools, proceeds to act its childish griefs and blandishments upon its doll. So I also made good use of my dumb companion and confidante; and whatever disease was most prevalent in Kingston, be sure my poor doll soon contracted it. I have had many medical triumphs in later days, and saved some valuable lives; but I really think that few have given me more real gratification than the rewarding glow of health which my fancy used to picture stealing over my patient's waxen face after long and precarious illness.

Before long it was very natural that I should seek to extend my practice; and so I found other patients in the dogs and cats around me. Many luckless brutes were made to simulate diseases which were raging among their owners, and had forced down their reluctant throats the remedies which I deemed most likely to suit their supposed complaints. And after a time I rose still higher in my ambition; and despairing of finding another human patient, I proceeded to try my simples and essences upon—myself.

When I was about 12 years old I was more frequently at my mother's house, and used to assist her in her duties; very often sharing with her the task of attending upon invalid officers or their wives, who came to her house from the adjacent camp at Up-Park, or the military station at Newcastle.

As I grew into womanhood, I began to indulge that longing to travel which will never leave me while I have health and vigour. I was never weary of tracing upon an old map the route to England; and never followed with my gaze the stately ships homeward bound without longing to be in them, and see the blue hills of Jamaica fade into the distance. At that time it seemed most improbable that these girlish wishes should be gratified; but circumstances, which I need not explain, enabled me to accompany some relatives to England while I was yet a very young woman.

I shall never forget my first impressions of London. Of course, I am not going to bore the reader with them; but they are as vivid now as though the year 18——(I had very nearly let my age slip then) had not been long ago numbered with the past. Strangely enough, some of the most vivid of my recollections are the efforts of the London streetboys to poke fun at my and my companion's complexion. I am only a little brown—a few shades duskier than the brunettes whom you all admire so much; but my companion was very dark, and a fair (if I can apply the term to her) subject for their rude wit. She was hot-tempered, poor thing! and as there were no policemen to awe the boys and turn our servants' heads in those days, our progress through the London streets was sometimes a rather chequered one.

I remained in England, upon the occasion of my first visit, about a year; and then returned to Kingston. Before long I again started for London, bringing with me this time a large stock of West Indian preserves and pickles for sale. After remaining two years here, I again started home; and on the way my life and adventures were very nearly brought to a premature conclusion. Christmas-day had been kept very merrily on board our ship the 'Velusia;' and on the following day a fire broke out in the hold. I dare say it would have resisted all the crew's efforts to put it out, had not another ship appeared in sight; upon which the fire quietly allowed itself to be extinguished. Although considerably alarmed, I did not lose my senses; but during the time when the contest between fire and water was doubtful, I entered into an amicable arrangement with the ship's cook, whereby, in consideration of two pounds—which I was not, however, to pay until the crisis arrived—he agreed to lash me on to a large hen-coop.

. . . Before I left Jamaica for Navy Bay . . . war had been declared against Russia, and we were all anxiously expecting news of a descent upon the Crimea. Now, no sooner had

I heard of war somewhere, than I longed to witness it; and when I was told that many of the regiments I had known so well in Jamaica had left England for the scene of action, the desire to join them became stronger than ever. I used to stand for hours in silent thought before an old map of the world, in a little corner of which some one had chalked a red cross, to enable me to distinguish where the Crimea was; and as I traced the route thither, all difficulties would vanish. But when I came to talk over the project with my friends, the best scheme I could devise seemed so wild and improbable, that I was fain to resign my hopes for a time, and so started for Navy Bay.

But all the way to England, from Navy Bay, I was turning my old wish over and over in my mind; and when I found myself in London, in the autumn of 1854, just after the battle of Alma had been fought, and my old friends were fairly before the walls of Sebastopol, how to join them there took up far more of my thoughts than that visionary gold-mining speculation on the river Palmilla, which seemed so feasible to us in New Granada, but was considered so wild and unprofitable a speculation in London. And, as time wore on, the inclination to join my old friends of the 97th, 48th, and other regiments, battling with worse foes than yellow fever or cholera, took such exclusive possession of my mind, that I threw over the gold speculation altogether, and devoted all my energies to my new scheme.

Heaven knows it was visionary enough! I had no friends who could help me in such a project—nay, who would understand why I desired to go, and what I desired to do when I got there. My funds, although they might, carefully husbanded, carry me over the three thousand miles, and land me at Balaclava, would not support me there long; while to persuade the public that an unknown Creole woman would be useful to their army before Sebastopol was too improbable an achievement to be thought of for an instant. Circumstances, however, assisted me.

As the winter wore on, came hints from various quarters of mismanagement, want, and suffering in the Crimea; and after the battle of Balaclava and Inkermann, and the fearful storm of the 14th of November, the worst anticipations were realized. Then we knew that the hospitals were full to suffocation, that scarcity and exposure were the fate of all in the camp, and that the brave fellows for whom any of us at home would have split our last shilling, and shared our last meal, were dying thousands of miles away from the active sympathy of their fellow-countrymen. Fast and thick upon the news of Inkermann, fought by a handful of fasting and enfeebled men against eight times their number of picked Russians, brought fresh and animated to the contest, and while all England was reeling beneath the shock of that fearful victory, came the sad news that hundreds were dying whom the Russian shot and sword had spared, and that the hospitals of Scutari were utterly unable to shelter, or their inadequate staff to attend to, the ship-loads of sick and wounded which were sent to them across the stormy Black Sea.

But directly England knew the worst, she set about repairing her past neglect. In every household busy fingers were working for the poor soldier—money flowed in golden streams wherever need was—and Christian ladies, mindful of the sublime example, 'I was sick, and ye visited me,' hastened to volunteer their services by those sickbeds which only women know how to soothe and bless.

Need I be ashamed to confess that I shared in the general enthusiasm, and longed more than ever to carry my busy (and the reader will not hesitate to add experienced) fingers where the sword or bullet had been busiest, and pestilence most rife. I had seen much of sorrow and death elsewhere, but they had never daunted me; and if I could feel happy binding up the wounds of quarrelsome Americans and treacherous Spaniards, what delight should I not experience if I could be useful to my own 'sons,' suffering for a cause it was so glorious to fight and bleed for! I never stayed to discuss probabilities, or enter into conjectures as to my chances of reaching the scene of action. I made up my mind that if the army wanted nurses, they would be glad of me, and with all the ardour of my nature, which ever carried me where inclination prompted, I decided that I *would* go to the Crimea; and go I did, as all the world knows.

. . . I made long and unwearied application at the War Office, in blissful ignorance of the labour and time I was throwing away. I have reason to believe that I considerably interfered with the repose of sundry messengers, and disturbed, to an alarming degree, the official gravity of some nice gentlemanly young fellows, who were working out their salaries in an easy, off-hand way. But my ridiculous endeavours to gain an interview with the Secretary-at-War of course failed, and glad at last to oblige a distracted messenger, I transferred my attentions to the Quartermaster-General's department. Here I saw another gentleman, who listened to me with a great deal of polite enjoyment, and—his amusement ended—hinted, had I not better apply to the Medical Department; and accordingly I attached myself to their quarters with the same unwearying ardour. But, of course, I grew tired at last, and then I changed my plans.

Now, I am not for a single instant going to blame the authorities who would not listen to the offer of a motherly yellow woman to go to the Crimea and nurse her 'sons' there, suffering from cholera, diarrhoea, and a host of lesser ills. In my country, where people know our use, it would have been different; but here it was natural enough—although I had references, and other voices spoke for me—that they should laugh, good-naturedly enough, at my offer. War, I know, is a serious game, but sometimes very humble actors are of great use in it, and if the reader, when he comes in time to peruse the evidence of those who had to do with the Sebastopol drama, of my share in it, will turn back to this chapter, he will confess perhaps that, after all, the impulse which led me to the War Department was not unnatural.

My new scheme was, I candidly confess, worse devised than the one which had failed. Miss Nightingale had left England for the Crimea, but other nurses were still to follow, and my new plan was simply to offer myself to Mrs. H——as a recruit. Feeling that I was one of the very women they most wanted, experienced and fond of the work, I jumped at once to the conclusion that they would gladly enrol me in their number. To go to Cox's, the army agents, who were most obliging to me, and obtain the Secretary-at-War's private address, did not take long; and that done, I laid the same pertinacious siege to his great house in————Square, as I had previously done to his place of business.

Many a long hour did I wait in his great hall, while scores passed in and out; many of them looking curiously at me. The flunkeys, noble creatures! marvelled exceedingly at the yellow woman whom no excuses could get rid of, nor impertinence dismay, and showed me very clearly that they resented my persisting in remaining there in mute appeal from their sovereign will. At last I gave that up, after a message from Mrs. H. that the full complement of nurses had been secured, and that my offer could not be entertained. Once again I tried, and had an interview this time with one of Miss Nightingale's companions. She gave me the same reply, and I read in her face the fact, that had there been a vacancy, I should not have been chosen to fill it.

. . . I had scarcely set my foot on board the 'Hollander,' before I met a friend. The supercargo was the brother of the Mr. S——, whose death in Jamaica the reader will not have forgotten, and he gave me a hearty welcome. I thought the meeting augured well, and when I told him my plans he gave me the most cheering encouragement. I was glad, indeed, of any support, for, beyond all doubt, my project was a hazardous one.

So cheered at the outset, I watched without a pang the shores of England sink beneath the smooth sea, and turned my gaze hopefully to the as yet landless horizon, beyond which lay that little peninsula to which the eyes and hearts of all England were so earnestly directed.

So, cheerily! the good ship ploughed its way eastward ho! for Turkey.

. . . And in the Crimea, where the doctors were so overworked, and sickness was so prevalent, I could not be long idle; for I never forgot that my intention in seeking the army was to help the kind-hearted doctors, to be useful to whom I have ever looked upon and still regard as so high a privilege.

But before very long I found myself surrounded with patients of my own, and this for two simple reasons. In the first place, the men (I am speaking of the 'ranks' now) had a very serious objection to going into hospital for any but urgent reasons, and the regimental doctors were rather fond of sending them there; and, in the second place, they could and did get at my store of sick-comforts and nourishing food, which the heads of the medical staff would sometimes find it difficult to procure. These reasons, with the additional one that I was very familiar with the diseases which they suffered most from and successful in their treatment (I say this in no spirit of vanity), were quite sufficient to account for the numbers who came daily to the British Hotel for medical treatment.

That the officers were glad of me as a doctress and nurse may be easily understood. When a poor fellow lay sickening in his cheerless hut and sent down to me, he knew very well that I should not ride up in answer to his message empty-handed. And although I did not hesitate to charge him with the value of the necessaries I took him, still he was thankful enough to be able to *purchase* them. When we lie ill at home surrounded with comfort, we never think of feeling any special gratitude for the sick-room delicacies which we accept as a consequence of our illness; but the poor officer lying ill and weary in his crazy hut, dependent for the mearest necessaries of existence upon a clumsy, ignorant soldier-cook, who would almost prefer eating his meat raw to having the trouble of cooking it (our English soldiers are bad campaigners), often finds his greatest troubles in the want of those little delicacies with which a weak stomach must be humoured into retaining nourishment. How often have I felt sad at the sight of poor lads who in England thought attending early parade a hardship, and felt harassed if their neckcloths set awry, or the natty little boots would not retain their polish, bearing, and bearing so nobly and bravely, trials and hardships to which the veteran campaigner frequently succumbed. Don't you think, reader, if you were lying, with parched lips and fading appetite, thousands of miles from mother, wife, or sister, loathing the rough food by your side, and thinking regretfully of that English home where nothing that could minister to your great need would be left untried—don't you think that you would welcome the familiar figure of the stout lady whose bony horse has just pulled up at the door of your hut, and whose panniers contain some cooling drink, a little broth, some homely cake, or a dish of jelly or blanc-mange—don't you think, under such circumstances, that you would heartily agree with my friend *Punch's* remark:—

> 'That berry-brown face, with a kind heart's trace
> Impressed on each wrinkle sly,
> Was a sight to behold, through the snow-clouds rolled
> Across that iron sky.'

I tell you, reader, I have seen many a bold fellow's eyes moisten at such a season, when a woman's voice and a woman's care have brought to their minds recollections of those happy English homes which some of them never saw again; but many did, who will re-member their woman-comrade upon the bleak and barren heights before Sebastopol.

. . . I shall now endeavour to describe my out-of-door life as much as possible, and write of those great events in the field of which I was a humble witness. But I shall con-tinue to speak from my own experience simply; and if the reader should be surprised at my leaving any memorable action of the army unnoticed, he may be sure that it is because I was mixing medicines or making good things in the kitchen of the British Hotel, and first heard the particulars of it, perhaps, from the newspapers which came from home. My readers must know, too, that they were much more familiar with the history of the camp at their own firesides, than we who lived in it. Just as a spectator seeing one of the battles from a hill, as I did the Tchernaya, knows more about it than the combatant in the valley below, who only thinks of the enemy whom it is his immediate duty to repel; so you, through the valuable aid of the cleverest man in the whole camp, read in the *Times'* columns the details of that great campaign, while we, the actors in it, had enough to do to discharge our own duties well, and rarely concerned ourselves in what seemed of such im-portance to you. And so very often a desperate skirmish or hard-fought action, the news of which created so much sensation in England, was but little regarded at Spring Hill.

My first experience of battle was pleasant enough. Before we had been long at Spring Hill, Omar Pasha got something for his Turks to do, and one fine morning they were marched away towards the Russian outposts on the road to Baidar. I accompanied them on horseback, and enjoyed the sight amazingly. English and French cavalry preceded the Turkish infantry over the plain yet full of memorials of the terrible Light Cavalry charge a few months before; and while one detachment of the Turks made a reconnaissance to the right of the Tchernaya, another pushed their way up the hill, towards Kamara, dri-ving in the Russian outposts, after what seemed but a slight resistance. It was very pretty to see them advance, and to watch how every now and then little clouds of white smoke puffed up from behind bushes and the crests of hills, and were answered by similar puffs from the long line of busy skirmishers that preceded the main body. This was my first experience of actual battle, and I felt that strange excitement which I do not remember on future occasions, coupled with an earnest longing to see more of warfare, and to share in its hazards. It was not long before my wish was gratified.

I do not know much of the second bombardment of Sebastopol in the month of April, although I was as assiduous as I could be in my attendance at Cathcart's Hill. I could judge of its severity by the long trains of wounded which passed the British Hotel. I had a stretcher laid near the door, and very often a poor fellow was laid upon it, out-wearied by the terrible conveyance from the front.

After this unsuccessful bombardment, it seemed to us that there was a sudden lull in the progress of the siege; and other things began to interest us. There were several arrivals to talk over. Miss Nightingale came to supervise the Balaclava hospitals, and, before long, she had practical experience of Crimean fever. After her, came the Duke of Newcastle, and the great high priest of the mysteries of cookery, Mons. Alexis Soyer. He was often at Spring Hill, with the most smiling of faces and in the most gorgeous of irregular uniforms, and never failed to praise my soups and dainties. I always flattered myself that I was his match, and with our West Indian dishes could of course beat him hollow, and more than once I challenged him to a trial of skill; but the gallant Frenchman only shrugged his shoulders, and disclaimed my challenge with many flourishes of his jewelled hands, de-claring that Madame proposed a contest where victory would cost him his reputation for gallantry, and be more disastrous than defeat. And all because I was a woman, forsooth. What nonsense to talk like that, when I was doing the work of half a dozen men. Then he would laugh and declare that, when our campaigns were over, we would render rivalry impossible, by combining to open the first restaurant in Europe. There was always fun in the store when the good-natured Frenchman was there.

One dark, tempestuous night, I was knocked up by the arrival of other visitors. These were the first regiment of Sardinian Grenadiers, who, benighted on their way to the position assigned them, remained at Spring Hill until the morning. We soon turned out our staff, and lighted up the store, and entertained the officers as well as we could inside, while the soldiers bivouacked in the yards around. Not a single thing was stolen or disturbed that night, although they had many opportunities. We all admired and liked the Sardinians; they were honest, well-disciplined fellows, and I wish there had been no worse men or soldiers in the Crimea.

The deaths in the trenches touched me deeply, perhaps for this reason. It was very usual, when a young officer was ordered into the trenches, for him to ride down to Spring Hill to dine, or obtain something more than his ordinary fare to brighten his weary hours in those fearful ditches. They seldom failed on these occasions to shake me by the hand at parting, and sometimes would say, 'You see, Mrs. Seacole, I can't say good-bye to the dear ones at home, so I'll bid you goodbye for them. Perhaps you'll see them some day, and if the Russians should knock me over, mother, just tell them I thought of them all—will you?' And although all this might be said in a light-hearted manner, it was rather solemn. I felt it to be so, for I never failed (although who was I, that I should preach?) to say something about God's providence and relying upon it; and they were very good. No army of parsons could be much better than my sons. They would listen very gravely, and shake me by the hand again, while I felt that there was nothing in the world I would not do for them. Then very often the men would say, 'I'm going in with my master to-night, Mrs. Seacole; come and look after him, if he's hit;' and so often as this happened I would pass the night restlessly, awaiting with anxiety the morning, and yet dreading to hear the news it held in store for me. I used to think it was like having a large family of children ill with fever, and dreading to hear which one had passed away in the night.

. . . I could give many other similar instances, but why should I sadden myself or my readers? Others have described the horrors of those fatal trenches; but their real history has never been written, and perhaps it is as well that so harrowing a tale should be left in oblivion. Such anecdotes as the following were very current in the Camp, but I have no means of answering for its truth. Two sergeants met in the trenches, who had been schoolmates in their youth; years had passed since they set out for the battle of life by different roads, and now they met again under the fire of a common enemy. With one impulse they started forward to exchange the hearty hand-shake and the mutual greetings, and while their hands were still clasped, a chance shot killed both.

———⁂———

Richard Cobden (1804–1865) was a cotton manufacturer, an MP, a leader of the Anti-Corn-Law League, and a relentless advocate of free trade. In the selection below he reflects on the role of Russia in the geopolitical landscape Britain was trying to control as the Crimean War drew both nations into a localized international conflict.

———

Richard Cobden, from *Russia and the Eastern Question* (1854)

. . . Russia comprises one-half of Europe, one-third of Asia, and a portion of America; and includes within its bounds nearly sixty millions, or a sixteenth portion of the human race. Its territory stretches, in length, from the Black Sea to the confines of Upper Canada; and from the border of China to the Arctic Sea, in width. The stupendous size of the Russian empire has excited the wonder and alarm of timid writers, who forget that "it is an identity of language, habits and character, and not the soil or the name of a master, which constitutes a great and powerful nation." Ruling over eighty different nations or tribes, the Autocrat of all the Russias claims the allegiance of people of every variety of race, tongue, and religion. Were it possible to transport to one common centre of his empire the gay opera lounger of St. Petersburg, habited in the Parisian mode; the fierce Bashkir of the Ural Mountain, clad in rude armor, and armed with bow and arrows; the Crimean, with his camel, from the southern steppes; and the Esquimaux, who traverses with his dogs the frozen regions of the north,—these fellow-subjects of one potentate would encounter each other with all the surprise and ignorance of individuals meeting from England, China, Peru, and New Holland; nor would the time or expense incurred in the journey be greater in the latter than the former interview. It must be obvious to every reflecting mind that vast deductions must be made from the written and statistical resources of a nation possessing no unison of religious or political feeling, when put in competition with other empires, identified in faith, language, and national characteristics. . . .

We may fairly assume that, were Russia to seize upon the capital of Turkey, the consequences would not, at least, be less favorable to humanity and civilization than those which succeeded to her conquests on the Gulf of Finland a century ago. The seraglio of the Sultan would be once more converted into the palace of a Christian monarch; the lasciviousness of the harem would disappear at the presence of his Christian empress; those walls which now resound only to the voice of the eunuch and the slave, and witness nothing but deeds of guilt and dishonor, would then echo the footsteps of travellers and the voices of men of learning, or behold the assemblage of high-souled and beautiful women, of exalted birth and rare accomplishments, the virtuous companions of ambassadors, tourists and merchants, from all the capitals of Europe. We may fairly and reasonably assume that such consequences would follow the conquest of Constantinople: and can any one doubt that, if the government of St. Petersburg were transferred to the shores of the Bosphorus, a splendid and substantial European city would, in less than twenty years, spring up, in the place of those huts which now constitute the capital of Turkey?—that noble public buildings would arise, learned societies flourish, and the arts prosper?—that, from its natural beauties and advantages, Constantinople would become an attractive resort for civilized Europeans?—that the Christian religion, operating instantly upon the laws and institutions of the country, would ameliorate the condition of its people?—that the slavemarket, which is now polluting the Ottoman capital, centuries after the odious traffic has been banished from the soil of Christian Europe, would be abolished?—that the demoralizing and unnatural law of polygamy, under which the fairest portion of the creation becomes an object of brutal lust and an article of daily traffic, would be discountenanced?—and that the plague, no longer fostered by the filth and indolence of the people, would cease to ravage countries placed in the healthiest latitudes and blessed with the finest climate in the world? Can any rational mind doubt that these changes would follow from the occupation of Constantinople by Russia, every one of which, so far as the difference in the cases permitted, has already been realized more than a century in St. Petersburg? But the interests of England, it is alleged, would be endangered by such changes. We deny that the progress of improvement and the advance of civilization can be inimical to the welfare of Great Britain. To assert that we, a commercial and manufacturing people, have an interest in retaining the fairest regions in Europe in barbarism and ignorance,—that we are benefited because poverty, slavery, polygamy, and the plague, abound in Turkey,—is a fallacy too gross even for refutation.

. . . By far the greater proportion of the writers and speakers upon the subject of the power of Russia either do not understand or lose sight of the all-important question, What is the true source of national greatness? The path by which alone modern empires can hope to rise to supreme power and grandeur (would that we could impress this sentiment upon the mind of every statesman in Europe!) is that of labor and improvement. They who, pointing to the chart of Russia, shudder at her expanse of impenetrable forests, her wastes of eternal snow, her howling wildernesses, frowning mountains, and solitary rivers,—or they who stand aghast at her boundless extent of fertile but uncultivated steppes, her millions of serfs, and her towns the abodes of poverty and filth,— know nothing of the true origin, in modern and future times, of national power and greatness. This question admits of an appropriate illustration, by putting the names of a couple of heroes of Russian aggression and violence in contrast with two of their contemporaries, the champions of improvement in England. At the very period when Potemkin and Suwarrow were engaged in effecting their important Russian conquests in Poland and the Crimea, and whilst those monsters of carnage were filling the world with the lustre of their fame, and lighting up one-half of Europe with the conflagrations of war, two obscure individuals, the one an optician, and the other a barber, both equally disregarded by the chroniclers of the day, were quietly gaining victories in the realms of science, which have produced a more abundant harvest of wealth and power to their native country than has been acquired by all the wars of Russia during the last two centuries. Those illustrious commanders in the war of improvement, Watt, and Arkwright, with a band of subalterns,—the thousand ingenious and practical discoverers who have followed in their train,—have, with their armies of artisans, conferred a power and consequence upon England, springing from successive triumphs in the physical sciences and the mechanical arts, and wholly independent of territorial increase, compared with which, all that she owes to the evanescent exploits of her warrior-heroes shrinks into insignificance and obscurity. If we look into futurity, and speculate upon the probable career of one of these inventions, may we not with safety predict that the steam-engine—the perfecting of which belongs to our own age, and which even now is exerting an influence in the four quarters of the globe—will at no distant day produce moral and physical changes, all over the world, of a magnitude and permanency surpassing the effects of all the wars and conquests which have convulsed mankind since the beginning of time? England owes to the peaceful exploits of Watt and Arkwright, and not to the deeds of Nelson and Wellington, her commerce, which now extends to every corner of the earth; and which casts into comparative obscurity, by the grandeur and extent of its operations, the peddling ventures of Tyre, Carthage and Venice, confined within the limits of an island sea.

If we were to trace, step by step, the opposite careers of aggrandizement, to which we can only thus hastily glance—of England, pursuing the march of improvement within the area of four of her counties, by exploring the recesses of her mines, by constructing canals, docks and railroads, by her mechanical inventions, and by the patience and ingenuity of her manufacturers in adapting their fabrics to meet the varying wants and tastes of every habitable latitude of the earth's surface; and of Russia, adhering to her policy of territorial conquest, by despoiling of provinces the empires of Turkey, Persia and Sweden, by subjugating in unwilling bondage the natives of Georgia and Circassia, and by seizing with robber hand the soil of Poland,—if we were to trace these opposite careers of aggrandizement, what should we find to be the relative consequences to these two empires? England, with her steam-engine and spinning-frame, has erected the standard of improvement, around which every nation of the world has already prepared to rally; she has, by the magic of her machinery, united forever two remote hemispheres in the bonds of peace, by placing Europe and America in absolute and inextricable dependence on each other. England's industrious classes, through the energy of their commercial enterprise, are, at this moment, influencing the civilization of the whole world, by stimulating the labor, exciting the curiosity, and promoting the taste for refinement, of barbarous communities, and, above all, by acquiring and teaching to surrounding nations the beneficent attachment to peace. Such are the moral effects of improvement in Britain, against which Russia can oppose comparatively little, but the example of violence, to which humanity points as a beacon to warn society from evil. And if we refer to the physical effects,—if, for the sake of convincing minds which do not recognize the far more potent moral influences, we descend to a comparison of mere brute forces,—we find still greater superiority resulting from ingenuity and labor. The manufacturing districts alone—even the four counties of England, comprising Lancashire, Yorkshire, Cheshire, and Staffordshire—could, at any moment, by means of the wealth drawn, by the skill and industry of its population, from the natural resources of this comparative speck of territory, combat with success the whole Russian empire! Liverpool and Hull, with their navies, and Manchester, Leeds and Birmingham, with their capitals, could blockade, within the waters of Cronstadt, the entire Russian marine, and annihilate the commerce of St. Petersburg! And, further, if we suppose that, during the next thirty years, Russia, adhering to her system of territorial aggrandizement, were to swallow up successively her neighbors Persia and Turkey, whilst England, which we have imagined to comprise only the area of four counties, still persevered in her present career of mechanical ingenuity, the relative forces would, at the end of that time, be yet more greatly in favor of the peaceful and industrious empire. This mere speck on the ocean—without colonies, which are but the costly appendage of an aristocratic government—without wars, which have ever been but another aristocratic mode of plundering and oppressing commerce—would, with only a few hundred square leagues of surface, by means of the wealth which by her arts and industry she had accumulated, be the arbitress of the destiny of Russia, with its millions of square miles of territory. Liverpool and Hull, with their thousands of vessels, would be in a condition to dictate laws to the possessor of one-fourth part of the surface of the globe: they would then be enabled to blockade Russia in the Sea of Marmora, as they could now do in the Gulf of Finland—to deny her the freedom of the seas, to deprive her proud nobles of every foreign commodity and luxury, and degrade them, amidst their thousands of serfs, to the barbarous state of their ancestors of the ancient Rousniacs, and to confine her Czar in his splendid prison of Constantinople. If such are the miracles of the mind, such the superiority of improvement over the efforts of brute force and violence, is not the writer of these pages justified in calling the attention of his countrymen elsewhere to the progress of another people, whose rapid adoption of the discoveries of the age, whose mechanical skill and unrivalled industry in all the arts of life,—as exemplified in their thousands of miles of railroads, their hundreds of steamboats, their ship-building, manufacturing, and patent inventions,—whose system of universal instruction, and, above all, whose inveterate attachment to peace, all proclaim America, by her competition in improvements, to be destined to affect more vitally than Russia by her aggrandizement of territory, the future interests of Great Britain? . . .

Karl Marx (1818–83) wrote a number of reports for the New York Daily News about the "outrages committed by the revolted sepoys" in India. They are an indictment of British rule, a sardonic commentary on the biases of the English press, and a graphic account of the violences visited on both sides.

Karl Marx on the events of 1857

The outrages committed by the revolted sepoys in India are indeed appalling, hideous, ineffable—such as one is prepared to meet only in wars of insurrection, of nationalities, of races, and above all of religion; in one word, such as respectable England used to applaud when perpetrated by the Vendeans on the "Blues," by the Spanish guerrillas on the infidel Frenchmen, by Serbians on their German and Hungarian neighbours, by Croats on Viennese rebels, by Cavaignac's Garde Mobile or Bonaparte's Decembrists on the sons and daughters of proletarian France. However infamous the conduct of the sepoys, it is only the reflex, in a concentrated form, of England's own conduct in India, not only during the epoch of the foundation of her Eastern Empire, but even during the last ten years of a long-settled rule. To characterize that rule, it suffices to say that torture formed an organic institution of its financial policy. There is something in human history like retribution; and it is a rule of historical retribution that its instrument be forged not by the offended, but by the offender himself.

The first blow dealt to the French monarchy proceeded from the nobility, not from the peasants. The Indian revolt does not commence with the ryots, tortured, dishonoured and stripped naked by the British, but with the sepoys, clad, fed, petted, fatted and pampered by them. To find parallels to the sepoy atrocities, we need not, as some London papers pretend, fall back on the middle ages, nor even wander beyond the history of contemporary England. All we want is to study the first Chinese war, an event, so to say, of yesterday. The English soldiery then committed abominations for the mere fun of it; their passions being neither sanctified by religious fanaticism nor exacerbated by hatred against an overbearing and conquering race, nor provoked by the stern resis-

tance of a heroic enemy. The violations of women, the spittings of children, the roast-
ings of whole villages, were then mere wanton sports, not recorded by mandarins, but
by British officers themselves.

Even at the present catastrophe it would be an unmitigated mistake to suppose that
all the cruelty is on the side of the sepoys, and all the milk of human kindness flows on
the side of the English. The letters of the British officers are redolent of malignity. An
officer writing from Peshawar gives a description of the disarming of the 10th Irregular
Cavalry for not charging the 55th Native Infantry when ordered to do so. He exults in
the fact that they were not only disarmed, but stripped of their coats and boots, and after
having received 12d. per man, were marched down to the riverside, and there embarked
in boats and sent down the Indus, where the writer is delighted to expect every mother's
son will have a chance of being drowned in the rapids. Another writer informs us that
some inhabitants of Peshawar having caused a night alarm by exploding little mines of
gunpowder in honour of a wedding (a national custom), the persons concerned were
tied up next morning, and "received such a flogging as they will not easily forget." News
arrived from Pindee that three native chiefs were plotting. Sir John Lawrence replied by
a message ordering a spy to attend to the meeting. On the spy's report, Sir John sent a
second message, "Hang them." The chiefs were hanged. An officer in the civil service,
from Allahabad, writes: "We have power of life and death in our hands, and we assure
you we spare not." Another, from the same place: "Not a day passes but we string up
from ten to fifteen of them (non-combatants)." One exulting officer writes: "Holmes is
hanging them by the score, like a 'brick'." Another, in allusion to the summary hanging
of a large body of the natives: "Then our fun commenced." A third: "We hold court-
martials on horseback, and every nigger we meet with we either string up or shoot."
From Benares we are informed that thirty zemindars were hanged on the mere suspicion
of sympathizing with their own countrymen, and whole villages were burned down on
the same plea. An officer from Benares, whose letter is printed in the London *Times,*
says: "The European troops have become fiends when opposed to natives."

And then it should not be forgotten that, while the cruelties of the English are related as acts of martial vigour, told simply, rapidly, without dwelling on disgusting details, the outrages of the natives, shocking as they are, are still deliberately exaggerated.
For instance, the circumstantial account first appearing in the *Times,* and then going
the round of the London press, of the atrocities perpetrated at Delhi and Meerut, from
whom did it proceed? From a cowardly parson residing at Bangalore, Mysore, more
than a thousand miles, as the bird flies, distant from the scene of action. Actual accounts of Delhi evince the imagination of an English parson to be capable of breeding
greater horrors than even the wild fancy of a Hindu mutineer. The cutting of noses,
breasts, etc., in one word, the horrid mutilations committed by the sepoys, are of
course more revolting to European feeling than the throwing of red-hot shell on Canton dwellings by a Secretary of the Manchester Peace Society, or the roasting of Arabs
pent up in a cave by a French Marshal, or the flaying alive of British soldiers by the cat-
o'-nine-tails under drum-head courtmartial, or any other of the philanthropical appli-
ances used in British penitentiary colonies. Cruelty, like every other thing, has its
fashion, changing according to time and place. Caesar, the accomplished scholar, candidly narrates how he ordered many thousand Gallic warriors to have their right hands
cut off. Napoleon would have been ashamed to do this. He preferred dispatching his
own French regiments, suspected of republicanism, to Santo Domingo, there to die of
the blacks and the plague.

The infamous mutilations committed by the sepoys remind one of the practices of the Christian Byzantine Empire, or the prescriptions of Emperor Charles V's criminal law, or the English punishments for high treason, as still recorded by Judge Blackstone. With Hindus, whom their religion has made virtuosi in the art of self-torturing, these tortures inflicted on the enemies of their race and creed appear quite natural, and must appear still more so to the English, who, only some years since, still used to draw revenues from the Juggernaut festivals, protecting and assisting the bloody rites of a religion of cruelty. . . .

Part II

Liberalizing Imperial Democracy:
Midcentury and After

A. Imagining an Imperial Polity

Lord Durham was despatched in 1838 to investigate the state of affairs in upper and lower Canada, where religious tensions and dissatisfaction with Crown government provoked riots and the specter of possible secession. The Report that ensued has been called "the Magna Carta of colonial liberty," at least for the white settler dominions.

Lord Durham, Report on Canada (1839)

. . . There are two modes by which a government may deal with a conquered territory. The first course open to it is that of respecting the rights and nationality of the actual oc- cupants; of recognizing the existing laws, and preserving established institutions; of giv- ing no encouragement to the influx of the conquering people, and, without attempting any change in the elements of the community, merely incorporating the Province under the general authority of the central Government. The second is that of treating the con- quered territory as one open to the conquerors, of encouraging their influx, of regarding the conquered race as entirely subordinate, and of endeavouring as speedily and as rapidly as possible to assimilate the character and institutions of its new subjects to those of the great body of its empire. In the case of an old and long settled country, in which the land is appropriated, in which little room is left for colonization, and in which the race of the actual occupants must continue to constitute the bulk of the future population of the province, policy as well as humanity render the well-being of the conquered people the first care of a just government, and recommend the adoption of the first-mentioned sys- tem; but in a new and unsettled country, a provident legislator would regard as his first object the interests not of the few individuals who happen at the moment to inhabit a portion of the soil, but those of that comparatively vast population by which he may rea- sonably expect that it will be filled; he would form his plans with a view of attracting and nourishing that future population, and he would therefore establish those institutions which would be most acceptable to the race by which he hoped to colonize the country. The course which I have described as best suited to an old and settled country, would have been impossible in the American continent, unless the conquering state meant to renounce the immediate use of the unsettled lands of the Province; and in this case such a course would have been additionally unadvisable, unless the British Government were prepared to abandon to the scanty population of French whom it found in Lower Canada, not merely the possession of the vast extent of rich soil which that Province contains, but also the mouth of the St. Lawrence, and all the facilities for trade which the entrance of that great river commands.

. . . In 1775 instructions were sent from England, directing that all grants of land within the Province of Quebec, then comprising Upper and Lower Canada, were to be made in fief and seigniory; and even the grants to the refugee loyalists, and officers and privates of the colonial corps, promised in 1786, were ordered to be made on the same tenure. In no instance was it more singularly exhibited than in the condition annexed to the grants of land in Prince Edward's Island, by which it was stipulated that the Island was to be settled by 'foreign Protestants'; as if they were to be foreign in order to separate them from the people of New England, and Protestants in order to keep them apart from the Canadian and Acadian Catholics. It was part of the same policy to separate the French of Canada from the British emigrants, and to conciliate the former by the retention of their language, laws, and religious institutions. For this purpose Canada was afterwards divided into two Provinces, the settled portion being allotted to the French, and the unsettled being destined to become the seat of British colonization. Thus, instead of availing itself of the means which the extent and nature of the Province afforded for the gradual introduction of such an English population into its various parts as might have easily placed the French in a minority, the Government deliberately constituted the French into a majority, and recognized and strengthened their indistinct national character. Had the sounder policy of making the Province English, in all its institutions, been adopted from the first, and steadily persevered in, the French would probably have been speedily outnumbered, and the beneficial operation of the free institutions of England would never have been impeded by the animosities of origin.

Not only, however, did the Government adopt the unwise course of dividing Canada, and forming in one of its divisions a French community, speaking the French language, and retaining French institutions, but it did not even carry this consistently into effect; for at the same time provision was made for encouraging the emigration of English into the very Province which was said to be assigned to the French. Even the French institutions were not extended over the whole of Lower Canada. The civil law of France, as a whole, and the legal provision for the Catholic clergy were limited to the portion of the country then settled by the French, and comprised in the seigniories; though some provision was made for the formation of new seigniories, almost the whole of the then unsettled portion of the Province was formed into townships, in which the law of England was partially established, and the Protestant religion alone endowed. Thus two populations of hostile origin and different characters, were brought into juxtaposition under a common government, but under different institutions; each was taught to cherish its own language, laws and habits, and each, at the same time, if it moved beyond its original limits, was brought under different institutions, and associated with a different people. The unenterprising character of the French population, and, above all, its attachment to its church (for the enlargement of which, in proportion to the increase or diffusion of the Catholic population, very inadequate provision was made) have produced the effect of confining it within its ancient limits. But the English were attracted into the seigniories, and especially into the cities, by the facilities of commerce afforded by the great rivers. To have effectually given the policy of retaining French institutions and a French population in Lower Canada a fair chance of success, no other institutions should have been allowed, and no other race should have received any encouragement to settle therein. The Province should have been set apart to be wholly French, if it was not to be rendered completely English. The attempt to encourage English emigration into a community, of which the French character was still to be preserved, was an error which planted the seeds of a contest of races in the very constitution of the Colony; this was an error, I mean, even on the assumption that it was possible to exclude the English race from French Canada. But it was quite impossible to exclude the English race from any part of the North American continent. It will be acknowledged by every one who has observed the progress of Anglo-Saxon colonization in America, that sooner or later the English race was sure to predominate even numerically in Lower Canada, as they predominate already, by their superior knowledge, energy, enterprise and wealth. The error, therefore, to which the present contest must be attributed, is the vain endeavour to preserve a French Canadian nationality in the midst of Anglo-American colonies and states. . . .

Perfectly aware of the value of our colonial possessions, and strongly impressed with the necessity of maintaining our connexion with them, I know not in what respect it can be desirable that we should interfere with [the Colonies'] internal legislation in matters which do not affect their relations with the mother country. The matters, which so concern us, are very few. The constitution of the form of government,—the regulation of foreign relations, and of trade with the mother country, the other British Colonies, and foreign nations,—and the disposal of the public lands, are the only points on which the mother country requires a control. This control is now sufficiently secured by the authority of the Imperial Legislature; by the protection which the Colony derives from us against foreign enemies; by the beneficial terms which our laws secure to its trade; and by its share of the reciprocal benefits which would be conferred by a wise system of colonization. A perfect subordination, on the part of the Colony, on these points, is secured by the advantages which it finds in the continuance of its connexion with the Empire. It certainly is not strengthened, but greatly weakened, by a vexatious interference on the part of the Home Government, with the enactment of laws for regulating the internal concerns of the Colony, or in the selection of the persons entrusted with their execution. The colonists may not always know what laws are best for them, or which of their countrymen are the fittest for conducting their affairs; but, at least, they have a greater interest in coming to a right judgement on these points, and will take greater pains to do so, than those whose welfare is very remotely and slightly affected by the good or bad legislation of these portions of the Empire. If the colonists make bad laws, and select improper persons to conduct their affairs, they will generally be the only, always the greatest, sufferers; and, like the people of other countries, they must bear the ills which they bring on themselves, until they choose to apply the remedy. But it surely cannot be the duty or the interest of Great Britain to keep a most expensive military possession of these Colonies, in order that a Governor or Secretary of State may be able to confer colonial appointments on one rather than another set of persons in the Colonies. For this is really the only question at issue. The slightest acquaintance with these Colonies proves the fallacy of the common notion, that any considerable amount of patronage in them is distributed among strangers from the mother country.

. . . I am well aware that many persons, both in the Colonies and at home, view the system which I recommend with considerable alarm, because they distrust the ulterior views of those by whom it was originally proposed, and whom they suspect of urging its adoption, with the intent only of enabling them more easily to subvert monarchical institutions, or assert the independence of the Colony. I believe, however, that the extent to which these ulterior views exist, has been greatly overrated. We must not take every rash expression of disappointment as an indication of a settled aversion to the existing constitution; and my own observation convinces me, that the predominant feeling of all the English population of the North American Colonies is that of devoted attachment to the mother country. I believe that neither the interests nor the feelings of the people are incompatible with a Colonial Government, wisely and popularly administered. The proofs, which many who are much dissatisfied with the existing administration of the Government, have given of their loyalty, are not to be denied or overlooked. The attachment constantly exhibited by the people of these Provinces towards the British Crown and Empire has all the characteristics of a strong national feeling. They value the institutions of their country, not merely from a sense of the practical advantages which they confer, but from sentiments of national pride; and they uphold them the more, because they are accustomed to view them as marks of nationality, which distinguish them from their Republican neighbours. I do not mean to affirm that this is a feeling which no impolicy on the part of the mother country will be unable to impair; but I do most confidently regard it as one which may, if rightly appreciated, be made the link of an enduring and advantageous connexion. The British people of the North American Colonies are a people on whom we may safely rely, and to whom we must not grudge power. For it is not to the individuals who have been loudest in demanding the change, that I propose to concede the responsibility of the Colonial administration, but to the people themselves. Nor can I conceive that any people, or any considerable portion of a people, will view with dissatisfaction a change which would amount simply to this, that the Crown would henceforth consult the wishes of the people in the choice of its servants.

. . . On these grounds, I believe that no permanent or efficient remedy can be devised for the disorders of Lower Canada, except a fusion of the Government in that of one or more of the surrounding Provinces; and as I am of opinion that the full establishment of responsible government can only be permanently secured by giving these Colonies an increased importance in the politics of the Empire, I find in union the only means of remedying at once and completely the two prominent causes of their present unsatisfactory condition. . . .

Thomas Carlyle (1795–1881) was a prolific essayist and critic. His "Occasional Discourse on the Negro Question" may be one of the most stylized examples of Victorian racialist discourse, but it also captures the complexities of contemporary racist thinking and sentiment in the wake of both Irish Catholic emancipation and the abolition of slavery.

Thomas Carlyle,
"Occasional Discourse on the Negro Question" (1849)

. . . My Philanthropic Friends,—It is my painful duty to address some words to you, this evening, on the Rights of Negroes. Taking, as we hope we do, an extensive survey of social affairs, which we find all in a state of the frightfullest embroilment, and as it were, of inextricable final bankruptcy, just at present; and being desirous to adjust ourselves in that huge upbreak, and unutterable welter of tumbling ruins, and to see well that our grand proposed Association of Associations, the UNIVERSAL ABOLITION-OF-PAIN Association, WHICH IS MEANT TO BE THE CONSUMMATE GOLDEN FLOWER AND SUMMARY OF MODERN PHILANTHROPISMS ALL IN ONE, DO *NOT* ISSUE AS A UNIVERSAL 'SLUGGARD-AND-SCOUNDREL PROTECTION SOCIETY,'—WE HAVE JUDGED THAT, BEFORE CONSTITUTING OURSELVES, IT WOULD BE VERY PROPER TO COMMUNE EARNESTLY WITH ONE ANOTHER, AND DISCOURSE TOGETHER ON THE LEADING ELEMENTS OF OUR GREAT PROBLEM, WHICH SURELY IS ONE OF THE GREATEST. WITH THIS VIEW THE COUNCIL HAS DECIDED, BOTH THAT THE NEGRO QUESTION, AS LYING AT THE BOTTOM, WAS TO BE THE FIRST HANDLED, AND IF POSSIBLE THE FIRST SETTLED; AND THEN ALSO, WHAT WAS OF MUCH MORE QUESTIONABLE WISDOM, THAT—THAT, IN SHORT, I WAS TO BE SPEAKER ON THE OCCASION. AN HONOURABLE DUTY; YET, AS I SAID, A PAINFUL ONE! WELL, YOU SHALL HEAR WHAT I HAVE TO SAY ON THE MATTER; AND YOU WILL NOT IN THE LEAST LIKE IT.

West-Indian affairs, as we all know, and some of us know to our cost, are in a rather troublous condition this good while. In regard to West Indian affairs, however, Lord John Russell is able to comfort us with one fact, indisputable where so many are dubious, That the Negroes are all very happy and doing well. A fact very comfortable indeed. West Indian Whites, it is admitted, are far enough from happy; West Indian Colonies not unlike sinking wholly into ruin: at home too, the British Whites are rather badly off; several millions of them hanging on the verge of continual famine; and in single towns, many thousands of them very sore put to it, at this time, not to live 'well,' or as a man should, in any sense temporal or spiritual, but to live at all:—these, again, are uncomfortable facts; and they are extremely extensive and important ones. But, thank Heaven, our interesting Black population—equalling almost in number of heads one of the Ridings of Yorkshire, and in *worth* (in quantity of intellect, faculty, docility, energy, and available human valour and value) perhaps one of the streets of Seven Dials—are all doing remarkably well. 'Sweet blighted lilies'—as the American epitaph on the Nigger child has it—sweet blighted lilies, they are holding up their heads again! How pleasant, in the universal bankruptcy abroad, and dim dreary stagnancy at home, as if for England too there remained nothing but to suppress Chartist riots, banish united Irishmen, vote the supplies, and *wait* with arms crossed till black Anarchy and Social Death devoured us also, as it has done the others; how pleasant to have always this fact to fall back upon: Our beautiful Black darlings are at last happy; with little labour except to the teeth, *which* surely, in those excellent horse-jaws of theirs, will not fail!

Exeter Hall, my philanthropic friends, has had its way in this matter. The Twenty Millions, a mere trifle despatched with a single dash of the pen, are paid; and far over the sea, we have a few black persons rendered extremely 'free' indeed. Sitting yonder with their beautiful muzzles up to the ears in pumpkins, imbibing sweet pulps and juices; the grinder and incisor teeth ready for every new work, and the pumpkins cheap as grass in those rich climates: while the sugar-crops rot round them uncut, because labour cannot be hired, so cheap are the pumpkins;—and at home we are but required to rasp from the breakfast loaves of our own English labourers some slight 'differential sugar-duties,' and lend a poor half-million or a few poor millions now and then, to keep that beautiful state of matters going on. A state of matters lovely to contemplate, in these emancipated epochs of the human mind; which has earned us not only the praises of Exeter Hall, and loud long-eared hallelujahs of laudatory psalmody from the

Friends of Freedom everywhere, but lasting favour (it is hoped) from the Heavenly Powers themselves. . . .

Our West Indian Legislatings, with their spoutings, anti-spoutings and interminable jangle and babble; our Twenty millions down on the nail for Blacks of our own; Thirty gradual millions more, and many brave British lives to boot, in watching Blacks of other people's; and now at last our ruined sugar-estates, differential sugar-duties, 'immigration loan,' and beautiful Blacks sitting there up to the ears in pumpkins, and doleful Whites sitting here without potatoes to eat: never till now, I think, did the sun look down on such a jumble of human nonsenses;—of which, with the two hot nights of the Missing-Despatch Debate, God grant that the measure might now at last be full! But no, it is not yet full; we have a long way to travel back, and terrible flounderings to make, and in fact an immense load of nonsense to dislodge from our poor heads, and manifold cobwebs to rend from our poor eyes, before we get into the road again, and can begin to act as serious men that have work to do in this Universe, and no longer as windy sentimentalists that merely have speeches to deliver and despatches to write. Oh Heaven, in West-Indian matters, and in all manner of matters, it is so with us: the more is the sorrow!

Our own white or sallow Ireland, sluttishly starving from age to age on its act-of-parliament 'freedom,' was hitherto the flower of mismanagement among the nations: but what will this be to a Negro Ireland, with pumpkins themselves fallen scarce like potatoes! Imagination cannot fathom such an object; the belly of Chaos never held the like. The human mind, in its wide wanderings, has not dreamt yet of such a 'freedom' as that will be. Towards that, if Exeter Hall and science of supply and demand are to continue our guides in the matter, we are daily travelling, and even struggling, with loans of half-a-million and such-like, to accelerate ourselves.

Let me suggest another consideration withal. West India Islands, still full of waste fertility, produce abundant pumpkins; pumpkins, however, you will please to observe, are not the sole requisite for human wellbeing. No: for a pig they are the one thing needful; but for a man they are only the first of several things needful. And now, as to the right of chief management in cultivating those West India lands; as to the 'right of property' so-called, and of doing what you like with your own? The question is abstruse enough. Who it may be that has a right to raise pumpkins and other produce on those Islands, perhaps none can, except temporarily, decide. The Islands are good withal for pepper, for sugar, for sago, arrow-root, for coffee, perhaps for cinnamon and precious spices; things far nobler than pumpkins; and leading towards commerces, arts, politics, and social developments, which alone are the noble product, where men (and not pigs with pumpkins) are the parties concerned! Well, all this fruit too, fruit spicy and commercial, fruit spiritual and celestial, so far beyond the merely pumpkinish and grossly terrene, lies in the West India lands: and the ultimate 'proprietorship' of them—why, I suppose, it will vest in him who can the *best* educe from them whatever of noble produce they were created fit for yielding. He, I compute, is the real 'Vicegerent of the Maker' there; in him, better and better chosen, and not in another, is the 'property' vested by decree of Heaven's chancery itself!

Up to this time it is the Saxon British mainly; they hitherto have cultivated with some manfulness: and when a manfuller class of cultivators, stronger, worthier to have such land, abler to bring fruit from it, shall make their appearance—they, doubt it not, by fortune of war and other confused negociation and vicissitude, will be declared by Nature and Fact to *be* the worthier, and will become proprietors—perhaps also only for a time. That is the law, I take it; ultimate, supreme, for all lands in all countries under this sky. The one perfect eternal proprietor is the Maker who created them: the temporary better or worse proprietor is he whom the Maker has sent on that mission; he who the best hitherto can educe from said lands the beneficent gifts the Maker endowed them with; or, which is but another definition of the same person, he who leads hitherto the manfullest life on that bit of soil, doing, better than another yet found can do, the Eternal Purpose and Supreme Will there.

And now observe, my friends, it was not Black Quashee or those he represents that made those West India Islands what they are, or can by any hypothesis be considered to have the right of growing pumpkins there. For countless ages, since they first mounted oozy, on the back of earthquakes, from their dark bed in the Ocean deeps, and reeking saluted the tropical Sun, and ever onwards till the European white man first saw them some three short centuries ago, those Islands had produced mere jungle, savagery, poison-reptiles and swamp-malaria: till the white European first saw them, they were as if not yet created—their noble elements of cinnamon, sugar, coffee, pepper black and grey, lying all asleep, waiting the white Enchanter who should say to them, Awake! Till the end of human history and the sounding of the Trump of Doom, they might have lain so, had Quashee and the like of him been the only artists in the game. Swamps, fever-jungles, man-eating Caribs, rattle-snakes, and reeking waste and putrefaction, this had been the produce of them under the incompetent Caribal (what we call Cannibal) possessors till that time; and Quashee knows, himself, whether ever he could have introduced an improvement. Him, had he by a miraculous chance been wafted thither, the Caribals would have eaten, rolling him as a fat morsel under their tongue; for him, till the sounding of the Trump of Doom, the rattle-snakes and savageries would have held on their way. It was not he, then; it was another than he! Never by art of his could one pumpkin have grown there to solace any human throat; nothing but savagery and reeking putrefaction could have grown there. These plentiful pumpkins, I say therefore, are not his: no, they are another's; they are his only under conditions; conditions which Exeter Hall, for the present, has forgotten; but which Nature and the Eternal Powers have by no manner of means forgotten, but do at all moments keep in mind; and, at the right moment, will, with the due impressiveness, perhaps in a rather terrible manner, bring again to our mind also!

If Quashee will not honestly aid in bringing out those sugars, cinnamons, and nobler products of the West Indian Islands, for the benefit of all mankind, then I say neither will the Powers permit Quashee to continue growing pumpkins there for his own lazy benefit; but will sheer him out, by and by, like a lazy gourd overshadowing rich ground; him and all that partake with him—perhaps in a very terrible manner. For, under favour of Exeter Hall, the 'terrible manner' is not yet quite extinct with the Destinies in this Universe; nor will it quite cease, I apprehend, for soft sawder or philanthropic stump-oratory now or henceforth. No; the gods wish besides pumpkins, that spices and valuable products be grown in their West Indies; thus much they have declared in so making the West Indies:—infinitely more they wish, that manful industrious men occupy their West Indies, not indolent two-legged cattle, however 'happy' over their abundant pumpkins! Both these things, we may be assured, the immortal gods have decided upon, passed their eternal act of parliament for: and both of them, though all terrestrial Parliaments and entities oppose it to the death, shall be done. Quashee, if he will not help in bringing out the spices, will get himself made a slave again (which state will be a little less ugly, than his present one), and with beneficent whip, since other methods avail not, will be compelled to work. Or, alas, let him look across to Haiti, and trace a far sterner prophecy! Let him, by his ugliness, idleness, rebellion, banish all White men from the West Indies, and make it all one Haiti—with little or no sugar growing, black Peter exterminating black Paul, and where a garden of the Hesperides might be, nothing but a tropical dog-kennel and pestiferous jungle,—does he think that will for ever continue pleasant to gods and men? I see men, the rose-pink cant all peeled away from them, land one day on those black coasts; men *sent* by the Laws of this Universe, and the inexorable Course of Things; men hungry for gold, remorseless, fierce as old Buccaneers were;—and a doom for Quashee which I had rather not contemplate! The gods are long-suffering; but the law from the beginning was, He that will not work shall perish from the earth, and the patience of the gods has limits!

Before the West Indies could grow a pumpkin for any Negro, how much European heroism had to spend itself in obscure battle; to sink, in mortal agony, before the jungles, the putrescences and waste savageries could become arable, and the Devils be in some measure chained there! The West Indies grow pine-apples, and sweet fruits, and spices; we hope they will one day grow beautiful Heroic human Lives too, which is surely the ultimate object they were made for: beautiful souls and brave; sages, poets, what not; making the Earth nobler round them, as their kindred from of old have been doing; true 'splinters of the old Harz Rock;' heroic white men, worthy to be called old Saxons, browned with a mahogany tint in those new climates and conditions. But under the soil of Jamaica, before it could even produce spices or any pumpkin, the bones of many thousand British men had to be laid. Brave Colonel Fortescue, brave Colonel Sedgwick, brave Colonel Brayne—the dust of many thousand strong old English hearts lies there; worn down swiftly in frightful travail, chaining the Devils, which were manifold. Heroic Blake contributed a bit of his life to that Jamaica. A bit of the great Protector's own life lies there; beneath those pumpkins lies a bit of the life that was Oliver Cromwell's. How the great Protector would have rejoiced to think, that all this was to issue in growing pumpkins to keep Quashee in a comfortably idle condition! No; that is not the ultimate issue; not that.

The West Indian Whites, so soon as this bewilderment of philanthropic and other jargon abates from them, and their poor eyes get to discern a little what the Facts are and what the Laws are, will strike into another course, I apprehend! I apprehend they will, as a preliminary, resolutely *refuse* to permit the Black man any privilege whatever of pumpkins till he agree for work in return. Not a square inch of soil in those fruitful Isles, purchased by British blood, shall any Black man hold to grow pumpkins for him, except on terms that are fair towards Britain. Fair; see that they be not unfair, not towards ourselves, and still more, not towards him. For injustice is *for ever* accursed: and precisely our unfairness towards the enslaved black man has—by inevitable revulsion and fated turn of the wheel—brought about these present confusions. Fair towards Britain it will be, that Quashee give work for privilege to grow pumpkins. Not a pumpkin, Quashee, not a square yard of soil, till you agree to do the State so many days of service. Annually that soil will grow you pumpkins; but annually also without fail shall you, for the owner thereof, do your appointed days of labour. The State has plenty of waste soil; but the State will religiously give you none of it on other terms. The State wants sugar from these Islands, and means to have it; wants virtuous industry in these Islands, and must have it. The State demands of you such service as will bring these results, this latter result which includes all. Not a Black Ireland, by immigration, and boundless black supply for the demand; not that—may the gods forbid!—but a regulated West Indies, with black working population in adequate numbers; all 'happy,' if they find it possible; and *not* entirely unbeautiful to gods and men, which latter result they *must* find possible! All 'happy' enough; that is to say, all working according to the faculty they have got, making a little more divine this earth which the gods have given them. Is there any other 'happiness'—if it be not that of pigs fattening daily to the slaughter? So will the State speak by and by.

Any poor idle Black man, any idle White man, rich or poor, is a mere eye-sorrow to the State; a perpetual blister on the skin of the State. The State is taking measures, some of them rather extensive in Europe at this very time, and already as in Paris, Berlin, and elsewhere, rather tremendous measures, to *get* its rich white men set to work; for alas, they also have long sat Negro-like up to the ears in pumpkin, regardless of 'work,' and of a world all going to waste for their idleness! Extensive measures, I say; and already (as, in all European lands, this scandalous Year of street-barricades and fugitive sham-kings exhibits) *tremendous* measures; for the thing is instant to be done.

What then is practically to be done? Much, very much, my friends, to which it hardly falls to me to allude at present: but all this of perfect equality, of cutting quite loose from one another; all this, with 'immigration loan,' 'happiness of black peasantry,' and the other melancholy stuff that has followed from it, will first of all require to be *un*done, and have the ground cleared of it, by way of preliminary to 'doing!'

. . . On the whole it ought to be rendered possible, ought it not, for White men to live beside Black men, and in some just manner to command Black men, and produce West-Indian fruitfulness by means of them? West-Indian fruitfulness will need to be produced. If the English cannot find the method for that, they may rest assured there will another come (Brother Jonathan or still another) who can. He it is whom the gods will bid continue in the West Indies; bidding us ignominiously, Depart ye quack-ridden, incompetent!

John Stuart Mill (1806–73) was a Liberal MP from 1865–68, a leading advocate of women's political rights and, as the excerpt below suggests, a champion of "the negro," especially in comparison to the caricature of Carlyle's Quashee, above. Mill was a proponent of abolition in the American context and he opposed Governor Eyre's brutal response to the rebellion of blacks in Morant Bay in 1865, helping to establish the Jamaica Committee that formally protested Eyre's actions.

John Stuart Mill, "The Negro Question" (1850)

[IF all the meetings at Exeter Hall be not presided over by strictly impartial chairmen, they ought to be. We shall set an example to our pious brethren in this respect, by giving publicity to the following letter. Our readers have now both sides of the question before them, and can form their own opinions upon it.—EDITOR.]

To the Editor of Fraser's Magazine.

SIR,

YOUR last month's Number contains a speech against the 'rights of Negroes,' the doctrines and spirit of which ought not to pass without remonstrance. The author issues his opinions, or rather ordinances, under imposing auspices; no less than those of the 'immortal gods.' 'The Powers,' 'the Destinies,' announce through him, not only what *will* be, but what *shall* be done; what they 'have decided upon, passed their eternal act of parliament for.'

. . . He entirely misunderstands the great national revolt of the conscience of this country against slavery and the slave-trade, if he supposes it to have been an affair of sentiment. It depended no more on humane feelings than any cause which so irresistibly appealed to them must necessarily do. Its first victories were gained while the lash yet ruled uncontested in the barrack-yard and the rod in schools, and while men were still hanged by dozens for stealing to the value of forty shillings. It triumphed because it was the cause of justice; and, in the estimation of the great majority of its supporters, of religion. Its originators and leaders were persons of a stern sense of moral obligation, who, in the spirit of the religion of their time, seldom spoke much of benevolence and philanthropy, but often of duty, crime, and sin. For nearly two centuries had negroes, many thousands annually, been seized by force or treachery and carried off to the West Indies to be worked to death, literally to death; for it was the received maxim, the acknowledged dictate of good economy, to wear them out quickly and import more. In this fact every other possible cruelty, tyranny, and wanton oppression was by implication included. And the motive on the part of the slave-owners was the love of gold; or, to speak more truly, of vulgar and puerile ostentation. I have yet to learn that anything more detestable than this has been done by human beings towards human beings in any part of the earth. It is a mockery to talk of comparing it with Ireland. And this went on, not, like Irish beggary, because England had not the skill to prevent it,—not merely by the sufferance, but by the laws of the English nation. At last, however, there were found men, in growing number, who determined not to rest until the iniquity was extirpated; who made the destruction of it as much the business and end of their lives, as ordinary men make their private interests; who would not be content with softening its hideous features, and making it less intolerable to the sight, but would stop at nothing short of its utter and irrevocable extinction. I am so far from seeing anything contemptible in this resolution, that, in my sober opinion, the persons who formed and executed it deserve to be numbered among those, not numerous in any age, who have led noble lives according to their lights, and laid on mankind a debt of permanent gratitude.

After fifty years of toil and sacrifice, the object was accomplished, and the negroes, freed from the despotism of their fellow-beings, were left to themselves, and to the chances which the arrangements of existing society provide for those who have no resource but their labour. These chances proved favourable to them, and, for the last ten years, they afford the unusual spectacle of a labouring class whose labour bears so high a price that they can exist in comfort on the wages of a comparatively small quantity of work. This, to the ex-slave-owners, is an inconvenience; but I have not yet heard that any of them has been reduced to beg his bread, or even to dig for it, as the negro, however scandalously he enjoys himself, still must . . . at all events; it is an embarrassment out of which the nation is not called on to help them: if they cannot continue to realize their large incomes without more labourers, let them find them, and bring them from where they can best be procured, only not by force. Not so thinks your anti-philanthropic contributor. That negroes should exist, and enjoy existence, on so little work, is a scandal in his eyes, worse than their former slavery. It must be put a stop to at any price. He does not 'wish to see' them slaves again 'if it can be avoided;' but 'decidedly' they 'will have to be servants,' 'servants to the whites,' 'compelled to labour,' and 'not to go idle another minute.' 'Black Quashee,' 'up to the ears in pumpkins,' and 'working about half an hour a day,' is to him the abomination of abominations. I have so serious a quarrel with him about principles, that I have no time to spare for his facts; but let me remark, how easily he takes for granted those which fit his case. Because he reads in some blue-book of a strike for wages in Demerara, such as he may read of any day in Manchester, he draws a picture of negro inactivity, copied from the wildest prophecies of the slavery party before emancipation. If the negroes worked no more than 'half an hour a day,' would the sugar crops, in all except notoriously bad seasons, be so considerable, so little diminished from what they were in the time of slavery, as is proved by the Customhouse returns? But it is not the facts of the question, so much as the moralities of it, that I care to dispute with your contributor.

A black man working no more than your contributor affirms that they work, is, he says, 'an eye-sorrow,' a blister on the skin of the state,' and many other things equally disagreeable; to *work* being the grand duty of man. 'To do competent work, to labour honestly according to the ability given them; for that, and for no other purpose, was each one of us sent into this world.' Whoever prevents him from this his 'sacred appointment to labour while he lives on earth' is 'his deadliest enemy.' If it be 'his own indolence' that prevents him, 'the first *right* he has' is that all wiser and more industrious persons shall, 'by some wise means, compel him to do the work he is fit for.' Why not at once say that, by 'some wise means,' every thing should be made right in the world? While we are about it, wisdom may as well be suggested as the remedy for all evils, as for one only. Your contributor incessantly prays Heaven that all persons, black and white, may be put in possession of this 'divine right of being compelled, if permitted will not serve, to do what work they are appointed for.' But as this cannot be conveniently managed just yet, he will begin with the blacks, and will make them work *for* certain whites, those whites *not* working at all; that so 'the eternal purpose and supreme will' may be fulfilled, and 'injustice,' which is 'for ever accursed,' may cease.

This pet theory of your contributor about work, we all know well enough, though some persons might not be prepared for so bold an application of it. Let me say a few words on this 'gospel of work'—which, to my mind, as justly deserves the name of a cant as any of those which he has opposed, while the truth it contains is immeasurably farther from being the whole truth than that contained in the words Benevolence, Fraternity, or any other of his catalogue of contemptibilities. To give it a rational meaning, it must first be known what he means by work. Does work mean every thing which people *do?* No; or he would not reproach people with doing no work. Does it mean laborious exertion? No; for many a day spent in killing game, includes more muscular fatigue than a day's ploughing. Does it mean *useful* exertion? But your contributor always scoffs at the idea of utility. Does he mean that all persons ought to earn their living? But some earn their living by doing nothing, and some by doing mischief; and the negroes, whom he despises, still do earn by labour the 'pumpkins' they consume and the finery they wear.

Work, I imagine, is not a good in itself. There is nothing laudable in work for work's sake. To work voluntarily for a worthy object is laudable; but what constitutes a worthy object? On this matter, the oracle of which your contributor is the prophet has never yet been prevailed on to declare itself. He revolves in an eternal circle round the idea of work, as if turning up the earth, or driving a shuttle or a quill, were ends in themselves, and the ends of human existence. Yet, even in the case of the most sublime service to humanity, it is not because it is work that it is worthy; the worth lies in the service itself, and in the will to render it—the noble feelings of which it is the fruit; and if the nobleness of will is proved by other evidence than work, as for instance by danger or sacrifice, there is the same worthiness. While we talk only of work, and not of its object, we are far from the root of the matter; or if it may be called the root, it is a root without flower or fruit.

The worth of work does not surely consist in its leading to other work, and so on to work upon work without end. On the contrary, the multiplication of work, for purposes not worth caring about, is one of the evils of our present condition. When justice and reason shall be the rule of human affairs, one of the first things to which we may expect them to be applied is the question, How many of the so-called luxuries, conveniences, refinements, and ornaments of life, are *worth* the labour which must be undergone as the condition of producing them? The beautifying of existence is as worthy and useful an object as the sustaining of it; but only a vitiated taste can see any such result in those fopperies of so-called civilization, which myriads of hands are now occupied and lives wasted in providing. In opposition to the 'gospel of work,' I would assert the gospel of leisure, and maintain that human beings *cannot* rise to the finer attributes of their nature compatibly with a life filled with labour. I do not include under the name labour such work, if work it be called, as is done by writers and afforders of 'guidance,' an occupation which, let alone the vanity of the thing, cannot be called by the same name with the real labour, the exhausting, stiffening, stupefying toil of many kinds of agricultural and manufacturing labourers. To reduce very greatly the quantity of work required to carry on existence, is as needful as to distribute it more equally; and the progress of science, and the increasing ascendancy of justice and good sense, tend to this result.

. . . Every age has its faults, and is indebted to those who point them out. Our own age needs this service as much as others; but it is not to be concluded that it has degenerated from former ages, because its faults are different. We must beware, too, of mistaking its virtues for faults, merely because, as is inevitable, its faults mingle with its virtues and colour them. Your contributor thinks that the age has too much humanity, is too anxious to abolish pain. I affirm, on the contrary, that it has too little humanity—is most culpably indifferent to the subject: and I point to any day's police reports as the proof. I am not now accusing the brutal portion of the population, but the humane portion; if they were humane *enough,* they would have contrived long ago to prevent these daily atrocities. It is not by excess of a good quality that the age is in fault, but by deficiency—deficiency even of philanthropy, and still more of other qualities wherewith to balance and direct what philanthropy it has. . . . [A] 'Universal Abolition of Pain Association' may serve to point a sarcasm, but can any worthier object of endeavour be pointed out than that of diminishing pain? Is the labour which ends in growing spices noble, and not that which lessens the mass of suffering? We are told, with a triumphant air, as if it were a thing to be glad of, that 'the Destinies' proceed in a 'terrible manner;' and this manner will not cease 'for soft sawder or philanthrophic stump-oratory;' but whatever the means may be it *has* ceased in no inconsiderable degree, and in ceasing more and more every year the terrible manner. In some department or other, is made a little less terrible. Is our cholera comparable to the old pestilence—our hospitals to the old lazar-houses—our workhouses to the hanging of vagrants—our prisons to those visited by Howard? It is precisely *because* we have succeeded in abolishing so much pain, because pain and its infliction are no longer familiar as our daily bread, that we are so much more shocked by what remains of it than our ancestors were, or than in your contributor's opinion we ought to be.

. . . That this country should turn back, in the matter of negro slavery, I have not the smallest apprehension. There is, however, another place where that tyranny still flourishes, but now for the first time finds itself seriously in danger. At this crisis of American slavery, when the decisive conflict between right and iniquity seems about to commence, your contributor steps in, and flings this missile, loaded with the weight of his reputation, into the abolitionist camp. The words of English writers of celebrity are words of power on the other side of the ocean; and the owners of human flesh, who probably thought they had not an honest man on their side between the Atlantic and the Vistula, will welcome such an auxiliary. Circulated as his dissertation will probably be, by those whose interests profit by it, from one end of the American Union to the other, I hardly know of an act by which one person could have done so much mischief as this may possibly do; and I hold that by thus acting, he has made himself an instrument of what an able writer in the *Inquirer* justly calls 'a true work of the devil.'

Benjamin Disraeli (1805–81), who started his career as the Conservative MP for Maidstone, became the first Jewish Prime Minister in 1868. Here he makes a case for why franchise reform is and should be a Tory issue.

Benjamin Disraeli, Third Reading of the Reform Bill (1867)

SIR, the debate of this evening commenced with what may be described as two very violent speeches—that is, speeches very abusive of the measure before the House, and very abusive of the ministers who have introduced it. I am more anxious to vindicate the measure than to defend the Government. But it necessarily happens in questions of this character, which have occupied the attention of Parliament for a long term of years, that it is practically impossible to distinguish the measure from the ministry in any observations upon it. So much depends upon personal character and engagements, and upon the necessity of the time and the temper of the country, when a minister is called upon definitively to act, that it is perhaps impossible to separate in the remarks which I have to offer to the House a consideration of the conduct of the Government from the nature of the Bill which we now ask leave to read a third time. It is very easy for the noble lord the member for Stamford, while he treats of a question which has occupied the attention of Parliament for more than fifteen years, to quote some ambiguous expression which was used early in that period of fifteen years by Lord Derby, and then to cite some small passage in a speech made by myself in the year 1866. But I think that honourable gentlemen on both sides of the House will admit that to arrive at a just judgment of the conduct of public men, and of the character of the measures they propose, it is necessary to take larger and fuller views. Measures of this importance, and the conduct of those who may recommend them, are not to be decided by the quotation of a speech made in 1852, or of the remarks made in 1866.

. . . I have always said that the question of Parliamentary Reform was one which it was quite open to the Conservative party to deal with. I have said so in this House, and on the hustings, in the presence of my countrymen, a hundred times. I have always said, and I say so now, that when you come to a settlement of this question, you cannot be bound to any particular scheme, as if you were settling the duties on sugar, but dealing with the question on great constitutional principles, and which I hope to show have not been deviated from, you must deal with it also with a due regard to the spirit of the time and the requirements of the country. I will not dwell upon the excitement which then prevailed in the country, for I can say most sincerely that, without treating that excitement with contempt, or in any spirit analogous to contempt, we considered this question only with reference to the fair requirements of the country. But having to deal with this question, and being in office with a large majority against us, and finding that ministers of all colours of party and politics, with great majorities, had failed to deal with it successfully, and believing that another failure would be fatal not merely to the Conservative party, but most dangerous to the country, we resolved to settle it if we could. Having accepted office unpledged, what was the course we adopted? Believing that it was a matter of the first State necessity that the question should be settled; knowing the majority was against us, and knowing the difficulties we had to deal with, being in a minority—and even with a majority our predecessors had not succeeded—after due deliberation we were of opinion that the only mode of arriving at a settlement was to take the House into council with us, and by our united efforts, and the frank communication of ideas, to attain a satisfactory solution.

. . . The question, therefore, for us practically to consider was—whether we were to accept this settlement of the borough franchise, we will say at 5*l.*, or whether we should adhere to the conviction at which we had arrived in 1859—namely, that if you reduced the qualification there was no safe resting-place until you came to a household rating franchise? The noble lord says that immense dangers are to arise to this country because we have departed from the 10*l.* franchise. (Viscount Cranbourne: No!) Well, it was something like that, or because you have reduced the franchise. The noble lord is candid enough to see that if you had reduced it after what occurred in 1859, as you ought according to your pledges to have done, you would have had to reduce it again by this time. It is not likely that such a settlement of the difficulty would have been so statesmanlike that you could have allayed discontent or satisfied any great political demands by reducing the electoral qualification by 40*s.* or so. Then the question would arise—is there a greater danger from the number who would be admitted by a rating household franchise than from admitting the hundreds of thousands—the right honourable gentleman the member for South Lancashire calculated them at 300,000—who would come in under a 5*l.* franchise? I think that the danger would be less, that the feeling of the large number would be more national, than by only admitting what I call the Prætorian guard, a sort of class set aside, invested with peculiar privileges, looking with suspicion on their superiors, and with disdain on those beneath them, with no friendly feelings towards the institutions of their country and with great confidence in themselves. I think you would have a better chance of touching the popular heart, of evoking the national sentiment by embracing the great body of those men who occupy houses and fulfill the duties of citizenship by the payment of rates, than by the more limited and, in our opinion, more dangerous proposal.

. . . The right honourable gentleman told us that in the course we are pursuing there is infamy. The expression is strong; but I never quarrel with that sort of thing, nor do I like on that account to disturb an honourable gentleman in his speech, particularly when he happens to be approaching his peroration. Our conduct, however, according to him, is infamous—that is his statement—because in office we are supporting measures of Parliamentary Reform which we disapprove, and to which we have hitherto been opposed. Well, if we disapprove the Bill which we are recommending the House to accept and sanction to-night, our conduct certainly would be objectionable. If we, from the bottom of our hearts do not believe that the measure which we are now requesting you to pass is on the whole the wisest and best that could be passed under the circumstances, I would even admit that our conduct was infamous. But I want to know what the right honourable gentleman thinks of his own conduct when, having assisted in turning out the Government of Lord Derby in 1859, because they would not reduce the borough franchise, he—if I am not much mistaken, having been one of the most active managers in that intrigue—the right honourable gentleman accepted office in 1860 under the Government of Lord Palmerston, who, of course, brought forward a measure of Parliamentary Reform which, it would appear, the right honourable gentleman also disapproved of, and more than disapproved, inasmuch as, although a member of the Government, he privately and successfully solicited his political opponents to defeat it. And yet this is the right honourable gentleman who talks of infamy!

Sir, the prognostications of evil uttered by the noble lord I can respect, because I know that they are sincere; the warnings and prophecies of the right honourable gentleman I treat in another spirit. For my part, I do not believe that the country is in danger. I think England is safe in the race of men who inhabit her; that she is safe in something much more precious than her accumulated capital—her accumulated experience; she is safe in her national character, in her fame, in the traditions of a thousand years, and in that glorious future which I believe awaits her.

Here Auberon Herbert (1838–1906) lays out the structure of government in Canada in the wake of the British North America Act of 1867, which provided for the federation of Upper and Lower Canada, New Brunswick, and Nova Scotia. Herbert echoed the sentiments of many contemporaries in Britain when he rejoiced that "happy [is] the country, in which a revolution . . . may be carried out by the employment of no weapon more deadly than the oratory of the stump. . . ."

Auberon Herbert, "The Canadian Confederation" (1867)

IT is a happy peculiarity in our history of recent years that the constitutions which have been given to the colonies are the result of peaceful and deliberate discussion. The . . . present constitution under which Canada the Province has disappeared, and given place to Canada the Confederation, will stand hereafter in the story of representative government as leading instances of that frank demand and free gift, where the argument of the sword has not preceded and assisted the negotiations of the council-chamber. Happy the country, in which a revolution—and this action on the part of our North American Provinces is a revolution, the full outgrowth of which it is impossible at present to distinguish accurately—may be carried out by the employment of no weapon more deadly than the oratory of the stump, and the spilling of nothing more precious than the ink which has flowed in controversy. And yet the difficulties which had to be overcome were many and complicated. If the new constitution of Canada does not make any great addition to the sum of our constitutional learning, yet it will not fail to leave upon the mind of the reader an enduring impression of the wise and patriotic spirit of compromise in which the delegates of the different provinces approached their task, and by which alone they have succeeded in constructing a central power, above conflicting interests and in spite of the doubt and mistrust which always impede the surrender of separate independence. Scarcely any more interesting blue-book can be placed in the hands of an Englishman, than that which contains the debates on Confederation in the Legislative Council and Assembly of Canada; and one closes the volume with a feeling of justifiable pride that the good sense, the comprehensive views and careful constitutional thought which pervade many of the speeches, are the growth of that good seed which this country gave to her colony.

We have only to remember what we have ourselves seen in Europe, and what we have read, to realise the difficulties which beset the work of confederation. For many years we have watched with curiosity the petty jealousies and heart-burnings which have divided the States of Germany, and which continued successfully to defy the national enthusiasm for unity, until at last an irresistible pressure from outside brought a portion of them together, as it was said, "with a clash." It was the same story with the United States. The same causes impeded and nearly defeated their confederation. It is always an easy thing to arouse provincial selfishness, and when any general scheme is put forward to inspire a section with the belief that their interests are to be sacrificed for the sake of the rest of the community. I cannot conceal my impression that in the history of the present movement, all that was timorous and mistrustful allied itself with all that was absolutely unpatriotic and disloyal, and in this bad company sought to hold its ground by appealing to a narrow and mistaken selfishness. . . .

The central Parliament is to hold its sittings at Ottawa. The Lower House is called the House of Commons, as Lord Carnarvon said, "in affectionate remembrance of the noblest traditions of English history." It consists of 181 members, who are elected throughout the provinces on the basis of population. The Upper House or Senate is nominated by the Governor-General, and its members will in the first instance be chosen from the present Legislative Councils of the Provinces; an arrangement which on such occasions is generally found to facilitate the transfer of power. In the Senate the different provinces find equal representation; the numbers being twenty-four from Ontario, twenty-four from Quebec, and twenty-four from the two maritime provinces. The character of the two Houses therefore represents the compromise which has been made on both sides. Ontario in the House of Commons obtains what she has so strongly claimed during the last few years, representation by population; and Quebec and the Lower Provinces an equal representation in the Senate. Quebec clings with great tenacity to her own peculiar institutions, and shares with the Lower Provinces in the slight feeling of distrust that not unnaturally influences all minorities which wed themselves to a more populous and a rapidly increasing community, and in a common wish to give as much strength and power of resistance as is possible to the Upper House.

. . . This sense of protection afforded to the different minorities by the Upper House, probably helped to determine that the principle of nomination for life should be adopted in the place of election. No tide of popular feeling which might for the moment place Protestants in conflict with Roman Catholics, or oppose conflicting interests, such as those of the farmers and the shipping trade, would be likely to carry with it men named for life, and independent of all constituencies. A more distinct influence was the feeling that the best men in the country would not sit for the Senate, owing to the expense which would attend the canvassing of constituencies three times as large as those which returned the members of the Lower House; and it was argued that it was a loss of power not to take advantage of the existence of a class of men in the country possessed of experience and position, whose services could not be obtained if it was necessary for them to pass through the ordeal of election. The prospect of connecting with politics such men, independent in means, and not entering parliamentary life as a profession, held out the further hope of creating and preserving an interest in public affairs in the minds of the whole of that leisured and most highly educated class, who have always a tendency to withdraw themselves from the tumult of political life, and whose indifference in such matters is a serious check to the well-being of a country. . . .

There have been two points selected for criticism in the constitution of the Confederation. It has been urged by a friendly critic that no provision is made against a conflict between the local and central Legislatures. There is, however, a clause which vests the residue of power—that is, all power outside and beyond those powers specifically distributed under the constitution—in the central Legislature. This clause, which might have been strengthened but for provincial reasons, would seem to assert the authority of the centre over the parts, and offers a reasonable security against any such conflict of general and local claims. It would be for the Confederated Parliament to consider hereafter whether they would not be wise in agreeing to refer any difficulty in the reading of the constitution itself to some such tribunal as that of the Privy Council. The second matter of objection is that the Lieutenant-Governors are to be selected by the Governor-General. This it is impossible to discuss, for those who object, do so on the ground that it establishes another link between the Confederation and the mother country. To all who are impatient to sever the connection between the two countries, it must remain an objection.

The promise of a worthy national existence is thus given to the provinces. There are many direct advantages secured to them by their union. One code of criminal law will be established; all arrangements connected with the post-office, and telegraphs, and inter-provincial communication will be placed on the same footing; three different tariffs, and three different currencies are reduced to one; and three separate and disconnected provinces will receive, as it were, a vertebrate organisation by means of the inter-colonial railway. But the moral effect will work greater changes. By the mere passage from provincial to national life, the mind of the people will acquire new force and energy; the pride of empire will be kindled, and will replace old local jealousies and narrow ambitions. It is sufficient to recall the wavering and uncertain progress which the American States made before they completed the act of Confederation, and the rapid and unintermitting prosperity which succeeded that event, to feel assured that with the charter of 1867 a new sun dawns upon the fortunes of British North America. The shadow of the great Republic has hitherto rested heavily upon these provinces, but they have already begun, and will continue, to free themselves from this. They have given substantial signs that the words freedom and independence have the same meaning to their people as they had in old days to those from whom they are sprung, and they have answered, in the manner which least admits of controversy, the imputation of being unwilling to help themselves.

. . . There remains one matter to be spoken of, which may prove a source of some difference of feeling between the new Canada and the mother country. I earnestly hope that this may not be the case, but I think it probable that a great battle is imminent between the free-traders and the protectionists of the colony. The adoption of a tariff—not for the purposes of revenue but of protection—would be a very unfortunate event in the interests of the province herself. Any barrier which tends to shut off a new country from older civilisations must be hurtful; the material seclusion is followed by a moral seclusion; and she not only keeps out the wares and manufactures, but gradually that also which is their invariable companion,—the feelings and ideas which are moving the mind of other nations. That this is not imaginary may be seen by observing the cosmopolitan character of all centres of trade. The stronger argument—on which all free-traders rest—that protection means taking a country from its natural occupation, applies peculiarly to Canada. Her growth and expansion depend upon her population pushing constantly on into unsettled districts, and availing themselves greedily of that best of all gifts, an unlimited soil. Any artificial stimulus which should draw the population towards the cities instead of sending them a-field would check the national well-being at the very fountain-head. And the injury would be aggravated by the peculiarities of climate, for if once large numbers of workmen were brought together in manufactories, it cannot be doubted that a great deal of suffering would result, whenever the inevitable depressions of trade took place during the months of the severe Canadian winter. Agriculture, though yielding smaller profits, and these profits as the reward of hard labour, is far more reliable, far less fluctuating than manufactures are. If Canada is sufficiently stout-hearted to resist the allurements of protection, it is probable that the cheapness of the necessaries of life—which is always the result of free trade—will help hereafter to attract those emigrants to her, who are the truest wealth of a new country. . . .

One last word as to what is not the least important part of my subject. In the midst of all ties and considerations one asks, How is the Empire to be organised? How is the England of the West and the England of the East to be made really one with that little island which now receives the allegiance of both? . . . No representation of colonies in the House of Commons, as it is at present constituted, is either desirable or possible. It has been forcibly shown that a mere sprinkling of colonists in the House would not fairly represent the colonies, and would not therefore secure the great object in view, the perfect welding of all the parts into one nation. But there are other schemes which seem practicable. The House of Commons might separate the administration of Foreign Affairs, Army and Navy, India and the Colonies, from the other business of the House, and place these departments under the control of a certain number of their own members, whom they would elect with proper precautions taken for the representation of the minority. These elected members would sit with a just proportion of colonial members in an Imperial Chamber, on days when the House of Commons was not sitting, and would control the departments which have been mentioned. They would be elected for a short term of years, and would retain their seats independently of any crisis in the House of Commons, but would be liable at any moment to be dissolved, and sent back for re-election to their own constituency, the House of Commons. Another solution has been put forward, which proposes that all home questions should be relegated to a

Provincial House, and all imperial questions to an Imperial House; each House being elected by the constituencies of the country. In some respects this plan is preferable; but as the number of English members in an Imperial House must be small, the enormous size of the constituencies seems an almost fatal objection. It is to be remembered that the number of English members has to be limited by considerations of the smaller class of highly educated men, from which a new country has to supply her political necessities; of the expense which the sending of many members would impose upon the colonies; and of the general desire to talk which will prevail in a House of such varied elements. This latter plan would be most opposed, as it would make a greater revolution in our present system. In either case the Upper House might be composed of a certain number of peers elected by themselves, and of colonial members nominated for life, or a long term of years, by the Governments of the different colonies. . . .

The year 1867 was an important one for politics in Ireland as well as in Canada and England. The Irish Republican Brotherhood, which had unsuccessfully tried to foment revolution in the United States and Canada, mounted campaigns of violence in Irish cities and in Manchester as well, where attacks on the constabulary there resulted in the execution of three Fenians. These "Manchester Martyrs"—W. P. Allen, Michael Larkin, and Michael O'Brien—popularized the cause in Ireland but embittered many in England. Below is the declaration of Fenian republicanism, which echoes both Tom Paine and Karl Marx in its call for equal rights for the support of sympathizers across "the entire world."

Proclamation of an Irish Republic (1867)

Proclamation to

The Irish People of the World

We have suffered centuries of outrage, enforced poverty, and bitter misery. Our rights and liberties have been trampled on by an alien aristocracy, who treating us as foes, usurped our lands, and drew away from our unfortunate country all material riches. The real owners of the soil were removed to make room for cattle, and driven across the ocean to seek the means of living, and the political rights denied to them at home, while our men of thought and action were condemned to loss of life and liberty. But we never lost the memory and hope of a national existence. We appealed in vain to the reason and sense of justice of the dominant powers.

Our mildest remonstrances were met with sneers and contempt. Our appeals to arms were always unsuccessful.

Today, having no honourable alternative left, we again appeal to force as our last resource. We accept the conditions of appeal, manfully deeming it better to die in the struggle for freedom than to continue an existence of utter serfdom.

All men are born with equal rights, and in associating to protect one another and share public burdens, justice demands that such associations should rest upon a basis which maintains equality instead of destroying it.

We therefore declare that, unable longer to endure the curse of Monarchical Government, we aim at founding a Republic based on universal suffrage, which shall secure to all the intrinsic value of their labour.

The soil of Ireland, at present in the possession of an oligarchy, belongs to us, the Irish people, and to us it must be restored.

We declare, also, in favour of absolute liberty of conscience, and complete separation of Church and State.

We appeal to the Highest Tribunal for evidence of the justness of our cause. History bears testimony to the integrity of our sufferings, and we declare, in the face of our brethren, that we intend no war against the people of England—our war is against the aristocratic locusts, whether English or Irish, who have eaten the verdure of our fields— against the aristocratic leeches who drain alike our fields and theirs.

Republicans of the entire world, our cause is your cause. Our enemy is your enemy. Let your hearts be with us. As for you, workmen of England, it is not only your hearts we wish, but your arms. Remember the starvation and degradation brought to your firesides by the oppression of labour. Remember the past, look well to the future, and avenge yourselves by giving liberty to your children in the coming struggle for human liberty. Herewith we proclaim the Irish Republic.

The Provisional Government

The 1860s witnessed a spate of legislation aimed at both domestic and colonial prostitution known as the Contagious Diseases Acts. Four years after the first "British" Act (1864) was introduced in England and Ireland to regulate the behavior of women deemed to be prostitutes, Act XIV of 1868 laid down similar provisions for prostitutes in Indian cities and ports. This was part of an empire-wide effort to protect British military men from contracting venereal disease and, of course, to secure the continued health of the British military presence on the subcontinent in the post-Mutiny era.

East India Contagious Diseases Acts (1868)
ACT NO. XIV. of 1868.

Passed by the Governor General of India in Council.

(*Received the Assent of the Governor General on the 17th April* 1868.)

An Act of the Prevention of certain Contagious Diseases.

Whereas it is expedient to provide for the better prevention of certain contagious diseases; it is hereby enacted as follows:—

Preliminary.

1. This Act may be cited as "The Indian Contagious Diseases Act, 1868."

2. In this Act—

"Magistrate" means any person exercising the powers of a magistrate or of a subordinate magistrate of the first class, and includes a magistrate of police in a Presidency town.

"Contagious disease" means any contagious venereal disease.

"Brothel-keeper" means the occupier of any house, room or place to or in which women resort or are for the purpose of prostitution, and every person managing or assisting in the management of any such house, room or place.

3. The places to which this Act applies shall be such places as the Local Government shall from time to time, with the previous sanction of the Governor General of India in Council, specify by Notification in the Official Gazette. The limits of such places shall, for the purposes of this Act, be such as are defined in the said Notification, and may from time to time, with such sanction as aforesaid, be altered by a like Notification.

Unregistered Prostitutes and Brothel-keepers.

4. In any place to which this Act applies, no woman shall carry on the business of a common prostitute, and no person shall carry on the business of a brothel-keeper without being registered under this Act at such place, and without having in her or his possession such evidence of registration as herein-after provided.

Any woman carrying on the business of a common prostitute, and any person carrying on the business of a brothel-keeper, without having been registered as aforesaid, or without having in her or his possession such evidence as aforesaid, shall, on conviction before a magistrate, be punished with imprisonment for a term which may extend to one month, or with fine not exceeding 100 rupees, or with both.

Registration of Prostitutes and Brothel-keepers.

5. The Local Government shall make rules for the registration of common prostitutes and of brothel-keepers, and shall appoint officers for the conduct of such registration, and may, with the previous sanction of the Governor General of India in Council, assign salaries and establishments to the said officers. The Local Government shall also provide such books and forms as may be necessary for the purposes of this Act.

Every woman complying with such rules (so far as they relate to prostitutes) and every brothel-keeper complying with such rules (so far as they relate to brothel-keepers) shall be deemed to be registered under this Act, and the registering officer shall furnish her or him with such evidence of registration as the Local Government shall from time to time direct.

The name, age, caste (if any) and residence of every such woman and such other particulars respecting her as the Local Government shall from time to time direct, shall be entered in a book to be kept for that purpose.

The name and residence of every such brothel-keeper and the situation of the house, room or place in which he carries on his business shall be entered in a book to be kept for that purpose.

6. Whenever any such woman changes her residence, she shall give notice thereof to such person and in such manner as the Local Government shall from time to time direct,

and the necessary alterations shall be made in the said book and in the evidence of registration furnished to her as aforesaid.

Any such woman failing to give notice as foresaid shall, on conviction before a magistrate, be punished with imprisonment for a term which may extend to 14 days, or with fine not exceeding 50 rupees, or with both.

Whenever any brothel-keeper changes his residence or acquires or enters into the occupation of any such house, room or place as last aforesaid, other than the house, room or place of which the situation has been registered as aforesaid, he shall give notice thereof to such person and in such manner as the Local Government shall from time to time direct, and the necessary alterations or additions shall be made in or to the said book and in the evidence of registration furnished to him as aforesaid.

Any such brothel-keeper failing to give notice as last aforesaid shall, on conviction before a magistrate, be punished with imprisonment for a term which may extend to one month, or with fine not exceeding 100 rupees, or with both.

Refusal to show Evidence of Registration.

7. Any registered woman or brothel-keeper who, without reasonable excuse, neglects or refuses to produce and show the evidence of her or his registration with which she or he shall have been furnished as aforesaid, when required so to do by such officer as the Local Government shall from time to time appoint in this behalf, shall, on conviction before a magistrate, be punished with imprisonment for a term which may extend to fourteen days, or with fine not exceeding 50 rupees, or with both.

Information of the class of officers for the time being authorized to make requisitions under this section shall be furnished to registered women and brothel-keepers, under such rules as the Local Government shall from time to time prescribe.

Special Provisions relating to Brothels.

8. If any brothel-keeper, whether registered as such under this Act or not, has reasonable cause to believe any woman to be a prostitute and not to be registered under this Act, and induces or suffers her to resort or be, for the purpose of prostitution, to or in the house, room or place in which he carries on his said business, he shall, on conviction before a magistrate, be punished with imprisonment for a term which may extend to six months, or with fine which may extend to 1,000 rupees, or with both.

Provided that nothing in this or any other section of this Act shall exempt the offender from any penal or other consequences to which he may be liable for keeping or being concerned in keeping a brothel or disorderly house or for the nuisance thereby occasioned.

9. Every such brothel-keeper shall be legally bound to furnish information on any subject relating to his business to such officers and in such manner and at such times as the Local Government shall from time to time prescribe in this behalf. Every such officer shall, for the purposes of this section, be deemed to be a public servant.

Examination of Prostitutes.

10. The Local Government shall have power to appoint persons to make periodical examinations of registered women in order to ascertain whether at the time of each such examination they are affected with contagious disease.

11. For each of the places to which this Act applies, the Local Government may make rules consistent with this Act respecting the times and places of examination under this

Act at that place, and generally respecting the arrangements for the conduct of those examinations and for recording the results thereof; and a copy of rules purporting to be rules under this section shall, if signed by a Secretary to such Government, be evidence of such rules for the purposes of this Act.

The Local Government may also require the persons making such examination to send in reports to such persons at such times and in such form as the Local Government shall from time to time prescribe.

Any person not a medical officer appointed to make such examination, and any registered woman, disobeying any rule made under this section, shall, on conviction before a magistrate, be punished with simple imprisonment for a term which may extend to one month, or with fine not exceeding 100 rupees, or with both.

Certified Hospitals.

12. The Local Government may from time to time provide any buildings or parts of buildings as hospitals for the purposes of this Act.

Any building or part of a building so provided and certified in writing by a Secretary to the Local Government to be so provided, shall be deemed a certified hospital under this Act.

Every certified hospital so provided shall be placed under the control and management of such persons as to the Local Government shall from time to time see fit.

13. The Local Government shall make regulations for the inspection, management, and government of the hospitals as far as regards women authorized by this Act to be detained therein for medical treatment or being therein under medical treatment for a contagious disease.

A copy of regulations purporting to be regulations made under this section shall, if signed by a Secretary to such Government, be evidence of such regulations for the purposes of this Act.

14. Any woman registered under this Act shall, on receiving notice from any such officer as the Local Government shall from time to time appoint in this behalf, proceed to the certified hospital named in such notice and place herself there for medical treatment.

If after the notice is delivered to her, she neglects or refuses to proceed to the said hospital within the time specified in the said notice, an officer of police shall apprehend her and convey her with all practicable speed to such hospital, and place her there for medical treatment.

15. Whenever any such woman affected with contagious disease places herself or is placed as aforesaid in a certified hospital for medical treatment, she shall be detained there for that purpose by such medical officer of the hospital as the Local Government shall from time to time appoint in this behalf until discharged by him by writing under his hand.

Medical treatment, lodging, clothing and food shall be provided gratis for every such woman during her detention in the hospital.

16. If any woman authorized by such medical officer to be detained in a certified hospital for medical treatment, quits the hospital without being discharged therefrom by the chief medical officer thereof, by writing under his hand (the proof whereof shall lie on the accused), or

If any woman authorized by this Act to be detained in a certified hospital for medical treatment, or any woman being in a certified hospital under medical treatment for a contagious disease, refuses or wilfully neglects while in the hospital to conform to the regulations thereof approved under this Act,

Then and in every such case such woman shall, on conviction before a magistrate, be punished with imprisonment, in the case of a first offence, for any term not exceeding one month, and in the case of a second or any subsequent offence, for any term not exceeding three months; and in case she quits the hospital without being discharged as aforesaid, she may be taken into custody without warrant by any officer of police.

On the expiration of her term of imprisonment under this section, such woman shall be sent back from the prison to the certified hospital, and shall be detained there unless the medical officer of the prison at the time of her discharge from imprisonment certifies in writing that she is free from contagious disease (the proof of which certificate shall lie on her).

Out-door Treatment of Prostitutes.

17. It shall be lawful for the Local Government to empower such surgeons or other persons as it shall from time to time appoint, to prescribe, by order to be served on any woman registered under this Act, who has not received a notice under Section 14, the times and places at which she shall attend for medical treatment, and, if necessary, the medical treatment to which she shall submit.

Every such woman disobeying or failing to comply with any such order shall, on conviction before a magistrate, be punished with imprisonment for a term which may extend to a month, or with fine not exceeding 100 rupees, or with both.

18. If any registered woman on whom such order as last aforesaid shall have been served conducts herself as a common prostitute before such surgeon or other person empowered as last aforesaid certifies in writing to the effect that she is then free from a contagious disease (the proof of which certificate shall lie on her), she shall, on conviction before a magistrate, be punished with imprisonment for a term which may extend to six months, or with fine not exceeding 500 rupees, or with both.

19. During the interval between the service of such order upon any registered woman and the granting of such certificate, an allowance for her subsistence shall be provided of such amount and in such manner as the Local Government shall from time to time prescribe.

Segregation of Prostitutes.

20. In any place to which the Local Government shall, by Notification in the Official Gazette, have specially extended this section, it shall be lawful for such officer as the Local Government shall from time to time appoint in this behalf, to cause a notice to be served on any registered woman, requiring her, after an interval of not less than seven days to be mentioned in the notice, not to reside in any street or place therein specified.

Any registered woman on whom such notice shall have been served disobeying the requisition therein contained shall, on conviction before a magistrate, be punished with imprisonment, in the case of a first offence, for any term not exceeding one month, and in the case of a second or any subsequent offence, for any term not exceeding three months. . . .

In this speech, which lays out what he perceives as some of the differences between conservatives and liberals, Disraeli (see p. 119) argues that "no minister in this country will do his duty who neglects any opportunity of reconstructing as much as possible our Colonial Empire, and of responding to those distant sympathies which may become the source of incalculable strength and happiness to this land."

Benjamin Disraeli, "Conservative and Liberal Principles" (1872)

MY LORD DUKE AND GENTLEMEN,—I am very sensible of the honour which you have done me in requesting that I should be your guest to-day, and still more for your having associated my name with the important toast which has been proposed by the Lord Mayor. In the few observations that I shall presume to make on this occasion I will confine myself to some suggestions as to the present state of the Constitutional cause and the prospects which you, as a great Constitutional party, have before you. . . . Gentlemen, the Tory party, unless it is a national party, is nothing. It is not a confederacy of nobles, it is not a democratic multitude; it is a party formed from all the numerous classes in the realm—classes alike and equal before the law, but whose different conditions and different aims give vigour and variety to our national life.

Gentlemen, a body of public men distinguished by their capacity took advantage of these circumstances. They seized the helm of affairs in a manner the honour of which I do not for a moment question, but they introduced a new system into our political life. Influenced in a great degree by the philosophy and the politics of the Continent, they endeavoured to substitute cosmopolitan for national principles; and they baptized the new scheme of politics with the plausible name of 'Liberalism.' Far be it from me for a moment to intimate that a country like England should not profit by the political experience of Continental nations of not inferior civilisation; far be it from me for a moment to maintain that the party which then obtained power and which has since generally possessed it did not make many suggestions for our public life that were of great value, and bring forward many measures which, though changes, were nevertheless improvements. But the tone and tendency of Liberalism cannot be long concealed. It is to attack the institutions of the country under the name of Reform, and to make war on the manners and customs of the people of this country under the pretext of Progress. During the forty years that have elapsed since the commencement of this new system—although the superficial have seen upon its surface only the contentions of political parties—the real state of affairs has been this: the attempt of one party to establish in this country cosmopolitan ideas, and the efforts of another—unconscious efforts, sometimes, but always continued—to recur to and resume those national principles to which they attribute the greatness and glory of the country.

The Liberal party cannot complain that they have not had fair play. Never had a political party such advantages, never such opportunities. They are still in power; they have been for a long period in power. And yet what is the result? I speak not I am sure the language of exaggeration when I say that they are viewed by the community with distrust and, I might even say, with repugnance. And, now, what is the present prospect of the national party? I have ventured to say that in my opinion Liberalism, from its essential elements, notwithstanding all the energy and ability with which its tenets have been advocated by its friends—notwithstanding the advantage which has accrued to them, as I will confess, from all the mistakes of their opponents, is viewed by the country with distrust. Now in what light is the party of which we are members viewed by the country, and what relation does public opinion bear to our opinions and our policy? . . .

Now, I have always been of opinion that the Tory party has three great objects. The first is to maintain the institutions of the country—not from any sentiment of political superstition, but because we believe that they embody the principles upon which a community like England can alone safely rest. The principles of liberty, of order, of law, and of religion ought not to be entrusted to individual opinion or to the caprice and passion of multitudes, but should be embodied in a form of permanence and power. We associate with the Monarchy the ideas which it represents—the majesty of law, the administration of justice, the fountain of mercy and of honour. We know that in the Estates of the Realm and the privileges they enjoy, is the best security for public liberty and good government. We believe that a national profession of faith can only be maintained by an Established Church, and that no society is safe unless there is a public recognition of the Providential government of the world, and of the future responsibility of man. Well, it is a curious circumstance that during all these some forty years of triumphant Liberalism, every one of these institutions has been attacked and assailed—I say, continuously attacked and assailed. And what, gentlemen, has been the result? For the last forty years the most depreciating comparisons have been instituted between the Sovereignty of England and the Sovereignty of a great Republic. We have been called upon in every way, in Parliament, in the Press, by articles in newspapers, by pamphlets, by every means which can influence opinion, to contrast the simplicity and economy of the Sovereignty of the United States with the cumbrous cost of the Sovereignty of England.

One of the most distinguishing features of the great change effected in 1832 was that those who brought it about at once abolished all the franchises of the working classes. They were franchises as ancient as those of the Baronage of England; and, while they abolished them, they proposed no substitute. The discontent upon the subject of the representation which has from that time more or less pervaded our society dates from that period, and that discontent, all will admit, has now ceased. It was terminated by the Act of Parliamentary Reform of 1867–8. That Act was founded on a confidence that the great body of the people of this country were 'Conservative.' When I say 'Conservative,' I use the word in its purest and loftiest sense. I mean that the people of England, and especially the working classes of England, are proud of belonging to a great country, and wish to maintain its greatness—that they are proud of belonging to an Imperial country, and are resolved to maintain, if they can, their empire—that they believe, on the whole, that the greatness and the empire of England are to be attributed to the ancient institutions of the land. . . .

If you look to the history of this country since the advent of Liberalism—forty years ago—you will find that there has been no effort so continuous, so subtle, supported by so much energy, and carried on with so much ability and acumen, as the attempts of

Liberalism to effect the disintegration of the Empire of England. . . . [And] what has been the result of this attempt during the reign of Liberalism for the disintegration of the Empire? It has entirely failed. But how has it failed? Through the sympathy of the Colonies with the Mother Country. They have decided that the Empire shall not be destroyed, and in my opinion no minister in this country will do his duty who neglects any opportunity of reconstructing as much as possible our Colonial Empire, and of responding to those distant sympathies which may become the source of incalculable strength and happiness to this land. Therefore, gentlemen, with respect to the second great object of the Tory party also—the maintenance of the Empire—public opinion appears to be in favour of our principles—that public opinion which, I am bound to say, thirty years ago, was not favourable to our principles, and which, during a long interval of controversy, in the interval had been doubtful.

Gentlemen, another great object of the Tory party, and one not inferior to the maintenance of the Empire, or the upholding of our institutions, is the elevation of the condition of the people. Let us see in this great struggle between Toryism and Liberalism that has prevailed in this country during the last forty years what are the salient features. It must be obvious to all who consider the condition of the multitude with a desire to improve and elevate it, that no important step can be gained unless you can effect some reduction of their hours of labour and humanise their toil. The great problem is to be able to achieve such results without violating those principles of economic truth upon which the prosperity of all States depends. You recollect well that many years ago the Tory party believed that these two results might be obtained—that you might elevate the condition of the people by the reduction of their toil and the mitigation of their labour, and at the same time inflict no injury on the wealth of the nation. You know how that effort was encountered—how these views and principles were met by the triumphant statesmen of Liberalism. They told you that the inevitable consequence of your policy was to diminish capital, that this, again, would lead to the lowering of wages, to a great diminution of the employment of the people, and ultimately to the impoverishment of the kingdom.

These were not merely the opinions of Ministers of State, but those of the most blatant and loud-mouthed leaders of the Liberal party. And what has been the result? Those measures were carried, but carried, as I can bear witness, with great difficulty and after much labour and a long struggle. Yet they were carried; and what do we now find? That capital was never accumulated so quickly, that wages were never higher, that the employment of the people was never greater, and the country never wealthier. I ventured to say a short time ago, speaking in one of the great cities of this country, that the health of the people was the most important question for a statesman. It is, gentlemen, a large subject. It has many branches. It involves the state of the dwellings of the people, the moral consequences of which are not less considerable than the physical. It involves their enjoyment of some of the chief elements of nature—air, light, and water. It involves the regulation of their industry, the inspection of their toil. It involves the purity of their provisions, and it touches upon all the means by which you may wean them from habits of excess and of brutality. Now, what is the feeling upon these subjects of the Liberal party—that Liberal party who opposed the Tory party when, even in their weakness, they advocated a diminution of the toil of the people, and introduced and supported those Factory Laws, the principles of which they extended, in the brief period when they possessed power, to every other trade in the country? What is the opinion of the great

Liberal party—the party that seeks to substitute cosmopolitan for national principles in the government of this country—on this subject? Why, the views which I expressed in the great capital of the county of Lancaster have been held up to derision by the Liberal Press. A leading member—a very rising member, at least, among the new Liberal members—denounced them the other day as the 'policy of sewage.'

Why, the people of England would be greater idiots than the Jacobinical leaders of London even suppose, if, with their experience and acuteness, they should not long have seen that the time had arrived when social, and not political improvement is the object which they ought to pursue. I have touched, gentlemen, on the three great objects of the Tory party. I told you I would try to ascertain what was the position of the Tory party with reference to the country now. I have told you . . . with frankness what I believe the position of the Liberal party to be. Notwithstanding their proud position, I believe they are viewed by the country with mistrust and repugnance. But on all the three great objects which are sought by Toryism—the maintenance of our institutions, the preservation of our Empire, and the improvement of the condition of the people—I find a rising opinion in the country sympathising with our tenets, and prepared, I believe, if the opportunity offers, to uphold them until they prevail.

Before sitting down, I would make one remark particularly applicable to those whom I am now addressing. This is a numerous assembly; this is an assembly individually influential; but it is not on account of its numbers, it is not on account of its individual influence, that I find it to me deeply interesting. It is because I know that I am addressing a representative assembly. It is because I know that there are men here who come from all districts and all quarters of England, who represent classes and powerful societies, and who meet here not merely for the pleasure of a festival, but because they believe that our assembling together may lead to national advantage. Yes, I tell all who are here present that there is a responsibility which you have incurred to-day, and which you must meet like men. When you return to your homes, when you return to your counties and to your cities, you must tell to all those whom *you* can influence that the time is at hand, that, at least, it cannot be far distant, when England will have to decide between national and cosmopolitan principles. The issue . . . is whether you will be content to be a comfortable England, modelled and moulded upon Continental principles and meeting in due course an inevitable fate, or whether you will be a great country,— an Imperial country—a country where your sons, when they rise, rise to paramount position, and obtain not merely the esteem of their countrymen, but command the respect of the world.

Upon you depends the issue. Whatever may be the general feeling, you must remember that in fighting against Liberalism or the Continental system you are fighting against those who have the advantage of power—against those who have been in high places for nearly half a century. . . . You must act as if everything depended on your individual efforts. The secret of success is constancy of purpose. Go to your homes, and teach there these truths, which will soon be imprinted on the conscience of the land. Make each man feel how much rests on his own exertions. The highest, like my noble friend the chairman, may lend us his great aid. But rest assured that the assistance of the humblest is not less efficient. Act in this spirit, and you will succeed. You will maintain your country in its present position. But you will do more than that—you will deliver to your posterity a land of liberty, of prosperity, of power, and of glory.

William Gladstone (1809–98) did not disagree with Disraeli on the necessity of empire—his speech turns on the conviction that "the sentiment of empire may be called innate in every Briton"—but for him the stakes of imperial policy are different from the point of view of English liberalism.

William Gladstone, "England's Mission" (1878)

. . . The sentiment of empire may be called innate in every Briton. If there are exceptions, they are like those of men born blind or lame among us. It is part of our patrimony: born with our birth, dying only with our death; incorporating itself in the first elements of our knowledge, and interwoven with all our habits of mental action upon public affairs. It is a portion of our national stock, which has never been deficient, but which has more than once run to rank excess, and brought us to mischief accordingly, mischief that for a time we have weakly thought was ruin. In its normal action, it made for us the American colonies, the grandest monument ever erected by a people of modern times, and second only to the Greek colonisation in the whole history of the world. In its domineering excess, always under the name of British interests and British honour, it lost them by obstinacy and pride. Lord Chatham who forbade us to tax, Mr. Burke who forbade us to legislate for them, would have saved them. But they had to argue for a limitation of English power; and to meet the reproach of the political wiseacres, who first blustered on our greatness, and then, when they reaped as they had sown, whined over our calamities. Undoubtedly the peace of 1782–3, with its adjuncts in exasperated feeling, was a terrible dismemberment. But England was England still: and one of the damning signs of the politics of the school is their total blindness to the fact, that the central strength of England lies in England. Their eye travels with satisfaction over the wide space upon the map covered by the huge ice-bound deserts of North America or the unpenetrated wastes of Australasia, but rests with mortification on the narrow bounds of latitude and longitude marked by nature for the United Kingdom. They are the materialists of politics: their faith is in acres and in leagues, in sounding titles and long lists of territories. They forget that the entire fabric of the British Empire was reared and consolidated by the energies of a people, which was (though it is not now) insignificant in numbers, when compared with the leading States of the Continent; and that if by some vast convulsion our transmarine possessions could be all submerged, the very same energies of that very same people would either discover other inhabited or inhabitable spaces of the globe on which to repeat its work, or would without them in other modes assert its undiminished greatness. Of all the opinions disparaging to England, there is not one which can lower her like that which teaches that the source of strength for this almost measureless body lies in its extremities, and not in the heart which has so long propelled the blood through all its regions, and in the brain which has bound and binds them into one.

. . . The truth is, that England has had a position in Europe unrivalled alike for its moral elevation and contingently for its material power. Long ago M. Guizot, in describing the attitudes of the several states and their several ambitions, aimed his indictment against England only in her policy hors d'Europe, and allowed that in European questions she had clean hands. We have a true superiority, as to moral questions, in European affairs, over the other great Powers of this quarter of the globe. Not perhaps because we are less 'far gone from original righteousness,' but because the inestimable boon of our insular position has, ever since the consolidation of France into a kingdom, relieved us from temptation. We would not, because we cannot; what was at first a conclusion of mere necessity has grown by long tract of time into our mental and even our moral habit. Unhappy Turkey apart, we have become tolerably impartial in European questions. The only selfish interest which we had, or believed we had, was in the Ionian Islands; and with that we have parted company. Our own misdeeds, if they exist, are distant; and on the whole we are admirably placed for upholding, by voice and influence, the interests which are so cruelly traversed by the emotions of selfishness, those, namely, of sheer justice and humanity.

There could not be a fairer or a wider field for the discharge of this noble duty, than in Turkey. The Crimean War had not impaired the dignity of our position, for it was made in the name of public law and European concert; not by single-handed action, not in order to maintain a Turkish Empire as a barrier thrown across the 'road to India.' We held it in 1875. But, from that time onwards, the policy of the Government has been avowedly addressed to the purpose of maintaining the Ottoman Empire in spite of its vices, because its destruction would be detrimental to our interest in the maintenance of our Indian rule. The first effect of this superlative egoism is to emasculate all our representations on behalf of humanity in Turkey. In vain we denounce the loathsome crimes, committed in Bulgaria or elsewhere by the Turkish forces, and advisedly covered, or even rewarded, by the Government. For the Pashas have been told all along, especially from the mouths of our Ambassadors, that we are bound by our own interests to maintain their dominion over the subject races while it stands, and to restore it as best we may when it falls. So that our verbal protestations are smitten with impotence from their birth: and it might even be conceived that they form the subject of smiles and winks between the agents of the Porte and those who, under instructions from London, recite the formula of remonstrance. It is not only on the Turk, however, that we have lost our hold. Over the entire field of the Eastern Question, this doctrine, pushed under the auspices of the Ministry into superlative extravagance, has altered our presumptive character of an umpire into that of a partisan. We are at this moment led to anticipate the appearance of a Report to proceed from an international Commission on the conduct of the Bulgarians to their Mohammedan neighbours during the Russian occupation. We are told to expect a tale of horror worthy of the Turks themselves: of outrages tolerated, or even shared in, by the Russian forces. If this terrible anticipation shall be realised, if the name of Christianity has been shamed, and the work of liberation tainted, by deeds loathsome in proportion to what we think the superiority of our creed, who does not at once perceive with what power we might have interposed had we upheld our impartial character intact, and how that power is crippled by the fact that British interests will be alleged, and may be believed, to be at the back of every remonstrance and complaint?

. . . The heroic mood cannot be the standard of ordinary national conduct; and for the Continental nations, separated as they are by slight boundaries or even imaginary lines, it would require nothing less than heroism, to raise themselves above the power and the suspicion of selfish aims in Continental questions.

The truth is that, turn where we will, we are met on every side with proofs that the cares and calls of the British Empire are already beyond the strength of those who govern and have governed it. A protracted experience of public affairs, not unattended with a high estimate of the general diligence, devotion, and ability of the Parliamentary as well as the civil servants of the Crown, has long convinced me that of the more difficult descriptions of the public business, apart from simple routine, it is only a small part that is transacted with the requisite knowledge, care, and thoroughness. We have undertaken, in the matter of government, far more than ever in the history of the world has been previously attempted by the children of men. None of the great continuous Empires of ancient or modern times ever grappled with such a task: the difference of discontinuity, even if it stood alone, is an essential difference. The nearest approach to our case was perhaps that of the Macedonian conqueror, to whose organising power posterity has not always done justice. But he did not rule the vast countries under his sway from Pella, as we do from London. He accepted the change in the centre of gravity, and became, as he could not but become, an Asiatic sovereign: a transformation for which it may be presumed that the line of British monarchs is not by any means prepared. Nor does it appear that our task is likely to be attenuated by the tendencies of the times; for, with the advancing development of civilisation, it seems too plain that they multiply, instead of reducing, the demands legitimately made on the time and care of governors. Our Colonial Empire rests so largely on devolution of legislative power and practical self-government, that of the four great branches of our office or mission, this is the one in which our performances fall least short of its normal standard. And yet here too we have had great and egregious failures. We failed to manage the Ionian Islands; and when we reproached Austria with her arbitrary conduct, she was able to retort by pointing to our own undoubted illegalities and excesses. We did not give to Canada the self-government now found so harmless and beneficial, until we had been warned by two rebellions. The Negro emancipation was a great and noble deed; but the slovenly manner in which it was worked out, and the material retrogression of what were the slave Colonies, if they do not indicate an exhausted patience, show that the rushing mill-stream of our affairs, when once the popular demand had been met, and the excitement had died away, prevented the expenditure of care needful in order to secure the elevating and civilising aims of the emancipation. It was a wretched consummation when, some ten years ago, we handed over Jamaica to arbitrary power. Nor has experience shown that the vices of a despotic system have been neutralised by the very high character and abilities of them who were charged with its administration. If any Englishman will take the pains to read the official Report, dated December 19, 1877, on the condition of the great Reformatory at Stony Hill, in Jamaica, for a series of years, he will see that under the mild sway of the British Government abuses may prevail, such as ought to raise a blush upon the cheek of any despot in the world.

Of all the Empires whose rise and fall have been recorded in history, there is not one that has owed its ruin or decay to checking the lust of unmeasured territorial acquisition. The wisest of the Roman Emperors was also the one, who even recalled the boundaries of his dominions from beyond the Danube. Every one can discern and denounce the private folly of the farmer who covets more and more land, when he has neither capital nor skill to turn to account what he has already got; though he does not commonly proceed by covenants taken in the dark lest his landlord should come to know what sort of deed he is signing. But it requires a steady eye and a firm resolution to maintain the good tradition of all our bygone statesmen at a juncture when all tradition is discarded for new-fangled, or, as Mr. Roebuck calls them, 'original' devices, and the mind of folly finds utterance through the voice of authority. England, which has grown so great, may easily become little; through the effeminate selfishness of luxurious living; through neglecting realities at home to amuse herself everywhere else in stalking phantoms; through putting again on her resources a strain like that of the great French war, which brought her people to misery, and her Throne to peril; through that denial of equal rights to others, which taught us so severe a lesson at the epoch of the Armed Neutrality. But she will never lose by the modesty in thought and language, which most of all beseems the greatest of mankind; never by forwardness to allow, and to assert, the equal rights of all states and nations; never by refusing to be made the tool of foreign cunning, for ends alien to her principles and feelings; never by keeping her engagements in due relation to her means, or by husbanding those means for the day of need, and for the noble duty of defending, as occasion offers, the cause of public right, and of rational freedom, over the broad expanse of Christendom.

B. Women, Politics, and Empire

⁓⁂⁓

Helen Taylor (1831–1907) was the daughter of Harriet Taylor and the stepdaughter of John Stuart Mill. An ardent supporter of women's rights, she was a radical member of the London School Board who helped to found the Democratic Federation in 1881. She attempted to gain a parliamentary seat for Camberwell in 1885 but her nomination was refused. Here she explains how and why petitioners for women's suffrage ground their request "on the principles of the British Constitution."

⁓⁂⁓

Helen Taylor,
"The Ladies' Petition [to the Commons for the Right to Vote]" (1867)

AMONG the demonstrations of opinion which the discussions on Parliamentary Reform have drawn forth during the past session, no one was more remarkable than the petition signed by fifteen hundred ladies, which was presented to the House of Commons by Mr. J. Stuart Mill. This petition is comprised in a few short sentences, and sets forth that the possession of property in this country carries with it the right to vote in the election of representatives in Parliament; that the exclusion from this right of women holding property is therefore anomalous; and that the petitioners pray that the representation of householders may be provided for without distinction of sex.

This claim, that since women are permitted to hold property they should also be permitted to exercise all the rights which, by our laws, the possession of property brings with it, is put forward in this petition on such strictly constitutional grounds, and is advanced so entirely without reference to any abstract rights, or fundamental changes in the institutions of English society, that it is impossible not to feel that the ladies who make it have done so with a practical purpose in view, and that they conceive themselves to be asking only for the recognition of rights which flow naturally from the existing laws and institutions of the country.

That a considerable number of ladies should think it worth while to examine into their actual political status, and finding it to all appearance inconsistent with the principles of the British Constitution, should proceed to lay what they term the 'anomaly' before the House of Commons, is assuredly an important symptom of our national condition; an evidence that the minds of English people, men and women, are actively at work in many directions where they might have been but little expected to penetrate. It is, at the same time, a sign of that disposition which various causes (partly political and partly philosophical) have tended to foster of late years, to seek the reform of existing evils rather in the development than in the overthrow of the present order of things.

. . . The petitioners ground their request on the principles of the British Constitution. They assert that certain facts in our existing system establish that women cannot be considered to be without the pale of the Constitution, for that there are precedents to show that its general principles have already been applied to women in some particular cases. They point out that in this country the franchise is dependent upon property, and that the acknowledgment of women as sovereigns among us shows that women are not considered disqualified for government. From these two principles, both of which are undoubted parts of the British Constitution as it stands at this day—the representation of property, and government by female sovereigns—the petitioners draw the evident inference that where the female sex is no bar to the higher, it cannot reasonably be to the lower privileges of political life, when those privileges are dependent upon conditions (such as the possession of property) which women actually fulfill. And they characterize the exclusion of half the human race from any share in self-government as an 'anomaly' in our representative system.

Whether this way of treating the subject arises from the petitioners themselves only looking at it from this peculiarly English point of view, or whether it is adopted as the one likely to meet with the most general support and the smallest amount of dissent, it is equally a sign of the times. If the idea of the political representation of women has now made its appearance among us in a peculiarly English dress, and one adapted to the exigencies of the reform discussions of the past session (which have turned so specially on the representation of property, and a suitable property qualification), we cannot refuse to admit that it is all the fitter to take its place among the political ideas of the day; and that it has thereby assumed a more practical character than if it had been attempted to establish it on the grounds of any more general or philosophical systems of representation. Without attempting to go at length into the subject, it will be easily seen that the representation of women might be urged with considerable force on almost any of these systems; but it is itself more in harmony with our present institutions than they are. Nothing can be more entirely foreign to our whole English system than Universal Suffrage, or than either Personal or Class Representation. All these systems, whether we hold them to be in the abstract pernicious or beneficial, are so entirely unable to coalesce with that already prevailing among us, that if they are to be tried it would be a wise policy to introduce them *parallel*, so to speak, to our present institutions, of which they are not the development, but properly and literally a re-form. But if any of these systems be admitted, either partially or entirely, either in theory or in practice, women would find a place under them equally with men. Universal Suffrage by its very name includes them; personal representation, if carried out on principle, has for its necessary consequences the representation of women, since the leading idea of personal representation is the effort to secure a hearing to every individual interest or opinion in the nation, however insignificant or obscure. And the totally opposite principle, of class representation, is in the highest degree favourable to the political interests of women, who, if considered as a class, are the most numerous class in the country. Indeed, no advocate of the system of class representation can for a moment refuse in consistency to recognise the claims of so important a class, and of one which is certainly bound together by a community of interests in many of the largest branches of human affairs. Those who disapprove of all attempts at class representation, and believe them to be a lingering remains of an effete state of society, and those who disapprove of special legislation grounded on difference of sex and enforcing by law the exclusion of women from all masculine occupations or privileges, may consistently object to consider women as a class, or to make any claim for them as such. But this is not possible for those who group all women together, as actual or potential wives and mothers. They, on the contrary, must in consistency admit that the wives and mothers of the nation, regarded as a class, form one before whose vital importance, and overwhelming numbers, all other classes shrink into insignificance. For independently of the consideration that women are in this country more numerous absolutely than the sum of all the many classes into which men are divided by their occupations, it is evident that if women are permitted no other interests than those which they hold in common with all women by virtue of their sex, these interests must be of proportionately greater consequence to women than the equivalent interests are to men, since men have other interests in life as well.

If therefore the lady petitioners had chosen to urge their claims simply as women, and not as English women, they would, on the theory of class representation, have been able to take up very strong ground. But, apart from all consideration of the abstract truth of this theory, it seems to us that they have done well to leave it aside. For it is, as we have indicated, diametrically opposed to the English political system, and indeed more fundamentally so than personal representation. For if the English system refuses to recognise the mere individual as a political unit, and if it insists that he must have palpable evidence that he requires protection for something more precious (we presume) than life or honour, before it admits him to any share in protecting himself; still more does it refuse to protect interests which do not belong to any one in particular, but which are diffused over vast numbers of men, grouped together under the merely ideal definition of a class. Property represented by an individual is the true political unit among us; and in this we recognise the influence of those mediæval habits of thought, which, putting forward living persons as the representatives of rights supposed to be inherent in particular functions or particular localities, was itself practically an advance on those Oriental ideas of caste which survive in the privileges of class, sex, or colour. . . . There can be no doubt that the principle underlying our English system of government, is that men are endowed with the privilege of voting in the election of members of the Legislature, in order to enable them to protect their property against undue taxation, or other legislative enactments that might injuriously affect it. So deeply is this idea rooted in the English mind, that long after the separation of the American colonies we find American politicians arguing against conferring votes on negro slaves, upon the express ground that slaves, not being able to hold property, do not require political representation; and for authority for this point of view we find them referring to the acknowledged principles of the British system of law, which, it is well known, is considered as the foundation of the institutions of the United States, wherever not abrogated by the American Constitution or by special legislation.

. . . Turning now to the question, what harm could be done by . . . [women's] admission? we are embarrassed by the difficulty of finding any answer whatever, unless we go out of the bounds we have prescribed to ourselves, and get beyond the limits of the constitutional point of view. Revolutionary violence is out of the question from them, and their numbers are not such as to give rise to any of the apprehensions of a disturbance of the balance of power which have been excited in some minds by the claims of the working classes. There would probably be found some duly qualified female voters in every rank of society, and among them some members of almost every religious system or political party, so that the existing interests of no single class or party or religious body could have anything to fear from them. It seems difficult to imagine a case where the principles of the Constitution could be applied with more absolute freedom from the slightest shadow of danger.

Can it be said that, although there would be no danger to the State, nor to anybody within the State, yet that private interests might suffer? We confess we do not see how this is to be maintained. If we consider the private interests of men, they cannot be concerned in the political action of independent women. Their political interests may be; but we have just seen that for these there is no danger. If it be urged that the power of voting may make women more independent than it is thought they ought to be, it appears to us, once again, that English law has already decided that women may be independent, and that a woman who is absolute mistress of her own life, person, and property, will not be rendered more independent of men by the power of giving all occasional vote for a member of Parliament. There are some who think that by giving to any women whatever the power politically to protect their own interests, we should diminish that generous, disinterested, and romantic character which is so charming in women, and which indeed we all like to see in others, and most of us even to encourage in ourselves, so long as it does not expose us too defenceless to the selfishness of the selfish. Yet the remarks we have already made on the legal ability of women to defend their own pecuniary interests will apply even more appositely here. For if the sole responsibility of all their own private pecuniary affairs does not unsex spinsters and widows, and make them coarse, worldly, avaricious, grasping, and selfish, the addition of a vote, giving them a very slight direct influence on public affairs, is not likely to have so extraordinary an effect upon the most gentle and amiable half of mankind; on the contrary, as we find that the names of ladies abound on all charitable and philanthropic subscription lists, showing how kindly and generous a use they are disposed to make of their property, so we might reasonably expect that such little direct influence on politics as the possession of a vote would give to women, would probably be chiefly used in the direction of what we may call philanthropic legislation; in any case, politics in themselves certainly afford more scope for exalted and generous feeling than private business affairs. Ladies accustomed to the government of households and the management of their families, will scarcely find political affairs petty, or calculated to exercise a narrowing influence on their sympathies. Whether we consider that women ought to be especially devoted to what is beautiful or to what is good, there is much work in the interests of either to be done in politics; and if the ladies were only to take schools, workhouses, public buildings, parks, gardens, and picture galleries under their special protection, and try to send to Parliament a few members who would work efficiently at such subjects, the rest of the community would have cause to be glad of their help, without their being themselves in the smallest degree vulgarized by such a task. . . .

The fear that a womanly nature could be corrupted or hardened by politics, would strike at the root of our Western and Christian civilization, which owes much of its progress to having devolved upon women a share of the commonplace practical cares and duties which go to make up the sum of ordinary human life, whether domestic or political. The ingenuity, the love of luxury, the taste, and the housewifely instincts of women, have contributed much to the comforts of modern civilization; a more rapid and efficient adaptation of these same comforts to prisons, schools, barracks, and workhouses, would be a useful and probable result of the extension of women's energies to political life. It is, indeed, remarkable how large a part of the subjects which occupy most attention in modern politics are of this quasi-domestic character; and how growing a tendency there is for them to become ever more so. The homes of the working classes, education, Factory Acts (regulating the labour of women and children), sanitary laws, water supplies, drainage (all municipal legislation in fact), the whole administration of the poor-laws, with its various subdivisions—care of the pauper sick, pauper schools, etc.—all these are subjects which already, by common consent, are included in the peculiarly feminine province of home and charity. If the possession of a vote should induce more women to extend their interest to the comfort and happiness of other homes beside their own, it will certainly not have exercised a deteriorating influence on their character.

Josephine Butler (1828–1904) was one of the most celebrated female reformers of the Victorian era. Her father John was a supporter of Whig social reform who was involved in the campaign for the 1832 Reform Act and the repeal of the Corn Laws. Deeply affected by the death of her six-year-old daughter Eva in 1863, she threw herself into charity work and eventually all manner of social reform, her leadership of the repeal of the Contagious Diseases Acts (1869) being the most famous. Her address to the Ladies National Association, which she helped to found, underscores the moral outrage that repealers used as their basis for a critique of the sexual double standard that motivated the Acts.

Josephine Butler,
Annual Address to the Ladies National Association (1871)

Friends and Fellow-Workers,

The conflict deepens! That we are, and have been all along, contending for more than the mere repeal of these unjust and unholy Acts of Parliament, is proved by certain signs, which are becoming more and more clear and frequent. We were, perhaps, ourselves unconscious, some of us are probably yet unconscious, how great is the undertaking upon which we have entered. It only very gradually dawned with perfect clearness on my own mind, that it is the old, the inveterate, the deeply-rooted evil of prostitution itself against which we are destined to make war. Had some one arisen in 1863, or at any time before this legislation was enacted, and called upon us to arise and join in a great crusade against this national, and socially-sanctioned abomination, we should scarcely have responded. Few, at least, would have had courage to respond. It would have appeared too herculean a task to dream of. God knew that He should not then find faith on the earth to this extent; and the way for the preparation of the needful faith and energy was opened up by the permission of an evil, terrible in itself, but out of which good will arise. The Contagious Diseases Acts were enacted; the fact became public; it was the harsh grating of the closing prison door which was to shut us in, as a nation, to our present state of moral wretchedness; it was the clank of the chain, dexterously fastened upon the prisoner, while as yet he had scarcely realized his own captivity. It woke us up. Still blind to the vast issues and meaning of the conflict for which we were arming ourselves, we arose, and demanded that, however sunk in depravity our nation might be, its depravity should at least not be sealed with the seal of legal sanction and State approval. We have been educated by the labours of the last two years. In opposing this legislation, we have gained enlightenment, faith, and courage. We perceive that the repeal of these Acts is the key to our future work, as our opposition to them has been the needful training for that work. We now see that all things are possible with God; that nothing can resist the progressive force of a pure principle, and the aroused conscience of a great nation; and we are led on, step by step, to contemplate a victory far beyond the defeat of this unholy law—*i.e.,* the overthrow of that permitted, systematic vice in the midst of us, which necessitates a permitted and systematic sacrifice to destruction of a section of the community for whom Christ died.

"What!" some will ask, "are we to believe that there will ever be a time when sexual vice will be put down; when that which has been from the beginning shall cease to be?" In reply I should wish to shew you that I do not indulge in any utopian dream. The perfectibility of the human race, in the sense in which some regard it, appears to me in the light of a utopian dream. I believe that the same tendencies will continue to exist in human nature which have existed in it from the beginning of the struggle between good and evil. "He that letteth, will let, until he be taken out of the way." Men and women will lapse into error, into sin. I believe that the conflict between good and evil, so far from dying out, will become keener and fiercer as time goes on; but that the faithful and uninterrupted efforts of the servants of God to establish the supremacy of conscience, and to bring every impulse of man's lower nature into subjection to God's laws, will be finally crowned by an act of the Divine will, whereby the original principle of evil itself will be expelled from the earth, and the reign of righteousness will be established. . . .

The assertion, that "prostitution has existed ever since the world began," upon which is based the assumption that it must for ever exist, has gone forth unchallenged. It requires to be examined. That the world has never been free from sexual irregularity, in some form and degree, I allow; but I know enough of history to be aware that there have been times in the world, countries in the world where prostitution, as an allowed, a recognised, and an encouraged evil, has been unknown. Some will aver, that grosser or more secret evils must have prevailed where such was the case. Not so. Those periods to which I refer were marked by a general simplicity of life and purity of manners, and by the exhibition of manly and womanly virtues; and I must observe, in passing, that such periods were ever distinguished by this one mark—the mark of a common standard of purity, and an equal judgment of the sin of impurity for both sexes alike; of a just severity towards the man as towards the woman, of Christian forbearance and tenderness towards the woman as towards the man. Nevertheless, if this could be disproved, and the dedication of a portion of female society to the service of the lusts of men could be proved to have been an institution established in each succeeding nation and generation, in one unbroken chain, I would not suffer such proof, for one moment, as an argument on which to base the assertion that the chain must still continue unbroken; rather, I will undertake to argue from this very ground, to the overthrow of this wickedness—to prove to you that, simply because the shameful thing had existed since the world began, *therefore it shall no longer exist.*

. . . When speaking of the future, and of possible agencies which may be needful to complete our victory, yet of which we ourselves would not have made choice, I have sometimes been misunderstood. It has been supposed that I aimed at some popular movement other than that which rests upon moral suasion alone; that I would "set class against class," and encourage some revolution very different from that silent revolution in the thoughts and sentiments of the people for which we are labouring. I should like to say here emphatically that such things are very far from my thoughts; and that I believe that, if we were to begin to base our hopes and endeavours on anything else except the force of the awakened conscience of the people, from that hour we should cease to advance: failure would mark all our projects. With all my heart and with the deepest faith in the invisible forces upon which alone I rely, I endorse the noble words of the American abolitionists, (and we too are contending for the abolition of slavery in its most hideous form,) "*When the necessary revolution in the mind of the people is completed, that in the institutions of the country will follow as the day the night.* Although we cannot foresee the exact time, nor the precise way in which slavery will be abolished, we know that its doom is sealed, for we believe that God is just. The abolition of slavery we recognise as the great task assigned to this generation in this country. We accept it as our appointed work, and are grateful to be permitted to assist in the evolution of this magnificent event. The scorn of the world, the anathemas of the Church, the sacrifice of all vulgar objects of ambition, may be well endured for the promotion of a cause, in the issues of which are involved the deliverance of the slave, the redemption of the country, and the progress of the race."

. . . It would be unwise to shrink from the contemplation of all the possible consequences of the "moral uprising" in which we are taking part. All evil things, I have said, are suicidal. We may endeavour to slay any particular evil quietly and gently, or we may desire that it should silently wither away before the breath of the Spirit of God. But how can we look back on history, or study the progress and completion of any great moral reform, without being struck by the fact that the upholders of any abuse, in their effort to retain their position and privileges, have again and again plunged the whole of the society in which the struggle was maintained, into woes which the reformers neither created nor foresaw? May it not be so again? It may be that those who rebel against moral restraints, and the stern purity required by Christ, who secretly desire the continuance of a social system which would secure license to those who desire license;—it may be that this now powerful section of society will prove so strong in its opposition that, refusing to yield to moral pressure and the demands of those who shall attempt to embody a purer morality in purer laws, they will so act as to bring down vengeance, in one form or another, not only on their own heads, but on the whole country, on ourselves and on our children. Partakers of the outward woe we will be, if God so wills; but never, even to save our country from temporary, necessary, and purifying calamity, will we consent to be partakers of their inward corruption, or to cease to charge them openly with their evil deeds. We pray God that these evils may be averted, and that our national sins may not have to be washed out in blood; and trusting in His arm alone, we never will consent to accept the aid of any arm of flesh: but it is well not to be unprepared for all that we may yet live to see; and those are mistaken in their judgment of us who call us revolutionary when we speak thus, and when we think it right to remind you how repeatedly the words have been fulfilled in the history of the world, which God spake through the mouth of the Jewish prophet—"Therefore thus saith the Lord; ye have not hearkened unto me in proclaiming liberty, every one to his brother, and every man to his neighbour; behold, therefore, I proclaim a liberty for you, saith the Lord, to the sword, to the pestilence, and to the famine."

This movement has awakened echoes in distant parts of the earth. In many countries besides our own, there is a sound of the restless shaking of long-worn chains. It is a movement, as I said, far, far beyond the obtaining of the repeal of certain Acts of Parliament passed by the English House of Commons. Great and noble things are about to be accomplished, and the more surely, the longer and more agonizing is our struggle. The heart and mind of a nation are never stirred from their foundations without manifold good fruits. "Whatever happens in the world has its sign which precedes it. When the sun is about to rise, the horizon assumes an infinite gradation of colours, and the East seems on fire. When the tempest is coming, a hollow sound is heard on the shore, and the waves heave as if stirred by some strange impulse. The innumerable and diversified thoughts which conflict and mingle on the horizon of the spiritual world, are the sign announcing the rising of the Sun of Righteousness. The confused murmur and the internal movement of peoples aroused, is the heralding sign of the tempest destined soon to pass over trembling nations. Hold yourselves ready, for the time approaches."

I said that the far reaching character of our agitation is indicated by certain signs, which at the first were lacking, but have now become evident. Of one such sign I cannot speak without sadness. Some men who worked with us at the beginning, shocked with the cruelty and illegality of the Acts, fall off when they understand the thoroughness of our crusade, and that it is directed not only against a chance cruel result of vice, but against the tacit permission—the indisputable right, as some have learned to regard it—granted to men to be impure at all. The touchstone of the central principle of our movement is too severe a test for such men, and they fall away. Let them leave us! Sad as such defection is, the cause we labour for is worth a double and a treble sifting of the means and forces employed in it.

The increased anger of our opponents—which finds expression in a portion of the Press of this country—is another sign of the recognition that it is not only against unjust and immoral legislation that we are at war, but against the guilt of society at large, in permitting and conniving at the regular and constant sacrifice of a multitude of women to the basest and most shameful uses.

. . . See the signs of terror in these writers of the present day! At first they said we were a despicable little clique, whose crotchet would soon be laughed to the winds. Now they are telling to the world our "extraordinary success," and that we "have roused every town and village in the land." Falling from one extreme to another, in neither case do they speak precisely within the bounds of truth. I could mention a few villages in the land which have not yet been roused; but fear suggests to them the sound of gathering forces on every hand, and the approach of an invincible foe—and truly we are an invincible foe. But the source of our power is hidden from them; they are perplexed, amazed; they seek hither and thither for the cause of our success, but cannot perceive it. How, indeed, should they perceive or understand it—men without faith? For the weapons of our warfare are not carnal, but spiritual, invisible, impalpable, and mighty to the pulling down of strongholds. How should they read the secrets of God, or rejoice in the steady and awful progression of a moral idea, which has taken root in the conscience of the mass of the people? We may say, equally with the social reformer I have already quoted; "the truth that we utter is impalpable, yet real; it cannot be thrust down by brute force, nor pierced with a dagger, nor bribed with gold;" nor can it be silenced by angry speech, invective, or calumny, nor yet by the silencing of our own voices in death.

. . . When I look back upon what *was* ten years ago; when I recollect how little opposition the great "social evil" met with, how careful most persons were never to mention its existence; when I recall the facts which, from time to time, stared up in their naked ugliness through the smooth fair surface of society; when I remember how a catering, as regular and remunerative as for any other market, was carried on for the markets of lust; how in all our great towns and cities there were, as now, well-known acknowledged temples of Venus of every grade, in which every class of man might prostitute himself, with just so much of the surroundings of refinement and luxury as he was rich enough to pay for, or so much of squalor and misery as his poverty reduced him to; of how, for years and years, before the Acts were introduced, the emissaries of high-class profligacy scoured the continent of Europe in search of attractive maidens for the London market; how virtuous women even encouraged the existence of these abominations by their cowardly terror, their real, or affected ignorance of the subject, and, it must also be confessed, their moral obliquity, in the admission of the doctrine, promulgated by the father of lies, that it is necessary for men to be unchaste, and for women to be ruined. When I recall these things, I cannot feel any wonder at all that the Contagious Diseases Acts came into being: they were the natural offspring of such a course of national depravity. The whole nation ought to sit in sackcloth and ashes. Kings, dukes, lords and ladies, officers of the army and navy, learned men and philosophers, (ignorant of the true philosophy,) cultivated men and women, teachers of youth, physicians, and ministers of religion, as well as the coarse and ignorant plebeian, all—all have been guilty in this matter. All have contributed their share, directly or indirectly, to the existence of this accursed thing, this permitted evil in our midst. I call it a permitted evil; for it was permitted before it was legalised by the Acts; it was more than permitted, it was encouraged, consciously fostered, and influentially patronised. Nothing is more untrue than to pretend that men who now indulge in profligate habits, would cease to do so simply on account of the removal of solicitation from the street—(by which is meant the solicitation of women only, for we hear of no plan for the suppression of the solicitation of men, which is so great and growing an evil)—inasmuch as it is well known to all who have taken any steps for the rescue of women, that large numbers of men constantly promote the evil of prostitution by deliberate and premeditated acts.

Mary Carpenter (1807–77) made four trips to India in the 1860s and 1870s in connection with her interest in prison reform, female education, and the condition of Indian women. In her letter to Lord Salisbury she makes a case for the training of female teachers for India through the foundation of Normal Schools designed specifically with colonial reformers mind.

Mary Carpenter, Letter to the Marquis of Salisbury (1876)

To The Right Hon. the MARQUIS OF SALISBURY,
H.M. Secretary of State for India.
My Lord,
    In compliance with the expressed wish of your Lordship, I beg respectfully to lay before you the following statement respecting the education of the female sex, with the

consequent emancipation and elevation of woman in her social position. To promote this was my chief object in visiting India.

In order to explain my objects and observations in my last and fourth journey in 1875–6 it is necessary for me to refer to my first, in 1866–7. This will be most concisely done by laying before you the report and recommendations then presented to the Governor in Council, Sir John Lawrence. It is as follows:—

The present condition of female education in India can be improved solely by the introduction of female teachers, and these can be supplied only by the establishment of Female Normal Training Schools.

The Government of India has long adopted this course to supply male teachers to boys' schools. The boys' schools are provided with good and efficient teachers, and are producing excellent results. If the same course is pursued for the girls' schools, there can be no doubt that similar results will follow after the system has had time to work. Isolated efforts have been made in some parts of Bengal to supply teachers by the establishment of Normal Schools; but these only prove the necessity of a more complete system.

Feeling assured that the Government has hitherto held back from taking this course, not through any apathy respecting female education, but from a desire to be assured that the want is actually felt by enlightened Natives, before taking any initiatory steps in the matter, I have, in the Madras and Bombay Presidencies, ascertained that enlightened Native gentlemen are most anxious for the establishment of such schools, as they have testified to me in writing; in Ahmedabad and Madras steps have been already taken by them in memorializing their respective Governments. In Calcutta I have ascertained that many respectable persons are desirous of the establishment of such schools, and have memorialized Government on the subject ;—the want of them is very strongly felt also in many important places in the mofussil.

I am well aware that the difficulties to be encountered in establishing Training Schools for female teachers are much greater than those attending Male Normal Training Schools. The ignorance of Hindu women of a suitable age is one great impediment, and the difficulty of finding any such, except widows, who would be able and willing to be trained for teachers, is another. I have fully considered these and many other obstacles, and having done this, and consulted persons of considerable experience in different parts of the country, I am persuaded that they may be surmounted.

The following are suggestions which I would beg to offer as to the general features of such a school as I desire to see established. It will, of course, be clearly understood that in these proposed Institutions the Government principle of non-interference in religious matters is to be strictly adhered to. While the personal religious liberty of every inmate of the Institution is to be respected, no one, while in it, is to attempt any religious proselytism. Different localities will have different requirements and adaptation to special circumstances. It will, therefore, be better in every case to commence on a small scale, and with as much attention to economy as is consistent with the proper development of the Institution.

Suggestions for the establishment of a Female Normal Training School.

First.—A house should be procured, adapted to furnish a comfortable residence for about a dozen Christian students, with a Lady Superintendent. Arrangements should be made for the separate boarding of non-Christian Native students when required. Arrangements for necessary furniture, board and attendance, to be made by the Inspector of Schools.

Secondly.—A Lady Superintendent, who should be responsible to Government for the entire management of the Institution, should be obtained from England (at a salary probably of about 200 Rupees a month, in addition to board and lodging); and a superior Mistress for training (at about 150 Rupees a month, in addition to board and lodging). In each case the passage money to be paid under certain conditions.

Thirdly.—Persons who wish to become students in training must apply to the Inspector, and must satisfy him that it is their intention to study and faithfully to prepare to be teachers. . . .

The Institution should be arranged as follows:—

The *House* provided must contain not only suitable class rooms, but comfortable accommodation for the Lady Superintendent, Training Mistress, and Students, (any non-Christian Native Students who may require to board in the Institution must have separate arrangements made for them), servants, conveyance, and whatever else is needed for a respectable household, to be provided also.

The *Lady Superintendent* will have the general management of the Institution, provide the board, and in every way be the head of the household. She will make all arrangements necessary for developing the objects of the Institution; confer with the Managers of Schools desirous of obtaining the assistance of the Mistress and Students; conduct all correspondence; and in all respects be responsible for the due carrying out of the intentions of the Government, to which only she will be responsible.

The *Training Mistress,* who is to be an English Certificated Teacher, will have the entire responsibility of training the Students; she will spend a portion of each day with them in the Schools; give them such separate instruction as may be needed; and with them receive daily lessons of a Master in the vernacular, to the acquisition of which she shall give careful attention. While teaching in any School she shall in no respect interfere with the regulations or wishes of the Managers.

Persons desirous of entering the Normal School as *Students* must satisfy the Lady Superintendent that their character and general qualifications are such as to render them suitable for Teachers, and also undergo an examination fixed by the Government. They must conform in all respects to the regulations while in the Institution, and must receive a certificate of qualification from the Lady Superintendent, signed by the Inspector, before leaving the School to take an engagement as a Teacher.

Though the preparation of Hindu women as Teachers should be always kept in view, and should be our ultimate object, yet to solve the problem of providing female Teachers for Girls' Schools, it appeared necessary to avail ourselves of the help of Europeans and Eurasians ;—and this for the following among other reasons:—

I. The difficulty of finding any number of Hindu women who would be willing to be trained as Teachers. None in fact appeared to be available, except widows, as all Hindu girls are married very young. With respect to the widows, great difficulties existed, so that we could not hope for some time to find many.

II. The introduction of them into Girls' Schools to learn the art of teaching, and to acquire it by practising, would in the existing state of Schools, involve their coming into contact with the other sex, which would be against their social custom.

III. The mental condition of adult widows who might be willing to be trained would be generally such as to render it impossible that a few years' tuition should fit them to be teachers.

It appeared, therefore, that it would be preferable at first to train as Teachers educated European and Eurasian young ladies to be Teachers, by giving such as might present themselves a good training from English Certificated Teachers. No such training or Normal School had been established by the Government, nor did I hear of any but one School where the attempt was even made to afford it. . . .

Annie Besant (1847–1933) was a radical and a freethinker (known as "Red Annie") who was elected to the presidency of the Indian National Congress in 1916. Here she uses the occasion of the passage of the 1884 Reform Act to reflect on what the effects of political reform have been since 1832.

Annie Besant, "The Redistribution of Political Power" (1885)

STANDING as we do face to face with the enfranchisement of two million men and the redistribution of electoral power in the community, it seems well to look back on earlier Reform Bills and to endeavor to judge of the probable results of the present measures from the results that have followed their predecessors. My object in the following pages is to trace out the most important tendencies which have shown themselves after each Reform Bill; to mark the chief activities manifested after each "infusion of new blood"; to present a picture of certain steadily developing modifications of the national organism, modifications which are likely to become very pronounced in the near future. I am not aware that any attempt has been made to distinguish the transitory from the permanent tendencies, the reforms done once for all amid great excitement from the apparently less important measures which none the less initiate new eras and serve as the starting-point for new developments. Yet in sociology as in geology, the most far-reaching changes are not made by the volcanoes and the earthquakes, but by the slow action of countless silent ever-working forces.

. . . One marked change has come over the nation apart from any legislative enactment—the decrease of the power of the hereditary peers after each Reform Bill. That of '32 swept away from them their control of the House of Commons; after '67, their legislative chamber became less and less able to hold its own against the increased power of the popular representatives; on the Bill of '84 they nearly shipwrecked their House, and when the new constituencies have had their say we may hope that the abolition of their hereditary right of obstruction will be within measurable distance.

Even when at last a Reform Bill was introduced, it met with bitter opposition. Sir Charles Wetherell railed against it in the true Tory style, prophesying all sorts of mischiefs as the consequences of Reform. "I say that the principle of the Bill is Republican at the basis; I say that it is destructive of all property, of all right, of all privilege; and that the same arbitrary violence which expelled a majority of members from that House at the time of the Commonwealth, is now, after the lapse of a century from the Revolution, during which the population has enjoyed greater happiness than has been enjoyed by any population under heaven, proceeding to expose the House of Commons again to the nauseous experiment of a repetition of Pride's purge." Despite of all these terrible forebodings the Bill passed into law, receiving the Royal Assent on June 7th, 1832.

The general result of the Act was to throw political power into the hands of manufacturers and capitalists, in a phrase to "enfranchise the middle classes." The direct influence of the working classes was, if anything, slightly diminished by the Act, since it disenfranchised a few places in which they had previously possessed the suffrage. It struck a fatal blow at the privileges of the possessors of hereditary authority, and gave representation to the commercial interests of the nation. One striking proof was given that the class which then won political power was not unworthy of the freedom it had gained. One of its first reforms was the introduction of a Factory Act to protect the more helpless of the operative class, and it ought never to be forgotten that effective legislative interference with employers was due to a Parliament elected principally by that very same *bourgeois* class which it is now the fashion to so unsparingly denounce. . . .

Results of the Reform Bill of 1867.

The question of Parliamentary Reform again took definite shape in 1858, after the convulsions caused by the Crimean War and the Indian Mutiny. In that year, the Tories being in power, Mr. John Bright formulated a new scheme of Reform, which proposed to give the franchise to all who paid the poor-rate in boroughs, to all who paid a £10 rental in counties, and to lodgers paying a similar rental. Voting by ballot was also adopted by the Reformers, for the protection of the poorer voters who were subjected to intimidation by their employers. In 1859 Mr. Disraeli introduced a Reform Bill containing a most extraordinary collection of fancy property franchises, and on this the Government was defeated, and Lord Derby went to the country. After the general election Lord Palmerston came into power, and in the following year, 1860, Lord John Russell introduced a measure which gave a £6 franchise in boroughs, and a £10 in counties; in this Bill appeared for the first time the proposal to make "three-cornered constituencies," in which a minority might secure representation by electing one member out of three. The Bill made but slow progress in the House, and excited no enthusiasm out-of-doors, and it was finally withdrawn by the Government on June 11th. The question of Reform then slept until 1865, when Mr. Baines brought up some resolutions in its favor, and the Government declined to take any action in the matter; the feeling outside had, however, been growing steadily, and after the general election of 1865—in which Mr. Gladstone was defeated at Oxford and returned for South Lancashire—the Liberal party found itself stronger than ever. On the assembling of Parliament, Earl Russell being Premier, Parliamentary Reform found a place in the Queen's speech, and Mr. Gladstone introduced the Government Bill on March 13th; the proposed was by no means a Radical one, the county franchise being fixed at £14, and the borough at £10, but . . . the Whigs and Tories together defeated the Government. Lord Derby took office at the end of June, and the agitation in favor of Reform now rose to fever heat; the Government tried at first to coerce the people, but succeeded only in irritating them, as when it closed the gates of Hyde Park against a meeting of the Reform League, and a new way was made into the Park over the pulled-down railings. On this the Government decided to yield to the popular demand, and in March, 1867, Mr. Disraeli, after bringing forward some abortive resolutions, startled Whigs, Tories, Liberals, and Radicals by introducing his famous Reform Bill which gave household suffrage to ratepayers in the boroughs, and reduced the county franchise to a £15 qualification. The latter was further reduced to £10, and householders who paid their rates in their rents received also the franchise. The Bill, characterised by Lord Derby as "a leap in the dark," passed the House of Lords in August, and thus the second great Reform Bill of the century became law, the working classes in the towns winning their enfranchisement and becoming, so far as the boroughs were concerned, the real depositories of political power. . . .

Results of the Reform Bill of 1884.

. . . As in the past, so in the future, the new Parliament will be full of reforming energy; again we stand on the threshold of great changes, changes to which some look with fear and some with hope.

We have already seen that the principle of legislative interference between employers and employed has been largely acted on by Parliament since 1832. There is no reason to suppose that the new Parliament will be more careless of the interests of the workers than its predecessors have been; indeed, elected as it will be, by a larger number of handworkers than have ever before taken part in the choice of representatives of the Commons, it will probably be more inclined to legislate in the interests of Labor than any Parliament we have yet seen.

The hours of labor have been shortened at successive intervals since 1801, and it is not unreasonable to suppose that a further shortening of these hours will soon be made. The ordinary London operative now works for a ten hours' day, from 6 a.m. to 5 p.m. with an hour's interval for dinner. Mr. Howell says on this: "If we take the metropolis we shall find that a building operative has to be at his work at six o'clock in the morning, and he now leaves at five o'clock at night. But he has often to walk four or five miles to his work, so that he has to leave home at five and cannot reach home again until six, making a total of thirteen hours. . . . An hour's walk is often very exhilarating to a business man, shut up in an office all day, but to a mason, carpenter, bricklayer, or plasterer, who has frequently to plod through the rain or drifting snow, it is painfully exhausting, especially when it has to be done before six o'clock in the morning."

There can be no doubt in the minds of reasonable people that a ten hours' day is too long. But if that be so, what shall we say to the hours of labor of shopmen and shopwomen, who in most large shops in London begin at 8 a.m. or 9 a.m. and continue at work until 7 p.m. or 8 p.m.? In the smaller shops things are still worse, and, going through a poor neighborhood, we see provision shops open until 10 p.m. or even 11 p.m. served by exhausted men and women, whose pale cheeks and languid movements tell of the strain which is destroying their vitality. The new Parliament should pass an Eight Hours Bill, making the legal day a day of eight hours only, and giving one half-holiday in the week, so that the weekly hours of labor shall not exceed forty-four. In time to come I trust that the hours of labor will be yet further shortened, but the passage of an Eight Hours Bill would mark a good step forward. Looking at the question from a rational point of view, it is surely clear that a human being should not be required to give more than eight hours out of the twenty-four—one third of his time—for absolute breadwinning. Another seven or eight hours must be given to sleep, leaving eight for meals, exercise, recreation, and study. The last eight are short enough for their varied uses, and I look forward to a time when the first section shall be shortened and the third lengthened; but if every worker had even eight hours of freedom in the day, his life would be a far more human and far more beautiful thing than it is at the present time.

The establishment of an eight hours' day would also help to distribute toil a little more evenly than it is distributed now; the same amount of work will have to be performed, and if each pair of hands only does 4/3 of the work it now does, additional pairs of hands must execute the remainder. At present some are being worn out with excessive labor, while others are clamoring for employment; shorter hours for the present workers mean work for the now idle hands.

. . . The lines here sketched are not likely to be followed out in any one Parliament, however great the impulse for improvement, but it is along these lines that the reforming energy will travel, if the study of the past shed any light upon the future of Reform.

Pandita Ramabai (1858–1922) was a Hindu widow who converted to Christianity shortly after her arrival in Britain to study at Cheltenham Ladies College in 1886. Her determination to establish a school for Hindu widows in India brought the wrath of orthodox Hindus down on her head, but this did not prevent her from traveling to the United States to raise money for her cause. In this excerpt from her book, *The High-Caste Hindu Woman*, the sales of which helped to finance her trip to the United States, Ramabai describes the life of the Hindu girl-child and the impact on her of the Hindu marriage system.

Pandita Ramabai, from *The High-Caste Hindu Woman* (1888)

ALTHOUGH the code of Manu contains a single passage in which it is written "A daughter is equal to a son," (See *Manu* ix., 130), the context expressly declares that equality to be founded upon the results attainable through her son; the passage therefore cannot be regarded as an exception to the statement that the ancient code establishes the superiority of male children. A son is the most coveted of all blessings that a Hindu craves, for it is by a son's birth in the family that the father is redeemed.

"Through a son he conquers the worlds, through a son's son he obtains immortality, but through his son's grandson he gains the world of the sun."—*Manu*, ix., 137.

"There is no place for a man (in Heaven) who is destitute of male offspring."—*Vasishtha*, xvii. 2.

If a man is sonless, it is desirable that he should have a daughter, for her *son* stands in the place of a son to his grandfather, through whom the grandfather may obtain salvation.

"Between a son's son and the son of a daughter there exists in this world no difference; for even the son of a daughter saves him who has no sons, in the next world, like the son's son."—*Manu*, ix. 139.

. . . In no other country is the mother so laden with care and anxiety on the approach of childbirth as in India. In most cases her hope of winning her husband to herself hangs solely on her bearing sons. Women of the poorest as well as of the richest families, are almost invariably subjected to this trial. Many are the sad and heart-rending stories heard from the lips of unhappy women who have lost their husband's favor by bringing forth daughters only, or by having no children at all. Never shall I forget a sorrowful scene that I witnessed in my childhood. When about thirteen years of age I accompanied my mother and sister to a royal harem where they had been invited to pay a visit. The Prince had four wives, three of whom were childless. The eldest having been blessed with two sons, was of course the favorite of her husband, and her face beamed with happiness.

. . . A lady friend of mine in Calcutta told me that her husband had warned her not to give birth to a girl, the first time, or he would never see her face again, but happily for this wife and for her husband also, she had two sons before the daughter came. In the same family there was another woman, the sister-in-law of my friend, whose first-born had been a daughter. She longed unceasingly to have a son, in order to win her husband's favor, and when I went to the house, constantly besought me to foretell whether this time she should have a son! Poor woman! she had been notified by her husband that if she persisted in bearing daughters she should be superseded by another wife, have coarse clothes to wear and scanty food to eat, should have no ornaments, save those which are necessary to show the existence of a husband, and she should be made the drudge of the whole household. Not unfrequently, it is asserted, that bad luck attends a girl's advent, and poor superstitious mothers in order to avert such a catastrophe, attempt to convert the unborn child into a boy, if unhappily it be a girl.

Rosaries used by mothers of sons are procured to pray with; herbs and roots celebrated for their virtue are eagerly and regularly swallowed; trees and son-giving gods are devoutly worshipped. There is a curious ceremony, honored with the name of "sacrament," which is administered to the mother between the third and the fourth month of her pregnancy for the purpose of converting the embryo into a boy.

In spite of all these precautions girls will come into Hindu households as ill-luck, or rather nature, will have it. After the birth of one or more sons girls are not unwelcome, and under such circumstances, mothers very often long to have a daughter. And after her birth both parents lavish love and tenderness upon her, for natural affection, though modified and blunted by cruel custom, is still strong in the parent's heart. Especially may this be the case with the Hindu *mother.* That maternal affection, sweet and strong, before which "there is neither male nor female," asserts itself not unfrequently in Hindu homes, and overcomes selfishness and false fear of popular custom. A loving mother will sacrifice her own happiness by braving the displeasure of her lord, and will treat her little daughter as the best of all treasures. Such heroism is truly praiseworthy in a woman; any country might be proud of her. But alas! the dark side is too conspicuous to be passed over in silence.

In a home shadowed by adherence to cruel custom and prejudice, a child is born into the world; the poor mother is greatly distressed to learn that the little stranger is a daughter, and the neighbors turn their noses in all directions to manifest their disgust and indignation at the occurrence of such a phenomenon. The innocent babe is happily unconscious of all that is going on around her, for a time at least. The mother, who has lost the favor of her husband and relatives because of the girl's birth, may selfishly avenge herself by showing disregard to infantile needs and slighting babyish requests. Under such a mother the baby soon begins to *feel* her misery, although she does not understand how or why she is caused to suffer this cruel injustice.

If a girl is born after her brother's death, or if, soon after her birth, a boy in the family dies, she is in either case regarded by her parents and neighbors as the cause of the boy's death. She is then constantly addressed with some unpleasant name, slighted, beaten, cursed, persecuted and despised by all. Strange to say, some parents, instead of thinking of her as a comfort left to them, find it in their hearts, in the constant manifestation of their grief for the dear lost boy, to address the innocent girl with words such as these: "Wretched girl, why didst thou not die instead of our darling boy? Why didst thou crowd him out of the house by coming to us; or why didst not thou thyself become a boy?" "It would have been good for all of us if thou hadst died and thy brother lived!" I have myself several times heard parents say such things to their daughters, who, in their turn, looked sadly and wonderingly into the parents' faces, not comprehending why such cruel speeches should be heaped upon their heads when they had not done any harm to their brothers. If there is a boy remaining in the family, all the caresses and sweet words, the comforts and gifts, the blessings and praises are lavished upon him by parents and neighbors, and even by servants, who fully sympathize with the parents in their grief. On every occasion the poor girl is made to feel that she has no right to share her brother's good fortune, and that she is an unwelcome, unbidden guest in the family.

. . . I have mentioned earlier the strictness of the modern caste system in regard to marriage. Intelligent readers may, therefore, have already guessed that this reason lies at the bottom of the disfavor shown to girls in Hindu homes. From the first moment of the daughter's birth, the parents are tormented incessantly with anxiety in regard to her future, and the responsibilities of their position. Marriage is the most expensive of all Hindu festivities and ceremonies. The marriage of a girl of a high caste family involves an expenditure of two hundred dollars at the very least. Poverty in India is so great that not many fathers are able to incur this expense; if there are more than two daughters in a family, his ruin is inevitable. For, it should be remembered, the bread-winner of the house in Hindu society not only has to feed his own wife and children, but also his parents, his brothers unable to work either through ignorance or idleness, their families and the nearest widowed relatives, all of whom very often depend upon one man for their support; besides these, there are the family priests, religious beggars and others, who expect much from him. Thus, fettered hand and foot by barbarously cruel customs which threaten to strip him of everything he has, starvation and death staring him in the face, the wretched father of many girls is truly an object of pity. Religion enjoins that every girl must be given in marriage; the neglect of this duty means for the father unpardonable sin, public ridicule and caste ex-communication. But this is not all. The girl must be married within a fixed period, the caste of the future husband must be the same, and the clan either equal or superior, *but never inferior,* to that of her father.

The Brahmans of Eastern India have observed successfully their clan prejudice for hundreds of years despite poverty; they have done this in part by taking advantage of the custom of polygamy. A Brahman of a high clan will marry ten, eleven, twenty, or even one hundred and fifty girls. He makes a business of it. He goes up and down the land marrying girls, receiving presents from their parents, and immediately thereafter bidding good-bye to the brides; going home, he never returns to them. The illustrious Brahman need not bother himself with the care of supporting so many wives, for the parents pledge themselves to maintain the daughter all her life, if she stays with them a married virgin to the end. In case of such a marriage as this, the father is not required to spend money beyond his means, nor is it difficult for him to support the daughter, for she is useful to the family in doing the cooking and other household work; moreover, the father has the satisfaction *first,* of having given his daughter in marriage, and thereby having escaped disgrace and the ridicule of society; *secondly,* of having obtained for himself the bright mansions of the gods, since his daughter's husband is a Brahman of high clan.

But this form of polygamy does not exist among the Kshatriyas, because, as a member of the non-Brahman caste, a man is not allowed by religion, to beg or to receive gifts from others, except from friends; he therefore cannot support either many wives or many daughters. Caste and clan prejudice tyrannized the Rajputs of North and Northwestern and Central India, who belong to the Kshatriyas or warrior caste, to such an extent that they were driven to introduce the inhuman and irreligious custom of female infanticide into their society. This cruel act was performed by the fathers themselves, or even by mothers, at the command of the husband whom they are bound to obey in *all* things.

It is a universal custom among the Rajputs for neighbors and friends to assemble to congratulate the father upon the birth of a child. If a boy is born, his birth is announced with music, glad songs and by distributing sweetmeats. If a daughter, the father coolly announces that "nothing" has been born into his family, by which expression it is understood that the child is a girl, and that she is very likely to be *nothing* in this world, and the friends go home grave and quiet.

After considering how many girls could safely be allowed to live, the father took good care to defend himself from caste and clan tyranny by killing the extra girls at birth, which was as easily accomplished as destroying a mosquito or other annoying insect. Who can save a babe if the parents are determined to slay her, and eagerly watch for a suitable opportunity? Opium is generally used to keep the crying child quiet, and a small pill of this drug is sufficient to accomplish the cruel task; a skillful pressure upon the neck, which is known as the "putting nail to the throat," also answers the purpose. There are several other nameless methods that may be employed in sacrificing the innocents upon the unholy altar of the caste and clan system. Then there are not a few child-thieves who generally steal girls; even the wild animals are so intelligent and of such refined taste that they mock at British law, and almost always steal girls to satisfy their hunger. . . .

―――

Millicent Garrett Fawcett (1847–1929) was the leader of the constitutional suffragists and one of the founders of the National Union of Women Suffrage Societies in 1897. In this essay she defends the need for a women's suffrage bill, invoking a variety of imperial references along the way.

―――

Millicent Garrett Fawcett, "The Women's Suffrage Bill" (1889)

. . . It is extremely difficult to realise the point of view of those who are passionately opposed to the granting of the parliamentary franchise to single women and widows who are householders, and fulfill all the qualifications demanded by law of the male voter.

One would think, to hear these worthy people talk or to read what they write, that the Women's Suffrage Bill proposes to enfranchise a horde of savages of whom we know nothing, except that they are regardless of the honour of England, have no respect either for order or liberty, and are intent only in breaking down all those valued institutions of our country which it has taken so many generations of labour and sacrifice to erect.

Mr. Goldwin Smith, for instance, thinks it not improbable that one of the first acts of enfranchised Englishwomen will be to "set Hindostan on fire." Mrs. Lynn Linton thinks that women's suffrage would cause the English national character to change, and to "incorporate all the defects of the French nature." Neither of them explains why. If the effort of Englishwomen in India had at any period of our history been directed to "setting Hindostan on fire," there would be some reasonable colour for refusing any extension of power to these dangerous firebrands. If the special "defects of the French nature" could be traced in any sense to women' suffrage, it might be reasonable to fear that what had worked ill in France would work ill here. But women's suffrage is not even heard of in France; it does not exist there as a practical political subject. One of Gambetta's sayings, in contrasting the political situations of England and France, was to the effect that England had the advantage of France in this respect, that here the enfranchisement of women was possible and desirable, while in his own country it was entirely out of the question. Englishwomen in India, so far as they have identified themselves with social and political subjects at all in that country, have done what in them lay to improve the education of Indian women, and to provide them with medical attendants of their own sex. Some women, too, have joined the little band of men who have protested against the association of English Christianity in India with the grossest forms of immorality. None of these things justifies, or indeed gives the smallest foundation for the baseless fabric of the vision that Englishwomen are intent on "setting Hindostan on fire."

If Englishwomen have, on the whole, been faithful and conscientious in the discharge of the duties and responsibilities already entrusted to them, if they have cared to make some little corner of the world better and happier than they found it, if their gradual introduction into some departments of public life, since the beginning of this century, has made prison life less degrading, has given workhouse children a better chance, has improved the quality of sick nursing, has contributed any solution to the problems of pauperism, has extended and improved education, then we may confidently appeal to the past as the best guarantee of what we hope for in the future. The subjects here briefly alluded to suggest the names of Elizabeth Fry, Mary Carpenter, the Miss Davenport Hills, Mrs. Nassau Senior, Miss Nightingale, Miss Octavia Hill, Mrs. William Grey and others, too numerous to mention. All the truly womanly work, to which they have devoted themselves, forms a body of tradition that will have a powerful influence in directing women's work in the future. The women I have mentioned and many others have come more or less into public life; they have produced social changes of the greatest importance; but the way in which they have worked affords no justification for the accusation that women in public life will give painful examples of "febrile exaltation," "of preference for persons over principles, and spasmotic attacks of suspicion, anger, and unreasonable national 'breaking out,'" which Mrs. Lynn Linton dreads as the result of women's suffrage. It need hardly be said that it is not expected that the rank and file of women will be equal to the leaders and inaugurators of the important social reforms I have mentioned, any more than the rank and file of men will be equal to Burke or Wilberforce. But when it is seen that a large body of representative Englishwomen for nearly a century have worked for definite purposes with persistence and devotion, when they have been uniformly reasonable in their demands, moderate in their arguments, and accurate in their statements, when the result of their work has been of such self-evident utility as to completely annihilate all opposition to it, then I think it is not unreasonable to claim that the national characteristics of the English people, such as practical moderation, common sense and honesty, are not the exclusive property of one sex.

Mrs. Lynn Linton and Mr. Goldwin Smith both talk of a nation in which women are allowed to vote for Members of Parliament, ceasing to be masculine. "We may bid adieu," says the lady, "to our place among the masculine nations of Europe;" and the professor takes up the wondrous tale by saying, "In the conflict of nations, what chance will a nation under female influence have against countries like Russia and Germany, with thoroughly masculine Governments?" Ever since the time when "Male and female created He them; and blessed them, and called their name Adam," no nation has ever been exclusively masculine, and no government even has been really free from feminine influences. We wish to see the influence of women in politics recognised and made responsible. It is a potent factor in politics not only in our own country and in the era of primrose leagues and women's political associations of every shade, but everywhere; and those countries which are now in the first rank of modern civilization are there, according to Sir Henry Maine, chiefly because they have frankly accepted and steadily carried forward all that series of changes which have gradually put an end to the seclusion and degradation of women.

There are nations whose civilisation offers a great contrast to our own, where the progress of women towards emancipation has been successfully resisted. Are these what Mrs. Lynn Linton means when she speaks of "masculine nations"? Is Turkey a masculine nation? If there is one adjective more than another in request in speaking of Turkey, it is "effeminate;" and yet it is in Turkey, of all European nations, that the emancipation of women has made the least progress. Is not the conclusion almost irresistible that ordered freedom develops the best qualities of both men and women, and that those nations will be richest in worthy citizens where this fact is frankly recognised?

Nothing astonishes Orientals more than the position of women in England. A Chinese mandarin has lately published his views on this subject. Women, he says, are even helped at meals before men; in his own country the men eat first, and when they have quite finished, if anything is left, the women are allowed to have it. Another Eastern, Syed Ahmed Khan, was amazed to find that the servant-girl who waited upon him in his lodgings in London could read and write; and he recorded his deliberate opinion that the little scrub in a London lodging, "compelled to work as a maid-servant for her living," was in reality superior in nearly all respects to Indian ladies of the highest rank. "Such," he adds solemnly, "is the effect of education."

. . . Great men do not spring from feeble mothers. In this way, through the principle of heredity, the general average of mental, moral and physical development of both sexes in any country is kept pretty much on a par. If it were not for this, when we consider the enormous advantages men have had over women in times past, in training, in power, and in the sobering effect of responsibility, we might expect to see as much difference between the men and women of the same country, as there is between the average Asiatic and the average European. But boys and girls, inheriting equally from both parents, the difference of circumstances between the sexes is prevented from exercising its full effect in producing permanent differences between them in mental and moral development.

Can anyone honestly feel that women's characters are incapable of benefiting by these ennobling influences? Caring only for their own domestic interests, and nothing for the great community of which they are a fragment, is merely selfishness writ large. I once heard a lady, the wife of a Member of Parliament, say, at a moment when we seemed to be on the brink of a war with Russia, that she would rather there were a war than a general election. She would rather, that is, than that her own domestic comfort and ease should be interrupted, and her husband's digestion upset, that thousands of homes should be made desolate, that tens of thousands of brave men should lose their lives, and their wives and children should taste the bitterness of widow and orphanhood. The first thing that women learn from bearing some part, however humble, in national life, is to care for other homes besides their own, to learn how law and social customs affect other people's children, and to test every proposed alteration in the law, not as it may affect their personal interests, but according to its bearing on the well-being of others. In a word, it extends their sympathies and enlarges their horizon.

. . . Some people are afraid that the enfranchisement of women will add to the impulsiveness and sentimentality of the electorate, and increase the risk of ill-considered legislation. They appear to forget that the women it is proposed to enfranchise are not of the "beloved Araminta" type or age. It is not certain indeed that the "beloved Araminta" type has not become extinct, like the Dodo. But however this may be, the single woman or widow who is a householder or owner of property, is not usually a person much given to gush and sentimentality. It is generally observed that knowledge of the facts and practical work are the best cure for sentimentality on a given subject, while at the same time this remedy for sentimentality gives a decided stimulus to what is valuable in feeling and sympathy. It is certainly not true that in practical affairs Englishwomen have been overmuch guided by silly sentiment. Miss Nightingale has not gone into heroics about nursing the sick: Miss Octavia Hill and the Miss Davenport Hills are the most practical of workers; a vast army of women is silently and diligently working for charity organisation, filled with a true wish to help their poorer neighbours to a happier and more satisfactory life, but utterly free from the gush of mere impulsive benevolence. Have boards of guardians, since the time when women were admitted as part of their electorate, shown any disposition to throw the safeguards and precautions of poor-law administration to the winds? A glance over the yearly reports issued by the Local Government Board shows that this is not the case; and that the twenty years during which women have voted in these elections have been characterised by very marked improvements in poor-law administration: the changes have been all in the direction which experience and political economy have shown to check the growth of voluntary pauperism, and to cut off the supply of hereditary paupers. Many of these improvements, perhaps most of them, have been initiated and carried through by men, but they have certainly been aided and supported, and not thwarted, by women, both as guardians and voters. One great branch of poor-law administration women may be said to have made their own; I mean the improved methods of bringing up pauper children. By improvements in the domestic arrangements in schools, in cottage industrial homes, in boarding out, in the much-needed auxiliary work of the Metropolitan Association for Befriending Young Servants, founded by Mrs. Nassau Senior, women have come in with their practical knowledge of home-life and child-nature, and have begun an altogether new era of hope for the quarter of a million of pauper children in our midst. Here we have an actual example, in a definite, tangible form, of women's suffrage and its consequences. It has resulted not in effusive sentiment, but in the application to a difficult social problem of good sense and good feeling, combined with good practical knowledge of the matter in hand. The children have enormously benefited by the change; the proportion of them that become respectable, self-supporting citizens has largely increased.

The benefit to the whole of society from this improvement is too obvious to need insisting on. What is now asked for as regards the parliamentary franchise, is that it should be extended to the same women, who, for twenty years, have been voting for poor-law guardians and in other local elections.

. . . There seems to be much reason to hope that the enfranchisement of women will at least have the effect on all parties of making the caucuses careful as to the character of the men chosen as candidates. The party managers will soon learn that the majority of women electors will refuse to support men of notoriously bad character. We have had a recent illustration of this in the selection of the London aldermen. There was a decided indication of the same feeling on the part of women in the late municipal elections in Kansas, where women voted for the first time. The party wire-pullers there were horrified to find that the women were guilty of the enormity of "scratching their ticket," that is, of not voting for the whole of the list put out by their party, if any man upon it was notorious for evil ways of any kind. After the manner of Americans, male and female, the women of Kansas are great at drawing resolutions, and it is refreshing to find them, in one of the townships of Kansas, solemnly demanding of their party, respectable men to vote for. Here is their declaration of independence: "Whereas the privilege of voting in municipalities has been granted to the women of Kansas; and whereas heretofore too many men of doubtful honesty and immoral character have been exalted to offices of public trust; therefore—Resolved: That we, the women voters of Atchison, demand that only those men be nominated for city and school offices that are recognised as persons of honesty, sobriety, and good moral character. Resolved: That we care less for parties than for principles, and political parties that expect our votes must give us good men for whom to vote." If the women voters, to whatever party they may belong, will just live up to this, caring less for parties than for principles and demanding good men for whom to vote, they may be the very salt of electioneering, purifying and sweetening the whole.

The much-publicized travels of Mary Kingsley (1862–1900) in Africa made her name a household word in fin-de-siècle Britain. Despite the fact that Victorians saw her as a pioneering woman, Kingsley rejected attempts to harness her to the women's rights movement, preferring to see herself as a "friend of Africa" rather than as a feminist. When the Boer War broke out in 1899 she hastened to South Africa, where she died shortly afterward of typhoid.

Mary Kingsley, from *Travels in West Africa* (1897)

. . . IT was in 1893 that, for the first time in my life, I found myself in possession of five or six months which were not heavily forestalled, and feeling like a boy with a new half-crown, I lay about in my mind, as Mr. Bunyan would say, as to what to do with them. "Go and learn your tropics," said Science. Where on earth am I to go, I wondered, for tropics are tropics wherever found, so I got down an atlas and saw that either South America or West Africa must be my destination, for the Malayan region was too far off and too expensive. . . . All my informants referred me to the missionaries. "There were," they said, in an airy way, "lots of them down there, and had been for years." So to missionary literature I addressed myself with great ardour . . . [and there] I got my first idea about the social condition of West Africa. I gathered that there existed there, firstly the native human beings—the raw material, as it were—and that these were led either to good or bad respectively by the missionary and the trader. There were also the Government representatives, whose chief business it was to strengthen and consolidate the missionary's work, a function they carried on but indifferently well. But as for those traders! well, I put them down under the dangers of West Africa at once. Subsequently I came across the good old coast yarn of how, when a trader from that region went thence, it goes without saying where, the Fallen Angel without a moment's hesitation vacated the infernal throne (Milton) in his favour. This, I beg to note, is the marine form of the legend. When it occurs terrestrially the trader becomes a Liverpool mate. But of course no one need believe it either way—it is not a missionary's story.

. . . It was the beginning of August '93 when I first left England for "the Coast." Preparations of quinine with postage partially paid arrived up to the last moment, and a friend hastily sent two newspaper clippings, one entitled "A Week in a Palm-oil Tub," which was supposed to describe the sort of accommodation, companions, and fauna likely to be met with on a steamer going to West Africa. . . . With a feeling of foreboding gloom I left London for Liverpool—none the more cheerful for the matter-of-fact manner in which the steamboat agents had informed me that they did not issue return tickets by the West African lines of steamers.

. . . *August* 10*th*.—The morning breaks gray, cheerless and chilly, the sea looks angry and wicked. For half-an-hour, while the crew are getting things straight, I comb my tangled hair and meditate on the problem "Why did I come to Africa?" This done we heave up anchor and shove off at about 5.30 A.M. and from that time till 1.45 go along near in-shore on the land breeze, among the rollers. I do not cite this as the proper course to lay, but give it as an example of the impossibility of getting a black crew to run out of smell of land; they always like to hug the shore, as not only my own experiences but those of sympathetic friends with whom I have interchanged experiences demonstrate. Let the shore be what it may they cling to it. Poor Mr. S., going from Gaboon to Eloby, got run well up the Moondah River on one occasion, owing to this persistent habit, and other adventurers have fared no better.

The shore along from Akanda to Cape Clara is one to which any white seaman would give a lot of room. Immediately south of our anchorage it begins to rise into dwarf vertical cliffs overhung by bush and trailing plants between which the cliff-face shows strange-looking slabs of white clay and rock. The sea plays furiously against them at high tide, and at low leaves a very narrow beach heavily strewn with immense rock boulders. By 1.30 we find we cannot get round Cape Esterias, so run in under the shallow lea of its northern side. There is here a narrow sand-beach, with plenty of rock on it, and a semi-vertical and supremely slippery path leading up to an ostentatiously European plank-built house. We fix up the *Lafayette* safely and all go ashore.

The inhabitants of this country have been watching us beating in, and taking a kindly interest in the performance, and so as soon as everything is all right they sing out in a chorus *Mboloani*. They did not do so before because it is not etiquette to distract people when they are engaged in the crucial occupation of landing a boat or canoe. I am taken possession of by a very comely-looking brown young lady, gracefully attired in my favourite coloured cloth, bright pink with a cardinal twill hem round it, and we go up the hill together. I note that she wears a tight rope of large green and white beads round her beautiful throat; she tells me her name is Agnes and that she is a subtrader for Messrs. Holt's factory at Eloby, and I find, thanks be! she talks fluent trade English, and further that on account of its European planks the ostentatious house is regarded by these kindly people as *ipso facto* my fit and proper dwelling for the time I may think good to stay at Cape Esterias. Its enterprising builder and owner apologises for its un-finished state; indeed, when at close quarters with it, I see it has merely got its walls up and its roof on. It is perched some four feet above the ground, on poles, and the owner has not yet decided what flight of stairs he will erect to the verandah. He has purchased an old ready-made flight, and has himself constructed a bamboo ladder, its cross pieces tied on to the uprights. I need hardly say, with tie-tie. This being done he has got both ladders lying on the ground beside each other, while he thinks the matter well out as to their respective advantages. Of course the additional fluster of my unexpected arrival renders him more than ever incapable of coming to a decision on their rival merits. I re-lieve his mind by ignoring them and swing up on to the verandah and enter the house. The furniture consists of shavings, tools, the skeleton of a native bedstead, and a bag of something which evidently serves as a bed. The owner proudly displays the charms of the establishment; he intends, he remarks, to paint the inside of the walls white, with the door and window frames a bright blue. . . . I recognise the good old cobalt in a pot. I applaud the idea, not that it is new on this Coast, but it is better than all white, or dunduckety mud-colour paint, the only other colour schemes in vogue for domestic decoration, and worlds an' away ahead of varnish, which acts as a "catch 'em alive oh" for all manner of insects, and your clothes when you hang them against it. I note there will be a heavy percentage of blue here, because in the fifteen feet square living room there are three doors and two windows—each one of which, from a determination to be quite the white man, is fitted with a lock and a bolt. The next room, there are only two, is particularly strong in windows, being provided with three. Out of the two to the north there is a lovely view of wooded valleys and low hills seen across that charming bright foreground of a banana plantation. The window to the east commands the line of back arrangements of one side of the little village, a view full of interest to the eth-nologist, only just at present I am too wet and tired for the soulful contemplation of sci-ence, or of scenic beauty, so I close all three windows up with their wooden shutters,—glass, of course, there is none—and having got my portmanteau, and a pud-ding basin of European origin—with a lively combination of blue, maroon, and gas greens all over it—full of water and, joy! a towel. . . .

The Roman Catholic Mission, the only representative of white men here, is on the southern face of Cape Esterias. Its buildings consist of a small residence and a large church. The church has a concrete floor and wooden benches, the white walls relieved by a frieze of framed prints of a religious character, a pretty altar with its array of bright brass candlesticks, and above it the tinted and gilt figure of the Virgin and Child. Every part of the place is sweet and clean, giving evidence of the loving care with which it is tended. As I pass the residence, the missionary, seeing me, sends one of his black retainers to fetch me in, and leads me on to the verandah, where I am most cordially received by the Père in charge, who has practical views on hospitality, and is anxious for me to have wine and many things else he can ill afford to spare from his own store. I thankfully confine my depredations to some sugar and a loaf of ex-cellent bread, but he insists on handing to Agnes for me a tin of beef and a lot of oranges. As I cannot speak French, nor he English, I do my best to convey my sense of his kindness and bow myself off.

Agnes, who is very proud of the Mission, tells me there is only one Père and one Frère stationed here, but she says "they are very good—good too much." They educate the children, teaching them to read French, &c., and should a child display any aptitude it is forwarded round to Gaboon to acquire a further training in the technical schools there in connection with the headquarters of the Mission. She herself, I gather, was educated primarily by the Mission, but she has continued her studies on her own account, for not only does she speak French grammatically, as the natives are taught to, and read and write it, but also English—Coast English no doubt, but comforting to the wanderer who falls in with her, while she claims an equal knowledge of Spanish; no mean range of accomplishments for a lady. I return to my abode and have a square meal and sugar in my coffee, thanks to the missionary, and so to bed, as Mr. Pepys would say. I am sure, by the way, Mr. Pepys would like Agnes, she is quite his style of beauty, plump and pleasant; I don't expect he would care for my seaweed bed though, unless he had been broken into it by African travel, for Mr. Pepys had great ideas of being comfortable in a conventional way.

. . . As the manœvre of placing your main-top up a tap is not mentioned, even in my friend *The Sailor's Sea Book,* I had better explain how the thing is done. The *Minerve* is an old line-of-battle ship, moored off Libreville to serve as a guard ship, a depot, and a hospital. She is by nature high out of water, on her gun deck is the hospital, on the main deck the officers' quarters and the exercise ground for the sailors and marines, and above this again is another structure with cisterns on, their taps projecting overside—why I do not know, unless they screw hoses on them, for I have never been aboard her or had her geography explained; above all is a roof of palm-leaf mats, in good old Coast style. The whole fabric, as Clark Russell would say, towers high into the air, just high enough about the cisterns for the lively *Lafayette* to get her precious spar up the nozzle of one of those taps, and of course it was a joke she could not resist trying on. I wish it clearly to be understood that I am not saying a syllable against the staid, stately *Minerve.* The only indiscretion she was ever guilty of was once leaving her moorings and going off with a heavy tornado, to the horror of Glass and Libreville, drifting away, hospital and all, to what seemed destruction. She was rescued, but what the feelings of those on board were, save that they had a lurid glow of glory in them and a determination that they would die in a manner creditable to La France, I know not. The feelings of those ashore I am faintly able to realise, and they must have been painful in the extreme, for the *Minerve* is beloved; many a man, nay, almost every man, knows that he owes his life to the skill and care he received on board her when he had "that attack." No man is, I think, regarded as being initiated into the inner life of Congo Français until he has been carried on board her in a dying condition from the fearful Coast fever, and duly pulled round. It would be an immense advantage to the other settlements along here had they such an institution. She is infinitely better than the so-called "Sanatorium" on higher ground. The idea of the efficacy of such stations is one of the most dangerous illusions rife on the West Coast—I even learn now that this Government is thinking of doing away with the floating hospital and building one ashore which will not have anything like so good a record to show as the wards of the *Minerve* now have.

After our incident with the authorities we pull ourselves together, and arrive at Hatton and Cookson's Wharf with a delusive dash, and glad I am to get there and return to all the comforts, society, and safety associated with it.

———✥———

Elizabeth Andrew (1845–1917) and Katharine Bushnell (1856–1946) were official Round-the-World missionaries for the World Women's Christian Temperance Union who both hailed from Evanston, Illinois. Though they had been to India and indeed had traveled throughout the British empire before, they went to the subcontinent in the late 1890s under the auspices of the Ladies National Association (Josephine Butler's organization, formed to combat the Contagious Diseases Acts; see above) to inspect the Indian cantonments, and especially to investigate the condition of Indian women who were subject to the system of regulated prostitution there.

———✥———

Elizabeth Andrew and Katharine Bushnell, from *The Queen's Daughters in India* (1899)

Dedicated
to
Josephine E. Butler,
Prophetess of the Truth in Christ Jesus; Lover of Holy Justice;
Friend of Outcast Women; Leader of "the New Abolitionists";
Whom God Hath Anointed with His Own Peculiar Joy.
Because, in the Spirit of Her Master, She Hath
"Loved Righteousness and Hated Iniquity."

A GENTLEMAN in India, who had spent many years in military service, told us the following tradition:—

"In the year 1856, before the Mutiny, Lady——was one evening riding out on horseback at Umballa, unattended, when the bridle of her horse was suddenly seized by a British soldier who was possessed of evil designs against her. Most earnestly she protested against his violence, and remonstrated with him that, besides the wrong to her, to injure one of her social rank would utterly ruin his entire future, as he would be flogged and dismissed from the army in disgrace. Thereupon ensued a conversation in which he pleaded extenuation for such a crime so successfully that she readily accepted his false statement that there was excuse for vice when soldiers were not allowed to marry. After that experience she sought opportunity to talk with high military officials concerning the necessity of protecting high-born ladies from such risks, by furnishing opportunities for sensual indulgence to the British soldiers, and the result was the elaboration and extension of a system for the apportionment of native women to regiments." We have never been able to verify the exact truth of this incident, but it probably has a basis in fact. Yet it has had its counterpart in a recent movement among the aristocratic women of England to re-introduce the same wicked legislation. It is on this account that the authors have considered it necessary to print a more extended account of the work in behalf of the women of India, in which they have had a large share. If the exceedingly simple style in which they give their story seems to some readers almost an insult to their intelligence, and lacking in the delicacy of touch that could be desired, it must not be forgotten for one moment that they are writing with special regard for those in the humblest ranks of life, who have often had scant opportunities for education; for it is upon the daughters of such that the oppressive laws for the licensing of prostitution fall; and in large part the supposed advantages of licensed prostitution accrue to the upper social classes, which are, in fact, the lower moral classes. The crusade against licensed fornication is a war between respectable daughters of the poor and rich and powerful men and women.

. . . There are about one hundred military Cantonments in India. Sometimes these Cantonments have few inhabitants besides the soldiers and a few traders in groceries, etc., for the soldiers; and again in some places a whole city has grown up within the Cantonment, and many Europeans reside therein, feeling more safe in case of threatened trouble from an uprising of the people against the Government, than outside under civil law only. All the land of a Cantonment belongs to the Government, and in case of war the military officials may seize, for residence, all the houses within the Cantonment without regard to the actual owners of the buildings, and the commanding officer has the power of expelling any one he pleases from the Cantonment, without assigning any reason for so doing.

. . . When a regiment came into a large Cantonment where there were barracks, there was generally a large Government brothel to which all the women were sent for residence, and a guard in uniform looked after them. When the soldiers were camped out in the open field, tents were set up for the women at the back part of the encampment. When the soldiers marched, the women were carried in carts, with British soldiers to guard them, or sent by train to the destination of the regiment. In charge of the women was placed a superintendent or brothel-keeper, called the "mahaldarni." She also was expected to procure women as desired; and we have ourselves read the official permits granted these women to go out to procure more women when needed.

On June 17, 1886, a military order, known among the opponents of State regulation as the "Infamous Circular Memorandum," was sent to all the Cantonments of India by Quartermaster-General Chapman, in the name of the Commander-in-Chief of the army in India (Lord Roberts). But during the course of the enquiry of the Departmental Committee of 1893, its real author was discovered to be Lord Roberts himself, not his Quartermaster-General.

. . . This order said (and military orders are well-nigh inexorable): "In the regimental bazaars it is necessary to have a sufficient number of women, to take care that they are sufficiently attractive, to provide them with proper houses, and, above all, to insist upon means of ablution being always available." It proceeds: "If young soldiers are carefully advised in regard to the advantage of ablution, and recognise that convenient arrangements exist in the regimental bazaar [that is, in the chakla], they may be expected to avoid the risks involved in association with women who are not recognised [that is, licensed] by the regimental authorities." In other words, young soldiers are not expected to be moral, but only to be instructed as to the safest way of practising immorality. This remarkable document goes on to suggest that young soldiers should be taught to consider it a "point of honour" to save each other from contagion by pointing out to their officers women with whom there was risk of disease. The document calls attention to the need of more women, and the necessity of making the free quarters "houses that will meet the wishes of the women"—in order, it is implied, that they may be the more easily lured to live in them.

... The British officials of India have not shown the slightest concern as to the spread of disease, even when introduced by their own race among the natives, but have actually sent these women abroad to scatter disease wherever they go. And what can a poor Army slave-woman do when thus turned out? Her caste is broken, because she has lived with foreigners, and her friends will seldom receive her back; she has been compelled to follow the soldiers on the march; and when dismissed may be hundreds of miles away from any human being who ever saw her face before. Practically almost every industrial door in India is closed to women, the nurse-girl to foreign children being so exceptional as not worthy of mention among the hundreds of millions of people. The Cantonment sometimes includes all there is of city life in the whole region, and the woman has no choice but the open fields or the jungle. God alone knows the fate of these helpless creatures, and few beside care to know.

... [These circumstances] drove us to God, our only helper. We were strangers in a strange land, carrying the burden of a sacred secret which weighed us to the earth. . . .

In March, 1892, we arrived at a huge Cantonment about midnight. As there was no dak bungalow at the place, we spread our rugs on the settees in the ladies' waiting-room, and slept till morning. The dak bungalow is an institution kept up by the Government for the convenience of military men and their families, although other travellers take advantage of its shelter, and was preferable to an hotel for our purpose, for our meals were served in our private rooms always, and we could lead a very retired life. After breakfast in the dining-room, we went out and engaged a cab, explaining, as was our custom, to the driver, that we were Christian missionaries, and in accordance with the teachings of our religion, we were searching out the most despised and disreputable of women, to tell them of God's care for them and to see what we could do for them; therefore we wished him to drive us to see the chakla women of the Cantonment. He looked a little bewildered, and then drove off with us.

After traversing a considerable distance, he entered a public garden, and began to drive slowly, that we might enjoy the flowers and foliage. We called to him, bidding him drive on rapidly, as we did not care to see the sights of the Cantonment. He nodded assent, and touching his horse with the whip, drove away in another direction. Presently he paused before another object to which he was accustomed to take visitors. Then we called him from his seat to the cab window, and told him that if he took us out of our way again, we should be obliged to leave his cab, call another, and dismiss him. We made sure he understood exactly what we wished, and he admitted that he did, but intimated that he scarcely thought it a proper place for us to visit. However, he consented, and drove off, and in a few moments brought us to an open field where two regiments were encamped. Fortunately, some drill of an unusual sort was going on, and a good many people had driven out to witness it; this, therefore, absorbed the attention of all. The Lord appointed all our seasons for us during our Indian investigations.

Taking a road leading to the back part of the camp, we left our cab and driver where several other cabs were standing, and walking along together, observed by no one, entered one of the ten little tents we found enclosed in a sort of fence of matting. The women received us cordially, although with real astonishment at such unusual visitors. The mahaldarni was not a bad-meaning woman in many regards, and she told us, with great satisfaction, of a sister of hers who had been promoted from the rank of a common soldiers' woman to be a mahaldarni, saying that she had left off her wickedness, prayed four times a day and read her Koran. She joined with her girls in expressions of utter abhorrence of the examinations to which the girls were subjected, saying, "Shame! Shame!"

She told us how the soldiers, when in drink, knocked the poor girls about in a most cruel manner, and reaching her own conclusion as to the meaning of our call, advised us not to join their number, telling us that the city was far preferable. She and the girls told of the heavy fines to which they would be liable if they did not go to the examinations, or attempted to leave the Lock Hospital when held there. She said if they made any fuss about the fine, then they would be imprisoned. A military guard was placed within the enclosure, in one of the tents; but he had either gone to sleep, or wandered out to get a view of the exercises that were going on near by. We gave a simple gospel talk through our interpreter, and she sang and prayed with the girls; then we made our way to the women of the adjoining Rest Camp.

. . . Returning to our cab, we told our driver to take us to the Lock Hospital; and after a long drive under the burning sun, we stopped before buildings enclosed within a very high brick wall with broken glass on its top to prevent the escape of inmates. A large, strongly-spiked gateway, with double doors, gave the impression of a veritable prison; and there, standing in the open gateway, was an uniformed armed guard. Previous experiences had not led us to expect anything quite so formidable, although there was generally some sort of a guard or watchman at hand, and the native physician usually resided on the premises. We had often said, and promised God, that, sacred as was the nature of the work, we would never prevaricate in order to cover up our real object, if closely questioned. We were not ordinary detectives, playing a part, but Christian women, and the difference was not to be lost sight of.

Our interpreter had not been instructed as to the full significance of our work, but was content to ask few questions if only she might be allowed to follow her bent freely and preach the gospel, which we gladly encouraged and helped in every way possible, for we should have felt that our mission was very incomplete had we met these women solely to hear their pitiful stories, and never utter a word to them of the love of the Heavenly Father, in the midst of such distressing surroundings. Our interpreter always carried religious tracts with her; and while we were hesitating to know how to encounter the armed sentinel, in the simplicity of her holy zeal she walked up to him, gave him a tract, and said a few words of a helpful nature. The guard noticed no more than that some ladies were being delayed at the gate, so he motioned us through, continuing his consideration of the leaflet, and forgetting to ask our errand. How easy for God to hide his own as He had hidden us again and again that day from guard and sentinel! We have frequently been asked how we escaped observation. We can only say that we made but little effort on our own part to do this, and trusted the Lord to do it all for us.

. . . The accounts we have given in previous pages reveal the extremely tender age at which some of these girls were thrust into a life of shame by court proceedings under the Contagious Diseases Acts, when they were openly enforced. Two Benares girls declared they were taken up by the police at fourteen, and one Sitapur girl said she was sold to a mahaldarni at eleven. Much has been said of the horrors of child-marriage in India, and these atrocities should not be minimized, even though we bear in mind the usually slender type of Eastern manhood; but what shall we say when the robust British soldier has had placed at his mercy a little girl of fourteen years old, of the delicate Oriental type; and this done by regular process of law "*to preserve his health*"?

Then again considering the heathen training of these women, we were led to expect that we should find blindness of the moral sense in relation to this sort of wrong-doing. On the contrary, they expressed great shame and humiliation, never tried to justify their sinful acts, spoke almost universally of their hatred of the life, shed bitter tears, and told us how burdened their hearts were in thinking of their sins. Unlike what we met elsewhere in speaking of religion to the natives, they had little desire for controversy. With not a single exception, we were made welcome, treated courteously, and listened to and blessed for our message. Even in the case of the mahaldarnis we found them not inaccessible, but inclined to expressions of contempt for the whole system of regulation, and of apology for being the hirelings of such a system—an excuse which must have more weight than in a country where industries are open to women. Rahiman of Meerut was an exception. She said she considered her business perfectly legitimate, because she was in a "Government position."

Several times we asked the women, "What do you wish us to do for you?" and were surprised at the answer. Desperately poor as many were, there was never an appeal for money; rather they said, "Pray for us;" or, "If you would build us homes, so that we could go to them, and not sin any more, what more could we ask?" and, "If you will help us to have the examinations stopped." Above all, we were astonished at the appeals made to us concerning the latter outrage. We told none of them our whole object in coming among them, yet with great care they described and expressed their abhorrence of the examinations, as well as the wickedness and illegality of them; and in two or three instances they mentioned that they had heard of ladies interested in their behalf, and suggested the possibility that we might do something for them. In one instance several of the women, after telling us of their humiliation, clasped their hands together, and lifting their eyes to heaven, prayed to God that He would "help us to help them." They invariably exonerated the Queen from all blame in this matter, saying, "She is a woman herself; she would not do this. She cares for her daughters in India."

Says Mrs. Josephine Butler: "It is impossible not to think of the fathers and mothers of the young Englishmen, mere boys, who go out to India as soldiers, and who are trained in this disgusting manner by the military authorities; not only in the indulgence of their vices, but in cowardly and brutal cruelties towards the weaker sex. It seemed a grand object indeed on the part of Lord Roberts and his subordinates to aim at sending back their discharged soldiers to England free from physical disease, regardless of their manliness, their moral character, their respect for women, and decent habits of life! Would not the loss of these be bought too dearly by the mere exemption from physical disease, even if this could be made possible?"

C. Varieties of National and Imperial Patriotism

———— ✧ ————

David Livingston (1813–1873) was virtually a household name in Britain—not just because of his African explorations and "discoveries," but because of the tremendous publicity his travel writing received at home. The letters below are drawn from his correspondence with the London Missionary Society well before his fame and suggest the kinds of delicate negotiations that had to be conducted with his sponsors as he made his way into "the interior" of the African continent.

———— ✧ ————

David Livingston, Missionary Correspondence (1841–42)

Kuruman
23rd Septr. 1841
Dear Sir,

That I might be able in my first communication to inform the Directors respecting my prospects of usefulness in the cause of Christ amongst the Heathen, I have delayed announcing my arrival at Kuruman for a period of nearly two months. We came hither on the 31st July, and received a most cordial welcome from the brethren Hamilton and Edwards. The warmth of it awakened in my bosom feelings of fraternal affection to both, and these subsequent intercourse has tended much to increase.

As it is in accordance with my own long cherished desire, and the intentions of the Directors, that my chief energies should be directed to the evangelization of the tribes in the interior, the mode in which this can best be effected has become a topic of intense interest in many conversations we have had together. The decision of the Directors, from judgements matured by long experience, is that an extensive native agency is the most efficient mode of spreading the gospel. In this decision most of the missionaries I have seen fully concur.

The question therefore, where are these to be got for the extensive field beyond us, has become to me one of peculiar interest. Whilst in England I had formed the opinion that great things might be done by means of this Mission—that it might be formed into a sort of focus, from which might diverge in every direction the beams of Divine truth. But after having personally inspected most of the surrounding localities in connexion with this station, I am compelled partially to relinquish the hope in so far as very extended operations are concerned. The great desideratum is a want of population. There is no want of success considering the smallness of the number who usually attend the preaching of the Word, nor can we consider even the attendance small when we remember the paucity of people actually within a reasonable distance of the church. What in England we should call a fair proportion pay respect to the gospel by their presence, and a larger proportion still give gratifying evidence of attachment to its principles by their walk and conversation. But, the population being small, even although there is a large proportion of believers there must be but a small number qualified, if with nothing more with only the willing mind to endure hardship for the benefit of their fellow men.

I should not have called your attention to this, which appears the only unfavourable feature in the Mission, had there been any probability of an increase of population. The cause of the steady decrease instead of augmentation of inhabitants has been in operation for a great number of years. The interior is quiet. As the gospel extends its influence peace will become more permanent, and unless the Bechuanas entirely relinquish their present mode of life, hold something else in estimation as their chief riches than cattle, we cannot expect that Kuruman will ever become populous. Regard for the welfare of their cattle will always lead them to choose more healthy locations for them than what this district presents.

That the Directors may judge whether my fears are well grounded, I may mention that within a circle of 8 or 10 miles around the station there are not a thousand inhabitants. The total number of native houses (occupied & unoccupied) on the station is 185. ± should be deducted for the unoccupied or used only as sort of store rooms and sleeping apartments for the unmarried females. But if we take this number, and take as an average the highest from frequent personal inspection I should say we can possibly give, viz. 5, we have only 925 as the total number of men, women, and children. The above average exceeds by 2 that usually taken by the French missionaries in estimating the population around them. There is however a much larger population about 16 miles off. Probably there are in that location 1,500 souls, amongst whom also the gospel has met with considerable success. In another direction, about 30 or 35 miles distant, there are two villages each containing from 150 to 200 inhabitants.

Although the population is small in this district, there is no want of inhabitants farther to the North and North-East. At Taons (pronounced Towns), which lies about East by North of this, Mr. Owen of the Church Missionary Society estimated the population at 15[000] or 20,000. The brethren itinerate thither although it is nearly 100 miles distant, and though but little positive success has attended their endeavours the prospect is cheering. The truth is working its way, and will soon prevail. Even the violent opposition manifested is encouraging, for anything is better than stupid indifference.

In view of the limited choice we are reduced to at this station, I may be allowed to suggest that we make the most of whatever agents we can find. Although desirable that they have somewhat more than decided piety, it is, I conceive, not absolutely necessary. Evils may arise from their ignorance and mistakes, but good will certainly be done, and I should hope it will abide, while the effects of their deficiencies will vanish before more efficient agents whom they themselves may now be instrumental in partially preparing. Making the most of every man under them seems to have been the reason, by the blessing of God, of the great success of the brethren at Griqua Town.

I purpose accompanying Br. Edwards in his journey to the interior, as I am informed by the brethren who are best able to judge it will be advantageous for me in many respects. I shall become better acquainted with the habits of the people [and] their language, and by exclusion from all European society for some time I hope to slip more readily into their mode of thinking, which is essentially different from ours. Mr. Edwards seems intimately acquainted with native character, and there is little fear but we shall be kindly received, more especially by those who have again & again sent messages for missionaries. There is reason to believe that the names of Hamilton, Edwards, & Moffat are well known hundreds of miles beyond us, as the nomadic habits of the people very much favours the transmission of news. We take with us two of the best qualified of our members here, for the purpose of planting them as native teachers in some promising locality, the expense of one of whom (if I do not receive in time the concurrence of Dr. Phillip) I shall endeavour to defray myself. The work is urgent. Souls are perishing, and what more efficient introduction can there be for the new missionaries, which I hope will soon follow us, than the residence for some months previously of one or two native teachers?

I am exceedingly gratified to observe the confidence which has been inspired into the minds of the Bechuanas of the efficacy of our medicines, by a very successful case of treatment which happened a day or two after our arrival. The brethren say it is altogether unprecedented, and an unsuccessful case since has not in the least abated their confidence. I feel thankful, and hope it will by the blessing of God enable me to win their attention to a much more important topic than the preservation of their bodies, even the salvation of their immortal souls.

Faithfully & affectionately yours,
David Livingston

To J. J. FREEMAN
Kuruman
22d Decr. 1841

The tribes within 100 miles North & North-East of this are all partially acquainted with the requirements of the gospel, but manifest the greatest hatred to them, and this is just what our knowledge of the human heart would lead us to expect. The same depravity exists everywhere, and this, although to Christians it may seem but the bare enunciation of a self-evident truth, ought to stand out prominently alongside the expectations of every young missionary. Those tribes however which lie at a greater distance, say 250 & 300 miles northward, are in quite a different condition. They know nothing of the gospel, & consequently form neither a good nor bad opinion of it. They know nothing more of missionaries than that they are a friendly race of whites who love all men, and in many respects we occupy the same position with respect to them as some of our missionaries have with the South Sea Islanders. There exists a strong impression in favour of Europeans, strongest among those not previously visited by missionaries, traders, &c, but only in a minor degree in the tribes nearer.

To account for this phenomenon, it is only necessary to remember the terrible scourging to which nearly all the Interior tribes have been in recent years subjected. They have experienced the cruelties of the invincible marauders who overan the whole country, and they have all heard of their successive repulses by mere handfuls of whites; and now the most distant are most anxious to secure the friendship of Europeans. The last marauder, the notorious Mosilekatsi, although obliged by the Boors to retire to the Eastern extremity of a lake in the Interior, has recently recommenced plundering, and the whole country is in a state of alarm. Those who dread him most have the greatest anxiety to obtain alliance with Europeans, and this feeling will induce them to receive either missionaries or teachers gladly.

Now if we can while this impression lasts confer on them a decided benefit, we may hope it will continue. But if we allow this opportunity to pass unimproved, it appears to me the time is not far distant when the Interior tribes will be in the same state of indifference & opposition to those nearer. Injurious influences are now in operation to effect this. The Boors of Port Natal have advanced right into the centre of the continent & seized most of the country & the best of the fountains towards the North-East. These on the one hand, and from this direction traders, Griqua hunters, & individuals from the tribes which hate the gospel, are every year passing in with more freedom, and in many instances they prove curses instead of blessings. (A Griqua has during this present year to my knowledge communicated the venereal disease to three tribes amongst whom it was unknown before. One of these has been visited by missionaries, but the other two have received one of the worst accompaniments of civilization before the missionaries came to give any of its blessings. This Griqua does not belong to any Mission station.)

May I beg an early intimation empowering us to make an effort immediately in behalf of the poor ignorant heathen in the Interior? If it is in accordance with the intentions of the Directors to form a new Mission in the Interior, I beg leave to call their attention to a tribe called the Bakhatla, the location of which is the best I have seen in the Interior. A large valley with a fountain about equal to this at Kuruman, & much more land, which by reason of the great height of the point from which the water comes out could be irrigated without any expense, abundance of pasture for cattle, with several other fountains at no great distance, and a manufacture of iron from ore found in abundance in the adjoining mountains, constitute the local attachments. Being a valley, however, it may be exposed to vicissitudes of temperature unfavourable to health, but it does not contain anything like the amount of decaying vegetable K[uruman] valley does, yet this is a healthy spot. I shall in my next furnish fuller information on this topic.

David Livingston

To John Arundel
Kuruman
22 Decr. 1841

Our journey was, in going & returning, at least 700 miles in length, but though so long we were not at any time more than 250 directly north. This however is farther in that direction than any missionaries have yet been. In one case the people had not before seen a white face, and in some others only one, viz. that of an enterprising trader who has frequently penetrated far beyond anyone else. We were however everywhere received with respect, and by those tribes situated farthest off even with kindness.

I was astonished at the difference observable near to Mission stations. Within a distance of 100 miles, the people who do not live actually on the stations are violent opponents of the gospel. They partially know the requirements of the gospel, they know they must put away their superfluous wives, &c &c, and on that account they hate it cordially. They won't listen. The chiefs to please the teachers call the people together, but the latter know the minds of the chiefs, & they refuse to come. They flock[e]d round the waggons for medicine, & would talk on any subject except that which of all others is the most important to be known, and I was pained to hear the scorn thrown on the name of Jesus when they thought I did not hear them. One chief got up a dance round Mr. Hamilton lately to drown his voice while preaching. This was an outrage that would not be committed by any other chief but himself, but though not openly opponents to that extent they are no less certainly unfavourable to preaching. When I say this I don't refer to those situated far beyond us. They know nothing of the gospel nor of missionaries, except that we are good people & friendly with all. But they, equally with those nearer & perhaps to a greater degree, possess an impression that Europeans are a decidedly superior race of people & it would be dangerous to provoke our enmity. In respect to their opinion of us, it must have undergone a complete revolution in the space of the last 20 years.

And to what are we to attribute this favourable change, by which any white man may travel through the length & breadth of the land without fear of molestation? It would be pleasant could we attribute it to the influence of the gospel which has so long, so affectionately & faithfully been preached to them. I expected this was the case, but when I have seen one impression over all the tribes, and this stronger in proportion as we recede from the regions where the gospel is known, I am compelled to give the credit of the change to a less lovely influence, viz. come & treated with great cruelty nearly all the Bechuanas, by a mere handful of Boors & Griquas.

But this impression, which exists in full force in all the tribes beyond 100 miles of this, will not long remain so. They are now purchasing guns themselves rapidly. They are visited by traders every year, and also by Griquas for the same purpose with the traders, and these latter are giving them the diseases of Europeans without any of their civilization. (The venereal disease was unknown amongst them until this same year it was taken into the Interior by a Griqua whom I know.) Persons also from the tribes adjoining us are passing in for the sake of getting game; and if a vigorous effort is not instantly made by us, I see no prospect left but that soon the tribes situated 200 & 250 miles distant will become as much opponents of the gospel as those within 100 miles of us.

Now you must not think me visionary when I say the effort could be made immediately. We don't need European missionaries to do it. They are good, but much can be done with far less expensive machinery. The whole of the tribes we visited could now be placed under effective instructors, had we only the means to employ them. The distant tribes would all receive them, not however from a desire to be instructed, for I could not ascertain that motive was present in the mind of a single individual we visited. It is not by any means like the South Sea Islands. One wishes a teacher because it will make him of more importance in the eyes of his neighbours, another expects a lot of guns with him, &c. But it is well they are willing at all to allow teachers to come amongst them. Some of the tribes nearer would not allow so much; they say if a white teacher comes we will listen to him, but we won't have a black one. This however is just an excuse, for they won't listen to a white teacher neither. The native teachers are really most efficient agents in the dissemination of religious truth, and if we had two with each of the Interior tribes I don't hesitate to affirm that as much would by the Divine blessing be effected by them, in the way of removing prejudice & enlightening & saving the people, as would be effected by any two Europeans for the first half dozen years at least.

That you may judge whether I am right or not, I shall mention some facts which I wish I could mention to the Directors without appearing to make an invidious comparison. The facts stare me every party feeling and anything like impeaching the wisdom of those who have preceded me in the work, & who are all greatly my superiors in prudence

& piety, I should certainly make them publicly known to the Directors. But knowing that they are fully aware of the value of native agents, & that they need nothing from me to strengthen their conviction on the subject, I do no more than mention them to you privately for your own information.

It has been the policy of the Griqua Town missionaries all along to employ native agents. The consequence has been, the believers have increased in a compound ratio. They have many imperfections, but God has blessed them wonderfully. On our way here we unexpectedly came upon a village on a Sunday morning, the want of water having compelled us to travel at that time. They knew nothing of us, & we were entirely ignorant of them. Yet we found that public worship & school for the children were regularly kept up, although from the illness of Mr. Hughs, & the distance being 60 or 80 miles from Griqua Town, they had been visited by no missionary for 10 months previously. This fact greatly strengthened my predilections in favour of employing as soon as possible all who are capable of making known the way of life. We had the best possible opportunity of observing their conduct, and who after seeing it would not wish to have a band of such assistants to aid on the cause of truth & holiness?

They have imperfections, but I see nothing else in the operations of the G. Town Mission to account for its success but these very imperfect instruments. The missionaries now can do little else than itinerate & superintend them, and they occupy not only what may be called their own field, but great part of ours. Am I sorry to see them stretching out on all sides & passing us as they are now doing W. by N.? No, I rejoice at it, & don't care though they hug us by & by in their arms & squeeze us out towards the North. If no other motive will send us north, their progress will. It is all the same whoever brings in sinners to Christ. It is common cause, & I am really glad to see the work going on. But unfortunately a little rivalry other than provoking to love & good works has got in amongst us, & those who have been longer in the work have local associations which prevent them seeing some things in the same light we do. They look at the subject from a different point of view, & consequently it appears in another form to them.

But native agency has been tried here too, as well as at Griqua Town. After Mr. Moffat went to England he seems to have changed a little his opinions on that subject, for he wrote back advising the brethren here to make a trial of two. These were appointed, and the consequence has been a large accession to the church. Each at his location has more members under him than are at the station . . . & the chief accessions . . . are always from their ministry. Add to this they are much more consistent in their deportment than those here, & so affectionate to us & to each other it is quite a treat to visit them. And this notwithstanding Mr. Edwards is an excellent Sicuana scholar, & an excellent preacher in it too. Since I understand him I am quite delighted to hear him. I believe this is the case too with the G[riquatown] Mission, for the truth seems so much more effectual & comes home to the heart better in proportion as it is divested of all that strangeness which attaches to foreigners in every country.

I am most anxious that more native teachers be employed, & in this anxiety the brethren E[dwards] & Hamilton now both cordially join. Along with this I make an application to the Directors, and I wait with much anxiety for an answer.

I should feel greatly obliged by a communication, however short. Please let me know how you are in health. My sheet is filled, & I have not said half of what I would, but I shall write you again I hope a more connected letter.

Yours affectionately,
D. Livingston

Kuruman
3rd July 1842
Dear Sir,

On the 10th of February last I left this station, and having proceeded into the interior of the Bechuana country remained there during the months March, April, May, and part of June. The whole of that period was characterised by the continued manifestation of the Divine goodness towards me, and now, with humble gratitude to Him whose Providential care watched over and brought me back in safety, I shall endeavour to state to you the objects for which this journey was undertaken, and the manner in which they were followed out.

The objects I had in view were the following: that I might by exclusive intercourse with the natives facilitate my labour in the acquisition of the language, that I might for a season be freed from all attention to medicine, and that, though still but imperfectly acquainted with their tongue, I might make an effort for the eternal welfare of the tribe or tribes with whom I should sojourn by means of native agents.

In order the more effectually to carry into operation the last & principal object I had in contemplation, I took with me two natives, members of the church in this place, and with two others connected with the management of the waggon we proceeded in a direction nearly North-East of Moteeto. This route brought us near to none of the tribes which lie East and West of it, and consequently we saw no people save a few of the Bakalihari and Bushmen, until after twelve days' travelling we arrived in the valley of the Bakhatla. There we saw three villages, each of which may be stated to contain a population of 400 souls. The situations of these are very inviting, for the valley is both beautiful and large, not less I think than forty miles in length and from two to four in breadth, and besides abundance of iron-stone it contains no fewer than seven fountains, each of which pours out a copious supply of excellent water.

As the people, however, are the sole manufacturers of the iron and wooden utensils in use among the Bechuanas, and in trading pass among all the tribes to the Southward, I thought it probable that they may have imbibed some of the prejudices to the gospel which prevail to such a lamentable extent among these, and consequently might not be in such a favourable state for the operations of native teachers as some tribes which live still farther to the North. We therefore only remained a few days with them. Their behaviour to us was, however, as kind as we could have expected. We found no difficulty in collecting them together, and when we addressed them on salvation by Christ they listened with respectful attention. I earnestly hope the time is not far distant when they shall hear statedly said with believing hearts the glad tidings of mercy.

Nearly directly North of the Bakhatla and a little more than one hundred miles distant lives Bubi, one of the chiefs of the Bakwain (Baquane), and one of the most sensible of his class I have yet seen. To him we next proceeded, and the very friendly reception Mr. Edwards and I met with from both him and his people last year, the very favourable character he bears among all the tribes, and the fact that Mr E. found them entirely ignorant of the gospel, induced me to prefer making a commencement for a native teacher with them.

. . . I proceeded Northward in order to visit the Bamangwato, Bakaa, and Makalaka, three tribes having their countries in Lat. 22° S. and stretching from 28° to 30° E. Long. The last-named is the smallest of the three, but it is a section of a people of very considerable numbers and who speak a language differing very decidedly from the Sitchuana. None of the Bechuanas I had with me could understand it. But from some of the words which I caught, I am inclined to think it belongs to the same root with their tongue. Their manners, too, are somewhat different from the Southern tribes, inasmuch as they are not entirely dependent on the rude kaross for covering, but manufacture cotton cloth for shawls &c. And besides the knowledge how to manufacture iron and copper, one of the five tribes into which the Makalaka are divided, called the Mashona, fight with guns instead of the assagai. These they obtain from the Portuguese on the Eastern coast, and from some circumstances which have come to my knowledge I am inclined to believe they procure them in exchange for slaves.

By conversation with many different individuals, and these of different grades, I ascertained the existence of no fewer than 28 tribes of people hitherto unknown to Europeans. Thirteen of these are reported to have another tongue, and the remainder speak Sitchuana. But as reports cannot (however carefully examined) be absolutely depended on, I shall turn to those which I myself visited.

Our route to the Bamangwato skirted the sandy desert which flanks the Bechuana country to the Westward. And as the sand proved very fatiguing for the oxen, when within 40 or 50 miles from that people they were unable to proceed farther, and I had to leave both oxen and waggon and perform my visit on foot. But I had not the least reason to regret having done so, for the chief (Sekomi) was evidently pleased that I had thrown myself on his bounty without the least appearance of distrust. Indeed, before I had been 10 minutes in his company, and while sitting surrounded by hundreds of his people, he began to shew his satisfaction by feeding me with the flesh of the rhinoceros and some other things which they consider dainties. He then took me to the house of his mother, presented me with a large elephant's tusk, more food, and, as we became better acquainted, he frequently and emphatically exclaimed, 'You have come to us just like rain', and 'If you had brought your waggon I should have detained you at least a month looking at you'.

Sekomi has a large number of people under him. In the town alone I numbered 600 houses, which is a number considerably larger than I have been able to count in any other Bechuana town in the country. But they are all very small, and cannot contain many individuals each. The one in which I lived was quite as large as any in the town, and three of us could not sleep in it without touching each other, unless we put out our fire.

The population is sunk into the very lowest state of both mental and moral degradation, so much so indeed it must be difficult or rather impossible for Christians at home to realize anything like an accurate notion of the grossness of the darkness which shrouds their minds. I could not ascertain that they had the least idea of a future state. And though they have some notions which seem to us to be connected with a belief in its existence, I have not met one who could put the necessary links together in the chain of reasoning so as to become possessed of the definite idea. Indeed, they all confess that they never think of anything connected with death, and do not wish the introduction of that subject. Their conceptions of Deity are of the most vague and contradictory nature, and his name conveys no more to their understanding than the idea of superiority. Hence they do not hesitate to apply the name of God to their chiefs, and I was every day shocked by being addressed by that title, and although it as often furnished me with a text from which to tell them of the only true God, and Jesus Christ whom He has sent, yet it deeply pained me, and I never felt so fully convinced of the lamentable deterioration of my species before. It is indeed a mournful truth that 'man has become like the beasts that perish'.

The country abounds with lions, and so much are they dreaded by the natives one man never goes out alone. The women have always some one to guard them when they go to their gardens, & they always go in companies to draw water, for the sake of the protection which numbers give. Nor are these precautions unnecessary. For a time I could not believe but that they were. But the earnestness with which the chief... [chided] me for going a few hundred yards from the town unattended, and the circumstance that he always sent an attendant if at any time he saw me going out afterwards, together with the fact that a woman was actually devoured in her garden during my visit, and that so near the town I had frequently walked far past it, fully convinced me that there are good grounds for their fears and precautions. It was most affecting to hear the cries of the orphan children of this woman. During the whole day after her death the surrounding rocks and valleys rung and re-echoed with their bitter cries.

I frequently thought, as I listened to the loud sobs painfully indicative of the sorrows of those who have no hope, that if some of our churches could have heard their sad wailings it would have awakened the firm resolution to do more for the Heathen than they have done. In some countries the light which the gospel once shed has gone out and darkness has succeeded. But though eighteen centuries have elapsed since life and immortality were brought to light, there is no certainty that these dark regions were ever before visited for the purpose of making known the light and liberty and peace of the glorious gospel. It would seem that the myriads who have peopled these regions have always passed away into darkness, and no ray from heaven ever beamed on their path. And with whom does the guilt rest if not with us who compose the church militant on earth?

You will, I am sure, bear with me in this digression from my narrative, for my mind is filled with sadness when I contemplate the prospects of these large masses of immortal souls. I see no hopes for them except in native agents. The more I see of the country, its large extent of surface, with its population scattered and each tribe separated by a formidable distance from almost every other, I feel the more convinced that it will be impossible if not impolitic for the church to supply them all with Europeans. Native Christians *can* make known the way of life. There are some in connection with both this and the church at Griqua Town who have done it effectually. Others too are rising up who will soon be capable of teaching, and if their energies are not brought into operation by taking up the field now open before us, I don't see where the benevolent spirit which we hope is springing up among the converts of the two Missions is to find an outlet. I conceive that even now the two Missions by cordial cooperation might at once supply with native teachers all the tribes within the range of our knowledge who are not inimical to claims of the gospel. It would not require more than six from each Mission to give two to each friendly tribe. And that this measure, or an attempt at it, would be advantageous to both churches, I need not refer you to the effects which increased benevolent exertions have on churches at home, and how often it happens that when churches have not work set before them in the cause of Christ, even more than they can actually perform, their benevolence degenerates into selfish quarreling. You will please to observe that I do not advance this proposition without diffidence, for I am sensible my sentiments, on account of want of experience, are entitled to much less deference than those of others in the same field.

With respect to the prospects for missions in the Interior, I think they are encouraging. There is no desire to have us, but there is security for both life & property with any of all the tribes we know, and scope for our labours provided we enter the field. Here on the outskirts we might remain without the probability of being disturbed, but we should not have scope so wide as in thousands of villages in England. We must I conceive go forward, and go forward far too, in order to get at the heathenism of this country.

7th July. I beg leave thankfully to acknowledge the receipt of your kind favour of the 18th February last, which has just come to hand. I look anxiously for your next, as I hope it will contain something definite respecting the Interior.

I beg leave to remain,
affectionately yours,
David Livingston

John Gibbs (1811–1875) was the son of an Irish captain of the Royal Cork Volunteers. He trained under Vincent Priessnitz, the father of the water cure, and then operated a hydropathic establishment himself at Barking around midcentury. There he oversaw water cures himself—a regime of hot and cold baths that were intended to produce a "crisis" in the patient who can then expel the disease or sickness through the skin. A teetotaler, anti-vaccinator, and medical reformer, Gibbs contributed to a variety of alternative medicine journals. In the pamphlet below he protests against state-sponsored vaccination as "bungling, tyrannical, un-English, and un-christian legislation."

John Gibbs, from *Our Medical Liberties* (1854)

. . . The Compulsory Vaccination Act, while dishonouring science, invades in the most odious, tyrannical, and, speaking as a Briton, unexampled manner the liberty of the subject, and the sanctity of home; unspeakably degrades the free-born Briton not only in depriving him of liberty of choice in a personal matter, but even in denying him the possession of reason; outrages some of the finest feelings and best affections of the human heart;—those feelings and affections which have their origin in parental love—that still bright spark of the Divine Nature breathed into man by his Heavenly Father;—sets at nought parental authority and responsibility, and coerces the parent either to violate his deliberate, cherished, and conscientious convictions, and even his religious scruples, or boldly to defy an unjust and tyrannous law.

This measure fails to satisfy even that body to whose prejudices it panders, whose selfish interests it subserves, and to whom its tyrannical clauses are especially grateful, and it is to undergo revision this session, not for the sake of consulting the interests and feelings of the subject, but with a view still further to gratify the prejudices, avarice, and vain-glory of grasping and usurping men. Nevertheless, this revision affords a favourable opportunity for the wronged, despised, and insulted laity to insist upon the repeal of the compulsory clauses. Last session the cabmen won the repeal of obnoxious enactments; are the friends of medical liberty less united, less numerous, or less influential?

. . . Once begun, where is such legislation to end? Is every presumed good thing in medical practice to be forced upon us? If one thing, why not another? Are we to be leeched, bled, blistered, burned, douched, frozen, pilled, potioned, lotioned, salivated, not only *secundum artem,* but by Act of Parliament? The glorious uncertainty of law wedded to the inglorious uncertainty of physic! What an union! Shall we be compelled to adopt that famous scientific remedy for enlargement of the heart—which cures the disease and kills the patient? or the wonderful remedies of any eminent specialist,—that is, when the learned gentleman shall have finally made up his mind what those shall be? It has been gravely proposed to inoculate with scarlatina as a protection from this disease; and also with the virus of the most loathsome of all diseases as a protection likewise from it; shall we have forced upon us these blessings too by Act of Parliament? Imagine Parliament the arena for discussing the merits of the conflicting doctrines and practices of the medical schools and sects! . . .

If it can be proved that vaccination is a blessing worthy of universal acceptance, let it be done. As a parent, I for one, shall greatly rejoice; and, doubtless, amongst those who now oppose it, will arise some of its most zealous and active advocates; but, in any event, let us have no bungling, tyrannical, un-English, and un-christian legislation. Let us leave compulsion to countries like Austria, where the number of hens a man may keep in his yard, or the number of bakers, or butchers, in a town, are alike regulated by law, and where the subject may be forcibly seized by the police, and carried off and vaccinated; or like Sweden, where prayers out of church, or out of canonical hours, are illegal; and where children are forcibly torn from their nurses' or parents' arms and triumphantly borne away to church and baptized. Compulsion does not suit England.

If Jenner were living now, I believe, that he, who himself suffered persecution, would be the first to raise his voice against compulsory vaccination. Be that as it may, let us remember that we do not derive our liberties from, or hold them by, the sufferance of our rulers, and that our rights are unalienable and cannot be confiscated by any earthly power. We had ancestors, who so loved liberty, that they would not surrender it for any material interests whatever; from the moment that we begin to weigh the latter against the former, and to falter in our choice, future historians will date the commencement of the decadence of public spirit and national greatness.

. . . Britons! guard well your hard-won precious rights. Surrender not even that one, which, in the immensity of your riches, may appear of but trivial value. Keep your medical liberties intact. You must preserve them all, or you must lose them all; and remember that with them must be lost, or preserved, no small portion of your civil and religious liberties as well; they are all intimately and inseparably united. Let no unhallowed tongue beguile you; let no unhallowed hand despoil you!

Isaac Butt (1813–1870) was one of the founders of the Home Rule League, whose object was winning self-government for Ireland. The Home Rule MPs created what was effectively an independent party at Westminster, with their own executive council, secretaries, and whips. Underscoring both the relative conservatism of his views and the long shadow that the Union continued to cast on British politics, Butt claimed that all he asked was that "the 100 Irish Members should be sent back again to a Parliament of their own, and the English Parliament might go on sitting as it was now."

Isaac Butt, Parliamentary speech (1874)

MR. BUTT rose to move the Resolution of which he had given Notice—

"That this House resolve itself into a Committee of the Whole House, to consider the present Parliamentary relations between Great Britain and Ireland."

The hon. and learned Member said, that as a large number of the people of Ireland entertained the opinion that the present relations between the two countries were un-satisfactory, he felt that those opinions ought to be submitted to the consideration of this House. In the difficulties in which he was placed in bringing the question forward, he certainly had this support—that he knew he was addressing an audience that would give him every indulgence. He had already read the Motion which he intended to sub-mit to the House, and if he were fortunate enough to obtain assent to it, and they went into Committee, he intended further to move—

"That it is expedient and just to restore to the Irish Nation the right and power of managing all exclusively Irish affairs in an Irish Parliament; and that provision should be made at the same time for maintaining the integrity of the Empire and the connection between the Countries by reserving to this Imperial Parliament full and exclusive con-trol over all Imperial affairs."

. . . He believed his duty was to put the House, as far as possible, in possession of the fullest and most complete information as to the plan he intended to submit, the new arrangement he proposed in the place of that which now existed, and which he main-tained was imperfect. He believed he was entitled to do this with some authority, for in the course of last autumn he and those who agreed with him in wishing for a new arrangement, as far as the present law of the land permitted them, took steps to obtain the general opinion of the people of Ireland. A requisition, signed by 25,000 persons fairly representing the middle classes, at all events, of three of the Provinces, and no in-considerable portion of the fourth, had been got up for the purpose of having a Con-ference in Dublin, where the plan he now proposed was fully and deliberately considered. At that Conference certain Resolutions were adopted, and 59 Irish Mem-bers who were returned to the present Parliament entirely assented to those Resolutions. After that there could no longer be any room for doubt as to what the Irish people de-sired, and whatever might be the decision of the House on that question, he was anx-ious that it should be distinctly understood that they were not seeking separation from England, but that, whether their plan was right or wrong, the object was to perpetuate and consolidate the connection between the two countries. In the Resolutions to which he referred, the Conference declared it to be their conviction that it was essential to the peace and prosperity of the people of Ireland that they should have the right of domes-tic legislation with respect to all Irish affairs; that the right of the Irish people to self-government by means of a Parliament assembled in that country was inalienable; that in asking for those rights he adopted the principle of a Federal arrangement which would secure to that Parliament the power of regulating all the internal affairs of the country, while leaving all Imperial questions to be decided by the Imperial Legislature, such as all matters relating to the defence of the Empire and the providing of supplies for Imperial purposes. The Resolutions which the Conference passed, embodying these views, laid down the principles of the party very distinctly, and, so far as he could see, there would be no difficulty in carrying them into effect. . . . In the next place, he would direct their attention to this fact—that they involved no change in the Constitution; and he was anxious that the House should clearly understand this. He proposed no change in the

Imperial Parliament, and if his scheme were adopted, the House would meet next year just as it had done this; there would not be a single change in Members or constituencies; there would be the Members for Leeds, Glasgow, Dublin, and Limerick—the only change would be to take from that Assembly some of the duties which it now discharged in reference to Irish business, and to relegate them to another.

. . . The Irish people had never given their assent to the surrender of their Parliamentary rights, and the authority of the United Parliament rested, so far as Ireland was concerned, upon crime as great as that which caused the disruption of Poland. He, as a friend of order, regretted that such was the case, and he thought it would be better for both countries that the authority should rest in the willing assent of the people, and not be supported, as now, by force. In weighing the desire of the people for restoration, they must not ignore the passions and the prejudices of the nation, their attachment to old principles, their indignation at the fraud perpetrated on them, and the wrong done them in wresting independent government from them. These were the forces at work which statesmen could not ignore. The Union having been carried there was no dissolution of the English Parliament, the 100 Irish Members simply took their seats in the English House of Commons, and there was an end of the matter. All he asked was that the 100 Irish Members should be sent back again to a Parliament of their own, and the English Parliament might go on sitting as it was now. Did the Representatives of English constituencies wish that Irish Members should vote on English questions? He believed they did not. The English Parliament, including the Scotch Members—he would perhaps have a word to say on the last point presently—would meet to discuss purely English affairs, and when there was any question affecting the Empire at large, Irish Members might be summoned to attend. He saw no difficulty in the matter. The English Parliament could manage English affairs as before the Union; but now the English Parliament undertook a duty it was unable to perform—namely, to manage the internal affairs of Ireland to the satisfaction of the Irish people. He did not seek to interfere with the right of taxing Ireland for Imperial purposes, providing always that Ireland had a voice in Imperial matters. He was asking only for a constitutional Government, and the benefit of those free institutions which had made England great. If he succeeded in showing that Ireland had not a Constitutional Government, then he thought he could rely on the justice and generosity of the English Parliament and of the Commons at large to give it to her. What was Constitutional Government? It consisted of adequate representation in Parliament—a control of the administration of affairs by a Representative Assembly of the people, so as to bring the Government of the country into harmony with the feeling, the wants, and the wishes of the people. Did the representation by 103 Irish Members in the English House of Commons amount to that? Could it be said that that House discharged the great function of Constitutional Government to Ireland? If it did not, then it followed that Ireland was deprived of that Constitutional Government which was its inherent right. He knew it might be said that this involved the question whether Ireland and England were not so blended into one nation, that the same House might discharge the duties of a Representative Assembly for both. That, again, was a matter of fact. The House might wish that they were all West Britons, but wishes would not alter facts. They should deal with things as they were.

. . . Would any hon. Member venture to say that Ireland had a Constitutional Government? Was there a department of the Irish Administration which did not consider it its highest policy to thwart the wishes of the Irish people? ["Oh!"] That he said deliberately. Apart from the office of Lord Chancellor there were five great and important administrative offices in Ireland:—that of the Chief Secretary, the Chief of the Irish Constabulary—that Irish Army of Occupation which was not placed in that country for the purposes of police—the First Commissioner of Police in Dublin, the Chief of the Local Government Board, and the chief of a very powerful, but anomalous Board—namely, the Board of Works. How many of these were Irishmen? Not a single one. And these were offices the owners of which were brought into daily contact with the life of the people. They were all filled at this moment by Englishmen or Scotchmen. He did not complain of Englishmen or Scotchmen holding offices in Ireland, but he thought it something more than a coincidence that five such offices should be so filled. He did not complain upon the administration of the foreign affairs of the Empire. On the contrary, he wished the Queen to have one Parliament to advise her upon foreign affairs, and to use the whole resources of the United Kingdom whenever it was necessary to do so; but he would try the Union by the administration of Irish affairs. At the end of 73 years of union with the richest country in the world, Ireland was, in proportion to its resources, the poorest country in Europe; and at the end of 73 years of union with the freest country in the world, Ireland laboured under a system of coercion more galling and oppressive than existed at that moment in any civilized European State. What had become of her population? In 1800 England contained 9,000,000 people, and Ireland about half that number. England had increased to 22,000,000, while Ireland had to point to destroyed houses and depopulated villages, and to a people flying across the Atlantic with hostile feelings, he regretted to say, towards the people and the Government of England.

. . . Was there an Englishman in the House who would not be glad to get rid of the opprobriums attaching to the Government of Ireland? If the wish was really entertained, the way to get rid of it was by allowing the Irish people an opportunity of trying to govern themselves. If they succeeded, great and glorious would be the reward of those who gave the opportunity; if they failed, theirs alone would be the blame. And where was there to be found any valid objection to granting what they asked? The Imperial Parliament would hold the Army, the Navy, and all that was connected with affairs purely Imperial, and no difficulty would be found in separating from Imperial questions those with which an Irish Parliament might properly deal. The United States of America afforded an illustration of a successful Federal Government with independent State Legislatures, and in some of our own Colonies they found instances of people owning the Imperial sway of England, but at the same time managing their own internal affairs. Even supposing that there might be some disaffected Members of an Irish Parliament— and this he did not admit—they would be in a miserable minority, and the fact of their disaffection being open to the light would give the strongest assurance of its speedy extinction. In two English Colonies were to be found men who, driven out of Ireland because they could no longer endure the system of Government existing there, had become Ministers under the British Crown, and were doing honour alike to the Colonies in which they served and to the Sovereign who had appointed them. Sir George Grey, the Governor of the Cape of Good Hope, wrote strongly in favour of giving a Federal Parliament to Ireland, and he believed in his soul that it would be the means of effecting a complete union with England. Wrong had driven a large proportion of the Irish people into the madness of insurrection or sympathy with insurrection. It was, indeed, the consciousness of this fact which made him set himself earnestly to work to devise a means of stopping this miserable series of abortive insurrections and revolts by which Ireland had been torn and some of the best and bravest of her sons driven into exile. He believed he had devised a plan which would satisfy the just demands of the people without pro-ducing a disintegration of the Empire; therefore, he had asked the people to give up the madness of revolt and join with him in constitutionally and peacefully making an ap-peal to England. Many of the people who supported this moderate proposal would waste their lives in useless struggles against England, if they saw no other redress for the sufferings of their country. Was any Irishman satisfied with the way in which Irish busi-ness was conducted in that House? Why, if it was only for the physical impossibility of the House transacting such business in a satisfactory manner he would have made out his case. Were Scotchmen satisfied with the way Scotch business was done, or indeed were Englishmen satisfied with the way English business was done? English business was hurried through at 2 or 3 o'clock in the morning, without discussion, because the House was overburdened with work. This was an injury to the character of the House. They were giving up something every day. He said nothing about the curtailment of the priv-ileges of Irish Members, and nothing about the shortening of discussions in order that business might be done. The House 30 years ago completely gave up the right of debate upon Petitions, which Lord Brougham said was one of the greatest blows that was ever struck at free discussions in the House, but it was inevitable.

   . . . It was idle to maintain that the Irish electors did not know what Home Rule meant. He did not mean to say that every man who voted for a Home Rule candidate knew all the details of the plan he had just explained, but neither did every voter who contributed to the Conservative reaction understand all the Conservative principles. But scarcely a man voted for Home Rule who did not perfectly understand he was voting to gain back to Ireland the management of Irish affairs, while pledging the country to sub-mit in all general concerns to the authority of this Parliament. He had passed very rapidly over a great many things, but he had endeavoured to show the plan which they proposed, and which had been adopted after long discussion and full deliberation, and he asked the House not lightly to reject the demand. He believed the Irish people were essentially Conservative. It was only misgovernment that had driven them into revolt. Give them fair play, and there was no people on earth who would be more attached to true Conservative principles than the Irish nation. The geographical position of Ireland made it her interest to be united with England. They were allied to England by ties of kindred and ties of self-interest, which bound them to maintain inviolate the connec-tion with this country, and the way to maintain that connection was to give them jus-tice in the management of their own internal affairs. Had they justice at present? Was the election franchise the same in the two countries? In Ireland one man in 25 had a vote; in England one in six. In Ireland a man must rent a house, paying £10 rent, to enjoy the municipal franchise; in England the renter of a £1 house could enjoy the fran-chise; and let them remember that it was since the Union the franchise was varied in the two countries. Give us—continued the hon. and learned Gentleman—a full participa-tion in your freedom, and make us sharers in those free institutions which have made England so great and glorious. Give us our share which we have not now in that great-est and best of all free institutions—a free Parliament, representing indifferently the whole people. . . . Are we under equal laws? Is there no trace in your policy of conquest? Give us a new participation in a new compact, carried, not by fraud and coercion, but founded on the free sanction of the Irish people. Backed as I am now by 60 Represen-tatives of the Irish people, in their name I offer you this compact, and I believe if it is accepted it will be, humanly speaking, eternal. Omniscience alone can foresee, and Om-nipotence alone can control the events of the far off and distant future; but speaking for us who can calculate and deal with the forces that move men in the present day, I believe that if you give Ireland the management of her own affairs, many a day will pass before there will be any change in the connection between the two countries. It is with reference to these views; it is in the confidence of these hopes; it is with an unwavering faith in these convictions that I now submit these Resolutions.

Charles Stewart Parnell (1846–91) came from an Anglican gentry family and became the Nationalist MP for County Meath in 1875 and Cork in 1880. He was the leading Irish Nationalist in Parliament from 1878, managing the difficult task of coordinating political bargaining at Westminster with radical movements and constituencies in Ireland.

Charles Stewart Parnell, Speech at Wicklow (1885)

It may appear preposterous, and it undoubtedly would be preposterous, to ask England to concede to us an engine which we announced our intention of using to bring about either separation of the two countries, or which we accepted silently with the intention of so using it; but there is great difference between having such an intention, or announcing such an intention, and giving counter guarantees against such an intention. It is not possible for human intelligence to forecast the future in these matters; but we can point to this—we can point to the fact that under 85 years of parliamentary connexion with England, Ireland has become intensely disloyal and intensely disaffected (*applause*); that notwithstanding the whig policy of so-called conciliation, alternative conciliation and coercion, and ameliorative measures, that disaffection has broadened, deepened and intensified from day to day (*cheers*). Am I not, then, entitled to assume that one of the roots of this disaffection and feeling of disloyalty is the assumption by England of the management of our affairs (*cheers*). It is admitted that the present system can't go on, and what are you going to put in its place? (Cries of '*Home Rule*') My advice to English statesmen considering this question would be this—trust the Irish people altogether or trust them not at all (*cheers*).Give with a full and open hand—give our people the power to legislate upon all their domestic concerns, and you may depend upon one thing, that the desire for separation, the means of winning separation at least, will not be increased or intensified (*cheers*). Whatever chance the English rulers may have of drawing to themselves the affection of the Irish people lies in destroying the abominable system of legislative union between the two countries by conceding fully and freely to Ireland the right to manage her own affairs. It is impossible for us to give guarantees, but we can point to the past; we can show that the record of English rule is a constant series from bad to worse (*cheers*), that the condition of English power is more insecure and more unstable at the present moment than it has ever been (*applause*). We can point to the example of other countries; of Austria and of Hungary—to the fact that Hungary having been conceded self-government became one of the strongest factors in the Austrian empire. We can show the powers that have been freely conceded to the colonies—to the greater colonies—including this very power to protect their own industries against and at the expense of those of England. We can show that disaffection had disappeared in all the greater English colonies, that while the Irishman who goes to the United States of America carries with him a burning hatred of English rule (*cheers*); that while that burning hatred constantly lives in his heart, never leaves him, and is bequeathed to his children, the Irishman coming from the same village, and from the same parish, and from the same townland, equally maltreated, cast out on the road by the relentless landlord, who goes to one of the colonies of Canada or one of the colonies of Australia, and finds there another and a different system of English rule to that which he has been accustomed to at home, becomes to a great extent a loyal citizen and a strength and a prop to the community amongst whom his lot has been cast; that he forgets the little memories of his experience of England at home, and that he no longer continues to look upon the name of England as a symbol of oppression, and the badge of the misfortunes of his country (*cheers*). I say that it is possible, and that it is the duty of English statesmen at the present day to inquire and examine into these facts for themselves with their eyes open; and to cease the impossible task, which they admit to be impossible, of going forward in the continued misgovernment of Ireland and persisting in the government of our people outside herself who know not her real wants (cheers); and if these lessons be learned, I am convinced that the English statesman who is great enough, and who is powerful enough to carry out these teachings, to enforce them on the acceptance, of his countrymen, to give to Ireland full legislative liberty, full power to manage her own domestic concerns, will be regarded in the future by his countrymen as one who has removed the greatest peril to the English empire (*hear, hear*)—a peril, I firmly believe, which if not removed will find some day, perhaps not in our time-some year, perhaps not for many years to come, but will certainly find sooner or later, and it may be sooner than later, an opportunity of revenging itself (*loud cheers*)—to the destruction of the British empire for the misfortunes, the oppressions, and the misgovernment of our country (*loud cheers:*).

Syed Ameer Ali (1849–1928) was a barrister by training and a judge of the Calcutta High Court with a specialty in Muslim law. He founded the National Mahommedan Association in 1877 in part because he believed that without a political organization India's Muslims would not be able to claim the rights and privileges they sought from the colonial administration.

Syed Ameer Ali, "A Cry from the Indian Mahommedans" (1882)

The over-sensitiveness of the Indian Government and its subordinate officers to outside criticism has the tendency to discourage, among the intellectual and educated classes of India, the frank expression of political feelings even when their publication is likely to prove of value to the Government itself. An honest criticism is often construed into a hostile attack; and outspoken comments on the policy of Government, however, legitimate in their character, are not unfrequently supposed to imply disloyalty. In Bengal, however, the Hindu community is enabled, by the wealth and education of its representative members, to ignore to some extent this liability to disfavour, and to express its views on important questions affecting its own interest with sufficient candour and emphasis to reach the ears of the governing classes. The Muslims possess neither the wealth nor the education of the Hindus; and, in consequence, have generally failed to attract the attention of the authorities to their grievances.

. . . Within the last twenty-five years great changes have taken place in India, and during this time every community under British rule has prospered, except the Muslim, which stands alone as the marked and disappointing exception. It is no exaggeration to say that English officials generally are at this day as far from understanding the real feelings of the Indian Muslims as they were half a century ago. Want of sufficient interest on one side, and absence of qualified exponents on the other, explain the imperfect knowledge possessed by the official world of India with regard to the Muslims. There is an increasing desire, however, to deal equitably and generously with them, and it therefore becomes important that the statesmen who at the present moment rule the destinies of India should be enabled to judge of the requirements of the Muslims in connection with their alleged grievances. That a homogeneous people like the Muslims of India, numbering fifty millions and having a common language and religion, should be discontented with the position they now occupy, is a matter for the serious consideration of the administrators of Indian policy.

. . . I now propose to offer a few practical suggestions, from a Muslim standpoint, for the solution of the great Muslim problem. The unsatisfactory condition of the Muslims has already forced itself on the attention of Government. It is necessary, therefore, that the views of the Muslims themselves, as to the remedial measures essential for their well-being, should be plainly and publicly stated. The time for mere sentimental expressions of sympathy and infructuous minutes and resolutions, leading to nothing, has gone by. Effectual measures are needed; words alone have no practical result. Government has for some time past expressed its sympathy for the Muslims, and the present Government is notably animated with a sincere desire to redress their wrongs and grievances. The Viceroy's reply to a recent address of the National Muhammadan Association lays special stress upon his desire to deal with all her Majesty's subjects on a footing of equality. In spite of all this, the condition of the Muslims, instead of improving, has within the last decade become worse. This, no doubt, arises from the fact that the same desire to deal equitably with the Muslims is not shared by the officers who really hold the threads of government in their hands. The first and foremost condition necessary for the prosperity of the Muslims is that the balance of state patronage between them and the Hindus should be restored. This however, cannot be achieved unless the officers with whom rest the actual distribution and dispensation of it lend their zealous support to the efforts of Government. Under the Treaty of 1765 the Muslims are fairly entitled to ask for greater consideration at the hands of the British than has latterly been shown to them, though perhaps it would be unreasonable of them to expect any such preponderating influence under the English Government as they possessed under their own sovereigns. But this is not, as Dr. Hunter in eloquent terms has pointed out, their petition and their complaint. 'It is not that they have ceased to retain the entire state patronage, but that they are gradually being excluded from it altogether. It is not that they must now take an equal chance with the Hindus in the race of life, but that, at least in Bengal, they have ceased to have a chance at all.' Under their own government the Muslims possessed several avenues to wealth and power. The army and police were officered by them; the administration of justice and the collection of the Imperial revenues were largely monopolised by Muslims. The department of education was exclusively in their hands. Long before the great Hindu Chancellor, Todar Mal, had introduced Persian into the subordinate departments, the Hindus had begun to learn the language of their masters with as much zeal as they now learn the English. Even towards the close of their empire, the Muslims represented the intellectual power of the land. Their system of education was 'infinitely superior to any other system of education then existing in India.' It was a reflex of the system which had been in vogue at Cordova and Baghdad, and which had enabled their ancestors to hold aloft the torch of knowledge, while all around them was lost in darkness. Their polish and their civilisation were by no means inferior to that of the Western nations, and their intellectual supremacy was as undisputed as their material power. Dr. Hunter remarks that 'during the first seventy-five years of our rule, we continued to make use of this (the Muslim system of education) as a means for producing officers to carry out our administration. But meanwhile we had introduced a scheme of public instruction of our own; and as soon as it trained up a generation of men on the new plan, we flung aside the old Muslim system, and the Muslim youth found every avenue of public life closed in their faces.' 'Had the Muslims been wise,' continues Dr. Hunter, 'they would have perceived the change and accepted their fate.' But they were not wise; they felt secure in a fool's paradise, and thus, when the old system was suddenly abolished, they either could not divest themselves of the traditions of their nobler days, or could not accustom themselves easily to the new order of things. They soon found themselves supplanted by men who had been specially trained according to the new method. The Muslims have simply been 'crowded off,' to use an expressive Americanism, from the public service and the independent professions. The entire government of the country, so far as it affects the natives of India, is virtually in the hands of the Hindus. Their influence is all-powerful in every department of State, and that influence is almost invariably exercised to exclude the Muslims, whom they regard as aliens, from their proper and legitimate share in official preferment. It will not be contended by the warmest advocate of the Hindu, that he is intellectually superior to, or possesses more stamina than the Muslim. The truth is, that for the last fifty years the Muslims have been, and still are, most grievously handicapped. The time has arrived when Government should insist upon all its officers giving loyal effect to the order recently passes, for the more extended employment of the Muslims in the service of the State. In the gazetted appointments also the present disproportion between Hindus and Muslims should be removed. Appointments to the subordinate judicial service are made, I understand, on the recommendation of the High Court, but for some reason the claims of the Muslims to a fair share of the patronage of the High Court have, for some years past, been so overlooked, that at the present moment the disproportion between Hindus and Muslims is probably greater in the subordinate judicial than in any other branch of the public service. The judicial service of the future must, from the necessity of things, be largely officered by the natives of India. Stamina and strength of character are as much needed in these offices as versatility. . . . Few can doubt that a larger introduction of the Muslim element into the judicial service will add strength to the administration of the country. . . .

 . . . The study of English is a vital question for the Muslims. It means whether the Muslims are to be enabled to emerge from the desperate condition into which they have fallen and take their proper place among the Indian nationalities, or whether they are to be allowed to sink still lower in material prosperity. At the present moment the Muslims are beginning to apprehend the proper causes of their decline and are making serious efforts to regain, to some extent, the ground already lost. Now that it is proposed to make the higher education of the natives of India self-supporting, it will be impossible for the Muslims to compete successfully or to keep pace with the Eurasians and the Hindus unless some extra assistance is rendered them. I would purpose that the purely vernacular schools should be abolished, and that the funds allotted to their support should be applied to promote high English as well as technical education. It seems unwise of the Government to maintain institutions for imparting a purely Oriental education, as this fosters in the old ideas of exclusiveness which are inconsistent with the exigencies of British rule.

. . . Lastly, I would urge upon Government the necessity of improving the administration of the Muslim law. At present the non-administration or mal-administration of the law of the Muslims is a fruitful source of discontent and dissatisfaction, and it is especially necessary, in the interests of the people as well as the Government, that this evil should be corrected. I would accordingly suggest the appointment in the Mofussil of a number of Muslim judges, qualified to expound the Muslim law; in fact, to sit as assessor-judges in the trial of Muslim cases. In the High Courts of Calcutta, Madras and Bombay, as well as in the Chief Court of Lahore, a Muslim judge should be appointed to assist the European and Hindu judges in administering the Muslim law. The mischief which occurs from the imperfect apprehension of the Muslim law, even by these superior tribunals, can hardly be over-rated. The administration of justice is the strongest and most favourable feature of the British Government, but for the last thirty years the Muslim law has been, in the majority of cases, misapplied. The appointment of Muslim assessor-judges in the Mofussil would entail very little additional expense on the Government. Justice in India is so heavily taxed that not only does it pay its own cost, but leaves a surplus of £45,000 a year. A small additional expenditure, incurred in conciliating and redressing the wrongs of a much-injured community, can be a matter of no very great moment. There is little doubt, I believe, that ultimately, under the system of taxation on justice which prevails in British India, the plan suggested would become self-supporting. As regards the appointment of Muslim judges in the High Courts of India, it is a matter respecting which the Muslims may fairly consider themselves aggrieved—for whilst several Hindu Judges have been appointed in Madras, in Bombay, and in Calcutta, no Muslim has yet obtained a seat on the bench of the superior tribunals. Sub-ventions also should be granted for the translation of the standard legal works into English. In this respect, the British Government may follow with advantage the example of the French Government in Algeria.

The remarks I have ventured to offer in the foregoing pages embody the result of much patient study and an anxious consideration of the entire subject of Muslim grievances. No one can attach greater importance to the permanence of British rule in India than myself, for I believe that upon it depends for a long time to come the well-being and progress of the country. I have stated my views frankly in the hope of evoking the interest of the English people on behalf of the Muslims, and of assisting the statesmen who are now charged with the conduct of affairs, both here and in England, to understand correctly Muslim feelings. I would, however, repeat the fact that the depressed and despairing condition of the Muslims demands the serious attention of Government, and should not be dealt with longer in the *dilettante* way which has hitherto been the fashion, but in a real, earnest manner. A nation consisting of upwards of fifty millions of souls, 'with great traditions but without a career', deprived by slow degrees of wealth and influence by a policy of mistaken sentimentalism, mixed with a contemptuous disregard for popular feelings, must ways constitute an important factor in the administration of India. It is this factor which cannot be ignored, and which must be taken into account by Government in all future projects for the well-being of India.

The Indian National Congress first met in 1885 in Bombay. In this, its first official resolution, the group called on the British Government to address issues that had been of concern to elite Indian men for several decades: reform of legislative councils, changes in the civil service examinations, and recognition of indigenous forms of political association.

The Indian National Congress: Resolutions (1885)

First Congress—Bombay—1885.

1. That this Congress earnestly recommends that the promised inquiry into the working of the Indian Administration, here and in England, should be entrusted to a Royal Commission, the people of India being adequately represented thereon, and evidence taken both in India and in England.

2. That this Congress considers the abolition of the Council of the Secretary of State for India, as at present constituted, the necessary preliminary to all other reforms.

3. That this Congress considers the reform and expansion of the Supreme and existing Local Legislative Councils, by the admission of a considerable proportion of elected members (and the creation of similar Councils for the North-Western Provinces and Oudh, and also for the Punjab) essential; and holds that all Budgets should be referred to these Councils for consideration, their members being moreover empowered to interpellate the Executive in regard to all branches of the administration; and that a Standing Committee of the House of Commons should be constituted to receive and consider any formal protests that may be recorded by majorities of such Councils against the exercise by the Executive of the power which would be vested in it, of overruling the decisions of such majorities.

4. That, in the opinion of this Congress, the competitive examinations now held in England for first appointments in various civil departments of the public service should henceforth, in accordance with the views of the India Office Committee of 1860, "be held simultaneously, one in England and one in India, both being as far as practicable identical in their nature, and those who compete in both countries being finally classified in one list according to merit," and that the successful candidates in India should be sent to England for further study, and subjected there to such further examinations as may seem needful. Further, that all other first appointments (excluding peonships, and the like) should be filled by competitive examinations held in India, under conditions calculated to secure such intellectual, moral, and physical qualifications as may be

decided by Government to be unnecessary. Lastly, that the maximum age of candidates for entrance into the Covenanted Civil Service be raised to not less than 23 years.

5.That in the opinion of this Congress, the proposed increase in the military expenditure of the empire is unnecessary, and, regard being had to the revenues of the empire and the existing circumstances of the country, excessive.

6.That in the opinion of this Congress, if the increased demands for military expenditure are not to be, as they ought to be, met by retrenchment, they ought to be met, firstly, by the re-imposition of the Customs duties; and, secondly, by the extension of the license tax to those classes of the community, official and non-official, at present exempted from it, care being taken that in the case of all classes a sufficiently high taxable minimum be maintained. And, further, that this Congress is of opinion that Great Britain should extend an imperial guarantee to the Indian debt.

7.That this Congress deprecates the annexation of Upper Burmah, and considers that if the Government unfortunately decide on annexation, the entire country of Burmah should be separated from the Indian Viceroyalty and constituted a Crown Colony, as distinct in all matters from the Government of the country as is Ceylon.

8.That the resolutions passed by this Congress be communicated to the Political Associations in each province, and that these Associations be requested, with the help of similar bodies and other agencies, within their respective provinces, to adopt such measures as they may consider calculated to advance the settlement of the various questions dealt with in these resolutions.

9.That the Indian National Congress re-resemble next year in Calcutta and sit on Tuesday, the 28th of December, 1886, and the next succeeding days.

In the general election of 1892 Dadhabai Naoroji (1825–1917), one-time Bombay mathematics professor and long-time Parsi merchant-entrepreneur, ran on the Liberal ticket for the constituency of Central Finsbury. He won the contest, thereby becoming the delegate of a colonial territory that many contemporaries, even those who were sympathetic to the cause of India, scarcely recognized as a legitimate nation, let alone as a viable electoral constituency. Naoroji was president of the Indian National Congress in 1886, 1893, and 1906.

Dadhabai Naoroji,
Speech at the second Indian National Congress, Calcutta (1886)

I need not tell you how sincerely thankful I am to you for placing me in this position of honour. I at first thought that I was to be elevated to this proud position as a return for what might be considered as a compliment paid by us to Bengal when Mr. Bonnerjee was elected President of the first Congress last year at Bombay. I can assure you however that that election was no mere compliment to Bengal, but arose out of the simple fact that we regarded Mr. Bonnerjee as a gentleman eminently qualified to take the place of

President, and we installed him, in that position in all sincerity as the proper man in the proper place. I now see however, that this election of my humble self is not intended as a return of compliment, but that, as both proposer and seconder have said, you have been kind enough to select me because I am supposed to be really qualified to undertake the task. I hope it may prove so and that I may be found really worthy of all the kind things said of me; but whether this be so, or not, when such kind things are said by those who occupy such high positions amongst us, I must say I feel exceedingly proud and am very grateful to all for the honour thus done me. (*Loud cheering.*)

Your late Chairman has heartily welcomed all the delegates who come from different parts of India, and with the same heartiness I return to him, and all our Bengal friends on my own behalf and on that of all the delegates from other Provinces, the most sincere thanks for the cordial manner in which we have been received. From what has been done already, and from what is in store for us during our short stay here, I have no doubt we shall carry away with us many and most pleasant reminiscences of our visit to Calcutta. (*Cheers.*) You will pardon me, and I beg your indulgence when I say that when I was asked only two days ago to become your President and to give an inaugural address, it was with no small trepidation that I agreed to undertake the task; and I hope that you will extend to me all that indulgence which my shortcomings may need. (*Loud cheers.*)

The assemblage of such a Congress is *an event of the utmost importance in Indian history.* I ask whether in the most glorious days of Hindu rule, in the days of Rajahs like the great Vikram, you could imagine the possibility of a meeting of this kind, where even Hindus of all different provinces of the kingdom could have collected and spoken as one nation. Coming down to the later Empire of our friends, the Mahomedans, who probably ruled over a larger territory at one time than any Hindu monarch, would it have been, even in the days of the great Akbar himself, possible for a meeting like this to assemble composed of all classes and communities, all speaking one language, and all having uniform and high aspirations of their own.

Well, then what is it for which we are now met on this occasion? We have assembled to consider questions upon which depend our future, whether glorious or inglorious. It is our good fortune that we are under a rule which makes it possible for us to meet in this manner. (*Cheers.*) It is under the civilizing rule of the Queen and people of England that we meet here together, hindered by none, and are freely allowed to speak our minds without the least fear and without the least hesitation. Such a thing is possible under British rule and British rule only. (*Loud cheers.*) Then I put the *question* plainly: Is this Congress a nursery for sedition and rebellion against the British Government *(cries of no, no);* or is it another stone in the foundation of the stability of that Government *(cries of yes, yes)*? There could be but one answer, and that you have already given, because we are thoroughly sensible of the numberless blessings conferred upon us, of which the very existence of this Congress is a proof in a nutshell. (*Cheers.*) Were it not for these blessings of British rule I could not have come here, as I have done, without the least hesitation and without the least fear that my children might be robbed and killed in my absence; nor could you have come from every corner of the land, having performed, within a few days, journeys, which in former days would have occupied as many months. (*Cheers.*) These simple facts bring home to all of us at once some of those great and numberless blessings which British rule has conferred upon us. But there remain even greater blessings for which we have to be grateful. It is to British rule that we owe the education we possess; the people of England were sincere in the declarations made more than half a century ago that India was a sacred charge entrusted to their care by Providence, and that they were bound to administer it for the good of India, to the glory of their own name, and the satisfaction of God. (*Prolonged cheering.*) When we have to acknowledge so many blessings as flowing from British rule—and I could descant on them for hours, because it would simply be recounting to you the history of the British Empire in India—is it possible that an assembly like this, every one of whose members is fully impressed with the knowledge of these blessings, could meet for any purpose inimical to that rule to which we owe so much? (*Cheers.*)

The thing is absurd. Let us speak out like men and proclaim that we are loyal to the backbone (*cheers*); that we understand the benefits English rule has conferred upon us; thus we thoroughly appreciate the education that has been given to us, the new light which has been poured upon us, turning us from darkness into light and teaching us the new lesson that kings are made for the people, not peoples for their kings; and this new lesson we have learned amidst the darkness of Asiatic despotism only by the light of free English civilization. (*Loud cheers.*) But the question is, do the Government believe us? Do they believe that we are really loyal to them; that we do truly appreciate and rely on British rule; that we veritably desire its permanent continuance; that our reason is satisfied and our sentimental feelings gratified as well as our self interest? It would be a great gratification to us if we could see in the inauguration of a great movement like this Congress, that what we do really mean and desire is thoroughly and truly so understood by our rulers. I have the good fortune to be able to place before you testimony which cannot be questioned, from which you will see that some at least of the most distinguished of our rulers do believe that what we say is sincere; and that we do *not* want to subvert British rule; that our outspoken utterances are as much for their good as for our good. They do believe, as Lord Ripon said, that what is good for India is good for England. I will give you first the testimony as regards the educated classes which was given 25 years ago by Sir Bartle Frere. He possessed an intimate knowledge of the people of this country, and with regard to the educated portion of them he gave this testimony. He said: 'And now wherever I go I find the best exponents of the policy of the English Government, and the most able co-adjutors in adjusting that policy to the peculiarities of the natives of India, among the ranks of the educated natives'. This much at least is testimony to our sincerity, and strongly corroborates our assertion that we, the educated classes, have become the true interpreters and mediators between the masses of our countrymen and our rulers. I shall now place before you the declaration of the Government of India itself, that they have confidence in the loyalty of the whole people, and do appreciate the sentiments of the educated classes in particular. I will read their very words. They say in a despatch addressed to the Secretary of State (8th June, 1880): 'But the people of India accept British rule without any need for appeal to arms, because we keep the peace and do justice, because we have done and are doing much material good to the country and the people, and because, there is not inside, or outside India any power that can adequately occupy our place.' Then they distinctly understand that we do believe the British power to be the only power that can, under existing circumstances, really keep the peace, and advance our future progress. This is testimony as to the feeling of the whole people. But of the educated classes this despatch says: To the minds of at least the educated among the people of India—and the number is rapidly increasing—any idea of the subversion of British power is abhorrent, from the consciousness that it must result in the wildest anarchy and confusion.' (*Loud cheers*).

We can, therefore, proceed with the utmost serenity and with every confidence that our rulers do understand us; that they do understand our motives, and give credit to our expressions of loyalty, and we need not in the least care for any impeachment of disloyalty or any charge of harbouring wild ideas of subverting the British power that may be put forth by ignorant, irresponsible or ill-disposed individuals or cliques. (*Loud cheers.*) We can therefore, quietly, calmly and with entire confidence in our rulers, speak as freely as we please, but of course in that spirit of the fairness and moderation which becomes wise and honest men, and in the tone which every gentleman, every reasonable being, would adopt when urging his rulers to make him some concession. (*Hear, hear.*) Now although, as I have said, the British Government have done much, very much for us, there is still a great deal more to be done if their noble work is to be fitly completed. They say this themselves; they show a desire to do what more may be required, and it is for us to ask for whatsoever, after due deliberation, we think that we ought to have. (*Cheers.*)

    . . . It has been asserted that this Congress ought to take up questions of social reforms (*cheers and cries of yes, yes*) and our failure to do this has been urged as a reproach against us. Certainly no member of this National Congress is more alive to the necessity of social reforms than I am; but, gentlemen, for everything there are proper times, proper circumstances, proper parties and proper places (*cheers*); we are met together as a political body to represent to our rulers our political aspirations, not to discuss social reforms, and if you blame us for ignoring these you should equally blame the House of Commons for not discussing the abstruser problems on mathematics or metaphysics. But, besides this, there are here Hindus of every caste, amongst whom, even in the same provinces, customs and social arrangements differ widely,—there are Mahomedans and Christians of various denominations, Parsees, Sikhs, Brahmos and what not—men indeed of each and all of those numerous classes which constitute in the aggregate the people of India. (*Loud cheers.*) How can this gathering of *all* classes discuss the social reforms needed in each individual class? What do any of us know of the internal home life, of the customs, traditions, feelings, prejudices of any class but our own? How could a gathering, a cosmopolitan gathering like this, discuss to any purpose the reforms needed in any one class? Only the members of that class can effectively deal with the reforms therein needed. A National Congress must confine itself to questions in which the entire nation has a direct participation, and it must leave the adjustment of social reforms and other class questions to class Congresses. But it does not follow that, because this national, political body does not presume to discuss social reforms, the delegates here present are not just as deeply, nay in many, cases far more deeply, interested in these questions than in those political questions we do discuss, or that those several communities whom those delegates represent are not doing their utmost to solve those complicated problems on which hinge the practical introduction of those reforms. Any man who has eyes and ears open must know what struggles towards higher and better things are going on in every community: and it could not be otherwise with the noble education we are receiving. Once you begin to think about your own actions, your duties and responsibilities to yourself, your neighbours and your nation, you cannot avoid looking round and observing much that is wrong amongst you; and we know as a fact that each community is now doing its best according to its lights, and the progress that it has made in education. I need not I think particularise. The Mahomedans know what is being done by persons of their community to push on the education their brethren so much need; the Hindus are everywhere doing what they *can* to reform those social institutions which they think require improvement. There is not one single community here represented of which the best and ablest men do not feel that much has to be done to improve the social, moral, religious status of their brethren, and in which, as a fact, they are not striving to effect, gradually those needful improvements; but these are essentially matters too delicate for a stranger's handling—matters which must be left to the guidance of those who alone fully understand them in all their bearings, and which are wholly unsuited to discussion in an assemblage like this in which all classes are intermingled. (*Loud cheers.*) . . .

In this excerpt from an anonymous article in the *Contemporary Review*, a Bengal magistrate evaluates the effects of British rule in Ireland and India, citing evictions and the presence of religious minorities as his basis for comparison. Indian nationalists and Irish radicals formed political alliances with each other throughout the 1880s and 1890s as part of their shared quest to secure for Home Rule from the imperial Parliament at Westminster.

A Bengal Magistrate,
"The Home Rule Movement in India and Ireland" (1890)

I HAVE spent nearly fifty years in Ireland and in India: in the latter I have represented Government in its dealings with populations varying between half a million and five millions.

The five millions, of different races and faiths, formerly bitterly inimical to each other, oppressing and oppressed, are now at peace. Peace has been maintained for many years without a single white soldier; for appearance sake a few companies of plump and idle sepoys are maintained, but no bayonet or bâton charge, no battering-ram, has, in my experience, been needed in a region larger than Ireland and Wales combined. There it has been my duty to practise the art of government; and seeing Ireland still garrisoned with 42,000 soldiers and military police, and noting the desire that it be so safeguarded from popular discontent for twenty years more, I would fain say a few words on the contrasts which British rule exhibits in the little island with its four millions of restless grumblers, and in the great Empire with its two hundred and fifty millions of peaceful toilers. Particularly I would note how errors in the administration of both have led to a cry for Home Rule. These demands may soon be heard on a united platform, and may herald a far-reaching federation; but I deal here with the striking and instructive contrasts in the causes which have led to the two agitations. The leaders, the machinery, the immediate objects, the official resistance hitherto offered are of very different types; the ultimate aims are probably the same, namely, the abolition of bureaucracy and the development of Imperial Federation by means of constitutional agitation.

The first question is, who pays for the agitation? For forty years it has been notorious that the Irish movement has depended on popular support: women have brought their mites, servant-girls their wages, wherever in Europe, America, or Australia the Irish race is found. They have given of their substance as freely as their sisters in Carthage contributed their hair in order to manufacture bowstrings. In India, on the other hand, out of its two hundred and fifty millions, those who subscribe at all in proportion to their means may be counted on one's fingers. In 1880 the expenses of the annual Congress and of the provincial agitation were very large: the sum of £15,000 was contributed by one retired English officer; a wealthy native barrister proffered £300; and a tax of fifteen shillings per head was levied upon each of the members of the Congress—upon the parliamentary representatives, in fact. These were the main sources of the income; the remaining contributions were few in number, and generally meagre in amount. Making every allowance for the shorter period during which the Indian agitation has been at work, and for the want of education among the masses, it is perfectly clear that, judged by the money test, the demand for Home Rule is a popular movement in Ireland, and is not so in India.

The other contrasted circumstances which I will indicate, point, I think, to the same conclusion: that the British administration in India has been far more gentle and gracious, far more sagacious and popular, than in Ireland. Famines, evictions, land laws, settlements, minorities once dominant but now dethroned—these forces have led the people towards Home Rule in Ireland: they have been quite powerless to do so in India. I will say nothing about contrasts between Indian and Irish religions, climates, or ancient histories. All students are aware that the caste system in India renders it almost impossible to create a unity of national feeling. But passing from such obstacles to Home Rule, I must first refer to one matter worthy of anxious contemplation by every loyal British Imperialist, that is, the comparative condition of the two units, Ireland and British India, during the reign of her present Majesty. Both have undergone great changes in the last fifty years, and it is noteworthy that the changes have been in opposite directions.

In 1838 Ireland had a population of eight millions, while England, Wales, and Scotland had only eighteen. At present there are less than five millions in Ireland, against about thirty-three millions in the others. The Irish population was one-third of the British aggregate; it has now sunk to one-eighth. For the Irish decrease, the Empire is so much the weaker: men have decayed, and so have soldiers; there need to be 70,000 Irishmen in the British army; last year there were only 31,000—a point of some significance when it is remembered that 150,000 men of Irish race fought in the American civil war.

While Ireland has decreased, British India has increased, not only in area, but in wealth, strength, and population, with great, nay startling, rapidity. Successive additions, each in itself a kingdom, one an empire, have swelled the crescent growth of this most marvellous political creation. Oudh, Burma, the Panjab, Scinde, Nagpur, besides numerous smaller fragments, have been annexed. These five alone cover 570,000 square miles, and have a population of fifty-eight millions. Their expanse is about equal to that of Germany, France, and Spain combined. From them have been raised Sikh infantry, and the cavalry which Sir Charles Dilke recently pronounced the finest in the world. Thus the star of India has waxed brighter and brighter, for its apparent and real strength has more than doubled, not only in the quantity of its material resources, but in the quality of its men from a soldier's point of view. British India formerly consisted of the littoral nearly all round the peninsula and of the Gangetic valley, but by the inclusion of the Panjab and Oudh—the nurseries of armies—and by treaty engagements with the Mahrattas, the Nizam, and the Ameer of Cabul, the Empress of India has become the only Sovereign whom the martial races of India regard with the loyalty which is a part of their nature and of their creed. British India has become much stronger, and is now a stupendous integer of the Empire, the biggest object in the statesman's outlook. Fifty years ago it was mainly regarded as the tropic home of toiling but effeminate millions, whose function was to produce cotton, indigo, and sugar, while ours was to shield them from fierce foes all around; now those foes have become subjects too. Wise and firm government command their loyal support; they will fight with us and for us. India has, then, abundantly redressed the balance, and replaced the deficit of three millions of Irishmen with nearly sixty millions of fairly loyal and tolerably contented Indo-British subjects. Lord Mayo once remarked to the present writer, when we were waiting in our howdahs for the outburst of a family of tigers, that the problems which he had to solve as Secretary at Dublin and as Governor-General at Calcutta, showed a great mutual resemblance. But I would dwell rather on the contrasts which the two countries present, because I consider them more instructive on the question of Home Rule, and more pregnant with emphatic lessons in the art of government. . . .

Evictions.

In both countries evictions by landlords have been closely watched by Government, but in Ireland rather because they are generally followed by outrages, and are often really sentences of death.

In Oudh, a province smaller than Ireland, there were in one year 37,000 eviction notices, of which about one-third resulted in actual loss of the farm; in other years there were as many as 50,000. In 1849 there were 19,949 evictions in Ireland, and this number has never been equalled since—at least, according to the statistics. They have now sunk to 800 (in 1888). So far the balance would appear to be in favour of the Irish tenant; this is, however, far from being the case. The province of Oudh is quite different from the rest of India. In Madras and Bombay the landlords have been evicted on a large scale, and the same policy was followed in North-west India to a limited extent, while in Bengal, with its sixty-six millions, and in the Panjab, successive enactments have been passed with the object of protecting the tenant. This course has quite recently been followed in Oudh too, though the assembled barons of that province declared that they would never consent to tenant-right, even if they were all to die in one day. But further, not only have evictions been checked and discouraged, but when they are permitted they present none of the harsh features in India which render them so repulsive in Ireland; for in India they can only be effected at one season of the year—in April, after the harvest has been cut. Further, the tenant resides in a village after eviction from his farm; he generally retains his house, and may get other fields, so that the double hardship of losing both house and land, the unroofing of the home under a wintry sky, never happens in India.

In Ireland there were 90,107 evictions during the thirty-one years 1849–80; of these 58,000 occurred in the years 1849–52, after the famine. Very possibly of those who were made homeless, many survived to become richer and happier in America; but still each eviction in those awful times involved risk of death to the sufferers, who took shelter in ditches, or crowded into poor-houses, to be swept off by typhus. That these 90,000 evictions resulted in many thousands of deaths is certain, and doubtless some forty or fifty of the agrarian murders which occurred during that period were the result of popular revenge.

In Oudh, though the numbers sent adrift were enormously larger, the hardships were much less, and the bloodshed was comparatively trifling. The economic evils of evictions—uncertainty of tenure, and discouragement of industry—remained, and Government has recently passed Acts in order to place the Oudh tenant on an equal footing with his brethren in the rest of India.

Throughout the peninsula, in fact, the cultivator is now protected, a result whose full completion has been achieved by ninety years of noble effort. It is only since 1881 that the Irish tenant has received any real protection, and up to 1870 the entire course of legislation was in the direction of facilitating eviction. That is, for three quarters of a century the aims of Irish and of Indian legislation were directly the reverse of each other, for from 1793 up to date the Indian legislator has been striving to destroy or curtail the landlord's oppressive powers. The three F's were always the main aim of the Indian Government; the means adopted varied in each case. In Madras and Bombay the land was nationalized as a rule. The landlords were evicted, and compensation in pensions or in freeholds was granted, calculated on the principle that they were entitled to ten per cent. of the rental.

In Northern India the landlords are retained to a large extent, but they have to pay half of their rental to the State, while the statute-book bristles with enactments designed to protect the tenant. Opinion varies somewhat among Indian statesmen as to whether this exploitation of the landlords was equitable, but all have agreed that the results have been most beneficial to one hundred and fifty millions of cultivators, whose rights have been protected and their industry encouraged, while the general interests of the State have been safeguarded by the retention of the land-tax. It yields annually twenty-one millions sterling, and the Indian people have through its means escaped taxes upon windows, paper, tea, coffee, sugar, tobacco, medicines, newspapers, such as have impeded civilization, and helped on one occasion to dismember the British Empire. . . .

The Religious Minority.

Religious animosities, however, do exist in India, and often cause much turmoil, requiring the assistance of the military. I must therefore briefly notice the contrast between the Protestant minority in Ireland and the Mussulman minority in India. The former numbers one-fifth, or about a million; Mussulmans number sixty millions, or about a quarter of the Indian total; both profess what they consider a purer faith, and both have waged war for centuries against the so-called idolatrous practices of their neighbours; there is hardly a temple in India of any antiquity which does not bear testimony in the broken noses of its gods to the iconoclastic zeal of the Moslem.

In both countries, for five hundred years, this minority possessed a political ascendency, which it exercised, however, very differently. The Moslem was haughty and overbearing, but tolerant enough of Hindu worship, save for occasional outbursts of bigotry; he has now been placed entirely on a level with the Hindus; he is nowhere and in no matter dominant. The Protestant, on the other hand, maintained in Ireland for 170 years a most galling system of religious persecution; the houses and the lands, the learned professions, the religious services, the priests and bishops, the very wives and children of the Catholics, were in constant peril according to law. These disabilities have been removed, but much remains which is not only offensive but injurious. The Protestant minority retain about three-quarters of the land, three-quarters of the unpaid magistracies: 56 of the 72 paid magistrates are Protestants; 228 out of 272 police-officers; 30 out of 32 lord-lieutenants; 36 out of 45 privy councillors; 35 out of 46 commissioners and other officials on Boards of Works and Local Government Boards; while all the high executive officials in Dublin, without a single exception, are Protestants.

The Moslem minority in India possesses no such monopoly. When deprived of their ascendency, they for many years held sullenly aloof from the English usurpers; bigotry, and fanaticism induced the more desperate of the faithful to become assassins, and the men who committed all the noted murders of English officers and governors, such as those of Fraser, Connolly, Macnaghten, Chief Justice Norman, Lord Mayo, were Moslems. These outbreaks of individuals did not lead to reprisals by the State upon the Moslem nation. No Coercion Acts were passed; increased energy was shown rather in sending the schoolmaster among the ignorant Pathans; the great imperial mosque was restored to them, and pains were taken so that they should get their fair share of public offices. The result has been that this minority has forgotten its old ascendancy, and its fancied wrongs; it clings to the British Government even after it has lost all monopoly and privilege, regarding the English as the natural protectors of the few against the many who might try for revenge, or at least for ransom, from their old oppressors.

The people in India, as in Ireland, are divided into two camps on the subject of Home Rule, the minority in each case being generally opposed to it, while the majority labour hard to persuade their ancient enemies that all old animosities are forgotten, and that Nationalists, when allowed to govern in domestic matters, will be tolerant and impartial. The Hindu would have apparently succeeded entirely; had it not been for an unfortunate occasion of strife. The calendars of the two faiths do not correspond: one is always overtaking and overlapping the other. The Moslem faith has one most mournful celebration, that of the martyrdom of Husn and Hosein, the Prophet's grandsons. The Hindus have a joyous festival in honour of the upspringing of the young rice, and of the victory of their deified King Ram; for two years in every thirty-five these two celebrations coincide, and unfortunately, in 1886–1887, the clashing of the rival processions, of the mourners and the revellers, caused bitterness between the two races everywhere, and bloodshed in many places. Moslems demand that idols and processions shall not be paraded past their holy mosques with fife, drum, and all the earsplitting harmonies dear to Hindus; for this cause battles have often raged round the shrines, and the deaths have numbered about 150 on more than one occasion.

There is no such rock of offence in Ireland. St. Patrick's Day never clashes with the 12th of July. The Protestant minority in Ireland have to dread matters more material; Home Rule would undoubtedly entail the loss of the ascendancy which they still enjoy in the way of State monopolies of place and power. It has been my lot on more than one occasion, as an Indian magistrate, to stand between rival masses numbering 30,000 on one side and 50,000 on the other, both yearning for hostilities; with the aid of a few policemen only, peace was preserved without even a bâton charge or a broken head. That moral suasion succeeded was certainly not due to the peaceful habits of the people, for when British magistrates were absent the butcher's bill at Vellore and Delhi far surpassed that at Belfast. The main reason undoubtedly was that both Hindu and Moslem respect their magistrates as just and impartial, and anything like defiance of their authority, much more any outrage upon their persons, even in a battle of mobs, would be avoided diligently by both sides; they would sacrifice even a religious orgy at the bidding of the just white man. Now, the impartial arbiter is exactly what the Irish people consider to be wanting in their country, and there is no doubt that the yearning for Irish Home Rule, though historically based upon race and religious differences, upon old sufferings, upon landlord wrong, evictions, famines, is at present nourished mainly by the popular abhorrence of their magistrates, police, and Coercion Acts. Nationalists think that the ancient ascendancy of the minority, rudely shattered by the abolition of the Church and land tyrannies, has been restored to former vigour by its alliance with the executive, whose officers, codes, and administrative principles have been adopted at the bidding of the English settlers, now more dominant than ever. They regard Home Rule not merely as the only means of national development, but as the only remedy for much galling injustice.

In Ireland, as already pointed out, the Nationalist majority has no share of State loaves and fishes; the national leaders are to be found oftener in the dock than on the bench. India, too, has men of similar type; Mandlik, Telang, Norton, Hume, Bonnerjee, Syed Ahmed, all are or were agitators; but they have been honoured by the State: not one of them has had personal experience of the plank bed or of the policeman's bâton. In its selection for the unpaid local magistracy, or the paid stipendiaries or police-officers, Government follows national feeling. The people revere Brahmins and Jeyuds, the holy men of the Hindu and Moslem faiths; Government respects and conciliates this sentiment, bigoted as it is; and high caste men, as they are called, if of good character and education, are preferred for official posts. So far, Indian government is according to Indian ideas, and its vast patronage is used so as to attract popular sympathy, which in Ireland is repelled. Curious to relate, though in every respect the Indian magistrates, paid and unpaid, are more popular, more effective and impartial, than in Ireland, and though there are only one or two relics of ascendancy policy in the administrative schemes, yet these little rifts in the lute injure the harmony. The demand for Home Rule in India is fostered mainly at present by the magisterial and executive posts being confined to foreigners in practice, though open to all in theory. . . .

Conclusion

In India a small minority only are discontented, for governors, magistrates, and police all work together in their proper places, aiming at no party objects, intent on the general good, and doubtless on those personal advantages also which men must always desire. In the reverse of this we find the main causes of the demand for Home Rule in Ireland. The people dislike with varying degrees of intensity their magistracy, their police, and the Coercion laws, which those bodies carry out; their minds dwell on secret Star Chamber inquiries, on benches of removables superseding juries, applying with clumsy ignorance ancient law which has descended from Edward III., and modern coercion, which has been obtained from the British Parliament through fictitious statistics and Pigott's forgeries. Generous and statesman-like has been much of State action, Liberal and Conservative, but the people as a whole have only heard of Lord Ashbourne's Acts; they have seen the bâton charge and the battering-ram, and heard the patter of buckshot; they have witnessed, they think, high-handed outrage by officials followed by no inquiry or redress; police in Ireland bear no numbers, so that civil actions are practically impossible. All this is galling, and they clamour for Home Rule, not because it will place a Parliament in College Green, but because it will sweep away the Castle and the removables, and place the police under control.

In India the nationalists have no such grievance, yet they, too, aim at Home Rule, and Congresses of twelve hundred delegates, with thousands of orations, but very few rupees, support the agitation. They demand that examinations for the Civil Service and the army shall be held simultaneously at London and Calcutta, so that their youth may compete on even terms; they ask to be allowed to volunteer, that men of good character may carry arms for sport or protection; that executive and judicial functions shall be separated; that some members of the legislative councils shall be elected by the people.

One reason, no doubt, for the temper and moderation with which these demands are pressed, is that Government has so far responded with successive reforms, and its tone has been cautious and conciliatory. Many thoughtful patriotic Indians, though content with their officials as individuals, think that authority should become less autocratic;

that the people should do more for themselves, and the bounds of liberty be broadened. Vast will be the task of responding to these requests, according to the varying needs of Indian nations, comprising all types of civilization. The Calcutta Government, inspired by traditions which have descended from warrior statesmen, such as Monro or the Lawrences, have refrained from stubborn refusals; conscious that the empire is God-given, they have not sought to maintain it by any alliance with a minority, or by any dependence upon privileged classes, and they have not become entangled in or discredited by partisan intrigues. Having recently pulverized great kingdoms, and treated land as national property, they are naturally chary of fastening such epithets as rapine or disintegration upon any constitutional agitation.

The Indian nationalists are conscious that they have received blessings which Ireland still lacks. The nationalized land pays easily a revenue of twenty-one millions sterling; rack-renting and evictions are rare and becoming rarer. The breakfast-table is free; the magistracy is able and impartial, freely chosen without favour from white and black; juries are not packed; there is no Coercion Act. The police are controlled, and efforts to correct their errors are ceaseless; there is no dominant minority ever galling the people with fresh instances of the monopoly of State powers and emoluments which they possess. In fact, the fabric of agitation wants the corner-stones which lie handy all over Ireland.

In India there is no angry discontent, there is hopeful, eager aspiration, for cautious concession is the motto of the rulers, not dogged denial. It is the fervent prayer of Indian Nationalists that the British Parliament will soon become representative of the Empire; that it will be relieved of petty domestic matters in Ireland, and will then take up the broad questions which concern two hundred and fifty millions of Indians; to them England has shown that she can be unselfish and benignant, and in their contentment has been her exceeding great reward. May the rulers of Ireland be of like mind. In their dealings with their magistracy and police, in holding the balance between rival parties, in special enactments for peace preservation, may they, as in the land question, not disdain to copy the wise men of the East, with their motto, "Be just and fear not."

'A. E.' (d. 1932) was the pseudonym for George William Russell, a poet, painter, editor, and mentor to many of the leading lights of the so-called Irish literary "renaissance." Here he confronts the cultural ramifications of English imperialism head on—"I confess I do not love England"—and argues that "if the stupefying influence of foreign control were removed" in Ireland it would mean "the starting up into sudden life of a thousand dormant energies, spiritual, intellectual, artistic, social, economic, and human."

A. E., "Nationality and Imperialism" (ca. 1900)

THE idea of the national being emerged at no recognisable point in our history. It is older than any name we know. It is not earth born, but the synthesis of many heroic and beautiful moments, and these, it must be remembered, are divine in their origin. Every heroic deed is an act of the spirit, and every perception of beauty is vision with the divine eye, and not with the mortal sense. The spirit was subtly intermingled with the shining of old romance, and it was no mere phantasy which shows Ireland at its dawn in a misty light thronged with divine figures, and beneath and nearer to us, demigods and heroes fading into recognisable men. The bards took cognisance only of the most notable personalities who preceded them; and of these only the acts which had a symbolic or spiritual significance; and these grew thrice refined as generations of poets in enraptured musings along by the mountains or in the woods, brooded upon their heritage of story until, as it passed from age to age, the accumulated beauty grew greater than the beauty of the hour, the dream began to enter into the children of our race, and their thoughts turned from earth to that world in which it had its inception.

It was a common belief among the ancient peoples that each had a national genius or deity who presided over them, in whose all-embracing mind they were enclosed, and by whom their destinies were shaped. We can conceive of the national spirit in Ireland as first manifesting itself through individual heroes or kings; and, as the history of famous warriors laid hold upon the people, extending its influence through the sentiment engendered in the popular mind until it created therein the germs of a kindred nature.

An aristocracy of lordly and chivalrous heroes is bound in time to create a great democracy by the reflection of their character in the mass, and the idea of the divine right of kings is succeeded by the idea of the divine right of the people. If this sequence cannot be traced in any one respect with historical regularity, it is because of the complexity of national life, its varied needs, and its infinite changes of sentiment; but the threads are all taken up in the end, and ideas which were forgotten and absent from the voices of men will be found, when recurred to, to have grown to a rarer and more spiritual beauty in their quiet abode in the heart. The seeds which are sown at the beginning of a race bear their flowers and fruits towards its close; and those antique names which already begin to stir us with their power, Angus, Lu, Deirdre, Finn, Ossian, and the rest, will be found to be each one the symbol of enduring qualities, and their story a trumpet through which will be blown the music of an eternal joy, the sentiment of an inexorable justice, the melting power of beauty in sorrow, the wisdom of age, and the longings of the spirit.

The question arises how this race inheritance can best be preserved and developed. To some it is of no value, but these are voices of dust. To some the natural outcome is coalition with another power, and a frank and full acceptance of the imperial ideal. To some the solution lies in a self-centred national life. I will not touch here upon the material advantages of one or other course, which can best be left to economists to discuss. The literary man, who is, or ought to be, concerned mainly with intellectual interests, should only intervene in politics when principles affecting the spiritual life of his country are involved. To me the imperial ideal seems to threaten the destruction of that national being which has been growing through centuries, and I ask myself, What can it profit my race if it gain the empire of the world and yet lose its own soul—a soul which is only now growing to self-consciousness, and this to be lost simply that we may help to build up a sordid trade federation between England and her Colonies? Was our divine origin for this end? Did the bards drop in song the seed of heroic virtues, and beget the mystic chivalry of the past, and flood our being with spiritual longings, that we might at last sink to clay and seek only to inherit the earth? The mere area of the empire bewitches the commonplace mind, and turns it from its own land; yet the State of Athens was not so large as the Province of Munster, and, though dead, the memory of it is brighter than the living light of any people on earth to-day. Some, to whom I would be the last to deny nobility of thought and sincere conviction, would lead us from ourselves through the belief that the moral purification of the empire could be accomplished by us. I wish I could believe it. I am afraid our own political and social ethics demand all the attention we can give. There is a reservoir of spiritual life in the land, but it is hardly strong enough to repel English materialism, while we are nominally hostile to English ideas; and shall it be triumphant when we have given over our hopes of a separate national existence, and merged our dreams and longings with a nation which has become a byword for materialism? Under no rule are people so free,—we are told. A little physical freedom more or less matters nothing. Men are as happy and as upright as we, in countries where a passport is necessary to travel from one town to another. No form of government we know is perfect, and none will be permanent. The federation of the world and its typical humanity, exists in germ in the spiritual and intellectual outcasts of our time, who can find no place in the present social order. A nation is sacred as it holds few or many of those to whom spiritual ideals are alone worth having; the mode of life, prosperous or unfortunate, which brings them to birth and enables them to live is the best of any; and the genius of our country has acted wisely in refusing any alliance offering only material prosperity and power. Every race must work out its own destiny. England and the Colonies will, as is fit and right, work out theirs without our moral guidance. They would resent it if offered, just as we resent it from them. It may be affirmed that the English form of government is, on the whole, a good one, but it does not matter. It may be good for Englishmen, but it is not the expression of our national life and ideas. I express my ideals in literature; you, perhaps, in social reform. Both may be good; yours, indeed, may be best, but I would feel it a bitter injustice if I was compelled to order my life in accordance with your aims. I would do poorly what you shine in. We ask the liberty of shaping the social order in Ireland to reflect our own ideals, and to embody that national soul which has been slowly incarnating in our race from its cloudy dawn. The twentieth century may carry us far from Finn and Oscar and the stately chieftains and heroes of their time, far even from the ideals of Tone, Mitchell, and Davis, but I hope it will not carry us into contented acceptance of the deadness, the dullness, the commonplace of English national sentiment, or what idealism remains in us; bequeathed from the past, range itself willingly under a banner which is regarded chiefly as a commercial asset by the most famous exponent of the imperial idea.

. . . I confess I do not love England. Love is a spirit which will not, with me at least, come at all. It bestows itself, and will not be commanded, having laws and an end of its own. But for that myriad humanity which throngs the cities of England I feel a profound pity; for it seems to me that in factory, in mine, in warehouse, the life they have chosen to live in the past, the lives those born into that country must almost inevitably lead now, is farther off from beauty, more remote from spirit, more alien from deity, than that led by any people hitherto in the memory of the world. I have no hatred for them. I do not think any of my countrymen have, however they may phrase the feeling in their hearts. I think it is a spiritual antagonism they feel which they translate into terms of the more limited conscious mind. I think their struggle is in reality not against flesh and blood, but is a portion of the everlasting battle against principalities and powers and spiritual wickedness in high places, which underlies every other battle which has been or will be fought by men. I do not say that everything English is stupid, invariably and inevitably wrong. But I do say that every act by which England would make our people other than they would be themselves, is stupid, invariably and inevitably wrong. Not invariably wrong, perhaps, when judged from the external point of view, but invariably wrong when judged from the interior spiritual standpoint. How terrible a thing it is to hinder the soul in its freedom, let the wild upheavals and the madness of protest bear witness.

Though we are old, ethnologically considered, yet as a nation, a collective unit, we are young or yet unborn. If the stupefying influence of foreign control were removed, if we had charge of our own national affairs, it would mean the starting up into sudden life of a thousand dormant energies, spiritual, intellectual, artistic, social, economic, and human. The national spirit, like a beautiful woman, cannot or will not reveal itself wholly while a coarse presence is near, an unwelcome stranger in possession of the home. It is shy, hiding itself away in remote valleys, or in haunted mountains, or deep in the quiet of hearts that do not reveal themselves. Only to its own will it come and sing its hopes and dreams; not selfishly for itself alone, but sharing in the universal human hopes, and desirous of solving some of the eternal problems. Being still so young as a nation, and before the true starting of our career, we might say of ourselves as the great American poet of his race, with which so many of our own have mingled—

> "Have the elder races halted?
> Do they droop and end their lesson, wearied, over there beyond the
> seas?
> We take up the task eternal, and the burden, and the lesson.
> Pioneers! Oh, pioneers!"

Mary Butler (1873–1920) was born in England to an Irish father and an Australian mother of Irish descent. Her father's aunt was married to Edward Carson's father so she was deeply enmeshed in Irish politics from the start. She was a prominent member of—and pamphleteer for—the Gaelic League (founded in 1893), which included some women among its members but was better known for the way it idealized the images of motherhood and home as repositories of the kinds of spiritual values that Irish cultural nationalism sought to reintroduce into Irish public life. As Butler wrote in the *United Irishman* in 1903, "the best of all schools is an Irish mother's knee."

Mary Butler, "Women's Role in Sustaining Gaelic Culture" (1901)

Some suggestions as to how Irishwomen may help the Irish Language Movement.

1. Realise what it means to be an Irishwoman, and make others realise what it means by being Irish in fact as well as in name.

2. Make the home atmosphere Irish.

3. Make the social atmosphere Irish.

4. Speak Irish if you know it, especially in the home circle, and if you have no knowledge of the language, set about acquiring it at once. If you only know a little, speak that little.

5. Insist on children learning to speak, read, and write Irish.

6. Insist on school authorities giving pupils the benefit of a thoroughly Irish education.

7. Use Irish at the family prayers.

8. Give Irish names to children.

9. Visit Irish-speaking districts. If Irish people who are students of the language go among their Irish-speaking fellow-country people in the right spirit and instill the right principles in them, they will be conferring a benefit on the people, and the people will in return confer a benefit on them by imparting their native knowledge of the spoken language to them.

10. Encourage Irish music and song.

11. Support Irish publications and Irish literature.

12. Employ Irish-speaking servants whenever possible.

13. Join the Gaelic League, and induce others to do so.

14. Spread the light among your acquaintances.

15. Consistently support everything Irish, and consistently withhold your support from everything un-Irish.

Sir Richard Temple (1826–1902) was educated at Rugby and Haileybury and was posted to India in 1847. He rose quickly in the ranks of the colonial administration and became a baronet in 1876; he was also a conservative M.P. for Evesham and then Kingston. In the passage below he surveys the Egyptian situation and argues that Egypt needs European "instruction and guidance" in civil administration if the peace and stability of the region is to be secured for British imperial hegemony.

Sir Richard Temple, "Principles of British Policy in Egypt" (1882)

The object of this article is not to discuss the causes which led to the British military operations in Egypt, but to examine the principles which should guide British policy when these operations have been crowned with success. Having extinguished by force the rebellion of Arabi and his party, England has for the moment a commanding opportunity; then how ought she to make use of it? That is the question.

Now this question is doubtless engaging the anxious attention of nearly all the Muhammadan world, that is, the Muhammadans in Turkey, in Persia, in Arabia, in Afghanistan, in India, in Northern Africa. There are still two important bodies of Muhammadans, namely, those dwelling in Central Asia, who are under Russian domination, and those inhabiting certain parts of the Chinese Empire, whose political thoughts can hardly be gauged. It is probable, however, that the Chinese Muhammadans do not trouble their minds on the subject. After all abatements, the number of Muhammadans who are seriously exercising their minds in this matter, must be great, comprising as it does a total population of nearly one hundred millions. There is no need for pausing to show how England has under her direct administration or her political control about half of this large aggregate. Her interest, then, in the Muhammadan world, if judged by the numerical standard of a census, would appear to be much greater than that of any other Power. Thus she has every motive to conciliate the Muhammadans, inducing them to confide in her benevolent will and loyal intentions.

It is important to bear this in mind when considering the main questions as above set forth. In reference to that question the first point is the maintenance of Muhammadan sovereignty and rule in Egypt. From the outset, then, the British authorities have proclaimed the maintenance of Muhammadan rule as represented by the Khedive. On his part the Khedive has commanded his subjects to loyally co-operate with the British authorities, and has declared Arabi a rebel in arms against his lawful master. The Sultan of Turkey is prepared to issue a proclamation to the effect that Arabi is a rebel. Further, to the Sultan there is allowed the option of sending a body of Turkish troops to co-operate with the British in Egypt at the seat of war. These proceedings certainly set England right with the Muhammadan world at large, and place her in the position of one who is battling for her Muhammadan allies (the Sultan and the Khedive) against an insurrectionary party. It also establishes the contention that Arabi is a rebel, notwithstanding any sentiments of nationality or feelings of fanaticism which may temporarily have gathered round him. There has undoubtedly been much in his conduct to attract the admiration and sympathy of many classes among Muhammadans generally. It is therefore of much consequence to so arrange the language of proclamations or other authoritative proceedings that he may be made to stand in his true position, namely, that of an insurgent against his legitimate lord. This is apparently being done quite effectually, and will produce a favourable effect upon Muhammadan opinion everywhere.

Happily the Khedive stands well in British opinion, as having played an exceptionally difficult part with loyalty and fidelity. But this public opinion has been dubious respecting the Khedive's suzerain, the Sultan of Turkey. On the one hand, all Englishmen who are acquainted with Constantinople, will considerately make allowance for the Sultan on account of the cruel difficulties which environ his political position. On the other hand, there is no disguising the violent probability that the recent troubles in Egypt have been indirectly encouraged by some classes in Turkey, and even fomented by some parties there. It . . . [would be] superfluous to recapitulate the reasons why the conduct of the Turkish Government during some stages of the negotiations is held to have been unsatisfactory, and to have been guided by the idea of impeding or retarding the British operations. These circumstances have injuriously affected Turkey's position, though it may yet be retrieved by behaviour which shall be worthy of acceptance as clearly good. If, then, it shall be found possible, with political consistency, to overlook the Sultan's shortcomings in the past, with a view to his co-operation in the immediate future, and thus to maintain the recognition of his suzerainty over Egypt—this will have a good effect upon the Muhammadan world, or more particularly upon that part of it with which England is directly concerned. The Sultan indeed holds a very high position among Muhammadans, though it is well to avoid making too much even of that position. He being (as will be readily remembered) of the Sunni sect, Persia, being of the Shia sect, will not pay reverence to him. Afghanistan too, as was proved by the experience of the last Afghan war, regards him but little. Still his office and person are venerated by most among the influential Muhammadans of India, his prestige is still maintained in Turkey, and probably there is a religious party on his side in Arabia. If then England shall find herself able, with the approval of Europe, to set the Khedive on a throne of real power, and to preserve the suzerainty of the Sultan, she will be held by the Muhammadan world to have done well. It would be a mere truism to state how many contingencies may hinder the accomplishment of any such design, as of many other good and wise designs.

Next, in the future settlement of Egypt it will be most desirable to obtain, not only the formal acceptance but also the cordial approval of the European Powers, and to avoid anything which may even bear the semblance of lawlessness or violence. Besides the high considerations which are too manifest to need recapitulation, it may be remarked that any step which should deviate from the comity of nations or from the best principles of international law, would be likely to produce bitter consequences hereafter. Aggressive ambition, on the part of one great Power, arouses similar tendencies among other Powers. It is obvious that there are several, perhaps many, Oriental regions which offer temptations and enticing opportunities to one or other of the great Powers for that sort of interposition which ultimately leads to domination. Though England is far from claiming any exclusive interest in the East, where other Powers also have interests, still such movements may prove embarrassing more or less to her, and occasionally might even be dangerous to her legitimate interest. She should therefore eschew giving the least encouragement to them by any example in her own conduct. If after being compelled to draw the sword in a just quarrel, and having secured advantages in Egypt of which the equitableness is unquestionable, England shall abstain from undue self-aggrandizement, shall carry with her the sentiments of the European Powers, and shall show that her work is done, not only for her own interest but for the interest of others also,—for the sake of the native ruler of Egypt, of the Egyptian people, and of all Europeans, to whatever nation belonging, who may carry on trade or industry in the Nile valley,— then she will possess an additional vantage-ground in political controversies hereafter. Her objections will continue to carry the moral force which happily they have always commanded, if in the future aggression shall be attempted by any Power upon those Oriental regions which are exposed to interference or to attack. Justice in argument does not indeed prevail invariably when such conjunctures arise, and material as well as moral forces are called into play. Still, the Power which has moral force on its side possesses a fulcrum which it is advantageous to keep and disadvantageous to lose.

. . . For the civil administration of the country the Egyptian Government will require instruction and guidance. The manner of affording such guidance will probably have to be decided by England, after consulting the other European Powers. Still, for conducting this administration, Egypt should be taught to rely on itself mainly; assistance it may have for a time, but it need not expect to be kept permanently in leading-strings. . . . It would not be possible to instruct the Egyptians in the art of government by introducing British officers into most of the important offices in the interior of Egypt, as has been done in British India. Such officers would doubtless effect much good, but they would virtually do the work, and the Egyptians would be inept at learning so long as a foreign agency was at hand to perform the business for them. It is the sense of responsibility which quickens the faculties of men, and necessity is the parent of self-help. Let the Egyptians be impressed with the consideration that there must be a decent administration, if they are to remain a nation, and that they must work out the problem for themselves, then they will soon begin to learn. The notion of a Ministry, in which each member is the responsible Minister for some Department of State, has taken some root in Egypt. Although some Khedives seem to have treated their Ministers as secretaries only, still the heads of State Departments will practically be the depositaries of much real power. Whatever may be the character of Egyptian statesmen generally, there have been honest and capable persons among them. Here then is a ready-made school for Egyptian statesmanship, and if the Khedive will really search for capable men, he will doubtless find them more and more among the rising generation of educated Egyptians.

Then there is the chamber of representatives, known as the Assembly of Notables or Delegates. The institution of this Assembly some years ago is one of the most noteworthy experiments yet made in any Oriental country. Whether the mode of election was rude and informal or not, the members were elected. When they first met they had only a vague notion of their future functions as virtually a controlling body in the State. They seem, however, by degrees to have warmed to their work, and to have passed some important votes on public questions, which votes were respected by the executive power. This chamber, like many other reformed bodies, must have been paralyzed by the recent events; still its resuscitation ought to be a primary object when a new settlement of Egypt comes to be made. There may be difficulty in arranging an efficient system for conducting the elections; but as the Egyptian Government had the courage to begin some years ago, it should persevere, when its general functions are restored after the conclusion of military operations. As all Englishmen know, institutions of this description do not attain any large growth in a generation, even in a century. Still, new constitutions have a great advantage in the dearly bought experience of the most advanced nations. There does not seem to be any clear evidence as to what the duties of the Egyptian Assembly have been. . . . [Nonetheless] the political growth of this Assembly may be judiciously fostered; and there is a hopeful chance of its voice being raised on behalf of the improvements already enumerated, most of which tell in favour of the people. It will ventilate grievances, and will give expression to the griefs of millions who are practically inarticulate. It will operate to some extent as a check on the corruption and peculation which are the prevailing vices in the official circles of almost all Eastern countries, and from which Egypt is not as yet exempt according to impartial testimony. It will probably be jealously opposed to all expenditure, without much regard to the reasons which may justify or necessitate the outlay; as experience in other Eastern countries, under foreign rule, has shown that whenever the natives are able to make their voice heard, they object unsparingly to the public expenses incurred by their rulers. It will be likely to follow the same method with the indigenous ruler, in the belief that the disposition to incur expense on improvements is really inspired by European example. Thus its financial influence, though in many respects tending to wise economy, will in some respects be harmful as hampering beneficent expenditure on public improvement. But it is not likely in the immediate future to be allowed by the Government to exercise a Parliamentary power over the State purse. Without, however, possessing such a power as that, it may by criticism of annual budgets, and on other occasions, obtain considerable influence over the finances. In British India the ultimate power in effect rests with the Government; still, new taxation cannot be imposed without votes by the Legislative Councils, of which non-official persons, both European and Native are members, and of which the debates are free and public. Though in practice the Government can appoint official members enough to ensure a majority, still the feelings of the non-official sections of the Councils are much regarded. A similar result would doubtless ensue if some plan of this sort were to be tried in Egypt. Either, as in British India, the Government might be empowered to appoint official members; or if that were deemed unsuitable for Egypt, the Government might retain the power of overruling the decision of the Assembly. This might primâ facie appear to be an arbitrary procedure; but the tendency would be for the assembly to win its way more and more, and for the Khedive to become less and less disposed to override its decisions. Moreover, the freedom and publicity of its debates would soon stamp a mark on State affairs, even though its decisions were not final. The consciousness that men may say publicly what they think and feel (within reasonable and well understood limits) must produce among Egyptians the same effect as that which it has long produced among European nations, and which it is beginning to produce in British India.

. . . Some administrators, possessing much old experience in the East, may be sceptical as to the practicability of inducing a Native State like that of Egypt to govern really well. But, in British India, the practicability of this is nowadays satisfactorily demonstrated. In past days, even during the preceding generation, there was much misrule in the Native Indian States. But during the present generation, owing to British influence, many of these Native States are fairly governed, and some few are managed nearly as well as the British territories. The number of States thus ruled respectably is increasing from time to time. Individual talent and personal originality are perhaps better educed in the Native States than in the British territories. These States have produced and are producing many native administrators of an excellent type, among whom some may even be termed statesmen. All this augurs well for Egypt, as showing that, with some judicious guidance at first, she may ultimately become proficient in the art of self-government.

. . . In conclusion, if hereafter the finances and resources of Egypt shall enable the Native Government to undertake enterprises beyond the limits of Lower Egypt, then magnificent schemes for utilising the river-water only await the means of execution in what may be termed the middle valley of the Nile. Beyond that again, in the upper valley of the great river, in the basins of the White Nile, the Blue Nile, and their tributaries, there is a productive area abounding in natural resources capable of sustaining a great population, but as yet scantily inhabited by tribes who, though now fierce, are not untameable. In this wondrous region a beneficent work can be performed, if the Egyptian Government shall fortunately acquire the power of performance. In this work Samuel Baker and Gordon have been the pioneers. If it languish for a while, it may be resumed hereafter. Then, if it be pursued to its legitimate conclusion, the results will be the suppression of slavery and the production of endless benefit to the human race in Northern Africa.

Though her embrace of Indian nationalism is best known, in fact Annie Besant (see above) was a critic of British imperial policy in Africa as well. Her litany against British imperial involvement in Egypt is in stark contrast to Temple, above. Her anti-imperialism is grounded in part in the cost to the average Briton ("When did England promise to make good rotten security with the blood of her children?"), in part in an objection to the ways in which foreign countries are "trampled under foot" in the name of Liberalism.

Annie Besant, "Egypt" (1882)

IN the general election of 1880, the nation pronounced a distinct vote of censure on the foreign policy of Lord Beaconsfield. That policy was a policy of aggression on weak countries, under pretence of safe-guarding British interests, a policy of endeavoring to control the government of semi-barbarous States for our own advantage, and for the supposed protection of India. For this Lord Beaconsfield invaded Afghanistan; for this he stole Cyprus; for this he brought Indian troops to the Mediterranean. Fortunately for England, the Liberals were then in opposition, and every Liberal platform rang with denunciations of "the Jingo policy." The immorality, the folly, the waste of money—all these were fertile themes for Liberal eloquence, and so well was its work performed that the nation hurled Lord Beaconsfield from power, and placed at its head the man whose policy was one of peace, of righteousness, and of respect for the rights of others. The new Cabinet performed well a large part of the duty entrusted to it. It withdrew our troops from Afghanistan; after some delay and vaccillation, it restored the Transvaal to independence; it is now engaged in trying to undo the mischief wrought in Zululand. On one portion only of the foreign policy of Lord Beaconsfield has the Cabinet failed in fulfilling the mission it received from the nation. His policy in Egypt was not repudiated by them. They allowed themselves—probably influenced by Mr. Goschen—to sanction by silence the responsibilities he had created, and the injustices his interference had wrought; the consequence of this dereliction from duty is the war in which we are involved, a war whose end the wisest cannot foresee.

. . . To me a war of aggression is wrong, even though—alas! that it should be so—it is covered by the justly-revered name of William Ewart Gladstone. I admit that the war is part of the fatal legacy of mischief left by Lord Beaconsfield to the nation, but I think that in this, as in other matters, Mr. Gladstone should have reversed, not continued, that policy. The nation condemned the policy, and Mr. Gladstone was not placed in power to continue it. . . . I propose . . . brief answers to the arguments advanced in defence of the English policy in Egypt.

. . . Let us glance at the excuses made for this iniquitous war, excuses similar in character to those made in defence of Lord Beaconfield's aggressions, and as futile as they.

It was said (1) that Arabi Pasha is "an unscrupulous and savage adventurer," and that "in vindicating the rights of its own subjects against a bandit chief, Great Britain is only discharging a duty of police to which the Khedive was unequal and which the Sultan refused to undertake." So far as we have evidence, Arabi Pasha has acted with moderation, courage and patriotism. He has been supported by all the chiefs of his own religion, by the representative chamber of his country, by the army, and by the people. One man cannot intimidate a nation, and Arabi is strong because he incarnates Egyptian nationality. He is now proclaimed a rebel, but the proclamation was made only when the Khedive was a helpless prisoner in our hands, and when his life and throne depended on his obedience to his foreign masters. The long struggle of the Sultan shows how his own lawful sovereign regards Arabi, and to speak of him as a rebel is merely to insult a gallant enemy in the most cowardly and unworthy fashion. But suppose that Arabi were all that his foes call him, by what right do we interfere? Who made us the "police" of Egypt? Until we can govern Ireland decently, the less we say about misgovernment abroad the better. Suppose Egypt claimed to discharge the "duty of police to which the Queen was unequal" in Ireland, what should we say? And if not Egypt in Ireland, why we in Egypt? Of course, the answer is that we have the strength on our side, but we scarcely expected to hear the Beaconsfield theory that "might is right" from the lips of William Ewart Gladstone.

It is said (2) that Egypt must not "claim a right to close" the Suez Canal (J. G. Rogers). But when has Egypt made any such claim, or attempted to close the Canal? The only closure of the Canal has been made by the English military authorities, they having broken through the rule of non-interference with the passage which has been kept by the "bandit chief," although he might have increased his chances of safety by wholly destroying the great engineering work.

It is said (3), still by Mr. Rogers, that the "bondholders are the creditors of the Egyptian Khedive and his people." True, although the Khedive who incurred the debt, was a reckless spendthrift, encouraged by the speculators, and the people gained nought by the millions which they are called upon to repay. But when did the English people engage to force the payment of high interest at the point of the bayonet? When did England promise to make good rotten security with the blood of her children? Are English wives to be made widows, and English babes to be rendered fatherless, in order that greedy gamblers in foreign stocks may play with dice loaded with English lives? If we are to fight to fill brokers' purses in Egypt, we had better send troops to Chili, to Peru, to Bolivia, to Spain, to every bankrupt State where greed of high interest has accepted bad security.

It is said (4) that we are acting in self-defence. Mr. Henry Richard has well answered this monstrous plea:—

> "But perhaps the hardiest, I may almost say the most audacious plea put forward is that the bombardment of Alexandria was a strict act of self-defence. Now, look at that plea for a moment. You send your fleet to the waters of a foreign nation, which nobody pretends had up to that time attacked or molested us in any way. You send it avowedly in a menacing attitude, and with hostile purpose, and when the Government and people of that country take some precautions to fortify their coasts against this invading force, that is treated as an affront, and you pour your internal fire upon them 'in strict self-defence.' I find a man prowling about my house with obviously felonious purpose. I hasten to get locks and bars, and to barricade my windows. He says that is an insult and threat to him, and he batters down my doors and declares that he does so only as an act of strict self-defence."

It is said (5) that we are strengthening the authority of the Khedive. Do we strengthen the Khedive's position by forcing him into the most odious of all positions, that of the monarch who crushes out the legitimate aspirations of his people in obedience to foreign dictation? And even suppose that we hold Tewfik on his throne by our troops, as Napoleon III. held the Pope on his against the will of his subjects. Why? and for how long? We sent no troops to reinstate Bomba—but then we had not learned that it was the duty of a great nation to become bailiffs to enforce a judgment-summons taken out by usurers.

In this invasion of Egypt the most sacred principles of Liberalism have been trampled under foot. We have commenced a war to enforce a foreign yoke on a people striving to break it; to crush back into slavery a nation trying to shake it off; to stifle the aspirations of a race awaking into national life; to re-establish a despotism over a community endeavoring to create a system of self-government. Sure am I that the English people who rose in righteous protest against the wrongs inflicted on Afghanistan, on Zululand, and on the Transvaal, will rise again to repeat that protest against the wrongs inflicted on Egypt, and to recall Mr. Gladstone to those principles of national righteousness which he proclaimed so boldly and so effectually in his magnificent stand against Tory Jingoism.

Nicknamed "Chinese Gordon" because of his exploits in China and Taiping, Charles George Gordon (1833–85) was a British general whose death at Khartoum made him a national hero and an imperial martyr. Gordon was sent to Egypt in 1884 to put down Sudanese rebels in Khartoum. He was killed in the siege, though as C. R. Haines's essay below suggests, the actual circumstances of his demise remained a matter of speculation in the press and among his supporters at home, some of whom viewed him as a victim of a government that failed to relieve the siege in time to save him.

C. R. Haines, "Gordon's Death: What is the Truth?" (1890)

THOUGH five long years have passed since the fall of Kartum, messages and scraps of news connected with that famous event still reach the ears of Europe from the deserts of Kordofan. On Easter Monday last a despatch from Kartum, dated just six years previously, was duly delivered in Cairo, as not very long before a similar letter was handed in to its destination at Rome. The Emin Relief Expedition has lately brought in one or two letters from Mahdist generals on the same subject, while the papers of January 21st, 1889, published an entirely new and in many respects most striking description of the closing scenes at Kartum from the mouth of a Greek who had served as a dervish in the Mahdi's army.

Every detail concerning Gordon's last moments has a wonderful fascination for those of his countrymen—and few know how many they are—who would fain make him their pattern to live and to die by, and this is sufficient excuse for endeavouring to evolve out of a mass of conflicting evidence the most probable and consistent story of how Gordon really met his death.

. . . On February 12th, 1885, after our victory at Kirbekan, there was discovered in the enemy's camp a letter from Mohammed El Khair, Emir of Berber, to a certain Abdul Mejid. In this it is stated, on the authority of a despatch from head-quarters, that Kartum was taken on January 26th, and "the traitor" Gordon killed. This, in itself conclusive, has been since confirmed by a letter (brought back by the Emin Relief Expedition) from Omar Saleh, the Mahdi's general in Equatorial Africa, to Emin Pasha. . . . Whoever was killed by the Mahdi's followers was at once consumed by fire, and this is one of the greatest wonders happening to confirm what is written as about to come to pass before the end of the world. There is just another wonder: the spears carried by the Mahdi's followers had a flame burning at their points, and this we have seen with our eyes, not heard only.

Neither of these communications says anything as to the manner of Gordon's death, which is the more to be regretted as the evidence which we have on that head is more abundant than consistent. A very candid, but prudently anonymous, friend of General Gordon, who wrote recently to the *Times,* seemingly finds no difficulty in the matter, for he gives the following as the "most trustworthy account and one which has become matter of history."

When Gordon heard the rebels in the town, he said, "It is all finished; to-day Gordon will be killed"; and went down stairs, followed by four sergeants, who took their rifles with them. He took a chair and sat down on the right of the palace door, the four sergeants standing on the left. All at once a sheikh galloped up with some Bagaree Arabs. The sergeants were on the point of firing, when Gordon, seizing one of the rifles, said,

"No need of rifles to-day; Gordon is to be killed." The sheikh told Gordon that he had been ordered by the Mahdi to bring him alive. Gordon refused to go, saying he would die where he was, adding that no harm was to be done to the four sergeants who had not fired on the rebels. The sheikh repeated the order three times, and each time Gordon gave the same answer. After a few words the sheikh drew his sword, and rushing up to Gordon cut him over the left shoulder, Gordon looking him straight in the face and offering no resistance.

It is hard to estimate the value of this "the most trustworthy" account, without knowing the source from which it is drawn, but one can, at all events, say that it is not in keeping with all that we know of General Gordon. The words "To-day Gordon will be killed," have not the true ring of Gordon's utterances. He was not accustomed to think and speak of himself thus. Moreover, they are directly inconsistent with his views on fatalism and suicide, as the following extracts from his *Letters to his Sister* will show:—

'We have nothing further to do, when the scroll of events is unrolled, than to accept them as being for the best; but, *before it is unrolled,* it is another matter, for you would not say "I sat still, and let things happen."'

'It (the body) is a necessary covering to you and me while we sojourn in the world: what God has joined together let not man put asunder.'

To provoke death in the manner described above would have been equivalent to committing suicide, and would have laid Gordon fairly open to the censure which his favourite writer, Marcus Aurelius, passes upon the Christians, when he says that a man should be always ready to die, "not from mere obstinacy as with the Christians, but considerately and with dignity." We can appeal, too, to Gordon's own expressed opinion. Discussing what he should probably do in the event of the city being taken, he says:—

'I toss up in my mind whether, if the place is taken, to blow up the palace and all in it, or else to be taken and, with God's help, to maintain the faith, and, if necessary, suffer for it (which is most probable). The blowing up of the palace is the simplest, while the other means long and weary suffering and humiliation of all sorts. I think I shall elect for the last, not from fear of death, but because the former has more or less the taint of suicide, as it can do no good to anyone, and is, in a way, taking things out of God's hands.'

. . . We may take it for granted then, that Gordon was killed at or near the palace, but how he was killed is not so clear. Herr Fricke, a German traveller, who was in Kartum at the time, asserts that he was killed by some of his own soldiers, who hurled their spears at him as he was going to inspect the lines with a cane only in his hand. This does not sound likely. For one thing, 3.30 A.M. was too early for such an inspection. But the whole of Herr Fricke's testimony is so confused and inconsistent that it cannot, unsupported as it is, be set against the weight of evidence opposed to it.

Ahmed Mohammed Saleh, a sergeant of the Egyptian army, who escaped from the massacre, affirms that the Governor-General was slain in the Palace after killing two of his assailants, but Abdullah Bey Ismail, commander of the irregulars in Kartum, gives the following particulars:—

'Gordon, with a European doctor, an interpreter, and two others, killed 200 Arabs at least from the Palace. When their ammunition was exhausted, the Eastern door was thrown open, and Gordon, calm and serene, smoking a cigarette, and carrying a sword in his right hand, appeared. There was a pause for a moment, but one near him raised a rifle and shot the General dead.'

Another native witness declares that a body of the enemy rushed to the Palace, intending apparently to take Gordon alive, but he sallied out against them, revolver in hand. After defending himself till his revolver was emptied, he was killed. Sergeant Ibrahim el Kadi, who served in Kartum, says that Gordon was called on to become a Mussulman, and, when he refused, slain with a sword after killing ten of his assailants.

Still another version states that Gordon was slain axe in one hand sword in the other, after he had accounted for three of his murderers.

We may dismiss the axe at once. There could be no conceivable object in carrying such a weapon when arms in plenty were to be had. It is more difficult to decide between revolver and sword. That Gordon sometimes carried the former weapon we know from an entry in his diary under date September 14, 1876, where he says:—

'I will carry my revolver to-morrow, though the native (he was in danger from ambushes) will have first shot if he does attack me.'

But Gordon had none of the Berserker spirit in him; his courage, as the *Standard* has remarked, was not of the wild-cat type. A revolver would better suit one who is swift to shed blood, which Gordon never was; and we cannot suppose that, when once he saw that the city was lost, he would wish to destroy life needlessly. Gordon, therefore, in all probability carried either his sword, as several witnesses aver, or if not his sword, then no arms at all, but only that little cane which constantly went with him into battle. Herr Fricke, indeed, expressly asserts that the latter was the case, but his evidence seems, on other grounds, to be untrustworthy. It is far more likely that Gordon did on this occasion wear his sword, as part of his official uniform, which, as we shall presently see, there is reason to believe he donned before his death. . . .

The head was then cut off by a Dugaine Arab, and exposed according to one authority on the Palace Gate, or, as is more likely, according to another, on a pole in an open space between the Mahdi's two camps at Omdurman. The body, after lying some time upon the ground, was, as some say, thrown into the Nile, but, according to others, buried in the ditch south of Khartoum. But Saporia mentions a report that the Zubair above mentioned carried off the body secretly and preserved it. So much credence was given to this report that Zubair was taken before the Mahdi, and his house searched. No coffin, however, was found. It is quite possible, however, that some native of Kartum may have secretly buried the body of one whom so many had reason to look upon as their benefactor; and we cannot but regret that no effort has been made to recover the precious relics. Even if considerations for his own safety and that of the men under him prevented Sir Charles Wilson from sending in a flag of truce for that purpose, one would think that this might have been done when he rejoined the troops at Korti. The Mahdi would certainly have returned the body for a ransom. All such considerations were forgotten. Our only endeavour seems to have been to scuttle away as fast as possible from the Soudan. Gordon's body lies somewhere far in the waste Soudan. His priceless journal, captured at the wreck of the *Abbas,* is in the Treasury at Omdurman, while Lupton, an Englishman and one of Gordon's governors, languishes still in captivity under the Mahdi's successor.

Perhaps we may be allowed to conclude with a wonderful tribute to Gordon's influence in the Mohammedan world, published in the *Jewish Intelligencer.* A correspondent mentions a conversation which he had with one of the Shereefs of Mecca. Being asked whether he had known Gordon, the latter answered, with tears in his eyes, "Did you also know that noble man of the Old Book (the Bible)? . . . How astonished and edified I always was with his conversation! How humble he was for so great a Pasha! The rich and the poor, the free and the slaves, were alike his children. He was one of those men to whom the verse of the Koran applies: 'The servants of the Merciful are those who walk meekly in the earth, and when the ignorant speak unto them answer Peace! and who pass the night adoring their Lord and standing up to pray unto Him' (cxxv., 66) . . . "Before I knew him," he added, "I hated the Christians, but Gordon has taught me to love them, and I see more clearly every day that a religion which makes such heroic, faithful, and disinterested men can only be a religion coming from the true God. And, believe me, the whole Mohammedan world has felt, and still feels every day, the painful loss of the noble defender of Kartum. We must not grieve; he is happier than we; he is in a better world; for the Koran says: 'How excellent is the reward of those who work righteousness.'"

Part III

At Home with Imperial Culture:
Toward the Twentieth Century

A. Empire's Civilizing Missions

Here Temple (see above) directly addresses late-Victorian critics of the civilizing mission and lays out a point-by-point defense of Christian proselytizing—cementing the connection between conversion and military conquest in the process.

Sir Richard Temple, "Religious Missions in the East" (1881)

I have been informed that there are certain objections, originating, apparently, from ladies and gentlemen recently arrived from India, which have a damping effect and a chilling influence upon the hearts and efforts of those in England who are labouring to obtain substantial support for the missions, and are advocating the sacred cause. I am not altogether surprised at hearing these objections here in Lincoln, because in May last I heard very similar objections mentioned in another part of England.

The first objection . . . is that missions are failures. I will ask you to consider in what does failure or success consist. What would you consider to be a successful result? What is the actual result? Why, that at this moment there are 390,000 native Christians in India, of whom 100,000 are communicants. Besides these there are 200,000 boys and girls at school, who, though not all of them Christians, are entrusted by heathen parents to the missionaries, and are receiving Christian instruction. Out of these no less than 40,000 are girls. So that, with converts and scholars, there are 590,000 persons, or, in round numbers, 600,000 altogether. Upon these, what with mission funds and educational grants from the State, there are being spent 400,000l. a year. That gives an average of less than 15s. per head and I venture to say no Government or State Department could do so grand a work at a cheaper cost.

. . . The second objection is that missionaries make no converts. Well, now I suppose that objection comes from the circumstance that the missionaries are largely engaged in educational work, which work concerns natives who are not necessarily Christian. How stand the facts about converts? Let me remind you that those figures of 390,000 have been gradually rising. In 1850 there were 92,000, in 1860 138,000, in 1870 230,000, and now there are 390,000, so you see that in those thirty years there has been a vast increase. How has that result been brought about unless the missionaries have made converts? The facts that I have mentioned cannot be gainsaid, for they are derived from official reports. There is no doubt some natural increase of the native Christian population, as happily that population has existed for two or more generations; still it cannot have been so prolific as to have produced all tills increase, which must be in a great part due to accessions from without by conversion.

The third objection is that the converts that are made come from the humblest class, intellectually and socially. I must say that this is not a very Christian objection, because we have divine authority for specially attending to this class, and one of the distinguishing marks of our religion is that it has to be preached to the poor, the degraded, and the miserable. But let us take the objection as it stands. You must bear in mind that in India the high-class people are to the lower class as one to ten. In other words, out of every ten in the population nine would be of the lower class and but one of the high; therefore if Christians were equally divided over the population we should expect to find nine men of the lower classes to one man of the high.

. . . The fourth objection is that among the converts many become Christians for the sake of making a livelihood thereby. You will kindly bear in mind that all the principal missionaries in India are Europeans—necessarily so, and that being the case most of the good salaries, the loaves and fishes that might be in the missionary service, necessarily go to our own countrymen and not to the native Christians at all.

Still there are 4500 natives in the service of the missions; and the converts, taken altogether, number about 400,000. So out of 400,000 Christians, the number employed is only 4500, or just one in ninety. But say the 400,000 includes the families, divide it by half and take the males only, 200,000, and divide by 4500. You will find that it gives them about one in 45, or that out of every 45 males who are native Christians in India one receives service under the missionaries and 44 do not. Where, then, is the strong temptation for the natives to embrace Christianity for the sake of earning a livelihood? The Government itself scrupulously abstains from offering service to Christians because they are Christians, and there is nothing to be gained in that way by adopting Christianity. Therefore you will see the worthlessness of this objection also.

The fifth objection is that native Christians are not morally better than heathens, but, on the contrary, worse. I am afraid that idea comes from reports that are spread about sometimes by ladies and gentlemen returning from India regarding the conduct of natives who have been domestic servants. Conceive the idea of judging a great community, numbering hundreds of thousands, by the isolated conduct of some domestic servant! Why, English servants are largely in service on the Continent, and suppose a Russian, because he was disappointed with one or two of his English servants, were to say that the English were a worthless nation. Yet that is the way in which you are asked to judge of native Indian Christianity. But as a matter of fact there are very few native Christians employed in the service of Europeans. For if an English master has a native Christian servant, while all the other servants are heathen, you can readily believe that the latter would make the place too hot for him. But I will suggest to you a better way of considering this question. The conduct of native Christians should be observed in their homes, in their villages extending over whole tracts of country. Thus viewed in the mass, they are found to be good and respectable people. . . .

. . . The next objection is that many of the missionaries are deficient in the culture necessary for the performance of their duties. I presume that this objection means that there are two classes of missionaries; one for practical and parochial work, and the other for controversial work among the highly educated natives. Now those are two distinct branches of duty. The first branch does not require a peculiar degree of culture. It is necessary that there should be practical zeal and energy, with a capacity for managing a vast amount of trivial business, business which becomes difficult because of its quantity. Now for that sort of work you may readily understand that we require missionaries of one stamp. But for arguing, and reasoning, and philosophising, highly cultured missionaries are required—missionaries of another stamp, such as some of those whose names have been already mentioned, and the younger men who are furnished by Cambridge to our Society's old Mission at Delhi, or by the Oxford mission to Calcutta. Thus you will readily see it is not the fact that any of the missionaries are unsuited to the duties which they have to perform. Those who are required for parish work receive proper training, and those who require higher culture obtain it at institutions like those just mentioned, and in connection with Oxford and Cambridge.

The eighth objection is that missionary reports transmitted to England present over-coloured and misleading views of success in work. It may be that those reports abound too much in anecdotes, which however illustrative do not afford proof, any more than two or three swallows make a summer. But the real, perhaps tile only, fault of the missionary reports is that they generally fail to give an adequate idea of tile magnitude of the work, and do not take quite so comprehensive a survey of the facts and figures as they might. You will see then that the reports are thus in some respects actually under-coloured.

The ninth objection is that labour in England for the support of missions abroad is not practical, but is little more than a romance, whereby good people amuse themselves. For one instant let me remind you of the result deducible from the facts which I will venture to marshal out for your consideration. The romance, if it be a romance, consists greatly, I might say sublimely, of the following array of figures. We have 400,000l. of annual expenditure, 432 mission stations, 500 European missionaries, and 3 missionary bishops, 4500 native assistants, 300 native ordained clergy, 85 training schools, and 4 normal institutions, from which are turned out 3000 students annually. We raise 20,000l. a year from poor native Christians. We have 24 mission presses, from which there issue three-quarters of a million of religious books annually, which are sold to the native public for a sum of 3800l. a year. We have 400,000 native Christians, and 200,000 boys and girls at school, of whom 1700 have at different times entered the universities established by law in India, and of whom again 700 have passed on to the taking of degrees. There are 40,000 girls at school and 1300 classes for the Zenana Missions in the apartments of the native ladies, and those classes are attended by 3000 lady students. I feel in giving those figures as if I were reading the record of some great State Department, and not of private enterprise such as this really is. I will say that it is truly honorable to British people and to the zeal of the Protestant Church. You must remember that it is a work which, if not done by our societies, cannot be done at all. It is a work from which Government are bound to abstain. I have always felt in India that the Government which I served might be able to make war with energy or conclude "peace with honour," or they might cover the country with a network of railways and canals, foster a world-wide commerce, spread industry and enterprise over the land, preserve order, dispense justice, diffuse secular education, and give ethical instruction; but with all those things there is one thing which the Government cannot give, and that is the light of Christian religion and morality. That sacred lamp it is for us to light and to carry aloft in distant regions. . . .

Then comes the tenth and last objection, which is that the delay in attaining missionary success has been so long protracted that people can hardly exert themselves on that account with so many pressing calls at home. I have shown you that success has already been vouchsafed. The Right Reverend Chairman has eloquently alluded to the great missionary Henry Martyn, a century ago. I wonder whether our forefathers foresaw the greatness of the success which a hundred years would produce. You will remember, too, that the result has been attained by an increase of 50 per cent. in each decade during the last thirty years, or one generation of man. If a similar result goes on, and we prosper equally during the generation upon which we are now entering, then the present number of converts will have increased by the end of that generation from 400,000 to 1,350,000, and the scholars to 625,000, total, 1,945,000, or, in round numbers, two millions. During the coming generation the result is likely to be even greater, because the work is now backed up, not only by European energy and the zeal of the Protestant Church, but also by the influence which education on the part of the State is producing throughout the land and amongst all classes of the people. Thus India is like a mighty bastion which is being battered by heavy artillery. We have given blow after blow, and thud after thud, and the effect is not at first very remarkable; but at last with a crash the mighty structure will come toppling down, and it is our hope that some day the heathen religions of India will in like manner succumb.

Written almost 20 years after the Treaty of Tietsin (1858) and in the very year when Queen Victoria accepted the title of "Empress of India" (1876), Edward Fry's essay captures the ongoing intersection of British imperial interests with the controversial trade in opium—especially where the commercial and strategic interests of India were concerned. His references to the Anti-opium Society and the comparisons he makes between the addictive properties of opium and whisky suggest how deeply the opium controversy reached into domestic reform movements, and how connected questions of imperial revenue and the civilizing mission might be.

Edward Fry, "China, England, and Opium" (1876)

It is impossible to think for a moment of our relations with China, without recurring to the opium question. In an interesting paper on those relations, in the November number of the *Fortnightly Review,* Dr. Bridges concluded with an almost despairing allusion to this question, as if it were one about which there is no real controversy as to the merits, and no hope of those merits being attended to, or allowed really to govern our counsels. There is too much ground for such a feeling; and yet I have such faith in the good feeling of my countrymen, that I believe that if they could once realize what it is that we have done and are doing as regards opium, they would rise as one man, and get rid of the accursed thing, which, as sure as there is a moral government in the world, will one day or the other find us out.

India is a long way off; China is still further; the Opium War was a long time ago; the opium question is continually referred to, and as continually passed over, so that most of us feel at once ignorant and weary of it, and so pass on to the things more ready to our hand. All these causes were operating to dull the consciences of most Englishmen as regards the opium question, when there was superadded yet another, which is greatly to be regretted. The Anti-Opium Society, which represents the last uncertain flicker of the national conscience on this subject, succeeded in bringing the matter before the House of Commons last session, and in doing so raised an absolutely false and irrelevant issue, and contrived to support it with some very unfortunate arguments. No doubt they will do better next time, but their indiscretion has interposed a new difficulty in the way of arousing the moral feelings of the nation on the subject, though their publications afford much useful information, for which I desire to express my obligation to the Society.

The real evil of our dealings with China is this: the Indian Government is interested in the sale of opium in two ways—first, as the proprietors of a certain quantity of opium raised in Bengal, and, secondly, as the owners of a transit-tax paid on other opium raised in native States and shipped at Bombay. In these two capacities we have long desired and still desire that China should buy opium. The Chinese Government has long believed and still believes opium to be prejudicial to its people, and desires to prohibit its growth and import; but, from the Opium War down to this hour, England has . . . produced and is producing in the minds of the Chinese authorities and people a sense of wrong and hostility to England. It is true that this is not the only source of hostile feelings, and that on some, though I fear not on all the other points in controversy, we are somewhat less in the wrong. But of all the sources of this feeling, opium is the principal, and therefore I aver that this feeling on the part of the Chinese is just and reasonable, and that in any quarrel which springs from that feeling, England's mouth is stopped from complaining, for England is the source and origin of that feeling.

The interest of the Indian Government in opium is very large. It retains, as I have said, in its own hands a monopoly of the right to grow and manufacture opium in Bengal; the gross revenue from this source in 1872–3, amounted to upwards of six millions sterling. Beyond this, there is a quantity of opium grown in Malwa, in the regions of Central India, and within the territory of native States, which is shipped at Bombay, and which is taxed on its transit through our territories. The amount of these pass-fees realized in 1872–3 was upwards of two and a-half millions sterling, and the produce of Malwa is stated to have trebled within the last three years.

This being the state of things, the motion of Mr. Mark Stewart in the House of Commons, made on behalf of the Anti-Opium Society, was addressed only to the evil produced by the monopoly; and what was proposed was, that England should abandon the monopoly practically in favour of private trade. This was a strangely erroneous issue to raise; for surely it is absolutely unimportant whether we raise revenue by a monopoly or by a tax. To me it seems idle, or very nearly idle, to harp on the difference between the Indian Government growing opium and permitting it to be grown; for the responsibilities of a despotic government are greater than those of a free State. To me it seems idle to suggest that there is any wrong in a Government deriving income from a poison; for, for my part, I would tax gin and whisky to the uttermost. Furthermore, it seems to me idle to complain of the tax and the monopoly in themselves, for both might be the means of lessening the growth and production of opium, just as in Bengal the tax on ganja (the spirit derived from hemp) has been levied so as in the course of fifteen years to double the income and lessen the consumption by a third. But what I do object to is that, being interested, as I have pointed out, in the sale of opium, the Government has worked both tax and monopoly alike for one purpose, and for one purpose only, viz., the acquisition of the largest amount of gain, and that without regard to the moral re-sults on China, and in defiance of the wishes of the Government and people of China.

. . . I believe, but I will not now urge, that opium is a poison, and that it ruins the bodies and souls of thousands of men. For my line of thought, no such proposition is needful; it is enough that the Chinese Government honestly objected to it. But I will carry my argument a step further, and without discussing whether some men can eat opium without harm, or whether it acts first on the mind or the body, or whether it is worse than gin or not so bad, this I will say, almost without fear of contradiction, that opium is a drug of such a character that the Chinese Government were at liberty, if they so determined, to hold it to be a poison, and that the Indian Government and English diplomacy had no right to say "You shall not hold it a poison." Just consider these four points: (1) that we English people have determined that in England opium is a poison, and have regulated its sale as such; (2) that in the treaties with Japan entered into by Lord Elgin we have agreed to a prohibition of opium as an article of commerce, the American treaty with Japan doing the same; (3) that our Indian Government has dis-couraged the consumption of opium in India, and that (to refer only to two eminent authorities) Sir George Campbell and Sir William Muir have both recently referred to a taste for this drug amongst our Indian fellow-subjects as a source of regret. . . .

An argument against interfering with the opium revenue, somewhat to the follow-ing effect, is often urged or suggested:—"It is very well," it is said, "for you to assume this high moral tone about the opium revenue; the revenue is not yours, but belongs to India, and with it England has nothing to do. To abolish the traffic is to throw some nine millions more of annual taxation on the already over-taxed population of India, and that for a scruple of some weak-minded philanthropists in England. Pray pay for your own philanthropy, and do not make another country pay for it." Let us consider this objection a little; and let us note, in the first place, that it may be taken to concede the justness of the objection to the revenue; it only objects to the person of the objec-tor. Let us note, in the next place, that the assumption of facts is entirely erroneous. The Indian budget is as much cognizable by the Imperial Parliament as the home bud-get, subject, of course, to this difference—that in one case the representatives of a na-tion settle its own taxation, and that, in the other, the representatives of one nation deliberate on the taxation of another. India is, as it were, a minor, under the guardian-ship of England, and England is, as it were, a trustee for India in the administration of Indian affairs. But in taking upon ourselves that burthen and that duty we have in-curred no obligation to do for India what we might not lawfully do for ourselves. If, in the course of our trusteeship, we have sold a poison wickedly, for the gain of a minor are we bound to continue so to do? Have we lost the right of repentance, because our sin enures to some one else's benefit? India cannot change the policy, for she is in tute-lage: England cannot change the policy, for she is a trustee; therefore the sin must go on for ever. Is that sound reasoning? The objection is, no doubt, sometimes put in a form which seems to assume that the question should be left to the Viceroy in Coun-cil, or to the Secretary of State in Council of India. But when we bear in mind the ex-tent and character of the interference of the Imperial Legislature in Indian affairs, such a proposition hardly bears stating.

But there is yet another reason why the question is an Imperial one. Our policy to-wards China is the policy, not of the Indian Government but of the Imperial Govern-ment; and India, which relies for its opium revenue on the pressure of England on China, can never assert that the question is not one of Imperial cognizance, and of di-rect interest to the English tax-payer. . . .

J. Ewing Ritchie goes even further than Fry—not just by insisting that "opium is to the Chinese what the quid is to the British tar, or the gin-bottle to the London charwoman," but by taking us into one of London's infamous opium dens. This graphic account, intended as an example of the corrupting effects of addiction, no doubt also offered middle-class readers an opportunity for a certain kind of arm-chair imperial exploration.

J. Ewing Ritchie, from *Days and Nights in London* (1880)

. . . AN effort is being made by a band of British philanthropists . . . to put down, if not the opium traffic, at any rate that part of it which is covered by the British flag. Opium is to the Chinese what the quid is to the British tar, or the gin-bottle to the London charwoman. But in reality, as I firmly believe, for the purpose of opening the door to all sorts of bribery and corruption, the traffic is prohibited as much as possible by the Chinese Government, for the ostensible object of preserving the health and morals of the people. This task is a very difficult one. A paternal Government is always in difficulties, and once we Christian people of England have gone to war with the Chinese in order to make them take our Indian-grown opium—a manufacture in which a large capital is invested, and the duty of which yields the British Government in India a magnificent revenue. It is a question for the moralist to decide how far a Government is justified in saying to a people: "We know so and so is bad, but as you will use it, you may as well pay a heavy tax on its use." That is the practical way in which statesmen look at it, and of course there is a good deal to be said for that view. But it is not pleasant to feel that money, even if it be used for State purposes, is made in a dirty manner; though I have been in countries where the minister of the religion of holiness and purity is content to take a part of his living from the brothel-keeper and the prostitute. Evidently there are many men as ready to take the devil's money as was Rowland Hill to accept the Bible at his hands.

. . . Have my readers ever been in Bluegate Fields, somewhere down Ratcliffe Highway? . . . The City missionary and the East London Railway between them have reformed the place. To the outward eye it is a waste howling spot, but it is a garden of Eden to what it was when a policeman dared not go by himself into its courts, and when respectability, if it ever strayed into that filthy quarter, generally emerged from it minus its watch and coat, and with a skull more or less cracked, and with a face more or less bloody.

"Thanks to you," said a surgeon to a City missionary who has been labouring in the spot some sixteen years, and is now recognised as a friend wherever he goes, "thanks to you," said the surgeon, "I can now walk along the place alone, and in safety, a thing I never expected to do;" and I believe that the testimony is true, and that it is in such districts the labours of the City missionary are simply invaluable. Down in those parts what we call the Gospel has very little power. It is a thing quite outside the mass. There are chapels and churches, it is true, but the people don't go into them. I pass a great Wesleyan chapel. "How is it attended?" I ask; and the answer is: "Very badly indeed." I hear that the nearest Independent chapel is turned into a School Board school; and there is Rehoboth,—I need not say it is a hyper place of worship, and was, when Bluegate Fields was a teeming mass of godless men and women, only attended by some dozen or so of the elect, who prayed their prayers, and read their Bible, and listened to their parsons with sublime indifference to the fact that there at their very door, under their very eyes, within reach of their very hands, were souls to be saved, and brands to be snatched from the burning, and jewels to be won for the Redeemer's crown. I can only hear of one preacher in this part who is really getting the people to hear him, and he is the Rev. Harry Jones, who deserves to be made a bishop, and who would be, if the Church of England was wise and knew its dangers, and was careful to avert the impending storm, which I, though I may not live to see the day, know to be near. But let us pass, on leaving Rehoboth, a black and ugly carcass, on the point of being pulled down by the navvy. I turn into a little court on my right, one of the very few the railway has spared for the present. It may be there are some dozen houses in the court. The population is, I should certainly imagine, quite up to the accommodation of the place. Indeed, if I might venture to make a remark, it would be to the effect that a little more elbow-room would be of great advantage to all. From every door across the court are ropes, and on these ropes the blankets and sheets and family linen are hanging up to dry. These I have to duck under as I walk along; but the people are all civil, though my appearance makes them stare, and all give a friendly and respectful greeting to the City missionary by my side.

All at once my conductor disappears in a little door, and I follow, walking, on this particular occasion, by faith, and not by sight; for the passage was dark, and I knew not my way. I climb up a flight of stairs, and find myself in a little crib—it would be an abuse of terms to call it a room. It is just about my height, and I fancy it is a great deal darker and dingier than the room in which a first-class misdemeanant like Colonel Baker was confined. The place is full of smoke. It is not at first that I take in its contents. As I stand by the door, there are two beds of an ancient character; between these beds is a very narrow passage, and it is in this passage I recognise the master of the house—a black-eyed, cheerful Chinaman, who has become so far naturalised amongst us as to do us the honour of taking the truly British name of Johnson. Johnson is but thinly clad. I see the perspiration glistening on his dark and shining skin; but Johnson seems as pleased to see me as if he had known me fifty years. In time, through the smoke, I see Johnson's friends—dark, perspiring figures curled on the beds around, one, for want of room, squatting, cross-legged, in a corner—each with a tube of the shape and size of a German flute in his hands. I look at this tube with some curiosity. In the middle of it is a little bowl. In that little bowl is the opium, which is placed there as if it were a little bit of tow dipped in tar, and which is set fire to by being held to the little lamps, of which there are three or four on the bed or in the room. This operation performed, the smoker reclines and draws up the smoke, and looks a very picture of happiness and ease. Of course I imitate the bad example; I like to do as the Romans do, and Johnson hands me a tube which I put into my mouth, while, as I hold it to the lamp, he inserts the heated opium into the bowl; and, as I pull, the thick smoke curls up and adds to the cloud which makes the room as oppressive as the atmosphere of a Turkish bath. How the little pig-eyes glisten! and already I feel that I may say: "Am I not a man and a brother?" The conversation becomes general. Here we are jolly companions every one. Ching tells me the Chinese don't send us the best tea; and grins all across his yellow face as I say that I know that, but intimate that they make us pay for it as if they did. Tsing smiles knowingly as I ask him what his wife does when he is so long away. Then we have a discussion as to the comparative merits of opium and beer, and my Chinese friends sagely observe that it is all a matter of taste. "You mans like beer, and we mans in our country like opium." All were unanimous in saying that they never had more than a few whiffs, and all that I could learn of its effects when taken in excess was that opium sent them off into a stupid sleep. With the somewhat doubtful confessions of De Quincey and Coleridge in my memory, I tried to get them to acknowledge sudden impulses, poetic inspirations, splendid dreams; but of such things these little fellows had never conceived; the highest eulogium I heard was: "You have pains—pain in de liver, pain in de head—you smoke—all de pains go." The most that I could learn was that opium is an expensive luxury for a poor man. Three-halfpenny-worth only gives you a few minutes' smoke, and these men say they don't smoke more at a time. Lascar Sall, a rather disreputable female, well known in the neighbourhood, would, they told me, smoke five shillings-worth of opium a day. Johnson's is the clubhouse of the Chinese. He buys the opium and prepares it for smoking, and they come and smoke and have a chat, and a cup of tea and a slice of bread and butter, and go back and sleep on board ship. Their little smoking seemed to do them no harm. The City missionary says he has never seen them intoxicated. It made them a little lazy and sleepy—that is all; but they had done their day's work, and had earned as much title to a little indulgence as the teetotaler, who regales himself with coffee; or the merchant, who smokes his cigar on his pleasant lawn on a summer's eve. I own when I left the room I felt a little giddy, that I had to walk the crowded streets with care; but then I was a novice, and the effect would not be so great on a second trial. I should have enjoyed a cup of good coffee after; but that is a blessing to which we in London, with all our boasted civilisation, have not attained. I frankly avow, as I walked to the railway station, I almost wished myself back in the opium den. There I heard no foul language, saw no men and women fighting, no sots reeling into the gutters, or for safety shored up against the wall. For it was thus the mob, through which I had to pass, was preparing itself for the services of the sanctuary, and the rest of the Sabbath.

China had been the site of the Christian civilizing mission since the Jesuits first arrived in the sixteenth century. British communities in China were varied: there were settlers connected to the treaty port service industries, expatriate businessmen and their families, and of course missionaries and mission workers. These latter were as a whole probably more directly in contact with Chinese people than other Britons of this "Chinese Raj," though they shared many of the imperial attitudes of proselytizing groups elsewhere in the empire. In the document below, Irene Barnes leads yet another kind of imperial tour "behind the Great Wall" and into the very interiors of Chinese life—with the hope that the images she brings to the sightline of metropolitan readers will inspire them to commit themselves to the redemption of this particular part of the "heathen world."

Irene H. Barnes, from *Behind the Great Wall* (1897)

GREAT China—the antipodes of Great Britain—teeming, million-peopled "Land of Sinim," how little we English men and women concern ourselves about it! Perhaps we drink its tea every afternoon; probably we wear its silk every day; and certainly, though we may not always recognise it, we are indebted in a thousand ways to that ingenious, industrious, enduring people so far away. But, widely separated as we are, and ignorant of each other as we remain, how can we grow enthusiastic over the eccentric and conservative Chinese family circle over the sea?

Shall we give a glance at the land three thousand miles Eastward Ho?

. . . Behind . . . [the] Great Wall exists a wondrous empire, the most ancient in the world. Its eighteen provinces cover an area of 5,300,000 square miles, a surface eighteen times as large as Great Britain. Its fourteen hundred and sixty walled cities, besides innumerable towns and villages, are so densely populated, its river-craft is so crowded with human life, that it would take nineteen years for all the Chinese to walk past a given point in single file at the rate of thirty a minute, day and night. For China contains nearly 400,000,000 souls. Behind the Great Wall lives ONE OUT OF EVERY THREE PERSONS BORN INTO THE WORLD!

. . . Glancing . . . at the people themselves, we find the Chinese workman content to live on rice and vegetables costing three-halfpence per diem, to dress in plain blue cotton blouses and roomy trousers (always of one shape and make), fastened with pieces of twisted calico for buttons, straw sandals, price one halfpenny a pair, and considering himself "passing rich" on wages varying from 3*d.* to 6*d.* a day. A broad-brimmed bamboo hat shields his shaven forehead from the sun, and a huge, stiff cape of palm-tree, fibre-like thatch protects him from the rain. Engage him as your "boy," and, winding his "pigtail" round his head, as a housemaid tucks up her skirt to scrub, or, funnier still, *pocketing* it, he will set to work, carrying out his favourite motto, "Can do."

Chinese men of the upper class are dressed in brilliant flowing robes, their feet encased in black satin boots with white felt soles, and their hair, shaven off their foreheads, is braided behind into one long tasselled queue, interwoven with coloured ribbons, reaching almost to the ground!

Women, no less than men, are the slaves of custom. Etiquette forbids a Chinese lady to walk out of doors. But it is unnecessary, since etiquette also has made her a cripple! For at six years of age almost every girl in China has to undergo the bandaging of both feet, in order to reduce them to the correct and fashionable size. A lady's shoe measures two and a half inches in length! To render them capable of wearing such minute cases, the feet are tightly bound, the four small toes being tucked under the sole of the foot, of which after a time they become a part, and the heel brought forward. The excruciating agony endured, while for two years the foot is crushed, stops growing, and practically dies, can better be imagined than described! When at last the process is complete, the Chinese lady, swaying and tottering along on her great-toe and heel, is considered as graceful in her movements as the "waving of the willow trees," and she is complimented on her "golden lily feet."

. . ."What a good mother she must have had!" say her friends, of a girl whose feet are particularly small. When a girl is to be married, the question is not, "Is she good, clever, beautiful?" but, "What is the size of her feet?"

Betrothed so early that it is no uncommon thing for a boy of eight to have as "wife" a baby-girl only six months old, the bride-elect is carried off by her future (generally unkind) mother-in-law to live with her. Once married, many Chinese women of good birth leave home for years together. It is improper for them to speak to a man. They have not been considered worth educating, and therefore their lives are spent in an endless, aimless round of embroidering their shoes, painting their faces, eyebrows and eyelashes, building up and decorating their hair, binding and rebinding their feet, cooking sweet-meats, nursing their children, and smoking—often, alas! though secretly, the opium pipe!

Throughout their careers, women are regarded as "moulded out of faults." If a husband is driven to make mention of his wife, he speaks of her as his "dull thorn," or by some equally uncomplimentary term. It is not at all uncommon for husbands to punish their wives severely; sometimes, no doubt, under great provocation, for Chinese women, untaught, unloved, uncared for, have all the faults and failings of unreclaimed natures; but at others for little or no reason. The question, "Does your husband beat you?" is very commonly put to English married ladies by Chinese women.

Obedience and propriety are the ideal, the religion of Chinese womanhood. Buddhism teaches her that there is no heaven for one so worthless as a woman; but there is the faint possibility that after a virtuous life and having passed through eighteen hells, she may be reborn on the earth as a little boy. She worships her ancestors on her bridal day by burning incense sticks before memorial tablets placed upon a shelf in her room, and perhaps prostrates herself from time to time in front of an "altar to heaven and earth" built in her garden.

The interior of the women's apartments, always at the back of the house, is never very inviting. No contrivance for warming the rooms by means of fires or stoves exists, except that found in the "*kang*," or brick bed, on which the inmates lie and sit. The Chinese know nothing of the enjoyment of their "ain fireside"; they rely on quilted and fur garments for warmth in winter. Even on a bright day the room is dim, and the absence of carpets and fireplaces, and of windows, renders it cheerless. Instead of being always rectangular, the doors are sometimes made round, leaf-shaped, or semi-circular; and it is thought desirable [that] they should not open opposite each other, lest evil spirits find their way in from the street! For this reason, too, the narrow Chinese streets are not laid out straight. Each house makes a slight angle with its neighbour, it being considered rather unlucky to have them exactly even. The general arrangement of a Chinese city presents a labyrinth of streets, alleys, and by-ways, very perplexing to a stranger who has neither plan nor directory to guide him, nor number upon the houses or shops to direct him.

Buddhism and Confucianism, the two idolatrous religions of China, as they are practised, foster all that is evil in the Chinese character, which by nature is essentially superstitious, cruel, cunning, and avaricious. However good the maxims of Buddha and Confucius may be, they have taken no moral hold upon their followers.

Yes, to the Asiatic traveller "Far Cathay" is an intensely interesting problem. Whether looked at from an historical, commercial or political point of view, it cannot fail to strike him as being the most remarkable country in the world. But to the CHRISTIAN MISSIONARY, China with its vast multitudes of heathen, its dark systems of religion, its degradation of woman, its disregard of human life, and the sin and suffering of its poorer classes—"stowed as ballast on steamers, crowded like cattle on sampan boats, from birth to old age"—is a heart-rending, soul-stirring spectacle.

A million a month are dying without GOD. Fourteen hundred of them have sunk into Christless graves during the last hour! Thirty-three thousand will pass to-day for ever beyond our reach! Despatch a missionary tomorrow, and one million and a quarter of immortal souls for whom Christ died will have passed to their final account before he can reach their shores. A low wail of helpless, hopeless misery, "a cry as of pain," is arising from China—one-half of the heathen world. What shall the answer be—from you? from me? Has it pierced our ears? Has it moved our hearts?

* * * *

Some among us have heard that cry, and "counting not their lives dear unto them" have entered the great walled land, prepared to lay them out or lay them down in winning China for Christ. In yonder glory there is a martyr-band whose crown of rejoicing in the day of the Lord Jesus will be a cluster of firstfruits of the Gospel from far Fuhkien. And to-day a little company of women are still teaching and winning, yearning over and bringing to the Saviour's feet their Chinese sisters who for long years have "sat in darkness and the shadow of death" BEHIND THE GREAT WALL.

Britons, and especially Londoners, did not have to travel to the colonies to see all manner of nomads, tribes, and "races," as Mayhew (1812–1887) details here. Though he was to become one of the Victorian era's most famous "philanthropic journalists" and indeed a pioneer of that genre, he began his career as a dramatist, traces of which can be found in this pseudoscientific account of the London street scene.

Henry Mayhew,
from *London Labour and the London Poor* (1861)

Of Wandering Tribes in General.

Of the thousand millions of human beings that are said to constitute the population of the entire globe, there are—socially, morally, and perhaps even physically considered—but two distinct and broadly marked races, viz., the wanderers and the settlers—the vagabond and the citizen—the nomadic and the civilized tribes. Between these two extremes, however, ethnologists recognize a mediate variety, partaking of the attributes of both. There is not only the race of hunters and manufacturers—those who live by shooting and fishing, and those who live by producing—but, say they, there are also the herdsmen, or those who live by tending and feeding, what they consume.

Each of these classes has its peculiar and distinctive physical as well as moral characteristics. "There are in mankind," says Dr. Pritchard, "three principal varieties in the form of the head and other physical characters. Among the rudest tribes of men—the hunters and savage inhabitants of forests, dependent for their supply of food on the accidental produce of the soil and the chase—a form of head is prevalent which is mostly distinguished by the term '*prognathous*,' indicating a prolongation or extension forward of the jaws. A second shape of the head belongs principally to such races as wander with their herds and flocks over vast plains; these nations have broad lozenge-shaped faces (owing to the great development of the cheek bones), and pyramidal skulls. The most civilized races, on the other hand—those who live by the arts of cultivated life,—have a shape of the head which differs from both of those above mentioned. The characteristic form of the skull among these nations may be termed oval or elliptical."

These three forms of head, however, clearly admit of being reduced to two broadly-marked varieties, according as the bones of the face or those of the skull are more highly developed. A greater relative development of the jaws and cheek bones, says the author of the "Natural History of Man," indicates a more ample extension of the organs sub-servient to sensation and the animal faculties. Such a configuration is adapted to the wandering tribes; whereas, the greater relative development of the bones of the skull—indicating as it does a greater expansion of the brain, and consequently of the intellectual faculties—is especially adapted to the civilized races or settlers, who depend mainly on their knowledge of the powers and properties of things for the necessaries and comforts of life.

Moreover it would appear, that not only are all races divisible into wanderers and settlers, but that each civilized or settled tribe has generally some wandering horde intermingled with, and in a measure preying upon, it.

According to Dr. Andrew Smith, who has recently made extensive observations in South Africa, almost every tribe of people who have submitted themselves to social laws, recognizing the rights of property and reciprocal social duties, and thus acquiring wealth and forming themselves into a respectable caste, are surrounded by hordes of vagabonds and outcasts from their own community. Such are the Bushmen and *Sonquas* of the Hottentot race—the term "*sonqua*" meaning literally *pauper*. But a similar condition in society produces similar results in regard to other races; and the Kafirs have their Bushmen as well as the Hottentots—these are called *Fingoes*—a word signifying wanderers, beggars, or outcasts. The Lappes seem to have borne a somewhat similar relation to the Finns; that is to say, they appear to have been a wild and predatory tribe who sought the desert like the Arabian Bedouins, while the Finns cultivated the soil like the industrious Fellahs.

But a phenomenon still more deserving of notice, is the difference of speech between the Bushmen and the Hottentots. The people of some hordes, Dr. Andrew Smith assures us, vary their speech designedly, and adopt new words, with the intent of rendering their ideas unintelligible to all but the members of their own community. For this last custom a peculiar name exists, which is called "*cuze-cat*." This is considered as greatly advantageous in assisting concealment of their designs.

Here, then, we have a series of facts of the utmost social importance. (1) There are two distinct races of men, viz.:—the wandering and the civilized tribes; (2) to each of these tribes a different form of head is peculiar, the wandering races being remarkable for the development of the bones of the face, as the jaws, cheek-bones, &c., and the civilized for the development of those of the head; (3) to each civilized tribe there is generally a wandering horde attached; (4) such wandering hordes have frequently a different language from the more civilized portion of the community, and that adopted with the intent of concealing their designs and exploits from them.

It is curious that no one has as yet applied the above facts to the explanation of certain anomalies in the present state of society among ourselves. That we, like the Kafirs, Fellahs, and Finns, are surrounded by wandering hordes—the "Sonquas" and the "Fingoes" of this country—paupers, beggars, and outcasts, possessing nothing but what they acquire by depredation from the industrious, provident, and civilized portion of the community;—that the heads of these nomads are remarkable for the greater development of the jaws and cheekbones rather than those of the head;—and that they have a secret language of their own—an English "*cuze-cat*" or "slang" as it is called—for the concealment of their designs: these are points of coincidence so striking that, when placed before the mind, make us marvel that the analogy should have remained thus long unnoticed.

The resemblance once discovered, however, becomes of great service in enabling us to use the moral characteristics of the nomad races of other countries, as a means of comprehending the more readily those of the vagabonds and outcasts of our own. Let us therefore, before entering upon the subject in hand, briefly run over the distinctive, moral, and intellectual features of the wandering tribes in general. . . .

Of the Wandering Tribes of this Country.

THE nomadic races of England are of many distinct kinds—from the habitual vagrant— half-beggar, half-thief—sleeping in barns, tents, and casual wards—to the mechanic or tramp, obtaining his bed and supper from the trade societies in the different towns, on his way to seek work. Between these two extremes there are several mediate varieties—consisting of pedlars, showmen, harvest-men, and all that large class who live by either selling, showing, or doing something through the country. These are, so to speak, the rural nomads—not confining their wanderings to any one particular locality, but ranging often from one end of the land to the other. Besides these, there are the urban and suburban wanderers, or those who follow some itinerant occupation in and round about the large towns. Such are, in the metropolis more particularly, the pickpockets—the beggars—the prostitutes—the street-sellers—the street-performers—the cabmen—the coachmen—the watermen—the sailors and such like. In each of these classes—according as they partake more or less of the purely vagabond, doing nothing whatsoever for their living, but moving from place to place preying upon the earnings of the more industrious portion of the community, so will the attributes of the nomad tribes be found to be more or less marked in them. Whether it be that in the mere act of wandering there is a greater determination of blood to the surface the body, and consequently a less quantity sent to the brain, the muscles being thus nourished at the expense of the mind, I leave physiologists to say. But certainly be the physical cause what it may, we must all allow that in each of the classes above-mentioned, there is a greater development of the animal than of the intellectual or moral nature of man, and that they are all more or less distinguished for their high cheek-bones and protruding jaws—for their use of a slang language—for their lax ideas of property—for their general improvidence—their repugnance to continuous labour—their disregard of female honour—their love of cruelty—their pugnacity—and their utter want of religion.

Of the London Street-folk.

THOSE who obtain their living in the streets of the metropolis are a very large and varied class; indeed, the means resorted to in order "to pick up a crust," as the people call it, in the public thoroughfares (and such in many instances it *literally* is,) are so multifarious that the mind is long baffled in its attempts to reduce them to scientific order or classification.

It would appear, however, that the street-people may be all arranged under six distinct genera or kinds.

These are severally:

I.   Street-sellers.
II. Street-buyers.

III. Street-Finders.

IV. Street-Performers, Artists, and Showmen.

V. Street-Artizans, or Working Pedlars; and

VI. Street-Labourers.

The first of these divisions—the STREET-SELLERS—includes many varieties; viz.—

1. *The Street-sellers of Fish,* &c.—"*wet,*" "*dry,*" and shell-fish—and poultry, game, and cheese.

2. *The Street-sellers of Vegetables,* fruit (both "green" and "dry"), flowers, trees, shrubs, seeds, and roots, and "green stuff" (as watercresses, chickweed and grun'sel, and turf).

3. *The Street-sellers of Eatables and Drinkables,*—including the vendors of fried fish, hot eels, pickled whelks, sheep's trotters, ham sandwiches, peas'-soup, hot green peas, penny pies, plum "duff," meat-puddings, baked potatoes, spicecakes, muffins and crumpets, Chelsea buns, sweetmeats, brandy-balls, cough drops, and cat and dog's meat—such constituting the principal eatables sold in the street; while under the head of street-drinkables may be specified tea and coffee, ginger-beer, lemonade, hot wine, new milk from the cow, asses milk, curds and whey, and occasionally water.

4. *The Street-sellers of Stationery, Literature, and the Fine Arts*—among whom are comprised the flying stationers, or standing and running patterers; the long-song-sellers; the wall-song-sellers (or "pinners-up," as they are technically termed); the ballad sellers; the vendors of playbills, second editions of newspapers, back numbers of periodicals and old books, almanacks, pocket books, memorandum books, note paper, sealing-wax, pens, pencils, stenographic cards, valentines, engravings, manuscript music, images, and gelatine poetry cards.

5. *The Street-sellers of Manufactured Articles,* which class comprises a large number of individuals, as, (a) the vendors of chemical articles of manufacture—viz., blacking, lucifers cornsalves, grease-removing compositions, platingballs, poison for rats, crackers, detonating-balls, and cigar-lights. (b) The vendors of metal articles of manufacture—razors and pen-knives, tea-trays, dog-collars, and key-rings, hardware, bird-cages, small coins, medals, jewellery, tinware, tools, card-counters, red-herring-toasters, trivets, gridirons, and Dutch ovens. (c) The vendors of china and stone articles of manufacture—as cups and saucers, jugs, vases, chimney ornaments, and stone fruit. (d) The vendors of linen, cotton, and silken articles of manufacture—as sheeting, table-covers, cotton, tapes and thread, boot and stay-laces, haberdashery, pretended smuggled goods, shirt-buttons, etc., etc.; and (e) the vendors of miscellaneous articles of manufacture—as cigars, pipes, and snuff-boxes, spectacles, combs, "lots," rhubarb, sponges, wash-leather, paper-hangings, dolls, Bristol toys, sawdust, and pin-cushions.

6. *The Street-sellers of Second-hand Articles,* of whom there are again four separate classes; as (a) those who sell old metal articles—viz. old knives and forks, keys, tin-ware, tools, and marine stores generally; (b) those who sell old linen articles—as old sheering for towels; (c) those who sell old glass and crockery—including bottles, old pans and pitchers, old looking glasses, &c.; and (d) those who sell old miscellaneous articles—as old shoes, old clothes, old saucepan lids, &c., &c.

7. *The Street-sellers of Live Animals*—including the dealers in dogs, squirrels, birds, gold and silver fish, and tortoises.
8. *The Street-sellers of Mineral Productions and Curiosities*—as red and white sand, silver sand, coals, coke, salt, spar ornaments, and shells.

These, so far as my experience goes, exhaust the whole class of street-sellers, and they appear to constitute nearly three-fourths of the entire number of individuals obtaining a subsistence in the streets of London. . . .

This excerpt from the celebrated narrative by Henry Stanley (1841–1904) recalls his en-counter with the Wangwana and his observations on traversing the African landscape. When he was refused help in Britain for his scheme for developing the Congo, he approached King Leopold II of Belgium and was thereby involved in the birth of the Congo State.

Henry Stanley, from *Through the Dark Continent* (1879)

THE sky was of a stainless blue, and the slumbering lake faithfully reflected its exquisite tint, for not a breath of wind was astir to vex its surface. With groves of palms and the evergreen fig-trees on either hand, and before us a fringe of tall cane-grass along the shores all juicy with verdure, the square tembés of Ugoy, and the conical cotes of Kawelé, embowered by banana and plantain, we emerged into the bay of Ujiji from the channel of Bangwé.

. . . Our Wangwana hurry to the beach to welcome us. The usual congratulations fol-low—hand-shakings, smiles, and glad expressions. Frank, however, is pale and sickly; a muffler is round his neck, and he wears a greatcoat. He looks very different from the strong, hearty man to whom I gave the charge of the camp during my absence. In a few words he informs me of his sufferings from the fever of Ujiji.

"I am so glad you have come, sir. I was beginning to feel very depressed. I have been down several times with severe attacks of the horrible fever. Yesterday is the first time I got up after seven days weary illness, and people are dying round me so fast that I was beginning to think I must soon die too. Now I am all right, and shall soon get strong again."

The news, when told to me in detail, was grievous. Five of our Wangwana were dead from small-pox; six others were seriously ill from the same cause. Among the Arab slaves, neither inoculated nor vaccinated, the mortality had been excessive from this fearful pest.

At Rosako, the second camp from Bagamoyo, I had foreseen some such event as this, and had vaccinated, as I had thought, all hands; but it transpired, on inquiry now, that there were several who had not responded to the call, through some silly prejudice against it. Five of those unvaccinated were dead, and five were ill, as also was one who had received the vaccine. When I examined the medicine-chest, I found the tubes bro-ken and the lymph dried up.

The Arabs were dismayed at the pest and its dreadful havoc among their families and slaves. Every house was full of mourning and woe. There were no more agreeable visits and social converse; each kept himself in strict seclusion, fearful of being stricken with it. Khamis the Baluch was dead, his house was closed, and his friends were sorrowing. Mohammed bin Gharib had lost two children; Muini Kheri was lamenting the deaths of three children. The mortality was increasing: it was now from fifty to seventy-five daily among a population of about three thousand. Bitter were the complainings against the hot season and close atmosphere, and fervent the prayers for rain!

. . . The general infidelity and instability of the Wangwana arises, in great part, from their weak minds becoming a prey to terror of imaginary dangers. Thus, the Johanna men deserted Livingston because they heard the terrible Mafitté were in the way; my runaways of Ujiji fled from the danger of being eaten by the Manyema.

The slaves of Sungoro, the coast trader at Kagehyi, Usukuma, informed my people that Lake Victoria spread as far as the Salt Sea, that it had no end, and that the people on its shores loved the flesh of man better than that of goats. This foolish report made it a most difficult matter to man the exploring boat, and over a hundred swore by Allah that they knew nothing of rowing.

A similar scene took place when about to circumnavigate the Tanganika, for the Arab slaves had spread such reports of Muzimus, hobgoblins, fiery meteors, terrible spirits, such as Kabogo, Katavi, Kateyé, and Wanpembé, that the teeth of Wanyamwezi and Wangwana chattered with fright. But no reports exercised such a terrible effect on their weak minds as the report of the Manyema cannibals, none were so greedily listened to, none more readily believed.

The path which traders and their caravans follow to Manyema begins at Mtowa, in Uguha, and, continuing south a few miles over a series of hills, descends into the plain of the Rugumba river about half-way between the Lukuga river and the traders' crossing-place.

The conduct of the first natives to whom we were introduced pleased us all. They showed themselves in a very amiable light, sold their corn cheaply and without fuss, behaved themselves decently and with propriety, though their principal men entertaining very strange ideas of the white men, carefully concealed themselves from view, and refused to be tempted to expose themselves within view or hearing of us.

Their doubts of our character were reported to us by a friendly young Arab as follows: "Kassanga, chief of Ruanda, says, 'How can the white men be good when they come for no trade, whose feet one never sees, who always go covered from head to foot with clothes? Do not tell me they are good and friendly. There is something very mysterious about them; perhaps wicked. Probably they are magicians; at any rate, it is better to leave them alone, and to keep close until they are gone.'"

From Ruanda, where we halted only for a day, we began in earnest the journey to Manyema, thankful that the Tanganika was safely crossed, and that the Expedition had lost no more of its strength.

. . . Travellers from Africa have often written about African villages, yet I am sure few of those at home have ever comprehended the reality. I now propose to lay it before them in this sketch of a village in the district of Uhombo. The village consists of a number of low, conical grass huts, ranged round a circular common, in the centre of which are three or four fig-trees kept for the double purpose of supplying shade to the community, and bark-cloth to the chief. The doorways to the huts are very low, scarcely 30 inches high. The common fenced round by the grass huts shows plainly the ochreous colour of the soil, and it is so well trodden that not a grass blade thrives upon it.

On presenting myself in the common, I attracted out of doors the owners and ordinary inhabitants of each hut, until I found myself the centre of quite a promiscuous population of naked men, women, children, and infants. Though I had appeared here for the purpose of studying the people of Uhombo, and making a treaty of friendship with the chief, the villagers seemed to think I had come merely to make a free exhibition of myself as some natural monstrosity.

I saw before me over a hundred beings of the most degraded, unpresentable type it is possible to conceive, and though I knew quite well that some thousands of years ago the beginning of this wretched humanity and myself were one and the same, a sneaking disinclination to believe it possessed me strongly, and I would even now willingly subscribe some small amount of silver money for him who could but assist me to controvert the discreditable fact.

But common-sense tells me not to take into undue consideration their squalor, their ugliness, or nakedness, but to gauge their true position among the human race by taking a view of the cultivated fields and gardens of Uhombo, and I am compelled to admit that these debased specimens of humanity only plant and sow such vegetables and grain as I myself should cultivate were I compelled to provide for my own sustenance. I see, too, that their huts, though of grass, are almost as well made as the materials will permit, and indeed I have often slept in worse. Speak with them in their own dialect of the law of *meum* and *tuum,* and it will soon appear that they are intelligent enough upon that point. Moreover, the muscles, tissues, and fibres of their bodies, and all the organs of sight, hearing, smell, or motion, are as well developed as in us. Only in taste and judgment, based upon larger experience, in the power of expression, in morals and intellectual culture, are we superior.

. . . The women, blessed with an abundance of hair, manufactured it with a stiffening of light cane into a bonnet-shaped head-dress, allowing the back hair to flow down to the waist in masses of ringlets. They seemed to do all the work of life, for at all hours they might be seen, with their large wicker baskets behind them, setting out for the rivers or creeks to catch fish, or returning with their fuel baskets strapped on across their foreheads.

Their villages consist of one or more broad streets from 100 to 150 feet wide, flanked by low square huts arranged in tolerably straight lines, and generally situated on swells of land, to secure rapid drainage. At the end of one of these streets is the council and gossip house, overlooking the length of the avenue. In the centre is a platform of tamped clay, with a heavy tree trunk sunk into it, and in the wood have been scooped out a number of troughs, so that several women may pound grain at once. It is a substitute for the village mill.

The houses are separated into two or more apartments, and on account of the compact nature of the clay and tamped floor are easily kept clean. The roofs are slimy with the reek of smoke, as though they had been painted with coal-tar. The household chattels or furniture are limited to food baskets, earthenware pots, an assortment of wickerwork dishes, the family shields, spears, knives, swords, and tools, and the fish-baskets lying outside.

. . . The Luama valley at Uzura at this season presents a waving extent of grass-grown downs, and while crossing over the higher swells of land, we enjoyed uninterrupted views of thirty or forty miles to the west and south.

From Mpungu we travelled through an interesting country (a distance of four miles), and suddenly from the crest of a low ridge saw the confluence of the Luama with the majestic Lualaba. The former appeared to have a breadth of 400 yards at the mouth; the latter was about 1400 yards wide, a broad river of a pale grey colour, winding slowly from south and by east.

We hailed its appearance with shouts of joy, and rested on the spot to enjoy the view. Across the river, beyond a tawny, grassy stretch towards the south-south-west, is Mount Kijima; about 1000 feet above the valley, to the south-south-east, across the Luama, runs the Luhye-ya ridge; from its base the plain slopes to the swift Luama. In the bed of the great river are two or three small islands, green with the verdure of trees and sedge. I likened it even here to the Mississippi, as it appears before the impetuous, full-volumed Missouri pours its rusty brown water into it.

A secret rapture filled my soul as I gazed upon the majestic stream. The great mystery that for all these centuries Nature had kept hidden away from the world of science was waiting to be solved. For two hundred and twenty miles I had followed one of the sources of the Livingston to the confluence, and now before me lay the superb river itself! My task was to follow it to the Ocean.

Sunity Devi (1864–1932) was the daughter of the Brahmo Samaj reformer Keshub Chunder Sen. His decision to marry her at the age of 14 to the minor Maharajah of Cooch Behar caused a sensation in India in part because Samajists professed to be against child-marriage. But Devi was more renowned in Britain because she was the first consort of an Indian ruler to accompany her husband to Britain—on the occasion of the Queen's Jubilee in 1887, as she describes below. Hers is a different kind of ethnography than Stanley's, perhaps, but offers a glimpse into "native" royalty in Britain nonetheless.

Sunity Devi, from *Autobiography of an Indian Princess* (1921)

The year 1887 was expected to be a memorable one for India, as our late beloved Queen-Empress would celebrate her Jubilee. India was anxious to show her loyalty to the Sovereign whose high ideals and humanity endeared her to all her people. Many of our princes therefore decided to render their homage in person. My husband made his plans for this eventful year long beforehand, but he cleverly kept all of us in the dark as to his intention that I should accompany him to England. It must be remembered that the conditions of life among Indian ladies were very different in 1887 from what they are today. The Maharani of Baroda, I believe, had once gone to Switzerland, but for the wife of a ruler to visit England with her husband caused quite a sensation. I think I am right in saying that I was the first Maharani to do such a thing, and I may as well confess that I was very apprehensive of what the visit would hold for me. I knew absolutely nothing about the journey. I was going to be a stranger in a strange land, and I was sensitive enough to dread being ogled at, for I well knew that this must be my fate in London. . . .

The glory of the sea enchanted me. When the boat was out on the ocean and no land could be seen, all Nature seemed to speak of the infinite God, and I felt so small. In the dark evenings when the water gleamed with phosphorescence, it looked as though there were thousands of stars under the sea responding to the stars above. It really was grand; a grandeur that no one could describe unless he had actually experienced it. Before we embarked, I tasted meat for the first time in my life, and I disliked the flavour so much that for the first few days of the voyage I ate nothing but a few vegetables. I often had fits of depression and sometimes left the dinner table to relieve my feelings with a good cry.

. . . It was May, but very cold for the time of year, and my first sight of London on a Sunday did nothing to lift my spirits. I saw half-deserted streets swept with a bitter wind which had already chapped my face, and I was heartily glad when at last we reached the Grosvenor Hotel. There all was brightness and animation. My husband was pleased to see me and the children and to show me the grand suite of rooms which had been reserved for us. The housekeeper at the Grosvenor had thought of everything that would make us comfortable, and my memory of her is of a pleasant woman with plenty of common sense. One thing I did not like. Our luxurious suite of rooms had no bathroom. I was told I was to have a bath in my room, but this I would not do. I was shown to a big bath, but was horrified when I was told that I must pass all those corridors each time I wanted a bath. I refused point-blank, and they finally prepared a small room as a bathroom for me.

Kind invitations poured in, and I was happy to see many old friends. I shall never forget the question Sir Ashley Eden put to me: "What do you think of our London fog?" for although it was May, I had experienced a yellow fog. I answered:

"Not much, Sir Ashley; I do not think I shall ever care for the London fog."

We dined at Sir Ashley's, and there I first met the present Lord Crewe. We had a large drawing-room at the hotel which I could never make cosy or comfortable; on rainy days especially, it felt damp and gloomy. When I went out for drives I used to see little children with their toy boats in Hyde Park, and I soon got a nice little sailing yacht for my Rajey, and both mother and son enjoyed floating this vessel on the Serpentine. Rajey's little face beamed with delight when he saw his boat cruising along. The late Lady Roseberry was most kind to my little ones; Rajey and Girlie spent some happy afternoons at her house. The present Lady Crewe was a little girl then, and her brother, Lord Dalmeny, made a great friend of dear Rajey and always remained the same. . . .

It had been intimated to me that Queen Victoria wished to see me privately before the Court, and it was arranged that I should go to Buckingham Palace for an audience. The question of what I was to wear had to be settled. The Maharajah, who always displayed the greatest interest in my wardrobe toilets, selected and ordered my gown for this great occasion. I was extremely nervous, and as I saw my reflection in the mirror in the pale grey dress I felt more terrified than ever. My maid, seeing me look so pale and shaken, brought me a glass of port. I never touch wine, except when it is absolutely necessary. My hand trembled so that I spilt half of the wine over my gown. Instantly a chorus of "How lucky" arose. But I gazed rather ruefully at the stains.

"Well, Sunity, it is time for us to start," said my husband, and I followed him to the carriage. Lord Cross, who was then Secretary of State for India, received us, and his wife whispered a few reassuring words to me before the officials escorted us down the corridors to the small room where Her Majesty was.

I cannot describe my feelings when I found myself in the presence of the Queen. To us Indians she was more or less a legendary figure endowed with wonderful attributes, an ideal ruler, and an ideal woman, linked to our hearts across "the black waters" by silken chains of love and loyalty. I looked at Her Majesty anxiously, and my first impression instantly dispelled my nervousness: a short, stout lady dressed in mourning who came forward and kissed me twice. I made a deep curtsy, and stepped back, and then my husband came forward and bent low over the Queen's hand. I experienced a feeling, as did everyone with whom Her late Majesty came in contact, that she possessed great personal magnetism, and she certainly was the embodiment of dignity. Her conversation was simple and kindly, and every word revealed her as a queen, woman and mother. I was delighted to find that I had not been disappointed in my ideal, and felt eager to go back to India that I might tell my country-women about our wonderful Empress. The audience occupied only a few minutes, but nothing could have exceeded Her Majesty's graciousness, and I came away proud and glad, and laughed at myself for my earlier apprehensions at being received by one so gracious. The Maharajah was very pleased at our reception and told me how proud he was of me.

The next day we attended the Drawing-room. I wore a white and gold brocade gown and a Crepe de Chine sari. I waited with the other ladies, and as it was a cold afternoon I was very glad to find a little cosy corner to sit down. I looked around me, and was admiring the pretty dresses and faces when I suddenly saw what I thought was a gentleman wearing a diamond tiara. I gazed at the face and then discovered it belonged to a lady who had a thick moustache. I went into the throne-room, and as I was told by Lady Cross that I need not kiss Her Majesty when I made my curtsy, as I had already been received privately, when Her Majesty wanted to kiss me I avoided her! But later I distinctly heard the Queen say to the Princess of Wales: "Why would not the Maharani kiss me?" This made me so nervous that I thought I would drop on the floor.

After I had finished making all my curtsies I went and stood near kind Lady Salisbury and watched the other ladies pass. One of the duchesses, an elderly woman in a very low-cut dress trimmed with old lace and wearing magnificent jewels, to my mind looked extremely miserable. I can still see her trembling as she curtsied; whether it was the cold or her aged body was tired I cannot say. I was greatly interested in all I saw; but shocked at the low-cut gowns worn by the ladies present. The cold was most trying to complexions and shoulders, the prevailing tints of which were either brick-red or a chilly reddish-blue. Now that the Courts are held in the evenings women's beauty is seen to greater advantage, but I shall never forget that May afternoon and the inartistic exposure of necks and arms. . . .

Life passed very swiftly and pleasantly for me during the Jubilee celebrations, and I was thoroughly spoiled, much to the delight of my husband. I have many recollections of that memorable year, and can picture to myself many of my kind and charming hostesses. I remember once in the supper room at Buckingham Palace my husband introduced the ex-Kaiser, then Prince William, to me, and the young prince bent down and kissed my hand. I blushed and my throat grew dry; my hand had never been kissed before by a man. After the Prince left us I tried to scold my husband in Bengali, but he laughed, and said: "Sunity, it is a great honour that your hand should be kissed by the future German Emperor; you ought to feel proud." I admired Prince William and the way in which the foreign Royalties showed their respect for ladies.

We went to Windsor Castle one day to present our gifts to Her Majesty. My husband chose a little diamond pendant with an uncut ruby in the middle, and told me to give it to Her Majesty. I said to my husband: "I shall be too nervous," but he urged me: "Just a few words, Sunity; it will please Her Majesty." Little did my husband know what those few words cost me. We went by special train to Windsor, and when we arrived at the Castle we were received by the equerries and high officials. It was the day for Indians to pay their homage to their Empress. Captain Muir was in command of the bodyguard on duty. We entered the throne-room where the Queen was, and I presented our little present with a few words to Her Majesty, who graciously accepted it and thanked me. I made a deep curtsy, but people who were present in the room said afterwards the Maharani of Cooch Behar's words were clear and her curtsy was most graceful. . . .

Booth (1829–1912) takes off explicitly and directly from Stanley's travelogue, leading us through the moral and spiritual desert of London's poor as if we were on an African expedition. In this excerpt he falls short of a call to arms, but brings together the traditions of colonial and investigative journalism articulated by Mayhew, Ritchie, and others in a highly provocative and even emotional exposé of the "heathen" interior at the heart of the empire.

General William Booth,
from *In Darkest England and the Way Out* (1890)

Why "Darkest England?"

. . . The attention of the civilized world has been arrested by the story which Mr. Stanley has told of "Darkest Africa," and his journeyings across the heart of the Lost Continent. In all that spirited narrative of heroic endeavor, nothing has so much impressed the imagination as his description of the immense forest, which offered an almost impenetrable barrier to his advance. The intrepid explorer, in his own phrase, "marched, tore, ploughed, and cut his way for one hundred and sixty days through this inner womb of the true tropical forest." The mind of man with difficulty endeavors to realize this immensity of wooded wilderness, covering a territory half as large again as the whole of France, where the rays of the sun never penetrate, where in the dark, dank air, filled with the steam of the heated morass, human beings, dwarfed into pygmies and brutalized into cannibals, lurk and live and die. . . .

It is a terrible picture, and one that has engraved itself deep on the heart of civilization. But while brooding over the awful presentation of life as it exists in the vast African forest, it seemed to me only too vivid a picture of many parts of our own land. As there is a darkest Africa, is there not also a darkest England? Civilization, which can breed its own barbarians, does it not also breed its own pygmies? May we not find a parallel at our own doors, and discover within a stone's throw of our cathedrals and palaces similar horrors to those which Stanley has found existing in the great Equatorial forest?

The more the mind dwells upon the subject, the closer the analogy appears. The ivory raiders who brutally traffic in the unfortunate denizens of the forest glades, what are they but the publicans who flourish on the weakness of our poor? The two tribes of savages, the human baboon and the handsome dwarf, who will not speak lest it impede him in his task, may be accepted as the two varieties who are continually present with us—the vicious, lazy lout, and the toiling slave. They, too, have lost all faith of life being other than it is and has been. As in Africa it is all trees, trees, trees, with no other world conceivable, so is it here—it is all vice and poverty and crime. To many the world is all slum, with the Workhouse as an intermediate purgatory before the grave. And just as Mr. Stanley's Zanzibaris lost faith, and could only be induced to plod on in brooding sullenness of dull despair, so the most of our social reformers, no matter how cheerily they may have started off, with forty pioneers swinging blithely their axes as they force their way into the wood, soon become depressed and despairing. Who can battle against the ten thousand million trees? Who can hope to make headway against the innumerable adverse conditions which doom the dweller in Darkest England to eternal and immutable misery? . . .

An analogy is as good as a suggestion; it becomes wearisome when it is pressed too far. But before leaving it, think for a moment how close the parallel is, and how strange it is that so much interest should be excited by a narrative of human squalor and human heroism in a distant continent, while greater squalor and heroism not less magnificent may be observed at our very doors.

The Equatorial Forest traversed by Stanley resembles that Darkest England of which I have to speak, alike in its vast extent—both stretch, in Stanley's phrase, "as far as from Plymouth to Peterhead;" its monotonous darkness, its malaria and its gloom, its dwarfish de-humanized inhabitants, the slavery to which they are subjected, their privations and their misery. That which sickens the stoutest heart, and causes many of our bravest and best to fold their hands in despair, is the apparent impossibility of doing more than merely to peck at the outside of the endless tangle of monotonous undergrowth; to let light into it, to make a road clear through it, that shall not be immediately choked up by the ooze of the morass and the luxuriant parasitical growth of the forest—who dare hope for that? At present, alas, it would seem as though no one dares even to hope! It is the great Slough of Despond of our time.

. . . The lot of a negress in the Equatorial Forest is not, perhaps, a very happy one, but is it so very much worse than that of many a pretty orphan girl in our Christian capital? We talk about the brutalities of the dark ages, and we profess to shudder as we read in books of the shameful exaction of the rights of feudal superior. And yet here, beneath our very eyes, in our theatres, in our restaurants, and in many other places, unspeakable though it be but to name it, the same hideous abuse flourishes unchecked. A young penniless girl, if she be pretty, is often hunted from pillar to post by her employers, confronted always by the alternative—Starve or Sin. And when once the poor girl has consented to buy the right to earn her living by the sacrifice of her virtue, then she is treated as a slave and an outcast by the very men who have ruined her. Her word becomes unbelievable, her life an ignominy, and she is swept downward, ever downward, into the bottomless perdition of prostitution. But there, even in the lowest depths, excommunicated by Humanity and outcast from God, she is far nearer the pitying heart of the One true Saviour than all the men who forced her down, aye, and than all the Pharisees and Scribes who stand silently by while these fiendish wrongs are perpetrated before their very eyes.

The blood boils with impotent rage at the sight of these enormities, callously inflicted, and silently borne by these miserable victims. Nor is it only women who are the victims, although their fate is the most tragic. Those firms which reduce sweating to a fine art, who systematically and deliberately defraud the workman of his pay, who grind the faces of the poor, and who rob the widow and the orphan, and who for a pretense make great professions of public spirit and philanthropy, these men nowadays are sent to Parliament to make laws for the people. The old prophets sent them to Hell—but we have changed all that. They send their victims to Hell, and are rewarded by all that wealth can do to make their lives comfortable. Read the House of Lords' Report on the Sweating System, and ask if any African slave system, making due allowance for the superior civilization, and therefore sensitiveness, of the victims, reveals more misery. . . .

But this book is no mere lamentation of despair. For Darkest England, as for Darkest Africa, there is a light beyond. I think I see my way out, a way by which these wretched ones may escape from the gloom of their miserable existence into a higher and happier life. Long wandering in the Forest of the Shadow of Death at our doors, has familiarized me with its horrors; but while the realization is a vigorous spur to action, it has never been so oppressive as to extinguish hope. Mr. Stanley never succumbed to the terrors which oppressed his followers. He had lived in a larger life, and knew that the forest, though long, was not interminable. Every step forward brought him nearer his destined goal, nearer to the light of the sun, the clear sky, and the rolling uplands of the grazing land. Therefore he did not despair. The Equatorial Forest was, after all, a mere corner of one quarter of the world. In the knowledge of the light outside, in the confidence begotten by past experience of successful endeavor, he pressed forward; and when the 160 days' struggle was over, he and his men came out into a pleasant place where the land smiled with peace and plenty, and their hardships and hunger were forgotten in the joy of a great deliverance.

. . . What a satire it is upon our Christianity and our civilization, that the existence of these colonies of heathens and savages in the heart of our capital should attract so little attention! . . . Before venturing to define the remedy, I begin by describing the malady. But even when presenting the dreary picture of our social ills, and describing the difficulties which confront us, I speak not in despondency, but in hope. "I know in whom I have believed." I know, therefore do I speak. "Darker England" is but a fractional part of "Greater England." There is wealth enough abundantly to minister to its social regeneration so far as wealth can, if there be but heart enough to set about the work in earnest. And I hope and believe that the heart will not be lacking when once the problem is manfully faced, and the method of its solution plainly pointed out.

Who are the Lost? I reply, not in a religious, but in a social sense, the lost are those who have gone under, who have lost their foothold in Society; those to whom the prayer to our Heavenly Father, "Give us day by day our daily bread," is either unfulfilled, or only fulfilled by the Devil's agency: by the earnings of vice, the proceeds of crime, or the contribution enforced by the threat of the law.

But I will be more precise. The denizens in Darkest England, for whom I appeal, are (1) those who, having no capital or income of their own, would in a month be dead from sheer starvation were they exclusively dependent upon the money earned by their own work; and (2) those who by their utmost exertions are unable to attain the regulation allowance of food which the law prescribes as indispensable even for the worst criminals in our jails.

. . . The first question, then, which confronts us is, what are the dimensions of the Evil? How many of our fellow-men dwell in this Darkest England? How can we take the census of those who have fallen below the Cab Horse standard to which it is our aim to elevate the most wretched of our countrymen?

. . . Darkest England, then, may be said to have a population about equal to that of Scotland. Three million men, women, and children, a vast despairing multitude in a condition nominally free, but really enslaved—these it is whom we have to save.

It is a large order. England emancipated her negroes sixty years ago, at a cost of £40,000,000, and has never ceased boasting about it since. But at our own doors, from "Plymouth to Peterhead," stretches this waste Continent of humanity—three million human beings who are enslaved—some of them to taskmasters as merciless as any West Indian overseer, all of them to destitution and despair. Is anything to be done with them? Can anything be done for them? Or is this million-headed mass to be regarded as offering a problem as insoluble as that of the London sewage, which, feculent and festering, swings heavily up and down the basin of the Thames with the ebb and flow of the tide?

. . . Darkest England may be described as consisting broadly of three circles, one within the other. The outer and widest circle is inhabited by the starving and the homeless, but honest, Poor; the second by those who live by Vice; and the third and innermost region at the center is peopled by those who exist by Crime. The whole of the three circles is sodden with Drink. Darkest England has many more public houses than the Forest of the Aruwimi has rivers, of which Mr. Stanley sometimes had to cross three in half an hour. The borders of this great lost land are not sharply defined. They are continually expanding or contracting. Whenever there is a period of depression in trade, they stretch; when prosperity returns, they contract. So far as individuals are concerned, there are none among the hundreds of thousands who live upon the outskirts of the dark forest who can truly say that they or their children are secure from being hopelessly entangled in its labyrinth. The death of the bread-winner, a long illness, a failure in the City, or any one of a thousand other causes which might be named, will bring within the first circle those who at present imagine themselves free from all danger of actual want. The death-rate in Darkest England is high. Death is the great jail-deliverer of the captives. But the dead are hardly in the grave before their places are taken by others. Some escape, but the majority, their health sapped by their surroundings, become weaker and weaker, until at last they fall by the way, perishing without hope at the very doors of the palatial mansions which, may be, some of them helped to build.

. . . The following are some statements taken down by [one of my] Officer[s] from twelve men whom he found sleeping on the Embankment on the nights of June 13th and 14th, 1890:

No. 1. "I've slept here two nights; I'm a confectioner by trade; I come from Dartford. I got turned off because I'm getting elderly. They can get young men cheaper, and I have the rheumatism so bad. I've earned nothing these two days; I thought I could get a job at Woolwich, so I walked there, but could get nothing. I found a bit of bread in the road wrapped up in a bit of newspaper; that did me for yesterday. I had a bit of bread and butter to-day. I'm fifty-four years old. When it's wet we stand about all night under the arches."

. . . No. 4. Elderly man; trembles visibly with excitement at mention of work; produces a card carefully wrapped in old newspaper, to the effect that Mr. J. R. is a member of the Trade Protection League. He is a waterside laborer; last job at that was a fortnight since. Has earned nothing for five days. Had a bit of bread this morning, but not a scrap since. Had a cup of tea and two slices of bread yesterday, and the same the day before; the deputy at a lodging-house gave it to him. He is fifty years old, and is still damp from sleeping out in the wet last night.

. . . No. 6. Had slept out four nights running. Was a distiller by trade; been out four months; unwilling to enter into details of leaving, but it was his own fault. (Very likely; a heavy, thick, stubborn, and senseless looking fellow, six feet high, thick neck, strong limbs, evidently destitute of ability.) Does odd jobs; earned 3d. for minding a horse, bought a cup of coffee and pen'orth of bread and butter. Has no money now. Slept under Waterloo Bridge last night.

. . . No. 10. Been out of work a month. Carman by trade. Arm withered, and cannot do work properly. Has slept here all the week; got an awful cold through the wet. Lives at odd jobs (they all do). Got sixpence yesterday for minding a cab and carrying a couple of parcels. Earned nothing to-day, but had one good meal; a lady gave it him. Has been walking about all day looking for work, and is tired out.

No. 11. Youth, aged 16. Sad case; Londoner. Works at odd jobs and selling matches. Has taken 3d. to-day—*i.e.,* net profit 1 1/2d. Has five boxes still. Has slept here every night for a month. Before that slept in Covent Garden Market or on door-steps. Been sleeping out six months, since he left Feltham Industrial School. Was sent there for playing truant. Has had one bit of bread to-day; yesterday had only some gooseberries and cherries—*i.e.,* bad ones that had been thrown away. Mother is alive. She "chucked him out" when he returned home on leaving Feltham because he couldn't find her money for drink.

No. 12. Old man, age 67. Seems to take rather a humorous view of the position. Kind of Mark Tapley. Says he can't say he does like it, but then he *must* like it! Ha, ha! Is a slater by trade. Been out of work some time; younger men naturally get the work. Gets a bit of bricklaying sometimes; can turn his hand to anything. Goes miles and gets nothing. Earned one and twopence this week at holding horses. Finds it hard, certainly. Used to care once, and get down-hearted, but that's no good; don't trouble now. Had a bit of bread and butter and cup of coffee to-day. Health is awful bad; not half the size he was; exposure and want of food is the cause; got wet last night, and is very stiff in consequence. Has been walking about since it was light, that is 3 A.M. Was so cold and wet and weak, scarcely knew what to do. Walked to Hyde Park, and got a little sleep there on a dry seat as soon as the park opened.

. . . Such are the stories gathered at random one Midsummer night this year under the shade of the plane trees of the Embankment. A month later, when one of my staff took the census of the sleepers out of doors along the line of the Thames from Blackfriars to Westminster, he found three hundred and sixty-eight persons sleeping in the open air. Of these, two hundred and seventy were on the Embankment proper, and ninety-eight in and about Covent Garden Market, while the recesses of Waterloo and Blackfriars Bridges were full of human misery.

The Saturday Review offered readers a detailed sketch of all the Courts at the Indian and Colonial Exhibition in the fall of 1886, laying out both the geography of the site and, at least in a virtual sense, of the West Indies as well.

Anon., " . . . the West Indian Court," *Saturday Review* (1886)

As one enters the West Indian Court from the northern side, the keynote is at once struck by a small compartment on the right, consisting entirely of sugar-canes exhibited by the Anglo-Continental Guano Company, and grown by the help of their manures in all parts of the Empire. These do not strike us as particularly fine specimens, but they are sufficient to show how this wonderful plant is able to adapt itself to different degrees of heat and rainfall, to flourish through the droughts of Queensland and the downpours of Penang as well as in the varying amount of moisture it obtains in the West Indian islands. This trustworthiness of the cane is the cause of the pertinacity with which its cultivation is maintained by the planters in spite of the fierce competition of European beet-sugar aided by bounties, and explains why it still holds its own over other products which the climate is also capable of producing. At first sight it would appear that Trinidad, whose court is on the opposite side, had abandoned everything in favour of Dr. Siegert's Angostura Bitters; but when the formidable case which contains these stimulants of a jaded appetite is passed, it will be found that besides sugar, and its concomitants rum, molasses, &c., Trinidad has a most interesting and varied show. Few of the islands possess such natural beauty of scenery and vegetation, and though photographs are inadequate to express the colouring of the tropics, it is worth while to linger over these, for they are artistically and carefully taken. The planting of cocoa has much extended of late years, and now occupies nearly half the acreage of the sugar-cane; the samples of this and of prepared chocolate are very numerous, and there is every reason to hope that the industry will become more developed and profitable as the consumption in England yearly increases. Cigars, too, are being gradually improved in manufacture, and have lately met with a ready sale, while coffee is also cultivated in suitable localities. It is clear, therefore, that Trinidad does not mean to be reproached with being at the mercy of the fortunes of a single product. The next few years will probably see a great development in the utilisation of the asphalte from the Pitch Lake, which even now contributes to the income of the island; and something might be done in the exportation of its timber; no fewer than 235 varieties of its woods are shown in the Exhibition, many of them of great beauty. Soap, honey, fibres, and lime-juice should not be passed over, nor that most common of all panaceas, "a certain cure for corns."

Totally different is the show of the Bahama Islands, which occupies the next bays of the section. Other colonies depend upon the land for their products; but the Bahamas lay the seas under contribution, and draw their chief spoils from it. The Executive Commissioner, Mr. Adderley, shows a magnificent collection of pink pearls, some in their natural state, others set with pearls and diamonds. They are found in the conch-shells which abound on the coast, and are of every shade, from the palest to the deepest pink; they are exported to the amount of about 3,000*l.* per annum, besides the value of the conch-shells themselves, which are used in Italy for cameos. After the Fisheries Exhibition of 1883, it occurred to Mr. Adderley that, with the materials on the spot, something ought to be done towards teaching the natives to carve cameos. Accordingly a School of Art was established at Nassau, with a competent Italian master, and the result is apparent in carvings which give promise of future excellence, and in many tasteful objects which are made from the pink shell. Sponge is another feature of the court, and forms a considerable item of the revenue of the islands, about 6,000*l.* worth being exported annually. A bold attempt has been made to popularize the Gorgonias or sea-fans, which abound here; they are pressed into various shapes, as coverings for handbags, baskets, cosies, and the like, and, under the auspices of a West End artiste, have been transformed into hats and bonnets. The star-fish coral and shell-work make a goodly show; and, if it were not for the beautiful paintings by Mrs. Blake of the Bahama flowers close by in the gallery, we should be tempted to forget that there were any products of the soil. Specimens of tobacco, cigars, and preserved fruits are, however, exhibited; but apparently the tastes or interests of the inhabitants lie in the direction of their maritime wares, for, although the soil and climate are suitable for the growth of fruit, cotton, and fibrous plants, labour and perseverance are at present wanting to develop the importance of these exports.

Crossing the picture gallery, we come to the space allotted to Jamaica, and here once more the sea gives place to the land. The manufacture of sugar has much improved of late years, and some good samples are shown, though not superior to those of other colonies. Jamaica rum, however, still holds the supremacy, and there is a wonderful display of it in this court of all ages and colours, from the purest white to the darkest tawny. Coffee, pimento, cinchona, spices, and starches are shown; but there is little attempt to display the fruits which now form a considerable item of export to the American market. Canada has shown us in this Exhibition how beautifully fruits can be preserved in syrup, and those of the tropics treated in this way would have been both decorative and instructive. Unhappily the West Indian mind seems content to reproduce them in wax, and there are some hideous examples of this mistaken art scattered through the section. The D'Oyleys and fans of Jamaica ferns pasted on the fibre of the lace-palm are now becoming well known in England, as they deserve to be, and some beautiful specimens are shown. On the opposite side, in the Grenada Court, is an exhibit of Jamaica which recalls to us the lively interest once taken by England in West Indian affairs; it is a sword of honour which bears the inscription—"Presented to Lord Crawford and Balcarres by the City of London in recognition of his services in the Maroon War."

Barbados occupies a much smaller space than its neighbour, but it makes a very neat show nevertheless. Sugar-canes are the dominant feature, two fine "stools" flanking the bays at the entrance, and cut canes being grouped round the central support of the court. Sugar is shown in various forms, and is conveniently placed both for the eye and for the nose, for Barbados prides itself on the sweetness of its cane-juice, and is only too delighted to invite comparison with its mortal enemy the beet. Two curious maps hang on the walls; one of them Ligon's, who was on the island from 1647 to 1650. This Exhibition, by-the-bye, has solved the long-vexed question of the earliest mention of Barbados, for it figures in the second Borgian Map, begun in the first years of the sixteenth century, as "La barbada," and this is almost certainly copied from Alexander VI.'s first map of 1494. A limb of the bearded fig-tree from which it is generally believed the island derived its name hangs in the inner court. Like the Bahamas, Barbados makes a display of its marine specimens, and some pink pearls are also shown, as well as many varieties of coral, for which the island is famous; pretty ornaments are made of the green-pea and rice shells. . . .

British Honduras, our sole settlement in Central America, is included in this section; the colony depends chiefly on its mahogany and logwood, and, besides samples of its magnificent woods, has little to display. These, however, have been most effectively arranged, and occupy a space perhaps disproportionate to the importance of the colony. Of the lesser islands it is not necessary to say much. Beyond a feeble joke about the jaws of a Barracouta, St. Vincent contributes little; Grenada shows her fruits in syrup to better advantage than the rest of the section, and there is an historical interest in the silver mace formerly used in her House of Assembly; St. Lucia tries to attract attention by placing a gaily-dressed figure of a black woman at her doors, but exhibits besides some fine samples of sugar from the usine; Tobago deserves attention for its birds' nests, and Montserrat for its lime-juice, of which there is a somewhat plaintive account in the official Catalogue; but Antigua makes a most effective display of strings of bright-coloured seeds, crab-eyes, job's tears, jumbies, and the like, which should meet with a ready sale, and find their way into Regent Street shop-windows; many, however, will think that Antigua's most interesting product is the turtle-soup which is to be found in one of Messrs. Spiers & Pond's restaurants. Of course each and every island exhibits sugar and rum, but, except St. Lucia, of inferior quality to those in the courts we have more minutely described.

A dreary tale of depression runs through the descriptive notices of the islands in the Catalogue, and the "Groans of the Plantations" are as loud now as in 1689. In spite of the opinion of British statesmen that Prince Bismarck is ignorant and foolish in this matter, the bounty system continues in flourish; and it is evident that only the strongest of the colonies can stand the struggle to the bitter end. Even these will have to meet the bounties in the only logical way, by the reduction of wages; and great suffering will be caused to the unfortunate negroes in order that the British consumer may have for the moment his sugar unnaturally and artificially cheap. Capital will not flow into colonies the price of whose products does not depend on the laws of supply and demand, but is at the mercy of any country which, as Russia did a few months ago, chooses to grant an enormous bounty for purposes of its own. These islands, it is true, are capable of producing almost anything; but it is hard that their supremacy in sugar should be wrested from them by an inferior article bolstered up by State aid; and any commercial man knows what years it takes to build up a new industry, even in prosperous times. It is on sugar that the population of the West Indies must mainly exist, if they continue to exist, for years to come.

T. N. Mukherji was an Indian official connected to the Indian and Colonial Exhibition who published an account of his time in London as part of a larger travelogue on Europe several years later. Here he recounts in lively and frank detail his experiences wandering the streets of London as a colonial native, and offers his opinions on English life and "civilization" in the process.

T. N. Mukherji,
Observations on the Indian and Colonial Exhibition (1889)

. . . Another place of considerable interest to the natives of England was the Indian Bazar where Hindu and Muhammadan artisans carried on their avocations, to witness which men, women and children flocked from all parts of the kingdom. A dense crowd always stood there, looking at our men as they wove the gold brocade, sang the patterns of the carpet and printed the calico with the hand. They were as much astonished to see the Indians produce works of art with the aid of rude apparatus they themselves had discarded long ago, as a Hindu would be to see a chimpanzee officiating as a priest in a funeral ceremony and reading out Sanskrit texts from a palm leaf book spread before him. We were very interesting beings no doubt, so were the Zulus before us, and so is the Sioux chief at the present time. Human nature everywhere thirsts for novelty, and measures out its favours in proportion to the rarity and oddity of a thing. It was from the ladies that we received the largest amount of patronage. We were pierced through and through by stares from eyes of all colours—green, gray, blue and black—and every movement and act of ours, walking, sitting, eating, reading, received its full share of "O, I, never!" The number of wives we left behind at home was also a constant theme of speculation among them, and shrewd guesses were sometimes made on this point, 250 being a favourite number. You could tell any amount of stories on this subject without exciting the slightest suspicion. Once, one of our number told a pretty waitress—"I am awfully pleased with you, and I want to marry you. Will you accept the fortieth wifeship in my household which became vacant just before I left my country?" She asked—"How many wives have you altogether?" "Two hundred and fifty, the usual number," was the ready answer. "What became of your wife, number 40?" "I killed her, because one morning she could not cook my porridge well." The poor girl was horrified, and exclaimed—"O you monster, O you wretch!" Then she narrated the sad fate of a friend of hers. She was a sweet little child, when an African student studying in Edinburgh came and wooed her. They got married in England and fondly loved each other. Everything went well as long as the pair lived in England, but after a short time he took his fair wife to his desert home in Liberia. Not a single white man or woman could she see there, and she felt very lonely. But the sight of her mother-in-law, who dressed in feathers and skins came dancing into the house half-tipsy, was more than she could bear. She pined for a short time and died.

Of course, every nation in the world considers other nations as savages or at least much inferior to itself. It was so from the beginning and it will be so as long as human nature will retain its present character. We did not therefore wonder that the common people should take us for barbarians, awkward as we were in every respect. They have very strict notions of dress, manners and the general bearing of a man, any deviation from which is seriously noticed. Utmost indulgence was however shewn to us everywhere. Her Majesty was graciously pleased to lay aside the usual rules, and this favour was shewn us wherever we went. Gentlemen and ladies of high education and culture, however, honoured us as the representatives of the most ancient nation now existing on the face of the earth. They would frequently ask us home, get up private parties and arrange for all sorts of amusements. In other houses we grew more intimate and formed part of the family party. To these we were always welcome, and could go and come whenever we liked. We got some friends among them, and these gentlemen would often come and fetch us home if we absented ourselves for more than the ordinary length of time. I fondly remember the happy days I passed with them, and feel thankful for the kindness they shewed me during my sojourn in their country.

In public matters non-official gentlemen were also very partial to us. "We want to hear the turbanned gentleman" was the wish often and often expressed. But we ceased not to be a prodigious wonder to strangers and to the common people. Would they discuss us so freely if they knew that we understood their language? It was very amusing to hear what they said about us. Often when fatigued with work, or when cares and anxieties cast a gloom upon our mind, we found such talks about us more refreshing than a glass of port wine. I wish I had the ability to do justice to the discussing power these ladies and gentlemen exercised in their kind notice of us, for in that case I could produce one of the most interesting books ever published. Or if I had known that I would be required to write an account of my visit to Europe, I would have taken notes of at least some of the remarkable hits on truth unconsciously made by ignorant people from the country, which are applicable to all nations and which set one to philosophise on the material difference that exists between our own estimate of ourselves and the estimate which others form of us.

If we were interesting beings in the eyes of the Londoners, who had oftener opportunities of seeing their fellow subjects from the far East, how much more would we be so to the simple villagers who came by thousands to see the wonders of the Exhibition. Their conduct towards us was always kind and respectful. They liked to talk to us, and whenever convenient we tried to satisfy their curiosity. Men, women and children, whose relations are in India serving as soldiers or in any other capacity, would come through the crowd, all panting, to shake hands with us and ask about their friends. Many queer incidents happened in this way. "Do you know Jim,—James Robinson you know of————Regiment?" asked a fat elderly woman, who one day came bustling through the crowd and took me by storm, without any of those preliminary manœuvres usually adopted to open a conversation with a stranger. I expressed my regret in not having the honour of Jim's acquaintance. The good old lady then explained to me that she was Jim's aunt, and gave me a long history of her nephew, and the circumstances which led to his enlistment as a soldier. If the truant nephew lost the golden opportunity of sending through us his dutiful message to his aunt, she on her part was not wanting in her affectionate remembrances of him. Among other things, most of which I did not understand, for she did not speak the English we ordinarily hear nor was her language quite coherent at the time, she begged me to carry to Jim the important intelligence that Mrs. Jones' fat pig obtained a prize at the Smithfield Agricultural Show. I shewed my alacrity to carry the message right off to Jim in the wilds of Upper Burma by immediately taking leave of the lady, who joined her friends and explained to them that I was a bosom friend of her nephew.

Once, I was sitting in one of the swellish restaurants at the Exhibition, glancing over a newspaper which I had no time to read in the morning. At a neighbouring table sat a respectable-looking family group evidently from the country, from which furtive glances were occasionally thrown in my direction. I thought I might do worse than having a little fun, if any could be made out of the notice that was being taken of me. I seemed to be suddenly aware that I was being looked at, which immediately scared away half a dozen eyes from my table. It took fully five minutes' deep undivided attention to my paper again to reassure and tempt out those eyes from the plates where they took refuge, and the glances from them, which at first flashed and flickered like lightning, became steadier the more my mind seemed to get absorbed in the subject I was reading. The closer inspection to which I submitted ended in my favour. Perhaps, no symptom being visible in my external appearance of the cannibalistic tendencies of my heart, or owing probably to the notion that I must have by that time got over my partiality for human flesh, or knowing at least that the place was safe enough against any treacherous spring which I might take into my head to make upon them, or owing to whatever other cause, the party gradually grew bolder, began to talk in whispers and actually tried to attract my attention towards them. The latter duty ultimately devolved upon the beauty of the party, a pretty girl of about seventeen. Of course it was not intended for my ears, but somehow I heard her say—"Oh, how I wish to speak to him!" Could I withstand such an appeal? I rose and approaching the little Curiosity asked—"Did you speak to me, young lady?" She blushed and hung down her head. Her papa came to the rescue. "My daughter, Sir, is delighted with the magnificent things brought from your country to this Exhibition. She saw some writing in your language on a few plates and shields, and is anxious to know its meaning. We did not know whom to ask, when we saw you. Will you take a seat here, and do me the honour to take a glass of something with me? What will it be? Sparkling moselle I find is good here; or shall it be champagne or anything stronger?" He said. The preferred glass was declined with thanks, but I took a chair and explained the meaning of some of the verses damascened on the Koftgari ware. The young lady soon got over her bashfulness, and talked with a vivacity which I did not expect from her. She was delighted with everything I said, expressed her astonishment at my knowledge of English, and complimented me for the performance of the band brought from *my country, viz.,* the West Indian band composed of Negroes and Mulattos, which compliment made me wince a little, but nevertheless I went on chattering for a quarter of an hour and furnishing her with sufficient means to annihilate her friend Minnie, Jane or Lizzy or whoever she might be, and to brag among her less fortunate relations for six months to come of her having actually seen and talked to a genuine "Blackie."

On another occasion in a poorer place called the Grill Room, where less elaborate food and cheaper refreshments were sold, a sailor came up to me and begged hard for the favour of my speaking to his wife. He said that he had returned from Australia the day before, and obtained a day's leave to bring his wife to the Exhibition. He wanted to please her and to satisfy her wishes as far as it lay in his power. The woman took into her head the fancy that she would not be happy nor would she enjoy the sights of the Exhibition unless I spoke to her. In utter vexation at the absurdity of the request I cried—"Nonsense, I can't speak to your wife!" But the man would take no denial, and his pleadings became more and more importunate as now and then he glanced at his petulant queen, who with downcast eyes gloomily sat at a distant table. Well, her ambassador succeeded in his mission, and I had to carry balm to the mind of the unhappy lady. She cheered up at once, and as a reward allowed her husband to have another glass of whisky. That settled him. With the assistance of his wife I had soon to pack him off to his home in a cab or otherwise he would have got into trouble.

How did the Anglo-Indians treat us? I am sure my countrymen would want to know that. They treated us as gentlemen would treat gentlemen. What kinder and warmer friend could any man hope to get than Sir George Birdwood? A fellow-feeling existed between the Anglo-Indians and ourselves as if they were our countrymen in that strange land. Here inequality of official position separated us, there we were guests. Their sojourn in an oriental land would have been for nothing if they had not learnt how honoured a guest is. Occasionally, however, we met with some queer characters who, specially if they had ladies with them, pompously displayed their acquaintance with the Hindi language, however slight it might be, and their power and superiority over us. That was as much as to tell the ladies—"Look, how great I am!" So far it was all right. And we did our best to look surprised at his unlimited command over the vernacular languages of India, and to look submissive before him to help him to be the Great Mogul he wished to look in the eyes of the ladies. The ladies would smile and giggle, his face would be all animation with pleasure and pride, his urbanity would know no bounds, and at the end, ten to one, it would end in an invitation. Lord, what villains we thought we were! But it was all done in charity. At any rate here is a hint for one or two swindling Indians we met in London, whose business was rather slack. Once, but once only, I met with a little rudeness from an Anglo-Indian. I do not give the *exact words* he used, but I give his meaning and materialise his tone into words. He majestically stalked towards me and said—"Slave, show me——'s office." "I am sorry I cannot obey your command just at this moment, Sir, as I am engaged, but if you go straight, turn to the right and then to the left, you will find yourself before that office," I replied. He got angry and said—"You must, Sir; who is your master?" "My master, Sir, is the Government of India. I cannot go with you for the reason that I am engaged with this gentleman, who is the Reporter for——." His rudeness did not annoy me more than his servility to the gentleman I named.

Outside the Exhibition we never experienced a single act of unkindness. We travelled alone in the East End, the West End and everywhere, and frequently got ourselves lost. Boys and girls would gather round, but they never molested us in any way. Beggars and bad women would no doubt be bolder with us than with the natives (of England), but they never gave us any trouble worth speaking of. No street Arab or London ruffian ever took advantage of our inexperience. On the other hand men who idly lounge about public houses in low quarters, were always ready to help us, and frequently shewed us the way when we got lost. Places where even cockneys would be afraid to go in the daytime we went to in search of adventures, but no adventure will happen to one who would keep clear of disreputable enticements. Once a villainous-looking Jew tried to cut a practical joke upon me. More than a dozen hands were at once raised in my protection, those hands belonged to English roughs, perfect strangers to me. At another time somebody called me a foreigner. "He is no foreigner!" cried several voices, "He is a British subject as you and I."

Author of two evangelical ethnographies of London (*The Asiatic in England*, 1873, and *The East in the West*, 1895), Joseph Salter was affiliated with the London City Mission for over 40 years. Though he was not a journalist, his writing is an echo of Mayhew's earlier work in *London Labour and the London Poor* (above), with a special emphasis on the Asian and African presence at the heart of the empire. In this chapter from *The East in the West*, Salter offers readers the kind of gothic sympathy that they would have found in fin-de-siècle social investigators like General William Booth (above), and others as well.

Joseph Salter, "Central Africans" (1895)

ON a beautiful morning in August we made our usual visit to the expatriated sons of Africa. We chose the Sabbath because they would be free from ship-duties. We mingled with about a hundred of "the remnant of the captivity"—those who, having outlived their wrongs, had reached the enchanted land of England—the land that had given them liberty. Midday produced tropical heat, and these liberados were almost as lightly clad as they would have been in their long-lost homes between the Nyanza and the Zambesi. They were all distinguished for muscle and bone, the weaker ones having died off, unable to sustain the endurance of servitude. Their broad breasts and curly heads were exposed to the glare of the sun; their tribal marks were visible on their faces and arms, and could be seen on their breasts also as the breeze blew their kanzu aside. These marks distinguish the various tribes of inland Africa. Some had foreheads equal to the Circassian, but with others the frontal bone retired at a considerable angle. The cheek-bone and lip varied from the Aryan form to the Negro—high and thick. The eyes of the Central African usually sparkle like polished gems when lighted up by some happy thought.

A few words of friendly salutation aroused all their native animation, and, as they displayed their teeth—white as the ivory of their own land—other tribal distinctions were noticeable. In some the two front teeth were cut so as to be at a right angle to each other, while others had their teeth cut to a point, giving them a saw-like appearance. These darkies belonged to Komango, and called themselves Wakomango. Among these hundred men were waifs from seven central tribes of the Wagindo, Wabusa and Wakua, etc., and each of them bore the brand of his clan. One informed us his home was sixteen days from Zanzibar, but he could not say in what direction. His calculation was based on the time it took the slave caravan to reach the coast. Another said he lived by the Great Lake, and, in his attempt to make us acquainted with the spot, said the tall palm tree on the other side of the water looked like a little boy. Ndugu said he lived on the banks of the "broad river" where the kiboko or hippopotamus laves and snorts, and where the mfalme who rules there marries twenty sable beauties every year, and kills five servants on the annual return of his father's death-day. But we were not sufficiently learned in African lore to determine from such data the place of their birth, except in the case of a few who claimed a home north of the Nyassa.

Saood narrated his capture very touchingly, while a mist seemed to come into his eyes. He was about fourteen years old when the Arab hunting party attacked his village with fire and bullets. He was captured and sold in the slave market of Zanzibar, but was finally released from the slave dhow by a British cruiser, and taken to Bombay. He was afterwards one of an expedition that passed near his home, but the town had become a desolate waste. He had had a mother and a brother, but his ardent desire to discover something about them was doomed to disappointment. As he told his tale the thought came to his mind that perhaps among the many Central Africans visited by the missionary he might some day see his brother, and so obtain news of his mother. So he said: "Write it all down. My brother's name is Musogo, and my mother's name is Karee Watangee; you see my tribal mark"—and he called attention to the scars under each eye. "My mother and brother have the same marks. Should you ever see Musayo, my younger brother, tell all about Saood, and inquire about mother." He also had a little sister, who he supposed was killed and buried in the ruins at the sacking of the village.

. . . Kasagaba was captured and sold to the Portuguese, by whom he was retained some years. He gave many harrowing accounts of the sufferings of himself and his companions in misery, but he also gave an account of his escape. The lash had cut pieces out of his back, and rough hands had removed the hanging fragments with the knife; then salt and chillies were applied to prevent a fatal result. But we pass by all the horrors of the ten years' servitude. His master died, and his slaves were all sold and shipped in a dhow, being packed below more like bags of sand for ballast than beings who were expected to breathe and live. Only small holes in the sides gave ventilation to the fainting human freight. These slaves, as far as their manacles and strength would let them, stood against the holes to catch the breeze and look across the broad expanse of blue, over which the wind and waves were taking them. One suddenly turned round and made an announcement which spread animation and excitement among all, and all who were able endeavoured to pass to the orifice to see the flag of hope. Strange that these pining prisoners, deported from Central Africa, should know the meaning and value of a British flag so well,—for such it was that had thrilled them. Noise, clamour, and activity betrayed the alarm of the crew. The doorway leading to the compartment where Kasagaba lay was barricaded with boards and lumber, but it was in vain. The lumber was soon removed, and the boarding was smashed in with an axe, wielded by the strong arm of a determined English tar; and the appearance of a British officer in uniform, sword in hand, was hailed with a wild African shout of delight and a flood of joyful tears. The dungeon was soon exchanged for daylight, and fetters for liberty. The diseased, the hungry, and the naked were attended to; and the *Water Witch*—the English ship which captured the slaver—took the dhow as a prize.

But Kasagaba was indebted to the *Water Witch* for more than the happy results just described. He learned something about the Saviour from the lips of the chaplain. On shore he again fell into Christian hands, where he learned more of the plan of grace and love, till, with glowing eyes and heart, he could tell how the *Water Witch* delivered him from slavery and death, and how the precious blood of the Saviour had saved him from the penalty of sin and the second death.

The Sabbath sun was fast declining, and about fifty Africans were ranging themselves for a dance on the quay. They formed a circle, outside of which two dusky musicians squatted. One of these had a guitar of homely manufacture, with three strings and the hard shell of the fruit called the Zeezee. The instrument of the other was extemporised, being made by thrusting a stout bamboo through a disused *bouilli bœuf* tin, on the side of which the dark musician kept beating with a marrow bone. To this music the Africans joined chorus, and sprang about. They all sang a monotonous repetition of the same few words, by no means all in unison, and the sentence was so divided that each one seemed to be a syllable behind his mate, so that some were on the first word of the strain while others were at the last! So it went round, occasionally varied by a change of the sentence and of the melody, but this was done so suddenly, without a break, as only to be noticeable to a trained ear.

Such a scene in London was romantic enough, and the singing not discordant. But the dancers did not continue long in motion. Suddenly they stopped for a moment, while the music went on. Then two from opposite sides reeled to the centre, and faced each other: all the interest was now on these. Their actions were lively, but one seemed to be the exact reproduction of the other, while a failure in this respect was signalled by a general clapping of hands. The two central figures would then reel back into their original position, the marrow bone was plied on the *bouilli bœuf* tin with fresh energy, and all recommenced the general dance.

The dance being over, these sons of Africa sought rest, squatting on the ground, spars, chains and barrels, while they listened to a song. The singer was above the average African, for he had been under European training. His weird strain was accompanied with an unmelodious kind of guitar. It was about slavery and ran somewhat thus:—

"I'm a slave, I'm a slave, on my brow
Grows the thick curly hair of my clan,
The badge of a slave
From a child to the grave;
I'm a slave, I'm a slave—not a man.
A man hath his kindred and friends,
His body and life are his own,

But the life of a slave
Is his master's, who gave
Full value for sinew and bone.
Aiwa, aiwa, ana ghulam wa.
"I'm a slave, I'm a slave, you can see,
And therefore you need not be told,
For all the world knows,
Where the sable skin grows,
There are muscle and bone to be sold.
Not a being that sits on his hearth,
Though it be but a kraal on the wold,
But a slave from my birth,
And my uttermost worth
Is my value in barter or gold.
Aiwa, aiwa, ana ghulam wa.
"I'm a slave, I'm a slave, for the whip
Has left its broad marks on my flesh;
You can count, if you will,
For I carry them still,
The scars of the terrible lash.
I toil with the rise of the sun
In childhood, in manhood, in age;
Or I'm bartered away
In the broad light of day,
I'm a slave, and my life is my wage.
Aiwa, aiwa, ana ghulam wa."

. . . To meet with Central African Christians in London is indeed pleasing. These dark diamonds sometimes emit most encouraging testimony to the labours of Christians abroad. There was Hamba, who had been seventeen months the servant of Dr. Kirk, our Consul at Zanzibar; Bejar, who had been servant to Dr. Robb, Hon. Physician at the Mission Station there; and another, who took the Christian name of William, and was one of the faithful band who attended Livingstone on his last journey, and carried his remains to the coast. The Nassick Orphanage, near Bombay, had the honour of educating William for his work. These all had a fair amount of Christian light and Bible information.

The African believes largely in charms, supposed to protect against lightning or storm. An African who owned one of these charms had passed through a storm of seven days' duration, in which one of his own men and an English sailor were washed overboard, and at the time he spoke several of the crew were lying in hospital injured. He said he had thrown "three of these powerful charms into the boiling sea, and such was the violence of the storm, it was seven days before they took effect!" That was one way of accounting for it.

The African's idea of England's power is very great. "You are a wonderful people," said one as we were walking and explaining the railway and the telegraph to him. "You live in a little island in the sea, and you rule India and Africa. All the world serves you and sends you its produce. If we put iron into the water it sinks to the bottom; but you make it carry your men and merchandise across the widest sea. We are afraid of the wind and the lightning, but you use them both: the wind drives your ships wherever you want to go, and the lightning carries your messages over the houses and under the sea, where you please, and your letters fly underground by some invisible carrier." This last wonder was owing to his seeing a letter dropped into a street pillar-post!

. . . The story of Saleem may fitly close this chapter. He was the son of African parents who had been freed from the Arab slave dhow. His father died, and the widowed mother took Saleem to Bishop (then Dr. Steere's orphanage). She had, however, a strong objection to the Christian faith, and made Saleem promise that he would never accept it. Three years and a half were passed at this school, after which he went to sea, where, among African heathen, he was in a fair way to carry out his mother's wishes. But one day, when in London, he found himself with others on board the vessel listening to the reading and exposition of the Swahili Scriptures. An awakened conscience by-and-by brought him to the Asiatic Rest for advice, where he acknowledged the truth of Christianity, and was in sore trouble to know what he should do regarding his old promise. It was explained that his mother had extorted, and he had given, the promise in entire ignorance of what Christianity was. About a year later he returned to London, but this time with a bright and happy face. "I'm a Christian! I'm a Christian!" were his first words, as he proceeded to tell us how it came about. His mother had died shortly after he had entered on his last voyage, and he considered that her death released him from his promise. At his urgent request he was baptized, he testifying to his faith in Jesus. We have often seen him since, and believe him to be a happy Christian. May he prove faithful unto death!

———

Echoing T. N. Mukherji's accounts of his travels through England in the 1880s (above), Merriman-Labor gives us a glimpse into what relations were like between black and white communities on the eve of World War I.

———

A. B. C. Merriman-Labor,
from *Britons Through Negro Spectacles* (1909)

When Blacks Meet Whites.

This want of relish for the colour of the Negro or ignorance about him and his colour, is more evidenced in the words or actions of the common people of the low class suburbs in Britain, by the actions of some thoughtless people of the better class, and amongst children of every class. A story or two will make this clear.

The present Alake of Abeokuta during his recent visit here, was so much annoyed by some thoughtless students of a certain British university, that prompt action was taken by the university authorities to punish the offenders.

As regards the treatment by white children to black people, an anecdote about a Negro bishop first suggests itself to in my mind. The late Bishop Crowther was once spending some time in England with a white clergyman, an evangelical missionary who had been out to West Africa. The black prelate was provided with a bed on which was a white sheet. Every morning the clergyman's little daughter would examine the sheet carefully to see whether some of the blackness of the good bishop was left on it.

This puts me in mind of a story I read not long ago in an English weekly magazine respecting a little fellow who returned home from school with his copy book covered all over with what seemed to be splashes of black ink. Asked by his father to explain the filthy condition of his book, the school boy replied that the splashes were caused by a Negro lad who, accidentally cutting his finger, used the copy book to wipe off his black blood.

The other story relates to my humble self. I was once spending a day with a respectable family at Stockwell in South London. The mother introduced me to her little daughter as a person who had come from Africa. The little child looked attentively at me for a while, and then turning to her mother, asked, "Mama! mama! is the African gentleman black all over his body, or only in his hands and face?" The mother replied "Well Mary, I have never seen his body, but I daresay it is black as well."

Little Mary, being a child who had been properly trained, did not bother to use her tongue and spittle on my hand to see if the blackness will come off. A queer white lady did use her spittle on a great-aunt of mine who was brought to England over sixty years ago.

As I speak of my late aunt, I call to mind a tragical story connected with her stay in the white man's country. Her mistress called with her to see a lady in the Midlands, a country woman who had never seen a Negro before. She was not told beforehand that she was to expect a Negro of the she-kind. In consequence, the country lady was so frightened on seeing my aunt suddenly, that, as she opened the door to her and her mistress, with one hand to the handle, she fell down dead.

Whilst this lady had a mortal dread for my aunt, both of them now far away, another lady, an elderly one, once a resident at delightful Dulwich in South-east London, was extremely fond of me. She wanted me always to visit her because, as she said, people with black hair, and black men more so, always brought her luck. On New Year's Eve, a few years ago, she asked me to call on her at twelve o'clock midnight, so that if I were her very first visitor, she would get luck during the whole year. I called on her as she desired. Strange to say, the year was a very lucky one to her. She became entirely free from her life-long rheumatism. Entirely free,—in fact, more than free, for the painful malady took her to a place where "there shall be no more death, neither sorrow, nor crying, neither shall there be any more pain, for the former things are passed away." She has now ceased to suffer. She is gone.

I am still here, suffering from some people's dislike of my colour, especially when I visit a low class suburb in Britain.

In the low class suburbs a black man stands the chance of being laughed at to scorn until he takes to his heels. And, in such low quarters, until the Diamond Jubilee of the late Queen Victoria which by bringing hundreds of black soldiers and others into Britain made black faces somewhat familiar, bad boys will not hesitate to shower stones or rotten eggs on any passing black man, however high he may be in his own estimation.

Pray that, even now, you never meet a troupe of children just from school. They will call you all kinds of names, sing you all sorts of songs, whilst following you about until a passing vehicle flies you out of their sight.

Pray also that you never encounter a band of factory girls just from their workshop. Some of these girls will make fun of you by throwing kisses to you when not making hisses at you, whilst others shout "Go wash your face guv'nor," or sometimes call out "nigger! nigger! nigger!"

. . . From the incidents which I have just related, you will see that the people's notion of black men is very limited, and even the limited very vague. A good many Britons believe that all Africans and even Indians in Britain, are from the same country, that they speak the same language, and are known to one another.

Of the black man's country, at least of West Africa, their knowledge is worse still. Apart from the statement that "Sierra Leone is the white man's grave"—a wrong statement indeed—few know anything of any other country in West Africa. Many fancy that the Colony of the Gold Coast is a part of the gold district of Australia. Even their learned men find it difficult to distinguish between Bathurst in New South Wales and Bathurst on the Gambia. The editor of a leading London newspaper could see no difference between Lagos in Southern Nigeria and Lagos in Portugal. Between Liberia in West Africa and Siberia in Russia is a distance of several thousand miles; but not a few believe that the former country is the same as the latter. Not a few believe, as the beggar thought, that inside the trousers of every Negro is a tail like that of a horse.

B. Work, Race, and Politics: Centers and Peripheries

~ಀ~

Flora Annie Steel (1847–1929) was primarily a short-story writer and novelist, but *The Complete Indian Housekeeper and Cook* was by far her most popular work. Revised and reprinted a dozen times between 1888 and the Great War, it served as a manual for several generations of Englishwomen who went "out" to India. Not only did Steel and her coauthor Gardner prescribe the duties of the Anglo-Indian housekeeper in great detail, they explicitly equated her domestic work the management of the British Empire.

~ಀ~

F. A. Steel and G. Gardner, from *The Complete Indian Housekeeper and Cook* (first edition, 1888)

The Duties of the Mistress

Housekeeping in India, when once the first strangeness has worn off, is a far easier task in many ways than it is in England, though it none the less requires time, and, in this present transitional period, an almost phenomenal patience; for, while one mistress enforces cleanliness according to European methods, the next may belong to the opposite faction, who, so long as the dinner is nicely served, thinks nothing of it being cooked in a kitchen which is also used as a latrine; the result being that the servants who serve one and then the other stamp of mistress, look on the desire for decency as a mere personal and distinctly disagreeable attribute of their employer, which, like a bad temper or stinginess, may be resented or evaded.

And, first, it must be distinctly understood that it is not necessary, or in the least degree desirable, that an educated woman should waste the best years of her life in scolding and petty supervision. Life holds higher duties, and it is indubitable that friction and over-zeal is a sure sign of a bad housekeeper. But there is an appreciable difference between the careworn Martha vexed with many things, and the absolute indifference displayed by many Indian mistresses, who put up with a degree of slovenliness and dirt which would disgrace a den in St. Giles, on the principle that it is no use attempting to teach the natives. . . . The Indian servant, it is true, learns more readily, and is guiltless of the sniffiness with which Mary Jane receives suggestions; but a few days of absence or neglect on the part of the mistress, results in the servants falling into their old habits with the inherited conservatism of dirt. This is, of course, disheartening, but it has to be faced as a necessary condition of life, until a few generations of training shall have started the Indian servant on a new inheritance of habit. It must never be forgotten that at present those mistresses who aim at anything beyond keeping a good table are in the minority, and that pioneering is always arduous work.

The first duty of a mistress is, of course, to be able to give intelligible orders to her servants; therefore it is necessary she should learn to speak Hindustani. No sane English-woman would dream of living, say, for twenty years, in Germany, Italy, or France, without making the *attempt,* at any rate, to learn the language. She would, in fact, feel that by neglecting to do so she would write herself down an ass. It would be well, therefore, if ladies in India were to ask themselves if a difference in longitude increases the latitude allowed in judging of a woman's intellect.

The next duty is obviously to insist on her orders being carried out. And here we come to the burning question, "How is this to be done?" Certainly, there is at present very little to which we can appeal in the average Indian servant, but then, until it is implanted by training, there is very little sense of duty in a child; yet in some well-regulated nurseries obedience is a foregone conclusion. The secret lies in making rules, and *keeping to them.* The Indian servant is a child in everything save age, and should be treated as a child; that is to say, kindly, but with the greatest firmness. The laws of the household should be those of the Medes and Persians, and first faults should never go unpunished. By overlooking a first offence, we lose the only opportunity we have of preventing it becoming a habit.

But it will be asked, How are we to punish our servants when we have no hold either on their minds or bodies?—when cutting their pay is illegal, and few, if any, have any real sense of shame?

The answer is obvious. Make a hold.

In their own experience the authors have found a system of rewards and punishments perfectly easy of attainment. One of them has for years adopted the plan of engaging her servants at so much a month—the lowest rate at which such servant is obtainable—and so much extra as *buksheesh,* conditional on good service. For instance, a *khitmutgâr* is engaged permanently on Rs. 9 a month, but the additional rupee which makes the wage up to that usually demanded by good servants is a fluctuating assessment! From it small fines are levied, beginning with one pice for forgetfulness, and running up, through degrees of culpability, to one rupee for lying. The money thus returned to imperial coffers may very well be spent on giving small rewards; so that each servant knows that by good service he can get back his own fines. That plan has never been objected to, and such a thing as a servant giving up his place has never been known in the author's experience. On the contrary, the household quite enters into the spirit of the idea, infinitely preferring it to volcanic eruptions of fault-finding.

To show what absolute children Indian servants are, the same author has for years adopted castor oil as an ultimatum in all obstinate cases, on the ground that there must be some physical cause for inability to learn or to remember. This is considered a great joke, and exposes the offender to much ridicule from his fellow-servants; so much so, that the words, *"Mem Sahib tum ko zuroor kâster ile pila dena hoga"* (*The Mem Sahib will have to give you castor oil*), is often heard in the mouths of the upper servants when new-comers give trouble!! In short, without kindly and reasonable devices of this kind, the usual complaint of a want of hold over servants *must* remain true until they are educated into some sense of duty. Of course, common-sense is required to adjust the balance of rewards and punishments, for here again Indian servants are like children, in that they have an acute sense of justice. A very good plan for securing a certain amount of truthfulness in a servant is to insist that any one who has been caught out in a distinct falsehood should invariably bring witnesses to prove the truth of the smallest detail. It is a great disgrace and worry, generally producing a request to be given another chance after a few days. These remarks, written fifteen years ago, are still applicable, though the Indian mistress has now to guard against the possibility of impertinence. This should never be overlooked for an instant.

The authors' advice is therefore—

"Never do work which an ordinarily good servant ought to be able to do. If the one you have will not or cannot do it, get another who can."

. . . Finally, when all is said and done, the whole duty of an Indian mistress towards her servants is neither more or less than it is in England. Here, as there, a little reasonable human sympathy is the best oil for the household machine. Here, as there, the end and object is not merely personal comfort, but the formation of a home—that unit of civilisation where father and children, master and servant, employer and employed, can learn their several duties. . . . We do not wish to advocate an unholy haughtiness; but an Indian household can no more be governed peacefully, without dignity and prestige, than an Indian Empire.

⁂

Inflected by Darwinian images of the struggle for existence, this account of the dock strike classifies working men as evidence of the "social wreckage" at the heart of the imperial capital, and assesses the financial costs of the industrial action that paralyzed London and threatened the commercial interests of the empire as a whole in 1889.

⁂

E. M. Clerke, "The Dock Labourers' Strike" (1889)

. . . The recent strike at the docks brought home to the consciousness of West London a startled sense of the precariousness of the artificial conditions of its daily life. . . . Few people in ordinary times cast a thought on the complex machinery constantly employed in the task of provisioning the great metropolis, or reflect on the army of carriers incessantly engaged in providing for the commissariat of its army or consumers. The general revolt of labour, promulgated by the leaders of the strike in the manifesto of August 30, would have reduced London to famine in a time measurable by the daily rations for its population, represented by its stored supplies of food. Fortunately the authors of the decree exaggerated their own power, and the threat, which could never have been more than a *brutum fulmen,* was retracted under pressure of public opinion. Its moral effect was to picture the West End as a community of drones, dependent for all that constitutes the physical basis of existence on the swarming hive of workers in the East.

... Rise early (says Miss [Beatrice] Potter) and watch the crowd at the St. Katharine's, or the West and East India Dock gates. The bell rings, the gate opens, and the struggling mass surge forward into the docks. The foremen and contractors stand behind the chain, or in the wooden boxes. The "ticket men" pass through, and those constantly preferred are taken on without dispute. Then the struggle for the last tickets begins. To watch it, one would think it was life and death to those concerned. But Jack having secured a ticket by savage fight, sells it to needier Tom for twopence, and goes off with the coppers to drink or to gamble. Or if the flush of business forces the employers to "clear the gates," many of those who on a slack morning would be most desperate in their demand for work, will break off after they have earned sufficient for a pint of beer and a pipe of tobacco and a night's lodging. Or take a day which offers no employment—watch the crowd as it disperses. The honest worker, not as yet attracted by the fascinations of East End social life, will return to his home with a heavy heart: there he will mind the baby while his wife seeks work; or, if not entirely hopeless, he trudges wearily along the streets searching vainly for permanent work. But the greater part of the crowd will lounge down the waterside, and stand outside the wharf and dock gates. As the day draws on, the more respectable element will disappear, while its place will be taken by the professional "cadger" and dock lounger. These men would work at no price. They gain their livelihood by petty theft, by cadging the earnings of their working friends, through gambling or drink, and by charitable assistance. I very much fear that these are the recipients of the free breakfasts with which the well-to-do West End, in times of social panic, soothes its own conscience and calms its own fears. But apart from this semi-criminal class, the staple of the dock and waterside population subsisting by means of the extreme fluctuation and irregularity of employment, is made up of those who are either mentally or physically unfit for worthful or persistent work. These men hang about for the "odd hour," or work one day in the seven. They live on stimulants and tobacco, varied by bread and tea and salt fish. Their passion is gambling. Sections of them are hereditary casuals; a larger portion of them drift from other trades. They have a constitutional hatred of regularity and forethought, and a need for paltry excitement. They are late risers, sharp-witted talkers, and, above all, they have that agreeable tolerance for their own and each other's vices which seems characteristic of a purely leisure class, whether it lies at the top or bottom of society.

The part played by dock labour in acting as a magnet to this floating and drifting mass of social wreckage, renders it one of the chief deteriorating influences in East London.

The strike, which had lasted in its active form for four weeks, has inflicted incalculable loss on the trade of London and all classes connected with it. It is said to have cost the metropolis, roughly speaking, not far from £2,000,000, the loss to the industries chiefly concerned having amounted to £70,000 a day. Dock share and debenture holders have had their property depreciated to the extent of another £1,000,000, these securities having fallen in no case less than 4, and generally as much as from 6 to 8 per cent. The general stagnation has been felt in industries quite unconnected with the shipping trade, and a blow has been dealt to the prosperity of London from which it will take long to recover. The higher rates which the dock companies must necessarily charge to shipping will drive it to seek a cheaper port, and though such a result may prove a corrective to the tendency to over-concentration displayed in the growth of London, the change cannot be effected save at a heavy cost of human suffering.

Nor is any permanent improvement in the position of the dock labourers themselves likely to ensue from the victory they have gained. Scarcity of work, not lowness of wages, was their real grievance against society, and the increased competition induced by higher pay will probably far outweigh the advantages accruing from the latter. Trade, too, it must be remembered, like the fowl that laid the golden eggs, may be destroyed, but not forced beyond its normal rate of productiveness, and the suffering caused by any interference with its functions falls most heavily on the lowest ranks of its hierarchy. A too-successful strike of ship carpenters some years ago finally drove the ship-building trade of the Thames to its northern rivals, the Clyde and Tyne, and the triumph proved most disastrous to those who achieved it. Should the dock strike produce any permanent effect in diverting the trade of London elsewhere, its consequences will first recoil on the heads of those who promoted or took part in it. The readjustments of the great commercial machine are as remorseless as the revolutions of the wheels of Juggernaut's car in crushing the human victims it encounters on its path.

But to Catholics at least, the great struggle will remain associated with a pleasing recollection—that of the part played in it by the Cardinal-Archbishop of Westminster. Not so much to his high ecclesiastical dignity as to his kindly human sympathy for all, but more especially for the poor of the great city, was due the personal influence which triumphed when all other advocates of conciliation had withdrawn in despair. Thus to him alone remains the glory of having played the part, so strangely fallen to a Roman Cardinal, of arbitrator between classes, as an Englishman among Englishmen, in the dispute which will be long remembered as the great strike of 1889.

Echoing many of the concerns of the Chartist movement, Thomas Burt (1837–1922) calls for the Labour MP to rise above class considerations. A former pit-worker, in the wake of the dock strike he advises against the formation of the Labour Party, urging Labour representatives to work for the interests of "the whole nation" instead.

Thomas Burt, "Labour in Parliament" (1889)

THOUGH labour representation has not as yet attained any great proportions, it is more than thirty years since the idea first took form in this country. In 1857, my friend G. J. Holyoake, himself an artisan in his youth, and a man who has never lost sympathy and touch with the work-people, was a candidate for the representation of the Tower Hamlets. John Stuart Mill then sent a generous subscription and a letter of hearty approval. The same distinguished Radical supported Mr. George Odger when he, some years afterwards, came forward for Southwark. Both Mr. Holyoake and Mr. Odger were defeated. The same fate befell Mr. Cremer, Mr. Howell, and other labour candidates in 1868, and it was not until 1874 that the late Mr. Macdonald and myself were returned as the first direct labour representatives to the House of Commons. The desire for special representation of the workmen, and the power to give effect to that desire, have alike increased since 1857. The extension of the suffrage in 1885 gave a new impetus to the movement in favour of labour representation, and in the present

Parliament there are nine members, including Mr. Cremer and Mr. Howell, who are recognized as coming under the category of working-class representatives. The term "labour representative," though not easy to define, perhaps requires some definition. It is sometimes contended that every member of Parliament who has himself been a workman is entitled to be called a labour representative. That would include men who have been fortunate speculators, who may have become millionaires, and large employers, and would be manifestly too wide. On the other hand, some deny that any labour member has yet found his way to the House of Commons. They maintain that it is not enough for a man to have been an artisan or labourer, but that he must continue to follow his calling when not attending to his parliamentary duties; others go so far as to contend that a man is not a labour member who does not continue his ordinary employment even when Parliament is in session. This, in theory, may look well enough, but in practice it is impossible.

. . . The best member, therefore, I repeat, is he who is free from class bias, who looks at every question on broad grounds of justice and humanity, who will speak and vote for what is right, though it may cut prejudice against the grain, and may militate against his own interests. Such members we have—mine-owners, railway directors, large employers of labour, who can be just and humane even when Mine Regulation Bills and Employers' Liability Bills are under consideration. Not only are these men in the House of Commons, but they come in increasing numbers, and there were never so many of them there as now. Do these admissions destroy or even weaken the claim for labour representation? I think not. The ideal to be aimed at is one thing, the actual realized is another. It may be desirable to get rid of classes and class distinctions. To abolish class animosities and class prejudices is certainly devoutly to be wished.

. . . The labour candidate, always a poor man, cannot easily cross the threshold of the House of Commons. That House has been called "a rich man's club." Money, no doubt, reckons for less now than formerly, but still it is hardly extravagant to say of the House of Commons that its "door is barred with gold and opens but to golden keys." The main difficulty of the rich man is overcome when he finds a constituency with the will and the power to elect him. The working-man has not only this preliminary obstacle to surmount, but he has to solve the problem of how his election expenses are to be paid, and to find the means of living, should his return prevent him from following his ordinary avocation.

The cost of elections has been greatly reduced by recent legislation, but it is still very high. At the last general election the amounts paid by candidates in scores of instances exceeded a thousand pounds, often reaching £1500, and rising to as much as £1700. The returning officer's fees alone, in numerous cases, were more than five hundred pounds, occasionally above six hundred, and reached as high a figure as seven hundred and thirty-four pounds. Two much-needed reforms are to relieve candidates of returning officers' charges, and to pay members of Parliament for their services.

. . . From its very constitution the House of Commons is a political assembly. Nine-tenths of the subjects which come before it are of a political character. Many of those that are not strictly labour questions are quite as important to the workman as those that are. Will any one pretend that questions of peace and war—which may involve not only vast expenditure of life and treasure, but justice and good-will between one nation and another—land law reform, and all that it embodies, are of less vital moment even to the workmen themselves than factory inspection, the liability of employers, or even State regulation of the hours of labour? By forming a labour party we should not get rid of the evils of party, but we should multiply and aggravate those evils. The labour member is called upon—by those who wish him to concern himself solely with labour questions—to give up his conscience and judgment on the great majority of the subjects that come before Parliament, and this he is asked to do, forsooth, in order that he may emancipate himself from the thraldom, the degradation, and the corruption of party! This view is not less insulting to the workman than it is absurd in itself. It assumes that the worker is something less than a man and a citizen; that, as a mere tool of industry, he should separate himself from humanity, from great controversies between individuals and between one nation and another, and concentrate all his energies upon matters that affect him as a manual labourer. As a temporary expedient that might be defensible, but it is utterly unsound, and therefore incapable of universal application. We should strive to unite, not to divide men; to efface, not to intensify class distinctions.

. . . If I have tried to prove, by an appeal to the facts of history and the teachings of experience, that the self-reliant policy of the British workman has been successful, and that it shows a record in the improved conditions of labour without a parallel elsewhere, it must not be imagined that I am preaching a complacent optimism. Because much has been done, it does not follow that everything is satisfactory. The wretchedness of some of our workers is appalling—not the idle, thriftless, and profligate only, but the industrious and provident. Let any one inclined to rest and be thankful read the report of Mr. Burnett on the condition of the chain and nail makers of Staffordshire, and the evidence given before the House of Lords' Committee on the sweating system. The strong hand of the law may have to be laid on the "sweater" of the East-end of London and upon the "fogger" of the Black Country. Evils so great and palpable must be attacked. With regard to the best mode of attack, opinions will differ. The strongest believers in the virtue of self-help will readily admit the need for occasional State intervention. Our factory legislation may require modification, and we must not be too pedantic. When warned against Socialism, we should remember that some of the most beneficent laws passed during the last fifty years have been more or less socialistic. After all, it is only a question of degree; we cannot draw a line and declare dogmatically that State interference is right on one side and wrong on the other. Each case must be judged on its merits. But it may be well for those of the workmen who are so ready to look to the State, to bear in mind that State help always means management, control, and discipline by the State, and can be had only at the sacrifice of individual liberty. . . .

The labour representatives, a mere handful of men, hardly more than one per cent. of the House of Commons, are utterly powerless, except so far as they act with or secure the co-operation of others. If they were much more numerous, I should still hesitate to recommend them to form themselves into a separate political party—especially into a party founded on the accident of class, a basis narrow and unstable—with the object, avowed or implied, of serving interests less broad than those of the whole nation. In principle I know that would be unsound; in practice I believe it would be either ineffective or mischievous. As to party, its evils, whatever they may be, cannot be cured by the creation of factions. Party, after all, is but the means to an end. Since it is an indispensable means, the true plan is to purify, to elevate, to ennoble it; to make it something better than a mean struggle for place or pay; to ensure that it is always—what I believe it usually is even now—the union of honest men, agreed on certain general principles, and banded together for the advancement of the public weal.

Emily Francis Strong (1840–1904) wrote works of art history and criticism during her first marriage to Mark Pattison. When she married the politician Sir Charles Dilke she changed her name to Emilia and became Lady Emilia Dilke—feminist, intellectual, and president of the Women's Trade Union League from 1886 until her death. As significant as her insistence on the role of women in the strike in the passage below is her use of the Melbourne factory women as a model for their English counterparts.

Emilia Dilke, "Trades Unionism for Women" (1890)

I HAVE heard that a lady once pestered the great Rothschild with inquiries as to the best means of making money, till, driven by her pertinacity into giving a direct answer, he impatiently exclaimed, "Matches, madam, matches are as good as anything—provided you have got enough of them!" Just so. The first requisite for the making of strong labour organisations, as for the making of great wealth, is to have abundance of material in your own hands. It is of no use to be prepared with all the machinery for organisation if no one will come to be organised. Yet this is the disheartening condition under which, until lately, I and others associated with me in the work of spreading Union principles amongst working women have been for many years carrying on our obscure and humble labours. We were united, as far back as 1874, by Mrs. Paterson, in a league now called the Women's Trades Union and Provident League, which has its office—where anyone may apply for help—at the Industrial Hall, Broad Street, Bloomsbury; and we have gone on ever since, distributing leaflets, handbills, pamphlets, by the thousand, in the many crowded centres of women's industry; yet, when we fondly hoped that the ground was thoroughly prepared, we have called meetings only to find ourselves face to face with so scant an audience that the platform had to be abandoned by the speakers, and the meeting, prepared with so much zeal, lapsed, of necessity, into a chat with the four or five anxious women who alone had ventured to respond to our invitations. Indeed we very soon came to regard such an experience as rather encouraging; for our four or five women, well indoctrinated, would come back to us at a later day, bringing as many more with them, and gradually the numbers would increase until, created by the efforts of the little band which had met us that first evening, there would arise a genuine trade society, soundly established, thoroughly independent, and self-governed, though numbering perhaps only a hundred or so. The nights we learnt to dread were our apparently successful nights, when, in reply to our call, we found a room packed with idlers, come out of curiosity, frightening away those we wanted to meet, and as certain to withhold all help as they were ready to give us their amused approval. Every now and again we were, however, cheered by some signs—such as were to be found in the strike of the Dewsbury weavers, so ably and successfully organised by Mrs. Ellis, herself a weaver—which showed that a few women, at any-rate, were thoroughly capable of understanding and applying the principles of trade organisation. Such occurrences were, alas! but few and far between. Nor did we, during those many years of which I speak, receive from the men's unions either countenance or support; rather was there a great unwillingness on their part to recognise the position of women in the trades, and to realise the fact that this position was likely to become a disturbing influence to their own industry precisely because of that neglect. They, as a body, neglected a plain duty towards their women-folk, and—as ever when duty is neglected—their neglect has recoiled on themselves, in too many instances taking a terrible vengeance.

In the Colonies—at least in Victoria—men were somewhat quicker than here to wake up to a sense of their responsibilities in this matter. The women of Melbourne, as late as 1882, were, indeed, no better off than their sisters in the Old World. The immense number of girls and women who found work in the factories, which rapidly arose after the law protecting native industries was passed, remained absolutely at the mercy of their employers, although their husbands and brothers had for thirty years previous enjoyed all the benefits of union. The natural consequence ensued. Steadily and surely the wages of the women were reduced to starvation point. At last they rebelled; a strike took place and the women appealed in their helplessness to the council of the men's Trades Hall. They did not appeal in vain. Their cause was vigorously advocated in the columns of the *Melbourne Age* by Mr. Julian Thomas, and the men's trade societies, together with the public, supported the women until satisfactory rates of pay for their labour were agreed to by the masters. Since the women of Melbourne won the day in 1882 they have remembered the means by which it was won. They did not rush together blindly to go on strike and then slink away as soon as the immediate object was obtained. Their English sisters may take a lesson from them, for they have kept up the organisation which served them in the day of trouble, and they are now actually represented on the council of the Trades Hall. They even possess their own hall, built by the trustees, at a cost of over £1,800, and known as the Female Operatives' Hall. These results could not, however, have been attained by the women unaided and unorganised. The successful termination of their struggle with the masters in the first instance, and the firm establishment of their unions on sound practical lines, could not have been achieved without the help and experience of the men.

Even in England there were, now and again, remarkable exceptions to the general indifference. Individual societies would sometimes come forward and give valuable help. The saddlers last year, for example, made friendly offers when the committee of the Women's Trades Union Provident League endeavoured, by means of their secretary, to induce the women employed in that trade to combine; and some years ago, when an effort was made through me to unite the tailoresses in Oxford, I received the most friendly assistance from the representatives of the Amalgamated Tailors in that town. The secretary and treasurer of the Oxford branch actually gave up their dinner-hour on several successive days in order to meet the girls as they left the factory, distributing our leaflets and doing their best to persuade them to come in. On the whole, however, the attitude of the more active and leading Trades Unionists has hitherto been, if not actually hostile, anything but friendly.

. . . Meanwhile, the story of the Great Strike in London was told us day by day. I do not here propose to touch on its general features, on its bearings on trade, or on any of the evils which it necessarily brought in its train, and which I am far from ignoring. I would, however, call attention to the fact that it was pregnant of results possibly unlooked for even by those whose long continued and persistent efforts had brought it about. Space will not allow me to do more than indicate the points at which it appears to me a very distinct and new impression has been made. In the first place, the Trades Unionist movement has received an amount of attention and sympathy from the lay public which is altogether unprecedented, and the large labour subscriptions which came in, especially from Australia, show a great advance in the direction of that general federation of all classes of industry which is an indispensable condition of efficient Unionism. This advance has brought with it, of necessity, the recognition of the fact that the problem of women's labour, as it stands to-day, can only be solved by the recognition of their claim to be included in the general organisation of industry; therefore, together with all those who have the condition of working women at heart, I am deeply grateful for the change of feeling which seems to have gathered volume and impetus from the circumstances attending the Great Strike. The question has, however, also begun to develop itself on a third line, which I have always expected it to take, which is of immense social importance, but which, as far as I know (with the exception of an excellent article in the *Economist,* September 21st, 1889, headed "Our Casual Labourer"), has received no notice from those who have been writing of the present crisis.

. . . If Unionism is to do its full and perfect work, and combination is to support, not injure, then there must be co-operation on the part of all classes in its service. Most strongly would I urge on women the claims of their labouring sisters. Not by mere talking, not by mere gifts of money, but by taking trouble; by taking trouble to master the grave problems of industry; by taking trouble to learn and know first, and then by the devotion of whole-hearted personal service to the work. This is the way in which all work of this kind, if it is to be effectual, must be carried on. It may be more pleasant, it is certainly easier to give individual alms and to receive thanks with a gratified sense of patronage. We want none of such charity; it is only by the intelligent and devoted service of heart and brain that the task we have in hand of spreading the principles of union can be wisely and serviceably prosecuted. We appeal to rich and idle women to help us; and what work can be more righteous, and, in so far as it regards our sisters, more womanly? The gospel of Trades Unionism, rightly understood, is the most Christian gospel that can be preached, but to preach it worthily there must be personal devotion and personal effort; not merely willingness to forego the pleasures of society and the pleasures of charity, but willingness to try to understand the true bearing of the difficult questions, economical and social, which are involved,—and which will often be found to affect the smallest details of a trade organisation,—and willingness to learn also what work really means. It is amiable of highly-cultured women to come now and again with pretty gowns and pleasant faces to talk kindly sentiment on our behalf from the chair at a public meeting, but it does not really help us who know what the labour and heat of the day mean. If they would only work at the work, if it were only one day a week, it would be better for them and better for those with whom they profess to sympathise. . . .

The specter of the East European Jew flooding British labor markets—and cities and leisure spaces and "domestic" life more generally—gave rise to a variety of discourses about what one historian has called the "anti-alien mentality" in the later nineteenth century. In this piece

David Schloss offers readers a view of the Jewish workman "in the flesh" in the wake of the dock strike, economic downturn, and industrial unrest at the fin-de-siècle.

―✥―

David F. Schloss, "The Jew as Workman" (1891)

THE renewed outburst of persecution, by which during the last few months the Jewish subjects of Russia have been assailed, has aroused in this country feelings of the deepest indignation—feelings in the expression of which Englishmen of every shade of religious belief and of all political parties have united. In terms of no superfluous politeness we have been told not to make ourselves ridiculous, but to mind our own business. But this question of the persecution of the Jews in Russia is emphatically our business. Experience has taught us that every fresh outburst of persecution in Russia is the signal for the departure to our own hospitable shores of large numbers of Jews whose existence in Russia has become, or threatens from day to day to become, one of absolutely intolerable hardship. For many of these exiles England is, no doubt, but a halfway house on their way to more distant countries. It is, however, impossible to deny the fact that there exists in England at this moment a considerable body of Jewish immigrants, the sole cause of whose presence here is the cruel treatment inflicted upon the Jewish subjects of the Tsar; and it seems certain that, if the persecution shall follow unchecked its relentless course, our industrial population will receive a further and in all likelihood a somewhat numerous accession of this foreign element.

It may be said that, if England desires to remain unaffected by the consequences of this Russian persecution, all that we have to do is to erect a legal barrier which shall effectually dam the tide of immigration. Into the question whether legislation such as this would be consistent with the honour, and is required in the interest, of England, I shall not enter. Far be it from me, myself a member of the Jewish race, to say one word that might in any way encourage the British nation, for the first time in its glorious history, to shut the door in the face of the victims of persecution. No less removed from my intention would it be to allow myself, led away by my natural commiseration with the oppressed Jews of Russia, to offer a factious and disloyal opposition to any measure which may be proved to be requisite for the welfare of the land of my birth.

In the meantime the Jew is with us, a factor in our social, and above all in our industrial, life by no means devoid of special interest for the thoughtful observer. The purpose of these pages is to present a faithful portrait of the Jewish workman, as he is to be found in London and in others of our great cities.

. . . Let us inspect these Jewish workpeople in the flesh. We cannot do better than book for Aldgate Station, and ask our way to Petticoat Lane, taking care to inquire for this classic thoroughfare by its modern appellation of Middlesex Street. In the immediate vicinity of this centre of Jewish working-class life, there is held, every Thursday and Friday, a market which, by reason of its extensive scale, as well as of the peculiarities of both purchasers and purchases, certainly deserves to be reckoned as one of the sights of London. The eye seeks in vain for a single face of the Anglo-Saxon type. The regular oval of the Sephardic countenance reminds you of those Latin nations among whom the ancestors of these 'Spanish and Portuguese' Jews dwelt in bygone days; here the flaming beard of an Ashkenaz recalls the Teuton; there the prominent cheek-bones and the peculiar set of the eyes, no less than the long coat and high boots, make one mistake for a moment yonder gaunt 'greener' for a full-blooded Slav; there is much that is very English about that young man who pushes through the dense crowd on his way to the Board-school close by, in which he is a teacher. But, look again! in the features of each and every one of these people we behold, proudly predominant over all minor accidents of physiognomy, the unmistakable stamp of the Israelite. Let us pick out the wife of one of the Jewish working men—the wig, by which the Jewess upon her marriage replaces her own hair, enables us to distinguish between the busy matron and the giddy girl upon gossip intent—and watch her catering. . . .

The most serious allegation made against the Jewish workman is his supposed willingness to work at a lower wage and for longer hours than the Gentile. The Jew who is working at fourpence per hour or less will almost invariably be found to be of foreign birth. Possessing in many cases, when he lands on our shores, little or no skill in any form of handicraft, he is, in order to learn a trade, forced to work, at first for his keep, and then for a few shillings a week. By-and-by his earnings increase, until they reach the level of those of our English casual labourers at the docks, of our chain- and nail-makers, of our Sheffield knife-blade-grinders, and so on. Very often the average wages received by the Jew of this type, taking one week with another, will, even when he has been here twenty years, amount to only fifteen shillings a week. The reason is not far to seek. In trades so greatly affected by seasonal variations and by spasmodic pressure of orders as are those in which most of these men are engaged, an income sufficient to support a family could not be earned by so incompetent a worker, except by working, when the trade is busy, for from fourteen to eighteen hours or even more out of the twenty-four. A few years of a life like this reduce the Jewish immigrant, in many instances, to a chronic condition of drowsy stolidity, utterly incompatible with the maintenance of anything like a reasonable speed in working—an average English workman being able with ease to perform in ten hours a task which would occupy one of these prematurely effete foreigners for eighteen. These poor fellows, in short, begin by ruining their earning power by overwork; and find themselves compelled, without any approach to willingness, to go on year after year toiling for the most beggarly pittance during hours of the most cruel length.

At the same time, it is, unfortunately, necessary to remark that a vast multitude of workers boasting the purest British blood have, until now, been 'willing' to work, often at a very low wage, for fully fifteen or sixteen hours out of the twenty-four. Many thousands of our tramcar and omnibus conductors regularly, some hundreds of thousands of our shop assistants frequently, work as long as this. Many of the bicycle-makers at Coventry put in about fifteen hours a day during the summer. Very many makers of fancy shoes in East London—I speak of men engaged on goods of the better class, none of which are made by Jewish artisans—are accustomed in the height of the 'sew-round' season to work day after day from twelve to fourteen hours. It is a common thing for English 'hand-sewn' bootmakers to devote, during many days of many weeks, to this extremely exhausting labour twelve or thirteen hours; and I am acquainted with some craftsmen with 'a good seat of work' who spend at the bench little less time than this from year's end to year's end, only taking a day off now and again when 'dead beat.' Toil for toil, I doubt whether the British puddler, working all the year round his twelve-hours shift, can properly be considered to take much less out of himself than the average Jewish tailor or bootmaker, who very often works much longer hours, but who invariably has a good deal of 'slack time.' Still, although the difference between Jew and Gentile in this respect is, perhaps, sometimes exaggerated, there can be no doubt that some Jewish workmen overtax their energies to an extent unparalleled among any class of Gentile workers. Many Jewish tailors have been accustomed very frequently to work during short spells of pressure for fifteen, sixteen, or even a much greater number of hours with scarcely a moment's break. In the workshops of the Jewish boot-finishers, before the recent strike, the normal hours worked during many successive weeks on the first five days of the seven were no less than eighteen. In another branch (the making of the lowest class of shoes) I have been in places in which some of the men (generally the 'sweating-masters' themselves) habitually worked even longer than this. I knew one man—and his is not an isolated case—who worked eighteen hours a day during half the year as a 'sweatee' in the 'finishing,' and some twenty as a 'sweater' in the 'sew-round' branch during the other half. 'What do you do on the Sabbath?' I asked him. 'Sleep from Friday afternoon until Sunday morning,' was his answer. Small wonder!

. . . The chief objection to their Jewish fellow-workmen that has hitherto been taken by the leaders of the English industrial classes is the alleged incapacity of the Jews for trade combination. From this reproach, however, the Jews have of late years done much to redeem themselves. Of the development of trade-unionism among the Jewish tailors, who both in Leeds, in Manchester, and in London have struck for, and have obtained, not unimportant concessions, there is no need to speak; but the story of the organisation of the Jews in the metropolitan boot trade is, in some respects, so remarkable as to demand a brief exposition. The manner in which the work has been given out by the manufacturers to 'middlemen,' or 'sweaters,' who themselves employed subordinate workmen, is well known. Now, the absolutely unique feature of the recent trade-union movement among the Jews is that, for some three years past, the unions both of the sweaters and of the sweatees have been engaged in a combination having for its aim the abolition of the sweating system. The middlemen have conspired to effect the extinction of the middleman. In all the history of labour I know of no parallel to this singular fact. . . .

Of the part played in this strike by the trade union of the 'sweatees' it remains to speak. From the first, in all the preliminary skirmishes, the Jewish journeymen had shown the most marvellous constancy; and when the final struggle began in earnest, the unsavoury purlieus of Spitalfields and Bethnal Green witnessed a sight strange indeed. At the rendezvous in Brick Lane there gathered together the most curious set of human beings that it has ever been my fortune to look upon—sallow, blear-eyed, stunted forms, clad in all manner of quaint varieties of the most piteous shabbiness. At mid-day these poor wretches fell in; their calico banners were proudly unfurled; their band struck up; and some six hundred members of the Jewish Journeymen's Union started on their march through the slums. Singly, in twos, and in threes—like the rats of Hamelin—from all sorts of cellars, garrets, and hutches, the finishers still at work came forth, and joined the ranks amid the cheers of their comrades, until, after a few days, no less than a thousand was the tale of the insurgents. The 100*l.* which, with how great self-denial may be imagined, the members of this trade-union had scraped together out of their most meagre earnings was soon spent, the more so, since in its distribution they generously invited the non-unionist workmen to participate. The public was appealed to for funds with very trifling success. But the Jewish tradesmen supplied food on credit to the value of 200*l.* Towards the end of the strike, indeed, everything—cash and credit alike—was exhausted. Still, these Jews fought on with the courage of the Maccabees; fought on, and at last won. Possessing some little personal acquaintance with strikers and strikes in many trades, I declare without hesitation that a better stand was never made by any body of workmen than by these unjustly despised scions of the Jewish race. . . .

Here the author links anti-alien discourse expressly with questions of imperial power and image, invoking the mythical John Bull as the right and proper guardian of the domestic nation's whiteness. In this instance, the colonies offer instructive lessons on how to handle the immigration "problem": for as MacArthur sees it, nothing less than "the whole weight of colonial opinion and experience is in the direction of imposing reasonable restrictions on the introduction of undesirable elements into . . . society."

W. A. MacArthur, from *The Destitute Alien* (1892)

THE average Englishman is very proud of his empire—perhaps, at times, even a little arrogant. He is never tired of telling the world how the sun never sets on his flag. He is always declaring his cheerful willingness to die for the empire at a moment's notice. He loves the poems which talk of the flag which has braved the storms of every sea, and which never floats over a slave. The unity of the empire has been a most successful electioneering cry. A new society has sprung into being, under most distinguished patronage, to forward the movement for the federation of the empire. Everybody joins it. Speakers find in the empire matter for glowing perorations—it is a safe subject for a leading article. Even among the politicians in the House of Commons, who have long since lost belief in most things, there may be found some who still hold to their faith in the empire.

All this indeed is to the good. No one who has seen with an intelligent eye the countries which make up the British Empire, can fail to return to England stirred to the very soul with a sense of the enormous possibilities which lie before these vast territories, which the courage and enterprise of Englishmen have added to their empire. And no impartial observer can fail to see that on the whole the empire of England is a factor in the world which makes for righteousness. Wherever our flag is planted there follow the arts of peace. And there follows also the spirit of fair play and of just dealings with native races which has made our government always tolerated, and in most cases welcomed by peoples the most diverse in race and religion and character.

All this is true, and it is well that the original John Bull at home should appreciate it, and be proud of it, and be always ready to cheer for his empire. But his testing time has yet to come. Up to the present he has had nothing to do for his empire but to cheer and to pay the bill. And this, to do him justice, he has always done cheerfully enough. But the world moves fast, and in matters of opinion it moves faster in the English world outside England than it does in England itself. And John Bull will find out that, if he is to realize his dream of a federation of the empire, he must do more than cheer for his colonies and pay some of their bills. It is good that he should cheer, and also, within limits, that he should pay. But he must also do violence to some of his opinions. He must give up some of his pet prejudices. He must be content to sink, to some extent, his own individuality. He can no longer pose as the all-powerful father. He must take his place as the wise elder brother of the English family. And he must admit that there are some things which his younger brothers can teach even him, and in which their experience may be a useful guide to him.

This is a hard saying for John Bull. No one, on the whole, has such useful prejudices as the good John. And he has found many of them serve him so well in the past that he clings to them with a dogged desperation which has become almost a part of his religion. We lay violent hands on the very Ark of the Covenant when we assail John Bull on any of these dear beliefs of his. And yet, if we are to make any progress with the subject of which this book treats, we shall have to attack John Bull on two of his most cherished illusions.

He believes in Free Trade as he does in the Thirty-nine Articles. He probably does not quite understand either, but he is convinced they are necessary for salvation. Protection he will not have in any shape. And for England itself no doubt he is right. Probably, also, for most of her colonies, though many of them have taken a different view, being under different conditions. But his belief in Free Trade, like all the beliefs he holds strongly, becomes to him a sort of fetish. He has blindly worshipped it so long and so ardently that, like Mr. Dick, who found it impossible to keep the head of Charles I. out of his memoirs, our good John finds an attack on Free Trade in every proposal for legislative interference with anybody or anything which comes into this country. He jumps to the conclusion that we are tampering with his most cherished principles in trying to exclude the pauper foreigner. But if he would learn from one of the most flourishing of his colonies, that of New South Wales, which is a free trade colony, he would find that she has long ago, despite her almost pedantic devotion to free trade, taken very strong steps indeed to shut out such immigrants from other countries as have seemed to her undesirable. I am not now referring to the Chinese. They are practically excluded from Australia also, though for a different reason, and I will return to their case later on. But I am referring now to instances in which Australia has refused to admit English subjects, natives of these islands, for reasons that have seemed to her to be sufficient. And, indeed, so strong has been her determination to keep her people free from moral contamination, that she has at times refused admission to English-born subjects even without the authority of a law to back her. When the Irish informers, after the trial of the Phœnix Park murderers, attempted to land in Australia, neither New South Wales nor Victoria would receive them. Their action was grossly illegal. It had no legal sanction. And yet the Home Government had no choice but to acquiesce in the decision of the Colonial Government, it being felt to be an impossible thing to attempt to coerce a great colony into receiving scoundrels of this class.

Most of the colonies have also taken steps to prevent the introduction of persons likely to become a charge upon the public or upon charitable institutions. And in so doing they have only followed the general practice of the world outside the British Isles. The whole weight of colonial opinion and experience is in the direction of imposing reasonable restrictions on the introduction of undesirable elements into their society. They acted in the case of the Irish informers upon moral grounds. They are acting in the case of the Chinese upon material as well as moral grounds. The Chinaman has about as low a standard of comfort as can be imagined. It is a standard which apparently cannot be raised to our level; at all events, not in Australia. And therefore they have been practically excluded from these colonies, in absolute defiance of treaties between England and China. I should like to see the English Colonial Secretary who would at this time of day attempt to interfere with the Anti-Chinese legislation of Australia. Sir Henry Parkes, the premier of New South Wales, when charged with having broken the laws of the land in excluding the Chinese, replied, "I care nothing about your cobweb of technical law; I am obeying a law far superior to any law which issued these permits, namely, the law of the preservation of society in New South Wales." That this is the right attitude no one who knows the habits of the Chinese can doubt. It is, of course, an attitude which shocks the pedantic free trader. It is an attitude which is not for the benefit of the consumer. If the be-all and end-all of government is to obtain unrestricted competition at the price of public morality and of decency of life, then no doubt Australia is wrong. But if it be a good thing to risk paying a shade more for a nation's goods, in order to exclude a moral plague which may turn a great city into a modern Sodom, then there is no friend of his kind who will not approve Sir Henry Parkes' declaration, and the action of the New South Wales and other Australian governments. I am justified in saying that the Imperial view—that is the view of almost the whole of the empire outside of England—is in favour of the restrictions we are seeking to obtain in England. Is it not a strange thing for England absolutely to refuse to listen to the teachings of the experience of almost every English-speaking community in the world except herself?

. . . Is it not, then, a strange thing for England to refuse to learn lessons which are the result of the experience of every other English-speaking nation in the world? For it must not be forgotten that the United States also have found the burden of undesirable immigrants intolerable. Twenty years ago America was inclined to be proud of the number of her immigrants, but within, comparatively speaking, the last few years, they have begun to pour in upon her in swarms from all parts of Europe, until she has become saturated, so to say, with very much the same class of immigrant whom we are seeking to exclude from England.

These immigrants—many of them—do not speak English, and do not assimilate with the population as do immigrants of the Scandinavian, German, and even Irish type. They bring with them a low standard of morals, and a low standard of physical comfort, and they therefore compete unfairly with existing labour in America, which has, for the most part, attained the enjoyment of a wage which enables it to live in tolerable comfort. There serious troubles have recently arisen from this very cause. They find that the lower class of foreign immigrants have secret societies of their own, with objects which are not compatible with the obligations of respectable citizenship. Some of these evils have recently come to light in the most marked manner during the Mafia Riots in New Orleans; and although the lynching of the Italians in New Orleans, whom the American citizens regarded as having been acquitted, owing to the terrorising or bribing of the jury by a secret Italian murder society, was no doubt grossly illegal, and ought to be repudiated in the name of law and order, yet there is not the slightest doubt that the entire current of American unofficial opinion is very strongly with the citizens of New Orleans, who are regarded as having on the whole taken the only course open to them to free themselves from the burden of an intolerable foreign tyranny. The presentment of the grand jury of New Orleans points out that there is no question more intimately connected with the subject matter of their investigation than immigration, and records its opinion "that the time has past when this country (America) can be made the dumping-ground for the worthless and depraved of every nation."

. . . The other argument which sorely oppresses John Bull is the argument in connection with political refugees. He fears that if legislation of this kind be passed, he may be found some day handing over continental political prisoners to the tender mercies of despotic governments. It is a fear which does him credit, but which, I think, is not well founded. Means might very well be devised to shield the political refugee. To begin with, very few of them come here as paupers, and still fewer come who are totally unknown, and whose cases could not therefore be enquired into before they were sent back.

Finally, I think John Bull should reflect that he owes a duty to his children. We believe the Anglo-Saxon race to be the finest of the world. Every Englishman, at home or abroad, or in America, is proud of his race, of his language, of his traditions, and of the great Anglo-Saxon stock from which he sprung. Kingsley has told us the touching story of the old warrior Wulf, who, on the point of submitting himself to Christian baptism, suddenly bethought him to inquire from the officiating bishop where were the souls of his heathen ancestors. "In hell!" replied the bishop. And Wulf drew back from the font. "He would prefer, if Adolf had no objection, to go to his own people."

So, I think, say we all. We prefer our own people and our own race. Let us see to it that we preserve its vigour and its noble characteristics, so that our colonial offspring may still bear themselves proudly when they think of the parent race from which they came. Let us be wise while yet there is time, lest in years to come our children should despise us. Surely they must despise us if they see us heedless alike of our own race traditions and of the experience with which they themselves have furnished us.

The Ngwato kingdom that Khama III (ca. 1835–1923) inherited from his father Sekgoma I was of enormous geographical importance, connecting Missionaries' Road from Mafeking to Bulawayo in western Zimbabwe. Khama offered an object lesson to Victorians about what the black man was capable of—especially if he converted to Christianity (he was baptized in 1860). His version of "Christian kingship" combined with his antipathy to the Boers, and the strategic centrality of his state, made him popular among British authorities as well as Cecil Rhodes's British South African Company—though he ultimately joined imperial forces to stop Rhodes's attempt to invade Matabeleland.

London *Times,* "Khama" (1893)

In sending nearly 1,800 of his men to join the combined force of Bechuanaland Border Police and the garrison of Fort Tuli, commanded by Major Goold Adams, Khama, the paramount chief of the Bamangwato, has given fresh evidence of his loyal devotion to Great Britain and of the important service that he can render to British interests in South Africa. By universal consent Khama is the most remarkable native chief south of the Zambesi, and indeed it may fairly be said in the whole of Africa. His personal appearance is striking. A recent traveller says that he "stands six feet in height, is of a slim wiry habit, and, although now verging on 60 years of age, might be taken for at least 12 or 15 years younger," and the impression made by him on a first meeting was that of a "tall, slim gentleman with a refined face, friendly smile, and shy yet self-possessed manner." Mrs. Knight-Bruce, wife of the Bishop of Mashonaland, bears equal testimony to the distinction and charm of Khama's character. He is, she says, "a radical reformer who yet develops both himself and his people on the natural lines of the race; he has made himself into a character that can be spoken of as a 'perfect English gentleman,' but without losing for a moment his self respect as an African; he has kept his position as a disciple, not a mimic, of white civilization, and he has shown how such a man can raise a nation. He has done it all, as he would tell us, because he is a Christian convert." In early life Khama was trained by the Rev. Robert Moffat and his son, John Moffat, and later in life was brought for many years into close contact with the Rev. John Mackenzie, the well-known missionary who was stationed at Shoshong, the then capital of the Bamangwato. Subsequently an able Scotch missionary named Hepburn became the chief's trusted friend and counsellor, so that all his life Khama has been fortunate in having the assistance and advice of men on whose judgment and disinterestedness he could place the utmost reliance. His life has been one of great activity and danger. At the age of 18 he incurred the displeasure of his father, Sekomo, by his firm refusal to take a second wife, and his love of reform and devotion to the ideas of the white men brought him into constant antagonism with his father and uncle, Sekomo and Macheng. Up to 1870 the Bamangwato were kept in a constant state of turmoil by the rival pretensions of Sekomo and Macheng to the chieftainship, but in that year the tribe chose Khama as chief. In a couple of years, however, he was driven by incessant intrigues to take refuge in the Botletli country, where he remained in exile for three years. In 1875 he was again called by the unanimous voice of the tribe to assume the chieftainship. "Since which time," says Mr. H. A. Bryden, whose recently published work, "Gun and Camera in Southern Africa," contains many interesting particulars of Khama and his country, "the Bamangwato have enjoyed perfect internal peace and have progressed materially and morally in an astonishing degree." During the 18 years of his rule Khama has abolished polygamy, and the practices of witchcraft and "smelling out" have disappeared; trial by jury has been introduced; European clothing has come into common use among the people; there is absolute freedom in the matter of religious observances; no man is forced to attend the mission services, but by his example Khama shows the value that he attaches to such matters. Yet he avoids the errors into which so many native Christians fall. His piety is not of the ostentatious kind—he never obtrudes his Christianity on the notice of white man or black. . . . In 1885 he offered his country to Sir Charles Warren in a document which is certainly among the most remarkable of its kind. The Government of that day did not accept the offer, but last year, without any warning and without consulting the chief, an Assistant-Commissioner—Mr. J. S. Moffat—was sent to Palapye with power to levy taxes, issue licences, hold courts, and perform other acts of government. To many men it appears that in this action on our part Khama has just ground of complaint. He formulates his case against us as follows:—"Years ago I offered to the British Government much of my country; I offered to throw it open to the English on certain conditions—in fact I gave them a free hand. I believed in the English, in their justice and good government. They declined my offer, and I heard no more of the matter. And now, without normal conclave and agreement, when I should have the opportunity of consulting my headmen, and putting all important matters fairly before my people, they proceed to place a ruler in my town, so that I myself, before I can buy a bag of gunpowder, have to go and obtain a permit. This is not fair or open-handed; it puts me in the wrong with my tribe, who say, 'How, then, is Khama no longer chief in his own country?' and I feel deeply that I am slighted and made small. All my life I have striven for the English, been the friend of the English, have even offered to fight for the English, and I am at last to be treated thus!" It speaks well for the magnanimity of Khama's nature that, notwithstanding this hurt to his dignity and feelings, he should have seized the opportunity afforded by the Matabele trouble to once more show the sincerity of his friendship for this country by himself leading a large contingent of his fighting men against Lobengula.

Perhaps the best known imperialist of the Victorian era, Cecil John Rhodes (1853–1902) made his fortune in the Kimberley diamond fields and helped to establish De Beers Mining Company in 1880. He was elected to the Cape Legislature in the same year, a seat he retained for life. As prime minister of the Cape from 1890–96, he was implicated in the failed Jameson Raid in support of uitlanders in the Transvaal—a scandal that forced him to resign the office of premier.

Cecil Rhodes, South African Speeches (1894)

Good Hope Hall at Cape Town, October 27, 1894

Your Excellency, Mr. Mayor, and Gentlemen,—You know this is rather a difficult toast to reply to, because I have to reply for the Ministry and the Houses of Parliament, and I happen to be a member of both. . . .

    If we were to talk further of external politics, Mr. Mayor, there is really one subject that I might say represents the politics of the country, and that is the native question. Now, you know I have been away for two months. I have been travelling the whole of that time continuously. I have been travelling for two months in a country that you are going to govern, and that your people are going to occupy. For two solitary months I have been continuously travelling, and, do you know, the one point that has come home to me is the question of native labour? It is a very interesting question. I feel I am detaining you, but I must mention it, because I want you to think over it. I start from here, where native labour is £3 or £4 a month and food, I get up to Bulawayo, and I find it 10s. a month and food, and the telegraph is going to Blantyre, where it is 4s. a month without the food. Then I come to Parliament, and I find that honourable members want irrigation schemes and fruit-cultivation schemes, and then I think it out. I find labour in England at 12s. a week, that is £2, 10s. a month, producing an export. I happened to go to Egypt the other day, and I found labour 2d. a day, that is 4s. a month, producing an export, and I find in India labour at 4s. a month, and food, producing an export. Then you talk to me about producing corn and sending it home, and you talk about fruit-cultivation, and you say the farmers are very lazy, and they won't do anything; but you don't really think over the question—the labour question—that is at the root of it all. You are paying these natives £3 or £4 a month, and here are the people of Blantyre, with whom we are just going to be connected by telegraph, paying 4s. a month, and you are going to ruin them. You are going to introduce £4 a month. Now, I am constantly meeting the gentleman who advises the Transvaal, and he made a proposition that those natives who don't work should pay a certain tax. Then, totally apart from that proposition, a gentleman who represented Her Majesty proposed that those who did not labour should pay a tax. Then I thought it out myself, and last session we passed a bill,—don't think I am going into party politics, for the whole House nearly approved of it; there were only three against it on the second reading.

On the subject of this bill I will tell you a story. I remember an excellent Dutch member came to me. He said, "I am going to vote for your bill, but I really think I am wrong." I said, "Why?" Well, this member represented Victoria West, his name is Mr. Le Roex, and he replied, "Why! I hear that the member for Fort Beaufort is going to vote for it." He added, "I am sure something is wrong; I must vote against it." You know, if I might put you a simile—I hope I am not saying anything which will subject me to subsequent criticism, but I think you will understand the feeling with which, and the reason why, I put it—really, if you want a simile, it is just as if those ethereal beings above voted with the ethereal beings below on a substantive proposition. Now, you may ask me why I put this proposition. I put it as being aloof from and above party politics, for the proposition you have got to think over is this, that we have got a great country, and while we cannot expect the neighbouring states to part with their independence, just in the same way as we will not part with our flag, yet on general questions like railway tariffs there is no need to go into a cut-throat competition detrimental to all of us.

It is just the same with regard to the labour question. We have all got to think out the proposition why the English labourer works at the rate of 12s. a week, why the Indian works at 2d. a day, why the Egyptian works at 2d. a day, and why we pay, including food, £4 a month? I represent two millions of natives, and they are lying idle. I know the best thing for them would be to understand the dignity of labour; and if you ask me for a big foreign policy, it is the question whether we can bring these natives to understand the dignity of labour, and whether we can make arrangements with the neighbouring states to co-operate in bringing that about. I have dealt with our railway question. I have dealt with our labour question, and others have dealt so ably with the development of the hinterland, that I will say very little on that point. It was a hobby. One went into Parliament fortunately with a hobby twelve years ago, and stuck steadily to it. One has had very unhappy times over it, but I find if you stick to a point which is a right point, a proper point, a point in the interests of the country, you gradually win the people to it. Tonight, I will not speak to you in an apologetic way, for in so far as our hinterland is concerned, the risks are over. I have kept clearly in my mind the idea of assimilation—the assimilation of men, the assimilation of territory—and I feel that the position is that one does not now wish to ask in a humble way for support; one wishes to ask the question, "Do you agree now?" I could not do that before. I can do it to-night. I will only give the pledge that the proposal I made twelve years ago, on the basis that there should be an amalgamation of laws and of people, will be carried out by myself, and I will add no more.

Election Speech of October 25, 1898
(made in Good Hope Hall to a Cape Town audience)

Now, gentlemen, the last time I met a Cape Town audience was during the Council elections, when we had a great fight, and we won. I met you in the hall close by, and we had a very successful meeting, and I felt that our case had your support. Since then, as far as I am personally concerned, there has been a good deal of work. I had to go home to get my Charter right, and I came back, and we fought another election, and in spite of having no organisation, and in spite of being taken by surprise, we had a tie. And a tie on what question? On the question of the proper representation of the people, because you must remember that the greater covers the less. If you get proper representation of the people, you will get those measures which you, as Progressive people, desire. If we don't have proper representation, we shall not get those measures, and therefore we have to do everything in our power to get a proper Redistribution Bill. Well, the speaker before me told you exactly what the position is, but I will even bore you by labouring the point again. You have a hundred and eight thousand voters in the country. Eighty per cent. voting would be eighty-six thousand. When I say eighty per cent. voting, I mean to say that if you made a careful calculation, and eighty-six thousand had recorded their votes, you would have fifty thousand votes, and the people who are in charge of this country thirty-six thousand. Well, that is a most anomalous condition. That is a most extraordinary position. But what do those people do who are in power? . . . They wish to keep us in a position which I call an application of Krugerism.

I will tell you what I mean by Krugerism. As you know, in the Transvaal the whole of the wealth, the greater portion of the population, practically the whole of the intelligence, is not represented at all, but they are lived upon by foreigners and an ignorant minority. Now, in this country they desire to apply Krugerism in this way. They are perfectly aware that the votes of the majority are for the party of progress, and they say, "We will not allow you to be fairly represented, we will evade it in every possible way, and allow the government of the country to be carried on by a minority, and we will prevent any fair redistribution, so as to prevent the majority having a voice." This is really Krugerism again in a minor form, and that is what we are fighting. And shall we win? Well, it will depend upon ourselves. Yes, if we keep united in the Cape Parliament, we shall win.

. . . I would just say a few words as to what we depend upon to get a Progressive majority in Parliament, and a Progressive Ministry. You must remember the whole of the issues of Africa are before you now. You are in an exceedingly pleasant and happy position, in so far as politics are concerned. A hundred years hence the whole of the races and relations of this country will be settled, and you have to assist. We have developed this new state in the North. We are just considering closer relations with Natal. We know the Republics must change on account of the enormous influx of Europeans. I know I have to be awfully careful about the Republics, so as not to hurt any one's feelings. But still we know that these two states are to change very rapidly, and it rests with the Colony at the base, it rests with us here, as to what will be the relations with the other states in South Africa. But when you think that, in addition to that, in the north of Africa the whole thing is changed by the conquest of Khartoum, and that what appeared to be imaginative madness five years ago is absolutely practicable now. And when we know absolutely that we are going to join—I know for myself and the state I represent that we shall join—the matter is beyond dispute. It is the agreement of all. Only the other day, I heard that the telegraph was nearly into Nyassa, that it will be completed to Tanganyika by the end of the year, and then I have only six hundred miles to Uganda, and we know that Kitchener is at Sobat. You see, it is a very little distance, and what you feel is that you will take a part in the whole work. And then we are opposed by this non-Progressive party who hate any expansion, because they think that it means their annihilation. We must remember that it is not the Dutch people, for this non-Progressive party consists of just a few. It is Camp Street; it is Pretoria. It is not the people, it is not the Dutch people. It is a little coterie who hate expansion, and who wish to keep in their own narrow groove of misrepresentation and libel to maintain their position. Not having the decision to face the people, and not having the courage to face Parliament, they have to do it by subterranean alleys. Gentlemen, we are not fighting the Dutch people, but the coterie, and I believe we shall succeed—and we shall succeed through this expansion that is going on, and which you all share in the satisfaction of working for. As I said just now, you believe now we are going to join from north to south. You hope you will share in that. You believe now thoroughly in federation in South Africa, in the union of the neighbouring states. Now, these are all principles of the Progressive party.

This celebration of empire as the export of Englishness was published in the same year as the Queen's Diamond Jubilee and embodies a pre - Boer War optimism about Britain's imperial destiny that would be unimaginable only a few short years later.

From *The Queen's Empire: A Pictorial And Descriptive Record* (1897)

NOT long ago a visitor to a public elementary school in the North of England had the curiosity to ask the head teacher whether he could tell him what became of the boys who had passed through his school. The teacher was equal to the demand. "Here," said he, "are the names of twelve boys who lived in this village and attended this school twelve years ago. They are still friends of mine, and I have corresponded with them all. Of the twelve, five only are living in their native country; one is doing well in Canada; a second is in the Royal Navy, serving in the West Indies; a third is with his regiment, a soldier in South Africa; a fourth has found a home in Australia; a fifth writes to me from Fiji, where he is employed under the Government; a sixth is in India; while one is settled in the Western part of the United States." Such was the roll-call of a little Yorkshire village.

Go where we please, throughout the length and breadth of the United Kingdom, the same story, or something very like it, will be told. From the Old Country, people still go out to the uttermost ends of the earth; there to plant their homes, to live their lives, and to extend the dominion of their race and speech. Where race and speech are the same as of old, much that came from the Old Country remains, and must always remain, unaltered and unalterable.

But climate, occupation, circumstance, the pressure and neighbourhood of other races, and above all the change from an old community to a new one, combine slowly but surely to modify in many respects the characteristics of the race in distant lands, and to produce new qualities which were unknown under the old conditions.

And so it has come about that in the British Empire there exist side by side, wherever we look, points of identity and points of divergence—the same yet different, one and yet many, united yet divided—each part separated from every other by distance, by local peculiarities, by forms of government, and yet each part bound to every other by a common speech, a common history, a common literature. Where the differences will end no man knows; how far the interests which are common will in the long run prevail over those which are separate, no man can say. The people who live among the vast lakes and rivers of Canada, in a country where Nature is on a scale so gigantic as compared with the limits of the United Kingdom, may some day develop into a race entirely unlike that which inhabits the British Islands. But that day is at present far off; and though the marked qualities of Canadian nationality are becoming every year more known and more respected, there is nothing in the Canadian character to distinguish it in essentials from that of any other English-speaking citizen of the British Empire. In the Southern Hemisphere the warm suns of Australia and of South Africa are without doubt developing a race which must in many essential particulars differ from that which inhabits the foggy and sea-swept islands which lie north of the 50th parallel, and whose furthest extremity is but six degrees south of the Arctic Circle.

But while the conditions of climate and occupation are at work to modify the type, a common language and a thousand common interests—habits ingrained in the race, qualities inherent in the blood—are also at work to counteract the effects of geographical separation and climatic difference.

Thus it is that throughout the whole of that part of the British Empire which is principally inhabited by English-speaking men and women, there is going on a perpetual expansion of the new and the old, the familiar and the unfamiliar, side by side. Go where he will, the traveller starting from the Old Country will find that he knows not whether to wonder most at the familiarity or at the novelty of what he sees. The speech, the buildings, the social life, the appearance of the people, all are the same wherever he wanders, and yet not the same, but different in a score of ways not always easy to define or to describe, but which can be felt and appreciated even by the most careless observer.

Or it may well be that it is the differences which first strike, and most forcibly strike, the mind and the imagination of the observer. How unlike is Canada to the United Kingdom! How widely different are Australia or New Zealand from the great Dominion! What a world apart is South Africa, even those parts of it where the English race is predominant! Yet he who begins with finding out the differences will in the long run not less surely find the similarities.

Hitherto we have only spoken of those portions of our great Empire which are inhabited wholly or to a large extent by men of our own race and speech. But this wonderful and complex Empire of ours contains, as we know, tens of millions of men and women of races alien to our own, speaking a speech not ours, obeying a religion whose sanctions we do not admit, and living in pursuance of social codes totally different in origin or character from that to which we give our adhesion.

Varied as are the conditions of human life upon the globe, infinite as are the degrees of civilisation attained by various men in various climates, it is true to say that there is scarcely a single condition of life, a degree of civilisation, which has not its example within the limits of The Empire; and with the variations of habit, thought, and feeling go all the outward manifestations of habit, thought, and feeling. The strange and picturesque customs of India, the peculiarities of African native ceremonial, the sports and occupations, the pastimes of native races in all parts of our dominion, combine to furnish a series of strange and delightful pictures capable of affording endless pleasure to the eye accustomed to the familiar round of Anglo-Saxon civilisation.

———

The Khaki election of 1900 occasioned many reflections on the fate of the empire, imperial policy, and jingoism. Taking a Fabian socialist position, George Bernard Shaw (1856–1950) calls for "a definite constitutional policy" for the "provinces" of the British Empire and outlines, among other things, the stakes of the election for South Africa's political future and the fate of free trade.

———

George Bernard Shaw, from *Fabianism and the Empire* (1900)

THE forthcoming General Election will turn, we are told, mainly on the popularity of Imperialism. If this be so, it is important that voters should make up their minds what Imperialism means. If it is a mere catchword vaguely denoting our insular self-conceit, then its victory at a General Election would be a grave symptom of national infatuation. But if it means a well-considered policy to be pursued by a Commonwealth of the communities flying the British flag, then it is as worthy and as weighty an issue as an election could turn on. Only, in that case, we must ask for a clear statement of the questions which have been considered, and the solutions proposed for them. . . .

Imperial Policy

THE best chance for Khaki at this election is not its own popularity, but the absence of any alternative. The Opposition front bench, having no ideas and no program (any more than the Government), will fall back on recrimination about irrevocable bygones in South Africa, instead of accepting the situation which has been created, rightly or wrongly, and facing it. Whether the electorate shares President Kruger's political ideas, or believes them to be as obsolete as his theology, it probably suspects that if the Government had been as earnest in its efforts to stave off war as in its efforts to stave off Old Age Pensions there would have been no war. But the electorate does not believe, and has not the slightest reason to believe, that if the Opposition had been in power, it would have been a whit less capitalist-ridden than the Government. . . .

What is needed now is a definite constitutional policy to be pursued by the Empire towards its provinces. The real danger against which such a policy must be directed is not the danger of attack on the Empire from without, but of mismanagement and disruption from within. The British Empire, wisely governed, is invincible. The British Empire, handled as we handled Ireland and the American colonies, and as we may handle South Africa if we are not careful, will fall to pieces without the firing of a foreign shot.

The primary conditions of Imperial stability are not the same throughout the Empire. The democratic institutions that mean freedom in Australasia and Canada would mean slavery in India and the Soudan. We are no longer a Commonwealth of white men and baptized Christians: the vast majority of our fellow-subjects are black, brown, or yellow; and their creed is Mahometan, Buddhist, or Hindoo. We forbid the sale of the

Bible in Khartoum, and punish British subjects in India for blasphemy against Vishnu. We rule these vast areas and populations by a bureaucracy as undemocratic as that of Russia. And if we substituted for that bureaucracy local self-government by the white traders, we should get black slavery, and, in some places, frank black extermination, as we have had in the "back blocks" of Australia. As for parliamentary institutions for native races, that dream has been disposed of by the American experiments after the Civil War. They are as useless to them as a dynamo to a Caribbean. We thus have two Imperial policies: a democratic policy for provinces in which the white colonists are in a large majority, and a bureaucratic policy where the majority consists of colored natives. Consequently the Empire cannot be governed either on Liberal or Conservative, democratic or aristocratic principles exclusively; and cannot be governed on Church of England or Nonconformist principles at all. An Imperial issue between these parties and creeds is necessarily a false issue.

... IN South Africa—and Imperial policy at the coming election will mean South Africa—the problem is still more complicated than in India; for in it neither democracy nor bureaucracy will serve alone, however modified. We are confronted there with colonies demanding democratic institutions in the midst of native races who must be protected despotically by the Empire or abandoned to slavery and extermination. And it is the Conservative party which has gone to war professedly on behalf of democracy; whilst the anti-Imperialist Liberals have the appearance of supporting the Boer oligarchy against it. What has really happened, however, is that a troublesome and poor territory, which the Empire cast off into the hands of a little community of farmer emigrants, has unexpectedly turned out to be a gold-reef; and the Empire, accordingly, takes it back again from the farmers. If the Empire were a piece of private property belonging to England (as most Englishmen think), and the Transvaal a farm privately owned by President Kruger (as the President explicitly affirmed without contradiction from Sir Alfred Milner at the Bloemfontein Conference), the transaction would be mere brigandage. And it may be conceded that to citizens and statesmen who are dominated by the morality of private property, the war must be demoralizing if they are on the side of the Empire, and shocking if they are on the side of the farmers. But it is impossible for a great Commonwealth to be bound by any such individualist superstition. However ignorantly its politicians may argue about it, reviling one another from the one side as brigands, and defending themselves from the other with quibbles from waste-paper treaties and childish slanders against a brave enemy, the fact remains that a Great Power, consciously or unconsciously, must govern in the interests of civilization as a whole; and it is not to those interests that such mighty forces as gold-fields, and the formidable armaments that can be built upon them, should be wielded irresponsibly by small communities of frontiersmen. Theoretically, they should be internationalized, not British-Imperialized; but until the Federation of the World becomes an accomplished fact, we must accept the most responsible Imperial federations available as a substitute for it. This is the best answer, for the purpose of excusing the war, to President Kruger's statement at Bloemfontein that, in demanding the franchise for the Outlanders, we were asking him to give the title-deeds of "his" land to the laborers on it. Sir Alfred Milner had no reply at all, because, not being a Socialist, he quite agreed with the President's fundamental position, and so had to argue in the manner of the wolf with the lamb.

... THE most obvious difficulty raised by the Chinese question has not as yet been mentioned by any English statesman. China, like Turkey, maintains a civilization which differs from European and American civilization. Without begging the question as to whether the Chinese civilization is a lower or higher one than ours, we have to face the fact that its effect is to prevent Europeans from trading in China, or from making railway and postal and telegraph routes across it for the convenience of the world in general. Now the notion that a nation has a right to do what it pleases with its own territory, without reference to the interests of the rest of the world, is no more tenable from the International Socialist point of view—that is, the point of view of the twentieth century—than the notion that a landlord has a right to do what he likes with his estate without reference to the interests of his neighbours. Nearly half a century ago we made war on China and forced her to admit our ships and give us a footing in certain ports. In concert with the Powers, we have just had to send an armed expedition to the Chinese capital to force them to tolerate the presence and the commercial and political activity of Europeans. Here we are asserting and enforcing international rights of travel and trade. But the right to trade is a very comprehensive one: it involves a right to insist upon a settled government which can keep the peace and enforce agreements. When a native government of this order is impossible, the foreign trading power must set one up. This is a common historical origin of colonies and annexations; and it may, for practical purposes, be regarded as an irresistible natural force, which will lead sooner or later to the imposition by the Powers of commercial civilization on all countries which are still refractory to it.

Unfortunately, the Powers, not excluding the British Empire, are apt to make this an excuse for purely piratical conquests of weaker States. Against this tendency it is necessary to protest. The value of a State to the world lies in the quality of its civilization, not in the magnitude of its armaments. If such an event as the annexation and assimilation of Switzerland by Russia were possible, it would be a calamity which the rest of Europe would be justified in peremptorily preventing, whereas if Switzerland were to annex Russia and liberalize her institutions, the rest of Europe would breathe more freely. There is therefore no question of the steam-rollering of little States because they are little, any more than of their maintenance in deference to romantic nationalism. The State which obstructs international civilization will have to go, be it big or little. That which advances it should be defended by all the Western Powers. Thus huge China and little Monaco may share the same fate, little Switzerland and the vast United States the same fortune.

The fate of China, however, is far from sealed. The Powers, including ourselves, have been guilty of flat piracy in China, and that, too, under the white flag of their legations instead of the black one. They tried to partition China; and it was not until they found that they were more likely to fight over the division of the spoils than to secure them that they drew back and professed the policy of the Open Door. Our attitude in the matter is perhaps best shown by the fact that we call the national movement in China to resist partition "the Boxer rebellion." It is no more a rebellion than the destruction of the Armada was.

Still, there remain our international rights of travel and trade, with the right to settled government which they involve. With these the present institutions of the Chinese Empire are incompatible; and these institutions, accordingly, must go. If the Chinese themselves cannot establish order in our sense, the Powers must establish it for them. And in undertaking our share of that establishment, we must proceed on the principle, directly opposed to that of Non-Interference, that we have international rights of travelling, trading, efficient police protection, and communication by road, rail, and telegraph in every part of the globe. Free Trade enables us to claim these rights with a better countenance than any other Power; but all the Powers claim them implicitly, and must finally do so explicitly, if only to put themselves in an intelligible moral position.

Clearly, however, these claims are reciprocal. If we have a right to go to China, the Chinaman has a right to come to us. But the huge Australasian section of the British Empire excludes Chinese, not as foreign devils, but, let us politely admit, as men so industrious, so docile, so skillful and so frugal, that they cheapen labour to a point at which the more expensive white man starves. The Australasians argue that whether the white man is worth his extra cost or not, they must not degrade his standard of life, and must therefore exclude the Chinaman under existing circumstances. Now, even if we forbear the obvious retort that the existing circumstances can and should be altered by establishing and enforcing a minimum standard of sanitation housing and remuneration for yellow and white men alike, we had better not shirk the fact that to exclude a subject of the Son of Heaven from our dominions is one thing: to exclude a subject of a Government established and guaranteed by the British, Russian, German, French, and American Powers is quite another. Clearly, if we meddle with China, and our interference does not relieve the poverty that produces emigration, we shall find ourselves in a Yellow Muddle that may bring the Chinese War into our own streets. If the Powers, to avert this danger, agree to deny to the Chinaman the international rights they force him to concede to Europe, competitive capitalistic exploitation of Chinese cheap labour on the spot will lead to a clamor in this country for protection against imports from China. On this point Imperialist statesmen must make up their minds promptly; for imports produced by foreign sweated labor have been in the past the most potent instruments of the downfall of Empires through Imperialism.

Free Trade.

... Socialism has demolished the Manchester School and discredited the Free Trade Utopia of its economists and dreamers; but all the king's horses and all the king's men can no more set up import duties again than Napoleon could bring back the marquises. What Socialism can do is to guide and develop export trade on the one hand, and on the other to nationalize such necessary trades as agriculture, engineering, etc., if the course of free trade threatens to take them abroad (as it might take abroad the business of national defence if we put up our military expeditions to be tendered for by competing contractors). Foreign imports cannot harm English industry as a whole: what they can do, often very beneficially, is to drive capital and labor out of one method or one trade into another. Thus employers may be driven from the sweating-den method, which is wasteful and cruel, into the regulated factory method, which is cheaper and better, though it requires abler direction and larger capitals. Or a trade may be exterminated by the fact that it can be done better abroad than at home. It is, of course, our business to see that the superiority of the foreign product in quality or cheapness is not due to the superiority of foreign education or consular organization and activity; but when a trade is fairly beaten, and is not a necessary part of a complete communal life, its capital and labor must seek a new outlet, and should not be encouraged to sit down and cry vainly for a protective tax on consumers. Now it may prove that the qualities which have made the Chinaman so dreaded a competitor in British and American labor markets may enable him in his own country, even under the lee of a Labor Code, to maintain his health, self-respect, and industrial efficiency, and bring up his family well, on a smaller wage than the Englishman in England can. If by doing so he can exterminate the wretched trades typified in Hood's

Song of the Shirt (which is as true to-day as it was when it was written, in spite of all the cultured tears that have dropped on it), giving us the articles these simple trades produce without the misery they now cost, so much the better for us. The labor they now degrade and the capital they waste will then produce exports to pay for them; and the various English industries will compete with each other for this export trade. And as production for export depends for its success mainly on quality of product, knowledge of foreign markets, and organization of production, whilst production of cheap sweated articles for consumption on the spot demands no higher qualifications than the common East End sweater possesses, the extermination of a sweated trade by Chinese competition, and its replacement by an extension of export trade, is an advantage to be courted and not a calamity to be staved off.

C. The Boer War and the New Century

Besant's criticisms of British activity in the Transvaal anticipate by almost two decades the kind of opposition to the Boer War that many in Britain came to articulate.

Annie Besant, "The Transvaal" (1881)

At the meeting of the Executive of the National Secular Society on February 23rd, it was decided to formally protest against the violation of public faith in proclaiming the annexation of the South African Republic, and the disregard of public morals shown in persisting in the path of wrong-doing. As one of the vice-presidents of the N. S. S. I sketch here an outline of British policy towards the Dutch South African Republic, thinking that it may be well to place in the hands of our branches facts which they may find it impossible to collect for themselves.

It is well known to every reader of history that the Dutch settled in Southern Africa before the English founded any colonies therein; the English, however, after awhile got the upper hand, and those Dutch who cared for independence retreated before them from time to time. The Cape of Good Hope and the Colony of Natal thus passed beneath British rule, many Dutch remaining as colonists, many "trekking" to live elsewhere in freedom. The Orange Free State was founded by some of these liberty-loving Dutch, and still exists independently, with a President at its head. Others of the travellers crossed the Vaal river, into a country which was uninhabited in some districts, and in others sparsely habited by various native tribes. . . .

It is clear that the Boers were here doing wrong to no man; they were settling on free land, land without occupants. They established a Republican form of Government, increased and prospered. From time to time this Government made grants of farms outside the uninhabited districts first colonised, and the Boers came into contact with the natives. Mr. Blencowe says on this:

"Those Boers who had obtained grants of farms in these parts, and who only occupied them for winter grazing, have for many years paid a tax to the natives of two heifers or two oxen per annum per farm."

This testimony is important as showing that the Dutch settlers were not oblivious of native rights when they came into contact with the original owners of the soil, and the same honorable fact is borne witness to by the Rev. A. Merensky, superintendent of the Berlin Missionary Society, a twenty years' resident in the Transvaal, in a letter to Sir W. O. Lanyou, dated August 10th, 1880 (*loc. cit.,* p. 19, Enclosure 2 in No. 52); he is speaking of the North Transvaal, in which the Boers ruled over the natives, and says:—

"The fact is that when they arrived they could do with the natives almost what they pleased, as the latter were not in possession of guns. . . . Although the natives were entirely left to the mercy of the Boers, and considered themselves their subjects in the first years after the arrival of the latter, they soon augmented in numbers, accumulated wealth, and came into the possession of guns, by means of which single tribes managed to hold their own against the Boers in the quarrels which arose."

. . . In 1877 the Government of Jingoism was in power in England, and Lord Carnarvon hit upon the notable plan of forcing confederation on the various colonies and states in South Africa. The Government cast greedy eyes at the little Republic across the Vaal, and made up its mind to annex it. Sir Theophilus Shepstone was appointed Commissioner, and was empowered to proclaim her Majesty's authority over the Transvaal on obtaining the consent of the Volksraad (Parliament of the Republic). But the Volksraad would give no consent, and on April 9th, 1877, Sir T. Shepstone wrote to the Executive Council of the Republic, saying that he was going at once to proclaim British sovereignty over the Transvaal. In answer, the Executive Council, on April 11th, resolved that her Majesty's Government had no right to disregard the convention of 1852, that the people of the Republic had by a large majority shown their dislike to the destruction of their independence, and concluded their resolutions as follows (Despatches No. 20):—

"The Government most strongly protests against the action of Her Majesty's Special Commissioner, resolving further to despatch immediately a commission of representatives to Europe and America with power and instructions to add to itself, if necessary, a third person, to try in the first instance to appeal to Her Majesty's Government, and if this should have no result, which the Government should regret and can as yet not believe, then to try and invoke the friendly help and assistance of other powers, foremost of those who have acknowledged the independence of this country."

Sir Theophilus Shepstone, however, pursued his way, and in defiance of treaty and of justice, he proclaimed in the Queen's name the annexation of the Transvaal, on April 12, 1877. The President of the Republic thereupon issued the following document:—

"PROCLAMATION.

"Whereas Her British Majesty's Special Commissioner, Sir Theophilus Shepstone, notwithstanding my solemn protest of yesterday entered against his purposes, communicated to me by his letter of 9th April, has been pleased to execute his designs, and has this day proclaimed Her British Majesty's Government over the South African Republic; and whereas the Government has decided to acquiesce for the present, under protest, for the purpose of despatching meanwhile a deputation to Europe and America, in the persons of Messrs. S. J. P. Kruger and E. P. Jorrisen, for the purpose there to defend the rights of the people, and to try to obtain a *peaceful* solution of the case:

"So it is that I, Thomas Francois Burgers, State President of the South African Republic, proclaim and make hereby known, with consent and advice of the Executive Council, to all officials, citizens, and inhabitants, to abstain from every word or deed calculated to frustrate the work of the mission.

"And I admonish all burghers and inhabitants to help carry out this decision of the Government for the preservation of order and the avoidance of bloodshed.

"Thomas Burgers,
"Government Office, Pretoria,
"State President.
12th April, 1877."

The protest could scarcely be more dignified and more moderate. The Republic was small, the oppressor was mighty, and, in addition to this disparity of strength, we note all through the desire of the Boers to avoid a conflict which might result in a war of black against white throughout Southern Africa. In 1877 and 1878 deputations were sent to England, but the Tory Government would not give way. Representatives from 4,000 burghers assembled in camp were sent to meet Sir Bartle Frere, and while this gentleman accepted their memorial to the Queen, and deceived them with professions of friendship, he wrote home expressing his regret that he had not artillery enough to destroy their camp. No answer was ever given to the memorial; the patience of the Boers was misinterpreted into submission, their payment of taxes into acceptance of British authority, and at last a general meeting of the people was held (December 10–17, 1879), and it was decided to call together the Volksraad.

Small excuse has ever been made for the high-handed violence of England towards the little Republic. It has been alleged that the Boers kept slaves, and although slavery among them consisted of indenturing natives for terms of service, it has been fairly argued that to indenture for years those who could not resist, was really to enslave them. I admit it. But the fact does not justify us in abolishing the Boer Republic. We have no right to annex Spain because the Spaniards hold slaves in Cuba. And the less have we the right in South Africa, since we follow the same abominable custom, and indenture helpless natives just as did the Boers. Mr. J. N. P. de Villiers, Civil Commissioner, writes as follows to the Secretary for Native Affairs, Cape Town, on August 18, 1880 (Further Correspondence, C 2740, Enc. 4 in No. 33):—

"The prisoners of both sexes sent hither from Koegas in November, 1878 (the adults being principally women), were indentured by me during the period from December, 1878, to November, 1879 (both months inclusive), to persons of known respectability. . . . With the exception of those apprentices who have since absconded (and these form, I believe, a large portion of their number), the natives before mentioned are still in service; the shortest terms stipulated under the regulations, that for adults, being three years. . . . Many of these [natives coming into the colony from outlying districts—A. B.] now appear to have been the reputed fathers and husbands of those under contracts of service who readily found their way to them; and it is to this circumstance that the numerous instances of desertion above alluded to must be attributed."

At Koegas a massacre of natives had occurred, women and children being shot by the gallant colonists. The murderers were not punished, and the women and children who escaped were indentured. That is, helpless prisoners were turned into slaves. It is instructive to note that many "absconded," and that "reputed husbands and fathers" were wicked enough to try and free the female slaves related to them. Mr. Villiers asks that some check shall be put on the arrival of free natives in the district, as they disturb the happy apprentices with their kind masters of "known respectability." The same gentleman writes, under date December 8th, 1879:—

"About 99 natives, being 46 adults and 53 children, have been placed under contracts of service between the 4th of December, 1878, and the 17th of November, 1879. . . . In pursuance of the approval which you were pleased to give to my suggestion previously made, parents and their younger children were kept together as far as possible when indentured."

And when not possible, Mr. Villiers? Looking at the list of these 99 natives, we observe that one is indentured only for six months, the rest for 3, 4, 5, 6, 9, 10, 11, 12, 13 or 15 years. Most of them are indentured to Dutchmen, so that while indenturing to Dutchmen by Dutchmen is a crime justifying annexation of the offenders, indenturing to Dutchmen by Englishmen is a highly moral action. Two slaves were sold—I beg pardon, two apprentices were indentured—to Mr. C. J. Esterhingen; the man absconded, the woman was "reported to have been found dead on the farm of Mr. Esterhingen." Unfortunate, very. On the whole, perhaps we had better not say too much regarding "indenturing" in the Boer Republic. It is right to add that I do not know whether the allegation that the Boers countenance this modified form of slavery is true or not. But one thing is certain: under the Boers the natives multiplied and grew wealthy . . . while we are constantly troubled with native revolts.

Since April 12th, 1879, the Transvaal had been in a state of suppressed excitement, fondly awaiting the news that the Home authorities had reversed the iniquitous acts of their colonial representatives. The downfall of the Jingo Government and the accession to power of Mr. Gladstone seemed to carry a message to the oppressed and injured Dutch that at length right should be done. They waited. The meeting of the Volksraad, decided on in December, 1879, did not take place until December, 1880, no good news having reached the patient petitioners for justice. At last it met, and on December 13th, 1880, it appointed Messrs. Kruger, Pretorius and Joubert as a triumvirate, to take more vigorous steps for the attaining of the righteous wish of the people. These gentlemen republished the Sandriver Convention, adding to it a pathetic declaration of the good faith kept by the Republic, and saying that the

"Government and people of the Republic have not then made use of their right to take up arms, being convinced that her Majesty's Government, better informed, would disapprove of the action of her official, and as the threats of that official made them fear that armed resistance would cause a civil war amongst the Colonists in South Africa, and war of extermination between the white and black race. The Government of the South African Republic has allowed this act of violence to be committed under protest, and the people have kept quiet in obedience to the lawful authority."

. . . On this same December 16th a patrol of eight Boers ride into Potchefstroom to carry the proclamation to the printing office. The English soldiers in Potchefstroom fire on them—war not having been proclaimed. The Boers retort, and the English bombard the town. On the same day the Boers send their demands to Sir O. Lanyon, allowing forty-eight hours for reply, and saying that any advance of troops will be regarded as a declaration of war. On the 17th they write to Sir G. Colley, to send him their proclamation, but dryly add as a postscript: "We are unable to send your Excellency the proclamation, as coming into Potchefstroom to have it printed, our patrol was fired upon by the troops." On the 18th Sir O. Lanyon proclaims the Boers as rebels, and they receive his answer on December 19th. On December 20th a detachment of English troops advances from Lydenburg towards Pretoria, and is attacked and defeated by the Boers. In England cries of "treachery" and "massacre" are raised, but the authorities in South Africa state that the Boers warned them that any advance of troops would be resisted; and the Colonel Commanding reports: "I have warned [the soldiers] to expect attack." So far from behaving with cruelty, as pretended, the Boers sent the wounded men on to their friends in Pretoria, and Major General Sir G. Colley reports: "They have acted with courtesy and humanity in the matter of our wounded," and have "released most of the prisoners taken from us." In the proclamation issued by the Republic on January 13th, 1881, respectful mention is made of the courage of the British troops, who "promptly went into larger, and proceeded to battle with the band playing." This proclamation charges Sir O. Lanyon:

"(1) With having commenced war without notice; (2) with carrying on this war against all rules of civilised warfare; and (3) particularly with the barbarous cruelties at Potchefstroom, bombarding an exposed town without warning."

Here the official information ends, and we await with keen anxiety the decision of the Ministry.

We ask that the South African Republic may be left undisturbed in freedom and independence. We ask that the three and a-half years' patient forbearance of the Boers may meet with its just reward. We ask that the English name may not be dishonored by the endorsement of the unrighteous act of an unscrupulous official. The Boers are weak; England is strong. So much the more reason that those who cannot be compelled by force should feel compelled by duty to do the right. We, who have not, like Sir Bartle Frere, "deep religious feelings;" we, who do not believe in God, but who do believe in justice, in truth, and in righteous dealing; we, who maintain that the prestige of a nation depends on its honor and its virtue and not on its armies and its navies; we plead that the right may be done by our Liberal leaders, and if they persist in wrong and in disregard of justice, we then dissever ourselves from, and publicly protest against, a policy which makes strength the excuse for oppression, and past error a plea for present wrong.

A self-styled "South African colonist," Reverend Wirgman proffers his views on the true cause of the war—the "natives" of South Africa, on whose behalf the British must be understood to be waging nothing less than a "holy war." As a clergyman he might have been expected to use such charged religious language, though his views were not unique in Britain among those who favored British military aggression against the Boers.

A. T. Wirgman, "The Boers and the Native Question" (1900)

WE are face to face with the most serious conflict that the British Empire has been compelled to wage during the course of the present century. The loss of South Africa would involve the disruption of the Empire. Our first plain duty is to set our teeth, square our shoulders, and bring the war to a successful termination.

We shall do this none the worse for the checks we have received. Writing as a South African colonist, I confess to a feeling of uneasiness as we entered into the war with so light a heart last October. One of the most thoughtful and able of our South African public men said to me, just before the Boers declared war, that he feared the consequences of too easy a victory. We both agreed that a walk over to Pretoria might involve a repetition of the Majuba policy, and a settlement which would curtail the power of South African Republicanism without making a final end of the Republics and their Flags. This would have meant a postponement of the conflict to a more convenient season for the Boers, and not its final ending.

The temporarily crippled Republics would have waited in patience until England was involved in foreign complications, and then their hour would have come. They would have struck, and struck hard, in a final desperate effort to banish the British Flag from South Africa. But we are beyond the reach of such future contingencies now. The verdict of the British Parliament and of the whole Empire has been given with no uncertain voice. The Republics and their Flags must go, and the British Flag must take their place.

The Flags of the Boer Republics and the Flag of Great Britain represent two entirely incompatible ideals of right and wrong, justice and injustice. They cannot coexist any longer upon this sub-continent of South Africa. It is a question of the survival of the fittest, and, quite apart from national feeling and patriotic fervour, there is no doubt in the mind of any right-minded man, who knows the facts, that peace, order, and justice to the natives can only be secured in South Africa under the Union Jack, as the symbol of political and religious liberty.

. . . I will go straight to the real underlying cause of this war. It is the *native question.* Here is the true parting of the ways between Briton and Boer. To the Briton the overwhelming multitude of natives in South Africa form a subject race bound to him by the ties of a common humanity. To the Boer the native is a 'zwart schepsel,' 'a black creature' who was created to be a hewer of wood and a drawer of water for his white master. The 'schepsel' cannot legally own land, ought not to be allowed to learn to read and write, must not be married by a minister of religion in such a way as to claim the recognition of the State for his marriage, like a white man's marriage, and above all must never under any circumstances be permitted to claim the franchise as a political unit of the State. I remember many years ago meeting a native who could read and write a little. He was working as a labourer on a Boer farm, and for some time got on well with his master until on one unlucky day the Boer farmer caught him in the act of reading a book. 'You can *read,* eh!' said the enraged farmer.

'Yes, *Baas,* a little,' replied the trembling native.

'Go,' roared the Boer, 'get off at once, and don't let me catch you here again.' The man took his dismissal for the serious crime (in Boer eyes) of knowing how to read, and had to seek work elsewhere. I have told the man's story just as he told it to me. No British farmer in South Africa would have turned off a decent farm labourer for the crime of knowing how to read, although he would be on his guard against any misconduct on the part of a semi-educated native, who, if he is inclined to be bad, is more difficult to deal with than an uneducated savage, because knowledge is power.

The difference between Briton and Boer in dealing with natives is irreconcilable and fundamental.

A Scottish Independent minister, who had been acting minister to a Boer congregation for some years, told me the other day that he believed that the Boers would have been reconciled to British rule years ago if they had not realised that the British Flag was in flat antagonism to their whole native policy.

Their native policy is one of their most cherished ideals, and the chief ingredient in the Boer ambition of a universal Afrikaner Republic is the thought that the Boer view of native policy would predominate in South Africa with the disappearance of the British Flag.

Over 250 years ago the Boers colonised South Africa in the spirit of the stern and harsh Calvinism of the Synod of Dort. They look upon themselves as the chosen people of God, the predestinated lords of the soil, whose destiny is to possess the whole of Southern and Central Africa. To them South Africa is the Land of Promise which, like the Israelites of old, they have to win for themselves by the sword. The native races are the Canaanites who have to be driven out and extirpated by their commandoes as Joshua smote the men of Jericho. Joshua allowed the remnant of the Canaanites no civil rights, and found no place for them, save as hewers of wood and drawers of water for his victorious host. The Boer leaders take Joshua as their model in dealing with the native races. And if an alien white race, like the English, comes and settles in South Africa, with its newfangled notions that slavery is wicked and that natives are human beings, so much the worse for the meddlesome strangers. If they settle in the land they must adopt Boer policy and Boer methods, or else they will be treated as an inferior race, so far as the Boer's rifle can enforce his superiority, and minister to his Calvinistic self-esteem. . . .

The black man must carry the Boer's burden, and think himself highly privileged that he is allowed to exist at all on consideration of his being a submissive beast of burden for the Boer. Dr. Livingstone found this out some forty years ago, when the Boers looted and destroyed his Mission station at Kuruman, and sent him forth a wanderer without a home.

Mr. Morley is making precisely the same mistake about the Boer war as Mr. Gladstone made in espousing the cause of the South in the American Civil War. The Southern armies fought with admirable skill and valour. So do the Boers. The South fought hard for its absolute independence, against the supremacy of the more powerful North. So are the Boers now fighting hard against British supremacy.

But the gallant fight of the South was in a bad cause, and the successful assertion of Southern independence would have meant the triumph of slavery and the victory of principles inherently evil and absolutely opposed to all true human progress. In like manner the Boer is fighting for an independence which he has abused, and struggling for a freedom to carry on a native policy that is far worse than the slavery once practised in the Southern States of America. The cause of the Boer is *inherently* unholy and unjust, and is fundamentally opposed to all true progress and civilisation. . . .

The relief of Kimberley may prove to be a turning point in the history of the war, and we may see the beginning of the end in the quiet acceptance of our rule by the occupied districts of the Free State, an acceptance made all the easier by the iron discipline enforced by Lord Roberts upon the troops occupying the enemy's country. When the Free Staters find by experience that the British Army respects private property, and acts throughout the country as it has acted in the occupation of Jacobsdal, peace will be speedily established with the gradual advance of the British Flag.

Our cause is righteous and true. I am not afraid to make Bishop Key's words my own, and to say with him that the British Empire is waging a holy war for the cause of freedom and justice to the native races of South Africa.

— ·ᴖ·ᴖ· —

Solomon Plaatje (1876–1932) was one of the founders of the South African Native National Congress (later, the African National Congress) and a newspaper editor, political writer, and novelist as well. Employed as a clerk and court interpreter in Mafeking in 1898, Plaatje was studying for the Cape Civil Service examinations when the Boer War broke out in 1899. This extract from his eyewitness account of the siege of Mafeking reminds us of what role Africans played in the conflict, as well the kind of guerilla warfare the Boers carried out against an imperial army and its allies.

— ·ᴖ·ᴖ· —

Sol Plaatje, from *Mafeking Diary* (1899–1900)

October–November 1899

Sunday, 29th

Divine Services. No thunder. Haikonna terror; and I have therefore got ample opportunity to sit down and think before I jot down anything about my experiences of the past week. I have discovered nearly everything about war and find that artillery in war is of no use. The Boers seem to have started hostilities, the whole of their reliance leaning on the strength and number of their cannons—and they are now surely discovering their mistake. I do not think that they will have more pluck to do anything better than what they did on Wednesday and we can therefore expect that they will either go away or settle round us until the troops arrive.

To give a short account of what I found war to be, I can say: no music is as thrilling and as immensely captivating as to listen to the firing of the guns on your own side. It is like enjoying supernatural melodies in a paradise to hear one or two shots fired off the armoured train; but no words can suitably depict the fascination of the music produced by the action of a Maxim, which to Boer ears, I am sure, is an exasperation which not only disturbs the ear but also disorganizes the free circulation of the listener's blood. At the city of Kanya they have been entertained (I learn from one just arrived) with the melodious tones of big guns, sounding the 'Grand Jeu' of war, like a gentle subterranean instrument, some thirty fathoms beneath their feet and not as remote as Mafeking; they have listened to it, I am told, with cheerful hearts, for they just mistook it for what it is not. Undoubtedly the enrapturing charm of this delectable music will give place to a most irritating discord when they have discovered that, so far from it being the action of the modern Britisher's workmanship going for the Dutch, it is the 'boom' of the state artillerist giving us thunder and lightning with his guns.

I was roaming along the river at 12 o'clock with David yesterday when we were disgusted by the incessant sounds and clappering of Mausers to the north of the town: and all of a sudden four or five 'booms' from the armoured train quenched their metal. It was like a member of the Payne family silencing a boisterous crowd with the prelude of a selection she is going to give on the violin. When their beastly fire 'shut up' the Maxim began to play: it was like listening to the Kimberley R.C. choir with their organ, rendering one of their mellifluous carols on Christmas Eve; and its charm could justly be compared with that of the Jubilee Singers performing one of their many quaint and classical oratories. But like everything desirable it ceased almost immediately. The Maxim is everybody's favourite here. Whenever there is an almost sickening rattle of Mausers you can hear them enquiring amongst themselves when 'makasono' is going to 'kgalema'. Boers are fond of shooting. They do not wait until they see anything but let go at the rate of 100 rounds per minute at the least provocation. I am afraid if they could somehow or other lay their hands on a Maxim they would simply shake it until there is not a single round left to mourn the loss of the others. One can almost fancy that prior to their leaving the State their weapons were imprecated by empyrean authority—and the following are my reasons for believing that the State ammunition has been cursed: when I passed the gaol yesterday afternoon Phil told me that while some prisoners were working in front of the gaol one of them was hit by a Mauser bullet (from the Boer lines) on the ribs. They expected the man to drop down dead, but the bullet dropped down (dead) instead. Immediately after, another hit a European's thigh. It penetrated the clothes but failed to pierce his skin; and just as if to verify this statement, another came round and struck the shoulder of a white man, who was shocked but stood as firm as though nothing had happened, when the bullet dropped down in front of him. . . .

Yesterday 22 Fingoes went out to the brickfields, which may be said to be exactly on 'disputed territory': they took shelter among the bricks and killed several of them, which vexed the latter to such an extent that they fetched one of their 7-pounders and cocked it right into the kilns. Our men lay flat against the bricks, 7-pounder shells crashing amongst them with the liberty of the elements. They went for the bricks, knocked spots out of the ground they lay on, and shattered the woodworks of their rifles between and alongside them; in fact they wrecked everything except the flesh of human beings. It affused several of its mortal discharges over them and when convinced that every one of them was dead, cleared away leaving the 22 men quite sound, but so badly armed that if the Boers had the courage to come near they would have led them away by the hands. The gunsmith is very busy mending their rifles, two of which are quite irreparable, and the men are having holidays in consequence.

Our ears cannot stand anything like the bang of a door: the rattat of some stones nearby shakes one inwardly. All of these things have assumed the attitude of death-dealing instruments and they almost invariably resemble Mausers or Dutch cannons. We often hear the alarm and run outside to find nothing wrong; and such alarm was often the motion of the pillow if one was lying down. David was yesterday grumbling: 'Oh, what a restless life; if I knew that things were going to turn out this way I would never have left Aliwal North.'

After I left Mr Mahlelebe yesterday I came through the gaol yard onto the Railway Reserve's fence. Mauser bullets were just like hail on the main road to our village. I had just left the fence when one flew close to my cap with a 'ping'—giving me such a fright as caused me to sit down on the footpath. Someone behind me exclaimed that I was nearly killed and I looked round to see who my sympathizer was. When I did so another screeched through his legs with a 'whiz-z-z-z' and dropped between the two of us. I continued my journey in company with this man, during which I heard a screech and a tap behind my ear: it was a Mauser bullet and as there can be no question about a fellow's death when it enters his brain through the lobe, I knew at the moment that I had been transmitted from this temporary life on to eternity. I imagined I held a nickel bullet in my heart. That was merely the faculty of the soul recognizing (in ordinary post-mortal dream) who occasioned its departure—for I was dead! Dead, to rise no more. A few seconds elapsed after which I found myself scanning the bullet between my finger and thumb, to realise that it was but a horsefly.

It is very difficult to remember the days of the week in times of war. When I returned from the river early this morning I found David still in bed, and he asked me if there is any sign of their advance. He was dumbfounded when I said that they were not likely to advance as today was Sunday. What, Sunday? He thought it was Thursday (Ha! Ha!). . . .

Tuesday, 31st

Long before 5 o'clock we were aroused by reports of Ben going as rapidly as she did last week. She was accompanied by the enemy's 7-pounder and all other pounders. We woke, dressed in a hurry, and went to the rocks to find things really very serious at Makane. They were shelling Makane and the dust was simply like a cloud around our little fort. The Boers were advancing towards the koppie like a swarm of voetgangers: they came creeping under cover of their shells, which were flying over their heads and preceding them like a lot of lifeless but terrific vanguards, until they opened fire with their muskets at long range. Their fire was very heavy, for the whole of the Dutch army had come from all round Mafeking and turned their attention towards our little fort at Makane. They have evidently discovered that to capture the whole place at once was a hopeless task and they had therefore decided on capturing one by one of our forts until they have nipped every one of them in the bud.

. . . To return to the subject. I think I have already stated that the Boers attributed their failure to the fact that we never leave our trenches to give them a chance of tackling us in the open. This morning they must have thought that they would easily compel us to do so by weakening Makane and naturally getting us to run to her assistance, thereby affording them an opportunity of going for us in the plain between this and there. If this was their expectation they were sorely disappointed, for nobody cared. They went for the little fort from east, south and west with muskets and artillery, the former being volleys from about 800 hands. But nobody in town, or anywhere else, troubled his soul about it. The volunteers round the place, seeing that all of the guns were turned towards Makane, stood up and admired the operation as though it was a performance on a theatre stage. It must have given them a headache to find such a multitude of them advancing towards a fort occupied by 70 officers and men of the B.S.A. Police—and nobody caring to go to their assistance. But this was not all: the enemy came quite close and still not a shot came from within the mysterious little fort. I believe the Boers (who always let off a number of rounds unnecessarily) must have thought that everyone was dead, for nearly 20 tons of bombs had already been plugged into the fort. The fortifications looked quite old and ragged in consequence. All of a sudden there came volley after volley from the dumb fort and we could see them fall when the Maxim began to play; some dead, some wounded and some presumably to wait until dark. Their officers, who were mounted behind them and urging them on, were—with one exception—the first to run and at 9 o'clock they hoisted the Red Cross. Their ambulances and Natives were busy 'tutaing' till about midday. Our losses were two officers and five men killed, and six wounded.

This engagement was very unfortunate to me as it deprived me of one of my dearest friends in the place, in the person of the Hon. Captain Marsham. These experienced sol-

diers never care how fast bullets may whizz about them: they stroll about in a heavy volley far more recklessly than we walk through a shower of rain, and that is how he
wrecked a career that was going to give him a name almost too heavy for his youth.

The enemy having had the reverse of this morning's attack, we had a very quiet
day. . . .

Sunday, 5th

Guy Fawkes's day. The usual prayers and thanksgivings. Late last evening about 1000
Boers were seen crossing from the southern laars over to the north of the town, but as
it soon became dark we lost sight of them. Just about the time 'Au Sanna' always fires
her 'bad-night' shot we heard the report coming from the north instead of the south;
we, however, thought little of it as it might have been that our ears were mistaken. This
morning, however, it was discovered that it was a dynamite explosion that went off.

The railway line being on a gradient a few miles north of the town, the Boers filled
the trolley with dynamite, tied a fuse to it, lighted the fuse, and pushed it down the re-
clining line into town. Their intention was apparently to wait until the dynamite exploded somewhere about the railway station and killed everybody, when they would
walk in and then publish to the civilized world that they had taken Mafeking at the barrel of the Mauser. But God forbade it and their determinations had been frustrated. The
dynamite exploded a half-mile beyond the graveyard, smashed the trolley that carried it,
tore up the line and blew up the ground. While some of us were paying homage to the
All-Father in places of worship, some were busy arranging the line to prevent a re-oc-
currence. A very fine day. Soft and pleasant rains till eve. . . .

Sunday, 12th

We have a black Sherlock Holmes in the person of Manomphe's son, Freddy. He arrived
from Kanya with some despatches this morning in company with Malno's brother-in-
law: the latter was on horseback, which is very risky to cross the enemy lines with. On
Friday the horseman remained behind and Freddy came across a party of 60 Boers at
Tlapeng. He hid the letters and went straight up to them. They searched him for letters,
and on finding nothing on his person, they became very friendly—more so when one
of the party recognized him as an old good servant of his. They gave him a quantity of
mutton which he roasted on the spot and had a fine repast at the same time as his Dutch
friends. They left the place at 5 p.m. giving him an opportunity of fetching his letters.
He reached his home (Ga-molimola) in the evening and hid his letters in an ant-heap
close by. Our friend the horseman, who met no Boers, arrived the same evening. Freddy
advised him to return to the bush and hide his horse all day next day (yesterday) until
dark, when they would plan the best way of getting into town. Freddy became doubtful of the man's aptitude and requested him to hand over his letters to him for safe-
keeping, which he did.

In the morning a party of 40 Boers rode past Modimola and asked Freddy where the
cattle were. Subsequently another party (of 90 this time) also came past. After leaving
Freddy's place, this last party observed the spoor of a horse. They traced it to a small village a little beyond. (Instead of going to where Freddy showed him, our foolish friend
went to this village.) When the inhabitants perceived the party approaching along the
horse's spoor, they decided to give them to understand that it belonged to the owner of

the village, and that his son had been riding it looking for stray goats. There was an interpreter of some sort who promptly advanced to meet the ephemeral conquerors of Mafeking and related to them the history of the horse. The head of the village—the old fool—overheard this, and blurted out that he was lying. This infuriated the Boers, who sentenced the interpreter to receive 55 cuts with a stirrup leather for his lies, and made a prisoner of our foolish friend while the interpreter was undergoing the sentence. When Malno's brother-in-law got arrested he whined and begged the Boers not to take him alone as he was not the only offender: there was another man, ahead with the Magistrate's letters, and they came from Kanya together.

The Boers returned to Freddy, who lied so classically, and with such thoroughness and serenity, that they disbelieved their prisoner's statement. They searched his person, his house, nay everything, but failed to find them; and Freddy walked calmly in here with both despatches this morning. From Freddy's information, the reason why we are having such quiet days is because the Boers have gone in different parties to loot our stock. We hope that by the beginning of next year they will be purging them back to us in much the same manner as they did 14 years ago. . . .

December 1899

Tuesday, 5th

I had a busy time today. A white man was charged with committing rape on a Native girl. The police rescued her off him and made a prisoner of him. I interpreted in this case and just when the evidence was about to reach the filthiest, superior authorities (military) demanded my services and I departed only to return towards the conclusion when the interpreting in it had become quite ceremonious. The military court cares nought for any such cases: I believe we will keep the evidence until the roads are open and commit him for trial before the judge next quarter.

I did not return to town this afternoon, the heaviest rain of the season having graced us with a visit. Surely if things go on at this rate the few, with whose ploughing the effects of this war did not interfere, will have too much grain for house consumption. The shower was heavy but quiet—so quiet that I fell asleep and only woke at 4.10 p.m. to find the village in flood. As I happened to be away in dreamland, and do not know what took place, I will leave the *Mafeking Mail* to describe the affair:

'Dead puppies, stinking sprats, all drenched in mud, drowned cats and turnip tops came tumbling down the flood' is what Dean Swift said in his description of a city shower. We suppose from his mentioning dead puppies and drowned cats that he meant it was raining 'cats and dogs'. We don't know the origin of the 'cats and dogs' shower but, if its root is 'kata doros' as some learned writer suggested or 'contrary to experience' we think it rained 'cats and dogs' yesterday. A sprinkle of over eight inches in about one hour is decidedly contrary to experience. Fortunately we are so positioned that there is ample natural drainage to take away even the enormous quantity of water which fell yesterday, but the trenches were soon filled and from them the water could not run. More damage to property was done by the storm than the Boers could ever accomplish in their 'storming'. Rations were destroyed, kits washed away, and in one case a man was nearly drowned, or smothered in the mud. He slipped in, fortunately feet downwards, and had not two of his companions been near him and promptly 'hauled him back again' he would have been done for. At the hospital redan the underground kitchen was flooded with six feet of water, the dinner beef spoiled and various little 'extras' the men had subscribed to buy, were lost. The women's laager trench was an underground canal. The sisters were washed out from their 'bomb-proof' and the Cape Police had an hour's diving in the seven feet deep coffee coloured pool for Maxim ammunition; while everyone had an experience of wetness and discomfort, which it is to be hoped will remain unique, but which was borne by the whole garrison in the same cheery manner which has been shown during all the time of the siege. We hope our friend the enemy enjoyed himself, and to help cheer him up we should like to tell him that through his lack of nous and pluck he missed a chance yesterday to annoy us, which is never likely to present itself again.

Some people had been over to the Boer lines to 'thiba' cattle. They managed to get four—abnormally fat elephants. They gave one to the chief, slaughtered two, ate part of the meat, and retailed the balance. I did not avail myself of the opportunity of finding out what loot tastes like as Meko had slaughtered a fat hammel and the hard ox is not very desirable when palatable mutton is knocking about.

Wednesday, 6th

. . . One shell hit Mr Weil's store yesterday. The store was full of customers and shop employees. It entered through the roof, travelled between the roof and the ceiling, shattering the beams until it destroyed the ceiling and exited through the wholesale door. Fragments made a race for the railway station. During that race a Burghersdorp chap—a refugee from Johannesburg—came in contact with one and was killed. The crowd in the shop escaped without injury. Another shell came round in the afternoon. It entered the private house of our young Town Clerk, pierced the outer wall and went on to a room in which the Town Clerk was. It destroyed the room and wrecked everything inside except the Town Clerk—a marvellous escape: one fragment went to the kitchen, where the cook, a very stout bastard lady, was and shook her so vehemently that she nearly had the perfect circulation of her blood disorganized.

Thursday, 7th

I wonder why the Boers are so 'kwaai' today. During the last few days we seldom had a 'Sanna' shell during the forenoon, and then a day's complement was only between two and four, but this morning we had seven between 7.00 a.m. and 8.00 a.m. from 'Sanna' only, besides a heavy thunder from the smaller artillery and a shower of Mausers which played the accompaniment. The middle of the day was somewhat quiet but operations were resumed at 3.30 p.m. with great vigour. I was obliged to stop going to town this afternoon despite urgent private affairs. The afternoon fire lasted till sunset but 'Sanna', just to show that she is older and mightier than the lot, kept up her part as long as the moon was shining—till 8.30 p.m. It will be a serious business if the Boers are going to give us no more sleep while the moon is shining. We always had only one shell—the 'bad-night' shot—fired into us between 8.00 and 9.00 p.m.

This single one we find very inconvenient as it makes everyone imagine, at sunset, that he is either going to have his legs shattered or a few nambulatory escapes—if he is not annihilated to death; but if we are going to have them as regularly as we had them this day we might as well expect to be throwing up the sponge soon. Our patience is altogether exhausted. When the trouble commenced no one dreamt that we would still be beleaguered at the end of November: others gave the troops only up to 30th October to arrive here; I, however, gave them up to 30th October to reach Kimberley and to arrive here on 20th November, which was the most liberal of the lot. But here we are today, December 7th, losing people daily and not even able to tell where the troops are. Surely if everybody knew that this was going to be the case we would never have had the forebearance to start it. The result of yesterday afternoon's 'Sanna' outrage was two whites and a Native killed, and two whites wounded. If we are going to die at this rate I am sure there will only be wounded people hopping about single-armed and with amputated legs to tell the history of the siege.

One of the killed was in Mr Riesle's bar (Mafeking Hotel). They are dead against our poor ex-Mayor. When they shelled us with 12- and 7-pounders, on the 16th October, Mr Riesle was the only person who got his windows smashed; I have already described how they went for his sitting-room and wrecked the piano and goods therein being, but have not mentioned that when 'Sanna' (before she was christened) gave her début in Mafeking on October 23rd Mr Riesle was the first victim. It went for him in a quaint manner; some flames had to be put out, which has never been the case with any other explosion up till this day. They have since been going for his outhouses, back-cottages, servants' rooms and W.C.'s time after time in a most merciless manner.

Monday, 11th

I went to town early this morning to fetch Mr Hamilton to take pictures in our village for *Black and White,* which paper he represents besides the London *Times.* A shell burst while I was at the residency where I always feel comfortable even if the alarm-bells go. It flew overhead and travelled for miles away in a northwesterly direction. I went to Riesle's for Hamilton and the bells rang while he was still preparing. The discomfort I endured can easily be imagined, for Riesle's is a place which I always hurry to pass quickly—even if there is nothing in the wind. It, however, went towards the railway and exploded there. We then left. Mr Briscoe's drift is not the road to travel, being exposed to the eastern Mausers and shells, particularly when one is on horseback—so we went to cross by the missionaries' foot drift (Lekoko's new dam). While we were in the plain between the town and our village we observed some heavy firing to the south of the stadt: at the foot drift we were met by several women, who said they were nearly all hit by Mauser bullets while routing 'Lichachane' for fuel. They had to come home minus the wood during a hail of bullets, every one of which fortunately missed them.

When we reached Mr Lefenya's house, we showed the pressman where lives my old uncle, who kept 90 Boers off on Saturday. I had scarcely finished when the old dame came to meet us and informed me that he had just come home wounded. With the prudence and forethought of the European, Mr Hamilton had every requisite with him and after we had dismounted we went in and washed and dressed the wound, which was, however, not very bad—having entered by the left armpit and exited through the fleshy part of the breast, touching no bones. Little Tiego, chief of the younger corps, had one of his left toes slightly tipped off and two other fellows were wounded, each in the leg— none dangerously. This gives one the idea that the Dutch muskets, unlike their artillery, have had their curses taken off, for this is really the Barolong's first casualty since the war broke out. I am afraid they have given the Boers nothing in return, for directly they got a sufficient view of the Boers the latter retreated hurriedly.

We received news that two despatch-runners were trying to come in here on Thursday night but were fired at by Boers. During their run for dear life the despatches got lost and they have now gone back to Kanya. The man Samuel Lefenya, who cheated the

Boers at Ganyesa a few days back, was leaving Mafeking with his wife. They were fired at by Boers and he got dangerously hit in the stomach; his wife was shot in the thigh and they were both taken to the laager. The former is not expected to live. The Boers have been seen picking 130 men and horses for the purpose of reinforcing the north. They say the English are so numerous up there that it is feared they will build the line.

The Boers must have thought that we were now eating horses and were surrendering, because of the white flags leaving for all of the trenches round about us. It was Colonel Baden-Powell sending out copies of the accompanying circular to the burghers, as he says it is exclusively for them and not for the officers and colonial rebels. It is a stirring manifesto, at least to me, but I wonder what its effects will be on Boer ears. We had a quiet day. Some rains set in during the forenoon. . . .

Tuesday, 26th

Early this morning we were aroused by the sound of big guns, muskets and Maxims towards Game Tree. It lasted for nearly an hour, then all was quiet again. It was a good number of the garrison endeavouring to capture a Dutch fort at Game Tree. Fitz-Clarence figured among the ringleaders again and everyone was sure that—bullets failing—he would capture the Dutch fort at the point of the bayonet, but they unfortunately found it a tough business. They got up to the fort and were preparing to jump right into it amongst the Boers. But the walls were so high that only a few managed to get on top. Even here they could do nothing as the trench was too well roofed and the Boers, who meanwhile had their rifles through the loop-holes, played havoc with them until they hoisted the Red Cross. FitzClarence alone got inside and stabbed two or three. They shot him once but he proceeded to bayonet another when they shot a second time and he dropped down—though not dead. (Three who went to the door of the trench were taken prisoners.) He is now in the hospital improving. I think the wounding of FitzClarence incapacitates an eminent 'moguli' from taking part in future operations against the Transvaal, when the troops cross the border. The Boers never hit so hard a blow on Mafeking since they besieged us. Altogether we lost 23 men killed and 26 wounded. The rest of the day was quiet.

Of all the commentary about Queen Victoria toward the end of her long life and reign, there are few examples that accord her so much agency in the South African question. One of Britain's most prominent journalists, Stead (1849–1912) captures the quintessential paradox of the Victorian monarch who "reigns but does not rule."

William T. Stead, "What Kind of Sovereign is Queen Victoria?" (1900)

THE Queen reigns but does not rule. Constitutional monarchy reduces the element of personal sovereignty to a minimum. For two hundred years, no British monarch has ventured to refuse to accept every law passed by both Houses of Parliament. The Queen is as much bound to obey the law as the meanest of her subjects. She cannot interfere with the courts of justice, great or small. On the advice of the Home Secretary, she can exercise the royal prerogative of mercy; but as the Home Secretary must approve, even this lingering remnant of royal power is more of a shadow than a substance. Everything is done in her name, but the whole authority nominally vested in the Crown is really exercised by Ministers who are absolutely dependent for their continuance in office from day to day upon the support of a majority of the House of Commons. These constitutional truisms lead many people to imagine that, as the Queen has no authority, she is therefore of no account. They could not make a greater mistake. The Queen has no power by virtue of her throne. But she has immense influence owing to the opportunity which her position gives her of counseling, persuading, and sometimes even coercing her Ministers to adopt her view of a question. Owing to her unique experience, her extraordinary memory, and her keen interest in all affairs of state, Queen Victoria is probably more influential than any of her subjects, not excluding either her Prime Minister or her Colonial Secretary. She has become the balance-wheel of the Constitution. This extraordinary position is due solely to her personal qualities and the use she has made of her unique opportunities. . . .

The General Election of 1880 was a great surprise and disappointment to the Queen. She was devoted to Lord Beaconsfield, and she regarded Mr. Gladstone with scant sympathy. In common with most of the London papers and all London society, the Court assumed that the British electorate was dominated by the flamboyant imperialism of the Prime Minister. She was cruelly disillusioned when the General Election returned Mr. Gladstone to power with a majority of more than a hundred. There was no possibility of mistaking the significance of the national verdict. Lord Beaconsfield's policy in Turkey, in Afghanistan and in South Africa had been directly assailed. Mr. Gladstone's indictment of the Jingo policy of war and annexation was unsparing. The popular response was overwhelming. After a vain effort to secure as Liberal Prime Minister Lord Granville, or the Duke of Devonshire (then Lord Hartington), the Queen bowed to the national mandate, and reluctantly intrusted Mr. Gladstone with the duty of framing a Cabinet.

Mr. Gladstone speedily succeeded in forming an administration. It was not so easy a task to decide upon a policy. Logically, of course, Mr. Gladstone ought to have annulled the Anglo-Turkish Convention, and evacuated Cyprus. He ought also to have restored to the Boers, who were refusing to pay taxes and were actually in armed revolt, the independence of the Transvaal. But the most critical and pressing of all questions was the future of Afghanistan. The invasion of Afghanistan by Lord Lytton was one of those imperial crimes against which Mr. Gladstone had inveighed most fiercely. Despite his protests, the British armies had pierced the passes, and had occupied both Cabul and Candahar. From Cabul even Lord Beaconsfield proposed to withdraw. But the whole Jingo party was passionately in favor of the retention of Candahar and the annexation of southern Afghanistan. Lord Roberts, then in chief command at Cabul, was also of the same opinion, and so was the Queen.

Mr. Gladstone did not evacuate Cyprus; he did not restore the independence of the Transvaal. But he felt himself compelled to proclaim at the earliest possible moment his determination to evacuate Candahar, and recall the British army from Afghanistan. He had appealed to the nation to reverse the policy of Lord Beaconsfield, and as the nation had given him a decisive majority, it is obvious that no other course was possible. So Mr.

Gladstone believed, and he had the concurrence of his colleagues. They therefore decided to announce in the Queen's Speech that Candahar was to be evacuated.

The Queen, however, dissented. She believed that to evacuate Candahar would be to sacrifice the dearly bought fruit of the Afghan war. She was full of distrust of Russia, and reposed implicit confidence in the opinions of Lord Roberts and Lord Beaconsfield. So it came to pass that when her new Ministers submitted to her the draft of the Queen's Speech, in which, according to the British Constitutional custom, Ministers lay down their program at the beginning of the Parliamentary session, she objected to signing it. Her Majesty took strong exception to the paragraph about Candahar, and urged that it should be omitted or made less peremptory. Mr. Gladstone refused. For that refusal she was prepared. But she did not know how far Mr. Gladstone could count upon the support of the Whigs who formed the bulk of the Cabinet. She knew that they had acquiesced more or less reluctantly in the Gladstonian agitation. She did not know whether they might not be glad to back her up in her demand for postponing any decisive declaration on the subject of Candahar. So she tabled her non possumus and waited.

Mr. Gladstone, however, was on this occasion master of his Cabinet. The mandate of the country was too unmistakable and too emphatic for any of them to dare to play any tricks with it. So they rallied as one man round their chief, and insisted that the Candahar paragraph should stand. The Queen, however, still protested, and argued—as her wont is, with vehemence and much plain speech—against hauling down the flag in south Afghanistan. At last it was necessary to send the leading members of the Cabinet on special deputation to Osborne, to explain to her Majesty that, however much she might loathe the policy of retirement, the paragraph announcing it must appear in the Queen's Speech. But so stiffly did the Queen hold out, that the royal consent was obtained only a few hours before the Queen's Speech was read from the throne.

. . . Those who imagine that her Majesty takes no serious interest in the great business of state, would be immensely amazed if they could even glance at the Queen's correspondence. She has always claimed to exercise the right to communicate directly in her own hand with any Cabinet Minister. In most cases, her letters are addressed to the Prime Minister, and these royal missives are always considered before any other business at Cabinet councils. But besides these more or less official communications to the Prime Minister, the Queen never hesitates on occasion to write to individual Cabinet Ministers, in order to apprise them of her views and opinions. In the case of Candahar, the matter concerned the India and the War Office, and it was to her Secretaries of State for these Departments that the Queen naturally addressed herself. Her correspondence with them, if ever it came to be published, would convince even the most skeptical as to the vigorous hand her Majesty has ever taken in the affairs of her realm.

The present deplorable war in South Africa, the Queen endeavored in vain to avert, not only at the eleventh hour, but by the sagacious prevision with which, in 1858, she had energetically supported Sir George Grey in working for the federation of South Africa. In that year the Volksraad of the Orange Free State had passed a resolution in favor of union or alliance with the Cape. In 1859, in communicating this resolution to the Cape Parliament, Sir George Grey, then Governor of the Cape, recommended that the opportunity should be seized for the purpose of founding a Federal Union of the Dutch and English colonies in South Africa. For this statesmanlike proposal he was cashiered by the Tory government of the day, against the vehement and passionate remonstrances of the Queen. The moment the Tory government fell, she secured his reappointment by the new administration. But it was too late. Sir George Grey, speaking many years afterward of the part which the Queen played in that memorable crisis, paid the following public tribute to the far-sighted, statesmanlike sagacity of the Queen. He said:—

"When I was a representative of the Queen in Africa, I had arranged a federation of the different states there, all having agreed to come into it except one; but the plan was regarded with disfavor both by the Ministry and the Opposition of the day in England; and the consequence was that I was summarily dismissed. One person in the empire held that I was right in the action taken, and that person was the Queen. Upon her representation I was reinstated. Her Majesty, together with the Prince Consort, held that it was necessary to preserve to the empire an opening for the poor and adventurous, and experience had shown that the Queen better represented the feeling of the British people on that question than did the Ministers of the day. The Queen held rightly that the energies of the British race should spread the empire as instinct moved, so long as no wrong was done to other people."

If Sir George Grey had been allowed to have his way, the federation of South Africa would have long ago created a stable and pacific Anglo-Dutch commonwealth. The Queen, however, was foiled by her Ministers. Federation was rendered impossible, with results which we are witnessing to-day.

. . . The part played by the Queen in maintaining a high standard of morality in her court is so universally recognized that it need only be referred to as one of the least of the services which Victoria has rendered to the realm. Much less generally known, and therefore much less widely appreciated, is the extent to which she has kept the whole of her empire in hand. By constantly keeping in touch, by personal intercourse and by frequent correspondence, with all those who stand for England overseas, she has done more to give a sense of unity to the heterogeneous collection of miscellaneous territories which we call our empire, than can easily be realized. No important Governor departs for his colony without a personal interview with the Queen. All our Proconsuls report to her personally. She sees all the Ambassadors, and many of them, besides their official dispatches, write constantly long private reports to their royal mistress. Her correspondence with the sovereigns of Europe has never been intermitted. The King of Belgium has never allowed one Sunday to pass since he came to the throne that he has not written a letter to the Queen. Other and more important sovereigns, although not quite such constant correspondents, nevertheless write confidentially to her whenever important affairs are to be settled, as they would not write to any one outside the royal caste. The Queen has kept herself posted by continuous personal intercourse with all the ablest of her subjects, as well as the sovereigns and ambassadors of foreign powers. At this moment, although she has passed her eightieth year, and her eyes are dim with age, she has preserved unimpaired her mental faculties, and has displayed a courage, a composure and a resource which have put her councillors to shame.

To sum up the whole matter, I venture to submit that although I have made no attempt to claim for the Queen the possession of infallible wisdom or of political sagacity beyond that of other mortals, I may modestly claim to have shown that the Queen is a sovereign who brings to the discharge of the responsible duties of her exalted position, a keen political instinct which, combined with a deep sense of her obligations, impels her to take an active part in the handling of all the great questions of state. Anything farther removed than the Queen from a mere royal puppet, immersed in trivialities of etiquette and pageantry, can hardly be imagined. She may not be, as the present Czar affirmed, "the greatest statesman in Europe," but among all contemporary sovereigns and statesmen you may search in vain for any one who possesses to the same extent immense experience, unfailing memory, steady judgment, unwearying industry, and intense consciousness of personal responsibility. These qualities combined in Queen Victoria, have given her a position of influence in the British Empire of to-day which, although purely personal, could never have been wielded by any woman if she had not inherited a throne.

Jonathan Atkinson Hobson (1858–1940) was an economist whose major works before *Imperialism* were studies of industry and modern capitalism, with an special emphasis on consumption. Here he weighs the relationship between the terms and practices of nationalism, colonialism and imperialism in the wake of the Boer War.

J. A. Hobson, from *Imperialism: A Study* (1902)

AMID the welter of vague political abstractions to lay one's finger accurately upon any "ism" so as to pin it down and mark it out by definition seems impossible. Where meanings shift so quickly and so subtly, not only following changes of thought, but often manipulated artificially by political practitioners so as to obscure, expand, or distort, it is idle to demand the same rigour as is expected in the exact sciences. A certain broad consistency in its relations to other kindred terms is the nearest approach to definition which such a term as Imperialism admits. Nationalism, internationalism, colonialism, its three closest congeners, are equally elusive, equally shifty, and the changeful overlapping of all four demands the closest vigilance of students of modern politics. . . .

Colonialism, where it consists in the migration of part of a nation to vacant or sparsely peopled foreign lands, the emigrants carrying with them full rights of citizenship in the mother country, or else establishing local self-government in close conformity with her institutions and under her final control, may be considered a genuine expansion of nationality, a territorial enlargement of the stock, language and institutions of the nation. Few colonies in history have, however, long remained in this condition when they have been remote from the mother country. Either they have severed the connexion and set up for themselves as separate nationalities, or they have been kept in complete political bondage so far as all major processes of government are concerned, a condition to which the term Imperialism is at least as appropriate as colonialism. The only form of distant colony which can be regarded as a clear expansion of nationalism is the self-governing British colony in Australasia and Canada, and even in these cases local conditions may generate a separate nationalism based on a strong consolidation of colonial interests and sentiments alien from and conflicting with those of the mother nation. In other "self-governing" colonies, as in Cape Colony and Natal, where the majority of whites are not descended from British settlers, and where the presence of subject or "inferior" races in vastly preponderating numbers, and alien climatic and other natural conditions, mark out a civilization distinct from that of the "mother country," the conflict between the colonial and the imperial ideas has long been present in the forefront of the consciousness of politicians. When Lord Rosmead spoke of the permanent presence of the imperial factor as "simply an absurdity," and Mr. Rhodes spoke of its "elimination," they were championing a "colonialism" which is more certain in the course of time to develop by inner growth into a separate "nationalism" than in the case of the Australasian and Canadian colonies, because of the wider divergence, alike of interests and radical conditions of life, from the mother nation. Our other colonies are plainly representative of the spirit of Imperialism rather than of colonialism. No considerable proportion of the population consists of British settlers living with their families in conformity with the social and political customs and laws of their native land: in most instances they form a small minority wielding political or economic sway over a majority of alien and subject people, themselves under the despotic political control of the Imperial Government or its local nominees. This, the normal condition of a British colony, was well-nigh universal in the colonies of other European countries. The "colonies" which France and Germany established in Africa and Asia were in no real sense plantations of French and German national life beyond the seas; nowhere, not even in Algeria, did they represent true European civilization; their political and economic structure of society is wholly alien from that of the mother country.

Colonialism, in its best sense, is a natural overflow of nationality; its test is the power of colonists to transplant the civilization they represent to the new natural and social environment in which they find themselves. We must not be misled by names; the "colonial" party in Germany and France is identical in general aim and method with the "imperialist" party in England, and the latter is the truer title. Professor Seeley well marked the nature of Imperialism. "When a State advances beyond the limits of nationality its power becomes precarious and artificial. This is the condition of most empires, and it is the condition of our own. When a nation extends itself into other territories the chances are that it cannot destroy or completely drive out, even if it succeeds in conquering, them. When this happens it has a great and permanent difficulty to contend with, for the subject or rival nationalities cannot be properly assimilated, and remain as a permanent cause of weakness and danger."

The novelty of recent Imperialism regarded as a policy consists chiefly in its adoption by several nations. The notion of a number of competing empires is essentially modern. The root idea of empire in the ancient and mediæval world was that of a federation of States, under a hegemony, covering in general terms the entire known recognized world, such as was held by Rome under the so-called *pax Romana*. When Roman citizens, with full civic rights, were found all over the explored world, in Africa and Asia, as well as in Gaul and Britain, Imperialism contained a genuine element of internationalism. With the fall of Rome this conception of a single empire wielding political authority over the civilized world did not disappear. On the contrary, it survived all the fluctuations of the Holy Roman Empire. Even after the definite split between the Eastern and Western sections had taken place at the close of the fourth century, the theory of a single State, divided for administrative purposes, survived. Beneath every cleavage or antagonism, and notwithstanding the severance of many independent kingdoms and provinces, this ideal unity of the empire lived. It formed the conscious avowed ideal of Charlemagne, though as a practical ambition confined to Western Europe. Rudolph of Habsburg not merely revived the idea, but laboured to realize it through Central Europe, while his descendant Charles V gave a very real meaning to the term by gathering under the unity of his imperial rule the territories of Austria, Germany, Spain, the Netherlands, Sicily, and Naples. In later ages this dream of a European Empire animated the policy of Peter the

Great, Catherine, and Napoleon. Nor is it impossible that Kaiser Wilhelm III held a vision of such a world-power. . . .

Nationalism is a plain highway to internationalism, and if it manifests divergence we may well suspect a perversion of its nature and its purpose. Such a perversion is Imperialism, in which nations trespassing beyond the limits of facile assimilation transform the wholesome stimulative rivalry of varied national types into the cut-throat struggle of competing empires.

Not only does aggressive Imperialism defeat the movement towards internationalism by fostering animosities among competing empires: its attack upon the liberties and the existence of weaker or lower races stimulates in them a corresponding excess of national self-consciousness. A nationalism that bristles with resentment and is all astrain with the passion of self-defence is only less perverted from its natural genius than the nationalism which glows with the animus of greed and self-aggrandisement at the expense of others. From this aspect aggressive Imperialism is an artificial stimulation of nationalism in peoples too foreign to be absorbed and too compact to be permanently crushed. We welded Afrikanerdom into just such a strong dangerous nationalism, and we joined with other nations in creating a resentful nationalism until then unknown in China. The injury to nationalism in both cases consists in converting a cohesive, pacific internal force into an exclusive, hostile force, a perversion of the true power and use of nationality. The worst and most certain result is the retardation of internationalism. The older nationalism was primarily an inclusive sentiment; its natural relation to the same sentiment in another people was lack of sympathy, not open hostility; there was no inherent antagonism to prevent nationalities from growing and thriving side by side. Such in the main was the nationalism of the earlier nineteenth century, and the politicians of Free Trade had some foundation for their dream of a quick growth of effective, informal internationalism by peaceful, profitable intercommunication of goods and ideas among nations recognizing a just harmony of interests in free peoples.

The overflow of nationalism into imperial channels quenched all such hopes. While co-existent nationalities are capable of mutual aid involving no direct antagonism of interests, co-existent empires following each its own imperial career of territorial and industrial aggrandisement are natural necessary enemies. The full nature of this antagonism on its economic side is not intelligible without a close analysis of those conditions of modern capitalist production which compel an ever keener "fight for markets," but the political antagonism is obvious.

The scramble for Africa and Asia virtually recast the policy of all European nations, evoked alliances which cross all natural lines of sympathy and historical association, drove every continental nation to consume an ever-growing share of its material and human resources upon military and naval equipment, drew the great new power of the United States from its isolation into the full tide of competition; and, by the multitude, the magnitude, and the suddenness of the issues it had thrown on to the stage of politics, became a constant agent of menace and of perturbation to the peace and progress of mankind. The new policy exercised the most notable and formidable influence upon the conscious statecraft of the nations which indulge in it. While producing for popular consumption doctrines of national destiny and imperial missions of civilization, contradictory in their true import, but subsidiary to one another as supports of popular Imperialism, it evoked a calculating, greedy type of Machiavellianism, entitled "realpolitik" in Germany, where it was made, which remodelled the whole art of diplomacy and erected national aggrandisement without pity or scruple as the conscious motive force of foreign policy. Earth hunger and the scramble for markets were responsible for the openly avowed repudiation of treaty obligations which Germany, Russia, and England had not scrupled to defend. The sliding scale of diplomatic language, hinterland, sphere of interest, sphere of influence, paramountcy, suzerainty, protectorate, veiled or open, leading up to acts of forcible seizure or annexation which sometimes continue to be hidden under "lease," "rectification of frontier," "concession," and the like, was the invention and expression of this cynical spirit of Imperialism. While Germany and Russia were perhaps more open in their professed adoption of the material gain of their country as the sole criterion of public conduct, other nations were not slow to accept the standard. Though the conduct of nations in dealing with one another has commonly been determined at all times by selfish and shortsighted considerations, the conscious, deliberate adoption of this standard at an age when the intercourse of nations and their interdependence for all essentials of human life grow ever closer, is a retrograde step fraught with grave perils to the cause of civilization.

This commentary on the Royal Commission's findings takes the connection between physical strength and military prowess—connections that had been used unscientifically during the Boer War to explain Britain's military weakness—as a given, in part because of the results of the postwar Royal Commission that investigated the viability of Britain's racial stock. Here Smyth examines the data for Scotland as well as his recommendation that data collection on children continue in schools.

A. Watt Smyth, from *Physical Deterioration* (1904)

THE publication of the report of the Royal Commission on Physical Training in Scotland unquestionably produced a considerable effect on the public mind. Englishmen asked themselves whether the conclusion that physical degeneration existed in Scotland was not likely to be even more true of England. Attention was called to the matter in Parliament, and particularly to a statement contained in the report for 1902 of the Inspector-General of Recruiting, to the effect that "the one subject which causes anxiety in the future, as regards recruiting, is the gradual deterioration of the physique of the working classes, from which the bulk of the recruits must always be drawn." Finally, in April 1903, the Director-General, Army Medical Service, drew up a memorandum on the physical unfitness of men offering themselves for enlistment in the Army. In this memorandum the question is asked whether the impeachment of the national health by Sir Frederick Maurice and others has a solid foundation in fact, and whether it is true of the population as a whole, or only of a certain section of it. It is pointed out that in spite of the large proportion of men found physically unfit for service in the Army, the public health statistics appear to show progressive improvement in the national health, and that feats of strength, agility, and endurance would point at any rate to improvement in the physique of the well-to-do classes. Yet the question we have to face is, if this large proportion of the community is unfit for military service, what is to become of those rejected? For what occupation are they fit? According to the last census 25 millions out of 32 millions live in towns, the town population having increased 15 per cent. during the last decade. The bulk of our soldiers are drawn from the class of unskilled labourers, and the highest number of rejections are among men employed in indoor occupations. The deterioration of the physique of the urban poor is attributed to insufficient and poor quality of food, defective housing, overcrowding, and insanitary surroundings. Add to this want of thrift, illness or death of the breadwinner, alcoholic excess, and acquired disease.

. . . While it may be true that the Army is now compelled to draw a larger proportion of its recruits from the lowest classes of the working population, the casual labourer and the unemployed, it must be recollected that the physical standard has been lowered. In 1845 the standard height for admission to the Army was 5 ft. 6 in.; in 1883 it had been lowered to 5 ft. 3 in.; and in 1900 to 5 ft. In 1901 no fewer than 593.4 per 1000 were under the old standard height of 5 ft. 6 in., and 511.8 were under the chest measurement of 34 in. which was the minimum in 1883. The statistics also appear to indicate a progressive decline in the average weight, for whereas in 1871, 159.4 per mille were under 8 st. 8 lbs., in 1901, 325 per mille failed to attain this very moderate weight. Again, if the physical standard to which recruits now attain be compared with that of the race, it will be found that the average recruit of 1900 at the age of nearly 20 years was 2 in. shorter, an inch less in the chest measurement, and 15 lbs. lighter than the average youth of 19 years, according to the measurement of the Anthropometric Committee of the British Association. Whilst giving all due weight to the mitigating circumstances set out in the report of the College of Surgeons, the fact cannot be forgotten that in spite of the lowering of the standard in certain respects, there has been no clear decrease in the proportion of total rejections, and that the decreases which are to be noted relate to those very measurements for which the standard has been reduced. In Germany, on the other hand, the evidence available appears to show that the percentage of the recruits rejected tends to decrease. It must not be assumed that the standard is lower in Germany; on the contrary, statistics go to prove that the average German recruit is taller and heavier than the average British recruit, and that after he has entered the Army he is healthier, spends less time in hospital, and has a lower death-rate.

. . . Lord Wolseley has recently expressed the opinion that the Army will never be "in a very satisfactory condition, until we pay our soldiers, at least, according to the current rate of wages given for unskilled labour." This implies that we are at present recruiting from the lowest grades of the labour market. His remedy—to pay a higher rate and so attract a higher grade—might, if it found favour with the Chancellor of the Exchequer, go a long way towards solving the recruiting difficulty. But it would do nothing to improve the national physique. On the contrary, it would tend to still further deterioration. Sir William Taylor deserves the thanks of the nation for having had the courage to ask the question, "If these men are unfit for military service, what are they good for?" Let it be remembered that the Army ought to be, and under the more enlightened administration of the present day is, to a large extent, a school of physical development. The whole system—the adequate diet, the gymnastics, even the barrack-yard drill will make a raw lad into a well-set up man, if only he possesses the constitution and framework. The splendid results obtained, under the direction of Colonel Fox, from most unpromising material are sufficient proof of this. If it is not worth while to take a lad for the Army where there is every facility for developing his physical organisation, must we not echo the question, What is he good for? No other employer of labour can be expected to take ill-grown, underfed lads, to feed them and put them through a course of physical drill, in the hope that in a year or so they will turn into robust workmen. He chooses with an eye to the present, not to the future; he wants a man to dig a ditch or handle freight to-day, not this time next year.

What becomes of the lads and young men unfit for the Army? Physically unable to do a good day's work, they must sink to the level of the most casual of casual labourers; drawing the lowest rate of wages when in work, and thrown out of work by the first depression of trade. Flung upon the streets they hang about the public-houses cadging for odd jobs. They marry early, girls as shiftless and physically unfit as themselves, bringing children into the world, of whom, without postulating any theory of hereditary degeneration, it may safely be asserted, looking to the conditions under which they are born and brought up, that they are not likely to be physically, intellectually, or morally superior to their parents.

. . . Even now statistics are not being collected systematically or on a large scale. None of the school boards seem to have taken any steps to obtain such statistics. The National Society for the Prevention of Cruelty to Children has obtained leave to make a beginning in London and Liverpool, and is endeavouring by measurements made out of school hours to establish a standard of height, weight, and other physical conditions. But the work ought to be done by the Education Authority itself. A partial inquiry would be practically useless; it must be general, and must take into account the differences of race, for that such difference exists, say between the English and the Welsh— the latter, though strong and healthy as a whole, being a smaller people—is well known. Then there is the comparative poverty of different districts, the average physical development being lower in the poorer districts. The inquiry must therefore embrace all classes of schools, in order, in the first place, that the statistics may be sufficiently large to furnish a general standard, and, in the second, to allow comparisons to be made between sections of the population living under different conditions. Mr Seebohm Rowntree has realised the necessity for this. In discussing some statistics which he had collected, he writes: "It would have been interesting had we been able to compare the weights and heights of the children with some national standard, but for the purposes of this inquiry such a standard would have been unreliable. The average heights and weights vary in different parts of the country, and consequently a comparison of results in two districts might be due to racial differences, and not to the nourishment and physical condition of the people."

It may be objected that this innovation would take time and labour, but, as a matter of fact, if the children were only weighed and measured, the school teachers could undertake the task with very little expenditure of time or trouble.

The information obtained would be far more valuable if observations on the chest girth, on the sight and hearing, and on the general aspect and health of the child were made also, and it is to be hoped that when the medical supervision of schools is made effective, as it is in Sweden, these additional facts will be recorded.

This system of weighing and measuring would, if carried out in all the classes in a town, present many advantages. In the first place, it would be a guide to the teachers in deciding whether children who appeared to be underfed received a sufficient amount of nourishment. If a child failed to increase in weight and height it would be presumptive evidence that it was not receiving sufficient food or was being subjected to some other injurious conditions at home. It is no doubt true that some children remain thin and undergrown no matter how much food they get, but this is the exception, and as a general rule slow development is not due to congenital weakness, but may be traced to improper feeding. If this duty of periodically weighing and measuring the children in their classes were imposed upon the teachers, it could not fail to increase their interest in the physical development of their pupils. Class teachers should be taught to consider it as much to their honour to have a class of well-grown, healthy boys or girls, as to succeed in passing some young prodigies through Standard VII. before they are 13. Sir John Gorst has offered the excellent suggestion that it should be "the duty of every class teacher to make such a daily inspection of the children in the class as an officer in the Army and Navy makes of the men under his charge, and to record and report anything abnormal—hunger, nakedness, dirt, or disease." Thus daily inspection, coupled with periodical weighings, would train the teachers to recognise early the first signs of failure in health, and would help them to become skillful in detecting the earliest signs of the acuter diseases. To watch the health of the children should, indeed, be considered one of the ordinary duties of a teacher, and skill and care in its performance ought, as Sir John Gorst has also suggested, to be reckoned among qualifications for promotion. In the second place, the body of statistics obtained would deal with a very large number of children, and if properly analysed by a skilled statistician, would yield averages which would supply the standard demanded by the second question propounded at the beginning of this chapter. Finally, the statistics would render it possible to make comparisons between the rate of physical development in different classes of the population, and would thus help us to answer the first question.

. . . The infantile mortality, a much more sensitive test of the public health, which is, at the same time, free from fallacies difficult to avoid in dealing with the total death-rate, reveals facts still more favourable to the rural districts.

The mortality among infants is given by the Registrar General in relation to the number of births registered. The table [below] shows the rates in recent years for the rural districts, for the smaller towns, for the great towns, and for the whole of England and Wales; but owing to the change in the classification of towns, the figures for the first two years are not directly comparable with those for the later period. It is, however, safe to assume that the fall in the rate for the great towns to be observed in the year (1902), when forty-three additional towns were included in that category, is in part due to the fact that in some of them the general conditions approach those of the smaller towns and rural districts:—

. . . It can hardly be necessary to prove that, without extreme care to neutralise influences obviously injurious to the growth of a sound mind in a healthy body, the conditions

Table of the Rates of Infant Mortality per 1,000 Births in the Whole of England and Wales, in the Greater and Smaller Towns, and in Rural Districts

	1900	*1901*	*1902*	*1903*
England and Wales	154	151	133	132
Great towns	172	165	145	144
Smaller towns	166	163	135	135
Rural	138	138	119	118

of life in towns must produce deterioration of the individual child. The richer classes recognise that even under the most favourable circumstances, in homes where everything that the most anxious thought and unstinted expenditure can provide, it is not well to keep children continuously in towns. The annual holiday is now in these classes very generally supplemented by the country cottage, and the boys, at least, are usually sent to boarding schools in the country. The children of the labouring classes do not enjoy these advantages; at best, with good luck, they may escape from the long unlovely streets for a fortnight in the year, while among the very poorest who live in the most crowded tenements in the worst districts, those are fortunate who can spend even one day in fresh air, among country sights and sounds—a day of days in their lives, which will enable them to understand the descriptions they may read in books of country joys.

. . . It has been proved beyond doubt that the influx of the rural populations into towns is increasing at an enormous rate; it has been equally proved that the death-rate, especially the infantile mortality, is much larger, proportionately, in towns than in the country. It is admitted that a large number of those infants not swept away by death, survive severely maimed and damaged from diseases generated by ignorant feeding, mismanagement, overcrowding, and other insanitary conditions. It follows of necessity that there is increasing physical deterioration of the population as a whole, although, to the shame of those responsible, there are no statistics to prove it in black and white.

The federation of Australia in 1901 came 50 years after Canada's confederation in 1867 and just a decade short of the federation of South Africa in 1910. This contemporary account of the passage of the bill that legislated for an Australian constitution captures the web of imperial relations that had created and would help sustain Australian federation. The comparison to Canada, the nature of the party political debate in the imperial parliament, the referendum on Western Australia and the Queen's Proclamation—taken together they remind us that this constitutional rearrangement did not just occur on the cusp of the old century, but bore traces of the Victorian as well as the "modern" zeitgeist.

On the Australian Constitution (1901)

INTRODUCTION OF THE BILL.—On 14th May, Mr. Chamberlain introduced the Commonwealth Bill into the House of Commons.

In introducing the Bill, Mr. Chamberlain said, to a crowded and enthusiastic House, that it marked an era in the history of Australia, and a great and important step towards the organization of the British Empire. This Bill—the result of the careful and prolonged labours of the ablest statesmen of Australia—enabled that great island continent to enter at once the widening circle of English-speaking nations. It would be in the interests of Australia, and also of the Empire, rendering the relations between the colonies and the motherland more cordial, more frequent, and more unrestricted. "Therefore we all of us—independently of party—welcome the new birth of which we are witnesses, and anticipate for these great, free, and progressive communities a future even more prosperous than the past, and an honourable and important position in the history of the Anglo-Saxon race."

... He contrasted the Constitution with that of Canada, and briefly outlined its provisions. ... The principles on which the Imperial Government had dealt with the Bill were these. They had accepted without demur, and they asked the House to accept, every word, every line, every clause, which dealt exclusively with the interests of Australia. But where the Bill touched the interests of the Empire as a whole, or of Her Majesty's subjects or possessions outside Australia, the Imperial Parliament occupied a position of trust which it was not the desire of the Empire—nor, he believed, of Australia—that they should fulfill in a formal or perfunctory manner. In accordance with these principles they had made some amendments; but they had refused—even at the desire of Western Australia and New Zealand—to make amendments where Imperial interests were not affected.

... Sir Henry Campbell-Bannerman, leader of the Opposition, expressed regret and disappointment that the Government had not felt themselves obliged to accept the Bill in its entirety. He thought that any proposed amendments should have been formulated and submitted to Australia at an earlier stage, and that Conferences and Memoranda in the Jubilee Year were not enough, in view of the many subsequent opportunities for intervention. The Government, by reserving action, had in effect, though not in intention, flouted Australia. He deprecated the conduct of the Government in going behind the opinions of the accredited representatives of Australia.

Mr. George Denison Faber, the new member for York, spoke of the appeal clauses from an experience of nine years as Registrar of the Privy Council. He pointed out that the nominal strength of the Privy Council was greater than that of the House of Lords; the real trouble was when both were sitting. He opposed amalgamation, but thought that the time had come for the establishment of a new Court altogether, and the appointment of more paid Judges. Sir Charles Dilke was glad that the substantial amendments had been reduced to two, and thought that Mr. Chamberlain had failed to show any vital necessity for amending the Bill. Mr. Vicary Gibbs spoke in favour of the amendments. Mr. Haldane saw no necessity for postponing the amalgamation of the Judicial Committee and the House of Lords; and urged that so long as the jurisdiction of the House of Lords was retained, it would be impossible to preserve the status of the Privy Council. Whilst there were two tribunals, one was starved to keep up the other, and judicial strength inevitably gravitated to the House of Lords. Mr. Stanley Leighton agreed that the objections to the present constitution of the Judicial Committee were well founded. The first reading was carried on the voices, with cheers.

SECOND READING OF THE BILL.—On 21st May, Mr. Chamberlain moved the second reading of the Bill in the House of Commons. ... With regard to Privy Council appeals, he reaffirmed the principle of non-interference with purely Australian interests, and vigilance for Imperial interests. He pointed out that clause 74 of the draft Constitution recognized this distinction by making an exception where "the public interests" of some part of Her Majesty's dominions outside Australia were involved; but the distinction did not go far enough. It was uncertain whether the phrase "public interests" would cover, for instance, the private interests of investors, or of any body of Her Majesty's subjects. Moreover, foreign relations were of equal importance with Imperial relations. The proposals of the Imperial Government had been before Australia for a week, and had been in most cases favourably considered. The Delegates, too, finding it impossible to carry out what they believed to be their mandate to secure the passage of the Bill without amendment, had been most considerate, and he had now arrived at an absolute agreement with four of them. He then read and explained the proposed new clause. With regard to the power of the Federal Parliament to limit the right of appeal, the Delegates had pointed out to him that a similar power was inherent in the Parliaments of the Australian colonies, subject to the reservation of the Bill exercising such power. Accordingly, it was proposed to grant this right to the Commonwealth, subject to an absolute statutory requirement that such Bills should be reserved.

Mr. Asquith, for the Opposition, expressed his gratification at Mr. Chamberlain's announcement of a settlement. He admitted the trusteeship of the Imperial Parliament, but thought that the danger of clause 74 had been exaggerated in some quarters. Mr. Henniker Heaton, Mr. Blake, Mr. James Bryce, and Mr. S. Evans joined in the congratulations. The Attorney-General expressed his appreciation of the tone of the debate, which was concluded by Mr. W. Redmond and Mr. T. M. Healy declaring, on behalf of Ireland, their envy at the rights of self-government accorded to Australia. The Bill was then read a second time with cheers, and taken into Committee *pro forma*.

AUSTRALIAN CRITICISMS.—In Australia, however, the suggested compromise was received, first with hesitation, and then with distinct disapproval, both the drafting and the policy of the new clause being condemned. On 24th May, a telegram seems to have been sent by the Government of New South Wales to Mr. Chamberlain, indicating acceptance of the arrangement by the Premiers; but a study of the cabled text of the clause changed the situation. In Queensland, Sir Samuel Griffith pointed out that the provision that no constitutional question should be "capable of final decision except by the High Court" was a clumsy and inaccurate mode of saying that all appeals in such cases should be brought to the High Court alone. He also argued that this would be a restriction, and not an extension, of the right of appeal to the Privy Council given by the original clause—under which he contended that appeals, even in constitutional cases, would lie from the State Courts direct to the Privy Council.

. . . THE FINAL COMPROMISE.— . . . Mr. Chamberlain, in consultation with the Delegates, had at last resolved to make this further concession, and to offer clause 74 in the form in which it now stands in the Constitution. This was gladly accepted by the Delegates, including Mr. Dickson. The Queensland Government withdrew their protest, and offered no objection. The Government of Victoria expressed approval of the clause as altered; and the Government of South Australia, while reiterating their inability to accept any amendment, telegraphed that they did not anticipate any difficulty from the amendment now proposed. The Government of Western Australia telegraphed that the new proposal was preferable to the previous one, but that they would have preferred an appeal as a right, without leave. In New South Wales—the only colony in which Parliament was then sitting—the Government submitted to both Houses a resolution affirming that the amendment now proposed was not such an important departure from the original Bill as would justify any action which would further delay Federation. This was carried without division in the Assembly on 21st June, and in the Council on 27th June.

THE ROYAL ASSENT.—On 9th July, the Queen gave her assent to the Bill. At the request of the Delegates, Her Majesty signed the Commission, declaring her assent to the Bill, in duplicate, and gave Mr. Barton one of the copies, as well as the pen, inkstand, and table used by Her Majesty, to be preserved in the Federal Parliament Buildings. On the same day, in the House of Lords, the House of Commons having been summoned to the bar, the Lords Commissioners (the Earl of Halsbury, the Earl of Hopetoun, and the Earl of Kintore), announced the Royal assent to the Bill, which was received with cheers.

THE ROYAL PROCLAMATION.—The issue of the Queen's Proclamation fixing the day for the establishment of the Commonwealth had been withheld pending the issue of the referendum in Western Australia, in order to enable her Majesty to be "satisfied that the people of Western Australia have agreed" to join the Commonwealth. Meanwhile some telegraphic communications passed between the Imperial and Colonial Governments as to the date on which the Commonwealth should be established. The prevailing opinion was in favour of the 1st January, 1901, the first day of the twentieth century—a dramatic and significant date for the birth of Australian nationhood. The sentimental argument was reinforced by the practical one that the 1st January was the beginning of a financial half-year in all the colonies. On the other hand there was some advocacy of the 26th January—the anniversary of the foundation of New South Wales in 1788—which was celebrated in several of the colonies as the patriotic festival of the year. The date chosen was the 1st January; accordingly, on 17th September, 1900, the Queen signed the Proclamation declaring that on and after the first day of January, 1901, the people of New South Wales, Victoria, South Australia, Queensland, Tasmania, and Western Australia should be united in a Federal Commonwealth under the name of the Commonwealth of Australia.

Thus all the five colonies of the mainland of Australia, and also the adjacent island of Tasmania, become Original States of the Commonwealth which is to be inaugurated on the first day of the twentieth century. The Commonwealth, as few dared to hope it would, comes into existence complete from the first—"a nation for a continent, and a continent for a nation." The delays at which federalists have chafed have been tedious, and perhaps dangerous, but they have been providential; they have given time for the gradual but sure development of the national spirit in the great colonies of Queensland and Western Australia, and have prevented the establishment of a Commonwealth of Australia with half the continent of Australia left, for a time, outside.

But though Australian union has been completed, Australasian union has not. New Zealand—separated from Australia by 1,200 miles of sea, and correspondingly more self-contained and less in touch with the national sentiment of Australia—has not yet decided to enter the Commonwealth. The choice between union or isolation, which has not yet been directly presented to the people of New Zealand, cannot long be deferred. On 19th October, 1900, a resolution was passed by the New Zealand House of Representatives, on Mr. Seddon's motion, declaring it to be desirable (*a*) That a Royal Commission should be appointed to inquire into and report upon the desirability or otherwise of New Zealand becoming a State of the Commonwealth: (*b*) that if the Commissioners deem Federation for the present inadvisable or premature, they should report as to the establishment of a reciprocal treaty between the Commonwealth and New Zealand, and indicate the lines on which it should be based: (*c*) that the Commissioners entrusted with this all-important matter, affecting the national life and well-being of New Zealand, should be conversant with the agricultural, commercial, and industrial interests of the colony, and be otherwise eminently fitted for their high office: (*d*) that they should be empowered to proceed to Australia to take evidence: and (*e*) that their report should be presented to the New Zealand Parliament within ten days of the opening of the next session.

CONCLUSION.—During the past century the foundations of Australian nationhood have been laid; with the new century will begin the task of building the superstructure.

Political barriers have been broken down, and the constitutional compact which, politically speaking, creates the Australian people, has been framed, accepted, and established. But all this is only the beginning. The new national institutions of Australia have to be tested in the fire of experience; provincial jealousies have to be obliterated; national sentiment has to be consolidated; the fields of national legislation and national administration have to be occupied. Australian statesmanship and patriotism, which have proved equal to the task of constructing the Constitution, and of creating a new nation within the Empire, are now face to face with the greater and more responsible task of welding into a harmonious whole the elements of national unity, and of guiding the Australian people to their destiny—a destiny which, it may be hoped, will always be linked with that of the mighty Empire of which they form a part.

Rosa Campbell Praed (1851–1935) was a novelist and author of more than 40 books who went from the Australian outback to the London literary world when she moved to England with her husband in 1876. In this excerpt from her novel *Fugitive Anne*, she offers a fictional account of the encounter between an Aboriginal boy and a white girl who, masquerading as a lascar (seaman), seeks emancipation from the trappings of white bourgeois colonial life because (as she says elsewhere in the novel) "I am a Bush girl to the bones of me."

Rosa Campbell Praed,
from *Fugitive Anne: A Romance of the Unexplored Bush* (1902)

Black Boy and Lascar

A BLACK boy and a young Lascar were trudging along a rough track in the Bush, some distance from the coast—a track that could hardly be called a road; it had been made by the wool-drays coming in from a far-off Western station. The traffic was at all times small, and now the way seemed lonely and quite deserted, for the shearing season had barely begun, therefore the ruts and bog-holes made by the last bullock team which had trodden it, had already become grass-grown.

Both black-boy and Lascar were dressed according to their kind, the latter more fully than is customary among Indians and Malays in Australia, though his garments were wholly inappropriate to foot travelling in the Bush, and were torn in many places, stained with mud, and draggled and limp from the heavy dews. His small, lithe form was pretty well covered by a voluminous sarong, and only a small portion of brown ankle showed between it and his boots, while the upper part of the body was clothed by a sort of tunic in cotton, beneath the outer muslin drapery, which even hung over his arms. He wore a muslin turban twisted round his head, set far forward, and with loose ends, that, from a side view, almost hid his face. He trudged wearily, with a blue blanket strapped upon his shoulders, which seemed scarcely large enough for its weight. Indeed, he was so small and slender as to look hardly more than a child.

The black-boy, larger and more muscular than the ordinary native, seemed to have been a station hand employed by white men. Round the open collar of his Crimean shirt was a red handkerchief, neatly folded sailor-wise, above which his neck showed brawny and black. His trousers were of good material and cut, though they hung loosely, and were turned up in a big roll overlapping the tops of the boots. They had evidently been made for a gentleman, and indeed, any one acquainted with the wardrobe of Mr Elias Bedo might have recognised the garments as having been once his property. They were held up by a strap, from which hung several pouches, a knife, a tomahawk, and sundry articles of miscellaneous use. Round his Jim Crow hat a puggaree was twisted, and he bore on his back a very large swag.

The two had just struck the main road, having made their way across country, through scrub and over creeks, to a point whence a small digging township might be reached without difficulty. The direct dray road to this township branched off some distance back, but, from the present point, the diggings lay as at the apex of a triangle, and a miner's rude track led to it through the Bush. Presently, on the crest of a ridge in front of them, the black boy's quick eyes discerned two or three men on foot, also humping their swags. He knew that they were probably diggers, and this was the signal for him to call to his companion, who lagged a little, and to strike sideways into the Bush. They soon got behind another low ridge, and walked on in the direction they wished to go, but out of sight of the track. By-and-by, the black boy stopped, looked up at the sun, and peered around. Then he laid down his pack, while he made certain observations usual with the Australian native when he is not quite sure of his whereabouts. Presently, he gave a click of satisfaction with his tongue and teeth, and re-shouldered his swag, beckoning to the Lascar.

"That all right. Mine soon find—im old sheep-station, I b'lieve. Come along now; we go look for water-hole."

The Lascar, who had sunk down upon a log, and was idly plucking and smelling some gum-leaves from a young shoot which sprouted near, rose, and again followed the native guide.

"That all right," the black repeated. "Mine think-it we sit down along-a shepherd's humpey very soon now."

The Lascar nodded and smiled, and trudged on again with a springier step than before.

They went silently through a stretch of gum-forest, wild and utterly dreary. The great uncouth trees rose above them, stretching overhead a latticework of stems, vertical rather than horizontal, and giving little shade. The limbs of the iron-barks were rough and knotted, with perhaps a stalactite of gum, red as blood, dropping here and there from some wound or abrasion on their surface, and were hung with long withes of green-grey moss that gave them a strange look of hoary antiquity. The arms of the white gums were smooth and ghostly white. They had but little foliage, and flapped shreds of pale papery bark that fell from them like tattered garments. Among the gums, there might be seen an occasional wattle, long past blossom, or a weird-looking grass-tree with its jaggled tuft of grey-green blades, thin and unleaflike, and its dark spear as long as the rest of its body. All was dull green-grey, arid and shadeless, from the thin leaves of the gum-trees to the tussocks of coarse grass and prickly spinnifex. These often hurt the bare ankles of the young Lascar, and he would give a little cry, instantly stifled, and then would tramp bravely on.

The Bush sounds only seemed to intensify the loneliness. It was getting towards midday, and most of the birds were silent. Those that were awake, had discordant notes, and were mostly of the parrot kind. They chattered shrilly, their harsh cries rising above the tinny whizz of myriads of new-fledged locusts, whose cast-off husks made odd shining blobs on the trunks of the trees. Now and then, the black boy ahead would call to his mate, and point to where a herd of kangaroos were disappearing in ungainly bounds through the tangled gum vistas. Sometimes an iguana would scuttle through the under-growth, or the boy would stop and tremble for a moment at the treacherous rustle of a startled snake.

About dinner-time, the appearance of the country changed, and the stony ridges, covered chiefly with mournful brigalow scrub, gave place to a less timbered plain. The sun poured on them as they traversed it, and more than once the Lascar took a pull at his water-bag. But far in the distance their goal could be discerned. This was a dim belt of denser vegetation; and as they came closer, they saw a fringe of almost tropical green-ery—great scrub-trees, and river-palms, and luxuriant creepers.

Here was the deserted sheep-station of which the black boy had spoken. It stood on the borders of a plain, close to a water-hole, which could be seen in a clearing that had been made in a patch of scrub. The grass upon the old sheep-yard was bright-green; there were still some straggling pumpkin plants, and a rosella shrub almost choked with weeds. Broken hurdles lay around, and close to the clearing was a dilapidated hut. The travellers made their way through vines and weeds, and entered the hut by an aperture, where the slab door hung back on broken hinges. Inside was a plank table, nailed to two stumps set in the earthen floor. Another plank, also supported by two lower stumps, served as a bench on one side of the table, and a slab bunk was set opposite against the wall. The Lascar sat down on the bunk, heaving a weary sigh of satisfaction at having found rest at last. Then he took off his pack, unrolled the blankets, and spread them on the bunk, making a bed on which he stretched himself. The black boy undid his swag too—it was much larger and heavier—and seated himself on the table, grinning benev-olently at his companion.

"Bûjeri you, Missa Anne!"—the Blacks' commendatory formula. "Ba'al mine think-it you able to walk that long way. You very fine boy, Missa Anne." And Kombo gave a peal of laughter as he eyed the transformed woman.

Anne laughed too. In their keen sense of humour, she and Kombo were at one. It is the redeeming quality of even the most demoralised township black. She tore off the be-spattered turban which had covered her head, and showed a short crop of soft hair—dark, but not dark enough to accord with her pretended nationality. Never did Singalese or Malay possess locks so fine and feathery. There did not now seem much of the Lascar in the little brown face, oval of shape, with its delicate aquiline nose, its small, pointed chin, and pretty, finely-curved lips. The eyes were dark-brown, very velvety, with curly lashes and straight, pencilled brows. Only in the hue of her skin, was the girl a Lascar; and how Anne Bedo had contrived, during the hours of her last night on the steamer, to stain her-self the colour of a half-caste, was a mystery only known to herself and to Kombo, who had got the materials from a black medicine man in Thursday Island.

The girl's white teeth shone, as she laughed, between her red lips. Her weariness seemed to have gone; at this moment she only thought of the liberty bought, it seemed to her, so easily. For Anne Marley, in her Bush girlhood, had loved adventure, had been familiar with the Blacks and their ways, had known Kombo since her tenth year, and now alone with him in the wilds, felt no fear.

She got up from the bunk and looked down at her soiled muslin draperies—so un-suited to the life she had been leading during the last few days—and at the tattered sarong, between the rents of which a woman's longcloth under-petticoat could be seen.

She put out her slender feet, cased in laced boots, which had been originally made for them, and therefore had not galled the poor little stockingless extremities. She contemplated ruefully the scratches on her ankles, over which the blood had dried and caked with the dust of the Bush, and gave a very feminine shudder.

"Kombo, I'm dreadfully dirty. I want to bathe. Find me a place in the water-hole where I can have a swim."

Kombo shook his head. "Mine think-it alligator sit down there, Missa Anne."

The girl shuddered again.

"Well, let us have something to eat first. We'll see what the place is like when we go to get water for the billy. Now let us find some sticks and make a fire. Quick—Murra, make haste, Kombo. Poor fellow me plenty hungry. Give me the ration bags. Go cut me a sheet of bark, and I'll make a damper on it."

Kombo unstrapped his swag, which turned out to be two separate bundles, each rolled in a blanket, and both together enclosed in another blanket. From the dirtiest of the two—that which presumably held his own property—he produced some ration bags containing flour, tea, and sugar. These he set on the table, and then unfastened a blackened billy, and two pint pots which hung at his waist.

Anne laid hands on the other bundle, and carrying it to the bunk, undid it, gloating, like the girl she was, over certain feminine appurtenances, to which for several days she had been a stranger. Certainly, she had combed her short hair and washed her face, but that was the only sort of toilet she had made. Their one idea had been to push on, in order that as much ground as possible might lie between them and the possibility of recapture. So they had slept but for an hour or two at a time, for the first day and night, and had only breathed freely since yesterday. A bundle of pocket-handkerchiefs, a change of linen, a grey riding-skirt and jacket, with a crushable cap, a few toilet requisites, pencils and paper, needles and cottons, and some other necessaries, made up all the baggage which Anne Bedo had brought away from the steamer. It had not been easy to take more, and even now she dreaded lest her husband should discover that the garments were missing, and so guess that she had planned her escape. Round her neck, beneath her tunic, she wore a locket containing the portraits of her mother and sister, and also a little bag in which was all her worldly wealth in the way of money.

Kombo went out to find sticks, and make a fire in the bark lean-to which the shepherd had used for a kitchen. Anne lingered in the hut. She had taken a little note-book out of her pack, in which were a few entries—the date of their departure from England, an address or two, and the list of her boxes on the steamer. The last entry had been a memorandum concerning prices of cattle which her husband had desired her to make on Thursday Island. The sight of it brought home to her the reality of her present situation. She turned the page, and, with the pencil attached to the book, scribbled sentences one after the other, with no regard to composition, as a mere vent for the wild joy that possessed her in the thought that she was safe from Elias Bedo, and free henceforward to live her own life.

"Anne Marley, escaped from bondage, rejoices in her liberty."

"Better death in the wild woods than life in chains."

"Anne Marley hails Nature, the emancipator."

"How sweet is the taste of freedom! How intoxicating the joy of deliverance!"

And so on, till the page was covered. Anne looked at her scribblings with the naughty pleasure of a child which has amused itself out of school hours by scrawling over a clean copy-book. It was a very silly ebullition of feeling, which she had cause to regret later.

Vida Goldstein (1869–1949) was one of a trio of women (Bessie Rischbeith and Alice Henry being the other two) who professed to represent Australian feminism at the turn of the century. Goldstein traveled widely, including a trip to the United States to attend the International Women's Suffrage Conference in Washington, D.C. in 1902 and an invited tour of Britain sponsored by the Women's Social and Political Union in 1911. Below she recaps the achievements of women's suffrage workers in Australia and beyond in an effort to locate her own senate candidature in Victoria just two years after the first Australian parliament voted to enfranchise white women.

Vida Goldstein on her Senate Candidature (1904)

"The world moves slowly, my masters!" woman's world especially; but it does move, and that's something to be thankful for. It took a big step forward on April 24th, 1902, when the first Australian Parliament enfranchised the women of this great continent; it took another on December 16th, 1903, when, for the first time in the world's history, the women of a nation took part in the making of a National Parliament. For many years past women have exercised political power in various directions in most countries possessing some form of representative government. In England, Sweden and Norway, women have school and municipal suffrage; in the United States they have school suffrage in twenty-five States, municipal suffrage in one, and full suffrage in four; in Australia they have school and municipal suffrage in every State, parliamentary suffrage in four, and national suffrage in all States. In 1900 the women of South Australia and Western Australia voted in the Federal elections, because, according to the Federal Constitution Act, the electors in any State could not be deprived of any rights they possessed when the Commonwealth was created, and the women of these two States already possessed the State franchise. But last December was the first occasion on which the women of a whole nation wielded power in national affairs, even to the extent of running three women candidates—two for the State of New South Wales (Mrs. Martell and Mrs. Moore), one for Victoria (myself).

All the world will be wondering how the experiment answered—what exactly was the result of this bold recognition of the principle of democracy—government by the people—in the political affairs of a continent. It is a little unfortunate for the purposes of this article that, owing to the vast area covered by the operations of the Federal Electoral Act, with its provisions for voting by post, the final figures as to the number of electors who voted are not yet available, but it may be said at once that sufficient is known to enable me to make the statement that the women voted in as large numbers, proportionately, as the men. The statement is not so exhilarating as it sounds, for a very small number of the men recorded their votes. The progress returns show that, of the 1,700,000 voters on the electoral rolls, only 900,000 went to the poll, and of these 40,077 cast informal votes—a small percentage, however, considering that nearly half the electors were absolutely inexperienced in voting, and that a large number of the invalid votes were made through no fault of the voters, but through some of the returning officers marking the papers incorrectly. That only 52 per cent of the Federal electors voted must be a sad disappointment to the leading Federation apostles, the Prime Minister, Mr. Deakin, and the leader of the Opposition, Mr. G. H. Reid. Mr. Reid has already expressed something more than disappointment on the subject. As reported in "The Argus," of January 1st, Mr. Reid, speaking in Perth, severely censured the electors for their political apathy. "What words," he asked, "could be too strong in condemnation of that dense mass of individual voters, who had not shown a single principle of public policy strong enough to incur the slight inconvenience of recording their votes? It was one of the most ominous features of our new national life that such a dense, inert mass existed. It was one of the worst features of their public life that men who were supposed to represent enterprise in the highest form, who were supposed to be gifted with intelligence and education to a high extent, were the very men who never seemed capable of public spirit except when their own miserable personal interests were concerned."

Although I share Mr. Reid's disappointment, the small vote at this and also at the last Federal election, did not surprise me. Ever since I have taken an active part in social and political affairs, I have had reason to deplore the lack of public spirit among the Australian people. Lacking public spirit, they lack also the true national spirit. The people as a whole have not grasped even the faintest idea of the principle of nationhood. Again I say, I am not surprised. It is only emphatic proof of what I have maintained, what all women suffragists have maintained, in the struggle to secure the right of suffrage, that public-spirited citizens are not born of unpublic-spirited mothers. The people of a country are just what the mothers make them, and mothers who have no civic responsibilities cannot be expected to teach the political idea how to shoot—not knowing the duties of citizenship, how can they teach them to others? We have only just sown the seed of a true Australian public spirit; we must wait many years before we see the fruit. Politics at present are more or less personal. Most men are in politics not for their country's welfare, but for their own, and the mothers of Australia have a huge task ahead of them in endeavouring to teach their children, the citizens of the future, that national welfare means individual welfare, and is a nobler ideal than personal welfare.

But to get back to the elections themselves. How did the women who voted vote? The opponents of women suffrage have always harped on two tuneless, clanging strings—women would be degraded by going to the polls; women would be swayed by personal predilections rather than by political reasons in the selection of candidates. The lie direct was given to both these assertions at the elections. Women were not degraded, because there is nothing about a polling booth to degrade either man or woman—going to record one's vote is nothing like so objectionable as elbowing all sorts and conditions of men in a scramble for tickets for a theatre, or a Melba concert, or the races. As for the other assertion, the suffrage opponents were generous enough to admit that the women showed more political discrimination and knew more about the whole business than the men did.

All through the campaign it was amusing to see how persistently the rabid anti-suffragists wooed the political affections of the women. Before the suffrage was granted to the women these gentlemen said that women could not fail to be degraded by taking part in politics. Now they talk grandiloquently about the refining, elevating influence of women in the political arena, and urge them to perform the sacred duty of voting—"for us." It is more than satisfactory to note that the anti-suffrage candidates, of whom there were only a handful, were either defeated through the women's vote, or else had their previous large majorities turned into very small majorities. Where successful, the influence of money and social position carried them through. The attitude of men on the suffrage question is a fairly accurate test of their feelings towards other questions in which women are specially interested. A large number of women recognised this and voted accordingly. As the members of the Legislative Council who have hitherto opposed the passing of the Women's State Franchise Bill took good care that their women folk voted for the "Argus" Four, it is to be presumed that the next time the Bill comes before them they will vote for it.

It speaks well for the future development of the political woman in Australia that so many women did take the trouble to go to the poll, for practically nothing has been done in organising the Federal vote until the formation of the Women's Federal Political Association a few months before the elections. The fight for State Suffrage was prolonged until the action of the Irvine Government in abandoning the principle at the behest of the Legislative Council members in the conference between the two Houses over the Constitution Reform Bill, made it impossible for us to get the State franchise during the life of the present State Parliament. The time left for Federal organisation was so brief that the wonder is the women polled so largely. It shows that the long agitation for State suffrage has had good results in educating a considerable section of the women in their public responsibilities.

A word of praise must be paid to the women's branches of the Political Labour League for the activity they displayed during the campaign. When the movement was first started to organise the women's vote in Victoria, which resulted in the formation of the Women's Federal Political Association, it was hoped that the women of all classes would agree to differ on questions of party politics and work together, first and foremost, in the interests of women and children, of industrial peace, and financial stability. If members held strong party views they would be free to join existing party organisations—Free Trade or Protectionist, Labour or anti-Labour. But unfortunately a number of women with pronounced Labour convictions resolved to dissociate themselves from the Women's Federal Political Association and organise wholly on labour lines. Miss Lilian Locke, formerly secretary of the United Council for Women's Suffrage, was appointed organising secretary of a Women's branch of the Political Labour Council, and worked hard in the Labour interests. Although I regret that the broad basis of the Women's Federal Political Association is not acceptable to Labour women, I rejoice to see women organising on any lines, even on Conservative lines, for organisation means education and enlarged interests, and I would sooner see women educated in views diametrically opposed to mine than not educated at all, and displaying the too prevalent apathy and indifference to important social and political questions.

. . . As soon as my candidature was announced the enemy prophesied a physical breakdown, and humiliating insults from men at my meetings. From all accounts I stood the racket of the campaign better than most of the candidates. After one month's work the voices of many were tattered and torn; mine was as fresh and clear the night before the battle as it was when I started skirmishing three months previously. As for insults, I had not the semblance of one offered me until two nights before the election, when addressing an audience of 1200 people at the Fitzroy Town Hall. At the conclusion of my address the chairman called for questions. A man standing near the platform handed up three written questions, which the chairman passed to me. I read them, found them to be deliberate insults, and said, "These questions are insults, and I refuse to answer them." Immediately every man in that vast audience rose to his feet and shouted, "Throw him out! the cur! Insult a woman! The hound! Chuck him out!" Seeing that the man was likely to be roughly treated, I held up my hand; the tumult ceased in a moment. "Please do nothing further—the gentleman"—indignant cries, "The gentleman?" "No, not the gentleman—the elector." "The elector showed he had some fine feeling left by putting the questions in writing. You have shown him what you think of him—please let the matter end there." Had I not made this appeal the man would have had the worst quarter of an hour he had ever known. I have mentioned this incident simply to prove to those who fear that women will be insulted when they aspire to enter the political arena that a body of men can always be trusted to protect women against insult.

The chief lesson to be learned from the elections is the necessity for organisation. The Labour Party was the best organised party, and their success proves what enthusiasm for a cause will accomplish. To my mind the woman's cause—and after all "the woman's cause is man's"—is deserving of as much enthusiasm as the Labour cause. Indeed, I believe the two are closely allied. The Labour cause in its widest sense is the cause of humanity, so is the woman's cause; but Labour seeks to reach the goal mainly by material means; women, having due regard for the material, place a higher value on the spiritual. As we women of Australia proceed with out work of political education, studying the principles at the base of all legislation dealing with our social, domestic, industrial and international relations, we shall assuredly come to the point when we shall see that it is righteousness alone that exalteth a nation.

Arnold White (1848–1925) was a one-time coffee-planter in Ceylon who wrote extensively on social problems in the 1880s and 1890s. He was preoccupied with what he called "the cult of infirmity" and the role of "alien immigrants," especially Jews, as threats to the racial purity of late-Victorian society. After a number of failed attempts at parliamentary electoral campaigns (1886, 1892, 1895), White turned to journalism as a full-time career. In his quest to address the "problem" of Jewish emigration, he traveled to Russia to try to persuade the Tsar to support a colonization scheme for Jews in Argentina. He also testified before the Royal Commission on Alien Immigration, which eventuated in the Alien Immigration Act of 1905.

Arnold White, "The Alien Immigrant" (1903)

The Government are much to be congratulated, therefore, in our opinion, on having appointed a Royal Commission to investigate alien immigration, under the experienced presidency of Lord James of Hereford. They have secured impartiality by giving the Jews an unimpeachable representative in Lord Rothschild, while an active M.P. like Major Evans-Gordon looks after the native interests of the East End. . . .

Without attempting to anticipate the Report, we may do good service to this important Commission by summarising facts brought before them which have hitherto lurked obscurely upon the back pages of the daily press. They have failed, as was to be expected, in gaining an exact idea of the extent of the yearly invasion. This is a country of unexamined passengers as well as of untaxed commerce, and Mr Llewelyn Smith, of the Statistical Department of the Board of Trade, can only assert that, during the past twelvemonth, as regarded the movement of passengers between the United Kingdom and Europe there was an excess inwards of 89,000 persons. Very many of them, no doubt, must have gone on to America after a stay of a few days or weeks. . . . The local authorities have, at any rate, to deal with 135,377 foreigners in the area of the County of London. No less than 54,310 of them, as Mr Reginald Macleod, the Registrar-General, explains, are herded together in Stepney, giving a proportion of about 18.2 per cent to the whole population. Mr Shirley Murphy, Medical Officer of Health of the London County, goes into further and more disquieting detail. Of the four sanitary areas comprised in the Borough of Stepney, Whitechapel has witnessed an increase of the alien element from 24.1 per cent to 31.08 per cent between 1891 and 1901; St George's-in-the-East gives figures during the same period rising from 16.2 to 28.8; in Limehouse they were 2.1 and 3.7; in Mile-end Old Town they were 5.3 as against 18.2. Yet in Southwark hard by, a densely packed working-class quarter, the relations for the ten years are merely as 0.7 to 0.8. Westminster contains 11,831 foreigners, and St Pancras 8,456,—totals by no means surprising when the wide dispersion of the French, German, and Italian elements is remembered. Still alien immigration virtually resolves itself into an infliction in the East End; and its meaning to the East End can be grasped from the simple calculation that, though the whole population has only increased by 13,000 since the census of 1891, the foreigners have been augmented during the same period by 22,000. The displacement of native-born must, in other words, have been prodigious, more especially as it has been increased by the devotion of land formerly occupied by dwelling-houses to commercial purposes. Yet the Polish Jew occupies and replenishes Whitechapel and St George's-in-the East.

The evidence before the Commission, if candidly studied, will remove some prejudices and dissipate some apprehensions concerning these irrepressible immigrants. Uncleanly though they may be,—and certain of the foreign steamship companies appear to consider washing and ventilation as unattainable luxuries,—they are not accused by medical officers of health of bringing epidemics with them. Dr Tyrrell, of the Royal Ophthalmic Hospital, asserts, indeed, that cases of trachoma, a contagious disease of the eyes which is largely a disease of the Jewish race, are beginning to be localised in London, after the patients have been rejected by the United States. It would be unfair, however, to construct a plague-scare out of various unsavoury admissions, the general conclusion being that the owners of vessels are exercising more supervision over their passengers than was the case some nine or ten years ago. Once established in Whitechapel or St George's-in-the-East, the "Polak" also undeniably develops by degrees various civic virtues. He begins, after a bit, to comply according to his limited lights with what he regards as the unreasonable requirements of the sanitary authorities. Abstemious by choice as well as necessity, he avoids many of the British vices, while succumbing to the passion for gain in the form of gambling. Subdivisional Inspector Hyder asserts, with the police-court reports to confirm him, that he has never known a gaming-house that has not been kept by a foreigner, and that those nuisances increase with the increase of the alien element. Illicit stills—another secretive source of profit—are worked entirely by foreigners, though many of them have become naturalised. . . .

If the argument of "England for the English" carries any weight at all, the intrusion of a compact alien element into the heart of London cannot be considered, at the same time, other than a calamity. Its eviction of the former inhabitants is best considered in connection with overcrowding. There remains another grievance nearly as formidable, that, from the shopkeepers down to the earners of precarious wages, it is driving out all native competition. The Jews will only deal with their own people, even though they get thereby a much inferior article. A witness, who as an insurance agent should know, declares that of 267 shops in the Commercial Road, 142 are occupied by aliens, evidently meaning persons with foreign names. This exclusiveness is, of course, enjoined by the Hebrew religion in the case of "Kosher" meat. But in walks of life requiring less capital the stress of Hebrew tenacity makes itself still more severely felt. Mr Blake, ex-president of the Costermongers' Federation of Great Britain, complains that foreigners will not "play the game fair"; and he embraces in a sweeping malediction both Jews and Italians. They decline to recognise the sanctity of the "pitch," but will rise before dawn to oust an old occupant who has worked up a connection. They bring the local authorities down on the trade by obstinately sticking to prohibited spots, often feigning an ignorance of English. Mr Blake, we note, is absolutely borne out in this last accusation by Chief-Superintendent Mulvaney. Of the persons summoned for obstructing the roadway last year, 74 were British and 375 foreigners; for the early months of this year the record is 13 British and 16 foreigners. And throughout the East End there rises the same bitter cry—that the pauper alien has intensified tenfold the struggle for existence. Much of this testimony comes, no doubt, from those who have been beaten by economic or personal accident. Did not Carlyle lament in the 'Latter-Day Pamphlets' the piteous case of Mr Jopling of Reading, an imaginary upholsterer and paperhanger, who, having stocked his shop, found that the railways had taken away his customers? Such wreckage there must be as social conditions change. The Commission had before them an even sadder and equally irremediable failure, that of a blind piano-tuner whose patrons had been scattered over London by the impact of the alien.

. . . The pauper alien, as the Commission are pretty safe to explain on his behalf, cannot be called a pauper in the sense that he comes on the rates. The total number of foreigners relieved by the Poor Law authorities averages at 2000 a-year for the whole of London, and only half of this small number are described as Russian or Polish. They have frequent recourse to medical assistance at the ratepayers' expense, and that on the most trumpery pretexts. But the admirably managed Jewish charities provide, on the whole, for the wants of the necessitous. How far those institutions act as a magnet to the Russian Pale and the Ghettos of Poland must be an open question: all charity tends to create poverty as well as to cure it. At least they encourage self-help, and not unfrequently repatriate the worthless. The ratepayers' chief grievance consists, however, in the sums which are spent, often ineffectually, in attempting to enforce the sanitary and factory laws. Mr Belcher's revelations before the Commission of the state of affairs in Stepney, where he is municipal councillor, can only be received with blank astonishment. In one case twenty-seven foreigners were discovered working in two small rooms, with mattresses all round, and their food was black bread and coffee. In a second twenty-one women toiled in a kitchen 16 feet by 12 feet and 7 feet high, beds being all round the room; their food black bread and coffee, and their pay 8d. or 9d. a-week. In a third, three beds were found in a cellar, with eleven people sleeping in them, yet the place was quite unventilated. Such kennels would annihilate English people, but Russian and Polish Jews contrive to exist and even to increase in them. Mr Shirley Murphy shows that the death-rate for Stepney has declined, in spite of overcrowding, from 25 per thousand between 1886 and 1890 to 23.82 per thousand between 1896 to 1900. Stepney, as a whole, returned an increased birth-rate at the last census, the largest rise being in Whitechapel and St George's-in-the-East; but in London generally it fell. Even a crammed street like Bell Lane had much less than the usual amount of infant mortality. The wiriness of the race renders it exempt from consumption, the usual companion of overcrowding; it safeguards itself with hereditary science against disease; through its abstemiousness it begets healthy children, and the mothers look after them at home instead of packing off to factories. That, in brief, is the clue to the survival of the least fit, from the recruiting-sergeant's point of view, in an acute contest for existence. Even if immigration ceased altogether to-morrow, the denationalisation of the East End would continue until, as we might hope, with increase of comfort, came a decrease of improvident marriages.

Mr Shirley Murphy roundly contends that in Stepney 8300 Englishmen have been displaced by 22,000 foreigners within the last ten years. In other words, Jewish landlords gamble in house property, and then look to making their profits by breaking the law as to the number of tenants they may admit. They have certainly put up the rents as well,— thus tenements formerly let at 13s. or 14s. a-week are now fetching as much as 23s., 27s., and 30s. Some of this enhanced value must be due to clearances for railway purposes, and to the rise of large factories. Not the whole of it, however, since the census returns establish that between 1891 and 1901 the population of the western district of St George's did not dwindle, though the number of houses largely decreased; and that the proportion of natives to aliens in the former year—10,000 to 2000—was exactly reversed in the latter. Thus overcrowding on the spot has obviously been accompanied by an overflow into the neighbouring slums. Looked at in other ways, the phenomenon may be interpreted to mean that 107 streets are occupied by foreigners which had native tenants six years ago: in a single locality, Albert Square, where from thirty-eight to forty houses used to be inhabited by Englishmen, there is now left but a single English family. In this instance again the evicted have evidently been forced to seek shelter elsewhere. The decisiveness for the foreign influx becomes the more undeniable when we remember that, against the diminution of the number of houses in some parts of the East End, in others two-storeyed buildings have been replaced by lofty model dwellings which accommodate many more than have been displaced. Yet the human saturation spreads laterally—ascends and descends. The growing resort to underground rooms, both for living and working, is a most evil sign, for the habits of the primitive troglodyte cannot be reproduced in the heart of a city without serious peril to the whole community.

The federation of Australia renewed public debate about the pros and cons of all manner of imperial relationships. In this essay for the *Contemporary Review*, E. Farrer sketches the realities—costs and benefits—of Canada's relationship to Britain and its empire with special attention to the Canadian manufacturer and the question of preferential tariffs.

E. Farrer, "Canada and the New Imperialism" (1903)

In discussing the relations, existing or proposed, between England and her Colonies, Englishmen are apt to take for granted that the people of the Colonies are Englishmen like themselves, an error which probably accounts for their frequent inability to understand the Colonial attitude on such questions.

. . . Let us turn for a moment to the case of English Canada. . . . In early days British-born settlers, old soldiers usually, were planted on frontier farms to serve as a bulwark against the democratic spirit—the "fierce spirit of liberty," as Burke called it—already rushing in from New England, New York, and Pennsylvania. The Sedition Act excluded persons of doubtful loyalty; if any succeeded in entering they were driven out by the Loyalists—the British party, as they styled themselves, the Jacobites of the New World as they were styled by others—who enjoyed a monopoly of the offices and did their best to acquire a monopoly of the land. Meanwhile the British governors, together with the "family compact" of Loyalists who acted as their advisers, kept the settlers from imitating the "awful example of a neighbouring nation" by refusing them self-government, by censoring the Press, imprisoning agitators, prohibiting the playing of American airs, issuing Crown land patents as bribes, and propagating loyalty by various other paternal methods. . . . Canadians of the present generation try to shield their memory; we say that if they hated the Americans, their wounds were still raw; if they were greedy for money and lands, they had been beggared; if they upheld and practised tyranny, they were sincere obscurantists and honestly believed in the divine right of kings and viceroys to bedevil human affairs. Despite all, the American spirit entered and took possession. The insurrections in Upper and Lower Canada turned upon Responsible Government, one of the fundamental demands of the American Colonies. Mr. Gladstone described the struggle as being, for Canada, *articulus aut libertatis aut servitutis*. In the end, of course, the people won. Some of the descendants of the Loyalists strive to keep alive the old animosity, and warn England that she is estranging Canada by courting the friendship of the United States. In another generation or so, these adherents of a lost cause will no longer have power for mischief.

Nature is healing the schism of the race by her own slow but efficacious methods. Hundreds of families of the United Empire stock have gone back to the United States, in some instances to the very place of their origin. Upwards of a million native Canadians are now living in the States, the great majority as naturalised Americans; whilst American farmers, attracted by cheap land and good laws, are entering the Canadian North-West at the rate of 50,000 a year. The exodus, as migration across the line is called, is a heavy drain on Canada; like an ancient conqueror, it sweeps away the flower of both sexes, leaving the unfittest to survive. During the last 30 years we have spent $10,000,000 on immigration work in Europe, yet our population has not held its natural increase, has not, that is, grown as fast as the population of an old and overcrowded country like England. The Canadian lad thinks no more of transferring himself to Buffalo or Chicago than a Scotch youth of going up to London, perhaps not so much. On the other hand, American tourists, "drummers," lecturers, preachers, sportsmen and investors come and go in Canada precisely as if this were a State of the Union. When we produce a champion athlete, a clever journalist or eloquent divine, they annex him and advertise him next day as a Yankee. Marrying and giving in marriage is going on without the slightest regard for the doctrines of the Loyalists.

. . . Our business relations with the Americans are as close as our social connections. It is estimated that since the good times returned in 1897, upwards of $150,000,000 of American capital has been invested in Canadian industries, petroleum, lumber, iron and steel, farm implements, pulp and paper, street railways, electric works, cement, gold and silver-lead mines, etc. Formerly, England supplied all the outside capital we required, but the English investor was far away and capital, like electric power, loses by long-distance transmission. The American investor in Canada is near by, is dealing with people as much like himself as one pea is like another, and finds conditions to be the same as at home, nature being no respecter of political frontiers. Our Federal and Provincial debts are held in England, but New York finances occasionally for Canadian municipalities. In British Columbia most of the paying mines have been developed by Americans, who are also getting hold of the coal and lumber. In the Klondike they outnumber the rest of the population. Since 1898, 120,000 persons have migrated from the United States to the Canadian North-West, not all native Americans, but all more or less imbued with the American spirit. It is probable that this class of settlers will before long dominate the vast region lying between Manitoba and the Rocky Mountains. Some think they will ultimately carry the Territories and British Columbia into the United States, that Manitoba will follow, and Canada be reduced to her former dimensions, her western boundary stopping at Lake Superior. The present writer ventures to think differently. However that may be, their influence does not make for the development of Imperialist notions either in the West or at Ottawa.

. . . Such is the situation which, in dealing with Canada, Imperialists have to consider. They are asking England to depart from a policy under which she has prospered greatly, and adopt another, which, from the nature of the case, would militate against her foreign trade alike by taxing foreign products—*i.e.,* by diminishing imports from foreign countries, which are paid for with exports, and by increasing the cost of her food and raw material, on the chance that it may enable her to augment the lesser trade with the Colonies, notwithstanding that the bulk of Canada's trace might at any moment be captured by the United States, simply by relaxing the Dingley tariff. One of the fundamental mistakes they make is in assuming that, given a preference in Britain, the Colonies would be glad to make large concessions to the British manufacturer. I am certain that Canada, for one, would not. When the preferential system was in force before, the cry was that we Canadians were more delvers and grubbers of raw material for the British artisan; whereas our neighbours, with their protective tariff, were establishing factories of their own, and becoming a powerful nation in consequence. There were few factories in Canada then, none of the tariff-born, tariff-bred, tariff-fed sort; and, as I say, the objection was that the preferential policy, by letting in British goods at a low rate of duty, kept us from having any. To-day we have some thousands of factories, great and small, which, the owners declare, have not sufficient protection as it is against British goods, because the present Government admits such goods at rates 33 1/3 per cent. below those levied on similar wares coming from foreign countries. Let Sir Wilfrid Laurier propose a more substantial preference for British exports, and the cry will at once be raised that Canadian interests are being sacrificed; that we are being thrown back to the pastoral stage of existence for the benefit of Manchester and Birmingham; that our first duty is not to Englishmen 3,000 miles away, but to the Canadians who are being driven across the line because of the demolition of Canadian industries, and so on. I do not believe that Sir Wilfrid—the Conservative or Opposition Party are in the hands of the Canadian Manufacturers' Association—would venture to face such a clamour, or, if he did, that he could do so successfully.

. . . Let us imagine, however, that the Canadian manufacturer was ready to sacrifice himself for the greater glory of the Empire; the next step would be for Britain to name the Canadian articles that should receive preferential treatment. Depend on it, she would not be allowed a free choice; Canada would have a voice or know the reason why.

Wheat alone would not satisfy us. The North-West is the only part of Canada which grows wheat for export in any considerable quantity, and its population is but an eighth of the whole. Ontario, the chief manufacturing Province, the Province, therefore that would be hit hardest by a further reduction of duties in favour of Britain, would demand a preference for staple exports like cattle and beef, bacon and meats, eggs, peas, fruit, hay, cheese and butter, pine lumber, etc.; Quebec would demand one for spruce, potatoes, sheep and lambs; British Columbia for canned salmon and lead; the Maritime Provinces for deals, cod, coal and iron. No doubt the other Colonies would push their claims in the same vigorous fashion, Australia asking a preference for wool and wine, the West Indies for sugar, Ceylon for tea, Newfoundland for herring, together with bounties on cod to enable her to compete with the bounty-fed cod of the Miquelon. It is not too much to say that the British consumer would have his hands full, especially as the self-governing Colonies would be sure to back their demands with threats to secede from the Empire if he refused to imitate the example of the fabled pelican that fed its young upon its own entrails.

Then would come the task of making preferential arrangements between the Colonies themselves. Our trade with Australia and South Africa together is nothing like so great as our trade with the single American city of Buffalo, and no arrangement we could possibly devise would add much to it. Seventy years ago, when the Empire was supposed to be welded into "one harmonious whole" by the preference system then in vogue, American fish and lumber were excluded from the British West Indies in order to give Canadians a monopoly of the trade. The West Indians declared that we fleeced them; we retorted that we were fleeced through having to buy their sugar at a fancy price when Brazil and Cuba were offering a cheaper article; and there was nothing but bad blood between us and them. At last they took the matter into their own hands, and in defiance of Downing Street opened their markets to American competition.

It is said these troubles could be avoided by giving the Colonies representation at Westminster. That is an old panacea, but no one has yet hit on the right formula for giving effect to it. . . . The Canadian Parliament is elected on the principle of representation by population; so, of course, is Congress; we on this continent cannot conceive how any other rule could be got to work equitably. Yet if we applied it to representation at Westminster, one of the two things would happen—either the Colonies, with their eleven million whites, would be over-ruled by the greater representation from the United Kingdom; or, if the time came when their inhabitants outnumbered those of the United Kingdom, tariff issues as well as issues of peace and war would be dictated to England and the Empire at large by the Colonial representatives. It would be a singular sight to see the Mother Country accepting its legislation from the Colonies—an inversion of parts akin to that which took place on the licensed holiday of Athenian slaves—and one may reasonably doubt whether the British people would relish it on top of a fiscal policy designed to increase the cost of their food for the benefit of the Colonial producer.

. . . The whole theory of the New Imperialism rests on the flimsiest sort of underpinning. In the first place, the notion of a federated Empire, of a permanent union between the Mother Country and the Colonies, is based on the unsafe doctrine of "once a Colony always a Colony"; on the supposition that Canada, for instance, is never to enter upon full national life, but is to remain, what she is now, an imperfectly-developed organism. Disraeli, the father of modern Imperialism, used to pretend in public to believe this, but he wrote Lord Malmesbury a note one day when we were worrying him about the North Atlantic Fishery Question, in which he said:—"These wretched

Colonies will all be independent, too, in a few years, and are a mill-stone about our necks." No one can read the brief annals of Canada or observe how we have been casting off, one by one, the regulation swaddling bands of a British Colony, without coming to the same conclusion. Yet these gentlemen fancy they can interrupt the processes whereby the boy grows into a man. The boy is to remain a page dedicated to the service of his master; is never to become his own master or serve himself and his native land with undivided loyalty. As Burke said of a constitution-monger of his day:—"It costs them nothing to fight with nature, and to conquer the order of 'Providence.'"

. . . Imperialists sometimes allow that it would be to England's interest to live on terms of friendship with the United States; at other times, as when discussing this plan for transforming Canada into a military outpost of the Empire, they ignore the United States. Forty years ago the Americans ordered Napoleon and the piratical Second Empire out of Mexico, and they would soon tire of our company on this continent if we were to set up in business as the Hessians of the 20th century. As things are, we tax England's patience by our squabbles over boundaries, cod, and seals, and by the peremptory manner in which we call on her to take her life in her hands in our behalf. Manifestly, if we were a regularly constituted part of the Imperial fighting machine, paying an annual contribution of men and money, she would have to fight the United States whenever we felt that she ought to, or the federation of the Empire would go to pieces.

Sinn Féin grew out of the nationalist interests of Arthur Griffith, who edited the nationalist newspaper the *United Irishman* from 1899. Griffith saw the paper as the heir to the movement begun by O'Connell and the Young Irelanders, as the call for "National Self-Determination through the recognition of the duties and rights of citizenship on the part of the individual," below, suggests. He formed Sinn Fein ("for ourselves") out of a variety of loosely nationalist organizations in 1905.

The *United Irishman* and Sinn Féin (1905)

Readers of the *United Irishman* desirous of supporting the National Council are requested to fill in the form on page 8 of this issue and forward it to the Hon. Secretaries.

Policy: National Self-Determination through the recognition of the duties and rights of citizenship on the part of the individual, and by the aid and support of all movements originating from within Ireland, instinct with the National tradition, and not looking outside Ireland for the accomplishment of their aims.

Constitution and Rules

1. The National Council shall be composed of members who pledge themselves to its principles and who subscribe a minimum of 1s. annually to its funds.

2. Any ten members may form a branch which shall pay 10s. per annum affiliation fee, but not more than one branch shall be formed in any electoral district, except with the consent of the Executive Committee.

3. Members of the Council who are candidates for public representative positions shall before being adopted, pledge themselves in writing, that in case of their election they will act and vote in regard to any issue as may in council be decided.

4. Such decision to be arrived at only at meetings, specially summoned in writing, of all members of the Council who are members of local governing bodies.

5. Citizens wishing to join the National Council must be proposed and seconded by two members, and their nomination be sent to the Council or Branch Committee which shall accept or reject the nomination at its next meeting.

6. No member of the British armed forces, or pensioner therefrom, to be eligible for membership, nor shall any person who has otherwise taken an oath of allegiance to the British Crown be admitted as a member as long as he shall retain the office involving the oath.

7. Each year an Ard Comhairle (Congress) shall be held, which shall be the supreme governing body of the organisation, and at which the Executive shall be elected. The meeting to be held in the summer, the date to be fixed by the Executive.

8. The Ard Comhairle shall meet at least once a month, and shall deal with matters arising in connection with organisation, finance, Press, propaganda, and all matters of urgent public importance. Meetings of the Central Body shall also be held at least once a month.

Bibliography of Primary Sources

Part I:
Shaping the Imperial Body Politic, 1829–1857

————. Report of the Select Committee on Transportation, Parliamentary Papers 1837–38, v. XXII.

Anon. "Chinese Emigration." London *Times,* 7 September 1866.

Anon. "The Ministry and the New Parliament." *Edinburgh Review* 87 (January 1848): 138–69.

Archibald, W. A. *The Sugar Question: A Letter Addressed to the Right Honorable Lord John Russell.* London: McKewan Brothers, 1847.

Beeton, Isabella. *The Book of Household Management.* London: S. O. Beeton, 1861.

Children's Employment Commission. *Appendix to the First Report of Commissioners*—Mines. Part II: Reports and Evidence from Sub-Commissioners. London: William Clowes and Sons, 1842.

Chisholm, Caroline. *Emigration and Transportation.* London: John Ollivier, 1847.

Cobden, Richard. *Russia and the Eastern Question.* Cleveland, Ohio: Jewett Proctor & Worthington, 1854.

Foster, Thomas Campbell. *Letters on the Condition of the People of Ireland.* London: Chapman and Hall, 1847.

Greg, William. "Shall We Retain our Colonies?" *The Edinburgh Review* (April 1851): 475–98.

Lovett, William and John Collins. *Chartism: A New Organization of the People.* London: J. Watson, 1840, preface and pp. 1–23.

Macaulay, Thomas Babington. *Macaulay's Minutes Of Education in India in the Years 1835, 1836, and 1837 and Now First Collected From Records in The Department of Public Instruction.* Calcutta: C. B. Lewis, 1862.

————."A Speech Delivered to the House of Commons, 2nd March 1831." In *The Works of Lord Macaulay: Speeches, Poems and Miscellaneous Writings.* London: Longman's, 1898, pp. 407–26.

Martineau, Harriet. "Earl Spencer and Miss Florence Nightingale." *Daily News,* 15 August 1910.

————. Letter to the American Women's Rights Convention. *Liberator* 22 (1 November 1851).

————. *Poor Laws and Paupers Illustrated: The Parish—A Tale.* London: Charles Fox, 1833, pp. 1–18.

Marx, Karl. "The Indian Revolt." *New York Daily Tribune,* 16 September 1857.

Mayhew, Henry. *1851: or, the Adventures of Mr. and Mrs. Cursty Sandboys and Family, who Came Up to London, to "Enjoy Themselves," and to See the Great Exhibition* [with plates by George Cruikshank]. London: David Bogue, 1851.

O'Connell, Daniel. "Bill for the Removal of Jewish Disabilities." In *The Speeches and Public Letters of the Liberator,* ed. M. F. Cusack. McGlashan and Gill, 1875, pp. 59–62.

————. "Speech at the Bar." In *The Speeches and Public Letters of the Liberator.* ed. M. F. Cusack. Dublin: McGlashan and Gill, 1875. pp. 2–16.

————. Speech at Mullinger. *The Nation,* 20 May 1843.

Ouchterlony, John. *The Chinese War: An Account of all the Operations of the British Forces from the Commencement to the Treaty of Nanking.* London: Sanders and Otley, 1844.

Prince, Mary. *The History of Mary Prince.* Ann Arbor: University of Michigan Press, 1992. Edited with an introduction by Moira Ferguson.

Seacole, Mary. *The Wonderful Adventures of Mrs. Seacole in Many Lands.* London: James Blackwell, 1858.

Thomson, Robert. *Australian Nationalism: An Earnest Appeal to the Sons of Australia in Favour of the Federation and Independence of the States of our Country.* Sydney, 1888.

Twopenny, Richard. *Town Life in Australia.* London, 1883.

Wakefield, Edward Gibbon. *A Letter from Sydney and Other Writings.* London: M. J. Dent and Sons, 1929.

Webb, Sidney and Beatrice. *English Poor Law History Part II,* v. 1. Printed by the Authors, 1929.

Wedderburn, Robert. *The Horrors of Slavery.* West Smithfield: R. Wedderburn, 1824.

Part II
Liberalizing Imperial Democracy: Midcentury and After

'A.E.'. "Nationality and Imperialism." In *Ideals In Ireland,* Lady Gregory, ed. London: Unicorn, 1901.

Ali, Syed Ameer. "A Cry from the Indian Mahommedans." *Nineteenth Century* 12 (August 1882): 193–215.

Andrew, Elizabeth W. and Katharine C. Bushnell. *The Queen's Daughters in India.* London: Morgan and Scott, 1899, pp. 14–63.

'A Bengal Magistrate.' "The Home Rule Movement in India and Ireland." *Contemporary Review* 57 (January 1890): 78–97.

Besant, Annie. *Egypt.* London: Printed by Annie Besant and Charles Bradlaugh, 1882.

————. *The Redistribution of Political Power.* London: Freethought Publishing, Company, 1885.

Butler, Josephine. *Sursum Corda: Annual Address to the Ladies National Association.* Liverpool: T. Brakell, Printers, 1871.

Butler, Mary. "Women's Role in Sustaining Gaelic Culture." *Irish-women and the Home Language.* Dublin: Gaelic League [n.d].

Butt, Isaac. "Parliamentary Relations (Great Britain and Ireland)—Home Rule." In *Hansard's Parliamentary Debates 3rd series, 37 & 38 Victoriae,* 1874, pp. 710–18.

Carlyle, Thomas. "Occasional Discourse on the Negro Question." *Fraser's Magazine* (December 1849): 670–79.

Carpenter, Mary. *Letters to the Rt. Hon. Marquis of Salisbury, Secretary of State for India . . . being a Report of her Fourth Journey to India in 1875–76.* Printed for Private Circulation, 1876.

Disraeli, Benjamin. "Conservative and Liberal Principles." In *Selected Speeches of the Right Honourable the Earl of Beaconsfield,* v. II, ed. T. E. Kebbel. London: Longmans, Green and Co., 1882, pp. 523–35.

————. "Third Reading of the Reform Bill." In *Selected Speeches of the Right Honourable the Earl of Beaconsfield,* v. II, ed. T. E. Kebbel. London: Longmans, Green and Co., 1882, pp. 607–23.

Durham. Report on the Affairs of British North America. In *Selected Speeches and Documents in British Colonial Policy 1763–1917,* ed. Arthur Berridale Keith, Oxford University Press, 1929.

Fawcett, Millicent Garrett. "The Women's Suffrage Bill." *Fortnightly Review* 51 (March 1889): 555–67.

Gibbs, John. *Our Medical Liberties.* London: Draper and Sons, 1854.

Gladstone, William. "England's Mission." *The Nineteenth Century* 4 (1878): 560–84.

Government of India. East India Contagious Diseases Acts (1868).

Haines, C. A. "Gordon's Death: What is the Truth?" *The United Service Magazine* 2 (1890): 130–37.

Herbert, Auberon. "The Canadian Confederation." *Fortnightly Review* 7 (April 1867): 480–90.

Indian National Congress. Resolutions. In *Indian Politics,* ed. W. C. Bonnerjee. Madras: G. A. Natesan and Co., 1898.

Kingsley, Mary H. *Travels in West Africa: Congo Français, Corisco and Cameroons.* London: Macmillan and Co., 1897, pp. 1–10, 410–57.

Mill, John Stuart. "The Negro Question." *Fraser's Magazine* (January 1850): 25–31.

Naoroji, Dadhabai. Speech. In *Indian Politics,* ed. W. C. Bonnerjee. Madras: G. A. Natesan and Co., 1898.

Parnell, Charles Stewart. Speech at Wicklow. *The Freeman's Journal,* 6 October 1885.

Proclamation of an Irish Republic. *The Nation,* 5 December 1867.

Ramabai, Pandita. *The High-Caste Hindu Woman.* London: George Bell and Sons, 1888.

Schapera, I., ed. *Livingston's Missionary Correspondence 1841–1856.* Berkeley: University of California Press, 1961.

Taylor, Helen. "The Ladies Petition [to the Commons for the Right to Vote]." *Westminster Review* 87 (1867): 63–79.

Temple, Sir Richard. "Principles of British Policy in Egypt." In *Oriental Experience: A Selection of Essays and Addresses Delivered on Various Occasions,* ed. Sir Richard Temple. London: John Murray, 1883, pp. 415–34.

Part III
At Home with Imperial Culture: Toward the Twentieth Century

Anon. "Colonial and Indian Exhibition: The West Indian Court." *The Saturday Review,* 3 July 1886, pp. 16–17.

Anon. "Sinn Féin principles." *United Irishman,* 9 December 1905.

Anon. "Khama." *London Times,* 21 October, 1893.

Barnes, Irene H. *Behind The Great Wall: The Story Of The C.E.Z.M.S. Work and Workers in China.* London: Marshall Brothers, 1897.

Besant, Annie. *The Transvaal.* London: Annie Besant and Charles Bradlaugh, 1881.

Clerke, E. M. "The Dock Labourers' Strike—I. The Labour Market of East London." *Dublin Review* 105 (October 1889): 386–406.

Burt, Thomas. "Labour in Parliament." *Contemporary Review* 55 (May 1889): 678–91.

Booth, General William. *In Darkest England and the Way Out.* Chicago: Charles H. Sergel, 1890.

Devi, Sunity. *Autobiography of an Indian Princess.* London: John Murray, 1921.

Dilke, Emilia. "Trades Unionism for Women." *The New Review* 2 (1890): 43–53.

Farrer, E. "Canada and the New Imperialism." *Contemporary Review* 84 (December 1903): 761–74.

Fry, Edward. "China, England, and Opium." *Contemporary Review* 27 (February 1876): 447–59.

Goldstein, Vida. "The Australian Woman in Politics." *Review of Reviews* [Australian edition] (January 1904): 47–50.

Hobson, J. A. *Imperialism: A Study.* New York: J. Pott and Company, 1902.

MacArthur, W. A. In *The Destitute Alien in Great Britain: A Series of Papers Dealing with The Subject of Foreign Pauper Immigration,* ed. Arnold White. London and New York: Charles Scribner's Sons, 1892.

Mayhew, Henry. *London Labour and The London Poor, a cyclopaedia of the condition and earnings of those that will work, those that cannot work, and those that will not work.* London: Griffin, Bohn & Company, 1861.

Merriman-Labor, A. B. C. *Britons Through Negro Spectacles; or, a Negro on Britons.* London: The Imperial and Foreign Company, 1909.

Mukherji, T. N. *My Trip to Europe.* London: Edward Stanford. 1889.

Plaatje, Sol T. *Mafeking Diary: A Black Man's View of a White Man's War.* Ed. John Comaroff with Brian Willan and Andrew Reed. Athens: Ohio University Press, 1990.

Praed, Rosa Campbell. *Fugitive Anne: A Romance of the Unexplored Bush*. London: John Long, 1902.

The Queen's Empire: A Pictorial And Descriptive Record. London, Paris, and Melbourne: Cassell & Company Ltd., 1897.

Quick, John and Robert Randolph Garran. *The Annotated Constitution of the Australian Commonwealth*. London: Australian Book Company 1901.

Rhodes, Cecil. In Vindex, *Cecil Rhodes: His Political Life and Speeches, 1881–1900*. London: Chapman Hall, 1900.

Ritchie, J. Ewing. *Days and Nights in London*. London. Tinsley Brothers, 1880.

Salter, Joseph., "Central Africans," from *The East In The West; or Work Among The Asiatics and Africans in London*. London: S. W. Partridge & Co., 1895.

Shaw, George Bernard. *Fabianism and the Empire: A Manifesto by the Fabian Society*. London: Grant Richards, 1900.

Schloss, David F. "The Jew as a Workman." *Nineteenth Century* 29 (January 1891): 96–109.

Smyth, A. Watt. *Physical Deterioration: Its Causes and the Remedy*. New York: E. P. Dutton, 1904, pp. 13–53.

Stanley, Henry. *Through The Dark Continent or The Source of the Nile around the Great Lakes of Equatorial Africa and down the Livingstone River to the Atlantic Ocean*. New York: Harper & Brothers, 1879.

Stead, William T. "What Kind of Sovereign is Queen Victoria?" *The Cosmopolitan* (1900): 207–16.

Steel, Flora Annie and G. Gardner. *The Complete Indian Housekeeper and Cook*. London: William Heinemann and Company, 1888.

Temple, Sir Richard. "Religious Missions in the East." In Sir Richard Temple, *Oriental Experience: A Selection of Essays and Addresses Delivered on Various Occasions*. London: John Murray, 1883.

White, Arnold. "The Alien Immigrant." *Blackwood's Magazine* 173 (January 1903): 132–41.

Wirgman, A. T. "The Boers and the Native Question." *The Twentieth Century* v. 47 (April 1900): 593–602.

Select Bibliography of Secondary Sources

Alexander, Ziggy and Audre Dewjee, eds. *The Wonderful Adventures of Mrs. Seacole in Many Lands.* Falling Wall Press, 1984.

Auerbach, Jeffery A. *The Great Exhibition of 1851: A Nation on Display.* Yale University Press, 1999.

Ballhatchet, Kenneth. *Race, Sex and Class under the Raj: Imperial Attitudes and Policies and Their Critics, 1793–1905.* Weidenfeld and Nicholson, 1980.

Bayly, C. A. *Empire and Information: Intelligence Gathering and Social Communication in India, 1780–1870.* Cambridge University Press, 1999.

———. *Imperial Meridian: The British Empire and the World.* London: Longman, 1989.

———. *Raj: India and the British, 1600–1947.* Oxford University Press, 1991.

Boehmer, Elleke. *Empire Writing: An Anthology of Colonial Literature, 1870–1918.* Oxford University Press, 1998.

Bolt, Christine. *Victorian Attitudes Towards Race.* Routledge Kegan Paul, 1971.

Boyce, D. George. *Nationalism in Ireland.* Routledge, 1995.

Burton, Antoinette. *At the Heart of the Empire: Indians and the Colonial Encounter in Late-Victorian Britain.* University of California Press, 1998.

———. *Burdens of History: British Feminists, Indian Women and Imperial Culture, 1865–1915.* University of North Carolina Press, 1994.

Cain, P. G. and A. G. Hopkins. *British Imperialism: Innovation and Expansion, 1688–1914.* Longman, 1993.

Chatterjee, Ratnabali. "The Indian Prostitute as Colonial Subject: Bengal, 1864–1883." *Canadian Women's Studies/Les Cahiers de la Femme* 13, 1 (1992): 51–4.

Chaudhuri, Nupur and Margaret Strobel, eds. *Western Women and Imperialism: Complicity and Resistance.* Indiana University Press, 1992.

Clark, Anna. *The Struggle for the Breeches: Gender and the Making of the British Working Class.* University of California Press, 1995.

Colley, Linda. *Britons: Forging a Nation, 1707–1837.* Yale University Press, 1992.

Colls, Robert and Philip Dodd, eds. *Englishness: Politics and Culture, 1880–1920.* Croom Helm, 1986.

Cook, Scott B. *Colonial Encounters in the Age of High Imperialism.* Longman, 1996.

Coombes, Annie. *Reinventing Africa: Museums, Material Culture and Popular Imagination.* Yale University Press, 1994.

Corrigan, Philip and Derek Sayer. *The Great Arch: English State Formation as Cultural Revolution.* Basil Blackwell, 1985.

Crawford, E. Margaret. "Food and Famine." In *The Great Irish Famine,* ed. Cathal Póirtéir. Dufour Editions, 1997.

Curtis, Lionel. *Apes and Angels: The Irishman in Victorian Caricature.* Smithsonian Institution Press, 1971.

Davidoff, Leonore and Catherine Hall. *Family Fortunes: Men and Women of the English Middle Class, 1780–1850.* University of Chicago Press, 1987.

Davin, Anna. "Imperialism and Motherhood." *History Workshop Journal* 5 (Spring 1978): 9–65.

Dawson, Graham. *Soldier Heroes : British Adventure, Empire, and the Imagining of Masculinity.* Routledge, 1994.

Digby, Anne. *The Poor Law in Nineteenth Century England and Wales.* The Historical Association, 1982.

Drescher, Seymour. *Capitalism and Antislavery: British Mobilization in Comparative Perspective.* Oxford University Press, 1987.

———. "Whose Abolition? Popular Pressure and the Ending of the British Slave Trade." *Past and Present* 143 (1994): 136–66.

Eastwood, David. "Recasting Our Lot": Peel, the Nation, and the Politics of Interest. In *A Union of Multiple Identities: The British Isles, c. 1750–c.1850,* eds. Laurence Brockliss and David Eastman. Manchester University Press, 1997, pp. 29–43.

Edwards, Paul and David Dabydeen. *Black Writers in Britain, 1760–1890.* Edinburgh University Press, 1991.

Farwell, Byron. *The Great Anglo-Boer War.* W.W. Norton, 1976.

Feldman, David. *Englishmen and Jews: Social Relations and Political Culture 1840–1914.* Yale University Press, 1994.

Ferguson, Moira. *Subject to Others: British Women Writers and Colonial Slavery, 1670–1834.* Routledge, 1992.

Finn, Margot. *After Chartism: Class and Nation in English Radical Politics, 1848–1874.* Cambridge University Press, 1993.

Fisher, Michael F. *The First Indian Author in Britain: Dean Mahomet 1751–1851 in India, Ireland and England.* Oxford University Press, 1996.

Fladeland, Betty. "Our Cause Being One and the Same": Abolitionists and Chartism. In *Slavery and British Society, 1776–1846,* ed. James Walvin. Louisiana State University Press, 1982, pp. 69–99.

Fletcher, Ian Christopher, Laura E. Nym Mayhall, and Philippa Levine, eds., *Women's Suffrage in the British Empire: Citizenship, Nation and Race.* Routledge, 2000.

Foster, R. F. *Modern Ireland, 1600–1972.* Penguin, 1988.

Fryer, Peter. *Staying Power: The History of Black People in Britain.* Pluto, 1984.

Gilroy, Paul. *The Black Atlantic: Modernity and Double Consciousness.* Harvard University Press, 1993.

Gainor, Bernard. *The Alien Invasion: The Origins of the Aliens Act of 1905.* Crane, Russak and Co., Inc., 1972.

Gossman, Norbert J. "William Cuffay: London's Black Chartist." *Phylon* 44 (1983): 56–65.

Grimshaw, Patricia and Marilyn Lake, Ann McGrath and Marian Quartly. *Creating a Nation: 1788–1990.* Penguin Australia, 1994.

Grimshaw, Patricia, Susan Johnson and Marian Quartly, eds. *Freedom Bound I: Documents on Women in Colonial Australia.* Allen and Unwin, 1995.

Gundara, Jagdish and Ian Duffield, eds. *Essays on the History of Blacks in Britain, from Roman Times to the Mid-twentieth Century.* Avebury Press, 1992.

Hall, Catherine. "The Early Formation of Victorian Domestic Ideology." In *Fit Work for Women,* ed. Sandra Burman. New York: St. Martin's Press, 1979, pp. 15–32.

———. "Imperial Man: Edward Eyre in Australasia and the West Indies, 1833–66." In *The Expansion of England,* ed. Bill Schwarz. London: Routledge, 1996, pp. 130–70.

———. "Rethinking Imperial Histories: The Reform Act of 1867." *New Left Review* no. 208 (1994): 3–29.

———. *White, Male and Middle Class: Explorations in Feminist Historiography* Routledge, 1992.

Hall, Catherine, Keith McClelland and Jane Rendall. *Defining the Victorian Nation: Class, Race, Gender and the Reform Act of 1867.* Cambridge University Press, 2000.

Hall, Kim. *Things of Darkness: Economies of Race and Gender in Early Modern England.* Cornell University Press, 1995.

Hamer, D.A. *Liberal Politics in the Age of Gladstone: and Roseberry: a Study in Leadership and Policy.* Clarendon Press, 1972.

Harcourt, Freda. "Disraeli's Imperialism, 1866–68: A Question of Timing." *Historical Journal* 23, 1 (1980): 87–109.

———. "Gladstone, Monarchism and the 'New' Imperialism." *Journal of Imperial and Commonwealth History* 14 (1985): 20–51.

Harlow, Barbara and Mia Carter, eds., *Imperialism and Orientalism: A Documentary Sourcebook.* Blackwell, 1999.

Harrison, Robert T. *Gladstone's Imperialism in Egypt: Techniques of Domination.* Greenwood Press, 1995.

Harvie, Christopher. *Scotland and Nationalism: Scottish Politics 1707 to the Present.* Allen Unwin, 1977.

Holmes, Colin. *John Bull's Island: Immigration and British Society, 1871–1971.* Macmillan, 1988.

Holt, Thomas C. *The Problem of Freedom: Race, Labor and Politics in Jamaica and Britain, 1832–1938.* Johns Hopkins University Press, 1992.

Horgan, John J. *Parnell to Pearse: Some Recollections and Reflections.* The Richview Press, 1948.

Hyam, Ronald. *Britain's Imperial Century, 1815–1914.* Barnes and Noble, 1976.

———. "Empire and Sexual Opportunity." *Journal of Imperial and Commonwealth History* 14, 2 (1986): 40–75.

Ignatiev, Noel. *How the Irish Became White.* Routledge, 1992.

Jeffery, Keith, ed. *"An Irish Empire?" Aspects of Ireland and the British Empire.* Manchester University Press, 1996.

Joyce, Patrick. *Visions of the People: Industrial England and the Question of Class, 1848–1914.* Cambridge University Press, 1991.

Judd, Denis. *Empire: The British Imperial Experience from 1765 to the Present.* Basic Books, 1996.

Kale, Madhavi. *Fragments of Empire.* Philadelphia: University of Pennsylvania Press, 1998.

Kennedy, Dane. *The Magic Mountains: Hill Stations and the British Raj.* University of California, 1996.

Kent, Susan Kingsley. *Gender and Power in Britain, 1640–1990.* Routledge, 2000.

Krebs, Paul. *Gender, Race and the Writing of Empire.* Cambridge University Press, 1999.

Levine, Philippa. "Re-reading the 1890s: Venereal Disease as 'Constitutional Crisis' in Britain and British India." *Journal of Asian Studies* 55, 3 (1996): 585–612.

———. "Venereal Disease, Prostitution, and the Politics of Empire: The Case of British India." *Journal of the History of Sexuality* 4,4 (1994): 579–602.

———. *Victorian Feminism, 1850–1900.* Tallahassee: University of Florida Press, 1987.

Lewis, Jane, ed. *Before the Vote was Won: Arguments for and against Women's Suffrage, 1864–1896.* Routledge, 1987.

Lorimer, Douglas. *Colour, Class and the Victorians.* Leicester University Press, 1978.

Lotz, Rainer and Ian Pegg, eds. *Under the Imperial Carpet: Essays in Black History, 1780–1950.* Crawley, England: Rabbit Press, 1986.

MacCaffrey, Lawrence J. *The Irish Question: Two Centuries of Conflict.* The University of Kentucky Press, 1995.

MacDonagh, Oliver. "O'Connell's Ideology." In *A Union of Multiple Identities: The British Isles, c. 1750 - c.1850,* Laurence Brockliss and David Eastman, eds., Manchester University Press, 1997, pp. 147–61.

MacKenzie, John M., ed. *Imperialism and Popular Culture.* Manchester University, 1986.

———. *Propaganda and Empire.* Manchester University Press, 1984.

McCalman, Iain, ed. *The Horrors of Slavery and Other Writings, by Robert Wedderburn.* Edinburgh University Press, 1991.

McClintock, Anne. *Imperial Leather: Race, Gender and Sexuality in the Colonial Contest.* Routledge, 1995.

McDevitt, Patrick. "Muscular Catholicism: Nationalism, Masculinity and Gaelic Team Sports, 1884–1916." *Gender and History* 9, 2 (1997): 262–84.

Marshall, Peter J. *The Cambridge Illustrated History of the British Empire.* Cambridge University Press, 1996.

Mehta, Uday Singh. *Liberalism and Empire: A Study in Nineteenth Century British Liberal Thought.* University of Chicago Press, 1999.

Midgley, Clare. "Anti-Slavery and Feminism in Nineteenth-Century Britain." *Gender and History* 5, 3 Autumn (1993): 343–62.

———. "Female Emancipation in an Imperial Frame: English women and the campaign against sati widow-burning in India, 1813–30." *Women's History Review* 9, 1 (2000): 95–121.

———. *Women Against Slavery: The British Campaign, 1780–1870.* Routledge, 1992.

———, ed., *Gender and Imperialism.* Manchester University Press, 1998.

Mukherjee, Rudrangshu. "Satan Let Loose Upon the Earth": The Kanpur Massacres and the Revolt of 1857. *Past and Present* no. 128 (August 1990): 92–116.

———. *Spectre of Violence: The 1857 Kanpur Massacres.* Penguin, 1998.

Newsinger, John. *Fenianism in Mid-Victorian Britain.* Pluto Press, 1994.

O'Connor, Maura. *The Romance of Italy and the English Political Imagination.* St. Martin's, 1998.

Parry, Jonathan. *The Rise and Fall of Liberal Government in Victorian Britain.* New Haven: Yale University Press, 1993.

Parsons, Neil. *King Khama, Emperor Joe and the Great White Queen: Victorian Britain through African Eyes.* University of Chicago Press, 1998.

Paquet, Sandra Pouchet. "The Heartbeat of a West Indian Slave: *The History of Mary Prince.*" *African American Review* 26, 1 (1992): 131–46.

Paxton, Nancy. "Mobilizing Chivalry: Rape in British Novels about the Indian Uprising of 1857." *Victorian Studies* 36, 1 (1992): 5–30.

Peers, Douglas M. "Law and Discipline in 19th Century English State Formation: The Contagious Diseases Acts of 1864, 1866 and 1869." *Journal of Historical Sociology* 6,1 March (1993): 28–55.

Porter, Andrew N., ed. *The Oxford History of the British Empire, v. III: The Nineteenth Century.* Oxford University Press, 1999.

Ramdin, Ron. *The Making of the Black Working Class in Britain.* Gower Publishing Co., Ltd., 1987.

———. *Reimagining Britain: 500 years of Black and Asian History* Pluto, 1999.

Rehin, F. "Blackface Street Minstrels in Victorian London and its Resorts: Popular Culture and its Racial Connotations as Revealed in Polite Opinion." *Journal of Popular Culture* 15 (1981): 19–38.

Reynolds, Henry. *Aboriginal Sovereignty: Three Nations, One Australia?* Allen and Unwin, 1996.

Rich, Paul. *Race and Empire in British Politics.* Cambridge University Press, 1986.

Richards, Thomas. *The Commodity Culture of Victorian England: Advertising and Spectacle, 1851–1914.* London: Verso, 1990.

Roberts, Andrew. *Salisbury: Victorian Titan.* London: Weidenfeld and Nicholson, 1999.

Robbins, Keith. *Nineteenth-Century Britain: England, Scotland and Wales in the Making of a Nation.* Oxford University Press, 1988.

Robinson, Ronald and John Gallagher, with Alice Denny. *Africa and the Victorians: The Climax of Imperialism.* New York: Anchor Books, 1968.

Roper, Michael and John Tosh, eds. *Manful Assertions: Masculinities in Britain since 1800.* London: Routledge, 1991.

Ryan, James. *Picturing Empire: Photography and the Visualization of the British Empire.* University of Chicago Press, 1997.

Said, Edward. *Orientalism.* New York: Vintage Books, 1978.

Samuel, Raphael. "Four Nations History" In his *Island Stories: Unravelling Britain*. London: Verso, 1997.

———. "Introduction: Exciting to be English." In *Patriotism: The Making and Unmaking of British National Identity, v. I: History and Politics*, Raphael Samuel, ed. London: Routledge, 1989, pp. xviii - lxvii.

———. *Theatres of Memory*. Verso, 1995.

Schneer, Jonathan. *London 1900: The Imperial Metropolis*. Yale University Press, 1999.

Schwarz, Bill, ed. *The Expansion of England*. Routledge, 1996.

Scobie, Edward. *Black Britannia: A History of Blacks in Britain*. Johnson Publishing, 1972.

Seecombe, Wally. Patriarchy Stabilized: The Construction of the Male Breadwinner Wage Norm in 19th c. Britain. *Social History* 11 (1986): 53–76.

Semmel, Bernard. *Imperialism and Social Reform: English Social-Imperial Thought, 1895–1914*. New York: Anchor Books, 1968.

Sharpe, Jenny. *Allegories of Empire: The Figure of Woman in the Colonial Text*. University of Minnesota Press, 1993.

Sheehy, Jeanne. *The Rediscovery of Ireland's Past: The Celtic Revival 1830–1930*. London: Thames and Hudson, 1980.

Sinha, Mrinalini. *Colonial Masculinity: The "Manly Englishman" and the "Effeminate Bengali" in the Late Nineteenth Century*. Manchester University Press, 1995.

Spurr, David. *The Rhetoric of Empire: Colonial Discourse in Journalism, Travel Writing and Imperial Administration*. Duke University Press, 1994.

Stedman Jones, Gareth. "The 'Cockney' and the Nation, 1780–1988." *Metropolis London: Histories and Representations since 1800,* ed. David Feldman and Gareth Stedman Jones. Routledge, 1989, pp. 272–324.

———. "Rethinking Chartism." In his *Languages of Class: Studies in English Working-Class History, 1832–1982*. Cambridge University Press, 1983.

———. *Outcast London: A Study in the Relationship Between Classes in Victorian Society*. Pantheon Books, 1971.

Stocking, George. *Victorian Anthropology*. New York: Free Press, 1987.

Strang, Herbert, ed. *Stories of the Mutiny*. Mittal Publications, 1990.

Swift, Roger and Sheridan Gilley, eds. *The Irish in Britain 1815–1939*. Pinter Publishers, 1989.

Teale, Ruth, ed. *Colonial Eve: Sources on Women in Australia 1788–1914*. Oxford University Press, 1978.

Thompson, E. P. *The Making of the English Working Class*. Vintage Books, 1966.

Thompson, Dorothy. *Outsiders: Class, Gender and Nation*. London: Verso: 1993.

Thorne, Susan. *Congregational Missions and the Making of an Imperial Culture in Nineteenth-century England*. Stanford University Press, 1999.

Tidrick, Kathryn. *Empire and the English Character*. I. B. Tauris, 1992.

Trevor-Roper, Hugh. "The Invention of Tradition: The Highland Tradition of Scotland." In *The Invention of Tradition,* Eric Hobsbawm and Terence Ranger, eds. Cambridge University Press, 1993, pp. 14–42.

Turley, David. *The Culture of English Antislavery*. London: Routledge, 1991.

Valenze, Deborah. *The First Industrial Woman*. Oxford University Press, 1995.

Vernon, James, ed. *Re-Reading the Constitution: New Narratives in the Political History of England's Long Nineteenth Century*. Cambridge University Press, 1996.

Visram, Rozina. *Ayahs, Lascars and Princes: Indians in Britain, 1700–1947*. Pluto Press, 1986.

———. *Asians in Britain: 400 Years of History*. London: Pluto Press, forthcoming.

Walkowitz, Judith R. *City of Dreadful Delight: Narratives of Sexual Danger in Nineteenth Century London*. University of Chicago Press, 1992.

———. "The Indian Woman, the Flower Girl, and the Jew: Photojournalism in Edwardian London." *Victorian Studies* 42 (Autumn 1998/99): 3–46.

———. *Prostitution and Victorian Society*. Cambridge University Press, 1980.

Walvin, James. *Black and White: The Negro and English Society, 1555–1945*. Allen Lane, 1973.

———. *Black Ivory: A History of British Slavery*. Howard University Press, 1994.

———. *Fruits of Empire: Exotic Produce and British Taste, 1660–1800*. New York University Press, 1997.

———. *Passage to Britain: Immigration in British History and Politics*. Penguin Books, 1984.

———. "The Propaganda of Anti-slavery," in his *Slavery and British Society*. Baton Rouge: Louisiana State University, 1982, pp. 49–68.

Ward, Alan J. *The Easter Rising: Revolution and Irish Nationalism*. Prentice Hall, 1980.

Ward, J. R. "The Industrial Revolution and British Imperialism." *Economic History Review* 47, 1 (1994): 44–65.

Ware, Vron. *Beyond the Pale: White Women, Racism and History*. London: Verso, 1992.

Wahrman, Dror. *Imagining the Middle Class: The Political Representation of Class in Britain, c. 1780–1840*. Cambridge University Press, 1995.

West, Shearer, ed. *The Victorians and Race*. Aldershot: Scolar Press, 1996.

Williams, Eric. *Capitalism and Slavery*. Duke University Press, 1944/1994.

Williams, Gwyn. *When Was Wales?: A History of the Welsh*. Black Raven Press, 1985.

Wohl, Anthony. "'Dizzi-Ben-Dizzi': Disraeli as Alien." *Journal of British Studies* 34 (July 1995): 375–411.

Zaidi, A. M. *The Grand Little Man of India: Dadhabai Naoroji, Speeches and Writings*, v. I. S. Chand and Co., 1984.

Zastoupil, Lynn. *John Stuart Mill and India*. Stanford University Press, 1994.

Zlotnick, Susan. "Domesticating Imperialism: Curry and Cookbooks in Victorian England." *Frontiers: A Journal of Women's Studies* 16, 2/3 (1996): 51–68.

Index